Scotland's
Highlands & Islands

Joe Bindloss
Clay Lucas

LONELY PLANET PUBLICATIONS
Melbourne • Oakland • London • Paris

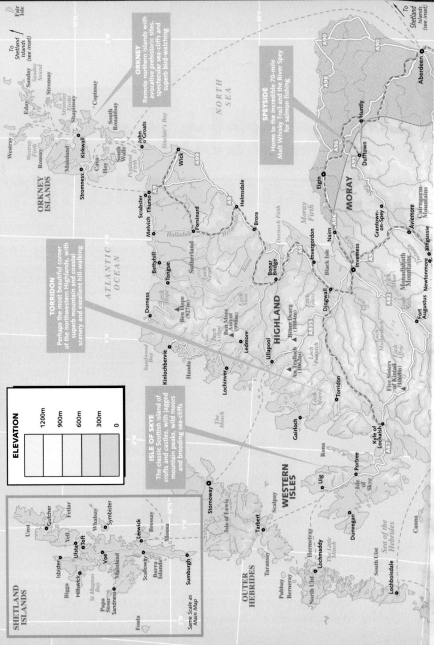

ORKNEY
Remote northern islands with evocative prehistoric sites, spectacular sea-cliffs and superb bird-watching

SPEYSIDE
Home to the incredible 70-mile Malt Whisky Trail and the River Spey for salmon fishing

TORRIDON
Perhaps the most beautiful corner of the northwestern Highlands, with superb mountain and coastal scenery and excellent hill-walking

ISLE OF SKYE
The classic Scottish island of crofts and castles, with jagged mountain peaks, wild moors and brooding sea-cliffs

ELEVATION

1200m	
900m	
600m	
300m	
0	

NORTH SEA

ATLANTIC OCEAN

ORKNEY ISLANDS

SHETLAND ISLANDS

Same Scale as Main Map

WESTERN ISLES

OUTER HEBRIDES

MORAY

HIGHLAND

Fair Isle

To Shetland Islands (see inset)

To Shetland Islands (see inset)

Aberdeen
Huntly
Dufftown
Elgin
Grantown-on-Spey
Aviemore
Nairn
Inverness
Kingussie
Newtonmore
Fort Augustus
Kyle of Lochalsh
Torridon
Five Sisters of Kintail (1068m)
Dingwall
Black Isle
Invergordon
Bonar Bridge
Ledmore
Ullapool
Lochinver
Kinlochbervie
Handa
Durness
Tongue
Bettyhill
Melvich
Thurso
Scrabster
Forsinard
Helmsdale
Brora
Wick
John o'Groats
Kirkwall
Stromness
Westray
Sanday
Stronsay
Eday
Rousay
Shapinsay
South Ronaldsay
Hoy
Copinsay
Gairloch
Portree
Uig
Isle of Skye
Dunvegan
Stornoway
Tarbert
Lochmaddy
Hermetray
North Uist
South Uist
Lochboisdale
Benbecula
Isle of Lewis
Scalpay
Rona
Canna
Ben Hope (927m)
Ben More Assynt (998m)
Ben Dearg (1084m)
An Teallach (1062m)
Cairngorm Mountains
Monadhliath Mountains
Mondhlath Mountains

Lerwick
Scalloway
Sumburgh
Unst
Yell
Fetlar
Gutcher
Whalsay
Symbister
Bressay
Mousa
Voe
Toft
Ulsta
Brae
Hillswick
Bigga
Isbister
Papa Stour
Sandness
Foula
Burra Islands
Mainland

Pentland Firth
Moray Firth
Dornoch Firth
Westray Firth
Stronsay Firth
Sinclair's Bay
Sandwood Bay
The Minch
Sea of the Hebrides
The Little Minch
St Magnus Bay

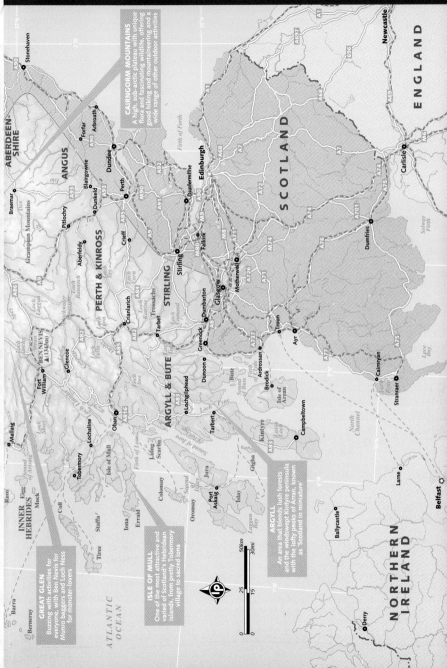

CAIRNGORM MOUNTAINS
A high, sub-arctic plateau with unique flora and fascinating wildlife, offering good hiking and mountaineering and a wide range of other outdoor activities

GREAT GLEN
Buzzing with activities for everyone, with Ben Nevis for Munro baggers and Loch Ness for monster-lovers

ISLE OF MULL
One of the most attractive and varied of Scotland's Hebridean islands, from pretty Tobermory village to sacred Iona

ARGYLL
An area that blends lush forests and the windswept Kintyre peninsula with the lofty peaks of Arran, known as 'Scotland in miniature'

ENGLAND

SCOTLAND

NORTHERN IRELAND

ATLANTIC OCEAN

INNER HEBRIDES

ABERDEEN-SHIRE

ANGUS

PERTH & KINROSS

STIRLING

ARGYLL & BUTE

Scotland's Highlands & Islands
1st edition – June 2002

Published by
Lonely Planet Publications Pty Ltd ABN 36 005 607 983
90 Maribyrnong St, Footscray, Victoria 3011, Australia

Lonely Planet offices
Australia Locked Bag 1, Footscray, Victoria 3011
USA 150 Linden St, Oakland, CA 94607
UK 10a Spring Place, London NW5 3BH
France 1 rue du Dahomey, 75011 Paris

Photographs
Many of the images in this guide are available for licensing from
Lonely Planet Images.
Web site: www.lonelyplanetimages.com

Front cover photograph
Kilchurn Castle near Loch Awe (John Lawrence, Tony Stone Images)

ISBN 1 74059 036 8

text & maps © Lonely Planet Publications Pty Ltd 2002
photos © photographers as indicated 2002

Printed by The Bookmaker International Ltd
Printed in China

Contents – Text

SKYE & THE WESTERN ISLES 232

THE NORTHWEST HIGHLANDS 272

ORKNEY & SHETLAND ISLANDS 315

LANGUAGE 368

GLOSSARY 371

INDEX 376

MAP LEGEND back page

METRIC CONVERSION inside back cover

Contents – Maps

MAP LEGEND   back page

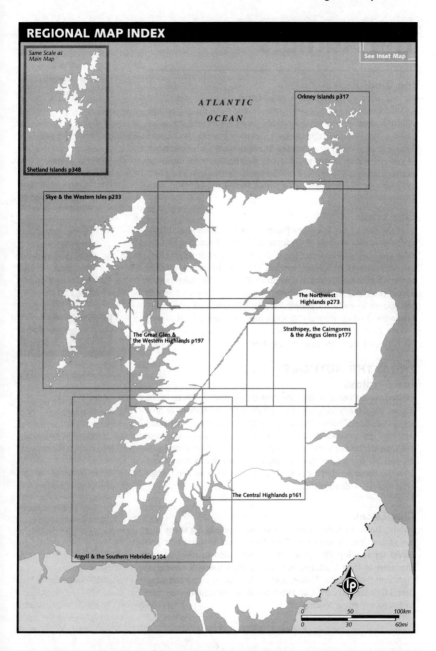

REGIONAL MAP INDEX

Same Scale as
Main Map

See Inset Map

ATLANTIC
OCEAN

Orkney Islands p317

Shetland Islands p348

Skye & the Western Isles p233

The Northwest
Highlands p273

The Great Glen &
the Western Highlands p197

Strathspey, the Cairngorms
& the Angus Glens p177

The Central Highlands p161

Argyll & the Southern Hebrides p104

| 0 | 50 | 100km |
| 0 | 30 | 60mi |

The Authors

Joe Bindloss
Joe was born in Cyprus, grew up in England and has since lived and worked in the USA, the Philippines and Australia, though he still calls London home. He first developed an incurable case of wanderlust on family trips through Europe in the old VW Kombi. After a degree in biology eliminated science from his future choice of careers, Joe moved through a string of occupations, including mural painting and sculpting, before finally settling on journalism. Joe has written for a number of Lonely Planet titles.

Clay Lucas
Born the same year as Lonely Planet, Clay began his working life as the office punchbag at Melbourne's GTV9 television station. When not being yelled at, Clay loaded videotapes and turned up the sound levels on advertisements. Deciding he wasn't strange enough for commercial TV, Clay sub-edited on *The Jakarta Post* during the dying days of the Suharto regime, before returning to Melbourne to write for Lonely Planet's Web site and coordinate Scoop travel news. He then travelled to Europe to work on various Lonely Planet guides before sub-editing on Dublin's *Evening Herald* newspaper. He now lives in Melbourne.

FROM THE AUTHORS
Joe Bindloss
Firstly I would like to thank the staff of the tourist offices in the region, particularly Sally Monro in Strathpeffer, for invaluable help and assistance. Thanks also to the staff of museums and B&Bs who opened up especially for me, and to the travellers I met along the way for their tips and appraisals of things to see and do (both on and off the beaten track). Finally, my thanks to the helpful drivers who stopped in the rain to help me with my broken fanbelt on a lonely Shetland hillside.

Clay Lucas
Special thanks to Sally Munro, David and Meagidh the sheep dog for getting me drenched at Glen Nevis, and to Charlotte and David for running The Lime Tree. Thanks also to Michael and Maureen at Iona Cottage; everyone should spend a couple of nights on their futons. Thanks also to my mother for all the wonderful CalMac ferry trips, to Peter and Anto for golfing bliss, and to Emma for going to Iona.

This Book

This is the 1st edition of Lonely Planet's *Scotland's Highlands & Islands* guide. It incorporates material written by Neil Wilson, Graeme Cornwallis and Tom Smallman for the 2nd edition of *Scotland*.

From the Publisher

This edition of *Scotland's Highlands & Islands* was produced in Lonely Planet's London office. Heather Dickson was the coordinating editor and Liam Molloy handled the mapping, design and layout. Abigail Hole, Arabella Shepherd, Craig MacKenzie, Emma Sangster and Jenny Lansbury helped with editing and proofing. Annika Roojun designed the cover, Jimi Ellis drew the climate chart and Lachlan Ross drew the back-cover map. Lonely Planet Images provided the photographs and illustrations were drawn by Asa Andersson, Jane Smith, Liam Molloy, Martin Harris and Patrick Watson.

Many thanks to Quentin Frayne for the handy language section and to Rachel Suddart for help with the Getting There & Away chapter. Thanks also to Amanda Canning, Paul Piaia and Messrs Bindloss and Lucas for all their hard work.

Foreword

ABOUT LONELY PLANET GUIDEBOOKS

The story begins with a classic travel adventure: Tony and Maureen Wheeler's 1972 journey across Europe and Asia to Australia. There was no useful information about the overland trail then, so Tony and Maureen published the first Lonely Planet guidebook to meet a growing need.

From a kitchen table, Lonely Planet has grown to become the largest independent travel publisher in the world, with offices in Melbourne (Australia), Oakland (USA), London (UK) and Paris (France).

Today Lonely Planet guidebooks cover the globe. There is an ever-growing list of books and information in a variety of media. Some things haven't changed. The main aim is still to make it possible for adventurous travellers to get out there – to explore and better understand the world.

At Lonely Planet we believe travellers can make a positive contribution to the countries they visit – if they respect their host communities and spend their money wisely. Since 1986 a percentage of the income from each book has been donated to aid projects and human rights campaigns, and, more recently, to wildlife conservation.

Although inclusion in a guidebook usually implies a recommendation we cannot list every good place. Exclusion does not necessarily imply criticism. In fact there are a number of reasons why we might exclude a place – sometimes it is simply inappropriate to encourage an influx of travellers.

UPDATES & READER FEEDBACK

Things change – prices go up, schedules change, good places go bad and bad places go bankrupt. Nothing stays the same. So, if you find things better or worse, recently opened or long-since closed, please tell us and help make the next edition even more accurate and useful.

Lonely Planet thoroughly updates each guidebook as often as possible – usually every two years, although for some destinations the gap can be longer. Between editions, up-to-date information is available in our free, quarterly *Planet Talk* newsletter and monthly email bulletin *Comet*. The *Upgrades* section of our website (W www.lonelyplanet.com) is also regularly updated by Lonely Planet authors, and the site's *Scoop* section covers news and current affairs relevant to travellers. Lastly, the *Thorn Tree* bulletin board and *Postcards* section carry unverified, but fascinating, reports from travellers.

Tell us about it! We genuinely value your feedback. A well-travelled team at Lonely Planet reads and acknowledges every email and letter we receive and ensures that every morsel of information finds its way to the relevant authors, editors and cartographers.

Everyone who writes to us will find their name listed in the next edition of the appropriate guidebook, and will receive the latest issue of *Comet* or *Planet Talk*. The very best contributions will be rewarded with a free guidebook.

We may edit, reproduce and incorporate your comments in Lonely Planet products such as guidebooks, websites and digital products, so let us know if you don't want your comments reproduced or your name acknowledged.

How to contact Lonely Planet:
Online: e talk2us@lonelyplanet.com.au, W www.lonelyplanet.com
Australia: Locked Bag 1, Footscray, Victoria 3011
UK: 10a Spring Place, London NW5 3BH
USA: 150 Linden St, Oakland, CA 94607

Introduction

My heart's in the Highlands, my heart is not here;
My heart's in the Highlands, a-chasing a deer;
A-chasing the wild deer, and following the roe,
My heart's in the Highlands wherever I go.
Robert Burns

Scots can be terrifyingly fond of Robbie Burns, and their favourite bard was, in turn, fiercely fond of the Highlands – taking it with him, as he says, wherever he did go. And you will too. Why? Because the Highlands and the sparkling, island-studded seas that surround them are incomprehensibly, indescribably beautiful. Catch them on a good day – when the sun is shining or a light fog is rolling in – and there's no more stunning place on earth.

This remote, rugged and romantic region is one of Europe's last great wildernesses, but experiencing it when the weather is fine is part of the challenge: a dependable climate is not the area's strong point. But with its stark mountains, windswept isles, heather-covered hills, bleak, empty moors and mysterious lochs, it is an exhilarating place to be at any time. And though the weather can be a curse, it can also be a blessing, because many Highland locales are made even more alluring by glum conditions. Awesome places such as Glen Coe or Rannoch Moor become eerily dramatic when shrouded in a light coating of mist, while the gruesome history of a place such as Culloden Moor – where in 1746 English soldiers slaughtered more than 1500 Jacobite troops – is in perfect keeping with miserable weather.

Miserable, of course, is the cliched reputation of the Highland demeanour. It's undeserved though, as Highlanders and their island counterparts are an inquisitive and jocular bunch. Some will make you work hard for their favour initially, but make it past their wariness and you'll find unfathomably generous and welcoming people with a wry sense of humour.

Saying that, people are exactly what you won't find in most of the Highlands and the far-flung islands that stretch as far north as the isolated and lonely Shetland. Even in peak season, the region is seldom overrun with tourists (with the exception of a few well-beaten tourist trails such as Loch Ness, and the isles of Skye and Mull). In many parts, the Highland Clearances – where the health and happiness of sheep was put ahead of Highlanders – crushed the 1000-year-old clan system and forced thousands to find new land to call home. Population numbers in many such places never recovered.

This decline saw the region's economy slowly become less dependent on environmentally low-impact ventures such as crofting, whisky distilling and fishing, and more dependent on damaging industries such as forestry and oil exploration. But with the growing awareness of the green tourism dollar, care is now being taken to ensure the region's future viability as one of the world's premier eco-friendly destinations – to encourage the legions of hikers, climbers, cyclists and canoeists who invade the region once winter's worst is done. The Highlands and islands are truly an outdoor-activity paradise.

If that all sounds like hard work, sipping a single-malt whisky in front of an open peat fire as the rain pounds down outside is probably more your thing.

Whichever you choose, it's a safe bet that part of your heart will stay in Scotland's Highlands and islands, even if you don't get round to a-chasing that deer.

Facts about Scotland's Highlands & Islands

HISTORY
First Immigrants

Scotland's first inhabitants were hunter-gatherers who crossed the ice bridge from northern Europe into Britain at the end of the last Ice Age around 10,000 BC. The first settlements were in southern Scotland, but over the next few thousand years these colonisers moved across the country in waves, spreading to the farthest reaches of the Highlands and islands.

Based on the study of stone tools found at Mesolithic sites, there are indications of Baltic and English cultures to the east, and Irish cultures on the west coast at Oban, as well as on the western islands of Rum, Islay, Jura and Arran. Mesolithic flints from northern France have also been found at numerous sites across the Highlands. Around 6000 BC, the land bridge between Britain and Europe was permanently broken, isolating the British Isles from mainland Europe.

Prehistoric Civilisations

Scotland was densely forested when the first hunter-gatherers arrived, but during the Neolithic era, beginning in the 4th millennium BC, people began to clear the land, cultivating the first crops and domesticating wild fowl, pigs and other animals. Trade sprang up between the individual family groups as meat, skins and stone became valuable commodities. As people began to take control of their environment, the population slowly increased, allowing more complex patterns of social organisation to evolve – most significantly, the creation of the first villages.

Only limited evidence of this early culture remains on the mainland, but on the treeless northern and western islands, stone was the principal building material, preserving a remarkable record of the domestic architecture of the first Britons, most impressively at Skara Brae in Orkney. All aspects of early life are represented, from primitive field systems and houses to ceremonial structures such as burial cairns and tribal halls.

At the end of the Neolithic period, around 2500 BC, the Beaker people reached the British Isles from mainland Europe, heralding the arrival of the Bronze Age. As well as bringing bronze and gold to northern Scotland, the Beakers introduced distinctive burial rites, including the burying of earthenware drinking vessels (known as *beakers*, hence their name) with the dead. The primitive stone tools of the Neolithic peoples were no match for the metal weapons of the invaders, and Beaker culture quickly came to dominate the British Isles. Many of the region's *cairns* (piles of stones used to mark a path) can be attributed to the Beakers, though there is evidence that in many cases they simply took over ceremonial sites that were used by native tribes.

The Celts

The Celts are another culture that has been heavily romanticised, although this tribal group were found throughout Europe, not just on the Celtic-fringe. The Celts who initially entered and conquered the Scottish Highlands were members of Indo-European tribes, who occupied England and Scotland from around 700 BC. As with their predecessors, the invaders were able to defeat the natives of the Highlands through a leap in weapons technology, this time the invention of iron – 'Men armed with iron entered Britain and killed the men of bronze,' was Winston Churchill's summary of their arrival. In fact, as had happened so many times in Scotland's history, the old tribes were mostly absorbed into the new tribes and things continued much as they had before.

The most lasting memorials of the Iron Age are the vast defensive *brochs* (fortified stone towers), which were erected across the region. This was a time of great uncertainty, with frequent raids by marauding European tribes, and villages pooled their resources to build these mighty lookouts, which reached 10m or 12m in height. Beneath the towers or individual houses were networks of tunnels known as *souterrains*, used to store food or as a last line of defence if marauders broke through the walls. The Iron-Age peoples lived in communal groups, in *crannogs* (wooden huts on artificial islands in lochs) in the southern Highlands or in stone wheel-houses (partitioned roundhouses) in the northern regions.

The Picts

For a long time, the culture of the Picts – named *pictus* (painted) by the Romans because of their body tattoos – was masked by the subsequent Gaelic culture, but the discovery of an ancient list of Pictish kings has allowed archaeologists to map the Pictish territory with some degree of accuracy. Southern Scotland was the preserve of the Celtic Britons, who also occupied most of northern England, but Pictland extended north from the Firth of Forth to the top of Caithness and across to Orkney and the Western Isles.

The Picts are believed to be descended from the Scottish Celts and were divided into at least seven tribal groups or king-doms on the mainland. The invading Gaels all but erased the Picts from the history books, but a record of this enigmatic culture was preserved in the form of intricately carved Pictish stones, featuring illustrations of stylised pagan symbols, men on horse-back and wild beasts.

Much of what we know about the Picts comes from the Romans, who invaded Scotland in AD 80. Resistance by the low-land British tribes collapsed comparatively quickly, but the northern province, which the Romans named Caledonia after the Caledones tribe, proved a tougher nut to crack. Eventually, the Roman general Agri-cola was able to advance along the eastern edge of the Highlands, supported from the sea by Roman battleships, defeating a vast

army of Picts at the decisive Battle of Mons Graupius in AD 84, thought to be near modern-day Inverness. Agricola went on to sail around the Orkneys, establishing for the first time that Britain was an island.

The history of the Highlands might have been very different if war hadn't broken out on the Romanian frontier in Europe. Roman legions were pulled out of northern Scotland for the European conflict, and the remaining Roman forts quickly succumbed to guerrilla raids by Pictish warriors. In 122, Emperor Hadrian pulled his troops back to northern England, building his famous wall to divide the conquered people from the indomitable Scots across a line between the Tyne and Solway Firths.

Emperor Antoninus Pius reclaimed south-ern Scotland, but sealed the abandonment of the north in AD 142 with the construction of the Antonine Wall, which divided Scotland in two along a line between the Clyde and Firth Forths. Apart from one more brief incursion by Septimus Severus early in the 3rd century AD, the Romans abandoned fur-ther attempts to subdue Scotland. Within a century they had abandoned the British Isles completely.

Over the next 300 years, the Picts faced attack from all sides as Angles from north-eastern England stormed the lowlands and Irish invaders established a foothold in Argyll. Simultaneously, Christianity began to spread northwards from the Romanised tribes of southern Scotland, aided by the arrival of St Ninian in 396 and more Irish missionaries in the mid-6th century. At var-ious times, the Picts fell under the influence of the Irish, the British and the Angles, before unifying under the northern king Bridei mac Máelchú in the late 7th century.

The 7th century was a golden period for Pictish culture and most of the carved Pic-tish stones found in northern Scotland were made at this time. However, Pictish unity only served to postpone the inevitable. The Picts held out against the Irish and the An-gles until the end of the 8th century, but in 793 Viking marauders from Scandinavia began to raid the north and west coasts and they were truly hemmed in from all sides.

In the following decades, the northern Picts were decimated and Caithness, the Western Isles, Orkney and Shetland were all absorbed into the Viking empire. The southern Picts retreated to Fife, before slowly being assimilated into the Irish kingdom of Dàl Riata. Pictish kings were granted limited autonomy as *mormaer* or earls by the Irish, but their language and religion was entirely suppressed. By the 9th century, Gaelic was the dominant language of the Highlands and the Celtic cross had replaced pagan symbols on all Pictish stones.

The Kingdom of Dàl Riata

Raiding parties from the Dàl Riata tribe in northern Ireland first crossed the North Channel in the early 6th century, establishing a power-base on the Mull of Kintyre under King Fergus Mór. Although part of the Celtic family of tribes, the Dàl Riata spoke Gaelic rather than Pictish and were aggressive missionaries for Christianity. It was these Irish Celts, known to the Romans as *Scotti*, who gave a Gaelic identity and a name to the people of Scotland.

The missionary movement really took off after 563, when the Irish missionary St Columba went into exile on the island of Iona, off the Isle of Mull, after waging a bloody war against the king of Ireland. Although an accomplished scholar, Columba was a firm believer in the proselytising power of the sword, ensuring that the conversion of Scotland proceeded with blood-thirsty zeal.

After centuries of tribal war between the Scotti and the Picts, it was the Norsemen who finally tipped the balance in favour of the Gaels. The destruction of the northern Picts created a power-vacuum, which the kings of Dàl Riata quickly exploited. Given the choice between joining the Scotti or dying at the hands of the Norsemen, many Pictish tribes capitulated to the Irish kings.

In 843 the Dàl Riata king Kenneth MacAlpin (Cináed mac Ailpín), who was the son of a Pictish princess, used the Pictish custom of matrilineal succession to formally take over the Pictish throne, uniting Scotland north of the Firth of Forth into a single kingdom. He made Scone (near Perth) his capital, and brought to it the sacred Stone of Destiny used in the coronation of Scottish kings. He also brought relics of St Columba to the monastery at Dunkeld, symbolising the importance of the Celtic Church. Thereafter the Scotti, and therefore Gaelic and Christianity, gained complete cultural and political ascendancy.

The Vikings

The first Viking longboats were seen off the shores of Orkney in the 780s and must have inspired horror in those who saw them. The marauders struck without warning, ransacking entire villages, butchering the occupants and carting anything of value back to Norway. For the next 500 years, the Norsemen pillaged the Scottish coast and islands, eventually taking control of Orkney, Shetland, the Western Isles and large parts of northern and western Scotland. Norse raiders sacked the religious settlement at Iona three times between 795 and 806, causing the monks to flee to Ireland with St Columba's bones.

The Viking reputation for brutality was well deserved, but the raids were primarily fund-raising expeditions to pay for their war against the forces of the French king Charlemagne. In reality, the Vikings were probably no more blood-thirsty than the Romans, Picts or Celts, but they made the fatal public relations error of attacking the monasteries, which produced all the history books from the medieval period!

Eventually the Viking colonies were ceded back to Scotland, but they always remained a culture apart from the mainland Scots. Aside from the Western Isles, which were subsequently settled by Gaelic-speakers, the Viking colonies were taken over by nobles from the lowlands and ended up speaking a mixture of Scots, English and Norn (ancient Viking).

Orkney was the first territory to be lost, falling under the care of the Scottish crown in 1231 after the death of the last Norse earl, but the west coast quickly followed suit, passing to the Scottish king Alexander III after the Battle of Largs in 1263. Three years later the Western Isles were gifted to Scotland in the Treaty of Perth, in exchange for an annual rent to the king of Norway.

Shetland remained a Norwegian possession right up until 1469, when it was mortgaged to King James III of Scotland in lieu of a dowry for his bride, Margaret, the daughter of the king of Denmark.

The MacAlpin Dynasty

The dynasty founded by Kenneth MacAlpin cemented its control over the Highlands during the 10th century, but it wasn't until the reign of Malcolm II (1005–18) that the Scots extended their control to the south of the country, defeating the Northumbrian Angles and King Canute at the Battle of Carham (1018) near Roxburgh. For the first time, there was a single unified Scottish nation, known first as Alba, and later as Scotia, extending as far south as the River Tweed.

Although the Angles were defeated at Carham, it was ultimately Anglo-Norman culture that came to dominate Scotland. Malcolm II's great-grandson, Malcolm III Canmore (1058–93), took a Saxon queen, Margaret, the granddaughter of the English king Edmund Ironside, and introduced Anglo-Norman systems of government and religious foundations.

Prior to Malcolm III's reign, kings were chosen by a system known as *tanistry*, in which the monarch was selected from a pool of nobles whose grandfathers had been kings, but Malcolm III threw the system into disarray by killing his predecessor, Macbeth (yes, *that* Macbeth!) and installing his son as his heir. For his part, Macbeth had obtained the throne by murdering Malcolm III's father, Duncan I, who himself reached the throne because his grandfather, Malcolm II, had murdered his main tanist rival. Sound like a Shakespeare play? Welcome to medieval Scottish history...

Malcolm III's heirs ruled Scotland fairly ineffectually until 1124, when his youngest son David I (1124–53) came to power. David I had been raised in England and drove a wedge between lowland and Highland Scots by adopting the Norman feudal system, granting land to noble Norman families in return for military service. Before long, the lowland Scots had even adopted a different language, Scots – akin to English,

Feudalism & the Scottish Clans

The feudal system introduced by David I gifted large tracts of Scotland to Anglo-Norman nobles, but in the Highlands, people were governed by the older clan system (from the Gaelic *clann*), which was based on common ancestry rather than land ownership. The clan was led by a chieftain, who inherited his position through tanistry, followed by a hierarchy of related nobles.

Although the clans had an organised system of government, the noble families frequently took devious steps to ensure that their candidates reached the highest positions, murdering tanist rivals and betraying their kinsmen to rival clans. The clans were initially opposed to feudalism, but soon grafted feudal law onto the traditional concept of kinship, becoming powerful landowners who could draw on vast private armies of their kinsmen for clan battles. In the following centuries clan wars raged across the Highlands and islands, many provoked by the Scottish crown to undermine the power of the Highland nobles.

The clan system was primarily a Gaelic invention – the Iron-Age peoples of Scotland followed a system of matrilineal inheritance – but some clans can trace their roots right back to the kingdom of Dàl Riata, including clan Donald, the ruling clan of the western islands. Of the other clans, the MacNeills were of Irish descent, while the MacLeods had Viking roots and the Campbells were descended from ancient Britons. Many noble families were also descended from Pictish *mormaer* or earls, who were kept on in positions of power under the kings of Dàl Riata, including the Macbeths.

with French, Norse and Gaelic influences. By 1212 Walter of Coventry remarked that the Scottish court was 'French in race and manner of life, in speech and in culture'.

Wars of Independence

The Canmore dynasty produced a string of able rulers, including Alexander III (1249–86), who drove the Vikings from mainland

Scotland, but the Canmore line ended in 1286 when Alexander III died after falling into the Firth of Forth. He was succeeded by his four-year-old granddaughter, Margaret (the Maid of Norway), who was engaged to the son of King Edward I of England.

Following Margaret's death in Kirkwall (Orkney) in 1290, some 13 tanists competed for the throne, but in the end it came down to a choice of two: Robert de Brus, lord of Annandale, and John de Balliol, the Norman lord of Galloway. Edward I of England, as the greatest feudal lord in Britain, was asked to arbitrate – he selected Balliol, over whom he had greater leverage – but rather than going home after the coronation, Edward set himself up as puppet ruler of Scotland, treating the Scots king as little more than a vassal. The humiliated Balliol finally turned against Edward, and allied Scotland with the French in 1295, beginning the enduring 'Auld Alliance'.

The English were then at war with the French and this open act of defiance was more than Edward could bear. In 1296 he besieged the lowlands, incarcerating Balliol in the Tower of London, demanding oaths of allegiance from Scottish nobles and removing the Stone of Destiny, the coronation stone of the kings of Scotland, from Scone to London.

The lowland nobles were used to switching their allegiance and many grudgingly accepted English rule, but the Highlanders had only limited allegiance to the lowland nobles and none at all to the English crown. A series of warlords harried the English occupiers, most famously the revolutionary army of William Wallace, which unusually for the time, included both Highland and lowland Scots.

Many people have a slightly skewed view of Wallace from Mel Gibson's rousing but largely fictitious *Braveheart*. The real Wallace was neither a commoner or a Highlander, but the son of the laird of Elderslie in Ayrshire. The law that English knights were allowed to ravage Scottish maidens on their wedding nights and the relationship between Wallace and Princess Isabelle of France, bride of Edward II, were also Hollywood inventions – Isabelle was only six years old at the time!

The legendry Scottish (and Hollywood) hero, William Wallace

When John de Balliol was imprisoned by Edward I, Wallace allied himself with Andrew de Moray, a highland laird from near Inverness, defeating the English roundly at the Battle of Stirling Bridge (1297). After the victory, Wallace was declared guardian of the realm but was defeated by the English at Falkirk in 1298. Wallace evaded Edward's troops for many years, but was betrayed by Sir John de Mentieth and taken to London where he was tried for treason, which he denied to the end – after all, he had never claimed allegiance to the English king!

Inspired by the example of men such as Wallace, the nobles slowly allied themselves behind Robert the Bruce, grandson of the same lord of Annandale who was rejected by Edward in 1292. Honouring an age-old tradition, Bruce murdered his rival, John Comyn, in February 1306 and had himself crowned king of Scotland at Scone the following month.

Bruce mounted a huge campaign to drive the English out of Scotland but suffered repeated defeats and was forced to go into hiding. Legend has it that while hiding from the English in a cave he witnessed a spider making repeated efforts to spin a web and was thus inspired to regroup his forces, going on to thoroughly rout the English forces of Edward II at the Battle of

Bannockburn in 1314. Continued raids on northern England forced Edward II to sue for peace, and, in 1328, the Treaty of Northampton gave Scotland its independence, with Robert I, the Bruce, as its king.

The Stewart Dynasty

Things were relatively stable until Robert I died in 1329, when Scotland returned to internal squabbling and ongoing border wars with England. Robert was succeeded by his five-year-old son, David II (1329–71), who had no heirs and passed the throne to his nephew, Robert II (1371–90), the child of his sister Marjory and her husband Walter the Steward. Thus was born the Stewart (from Steward) dynasty, which would rule Scotland and Britain for the next 300 years.

All this had little effect on the people of the Highlands and islands, who had long been marginalised by the ruling nobles. As the lowland families squabbled for power under a succession of weak Stewart kings, the clans cemented their power in the Highlands, most significantly the Donalds of the Hebrides, who came to wield almost regal power as lords of the Isles.

In 1493, James IV (1488–1513), the strongest of the Stewart monarchs, enforced his authority over the Highland clans, reclaiming the title of lord of the Isles. Protestantism was seen in Scotland for the first time, a reaction to the corrupt medieval Roman Catholic Church, and many of Scotland's universities were founded – all of course in the lowlands – establishing Scotland as a European centre of learning.

Although he restored the power of the Scottish crown, James IV became a pawn in the bigger game between France and England, marrying the daughter of Henry VII of England and then declaring war on the English at the suggestion of his French allies. James IV's reign came to a tragic end at the Battle of Flodden Field in 1513, in which 10,000 of his subjects also lost their lives.

Mary Queen of Scots & the Reformation

The next Scottish monarch, James V (1512–42), imprisoned and exiled many of the rebellious Highland chieftains, passing their lands to loyal clans such as the MacKenzies of Kintail, and also tried to wage war on the English, but died with no male heirs in 1542, following his defeat at Solway Moss. However, his French wife, Mary of Guise, bore him a daughter, Mary, just days before he died, and for the second time in its history, the throne of Scotland passed to a female monarch, Mary I (1542–67).

Mary was sent immediately to France and the country was ruled by regents, providing the nobles with yet another chance to cement their power bases across Scotland. Henry VIII of England urged the Scots to wed the infant queen to his son, Edward VI, but when his overtures were turned down, Henry tried more persuasive tactics, attacking Edinburgh and several abbeys in the Scottish borders. The Rough Wooing, as it was called, failed dismally; Mary married the French dauphin in 1558, becoming queen of France as well as Scotland.

Although Mary was Catholic, she was forced to bend to the will of John Knox, a pupil of the Swiss reformer Calvin, who turned lowland Scotland against the corrupt Catholic Church. In 1560 the Scottish parliament created a Protestant Church that was independent of Rome and the monarchy, abolishing Latin Mass and denying the pope's authority. This didn't sit well with the impoverished but staunchly Catholic Highlanders, who existed in a state of virtual warfare with the lowlands throughout the medieval period. The image of Highlanders as lawless cattle-rustlers persisted in the lowlands right up to the 18th century.

Mary's curious reign came to an end in 1567, following a scarcely believable train of events in which Mary's second husband Henry Stewart (Lord Darnley) was involved in the murder of her Italian secretary Rizzio (rumoured to be her lover) and was then himself murdered, probably by Mary's new lover and third husband-to-be, the earl of Bothwell, aided by the shady Gilbert Balfour of Orkney. After a rebellion by the nobles, Mary abdicated the throne in favour of her infant son, James VI (1567–1625) and threw herself at the mercy of Queen Elizabeth I of

England, who didn't show her any. Mary was imprisoned in the Tower of London and was beheaded in 1587 after being implicated in a plot to kill Elizabeth.

Although things didn't work out well for Mary, her son James VI took the Scottish throne and eventually inherited the English throne too when Queen Elizabeth I of England died childless in 1603 in the so-called Union of the Crowns, becoming James I of Great Britain (usually written as James VI/I).

The first king of Great Britain quickly moved his court to London, setting a tradition that continued, with only a few deviations, until Scottish devolution in 1997.

Covenanters & Civil War

During the 17th century, the Catholic ruler Charles I (1625–49) tried to impose episcopacy (the rule of bishops) and an English liturgy on the Scottish Presbyterian Church, triggering widespread unrest. In 1638, hundreds signed a National Covenant affirming their right to follow the Presbyterian faith. The same rights, however, did not extend to Catholics in the region, who were forcibly converted throughout the 17th century.

By the 1640s, Scotland had become divided between the Covenanters and those who supported the king, most notably the marquis of Montrose, a staunch Calvanist who nonetheless accumulated a fearsome army of Highlanders in defence of Charles I. Montrose was eventually defeated in 1650 at Carbisdale and betrayed to his enemies by the MacLeods of Assynt. In desperation, Charles I convened the English parliament, hoping to raise money for an army, but they refused to raise taxes, and in response Charles declared war on parliament, triggering the English Civil War.

Led by the charismatic but brutal Oliver Cromwell, the English Parliamentarians staged a dramatic coup d'etat, seizing control of the country and executing Charles I in 1649. Although the Scots opposed Charles' religious beliefs and autocratic rule, they were appalled by his execution and offered his son Charles II the Scottish crown as long as he signed the Covenant. Charles II (1649–85) was crowned at Scone

on 1 January 1651, but was quickly deposed by Cromwell, who pressed far into the Highlands and islands from his fortress at Inverness to track down Royalist sympathisers.

Cromwell died in 1658 and Charles II was restored to the throne two years later, immediately betraying his supporters by reneging on the Covenant. The episcopacy was reinstated and hardline Presbyterian ministers were replaced. Many clergymen rejected the bishops' authority and started holding outdoor services, or conventicles, until Charles' brother and successor, James VII/II (1685–9) made worshipping as a Covenanter a capital offence.

Union with England in 1707

The Protestant English rebelled against James VII/II in 1689, driving him into exile and replacing him with his Protestant daughter and her Dutch husband, William of Orange. Effectively king in his own right, William restored the Presbyterian structure in Scotland and took steps to suppress the Highland clans, conniving in the Glen Coe Massacre, in which 38 MacDonald Royalists were killed (see the boxed text in The Great Glen & the Western Highlands chapter). During the 1690s, Scotland was ravaged by famine, and cattle raids on lowland farms by desperate Highlanders became widespread, increasing the anti-Highland feeling among lowlanders. Almost a third of the population died in some Highland areas.

Feelings against the English also ran high – exacerbated by widespread bankruptcy in Scotland following a failed English investment scheme in Panama – but the powerful merchants of the lowlands soon realised that the only way to gain access to the lucrative markets of the developing colonies was through union with England. Despite popular opposition, the Act of Union – which brought England and Scotland under one parliament, one sovereign and one flag, but preserved the independence of the Scottish Church and legal system – took effect on 1 May 1707.

The Jacobites

From its inception, the union was resented by many Scots, particularly in the Highlands.

In the 18th century, a group called the Jacobites, supporters of James VII/II (the title comes from Jacob, the Latin form of James), sought to displace the Hanoverian monarchy (chosen by the English parliament in 1701 to succeed the House of Orange) and restore a Catholic Stuart king to the British throne. Jacobitism was mainly a Highland movement; it drew little support from the staunchly Presbyterian lowlands.

James Edward Stuart, known as the Old Pretender, was the son of James VII/II, and staged a failed attempt on Scotland in 1708 and another in 1715, with the aid of John Erskine of Mar, who seized Perth with an army of Highland volunteers. The rebellion was suppressed with the aid of Dutch troops and fizzled out after the inconclusive Battle of Sheriffmuir. Another Scottish folk hero from this time was Rob Roy, a MacGregor chief and sometime cattle-rustler who waged a campaign against the oppressive duke of Montrose in 1711.

In 1745 the Old Pretender's son, Charles Edward Stuart (better known as Bonnie Prince Charlie), landed in Scotland to claim the crown for his father. Supported by an army of Highlanders, he marched southwards and captured Edinburgh (except for the castle) in September 1745. He got as far south as Derby in England, but success was short-lived; a Hanoverian army led by the duke of Cumberland – later immortalised as 'Butcher' Cumberland – harried him all the way back to the Highlands, where Jacobite dreams were finally extinguished at the Battle of Culloden in 1746. Many injured Highlanders were executed by Cumberland following the battle. Charles fled to France via Skye, aided by Flora MacDonald, and later died in exile.

After 'the '45' (as it became known), the government sought to suppress the Highland clans, banning the keeping of private armies, Highland dress and the playing of the pipes. Many Jacobites were transported or executed, or died in prison, while others forfeited their lands or willingly emigrated to the developing colonies in North America. General Wade, and his successor General Roy, drove new military roads through the glens, and garrisons were established at Fort William, Fort Augustus and Fort George (near Inverness). The first Highland Regiments were created in the British Army, fighting alongside their former enemies in the war against Napoleon.

As a side effect, the new roads increased trade between the Highlands and the lowlands, reducing the traditional suspicion of Highlanders in the lowlands and exposing the Highland clan leaders for the first time to the wealth of the lowlands.

The Highland Clearances

The banning of Highland armies following the Jacobite rebellions led to a fundamental shift in the way that the Highland landowners viewed their estates. Clan leaders no longer needed the *cottars* (landless peasants) for private armies and the vast tenantry ceased to be an asset and became a worrying financial burden. Simultaneously, the tenant population went through a dramatic growth spurt with the introduction of the potato, almost doubling the number of dependents who relied on the clan leaders for support.

Unable or unwilling to foot the bill for the tenantry that had served them so well in the clan wars, many landowners encouraged migration to the colonies, shipping thousands to Canada, Australia and New Zealand. Others put the tenants to work fishing for herring or harvesting kelp for the chemical industry, providing an income that the workers could use to pay their ever-increasing rents. With the end of the Anglo-French war, the market for kelp dried up and landowners turned to large-scale sheep farming as a way to keep their lands profitable. Traditional black cattle of the Highlands were replaced with hardy Cheviot sheep, and many landowners began to evict the tenant farmers to smallholdings (crofts) on the coast to open up the land for massive sheep flocks.

So began the Highland Clearances, one of the most shameful episodes in Scottish history. At various times historians have laid the blame on the English, for suppressing the clan system, and on the mercenary lowland nobles who took over lands in the Highlands on the orders of the Scottish crown to break the power of the Highland clans. However, many ancestral clan leaders showed no more loyalty to their vassals than the southern landlords.

Some of the most brutal clearances were carried out on the Isle of Skye by the Mac-Donalds and MacLeods, who had been clan leaders of Skye ever since the days of Malcolm Canmore.

It is a testament to the callousness of the landlords that few bothered to keep records of the number of people they evicted from their land, but modern historians estimate that between 50,000 and 100,000 people were cleared from the Highlands and islands during the 19th century. A few cottars stayed to work the sheep farms, but most were relocated to desperate crofts on poor coastal land or fled to the cities in search of work. And many more emigrated – some willingly, some under duress – to the developing colonies. All over the region today, only a ruckle of stones among the bracken remains where once there were whole villages. The Mull of Oa on Islay, for example, once supported a population of 4000 – today there are barely 40 people.

Lowland Scotland saw a huge upsurge in its fortunes in the 18th and 19th centuries with the arrival of the Industrial Revolution, but this radical force for change had little influence on the Highlands and islands. Instead, many lowland Scots who made their fortunes from the new industries bought up vast estates in the Highlands, engaging in either brutal clearances or well-intentioned but ineffectual projects of social reform. The Potato Famine of the 1840s led to further mass evictions, though some landlords created so-called 'destitution' projects to provide work and food for their tenants.

As crofters were relocated to poorer land, rents soared. Some crofters rebelled against the evictions, most notably in Skye, Sutherland and Lewis, leading to the formation of the Crofters' Party and Highland Land League, who encouraged more acts of resistance throughout the region. The crofters' cause struck a chord in Edinburgh and London, and a number of judicial enquiries were held, but while most of the tenants who were

arrested for resisting eviction were freed, the judiciary found nothing illegal in the clearances themselves.

Eventually the ardent clamour for change reached the ears of the Liberal government of William Gladstone in London, which grudgingly appointed the Napier Commission to overhaul agrarian management in Scotland. In 1886, the government passed the Crofters' Holdings Act, guaranteeing fair rents, security of tenure and rights of inheritance for crofters, followed by the Land Settlement Act in 1919, which allowed for the creation of new and larger crofts.

Tourism & Politics

A romantic vision of Highland life had become prevalent in the lowlands during the 18th century, aided by the famous travelogue of Dr Johnson and James Boswell, who toured Skye in 1773, and the fraud of James MacPherson, who concocted an epic poem about the Celtic king Fingal, and attributed it to the ancient Gaelic bard Ossian. Highland chic really took off in the 19th century, encouraged by the writings of Sir Walter Scott, an ardent nationalist who wrote a series of incredibly popular novels set in the Highlands, including *Ivanhoe* and *The Pirate*. In 1822, Scott persuaded King George IV to make a state visit to Edinburgh, where he was greeted by Highlanders in traditional plaids (the traditional tartan costume of the Highlands) and quite a few non-traditional tartans, passed off as traditional colours. George even wore a kilt for the occasion, triggering Highland-mania amongst the English fashionable classes.

His successor Queen Victoria fell totally in love with the Highlands, buying a huge estate at Balmoral and sneaking around the Highlands incognito in the company of her Scottish ghillie, John Brown. With the spread of the railways, Scotland rapidly became a popular tourist destination and Highland lairds transformed their lands into sporting-estates where wealthy southerners could fish for salmon, shoot grouse, stalk red deer and indulge their Highland fantasies. Strathpeffer, near Inverness, became a fashionable spa town, known as 'Harrogate of the North', and the same period saw the creation of the Scottish Mountaineering Club and the beginnings of Munro bagging in the Highlands.

Elsewhere, the new urban society saw a growing bourgeoisie take precedence in politics over the still powerful landed aristocracy, and political life became more closely integrated with England. There was much constitutional and parliamentary reform during the Victorian era, including changes within the Church and improvements to the education system, setting the foundations for many of the remarkable scientific achievements by Scots in the 19th and 20th centuries.

The 20th Century

Many Highlanders were called upon to fight in the Boer War, WWI and WWII, with huge casualties that were felt keenly by small Highland communities. At the end of WWI, the German fleet was impounded in Scapa Flow in Orkney, where it was scuppered by the German admiral to prevent it falling into British hands. The lowlands escaped the German bombing that ravaged England, and industry profited from the demand for weapons and ships for the war effort. However, the Highlands and islands were crippled by the collapse of the Eastern European market for herring and the decline in demand for fish and farm produce during the Great Depression of the 1930s. The region saw a further wave of depopulation as more Highlanders went into self-imposed exile in the New World.

In the postwar years, the Forestry Commission brought much-needed income to the Highlands, as did the development of hydroelectric schemes in many of the glens. The worldwide growth in tourism led to an influx of Americans and Canadians of Scottish descent visiting the Highlands and islands in search of their cultural roots. The English continued to have a huge presence, of course, buying up many sporting-estates and Highland homes in their quest for the Scottish idyll. Although the welcome they received was often less than enthusiastic – the immigrants are still referred to as 'white-settlers' by many locals – the movement went into overdrive during the 1980s' Thatcherite economic boom in England. Locals were understandably resentful that the same economic policies that were crippling Scotland were allowing wealthy southerners to buy Scottish houses at rock-bottom prices.

The discovery of oil and gas in the North Sea in the 1970s brought new prosperity to Aberdeen and the surrounding area, and to Shetland, but much of the oil revenue was siphoned off to England. This, along with takeovers of Scots companies by English ones (which then closed the Scots operations, asset-stripped and transferred jobs to England), fuelled increasing nationalist sentiment in Scotland. The Scottish Nationalist Party (SNP) developed into a third force in Scottish politics, taking 30% of the popular vote in the 1974 General Election.

The first serious attempt to address the so-called 'Highland Problem' – characterised by low incomes, high unemployment and out-migration – was the creation of the Highlands and Islands Development Board in 1972, which built schools, fishing ports and community centres across the region. More funding arrived from Europe in the form of grants for community projects such as the advancement of Gaelic education. The fishing industry moved onto new catches, including cod and mackerel, but lost its competitive edge when Britain joined the European Union (EU), crippled by new fishing quotas and by over-fishing.

Today the fishing industry survives on a smaller scale, fishing for exclusive catches for the restaurant market. See Ecology & Environment later in the chapter for more details.

Self-Rule

The growing support for the SNP during the 1970s led both Labour and Conservative governments to toy with the idea of offering Scotland devolution, or at least some degree of self-government, and in 1979 a referendum was held on whether to set up a directly elected Scottish Assembly. Fifty-two per cent of those who voted said 'yes' to devolution but the Labour prime minister, James Callaghan, decided that everyone who didn't vote should be counted as a 'no'. By this reasoning, only 33% of the electorate voted 'yes', so the Scottish Assembly was rejected.

From 1979 to 1997, Scotland was ruled by a Conservative government in London, even though the majority of Scots had voted for Labour. For a while, the Scottish cause found a champion in Labour leader John Smith, a native of Dalmally, who was widely tipped to be the next prime minister, but he died unexpectedly in 1994 and was replaced by Tony Blair. Following the landslide victory of Tony Blair's Labour Party in May 1997, another referendum was held on the creation of a Scottish parliament. This time the result was overwhelmingly and unambiguously in favour.

Elections to the new parliament took place on 6 May 1999, and the Scottish parliament convened for the first time on 12 May in the Assembly Rooms of the Church of Scotland at the eastern end of the Royal Mile in Edinburgh; Sir Donald Dewar (1937–2000), formerly the Secretary of State for Scotland, was nominated as first minister (the Scottish parliament's equivalent of prime minister). The parliament was officially opened by Queen Elizabeth II on 1 July 1999. One of its first actions was to dissolve the feudal system of land tenure in 2000.

Following his untimely death in October that year, Donald Dewar was replaced by the Labour minister Henry McLeish, a career politician who slowly advanced the Scottish cause in Westminster and redistributed much needed funding from Westminster and Edinburgh to the Highlands and islands. McLeish failed to declare the income he received from subletting his constituency offices in Edinburgh, and was subsequently shot down in a hail of tabloid newspaper speculation, resigning in November 2001.

Scottish education minister Jack McConnell was elected to replace Henry McLeish and became Scotland's third First Minister on 26 November 2001, despite media revelations that he had previously used his parliamentary position to secure employment for his mistress.

Pending further developments, the Scottish parliament is set to move into new purpose-built premises in Holyrood in Edinburgh in spring 2003. Amongst other legislation are further changes to land-tenure laws, to alter the balance of land-ownership from private land-owners to community cooperatives. With Labour weakened by the revelations about two successive first ministers, the SNP have high hopes for the general election in 2005, when Scottish independence may become a very real possibility.

GEOGRAPHY & GEOLOGY

The mountainous Highlands and islands cover some 15,077 sq miles to the north of the Highland Boundary Fault, a geological divide which separates the rugged topography of the Highlands from the gentle lowland plains to the south and east. The north of Scotland was once separate from the rest of the British Isles, forming part of a supercontinent with Greenland, the USA and Canada, but as the Atlantic Ocean opened up, between 520 and 400 million years ago, Scotland and England collided, forcing up the land which later gave rise to the Grampian Mountains.

This was a time of great tectonic upheaval and much of the bedrock in the central Highlands is formed from volcanic basalt, which cooled to form blunt massifs and curious hexagonal columnar dolerite formations. In the northern Highlands and the islands, the faulted granite gives way to bedded sandstone and limestone, which was easily split into flagstones and building blocks by Scotland's prehistoric inhabitants. The buckling of the earth's crust along the Highland Boundary Fault forced many areas of the seabed above the water, creating many of the Scottish islands. The distinctive Highland glens (from the Gaelic *gleann* meaning valley) were gouged out by the action of glaciers during the last Ice Age.

The central and northwestern Highlands are mainly mountainous, with scoured glacial valleys and distinctive sandstone peaks, but the landscape becomes much flatter and greener towards the northeastern tip of the mainland. Offshore, Orkney is mainly lowlying and green, formed from the buckled bedrock of an ancient fossil seabed, while the Western Isles are a mixture of semi-submerged bog and moderate hills, edged by broad sands accumulated by longshore drift. Shetland is covered in peatland and has a somewhat Nordic landscape of glacial glens and sea lochs.

The region's most notable geological features are its Munros (see the boxed text 'Hill Terminology' in the Activities chapter). The region boasts some 284 Munros – including Britain's highest mountain, Ben Nevis, at 1343m – and climbing all 284 has become something of a hill-walkers' grail.

The region also has thousands of lochs and lochans, freshwater lakes created by the scouring action of the glacial ice sheets. Some, such as Loch Ness, hide a network of subterranean caverns, believed by many to be the hiding place of mythological beasties such as the Loch Ness Monster. The string of lochs in the Great Glen is strung together by the Caledonian Canal (see the boxed text 'Canal Plus' in The Great Glen & the Western Highlands chapter), built in 1882.

Although the Highlands comprise about two-thirds of the total area of Scotland, they are only home to around 4% of the country's population. This is only partly down to the inhospitable environment – a more crucial factor was the Highland Clearances (see the boxed text in The Northwest Highlands chapter). Today only 130 of Scotland's 790 islands are inhabited and more and more are being abandoned as young Scots move away to the mainland in search of employment.

The islands are broadly split into three groups: the Hebrides, Orkney and Shetland. The Hebrides comprise the Inner Hebrides, including the islands of Mull, Coll, Tiree, Colonsay, Iona, Islay and Jura, and the Outer Hebrides or Western Isles, which include Barra, Benbecula, North and South Uist, Berneray, Harris and Lewis. The other island groups lie due north of the Scottish mainland. Both the Orkney and Shetland groups consist of a large central island (known in both cases as 'Mainland') and a number of outlying islands, some far out to sea. The tip of Unst in Shetland is the northernmost point in the British Isles.

Inverness is the 'capital' of the Highlands and is far and away its largest settlement. The island groups each have their own regional capitals – Stornoway on Lewis is the principal city in the Western Isles, Kirkwall is the capital of Orkney and Lerwick is the main settlement in Shetland.

CLIMATE

Scottish weather is notoriously changeable, and the Highlands and islands can switch from brilliant sunshine to driving rain in an instant. 'Sunny spells' is an optimistic weatherman's phrase often used to describe this quirk of the Scottish weather, and translates in real terms to 'mostly rainy'.

In general, the Scottish climate is cooler and more temperate than in mainland Britain and the high ground of the Highlands ensures that the region gets more than its fair share of rainfall – ranging from 700mm to 3000mm per annum. The west coast is generally wetter than the east (rainfall averages around 650mm) and May, June and September are the driest months, though rain can fall at any time. In the height of summer, the weather can be delightfully warm and dry – at least as good as that on the English mainland – and the magnificent Scottish beaches on the north coast and the islands really come into their own.

The storm season runs from August to April and during this period vicious Atlantic storms can strike the coast at any time, often accompanied by strong winds. Public transport is frequently disrupted as aircraft are grounded, bridges are closed to traffic and ferries are stuck in port.

At any time of year, you should be prepared for rapid changes in the weather. It's a good policy to carry a lightweight raincoat whenever walking, even if you set out under clear skies. There are also wide variations over small distances; while one glen broods under cloud, the next may be basking in sunshine. Many visitors try and chase the patches of sun across the Highlands, but you're probably better off waiting for the bad weather to pass overhead; as the locals say, 'If you don't like the weather, just wait for five minutes'.

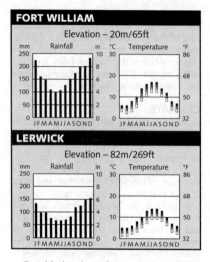

FORT WILLIAM

Elevation – 20m/65ft

LERWICK

Elevation – 82m/269ft

Considering how far north the country lies (Inverness is on the same latitude as Churchill in northern Canada), you might expect a colder climate, but the Gulf Stream keeps the temperature above freezing for most of the year. The east coast is often warmer in summer and colder in winter than the west coast. Temperatures rarely drop below 0°C on the coast, although winds off the North Sea can shake the fillings from your teeth. The west coast is milder and wetter, with over 1500mm of rain and average summer highs of 19°C. The western Highlands around Fort William are the wettest place in Britain, with annual rainfall as high as 3000mm.

ECOLOGY & ENVIRONMENT

When environmentalists talk about preserving Scotland's natural heritage, the environment they refer to is almost entirely man-made. Scotland was once covered in mainly deciduous forest, including trees such as birch, ash, oak and hazel, joined by Caledonian pine when the climate warmed about 4000 years ago. As successive cultures spread into the Highlands and islands from mainland Europe, they cleared the land for farming, ship-building and firewood, removing a staggering 99% of the natural tree cover. The exception to this is the windswept islands to the north and west, which were only ever able to support limited tree cover, though names such as the Forest of Harris indicate that coverage was once more extensive than it is today. The low scrubby heathland that covers most of the Highlands and islands is maintained by the managed grazing of sheep, cattle, deer and game birds.

Artificial or not, the heathland scenery has become synonymous with the Scottish Highlands, and has an untamed, wild beauty. Many native species, such as deer, grouse and eagles, are dependent on this low-lying vegetation for their survival, and over the centuries decaying heather and grasses have been compacted into peat, an important fuel source in the Highlands and islands. The most important region of peat bogland is the Flow Country in the far north of Sutherland and Caithness, which has been proposed for World Heritage status.

During the 1980s, under the tutelage of the Thatcher government in Westminster, attempts were made to reforest the peatlands and other areas with vast plantations of fast-growing conifers such as sitka spruce and lodgepole pine, but this recipe for quick cash had unforeseen – or ignored – environmental consequences. As well as destroying wildlife habitat, the conifers increased the local soil acidity, killing native plant species in the surrounding bogland. There is also evidence that these plantations are altering local weather patterns, producing negative conditions for native plants and animals.

Another infamous environmental blunder was the eradication of wolves in the 18th century. With their only natural predator out of the picture, the population of red deer exploded and many areas were grazed to the ground. The authorities imposed an annual cull of deer but this has proved to be a mixed blessing; the cull draws a huge crowd of stalkers (deer-hunters) every year, providing a much-needed boost to the Highland economy, but many other visitors are appalled by the slaughter. The Carnivore Trust has campaigned for the reintroduction of wolves as a natural control on deer numbers since 1977, but the proposal has faced widespread opposition from landowners who profit heavily from the cull.

Around 70% of the British fishing fleet operates out of Scotland, and since the collapse of the herring during the wars fishermen have moved from one species to another, trying to stay one step ahead of the fishing quota system (see Endangered Species later in this section).

In the 1980s, salmon farming seemed like the perfect answer to falling wild salmon stocks and growing unemployment in the fishing industry. Tax breaks were provided to landowners who made sea lochs on their land available for salmon and trout farms and for a while everyone was happy, until environmentalists discovered that excess food and pesticides from salmon cages were polluting the sea lochs and causing toxic algal booms.

Since then, the industry, which is worth more than £300 million a year to the Scottish economy, has been blamed for an epidemic of disease and parasite infestations among wild salmon, catches of which have dropped by 84% since 1986. The government has been slow to enforce environmental restrictions on what is still regarded as its biggest success story in the Highlands. Despite being protected by law, grey seals are another victim of salmon farming, being routinely shot by fish-farmers.

So-called 'superquarries' are another controversial development of recent decades. Plans for a vast, £70 million quarry on the island of Harris in the Outer Hebrides were finally blocked by the Scottish Executive in 2000, after a 10-year legal battle. A superquarry already scars the northwestern shore of Loch Linnhe at Glensanda, opposite the Isle of Lismore.

In Caithness, the Dounreay nuclear-waste reprocessing plant had a poor safety record over several decades. Following a series of accidents and disclosures about errors and cover-ups – among other revelations was the mysterious disappearance of around 170kg of weapons-grade uranium – the British government decided to close it down in 1998. However, reprocessing will continue

until about 2006 when the waste runs out; after that it'll take until 2095 to dismantle the plant safely, clean up the site and encase the remains in concrete.

The remote islands of St Kilda, 60 miles west of the Western Isles, set in a pristine ocean wilderness that supports 21 species of whale and dolphin, became Scotland's first World Heritage Site in 1986. Greenpeace claims the site is threatened by oil exploration and applied to put it on a Unesco list of sites in danger; the application was turned down in 1999.

Shetland appears to have pretty much recovered from the sinking of the oil tanker *Braer* in 1993; the coastline was spared serious damage because storms churned the spilled oil into a relatively harmless residue. Marine biologists are still monitoring what long-term effects the pollution has had on marine life. Numerous oil tankers ply the waters around Shetland and the Western Isles, and the area is notorious for shipwrecks, so the threat of a similar accident remains very real.

Five Scottish beaches have been awarded the coveted European Blue Flag award for water quality and environmental management, but only Nairn (near Inverness) is in the Highlands. The pristine beaches of the Western Isles are rarely considered for awards but are far cleaner than many Blue Flag beaches in Europe. The Highlands of Scotland Tourist Board publishes an annual ranking of beaches in the region.

The organisations listed below are concerned with the environment:

Friends of the Earth Scotland (FoE Scotland; ☎ 0131-554 9977, **W** www.foe-scotland.org.uk) 72 Newhaven Rd, Edinburgh EH6 5QG. This voluntary organisation campaigns on environmental issues and publishes an annual beach guide *Sand, Sea and Sewage* rating the cleanliness of Scotland's beaches.

John Muir Trust (JMT; ☎ 0131-554 0114, **W** www.jmt.org) 41 Commercial St, Leith, Edinburgh EH6 7EQ. This charity believes that the only way to protect and preserve public access to the wild areas of Scotland is to own them. It has purchased several properties, including Ben Nevis, and manages them in partnership with local communities.

National Trust for Scotland (NTS; ☎ 0131-243 9300, W www.nts.org.uk) Wemyss House, 28 Charlotte Square, Edinburgh EH2 4ET. This voluntary conservation body cares for around 187,175 acres of countryside (as well as owning historic buildings) and has reciprocal membership agreements with the National Trust for England, Wales and Northern Ireland.

Royal Society for the Protection of Birds (RSPB; ☎ 0131-311 6500, W www.rspb.org) Dunedin House, 25 Ravelston Terrace, Edinburgh EH4 3TP. The RSPB manages a number of nature reserves around Scotland that are open to the public.

Scottish Environment Protection Agency (SEPA; ☎ 01786-457700, W www.sepa.org.uk) Erskine Court, Castle Business Park, Stirling FK9 4TR. The SEPA is a public body responsible for environmental protection. It has an emergency hotline (☎ 0800 807060) for reporting pollution incidents.

Scottish Natural Heritage (SNH; ☎ 0131-447 4784, W www.snh.org.uk) 12 Hope Terrace, Edinburgh EH9 2AS. This government agency is responsible for the conservation of Scotland's wildlife, habitats and landscapes. It designates and manages National Nature Reserves (NNRs) and Sites of Special Scientific Interest (SSSIs), and will be responsible for the development of national parks in Scotland.

Scottish Wildlife Trust (SWT; ☎ 0131-312 7765, W www.swt.org.uk) Cramond House, 16 Cramond Glebe Rd, Edinburgh EH4 6NS. This voluntary agency owns or manages over 120 nature reserves.

The Woodland Trust Scotland (☎ 01476-581135, W www.woodland-trust.org.uk) Glenruthven Mill, Abbey Rd, Auchterarder, Perthshire PH3 1DP. This is the Scottish arm of a UK charity dedicated to conservating native woodlands.

FLORA

Although much of Scotland was originally covered by the Caledonian forest, deforestation has reduced this once-mighty forest to a few small pockets of indigenous trees; barely 1% remains. Almost three-quarters of the country is uncultivated bog, rock and heather. In mountainous areas, such as the Cairngorms, alpine plants thrive, while in the far north there are rare lichens and mosses. Acidic peat covers around two-million acres, most notably in Shetland and the Flow Country of Caithness and Sutherland, covering 1500 sq miles.

Although the thistle is commonly associated with Scotland, the flower was actually introduced by the Romans. Scotland's national flower is the Scottish bluebell (known in England as the harebell), which carpets the floor of native woodlands in spring.

Highland Plants

The exposed heathland is typically covered in heather, which produces tiny pink and purple flowers in August, and the damp conditions are ideal for insectivorous plants such as sundew and butterwort and bright-yellow bog asphodel. Other conspicuous flowering plants include vivid pink rhododendrons and bright yellow gorse (or whin), which both flower in May.

A few areas still contain wild woodland, including parts of the ancestral Caledonian forest, characterised by Scots pine, oak, silver birch, willow, alder and rowan; the best examples are at Abernethy, Rothiemurchus, Glen Affric and Strathfarrar. The forest floor is home to creeping lady's-tresses, orchids, bluebells and wintergreen, with it's pearl-like flowers. At higher altitudes, Alpine plants dominate, including prostrate juniper, dwarf willow, purple saxifrage and alpine clubmosses.

The unique geology of Shetland has produced unique areas such as the Keen of Hamar on Unst, home to rare species such as frog orchids, mountain everlasting and Edmonston's chickweed, found nowhere else in the world.

Coastal Plants

Much of the coast of the Highlands and islands is covered in machair, a fertile soil produced by the accumulation of lime-rich shell sand, which provides ideal conditions for wildflowers such as corn marigolds, red campion, primrose, dog-violet, thrift (which produces a carpet of pink flowers in summer), squill, meadow buttercups, gentian, wild thyme and heath-spotted orchids. The colours begin in spring and change from white and yellow to red and blue in the autumn. You may also spot the grey oysterplant, common on the Scandinavian fringe.

FAUNA

Although many native animals have become extinct in the region, the small human population and wilderness environment has preserved species which have long since vanished south of the border.

Mammals

The native mammal you're most likely to see in the Highlands and islands is the red deer, which is found in most wilderness areas. The population is controlled by an annual cull, but the hunting estates generally discourage trophy collecting and select the weakest animals of both genders for their deer-stalking clients. There is a small herd of introduced domestic reindeer living in a semiwild state in the Cairngorms, but the native reindeer, the elk, lynx, wild horse, brown bear, beaver wild boar and auroch (wild ox) are all long extinct. The last wolf was shot in Sutherland in 1745.

Scotland has a number of threatened native predators, the best known being the Scottish wildcat, though these elusive creatures are rarely seen. Similarly elusive are pine martens (a relative of the weasel), ermine stoats (whose coats turn white in winter) and otters, which are rare but less so than in England. Otters are famously hard to spot in the wild, though their footprints and droppings are often seen around the coast; you stand your best chance in the north-west Highlands, Orkney and Shetland. Foxes and red squirrels are found throughout the country and Scotland contains almost the entire British population of blue mountain hares.

The Highlands and islands are home to a wide variety of marine mammals, from occasional visitors such as hump-backed whales and orcas (killer whales), to relatively common species such as bottlenose dolphins, which are often seen in the Moray Firth. There are two species of seal, the common and grey seal, which can be seen all around the coast and throughout the islands (it's hard to avoid them in Orkney). Grey seals were once threatened but have recovered impressively with legal protection, today accounting for 50% of the world population.

Dolphins can often be spotted in the Moray Firth.

Some unusual farm breeds are still raised in the region, including black-faced and Jakob's sheep and the rare soay, the ancestral wild sheep of Scotland. You'll also see plenty of Highland cattle, diminutive hairy cows with lots of character but foul tempers. Also widespread are the legendary Aberdeen Angus cattle, said to produce the finest beef in the world. The Shetland Islands, Eriskay and Rum have semi-wild miniature horses, and Shetland is also known for its unique short-legged sheepdogs, known as Shelties.

Birds

Scotland has an immense variety of bird species ranging from native heathland birds to migratory seabirds who stop here annually to breed.

Heathland Birds Large numbers of grouse graze the heather on the moors, and gamekeepers burn vast areas to encourage the new shoots that attract this popular game bird. The rare capercaillie, a black, turkey-size member of the grouse family, is occasionally seen in wooded areas, while that master of disguise, the ptarmigan, lives on higher ground in the Cairngorms. Birds of prey, such as the golden eagle, osprey, peregrine falcon, merlin, short-eared owl and hen harrier are protected and hunt for mice and voles on the open moorland, particularly in the Flow Country of Caithness and Sutherland. Snowy owls are sometimes seen in northern Shetland. Other birds worth looking out for include curlews (whimbrels in Shetland), dunlin, crossbills, long-tailed tits and the rare corncrake. Throughout the region, you'll see the raven, which still has the same sense of foreboding it had in Macbeth's day.

Water Birds Since Scotland has 80% of Britain's coastline, it's not surprising to find huge populations of migratory seabirds. The most famous visitor is the puffin, which breeds in burrows dug into the cliffs from April to August; remarkably, these tiny characters spend the rest of the year far out to sea. Other seabirds which arrive in their millions every summer are great skuas, gannets, fulmars, razorbills, kittiwakes, shearwaters, shags, terns and guillemots. The best places for viewing are the cliff reserves in Orkney and Shetland, particularly the remote islands of North Ronaldsay (Orkney), Foula and Fair Isle (Shetland) and St Kilda, off the Western Isles.

There are also some very rare freshwater species to look out for, including red-necked phalaropes and red-throated divers, seen on some of the Orkney and Shetland Islands. Black-throated divers, greylag geese and whooper swans are more common, while the sandy beaches are fringed with oystercatchers, plovers and other waders.

Fish & Reptiles

The fabled wild Scottish salmon, sea trout and brown trout are found in many rivers and lochs. Native reptiles include the common adder (venomous) and the common lizard, but these are rarely seen.

Endangered Species

In spite of some commendable conservation work, many species in Scotland are coming under increasing threat from modern farming and fishing methods. The once common corncrake, for example, was almost completely destroyed by modern mowing techniques, but it is recovering under a subsidy scheme which rewards farmers for mowing in a corncrake-friendly fashion. Many birds of prey are at risk from egg collectors, while seabirds are threatened by oil spills and the vast amounts of fishing line abandoned by anglers.

Things are far worse below the water. Wild Scottish salmon stocks are on the verge of collapse due to disease and pollution caused by intensive fish-farming. Dozens of commercial fish species have been driven to the edge of extinction, including herring, mackerel, haddock and cod, which is now thought to be below the minimum population required for the species to survive in Scottish waters. The latest species to come under threat is the monkfish (also known as angler fish), which is being caught in ever increasing numbers for the restaurant trade. Things also aren't looking too rosy for the harbour porpoise, which isn't expected to survive long into the millennium. Wildlife species that were slaughtered to the point of extermination in the 19th century – golden eagles, buzzards, pine martens, polecats and wildcats among them – are protected by law and are only now recovering. However, many of these species are a natural enemy of game birds and in order to preserve the latter for sporting shooters, some unscrupulous estate owners and gamekeepers poison birds of prey and other predators.

To combat these threats, Scottish Natural Heritage (SNH) has established a Species Action Programme to restore populations of endangered species. Both the red kite and the white-tailed sea eagle, both absent from Scotland since the 19th century, have been successfully reintroduced.

Conservation Areas

Scotland's first ever national park, Loch Lomond and the Trossachs National Park, opened in April 2002. There are also plans to create a second national park in the Cairngorms.

National Nature Reserves (NNRs), also of national importance, protect habitats and specific animal and plant species. Sites of Special Scientific Interest (SSSIs) are significant for their geology, flora, fauna or habitats or combinations thereof. All NNRs are also SSSIs and are managed by SNH (Keeping up with the acronyms?). NNRs in the Highlands and islands include:

Foot-and-Mouth 2001

During 2001, the British Isles were hit by a catastrophic outbreak of foot-and-mouth disease, a debilitating condition of sheep, cattle and pigs. In an attempt to control the epidemic, walkers were banned from rural areas and farms, and whole herds of cattle and pigs were killed and then burned on huge pyres. The controversial move was primarily an economic decision – most animals recover from the disease and there is no risk to humans, but meat from infected animals cannot be sold in the UK under European laws. The UK was declared free of foot-and-mouth in December 2001, but many landowners are still restricting access to their land. Please respect signs prohibiting walkers and disinfect your boots in the footbaths provided.

Abernethy Forest (Nethybridge) – The largest surviving native pine wood in Scotland, home to capercaillie, crossbills, crested tits and ospreys

Ariundle (Strontian) – A moss-covered oak woodland, with many rare lichens and ferns

Beinn Eighe (Kinlochewe) – Britain's first NNR, featuring Caledonian woodland with arctic-alpine plant species, overlooking Loch Maree

Ben Lui (Tyndrum) – Alpine environment with saxifrages and other mountain plants

Ben Wyvis (Garve) – A towering mountain ridge with pine martens, golden eagles and rare shrubs

Claish Moss (Loch Sheil) – An ancient peatbog, home to many rare plant species

Corrieshalloch Gorge (12 miles south of Ullapool) – A scenic slot-sided gorge, 60m deep but only 10m wide

Creag Meagaidh (Laggan) – Mountainous reserve with native forest, golden eagles and ptarmigan

Glasdrum Wood (Loch Creran) – Native woodland with numerous butterfly and insect species

Glencripesdale (Loch Sunart) – A remote woodland reserve with otters, pine martens and Scottish wild cats

Glen Roy (Roy Bridge) – Spectacular glacial formations

Hermaness (Unst, Shetland) – A vast bird reserve overlooking Britain's most northerly point; home to over 100,000 seabirds, including puffins, gannets and great skuas

Keen of Hamar (Unst, Shetland) – Serpentine rock debris environment with unique plant species

Loch Druidibeg (South Uist) – A scenic area of machair (wild grassland); home to corncrakes and wildflowers in spring

Loch Fleet (Golspie) – Coastal reserve with large populations of wildfowl and waders

Moine Mhor (Kilmartin) – Wetland habitat with native plants and insects and Neolithic remains

North Rona & Sula Sgeir (off Lewis) – An island group with large populations of storm petrels, Leach's petrels, gannet and guillemot, plus breeding grey seals

Noss (off Bressay, Shetland) – Bird reserve with large populations of guillemots, gannets, fulmars, great skuas and kittiwakes; easily reached from Lerwick

Rum (Isle of Rum) – A tiny mountainous island with ospreys and Manx shearwaters

St Kilda (50 miles west of Lewis) – An incredibly remote and craggy island, home to vast populations of seabirds, marine mammals, Soay sheep (the wild sheep of Scotland) and deserted human settlements

Staffa (off Mull) – An uninhabited island with spectacular columnar basalt formations, including Fingal's Cave

Taynish (Tayvallich) – A deciduous woodland, home to 300 native plant species

The NNRs are supplemented by various Local Nature Reserves (LNRs) which cover sites of local conservation interest for public use. There are also Regional Parks, and smaller Country Parks, which are areas of countryside set aside for public recreation. National Scenic Areas (NSAs) are regions of exceptional natural beauty, especially in the Highlands, and are also considered of national significance.

GOVERNMENT & POLITICS

The Scottish parliament is a single-chamber system with 129 members (known as MSPs), elected through a system of proportional representation, and led by a first minister, currently Jack McDonnell. It sits for four-year terms (the next elections are in 2003) and is responsible for education, health, housing, transport, economic development and other domestic affairs. It also has the power (as yet unused) to increase or decrease the rate of income tax in Scotland by up to 3%.

The Scottish Executive – composed of the first minister, Scottish ministers, junior ministers and Scottish law officers – is the Scottish government, which proposes new laws and deals with the areas of responsibility outlined above, while the body of MSPs constitutes the Scottish legislature, which debates, amends and votes on new legislation.

The UK government in Westminster still controls defence, foreign affairs and social security. Scotland is represented in Westminster by 129 Scottish members of parliament (MPs) in the House of Commons, out of a total of 658. The Scotland Office, headed by the Secretary of State for Scotland, is the Westminster department charged with ensuring Scotland's interests are represented in the UK government.

In contrast to Westminster, where the main political contest is between the Labour and Conservative parties with the Liberal Democrats coming a poor third, Scotland has four main parties – the Labour Party, the SNP, the Scottish Conservative and Unionist Party (also known as the Tory Party, or just the Tories), and the Liberal Democrats (Lib Dems) – and the main struggle for power is between Labour and the SNP. The long-term goal of the Scottish Nationalists is complete independence for Scotland.

In the 1999 Scottish parliamentary elections, Labour won 56 seats, the SNP 35, Conservatives 18, and the Lib Dems 17; the Scottish Socialist Party and the Green Party took one seat each.

ECONOMY

Although the Scottish economy is generally experiencing a long-overdue upturn, the majority of Scotland's new-found wealth is still concentrated in the lowlands. However, the devolved Scottish parliament is giving increasing amounts of parliamentary time to Highland issues, including sweeping changes to the land-tenure laws. Earnings in the Highlands & Islands Enterprise (HIE) area are lower than for the rest of Scotland – the average weekly wage is 10% less than the UK average – but unemployment is actually slightly less than the Scottish average of 4% (impressive seeing as it once soared to 15%!).

There is a strong trend of seasonal unemployment due to the seasonal nature of the farming, fishing and tourism industries. Orkney and Shetland both have significantly higher employment than on the mainland. The per capita GDP for the HIE is around 78% of the GDP for the UK as a whole, with the exception of the Shetland Islands, where it is 119% of the UK average.

The primary industries here are fishing (accounting for 50% of the Scottish fish catch), agriculture (mainly sheep and cattle production) and forestry. These industries only employ 6% of the population but account for more than 15% of Scottish agricultural output. More than 27% of people are employed in tourism and nearly 29% in public administration, education and health. This figure is only likely to increase with the changeover from private to public ownership of land. The exponential growth of tourism and fish-farming is bringing much-needed investment in the Highlands and islands. The fastest-growing sector is the call-centre business, buoyed by the discovery that English consumers are more likely to trust callers with a Scottish accent!

Oil and gas production in the North Sea is still rising, and industry pundits predict that it will continue to rise for several decades to come. However, evidence from depleted North Sea oilfields suggests that far from extending the life of oilfields, technological advances are exhausting reserves far faster than predicted, with sharp declines predicted after 2006.

About 10% of people in the HIE are employed in manufacturing, exporting most of the produce to Europe and North America. HIE output is mainly accounted for by textiles and clothing (especially woollen knitwear), and food and drink – Scotch whisky is one of the country's most lucrative exports. Some traditional cottage industries, such as the weaving of Harris tweed, survive and thrive on a small scale.

POPULATION & PEOPLE

The Highlands and islands contain just 373,000 of Scotland's 5.1 million people, making them one of the most sparsely populated areas in the EU; the Highlands have just 23 persons per sq mile compared to an EU average of 290. About 30% of the population in the region live on around 90 islands off the Scottish coast.

The population of the Highlands and islands decreased massively during the Highland Clearances, and fell further after WWII as rural residents moved to the lowlands or England looking for work. The rural population is slowly increasing on the mainland, with 0.3% population growth between 1991 and 1998, but out-migration is still a problem in Orkney, Shetland and, most severely, in the Western Isles, where the population dropped by 5% in the same period. The population of Scotland as a whole is also decreasing due to economic migration to England and high mortality due to ill health, with 5000 more deaths than births in 1999.

However, there are some signs that the devolved Scottish government is providing new economic incentives for Highlanders to stay; Inverness is the UK's fastest-growing city, with a population increase from 41,800 in 1991 to 68,700 in 2001.

Ethnically, Scots are a mixture of Anglo-Saxon, Celtic and Scandinavian stock, with some distant ancestral traces of the Stone-Age tribes who occupied the region before the Celts. Immigration has added to Scotland's ethnic mix, though less so than south of the border.

Probably the largest immigrant community are the English, many of whom bought houses here during the English economic boom in the 1980s. Irish people also have a significant presence in Scotland, many of them descended from refugees who came to the western Highlands during the 19th century Potato Famine. There are also many smaller ethnic communities including Italians, Poles, Indians, Pakistanis and Chinese.

EDUCATION
Scots have always put a high value on education, largely due to the efforts of the Scottish Church, which made a conscious decision to spread literacy to every corner of the country in the 16th century. There was always a Highland-lowland imbalance though, and

the Highlands were never able to boast the almost 100% literacy of the central lowlands.

From its beginnings, the Scottish education system was meritocratic – it provided the opportunity for anyone, regardless of their social background, to progress to the highest levels if they had the ability, allowing some Highlanders to achieve positions out of all proportion to their social status. Nonetheless, a disproportionate number of the famous Scots who were responsible for so many of the innovations we take for granted today – including tarmac roads, Mackintosh raincoats and penicillin – were from privileged lowland families.

The modern education system in Scotland is separate from that in England and Wales. Primary education from the age of five to 12, and secondary education from 12 to 16, are compulsory; pre-school nursery education is optional. Scottish Certificate of Education (SCE) Standard Grade examinations are held at the end of the fourth year of secondary school.

Students can stay on at secondary school for a fifth and sixth year if they choose to sit SCE Higher Grade exams, which are required for entrance to further education, training and university. Honours degree courses in Scotland last four years.

State schools are supplemented by a number of independent, fee-paying schools. All of Scotland's universities are in the south, though the Highlands and islands have numerous community colleges and several Gaelic colleges.

In 2001, the Scottish parliament created the University of the Highlands and Islands Millennium Institute, which is currently trying to solve the problem of creating a new university that will cater to the needs of the remote rural communities of northern Scotland.

ARTS
The arts never seem to have caught the Scottish popular imagination – or at least not in a form recognised by modern culture vultures. Perhaps the need for creative expression took different, less elitist paths – in folk music and dance, and in oral poetry and folk stories. With the notable exception of literature, the

Highlands and islands are under-represented in the arts, though they have formed a popular subject matter for lowland artists.

Literature

Scotland has a long and distinguished literary history and this is one field where the people of the Highlands and islands really shone. The most famous poet to be inspired by the region was Hugh MacDiarmid, who lived for a while on the Isle of Whalsay (Shetland). A founder of the Scottish Nationalist Party, a dedicated communist and instigator of the 20th-century Scottish cultural renaissance, his most famous work is probably *A Drunk Man Looks At The Thistle*, a 2685-line Joycean monologue about the Scottish condition written in 1926.

The poet and storyteller George Mackay Brown (1917–96) was born in Stromness in the Orkney Islands, and lived there almost all his life. Although his poems and novels are rooted in Orkney, his work transcends local and national boundaries. His novel *Greenvoe* is a warm, witty and poetic evocation of everyday life in an Orkney community. Mackay Brown was prolific; other fine novels include *Beside the Ocean of Time* and *Vinland*, while his poetry has been published in collections such as *Travellers* and *Collected Poems: 1954–1992*.

Although born in Wales, Eric Linklater (1899–1974) viewed Orkney as his spiritual home, writing *White Maa's Saga* about the islands in 1928, as well as the highly regarded war novels *Private Angelo* and *The Dark of Summer*, partly set in Orkney and Shetland. Another Orcadian worth looking out for is poet Edwin Muir, who wrote longingly about Orkney from exile in Glasgow and wrote the interesting travelogue *Highland Journey* in 1935. The poet Norman McCaig (1910–96) was born in Edinburgh but came from a Harris family and wrote eloquently about the Highlands and islands – *Selected Poems* is probably the best collection of his work. Lewis poet Iain Crichton Smith (1928–98) is one of the most prolific writers of Gaelic poetry; his works include *Burn is aran* (Water and Bread) and *Na Guthan* (Voices) – his *Towards the Human* is

a fine collection of essays and poems on Gaelic life. The ancient Hebridean poet Alexander MacDonald wrote some interesting epics about the Clanranald including *Clanranald's Galley* in 1750.

The hugely popular writer Neil Munro (1863–1930), born in Inverarary in Argyll, is responsible for some of the most loved books about the region, including the humorous tales of Para Handy and his boat the *Vital Spark*, which have been repeatedly dramatised on television, radio and the stage.

Caithness resident Neil M Gunn (1891–1973), born in Dunbeath, is celebrated as the best Scottish novelist of the 20th century, penning such evocative tales as *Morning Tide* and *The Silver Darlings*, about the herring industry. Sir Compton MacKenzie (1883–1972) spent much of his life on the island of Barra, where he is buried; his famous comedy *Whisky Galore* is based on the true story of the wreck of a whisky cargo ship off the coast of Barra.

The author Gavin Maxwell, who wrote the popular children's book *Ring of Bright Water* lived for many years on Eilean Bàn, the island between Skye and the mainland, now supporting part of the Skye Bridge. Another famous children's author was Sir James Matthew Barrie of Kirriemuir, who wrote the perennially popular *Peter Pan*.

Architecture

The Highlands and islands are known for their ancient architecture, which includes some of the earliest buildings in the British Isles. There are relics from every period, from the Neolithic to the Highland Clearances.

Neolithic (5000 BC to 2500 BC) The ancient stone houses in the Western Isles, Orkney and Shetland are an incredible record of the dry-stone architecture of the original native peoples of Britain. An immense variety of structures have survived, from primitive farmsteads and huge stone cairns to complex ceremonial buildings.

An incredible concentration are found in Orkney, including the best-known and best-preserved site, the village of Skara Brae (from 3100 BC) just north of Stromness.

The Neolithic people also built numerous stone circles, including the famous circle at Calanais in Lewis, and hundreds of burial cairns across the region.

Bronze Age (2500 BC to 700 BC) The Bronze-Age Beaker people took over many Neolithic sites and built more cairns and stone circles, incising some stones with 'cup markings', such as the Ringing Stone on Tiree. Another structure invented by the Beakers was the crannog, a wood-and-stone fort constructed on an island in a loch. There are fine examples on Loch Tay (near Kenmore) and at Loch Finlaggan (Port Askaig).

Iron Age (c.700 BC to 600 AD) The Iron-Age Celts created possibly the most distinctive ancient building in the region, the characteristic stone broch; there are fine examples at Glenelg (south of Kyle of Lochalsh), Dun Carloway (Lewis) and Mousa (Shetland). Of a similar age are duns, small stone forts, typically found on artificial islands in lochs, and wheelhouses (partitioned communal roundhouses) of the northern and western islands. The most complete wheelhouses can be seen at Jarlshof in Shetland.

Pictish & Early Christian (4th to 12th Centuries) Few early-Christian monuments have survived in the region, but the Picts left a valuable record of their culture in the form of Pictish stones, which have been discovered across the region, from Argyll to Skye and Shetland. Many of the finest Pictish stones were carted off to Edinburgh, but the Shetland Museum in Lerwick, the Dunrobin Castle Museum in Sutherland and the Inverness Museum all have some striking examples.

There are a few relics of the early Celtic Church on the islands, most notably the beautiful Celtic crosses at Kildalton, Islay (8th century) and Iona (10th century). Shetland and Orkney have several ruined medieval kirks and a lone example of a round Celtic church tower survives at Egilsay (Orkney), dating from the 10th century.

Romanesque (12th Century) The Romanesque style – with its characteristic round arches and chevron decoration – was introduced to Scotland along with the monasteries that were founded during the reign of David I (1124–53). The most impressive example is the wonderful St Magnus Cathedral in Kirkwall, Orkney.

Medieval (12th to 16th Centuries) During the medieval period, the majority of the population were peasant farmers on the lands of the nobles and lived in simple thatched stone dwellings known as crofts or 'black-houses', which continued in a similar form right up until the 20th century.

Only the nobles and the Church were able to build more grandiose monuments, and many fine castles and ancient churches survive from this time. Famous castles include those at Eilean Donan, Dunstaffnage, Duart, Urquhart and Wick on the mainland, at Duntulm in Skye, at Muness and Scalloway in Shetland, and on Westray and Wyre in Orkney. Other fine buildings from this time include the Bishop's and Earl's Palaces in Kirkwall, Orkney.

After the Reformation many abbeys and cathedrals were deliberately damaged or destroyed, including those at Beauly and Fortrose.

Post-Reformation (16th to 19th Centuries) During this period the traditional fortified keeps were superseded by a new kind of castle, the towerhouse, which became a characteristic feature of the Scottish countryside, and many ancient castles were rebuilt in the Romantic style. Good examples include the castles at Brodick (Arran), Armadale and Dunvegan (Skye), Stornoway (Lewis), Kisimul (Barra), Balmoral (near Ballater) and Blair Atholl (near Pitlochry).

The 20th Century The architectural innovations of the 20th century were mostly confined to the lowlands. In the Highlands and islands the most significant new feature was the introduction of cheap-kit housing to replace the traditional stone crofts. It was not all bad news – attractive weatherboard houses were imported into Orkney and Shetland from Scandinavia – but in general, the majority of new buildings have been faceless concrete bungalows. Here and there, individuals have restored and modernised the traditional black-houses – at Gearrannan in Lewis for example – but a more common sight is whole villages of stone croft houses sitting abandoned on the edge of grey, impersonal housing estates.

Music
The Highlands and islands have a rich tradition of folk music and dance, and classical recitals are becoming more and more popular, though classical music is still mainly associated with festivals or religious services.

Classical While most classical music in the region is still at an amateur level, Hoy in Orkney is home to one of Scotland's musical greats, Sir Peter Maxwell Davies, the Composer Laureate of the Scottish Chamber Orchestra and the associate Conductor/ Composer of the Royal Philharmonic Orchestra in London. Among his compositions was *Into the Labyrinth*, set to the words of fellow Orcadian George Mackay Brown. His recent work has included *The Jacobite Uprising* (1997) and *Sea Elegy* (1998), set to more of George Mackay Brown's poetry.

Folk & Pop The Highlands and islands have always had a strong folk tradition and in the 1960s the roots revival provided a forum for the Gaelic songs of Cathy-Ann McPhee from Barra and Margaret Stewart from Lewis. Initially, most of the performers came from outside the region, but the arrival of the Boys of the Lough, headed by Shetland fiddler Aly Bain, introduced the world to authentic Highland folk music. Aly was probably the most influential folk musician Scotland has seen, and brought pipes, concertina, mandolins and other traditional instruments to a wide audience, recording with performers such as Tom Anderson and Phil Cunningham. Other reputable fiddlers include Scott Skinner, Willie Hunter and Catriona MacDonald, who studied under the same master fiddler

as Aly Bain. For the Highland pipes in all their untamed power, hunt down the work of John Burgess or the versatile piper Hamish Moore. Iain McLachlan is a skilled accordion player who has brought the music of the western islands to new listeners on the mainland.

Regional folk music reached a broader audience through the Gaelic compositions of North Uist band Runrig, who transformed island *ceilidh* music into stadium rock over two decades. Another powerful ambassador for Gaelic music was the band Capercaillie. Other Gaelic/Celtic 'big bands' include Ossian and the Battlefield Band, which have both seen plenty of Highlands and islands musicians in their line-ups. Seelyhoo are led by two Orcadian sisters and blend modern and traditional influences, while Shooglenifty are taking traditional rhythms to the clubs with a fusion sound they describe as 'acid croft'.

As well as cross-over bands such as Runrig, the region has produced some interesting pop music, most notably the whimsical Travis-esque melodies of the Mull Historical Society, originally from Tobermory.

Concerts take place regularly at community centres and pubs across the region, but probably the best forum for traditional music are the big music festivals – see Special Events in the Facts for the Visitor chapter for details. *Ceilidhs* are also a good place to see hear music – see the following section.

Dance
Another homespun artform that the Scots have made their own is dance. The most famous dances are the formal Highland dances performed at Highland Games, which date back to the foundation of Scotland. There are four official Highland dances: the Sword Dance, Seann Triubhas, the Reel of Tulloch and the Highland Fling. The Sword Dance or *gille calum* comes from the legend that Malcolm Canmore celebrated his victory over a Macbeth chieftain by dancing over a crucifix made from his *claymore* (sword) and the sword of his rival. The Sean Triubhas is attributed to the desire of Highlanders to shake off the hated

triubhas (trousers) they were forced to wear after the 1745 rebellion. A chilly congregation who danced to keep warm are credited with inventing the Reel of Tulloch, while the famous Highland Fling was invented in the 1790s to mimic the movements of a stag; clansmen reputedly danced the steps on their *targes* (leather-covered shield).

A less regimented forum for Highland dance is the traditional *ceilidh* (pronounced **kay**-lee). The name comes from the Gaelic word meaning a visit, dating back to the days when the end of the work day was celebrated by singing and dancing in the worker's homes. A local bard (poet) presided over the telling of folk stories and legends, and the accompanying dancing and song provided the young men and women of remote rural communities with an opportunity for some flirtation and courtship. In its current incarnation, the ceilidh is a folk dance, usually with pipe music and set dances led by a 'caller' who leads the dancers through their steps.

Storytelling

The oral tradition has been hugely influential in the development of Scottish culture, and this ancient artform has gained considerable recognition in recent years, with the creation of the Tall Tales for Short Days festival in Orkney in October and the Shetland Storytelling Festival in September.

Film

Scotland has never really had its own film industry, but in the last few years the government-funded agency Scottish Screen (☎ 0141-302 1730) has been created to nurture native talent and promote and develop all aspects of film and TV in Scotland. The Highlands have cropped up in the background of a few big blockbusters and plenty of independent films, but many directors turn to nearby Ireland for landscape footage due to the generous tax breaks offered by the Irish government.

Although the lowlands have produced such bright lights as Sir Sean Connery, few actors have come from the Highlands and islands. Perhaps the most famous face is Robert Shaw (1927–78), the cynical boat captain from *Jaws*; he grew up in Stromness, Orkney. His other film roles were in *The Sting* and *Black Sunday* and as the villain in *From Russia With Love*, playing opposite Sir Sean.

SCIENCE, EXPLORATION & POLITICAL THOUGHT

Although Scotland has produced more than 20% of Britain's leading scientists, philosophers, engineers and inventors, these advances were mostly the work of lowland Scots. Famous Highland scientists include Sir William Cheyne (1852–1932) of Fetlar in Shetland, who pioneered the use of antiseptics in medicine, and Dunkeld's John Rickard MacLeod (1876–1935), who discovered and isolated insulin in Toronto in 1921.

However, exploration was a field in which the hardy people of the islands excelled, mapping some of the harshest parts of the globe. The most famous Highland explorer is Dr John Rae of Stromness (Orkney), who discovered the Northwest Passage from the Atlantic to the Pacific and also the doomed expedition of Sir John Franklin, though Franklin was credited with Dr Rae's discovery for many decades by English historians! Another notable explorer was William Balfour Blaikie (1825–64) from Kirkwall in Orkney, who opened the River Niger in Africa to navigation.

A more questionable explorer was Earl Henry Sinclair, a 14th-century earl of Orkney; Scots nationalists claim he discovered America in 1398. This claim is based on a disputed 16th-century document and the Westford Knight rock carving in Massachusetts, reputed to be a knight belonging to clan Gunn (or a doodle carved by schoolchildren in 1800, according to US archaeologists).

The Highlands and islands have produced some notable politicians, most famously Viscount William Whitelaw, former British deputy prime minister, who grew up in Nairn. Former Labour leader John Smith, born in Dalmally, would probably be sitting where Tony Blair is now if he hadn't suffered a fatal heart attack in 1994. Another potent political figure was the communist and poet Hugh MacDiarmid who helped found the Scottish Nationalist Party.

All Things Scottish

The Highlands are romantically viewed as the seat of all traditional Scottish culture, a semi-mythical world of mist-shrouded glens, kilted Highlanders, caber tossing and the bass drone of the bagpipes. However, many of these Highland icons have origins from much farther afield.

Bagpipes Although no piece of film footage on Scotland is complete without the drone of the pipes, this curious instrument actually originated in ancient Egypt and was brought to Scotland by the Romans. Clan armies later adapted the pipes to accompany their warriors into battle, but bagpipes were banned by the English following the Jacobite Rebellion, and the instrument had fallen out of favour by the 19th century.

The pipes altered considerably from their original form over the centuries, giving rise to such instruments as the Highland war pipes (playing these monster pipes has been likened to wrestling a giant octopus), which echoed out across the glens during the clan wars. The Highland pipes comprise a leather bag kept inflated by a blowpipe and held under the arm; the piper forces air through the pipes by squeezing the bag, three of which are drones and play continuously, while the fourth or chanter pipe is used to play the melody.

Queen Victoria did much to repopularise the bagpipes, with her patronage of all things Scottish. When staying at Balmoral she liked to be wakened by a piper playing outside her window. These days, you're more likely to hear the quieter Chamber pipes and Northumbrian pipes, which are inflated using a pair of bellows rather than a blow pipe and are better for indoor performances. Competitive piping is still a popular pastime in the Highlands and islands – the sound of duelling bagpipes is quite an experience.

Highland Games According to oral tradition the Highland Games date back to the kingdom of Dàl Riata and were essentially war games, allowing clan leaders to select their most skilled warriors for battle. In the 11th century, Malcolm Canmore is believed to have staged a royal contest to find the fastest runners in the kingdom to carry his messages across the Highlands.

Historical evidence for a tradition of annual clan games is patchy but the games certainly took off in the 19th century with the creation of the first Highland Societies. In 1848 Queen Victoria patronised the Braemar Highland Games and the games were incorporated into the Highland legend.

Most of the activities in the games are based on equipment readily available to the average Highlander. The hammer throw was derived from the traditional *mell* used to drive fence-posts, while steelyard weights were thrown for distance and height. The caber (Gaelic for 'tree') was simply a tree trunk, and rounded river stones were used as *clachnearts* for putting the stone. Today, the games have a popularity that far outstrips their origins, cropping up everywhere from Auckland to Ottawa.

Tartan This distinctive patterned woollen material has become the definitive symbol of Scotland and the Highlands, inspiring blankets, kilts, ties and key-fobs and a thousand other saleable souvenirs. The tough, warm and water-resistant fabric is thought to date back to the Roman period, though it has become romantically associated with the Gaelic Celts, who arrived from Ireland in the 6th century. What is certain is that tartan had become the standard uniform of Highlanders by the 18th century. Following the Battle of Culloden, the use of tartan for any form of clothing was banned in an attempt to undermine the solidarity of the Highland clans.

However the ban was only enforced in the Highlands and did not apply to the armed services, which now included a large number of Highland Regiments. The weaver William Wilson established a factory at Bannockburn to supply the army with tartan, experimenting with a wide range of new

All Things Scottish

designs and colours. In 1778, the London Highland Society requested that the clans submit a piece of their traditional clan tartan to preserve the traditional designs but most of the tartans preserved by the society were actually designed and woven by the Wilsons.

In the 19th century, tartan got caught up in the so-called 'Cult of Balmorality' – Queen Victoria's patronage of Scottish culture – and many of the *setts* (tartan patterns) now associated with particular clans were created out of thin air by a pair of brothers known as the Sobieski Stuarts, who claimed to be descended from Bonnie Prince Charlie. The brothers' setts were based on a 'lost' document dating back to the 15th century and they published a hugely successful book of fraudulent tartans, *The Costume of the Clans*, which became established as the genuine tartans of many Highland clans before their elaborate fraud was exposed. Today every clan, and indeed every football team, has one or more distinctive tartans, though few date back more than 150 years.

The bagpipes, originally from Egypt, were brought to Scotland by the Romans.

The Kilt The original Scottish Highland dress was not the kilt but the warrior's *plaid* – a long length of warm tartan cloth wrapped around the body and over the shoulder which was very practical for Highland warfare.

The wearing of Highland dress was banned after the Jacobite rebellions but was revived after George IV's 1822 visit to Edinburgh, when Sir Walter dressed the king and his courtiers in kilts. The image of kilt, dirk and sporran was established in the 1850s under Queen Victoria. By a curious historical twist, the kilt was actually the creation of an English engineer, Thomas Rawlinson, who decided that *plaids* were impractical for the workers on his iron foundry in Invergarry!

The Scottish Flag Scots are divided over which flag to wave – the Saltire or the Lion Rampant. The Saltire – a diagonal white cross on a blue ground – is one of the oldest national flags in the world, dating from the 14th century, and is associated with the diagonal cross used to crucify St Andrew, Scotland's patron saint, although he never visited Scotland.

According to legend, white clouds in the form of a saltire appeared in a blue sky during the Battle of Nechtansmere between Scots and Saxons, urging the Scots to victory. It was incorporated in the Union Flag of the United Kingdom following the Act of Union in 1707.

The Lion Rampant – a red lion on a golden-yellow ground – is the Royal Banner of Scotland. It is thought to derive from the arms of King William I the Lion (1143–1214), and strictly speaking should be used only by a Scottish monarch. It is incorporated in the British Royal Standard, quartered with the three lions of England and the harp of Ireland.

SOCIETY & CONDUCT

Outside Scotland, Scots are often stereotyped as being a tight-fisted bunch, but you shouldn't believe this bit of old English propaganda. You'll find most Scots overwhelmingly generous, particularly if your car breaks down on a lonely road. The Scots are a dour people and may at first appear reserved, but they have a lively sense of humour, as you'll discover if you go into any pub in the Highlands and islands.

Visitors are generally treated very courteously, though English visitors may find a slightly terse reception in parts of the Western Isles. Much of the blame for this falls on the so-called 'white settlers', English immigrants who bought properties during the 1980s boom, contributing to the decline of Gaelic culture. However, the class distinctions that bedevil England are less prevalent in Scotland, if only because Scotland only ever really had two classes: the ruling nobles and everybody else.

The influence of religion is declining fast, but in the Western Isles it still affects everyday life, though sectarian tension between Protestants and Catholics is reserved for the Glasgow football terraces. The Scottish love of fighting should not be underestimated, however; whisky, the national drink, is notorious for producing violent, rather than happy, drunkenness.

Pub brawls are common in city-centre pubs in the depressed northern towns, but almost unheard of in rural pubs. The Scots take their drinking seriously, spending an average 9% of their weekly income on booze and cigarettes, the highest consumption in Britain, leading to a high incidence of drinking- and smoking-related illness and a high adult mortality rate.

The national taste for fried food has created another social problem in soaring levels of obesity and late-onset diabetes. The poor Scottish diet was long seen as yet another Scottish cliche, but Scotland now officially has the highest incidence of type-two diabetes (the obesity-related form of the disease) in Europe. A new case of this debilitating condition is discovered every five minutes. As result of poor diet, smoking and drinking, a quarter of Scots suffer some form of heart disease. The Scottish parliament has even debated creating a so-called 'Food Czar' to address the nation's health problems.

Dos & Don'ts

Though using the term 'British' is fine, the Scots understandably don't like being called English, particularly now that they have their own parliament. Subjects such as religion, Scottish nationalism and the Old Firm football clubs are also potential powder kegs – if these topics come up in pub conversation, it's probably best to practise your listening skills, at least until you're sure of the situation.

Treatment of Animals

As elsewhere in Britain, the people of the Highlands and islands have a huge love for domestic animals – dogs, cats and horses in particular – and an apparent disregard for wild animals such as game birds, deer and 'pest' species such as rabbits and seals. If you're squeamish about hunting, it's probably best to avoid the area during the deer-stalking season, from August to October.

RELIGION

Religion has always played an extremely important role in Scotland's history, and the Scots remain one of the most pious cultures in Britain. Some 10% of Scots regularly attend church services, as compared to 2% of people in England and Wales.

Scotland has swung from one version of Christianity to another during its long history, but each successive incarnation was equally thorough in removing all traces of the preceding faith. The Scotti tribes, after whom the nation was named, were strict Roman Catholics, but their religion was almost entirely suppressed by Presbyterians from southern Scotland, who forced their faith on the Highlanders from the 16th century onwards. A few small pockets of Catholicism were established in the southern Hebrides by covert missionary operations following the Reformation, but most of Scotland's 800,000 Roman Catholics are descended from 19th-century Irish immigrants to the south of the country.

Similarly, the Episcopal (Anglican) Church of Scotland, brought to Scotland by the descendents of Kenneth MacAlpin, now has only about 35,000 members, many of them in the Highlands and islands region.

Today, two-thirds of Scots belong to the Presbyterian Church (or Kirk) of Scotland, or its splinter groups the Free Church of Scotland (known as the Wee Frees) and the United Free Presbyterians. See the boxed text 'The Wee Frees & Other Island Creeds' in the Skye & The Western Isles chapter. The region also supports small communities of Chinese Buddhists, Indian Hindus and Pakistani Muslims.

LANGUAGE

The official language of Scotland is standard English, with a smattering of loan-words from ancient Scots, French and Gaelic, but there are several regional variations in the Highlands and islands. The people of Orkney and Shetland, for example, still use many Norn (ancient Viking) words, while the inhabitants of the Western Isles speak Gaelic first and English as a second language. Some of the Scottish accents in rural parts of the region are notoriously difficult for visitors to understand.

For information on Scottish Gaelic see the Language chapter at the end of the book.

Scots

From around the 8th to the 19th centuries the common language of lowland Scotland was the 'Scots tung' (sometimes called Lallans), which evolved, like modern English,

from the ancient language of the Angles. Over the centuries, Scots was moulded by Dutch, French, Gaelic, German and Scandinavian influences, and although there are certain similarities between Scots and English, the two languages are as different today as Norwegian is from Danish. Scots was the official language of the state in Scotland until the Act of Union in 1707. You're most likely to hear it today in the poetry of Robert Burns.

English rose to predominance as the language of government and of 'polite society' following the Union. However, you can still detect the influence of Scots in the northern isles, which were gifted to lowland Scots after the fall of the Viking empire. The spread of education and literacy in the 19th century had a firmly English slant, which eventually led to the Scots language being perceived as backward and unsophisticated – but with the recent revival of Scottish identity, the language is undergoing something of a renaissance – Scots language dictionaries have been published, there are university degree courses in Scots language and literature, and Scots is studied as part of the school curriculum.

Norn

Today, the ancient Viking language of Norn is no longer spoken in Scotland, though some Norn words are still used in Orkney and Shetland. Numerous place names have Norse origins, particularly in the northern and western islands and along the northwest coast. Place names containing 'dale', 'burg', 'wick', 'uig', 'ness', 'voe' or 'ay' are usually Norse in origin.

Activities

One of Europe's last great wildernesses, Scotland's Highlands and islands are spectacularly wide, empty and exhilarating, and brimming with outdoor pursuits in summer, and more than a few in winter. Innumerable glens to fish; huge sets of mountains to hike, ski, ride or climb; vast stretches of moorland to wander; dazzling oceans to swim, surf or dive; and, being the home of golf, the world's highest ratio of courses to swingers.

Many of the activities below aren't expensive – in fact doing them may end up being a cheaper way of seeing the country than not doing them – and many will let you see parts of this heart-wrenchingly beautiful place in a way lazier types won't.

Most activities are well organised and have clubs and associations that can give visitors invaluable information and, sometimes, substantial discounts. Many of these organisations have national or international affiliations, so check with local clubs before leaving home. The Scottish Tourist Board (STB; ☎ 0131-332 2433, ⓦ www.visit scotland.com), 23 Ravelston Terrace, Edinburgh EH4 3EU, has brochures on most activities, which can provide a starting point for further research, and their excellent activities Web site at ⓦ www.wannabethere .com has lots of great deals and information on jaunts in the region.

Bird-Watching

The Highlands and islands are a twitcher's paradise. There are more than 450 bird species recorded in Scotland, many extremely rare, and over 80 ornithologically important nature reserves managed by Scottish Natural Heritage (SNH), the Royal Society for the Protection of Birds (RSPB) and the Scottish Wildlife Trust (SWT). The Scottish Ornithologists Club (☎ 0131-556 6042, ⓦ www.the-soc.org.uk), 21 Regent Terrace, Edinburgh EH7 5BT, is your best bet for detailed information.

Some of the top locations to spot rare birds include: Handa Island, where there are skuas and puffins; the Treshnish Isles off Mull for shags, razorbills and guillemots; and Loch Garten by Boat of Garten for ospreys. Other spectacular birds of prey to be found in the region are peregrine falcons, golden eagles and the reintroduced red kite and white-tailed sea eagles.

There are huge concentrations of seabirds at Duncansby Head near John o'Groats and at the Clo Mor Cliffs on Cape Wrath. The islands are also home to thousands of seabirds as well as a stopover for migrating birds. In the Hebrides, Islay is a wintering ground for huge flocks of greylag and barnacle geese and Druidibeg in South Uist and Balranald in North Uist have large populations of migrant waders.

The best of Orkney's reserves are at Mull Head (Mainland), North Hoy, Noup Head (Westray) and the outlying island of North Ronaldsay – all of which attract huge populations of breeding seabirds and migratory birds.

The Shetland Islands are famous for their varied birdlife: on Sumburgh Head are puffins, kittiwakes, fulmars, guillemots, razorbills and shags; while Noss (Whalsay), Out Skerries, Fair Isle and Foula are in the path of thousands of migrating birds. See the boxed text 'Twitching in the Shetlands' in the Orkney & Shetland Islands chapter and Fauna in the Facts about Scotland's Highlands & Islands chapter for more details.

Canal Cruising

If you're stretching 'activity' to its broadest meaning, one peaceful and fun way to see the southern Highlands is via a canal.

Built at the beginning of the 19th century as a means of moving freight and as short cuts for seagoing vessels, canals went out of fashion with heavy industry in the early 20th century as road transport improved. However, unlike lowland canals that fell into ruin from disuse, the Highland fishing trade kept canals in good working order, and in recent decades they've been revived by the tourist industry. The 60-mile Caledonian Canal, with its mixture of canal reaches, open lochs and stunning scenery, slices through the Great Glen from Fort William to Inverness, and was built so boats could avoid the long and arduous passage around Cape Wrath. The 9-mile Crinan Canal in Argyll allowed them to avoid the Mull of Kintyre.

Both canals are owned and operated by the British Waterways Board (☎ 0141-332 6936, Ⓦ www.scottishcanals.co.uk), Canal House, 1 Applecross St, Glasgow G4 9SP, which publishes the free *Skippers' Guides* to canals (available online), as well as a list of hire-boat and canal-holiday companies.

The Caledonian Canal's main operator is Caley Cruisers (☎ 01463-236328, Ⓦ www .caleycruisers.com), Canal Rd, Inverness IV3 6NF, which has a fleet of 50 motor cruisers, ranging from two to eight berths, available for hire from March to October. In July and August, a 32-foot, two- to three-berth cruiser costs around £615 per week, and a 39-foot boat sleeping six to eight people costs £1825 per week. Early and late in the season these rates fall to around £330 and £1115 respectively.

No expertise or training is needed; you're normally given a quick once-over of the boat and an explanation of how things work, a brief foray out onto the loch or canal and then you're on your way. Before long you will find yourself working the locks like a veteran.

Canoeing & Kayaking

The Highland region, with its islands, sea lochs and indented coastline, is ideal for sea kayaking, while its inland lochs and rivers are great for both Canadian and white-water canoeing. Various activity centres offer kayaking, including Loch Earn, Glen Nevis,

Marybank and Applecross on the mainland, Kilmuir and Raasay on Skye and Lochmaddy on North Uist.

The Scottish Canoe Association (☎ 0131-317 7314, Ⓦ www.scot-canoe.org), Caledonia House, South Gyle, Edinburgh EH12 9DQ, organises beginner-level courses and also publishes coastal navigation sheets.

Cycling & Mountain Biking

The Highlands and islands are a remote, wild and simply unforgettable region to cycle. In the best, most isolated areas you'll find narrow, winding single-track roads that undulate across lonely purple moors, alongside long and narrow lochs, and around the dramatic coastline. Here, sheep and shaggy Highland cattle own the roads, and pretty white crofters' cottages dot the hillsides.

The relative absence of cars on its scenic single-track B-roads make cycling particularly special; in a world obsessed with going faster, motorists generally avoid the long winding drive on a single-track B-road in favour of evenly graded A-roads. Evenly graded, though, is what B-roads are not. While most A-road hills are long, steady climbs at worst, narrow B-roads and unclassified roads typically rock and roll with steeper gradients. The weather can also make cycling unpredictable – it can be as rugged and wild as the landscape, or warm and hospitable.

For those who prefer rougher terrain, there are over 500 miles of off-road routes in the Highlands designated for cyclists and walkers. Mountain biking in the Lochaber region – surrounding Ben Nevis and Fort William – is particularly good. To find out more, go to the activities section of the Web site at Ⓦ www.forestry.gov.uk or write to Forestry Enterprises (☎ 014630-232811), 21 Church St, Inverness IV1 1EL, for their free booklet detailing mountain-bike locales.

INFORMATION

The STB publishes a useful free booklet, *Cycle Scotland*, and many regional Tourist Information Centres (TICs) have details on local cycling routes and places to hire bikes.

The Cyclists' Touring Club (CTC; ☎ 014 83-417217, fax 426994, e cycling@ ctc.org.uk, w www.ctc.org.uk), Cotterell House, 69 Meadrow, Godalming, Surrey GU7 3HS, is Britain's biggest cycling organisation and has comprehensive information. It provides suggested routes, lists of local cycling contacts and clubs, recommended accommodation, organised cycling holidays, a cycle-hire directory and a mail-order service for maps and books.

For detailed and up-to-date information on Scotland's cycle-route network contact Sustrans (☎ 0117-929 0888, w www.sus trans.org.uk), 53 Cochrane St, Glasgow G1 1HL. Sustrans is a charity that promotes sustainable transport, and its flagship project is the National Cycle Network – around 5000 miles of traffic-free cycling routes all over Britain. In Scotland, the backbone of the network is the route from Carlisle (in northwestern England) to Inverness, via Pitlochry and Aviemore.

Throughout the Highlands, you'll find plenty of operators hiring out bikes from around £10 to £15 per day or £50 per week plus a deposit refundable when the bike is returned.

BICYCLE TRANSPORT

Scottish transport is well equipped for carrying bicycles, generally for free – remember, the bicycle was invented in Scotland.

On most Caledonian MacBrayne (Cal-Mac) and P&O ferries, your trusty steed will either travel free or for a £1 to £2 supplement; smaller ferries carry bikes for free.

Bicycles ride free on buses, provided there's enough room in the luggage compartment. In some cases, you'll be asked to remove pedals or a wheel or, if the driver is a real stickler, to put your bike in a box.

Generally, bikes can be taken free on Scot-Rail trains, provided space is available. However, on long-distance routes or the more popular routes such as Inverness to Aberdeen, the West Highland Railway or the Inverness to Kyle of Lochalsh line, it's essential to make a reservation (see the Getting Around chapter for ScotRail details) for your bike. Some trains carry only one or two bikes so make your reservation (and get your ticket) at least 24 hours before travelling. Check bike-carriage details with the rail company for the whole of your planned journey as far in advance as possible.

WHERE TO CYCLE

Cyclists in search of the wild and remote will love northwestern Scotland's majestic Highlands and mystical islands, which offer quiet pedalling through breathtaking mountainscapes. There are fewer roads in this part of Scotland and generally less traffic. The roads that are there are well graded but sometimes very remote, so carry plenty of food and plan ahead. Of the isles, Skye has a bridge to the mainland and suffers the worst seasonal traffic; good ferries between the islands offer easy escape routes.

Down south, the beautiful forests, lochs, glens and hills in the central areas of Scotland are more accessible and have a more intimate charm, while a pedal through the rugged Hebrides is an enchanting and unforgettable cycle. Cyclists can seek out the smaller roads and tracks to avoid traffic.

The Hebrides

The scenic Hebridean islands, linked by a comprehensive ferry system, provide superb cycling. The route outlined here comprises some 280 miles of cycling, and any tour will need to be planned around the times of ferry crossings; some are summer only.

Beginning on Arran, which has fantastic cycling along its mostly flat bays, you can link up to the Kintyre peninsula easily by catching the Lochranza-Claonaig ferry. Then head northwards through Lochgilphead to Oban and catch the ferry to Craignure on the Isle of Mull (or if you're lazy catch the Craignure ferry to Islay, do some riding there, then ferry on to Oban).

Mull is worth exploring before taking the ferry from Tobermory to Kilchoan. Cycle eastwards along the isolated Ardnamurchan peninsula to Salen then head northwards, past some truly wondrous Mediterranean-like beaches, to Mallaig. Ferries leave from here to Armadale on the Isle of Skye. You can then cycle northwards to Uig, or follow numerous other routes around the island.

From Uig, take a ferry to Tarbert (Isle of Harris) in the Outer Hebrides. These outer isles are wild and remote places with many quiet roads to explore. Cycle south to Benbecula and onto South Uist where you can catch the ferry back to Oban.

 Diving

Dipping a toe into Scotland's icy waters may be enough to send you running for dry land, but Scotland's rich maritime history has produced a spectacular array of shipwrecks for dedicated scuba divers. The marine landscape may not be the Great Barrier Reef, but there is plenty of fascinating marine life from soft corals and jewel anemones to mighty conger eels, lobsters, crabs, cuttlefish, sea urchins and starfish. You may also be lucky enough to spot seals and dolphins, though marine mammals tend to be scared off by scuba units. And the wrecks, particularly those from the Great Wars, are absolutely magnificent.

During summer you can get away with a wet suit, but in spring or autumn, or if you feel the cold, a dry suit is a good idea. You'll need to be dry-suit certified or take a dry-suit course while you're here; courses usually cost around £95. Most people dive on prebooked diving holidays, but day-trips can be arranged for around £30 to £40 including two dives. If you aren't certified, Open Water Diver courses will set you back around £265.

The most popular and accessible wreck diving is at Scapa Flow in Orkney but there are many other wrecks to explore off the coast of Skye, the Shetland Islands, the

JANE SMITH

Western Isles and along the northwest coast of Scotland.

The Lonely Planet/Pisces *Diving & Snorkelling Scotland* guide, by Lawson Wood, describes some of the best sites and lists operators offering dive services and boat charters. The Scottish governing body for diving, the Scottish Sub-Aqua Club, has extensive links on its Web site at W www.scotsac.com.

SCAPA FLOW WRECKS

With the wrecks of seven Imperial German warships on the seabed, Scapa Flow is unsurprisingly one of the most popular diving locations in Europe. Enclosed by Mainland Orkney, Hoy and South Ronaldsay, this is one of the world's largest natural harbours and has been used by vessels as diverse as King Haakon's Viking ships in the 13th century and the NATO fleet of today.

The British Home Fleet sailed from Scapa Flow to meet the German High Seas Fleet at the Battle of Jutland on 31 May 1916. After the war, 74 German ships were interned in Scapa. When the terms of the armistice were agreed on 6 May 1919, with the announcement of a severely reduced German navy, Admiral von Reuter, head of the German fleet in Scapa, set in play a pre-planned scheme to prevent these weapons of war falling into enemy hands. On 21 June, a secret signal to scuttle the ships was passed from vessel to vessel and the entire fleet disappeared into Scapa Flow. A few older local residents can still remember seeing the ships upend and slowly vanish beneath the waves.

Most of the ships were raised in an incredible operation by Ernest Cox, who bought the wrecks from the Admiralty in 1923, but the remaining wrecks sit at depths of 24m to 26m and are encrusted with marine growth. There are three battleships – the *König*, the *Kronprinz Wilhelm* and the *Markgraf* – which are all over 25,000 tonnes. The first two were subjected to blasting for scrap metal, but the *Markgraf* is undamaged and considered one of the best dives in the area. Four light cruisers (4400 to 5600 tonnes) – the *Karlsruhe*, *Dresden*,

Scapa Flow is one of the most popular diving locations in Europe.

Brummer and *Köln* – are particularly interesting as they lie on their sides and are very accessible to divers. The *Karlsruhe*, though severely damaged, is only 10m below the surface. Its twisted superstructure has now become a huge metal reef encrusted with diverse sea life.

As well as the German wrecks, numerous other relics rest on the seabed in Scapa Flow, including the Churchill Barrier ships, the U-boat *UB-116* and the 600-ton gun turrets of the *Bayern*. HMS *Royal Oak*, which was sunk by a German U-boat in October 1939, with the loss of 833 crew, is now an official war grave; the only diving allowed here is the annual wreath-laying ceremony on the wreck by the Royal Navy.

If you're interested in diving in Scapa Flow, contact the following:

The Diving Cellar (☎ 01856-850055,
  ☎/fax 850395, ℮ leigh@divescapaflow.co.uk),
  4 Victoria St, Stromness
European Technical Dive Centre (☎ 01856-
  731269, fax 731345, ℮ sue@technical
  divers.com), Garisle, Burray
Scapa Flow Dive Centre (☎ 831821, ℮ dave
  .scapaflowdivcentre@virgin.net), Cara 4,
  South Ronaldsay
Scapa Scuba (☎/fax 01856-851218, ℮ diving
  @scapascuba.co.uk), 13 Ness Rd,
  Stromness

For further details read *Dive Scapa Flow* by Rod MacDonald or visit the Web site at ⓦ atschool.eduweb.co.uk/jralston/rk/Scapa, which gives a breakdown of the wrecks.

Golf

As the tourist board never tires of telling us, Scotland is the home of golf. The game has been played here for centuries and there are more courses per capita in Scotland than in any other country.

The Highlands has fewer Championship courses than the lowlands, but there are still huge numbers of top-notch courses. Best in the Highlands is Royal Dornoch, in Sutherland. Other great courses (though virtually *every* course in Scotland has something to recommend it) include Machrihanish Golf Links in Kintyre, with what Jack Nicklaus once called the world's best ever opening hole, Machrie Golf Links in Islay, and the Braemar Golf Course, the highest in Britain. The course at Loch Lomond is home to the World Invitational Championship.

Be sure to check if there's a dress code; most courses will expect a collar and no jeans. Just about every Highlands course hires clubs (see costs below).

Courses are tested for their level of difficulty and most are playable year-round. Most clubs give members priority in booking tee-off times, so book in advance.

INFORMATION

The STB publishes the extremely thorough *Golf in Scotland* booklet, a free publication that's frequently updated and has course ratings, green fees, dress codes and contact details for just about every course in Scotland. Contact the STB, and they'll send you a copy. The Web site at ⓦ www.scottish golf.com has excellent information.

COSTS

A round on most courses costs between £10 and £15, though for posher courses you might pay £20 to £25; for the really well-known Highland courses such as Royal Dornoch you'll pay at least £45, and more at weekends.

Club hire should cost between £5 and £10 on top of your green fees; if they cost any more either don't play there or demand clubs a pro would be happy to play with.

Fishing

Fishing is enormously popular in the Highlands and islands, where the rivers and lochs are filled with salmon, trout (sea, brown and rainbow), pike, arctic char and many other species. The region's streams, rivers, lochs and firths probably have Europe's greatest variety of marine habitats and some of its cleanest waters.

If you're fishing for trout, remember that the wild brown trout season closes from early October to mid-March. The season closure for salmon and sea trout varies between districts; it's generally from early November to early February.

You don't need a licence to fish in Scotland but much of the land and fishing rights to most waters are privately owned, so you must obtain a permit from the owners or their agents. These are often readily available at local fishing-tackle shops or hotels. Permits usually cost around £15 per day but some salmon rivers – notably the Tweed, Tay and Spey – can be much more expensive.

The STB's booklet *Fish Scotland* is a good introduction stocked by all TICs. For more in-depth information you should try *Scotland for Game, Sea and Coarse Fishing*, available from Pastime Publications (☎ 0131-5561105), 6 York Place, Edinburgh EH1 3EP. The Scottish Anglers National Association, online at Ⓦ www.sana.org.uk, has lots of good information, or you can contact the Scottish National Anglers Association on ☎ 0131-339 8808.

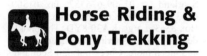

Horse Riding & Pony Trekking

Pony trekking has been going on in the region since the Dark Ages, admittedly not always for tourism – it was perhaps more your massacre-fleeing, peasant-subsistence means of getting about then, rather than the nouveau-riche pleasure it is today. Nevertheless, there's still hundreds of miles of beautiful coastline to be ridden, and seeing the country from the saddle is a wonderful experience, whether you're experienced or not. There are riding schools catering to all levels of proficiency. A half-day's pony trekking costs around £15, and riding hats are included. Many pony trekkers are novice riders so most rides are at walking speed with the occasional trot.

If you're an experienced horse rider there are numerous riding schools with horses for hire – TICs have details.

The STB publishes the unfailingly dependable *Riding & Trekking Scotland* booklet, which lists Scottish riding centres. Associations you can contact include: the Trekking & Riding Society of Scotland (☎ 01821-650210, Ⓦ www.ridinginscotland.com), Steadingfield, Wolfhill, Perthshire PH2 6DA, which is the main society for riders in Scotland; or the British Horse Society (☎ 0870 120 2244, Ⓦ www.bhs.org.uk), British Equestrian Centre, Stoneleigh Park, Kenilworth, Warwickshire CV8 2LR. The latter publishes *Where to Ride and Train* (£5.95), which lists places throughout the UK, and can send lists specific to a particular area.

Rock Climbing

Scotland is a climber's Mecca. Serious climbers will probably head for Glen Coe, Torridon or Ben Nevis.

The Cairngorms, Cuillin Ridge (see that section later in this chapter), Arrochar and Arran are favourites with climbers too, and there are also hundreds of smaller crags all over the country. Some of the more remote crags in the Highlands and Western Isles have only been explored in the last decade. One unusual feature of Scotland's rock-climbing scene is the sea stacks around the coast, most famously the 140m-high Old Man of Hoy in Orkney.

Rock Climbing in Scotland, by Kevin Howett, and the Scottish Mountaineering Club's regional *Rock & Ice Climbs* guides are excellent references. You can also pick up useful information in most climbing-equipment shops.

For more detailed information your best entry point is the Mountaineering Council of Scotland (☎ 01738-638227, W www .mountaineering-scotland.org.uk), The Old Granary, West Mill St, Perth PH1 5QP. It's the main body representing all mountaineering organisations, and if they can't help you they'll put you in touch with someone who can. Otherwise, check out the Scottish Mountaineering Club's Web site at W www.smc.org.uk.

CUILLIN RIDGE

For many visitors the Cuillin Ridge is the prime motivation for coming to Skye and it's a challenging but manageable traverse, with some basic rock-climbing and gripping sensations of exposure as you clamber around the unprotected bluffs. The full traverse includes over 30 peaks, with views over some spectacular corries (natural amphitheatres) to the ocean beyond. The Red Cuillin can mostly be climbed without special equipment, if you don't mind the odd vertiginous scramble, but the complete traverse of the Black Cuillin ridge is the definitive Munro excursion.

The traverse is usually attempted from Glenbrittle, and can be completed in 12 to 14 hours, though many groups bivouac on the ridge. It's four hours' hike from Glenbrittle to the top of Gars-bheinn (895m), at the southern end of the ridge. From here, the trail follows the colls and tops of the various Munros to Sgurr Nan Gillean (965m) at the ridge's northern end. You'll need to do some airy free-climbing or rope up for the descent of Thearlich-Dubh Gap and the King's Chimney. The rock spire of Inaccessible Pinnacle (986m), about halfway along the ridge, is a popular detour; it's an easy climb and you can abseil down from a fixed wire sling. The final descent from Sgurr Nan Gillean to Sligachan takes around three hours.

Several companies offer guided walks and climbs in the Cuillins. Cuillin Guides (☎ 01479-640289), Stone Lee, Glenbrittle, offers custom-made ascents of the peaks for £80 per day for up to two people (£40 per person for groups of three or more) and day packages to the Inaccessible Pinnacle for £40 per person. Skye Highs (☎ 01471-822116), 3 Luib, Broadford, offers five-day courses including the ascents of all 12 Munros on Skye – call for details.

If you're planning on tackling the route independently, you'll need one or two 50m ropes and a selection of long slings and protection to lead and abseil the harder sections. Make sure you are well prepared; bring plenty of drinking water, a good compass and OS Landranger sheet 32 or Harvey's *Cuillin Hills*, which has a 1:12,500 scale insert of the Cuillin Ridge. The definitive guide to the Cuillin is Noel Williams *Skye Scrambles* (£12.95). There's a live web-cam of conditions at the Cuillin at W www .camvista.com/scotland/scenic/skye.php3.

Sailing

The waters surrounding the Hebrides and southern Argyll are steeped in maritime history. The early settlers who colonised Scotland, and the Vikings who followed them, all knew the beauty and difficulties of navigating this region.

Today it's widely acknowledged as one of the world's finest cruising grounds, and its myriad islands, superb scenery and challenging winds and tides make it ideal for experienced sailors, while there are also an abundance of sheltered bays for beginners to learn in.

First step for anyone interested in taking to Scottish waters is getting hold of Sail Scotland's *Welcome Ashore* booklet, available in most TICs or by contacting Sail Scotland (☎ 01309-676757, fax 01309-673331, e info@sailscotland.co.uk) at PO Box 8363, Largs, KA30 8YD. The booklet details yacht chartering, beginners courses and much more. Check out Sail Scotland's excellent Web site at W www.sailscotland .co.uk.

The Kyles of Bute allegedly has Scotland's best sailing, and there's an array of sailing schools there. Tarbert, nearby, is also a sailing centre, and hosts the Scottish Series (Britain's second largest yacht race) each May.

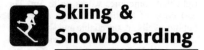

Skiing & Snowboarding

Scotland's five ski centres offer downhill skiing and snowboarding, as well as limited cross-country skiing. However, the downhill runs are far smaller and the weather considerably less reliable than anything you'll find in the Alps or Pyrenees. When there's a good cover and the sun's shining, though, it can be a very pleasant place to ski.

The high season runs from January to April but it's sometimes possible to ski from as early as November and as late as May. However, high winds and poor weather can make the winter-sports scene something of an endurance test.

Package holidays are available but it's easy to make your own arrangements, with all kinds of accommodation on offer in and around the ski centres. It can be extremely busy at weekends, especially if there's a good weather forecast, but mid-week you can sometimes have a slope all to yourself.

INFORMATION

Contact the STB (☎ 0131-332 2433, W www.skiscotland.net) for its detailed *Scottish Snow* brochure and accommodation list. General information can be obtained from Snowsport Scotland (☎ 0131-445 4151, W www.snsc.demon.co.uk), Hillend, Biggar Rd, Edinburgh EH10 7EF.

The Ski Hotline weather-report service can be useful. Phone ☎ 09001-654 followed by 654 for all centres, 660 for Nevis Range, 658 for Glen Coe, 656 for Glenshee, 657 for The Lecht and 655 for Cairngorm. For cross-country skiing the number is ☎ 0891-654659; calls cost 60p per minute. Check online at W www.ski-scotland.com, which is updated daily during the ski season.

RESORTS

Ski resorts in the Highlands include:

Cairngorm (1097m; ☎ 01479-861261, W www.cairngormmountain.com) – Popular with snowboarders, this resort has almost 30 runs spread over an extensive area and Aviemore, with its pubs, restaurants and shops, is nearby. A ski bus service links the slopes with surrounding villages.

Glen Coe (1108m; ☎ 01855-851226, W www.ski-glencoe.co.uk) – This is the oldest resort, with only five tows and two chairlifts, but it's easily accessible from Glasgow and has some spectacular scenery.

Glenshee (920m; ☎ 01339-741320, W www.ski-glenshee.co.uk) – Located on the A93 road between Perth and Braemar, Glenshee offers the largest network of lifts and widest range of runs in Scotland. It also has snow machines for periods when the real thing doesn't appear.

The Lecht (793m; ☎ 01975-651440, W www.lecht.co.uk) – This is the smallest and most remote centre, located on the A939 road between Ballater and Grantown-on-Spey. However, the short runs are good for beginners and families.

Nevis Range (1221m; ☎ 01397-705825, W www.nevis-range.co.uk) – Located near Fort William, Nevis Range offers the highest ski runs, grandest setting and some of the best off-piste potential in Scotland. A gondola takes you to the foot of the main skiing area, which has eight tows and three chairlifts.

Access to the centres is probably easiest by car and there are plenty of car parks. Slopes are graded in the usual way, from green (easy) through blue and red to black (very difficult); and each centre has a ski patrol. Make sure your travel insurance covers you for winter sports.

COSTS

It's easy to hire ski equipment and clothing when you arrive but if you want lessons then you will need to book them in advance. The prices vary but on average expect to pay £13 to £15 per day for hire of skis, boots and poles or snowboard and boots; and £8 to £12 per day for ski clothing.

Lift passes cost £15 to £20 per day, or £64 to £80 for a five-day pass (Monday to Friday only, passport photo required). In a group, ski lessons cost around £12 per person for two hours; private lessons cost £20 to £25 per hour. A one-day beginner's package, including lift pass, equipment hire and

ACTIVITIES

four hours' instruction, costs around £30 to £45, depending on the resort. Cairngorm is generally the most expensive of the lot, Lecht the cheapest.

CROSS-COUNTRY SKIING

There's terrific cross-country skiing near Braemar, going out to Inverey, as well as around Glenshee and the Cairngorms. Glen Mulliach, 5 miles west of the Lecht, is another Nordic skiing centre.

 # Surfing

Cold though the waters may be, the number of grommets clutching their boards and hitting the Highland surf has long been on the increase. Only hardy, well-wet-suited surfers do anything more than take a quick dip, but those that do are amply rewarded with truly magnificent coastline, beautiful sandy beaches and some of the best surfing breaks in Europe.

Summer water temperatures are around 13°C and winter temperatures are 5° to 6°C colder so getting in the water, at least in summer, is feasible if you have a wet suit. A 3mm full suit (steamer) and boots is sufficient in summer, while winter requires a 5mm suit, plus boots, hood and gloves.

The most unusual aspect of surfing here is the impact of the tides. The tidal range is large, which means there's often a completely different set of breaks at low and high tides. As is usually the case, the waves tend to be the biggest and best on an incoming tide. The waves in spring, autumn and winter tend to be bigger and more consistent than in summer; conditions in summer can be unreliable.

The entire Scottish coast has surf but it's the far north and west that has world-class possibilities, particularly the coastline between Bettyhill and Thurso and in the Outer Hebrides. Lewis has the best and most consistent surf in Britain, with around 120 recorded breaks and waves up to 5m. Thurso has a couple of famous breaks, one in front of the harbour wall with lefts and rights, known as Reef, and one at Beach. Thurso East (Castle Reef) is the big one – a huge

right that sometimes works up to 5m. The east coast of Scotland is easily accessible but the swells are unreliable and short-lived.

For more details contact Hebridean Surf (☎/fax 01851-705862, e hebsurf@madas afish.com, w www.hebrideansurf.co.uk), 28 Francis St, Stornoway, Lewis HS1 2ND.

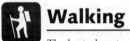 # Walking

The best place to appreciate the heart-wrenching beauty of the Highlands and islands is from a walking trail. The region is a walker's paradise, and you can spend a lifetime (and people do) walking its short and long-distance trails, and never come close to seeing it all.

The peak time for walking is May to September. Winter walking in the Highlands requires, at the very least, an ice axe, crampons and mountaineering experience. July and August is likely to be busier than normal – although only a few parts of the Highlands ever get really crowded (namely, Glen Nevis and parts of the West Highland and Speyside Ways). Midges can also be a problem at this time.

The most pleasant time is May to mid-June – before the midges start to emerge. September (and sometimes October) is also good, although the days are colder and shorter.

SAFETY & EQUIPMENT

Whatever time of the year you go, it's vital to be properly equipped: Highland weather can become vicious in an instant at any time of year, and many inexperienced walkers have died through lack of preparation.

Most of these deaths are due to exposure, so warm clothing is absolutely essential. Waterproofs and thermals are advisable, as are proper walking boots; tracks often start out beautifully maintained but quickly turn to mud in rough conditions. You'll also need ankle support for going up or down even the tiniest hill.

Proper maps are also vital, and should be at least 1:50,000, or larger if you're going off-track.

Carrying a little food can save your life: walkers should carry at least a few bare necessities, such as chocolate bars, muesli bars or nuts and dried fruit. Smarter walkers will carry a good deal more than this if they're doing more than a day walk.

The importance of carrying at least one litre of water at all times can't be overstated either; fresh water can sometimes be surprisingly hard to come by in the Highlands, and especially difficult to find on some islands. Sunscreen is also a good idea.

In winter, never go out without proper warm gear such as hats and gloves, as well as thermals and a good jacket.

ACCESS

Scotland has a formal system of rights of way, and there's a tradition of relatively free access to open country, especially on mountains and moorlands. There is much cooperation between organisations such as the Scottish Landowners' Federation, the Mountaineering Council of Scotland and the Ramblers' Association to promote responsible access to the countryside.

Providing you don't cause damage and that you leave the land if (in the unlikely event) you're asked to do so by the owner, you shouldn't have any trouble. You should, however, avoid areas where you might disrupt or disturb wildlife, lambing (generally mid-April to the end of May), and grouse shooting and deer stalking (mainly from 12 August to the third week in October – if you're walking around this time you *must* phone one of the 12 Hillphone lines that give information on where deer-stalking is happening; all TICs have a Hillphones brochure).

Rights of way exist but local authorities aren't required to list and map them so they're not shown on Ordnance Survey (OS) maps. However, in its guide, *Scottish Hill Tracks*, the Scottish Rights of Way & Access Society (SRWS) publicises those routes which have, or deserve to have, legal status and defends those under threat.

Access is free at all times to areas owned by the National Trust for Scotland (NTS) and to most owned by the Forestry Commission.

Hill Terminology

Before you head off into the hills to bag your first Munro, there are few essential terms you need to know. First of all, you'll need to be up on your mountain names: *Munros* are peaks over 914m and named after Sir Hugh Munro, who published his famous *Table of Heights over 3000ft* in 1891; *Corbetts* are peaks between 763m and 914m; and *Grahams* are peaks from 610m to 763m. Just so you know, all these peaks are also *Tops*.

Munro bagging is the slightly masochistic sport of ascending all 284 Munros – including many undramatic hummocks – and was invented by Reverend Robertson in 1901. And if you bag all the Munros and achieve *compleation* you can head for the 221 Corbetts and 224 Grahams.

Most ascents follow *burns* (streams) through *coires* (scooped out glacial valleys – pronounced cor-ees) to *bealachs* (mountain passes) or *colls* (ridges between the peaks). If you've followed your map correctly, you should now be in a position to *bag* (reach the summit of) the surrounding peaks.

A few climbing techniques you may need to employ are: *scrambling* – less a technique than a human instinct to stick close to the rock when dangling over precipitous drops; *bouldering* – basic rock-climbing but without the reassurance of a rope; and *chimneying* – climbing narrow gullies by bracing your body across the gap (if you ever climbed the door frame as a kid, you know what chimneying is!).

If a fellow walker asks you if you'll be using *protection* on a route, it's not a come-on – ropes are used to prevent falls on steep or exposed sections of many hill-walks. Often going down is harder than coming up, so *abseiling* (lowering yourself along a fixed rope using a belaying device) may get you down to solid ground.

For more details about Munros, Munro bagging and joining the Scottish Mountaineering Club visit the SMC Web site at W www.smc.org.uk.

INFORMATION

Every TIC is well versed in the walks around their area, and has brochure upon brochure (free or for a nominal charge) detailing suggested walks in the region. Other useful sources of information are:

Mountaineering Council of Scotland (☎ 01738-638227, W www.mountaineering-scotland .org.uk) The Old Granary, West Mill St, Perth PH1 5QP

Ramblers' Association Scotland (☎ 01577-861222, W www.ramblers.org.uk/scotland) Kingfisher House, Auld Mart Business Park, Milnathort, Kinross KY13 9DA

Scottish Rights of Way & Access Society (☎ 0131-558 1222, W www.scotways.co.uk) 24 Annandale St, Edinburgh EH7 4AN

GUIDEBOOKS

Scores of books are available describing walks ranging from half-hour strolls to week-long expeditions.

Lonely Planet's *Walking in Scotland* covers Highland and island walks in great depth, detailing both short walks and long-distance paths.

For general advice, the STB produces a *Walking Scotland* brochure, describing numerous routes. *Great Walks Scotland*, by Hamish Brown et al, describes a good range of routes of varying difficulty all over the country. Or try *100 Best Routes on Scottish Mountains*, by Ralph Storer.

The Scottish Mountaineering Club publishes *The Munros: Scottish Mountaineering Club Hillwalkers Guide*, the definitive guide to the peaks. Cameron McNeish's *Munro Almanac* is also useful.

The *High Mountains Companion* is a condensed text of Irvine Butterfield's *The High Mountains of Britain & Ireland*. Both books cover the British Isles but concentrate on the mountains of Scotland.

Highly recommended if you like mountains but can't stomach the intensity of Munro bagging is *The First Fifty*, by Muriel Gray. She likes to debunk the mystique and fastidiousness that envelops many others who write about walking in Scotland.

And just in case you thought all walks in Scotland were up the biggest mountains,

there's *Exploring Scottish Hill Tracks*, by Ralph Storer, with a marvellous range of circular routes and longer expeditions for walkers and mountain bikers, many following traditional cattle-drovers' routes through the glens.

MAPS

OS caters to walkers with a wide variety of maps at different scales. Its Landranger series at 1:50,000 (1¼ inches to 1 mile) is good, but if you want more detail it also publishes Explorer maps at 1:25,000 (2½ inches to 1 mile). TICs usually stock a selection. Alternatively, look out for the excellent walkers' maps published by Harveys; they're at scales of 1:40,000 and 1:25,000.

Munro baggers should check out Bartholomew's map of the Munros (£3.99).

ORGANISED WALKS

There are plenty of operators offering guided walks; the STB has a comprehensive list. Scot Trek (☎ 0141-334 9232, W www .scottrek.co.uk), 9 Lawrence St, Glasgow G11 5HH, organises walking holidays from June to November that include the Cairngorms and the West Highland Way.

WHERE TO WALK
Ben Lawers

Crouching like a lion over Loch Tay, Ben Lawers is one of the area's best day walks, with dazzling views from its peak towards the North Sea and the Atlantic. The ascent can take up to five hours, and you need wet weather gear, water (important for this walk) and at least a little food, even though the trail is well marked. Using a well-worn trail, the walk climbs 940m, and on its rocky summit you'll find the remnants of a 30-man attempt in 1878 to elevate Ben Lawers 5m to reach Scotland's elite 1200m club.

The walk starts at the Ben Lawers Visitor Centre (☎ 01567-820397), 5 miles east of Killin, about a mile up a well-marked road off the A827. Catch postbus No 212 or 213 to the start of this road.

From the visitor centre take the Nature Trail northeastwards. After the boardwalk protecting a bog, cross a stile. Fork left and ascend along a burn (right). At the next rise, fork right and cross the burn. A few minutes later ignore the Nature Trail's right turn and continue ascending parallel to the burn's left bank for just over half a mile. Leave the protected zone by another stile and steeply ascend Beinn Ghlas' shoulder. Reaching a couple of large rocks, ignore a northbound footpath and continue zigzagging uphill. The rest of the ascent is a straightforward succession of three false summits.

The last and steepest section alternates between erosion-sculpted rock and a meticulously crafted cobbled trail. A cairn marks the Beinn Ghlas (1103m) summit. Enjoy the great view of Ben Lawers ahead.

Descend northeastwards along the ridge crest for 20 minutes to the base of Ben Lawers. The initial segment of the half-mile (800m) ascent is made easier by the cobbled sections of path. After a brief plateau, the ascent continues along an eroded trail to the rocky summit, where the views (assuming it's clear!) are remarkable.

Ben Nevis

There's something irresistible about an attempt on Ben Nevis (1344m), the highest peak in the country, but the climb should not be undertaken lightly. You'll need warm clothes, food and something to drink, a detailed map and compass (and know how to use them!). See the boxed text 'Ben Nevis – An Extreme Climate'.

The path begins in Glen Nevis, either from the car park by Achintee Farm (on the northern side of the river and reached by the road through Claggan), or from the SYHA youth hostel on the road up the glen – these two trails join after about a mile. Follow the Red Burn before zigzagging up to the summit and the old observatory ruins, where there are fantastic views of the Mamores. It takes between four and five hours to reach the top and 2½ to three hours to descend.

Cairngorms

This extensive mountain range is popular with climbers and hillwalkers year-round. These are the wildest uplands anywhere in Britain, with arctic tundra, superb high corries and awesome rock formations. The wildlife is pretty good too.

Cairn Gorm (1245m) is the most accessible summit but the high plateau is not the place for a casual stroll. You're only about 650 miles from the Arctic Circle here, and at altitudes of 1000m or more you're certainly in an arctic environment. Weather conditions are notoriously bad and navigation on the featureless summit plateaus can be difficult. Unless you're an experienced mountaineer the routes should only be attempted in summer. Even then, walkers should be prepared for poor conditions.

The Cairn Gorm High Circuit is one of the most popular routes in the Cairngorms because of its easy access from Aviemore.

Ben Nevis – An Extreme Climate

As you'd expect, the weather atop Britain's highest mountain can be the country's most extreme. The temperature on the summit is typically 9°C colder than at the mountain's base, and this doesn't allow for wind chill – there's a delightful average of 261 gales at the summit per year. And let's not forget wind speeds well in excess of 100mph have been recorded up here.

Even if skies are clear when you set out, caution is still necessary because the weather can turn arctic at any time. The mean annual summit temperature is below 0°C and snow often lies until early summer – the summit is only about 60m below the permanent snow line. And, if attempting the climb in the winter months, remember to check what time it gets dark and give yourself enough time to get up and down.

And while we're banging on with this misery, let's give you one last cheery fact: the views from up here are superb, but your chances of seeing them ain't – the summit, on average, is cloud-covered six days out of seven. Best of luck.

From the ski-area car park (at 625m altitude) it takes about 1½ hours to climb up to the summit of Cairn Gorm at the start of the circuit, which runs around the rim of Coire an t-Sneachda and Cairn Lochan, then down the ridge that runs alongside Lurcher's Gully and back to the car park. The total distance is around 7 miles.

Glen Coe

The lofty peaks and ridges that flank Glen Coe should be left to the mountaineer, but there's a good rough walk through the remote, rugged landscape circumnavigating Buachaille Etive Beag. The 9-mile walk itself is quite a challenge and you might be glad of trekking poles for balance when negotiating stream crossings. Allow at least five hours.

Another great hike (allow six hours) leads through the Lost Valley to the top of Bidean nam Bian, which stands at 1150m. Cross the footbridge below Allt-na-reigh and follow the gorge up into the Lost Valley, continuing up to the rim, then along it, to the right, to the summit. You need to be very careful crossing to Stob Coire Nan Lochan as there are steep scree slopes. Descend the western side of this ridge and round into Coire nan Lochan, where a path heads back to the road.

For something less strenuous, hike this route only as far as the Lost Valley, a hidden mountain sanctuary still haunted by the ghosts of murdered MacDonalds. Allow three hours for this.

The Aonach Eagach, the glen's northern wall, is said to be the best ridge walk on the Scottish mainland, but it's difficult in places and you will need a good head for heights. Some parts could almost be graded a rock climb.

From Kingshouse Hotel, the view of Buachaille Etive Mór (1022m) will give you a sense of dèja vu, as it appears in photographs and adverts all over the world. The walking route to the top starts at Altnafeadh, 2½ miles west of the hotel. It takes only four hours, but it's not for casual hikers, as the higher part of the route leads up steep scree slopes in Coire na Tulaich.

Goatfell

Though this rock on the Isle of Arran falls short of being a Munro by 40m, Goatfell – at 874m – is still damn big. On a clear day, from its summit you can see Skiddaw in the Lake District, Ben Lomond to the northeast, the coast of Northern Ireland, and the conical mass of Holy Island rearing up from the sea in Lamlash Bay.

The Goatfell circuit can be done by relatively inexperienced walkers, though it's important to have proper waterproof gear, a compass and one of two maps – the Landranger map 1:50,000 No 69 (Isle of Arran) or the Outdoor Leisure map 1:25,000 No 37 (Isle of Arran).

The circuit starts and ends in Brodick, and its 11 miles take up to eight hours.

From Brodick head northwards along the main road for about 1½ miles to a major junction and turn left along the B880 towards Blackwaterfoot. About 100m farther turn right down the narrow 'Glen Rosa Cart Track' and follow this to the camp site. Continue along a clear vehicle track to the glen, with superb views of the precipitous peaks on the western side, culminating in Cir Mhór (798m).

The track becomes a path at the crossing of Garbh Allt. Aiming unerringly for the Saddle, the low point between Cir Mhór and Goatfell, the path climbs gently and you'll be treated to fine views of Glen Sannox.

To the right, the features of the next stage are clearly visible – bouldery West Ridge, leading steeply up to North Goatfell, and Stacach Ridge, crowned by four small, rocky peaks.

From the Saddle, a braided and eroded string of paths leads up the ridge towards North Goatfell. There are some narrow, exposed sections and a few near-vertical 'steps' where you'll need to use your hands. After about an hour the route nears the summit of North Goatfell (818m). The final section is a scramble but, if this is too intimidating, pass below the top, keeping it on your left, and return to the ridge. Turn back to gain the summit from the east, over large slabs and boulders.

From North Goatfell you can keep to the crest of the ridge, scrambling over the rocky knobs. Alternatively, drop down to the eastern side of the ridge and follow the less exposed paths below the knobs.

The final section involves hopping over giant boulders to the summit of Goatfell with its stunning views.

To return, take the path down the steep eastern face of the peak. At a path junction with a large cairn, turn right and follow the all-too-clear path southeast then south across moorland, down the valley of Cnocan Burn and into scattered woodland. Then, at a junction in a pine plantation, continue straight on and turn right at a T-junction. Go down through pines and the grounds of Brodick Castle.

Speyside Way

This is definitely a route that any serious walker will want to tick off in their journey book. A stunning lowland path running alongside the River Spey, which brims with salmon and anglers trying to snag them, the Way can be done from either Aviemore, in Strathspey, or from Buckie on the North Sea coast.

At only 66 miles, the Way can be done in four or five days. It's extremely well signposted and way-marked with the official thistle hexagon logo (see overleaf).

The Way closely follows the river for many miles and makes use of footpaths, cycle tracks, old railway formations, forest roads and quiet rural roads. It passes through Boat of Garten, Nethy Bridge, Grantown-on-Spey, Cromdale, Aberlour, Craigellachie, Fochabers and Spey Bay.

The Speyside Way Ranger Service (☎ 01 340-881266) publishes a free brochure with a great map of the walk and details of facilities along the route, and a public transport guide. For more details check out the Moray Council Web site at W www .moray.org and the extremely thorough W www.speysideway.org.

The Harvey Walker's 1:40,000 map *Speyside Way* is the official map for the route, while *The Speyside Way Guide*, published by Rucksack Readers, has easy to use 1:100,000 strip maps and lots of information.

West Highland Way

Officially Scotland's (and Britain's) most popular long-distance path, with a hefty 50,000 people walking it each year, the West Highland Way stretches 95 miles from Milngavie on the outskirts of Scotland's largest city, Glasgow, to the base of its highest mountain, Ben Nevis.

Beginning in the lowlands, the greater part of this glorious walk is among the mountains, lochs and fast-flowing rivers of the Highlands. After following the eastern shore of Loch Lomond, and passing Crianlarich and Tyndrum, the route crosses wild Rannoch Moor and reaches Fort William via beautiful Glen Nevis, in the shadow of Britain's highest peak, Ben Nevis.

Perhaps because you set out in bustling Glasgow, trek for six or seven days over dramatic scenery, and then arrive in homely Fort William, this rewarding walk really will feel like an epic journey.

Once you've done the walk you'll never be able to look at a map of Scotland again without tracing your finger over the little patch you covered on foot.

The path is very easy to follow and uses the old drove roads, along which cattle were herded in the past, an old military road (built by troops to help subdue the Highlands in the 18th century) and disused railway lines.

It's well signposted with a thistle and hexagon motif. The trail is best walked from south to north, and you must be properly equipped with good boots, maps, compass, food and drink for the northern part of the walk. Midge repellent is also essential.

Accommodation is easy to find, though between Bridge of Orchy and Kinlochleven it's limited. In summer, book B&Bs in advance. There are youth hostels on or near the path (which also fill up in summer), as well as bunkhouses, and it's also possible to camp in some parts.

When to Walk The route can be walked any time of year, though May is the most popular month as many try to avoid the midges. Spring and autumn can be particularly beautiful. One section, Conic Hill (358m) by Loch Lomond in the early part of

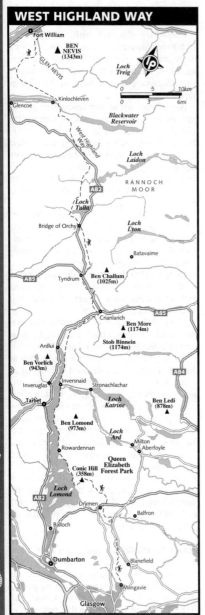

WEST HIGHLAND WAY

the walk, is closed for lambing during the last two weeks in April and the first two weeks in May. The Way itself is unaffected by deer stalking, but detours from the track should be avoided from August to October.

Walk Information Four OS Landranger maps cover the way:

Landranger 41: Ben Nevis, Fort William & Glen Coe
Landranger 50: Glen Orchy & Loch Etive
Landranger 56: Loch Lomond & Inveraray
Landranger 64: Glasgow, Motherwell & Airdrie

Harvey's *West Highland Way Map* is excellent and the best guide is the *West Highland Way* from Rucksack Readers (W www.rucsacs.com). The official guide is the more expensive *West Highland Way*, by Bob Aitken & Roger Smith, which comes with its own 1:50,000 OS route map.

For a free list of accommodation on the Way contact the Loch Lomond Park Ranger Service (☎ 01360-870470), the Glen Nevis Countryside Ranger Service (☎ 01397-705922) or the Scottish Tourist Board (☎ 0131-332 2433). The West Highland Way Web site at W www.west-highland-way.co.uk is very useful, offering practical information, accommodation listings and numerous useful Web links.

In case of an emergency, in the Glasgow area contact Strathclyde Police on ☎ 0141-532 2000 or, along the northern section of the Way, the Fort William police on ☎ 01397-702361.

Camping Pitching tents is only permitted on the Way in designated areas; there are several free, one-night only backpacker sites without facilities on the route, which operate a strict policy of no open fires. There are also restrictions on walking with dogs in certain areas – contact the information services listed for details.

The walk is well marked with this thistle motif.

Guided Walks & Baggage Services Several companies organise walking holidays on the Way with vehicle support. C-N-Do (☎ 01786-445703, ⓔ info@cndoscotland .com) and Lomond Walking Holidays (☎ 01786-447752, ⓔ paul@milligan.force9 .co.uk) are two of the larger ones.

Rather than taking a full tour, you can make the going easier by using a pack-carrying service. Travel-Lite (☎ 0141-956 6810) charges £32 to pick up your bag each morning and deliver it to your next B&B or hostel, ready for when you arrive (eight collections and deliveries maximum).

Facts for the Visitor

HIGHLIGHTS

There is certainly no shortage of things to see and do in the Highlands and islands, whether you feel like following in the footsteps of the first human beings to settle in the British Isles, combing the heathland for stags and eagles, bagging Scotland's highest peaks or just enjoying the exhilaration of this rugged landscape.

Historic Cities, Towns & Villages

Inverness
The capital of the Highlands has a scenic location between the River Noss and the Beauly Firth.

Lerwick
This splendid port has changed little in 200 years.

Stromness
An ancient Royal Burgh, Stromness is the quintessential fishing port.

Abbeys & Cathedrals

Iona Abbey
Dating back to 1200, this abbey played a huge role in the conversion of Scotland.

St Magnus Cathedral
This red-sandstone cathedral in Kirkwall (Orkney) was built by the same masons who built Durham Cathedral in England.

Museums & Galleries

Highland Folk Museum
Split between Newtonmore and Kingussie, this fascinating museum in Strathspey concentrates on the life of ordinary Highlanders.

Shetland Museum
This eccentric museum in Lerwick covers all aspects of Shetland's history.

Stromness Museum
This wonderful museum showcases the extraordinary maritime history of Stromness in Orkney.

West Highland Museum
For a real insight into the Jacobite rebellions, visit this museum of Highland history in Lochaber.

Castles & Stately Homes

Balmoral
The Highland house of the British royal family, Balmoral is an opulent pile and you might catch a glimpse of HRH.

Blair Castle
Probably Scotland's finest castle, Blair has sumptuous fittings and even its own private army (Pitlochry).

Dunrobin
Set in magnificent grounds in Golspie, this was the former home of the notorious duke of Sutherland.

Eilean Donan
This wonderful castle on an island off Glenelg is probably the definitive Highland castle.

Kisimul
This spectacular castle is set in a lake on the remote island of Barra and can only be reached by boat.

Urquhart
Although ruined, this castle overlooking Loch Ness is one of the most famous in Scotland.

Prehistoric Remains

Calanais Standing Stones
Perhaps Scotland's finest stone circle, set within a cross-shaped avenue of tall stones on a dramatic hillside in Lewis.

Jarlshof
This excavated village complex presents a window onto 5000 years of history, from the ancient Britons to the Vikings and Scots lairds.

Mousa Broch
Built by the ancient inhabitants of the Shetland Islands, this amazingly preserved *broch* (defensive tower) is Britain's finest.

Ring of Brodgar
This ancient stone circle in Orkney is part of an extensive ceremonial site that includes standing stones and a chambered tomb.

Skara Brae
The extraordinarily well-preserved remains of a village inhabited 5000 years ago – including stone dressers, fireplaces, beds and boxes – can be found in Orkney.

Train Journeys

Inverness-Kyle Line
Travel on this line for an excellent trip through wild moors and glens, leading to the bridge to Skye.

The West Highland Railway
This is Scotland's most famous railway line, with dramatic sections crossing Rannoch Moor and from Fort William to Mallaig; see the boxed text in the Getting Around chapter.

Beaches & Coastal Scenery

Beaches

North and South Uist, Barra, Harris, Lewis, and the north coast of the mainland have splendid beaches. Farther south, Nairn has the Highlands' only Blue Flag beach. Orkney has many fine beaches, particularly on Sanday, while Shetland has Britain's largest sand tombolo at St Ninian's Isle.

Cliffs

Spectacular cliffs can be found at Hoy (Orkney), Unst (Shetland), Clo Mor (Cape Wrath) and around Duncansby Head (John o'Groats).

Oban to John o'Groats

The scenery here is one of the world's greatest natural spectacles, with arches, caves, stacks and hidden coves in many places along the coast.

Activities

The Highlands and islands offer an astounding range of outdoor activities from hill-walking and mountaineering to bird-spotting, scuba diving and golf – see the Activities chapter for details.

SUGGESTED ITINERARIES

Depending on the time at your disposal, you might want to try some of the following:

Four days
Visit Glencoe, Inverness and Loch Ness
One week
Visit Glencoe, Ben Nevis, Oban, Fort William, Inverness and Loch Ness (or skip Inverness and Loch Ness and visit Skye, Islay or Mull)
Two weeks
Visit Glencoe, Ben Nevis, Oban, Fort William, Inverness, Loch Ness, Torridon and Skye, Islay, Mull or the Small Isles (alternatively head northwards to Thurso and Orkney)
One month
Start in the southwest and add the Cairngorms and some of the smaller, southern isles, see Inverness and Skye and follow the northwest coast via Ullapool to Thurso and cross to Orkney and/or Shetland (alternatively visit Lewis and Harris from Ullapool)
Two months
As for one month except explore Speyside and Argyll, the other Western Isles, climb some of the Munros in the northwest and spend more time in Orkney and Shetland

PLANNING

When to Go

The two most important things to plan for when visiting the Highlands and islands are rain and midges (small biting insects). The British summer, from June to August, is certainly the driest time to visit, but this is also peak midge season, particularly on the islands. It's also peak tourist season, and many attractions can be swamped by coach-tour groups. On the plus side, daylight hours are long; the midsummer sun sets around 11pm in the Shetland Islands and even on the mainland there are seemingly endless summer evenings.

April/May is probably the best window for visiting the region, when midge numbers are low and the rain is only a periodic inconvenience. September/October is another good time window, with few midges and spectacular autumnal colours.

Unless you're here for winter sports in the mountains, winter is probably best avoided. Days are almost uniformly dark, cold and damp. The sun never completely rises in the far northern islands and even on the mainland you'll be lucky to see more than a few hours of daylight. Ferry and airline schedules are routinely disrupted by high winds and high-altitude roads and even rail lines may be closed by snow and landslides. Most hostels, B&Bs, hotels, restaurants and visitor attractions shut, and buses slow to a trickle. That said, more places are staying open over the winter, and the Highlands have a desolate beauty in the winter snow.

Whenever you visit Scotland, you're likely to see both sun and rain, so pack accordingly.

What Kind of Trip

The Highlands and islands offer a staggering range of diversions, but most have a firmly outdoor bent. Your particular interests will have a large bearing on the kind of trip it'll be, as will the amount of time and money at your disposal. Hill-walking, for example, is free and the infrastructure of trails and places to stay and eat is extremely well organised, while skiing is easily as expensive as in Europe's top ski resorts.

The most important factor to allow for is time. There are no fast routes around the region; roads twist and turn endlessly and a journey that looks like 50 miles on the map will often be 150 miles once you factor in all the hairpin bends and detours. You'll get more out of your visit if you take time to explore some of the less touristy towns, and the wonderful remote parts of the Highlands are best appreciated on a longer stay. It's easy enough to get to the main centres by bus or train, but some attractions have no public transport, so walking, cycling or driving may be your only way to see them.

With limited time, your best bet might be to take a coach tour, or one of the hop-on, hop-off bus tours operated by Haggis Backpackers or MacBackpackers (see the Getting Around chapter for details).

Maps

For casual touring and driving around the Highlands and islands, you can get away with any of the road atlases of Britain. If you plan to go off the beaten track, you'll need one that shows at least 3 miles to the inch. For something a little more detailed, try the very good Scotland Tourist Map series (£3.99), published by the regional Highland tourist authorities in partnership with Estate Publications, which show hundreds of lesser-known historic sites, as well as the obvious attractions.

If you mean to do any walking, it's well worth shelling out for the Ordnance Survey (OS; W www.ordsvy.gov.uk) Landranger series at a scale of 1:50,000 or the Explorer series at a scale of 1:25,000. They cost £5.99 and £6.99 per sheet, respectively, and are produced by the British government's mapping agency. Landranger maps cover the entire region, from Argyll to the tip of Shetland. See the individual chapters for the maps covering each area.

Tourist offices usually provide basic maps of large towns.

What to Bring

While almost anything you think of can be bought in Scottish cities, you will pay a significant mark-up for most items in the islands and other remote rural areas, assuming you can find what you need. Bear in mind that Britain is one of the most expensive countries in Europe and many things may be cheaper at home.

The traditional backpack is still the most practical item for carrying gear around the region, particularly if you plan to do any walking. Do your back a favour and opt for a small pack (65L is a sensible size). Plastic carrier bags or zip-lock sandwich bags will keep things organised, and dry, inside your backpack.

If you bring a tent, make sure it is thoroughly waterproof and wind resistant. Bear in mind that most camp sites close from October to Easter, and camping out in the region during winter is strictly for masochists. Providing your own sleeping bag will save you a few pounds in many hostels, though some places insist that guests use the clean sheets and quilts provided by the hostel instead. If you're driving in winter, it's worth having a warm blanket and some emergency food in the car in case roads are closed by snow.

One almost essential item is a decent torch (flashlight). There is little street lighting in the more remote Highlands and islands and a small portable torch will let you explore any caves and cairns you come across on your travels. A padlock is handy for locking your bag to a train or a bus luggage rack, and may also be needed to secure your hostel locker. A Swiss Army knife (or any pocketknife that includes a bottle opener and strong corkscrew) is useful for all sorts of things.

Walkers are advised to carry a compass, maps and some emergency food, particularly if you head off the main walking trails. Carry plenty of water while walking to stave off dehydration; water from Highland burns may be polluted by livestock so water purification tablets are a sensible policy. It's a good idea to treat your walking boots with a waterproofing agent and don't forget some form of waterproof jacket with a hood (the Highland winds will make short work of umbrellas). A waterproof holder for maps is also a good idea.

RESPONSIBLE TOURISM

With so many of its natural resources exploited for tourism, Scotland is particularly at risk from irresponsible visitors. Remember that what may look like deserted heath or grassland to you may represent a fragile ecosystem. During the recent epidemic of foot-and-mouth disease (see the boxed text in the Facts about Scotland's Highlands & Islands chapter), many areas were closed off to walkers, and even though Scotland is now officially clear of the disease, many farmers are still nervous about letting walkers cross their land.

Tourists have picked up a bad reputation over the years for knocking over dry-stone walls, damaging fences, leaving gates open and creating shortcuts along walking trails, which soon become gushing courses for rainwater. You should follow the rules of the Comeback Code (a revised version of the country code): don't touch or feed animals, don't drop food scraps or litter, avoid entering enclosed fields or farmyards, don't park where animals gather, close gates behind you and obey signs placed by farmers.

TOURIST OFFICES
Local Tourist Offices

Tourist information in the Highlands and islands is handled through a series of regional tourist boards, all under the auspices of the Scottish Tourist Board/Visit Scotland (STB; ☎ 0131-332 2433, e info@stb.gov.uk, W www.visitscotland.com) in Edinburgh.

The Highlands and islands are divided between a number of smaller regional tourist boards:

Argyll, the Isles, Loch Lomond, Stirling & Trossachs Tourist Board
(☎ 01369 701000, W www.scottish.heart lands.org) 7 Alexandra Parade, Dunoon, Argyll

Highlands of Scotland Tourist Board
(☎ 01997 421160, e admin@host.co.uk, W www.highlandfreedom.com) Peffery House, Strathpeffer

Orkney Tourist Board
(☎ 01856 872856, e orkneytb@csi.com, W www.visitorkney.com) 6 Broad St, Kirkwall, Mainland Orkney

Shetland Islands Tourism
(☎ 01595 693434, e shetland.tourism@ zetnet.co.uk, W www.visitshetland.com) Market Cross, Lerwick

Western Isles Tourist Board
(☎ 01851 703088, e witb@sol.co.uk, W www.witb.co.uk) 26 Cromwell, Stornoway, Isle of Lewis

Information can also be obtained through the STB in London at 19 Cockspur St, London SW1 5BL, off Trafalgar Square. For telephone enquiries, you're best off calling the Edinburgh office.

Most towns have TICs that open 9am or 10am to 5pm weekdays year-round plus weekends in summer. In small places, particularly in the Highlands, TICs only open from Easter to September. Note that tourist offices only promote their members, who pay high fees for membership and may pass those fees on to visitors.

Tourist Offices Abroad

Overseas, the British Tourist Authority (BTA; W www.bta.org.uk) represents the STB and stocks masses of information, much of it free. For information in foreign languages you can check out the Web site at W www.visitbritain.com.

Contact the BTA before leaving home because some discounts are available only to people who have booked before arriving in Britain. Travellers with special needs (disability, diet and so on) should also contact the nearest BTA office. Addresses are listed on its Web site. Some overseas offices are:

Australia
(☎ 02-9377 4400, fax 9377 4499, e visit britainaus@bta.org.uk) Level 16, The Gateway, 1 Macquarie Place, Circular Quay, Sydney, NSW 2000
Canada
(toll-free ☎ 1-888 VISIT UK, ☎ 905-405 1720, fax 905-405 1835, e travelinfo@ bta.org.uk) 5915 Airport Rd, Suite 120, Mississauga, Ontario L4V 1T1
France
(☎ 01 44 51 56 20, fax 01 44 51 56 21) Maison de la Grande Bretagne, 19 Rue des Mathurins, F-75009 Paris (entrance in Rues Tronchet and Auber)
Germany
(☎ 069-97 1123, fax 97 112444, e gbinfo@ bta.org.uk) Westendstrasse 16–22, D-60325 Frankfurt
Ireland
(☎ 01-670 8000, fax 670 8244, e contactus@ bta.org.co.uk) 18–19 College Green, Dublin 2
Italy
(☎ 02 8808 151) Corso Magenta 32, Milano 20123

Netherlands
 (☎ 020-689 0002, fax 689 0003, ℮ BritInfo
 .NL@bta.org.uk) Aurora Gebouw (5e), Stad-
 houderskade 2, NL-1054 ES Amsterdam
New Zealand
 (☎ 09-303 1446, fax 377 6965, ℮ bta.nz@
 bta.org.uk) 17th Floor, NZI House, 151 Queen
 St, Auckland 1
Spain
 (☎ 0902 171 181) Calle Santiago de
 Compostela 100, 2, 28035 Madrid
USA
 (☎ 1 800 GO 2 BRITAIN, ℮ travelinfo@
 bta.org.uk) 625 N Michigan Ave, Suite 1001,
 Chicago IL 60611 (personal callers only); 551
 Fifth Ave, Suite 701, New York, NY 10176-
 0799

VISAS & DOCUMENTS
Passport
Your most important travel document is a
passport, which should remain valid until
well after your trip. If it's about to expire,
renew it before you go; many countries insist that your passport remains valid for up
to six months after your arrival.

Australian citizens can apply at post offices, or the passport office in their state capital; Canadians can apply at regional passport
offices; New Zealanders can apply at any
district office of the Department of Internal
Affairs; and US citizens must apply in person (but may usually renew by mail) at a US
Passport Agency office or some courthouses
and post offices.

Citizens of European Union (EU) countries just need a national identity card
(which usually involves less paperwork and
processing time) for travel to Britain, but
carrying a passport is still advisable.

Visas
While British citizens rarely have trouble
getting visas to travel abroad, the British Department of Immigration does not always extend the same courtesy to other nationalities.
It's essential to check the latest situation with
your local British embassy, high commission
or consulate before leaving home. Check the
Foreign Office Web site at W visa.fco.gov
.uk for the latest visa regulations.

No visas are required for Scotland if you
arrive from England, Wales or Northern

Ireland. If you arrive from the Republic of
Ireland or any other country, normal British
customs and immigration regulations apply.

Tourist Visas Currently, if you're a citizen
of Australia, Canada, New Zealand, South
Africa or the USA, you will be given leave
to enter Britain as a tourist at your port of arrival. Citizens of these countries are permitted to stay for up to six months, but are
prohibited from working and officials may
ask to see evidence that you can support
yourself while you are in the UK. People
have been refused entry because they happened to be carrying papers (such as references) that suggested they intended to work.
Part of the assessment of your ability to support yourself will be based on your appearance, so dress smartly when you enter the
country! A credit card is often accepted as
evidence of funds.

Visa Extensions To extend your stay in
the UK contact the Home Office, Immigration & Nationality Directorate (☎ 0870 606
7766), Block C, Whitgift Centre, Croydon,
London CR9 1AT, *before* your existing permit expires. You'll need to send your passport with your application.

Onward Tickets
Although you don't need an onward ticket
to be granted 'leave to enter' on arrival (see
Visas), this could help if there's any doubt
over whether you have sufficient funds to
support yourself and purchase an onward
ticket in Britain.

Travel Insurance
A travel-insurance policy to cover theft,
loss, medical problems and cancellations is
a good idea. However, there's a wide variety of policies available and you should
check the small print carefully.

• Some policies specifically exclude 'dangerous
 activities', which can include scuba diving,
 motorcycling, skiing and even trekking.
• A locally acquired motorcycle licence is not
 valid under some policies.
• You may prefer a policy which pays doctors or
 hospitals directly rather than you having to pay

on the spot and claim later. If you have to claim later make sure you keep all documentation.

- Some policies ask you to call back (reverse charges) to a centre in your home country where an assessment of your problem is made.
- Check that the policy covers ambulances or an emergency flight home.

Driving Licence & Permits

Citizens of the EU, Iceland, Norway and Liechtenstein can use their home driving licence until its expiry date. For non-EU citizens, home driving licences are legal for 12 months from the last date of entry to Britain; you can then apply for a British licence at post offices.

Many automobile associations worldwide have reciprocal programmes with the British Automobile Association (AA) or Royal Automobile Club (RAC). Ask your home automobile association for a letter of introduction, which will entitle you to services such as breakdown assistance, technical and legal advice and so on, usually free of charge.

Hostel Card

If you're travelling on a budget and intend to stay in hostels, membership of the Scottish Youth Hostel Association (SYHA) is a must. Membership costs £6 for over-18s, £2.50 for under-18s, and £60 for life membership. There are around 56 SYHA or SYHA-affiliated hostels in the Highlands and islands, and members are eligible for a wide list of discounts. Membership of Hostelling International (HI) entitles you to the same benefits, while SYHA membership will give you reciprocal benefits at HI-member hostels worldwide.

Student & Youth Cards

Most useful is the International Student Identity Card (ISIC), which displays your photograph. This can perform wonders, including producing discounts on many forms of transport. Even if you have your own transport, the card soon pays for itself through reduced or free admission to attractions and cheap meals in some student restaurants.

There's a worldwide industry in fake student cards, and many places now stipulate a maximum age for student discounts. If you're aged under 26 but not a student, you can apply for the Euro<26 card (W www.euro26.org), while under-25s have the GO25 card issued by the Federation of International Youth Travel Organisations (FIYTO; W www.fiyto.org). These cards are available through student unions, hostelling organisations or youth-oriented travel agencies. They don't automatically entitle you to discounts, but you won't find out until you flash the card.

If you live in Scotland and are aged 12 to 25, the Young Scot card (☎ 0870 513 4936, W www.youngscot.com) gives discounts on everything from fast-food meals to bus, train and ferry tickets.

Seniors Cards

Discount cards for over-60s are available for rail and bus travel. See the Getting Around chapter.

Other Documents

Nationals of EU countries should carry Form E111, which allows free emergency medical treatment in Scotland. Ask your national health service or travel agent for a form well in advance. Australian Medicare doesn't cover medical treatment in Scotland.

Copies

All important documents (passport data page and visa page, credit cards, travel insurance policy, air/bus/train tickets, driving licence and so on) should be photocopied before you leave home. Leave one copy with someone at home and keep another with you, separate from the originals.

It's a good idea to store details of your vital travel documents in Lonely Planet's free online Travel Vault in case you lose the copies (or can't be bothered with them). Your password-protected Travel Vault is accessible online anywhere in the world – create it at W www.ekno.lonelyplanet.com.

EMBASSIES & CONSULATES
Your Own Embassy

It's important to realise what your own embassy – the embassy of the country in which you are a citizen – can and can't do to help you if you get into trouble. Generally speaking, it won't be much help in emergencies if the trouble you're in is remotely your own fault. Remember that you are bound by the laws of the country you are in. Your embassy will not be sympathetic if you end up in jail after committing a crime locally, even if such actions are legal in your own country.

In genuine emergencies you might get some assistance, but only if other channels have been exhausted. For example, if you need to get home urgently, a free ticket home is exceedingly unlikely – the embassy would expect you to have insurance. If you have all your money and documents stolen, it might assist with getting a new passport, but a loan for onward travel is out of the question.

UK Embassies & Consulates Abroad

Some UK embassies abroad include:

Australia
High Commission: (☎ 02-6270 6666) Commonwealth Ave, Yarralumla, Canberra, ACT 2600
Canada
High Commission: (☎ 613-237 1530) 80 Elgin St, Ottawa, Ontario K1P 5K7
France
Embassy: (☎ 01 44 51 31 00) 35 rue du Faubourg St Honoré, 75383 Paris
Germany
Embassy: (☎ 030-20457 0) Wilhelmstrasse 70, 10117 Berlin
Italy
Embassy: (☎ 06 4220 2600) Via XX Settembre 80a, I-00187 Roma RM
Netherlands
Embassy: (☎ 70 427 0345) Lange Voorhout 10, De Hague 2514 ED
New Zealand
High Commission: (☎ 04-924 2888) 44 Hill St, Wellington 1
Spain
Embassy: (☎ 091 700 8200) Calle de Fernando el Santo 16, Madrid 28010
USA
Embassy: (☎ 202-588 6500) 3100 Massachusetts Ave NW, Washington DC 20008

Consulates in Scotland

Most foreign diplomatic missions are in London but a handful are located around Edinburgh (code ☎ 0131):

Australia
(☎ 624 3333) 69 George St, EH2 2JG (NB For emergencies contact the Australian High Commission in London on ☎ 0207-379 4334)
Canada
(☎ 220 4333) Standard Life House, 30 Lothian Rd, EH1 2DH
France
(☎ 225 7954) 11 Randolph Crescent, EH3 7TT
Germany
(☎ 337 2323) 16 Eglinton Crescent, EH12 5DG
Ireland
(☎ 226 7711) 16 Randolph Crescent, EH3 7TT
Italy
(☎ 226 3631) 32 Melville Street, EH3 7PG
Netherlands
(☎ 220 3226) Thistle Court, 1–2 Thistle St, EH2 2HT
New Zealand
(☎ 222 8109) 5 Rutland Square, EH1 2AS
Spain
(☎ 220 1843) 63 North Castle St, EH2 3LJ
USA
(☎ 556 8315) 3 Regent Terrace, EH7 5BW

CUSTOMS

Travellers arriving in the UK from other EU countries don't have to pay tax or duty on goods for personal use. The maximum amount of tobacco and alcohol that each person can bring into the country duty free are 800 cigarettes, 400 cigarillos, 200 cigars, 1kg of smoking tobacco, 10L of spirits, 20L of fortified wine (eg, port or sherry), 90L of wine and 110L of beer. Those aged under 17 are not allowed to import any alcohol or tobacco.

Travellers from outside the EU can bring in, duty free, a maximum of 200 cigarettes *or* 100 cigarillos OR 50 cigars *or* 250g of tobacco; 2L of still table wine; 1L of spirits *or* 2L of fortified wine, sparkling wine or liqueurs; 60mL of perfume; 250mL of toilet water; and £145 worth of all other goods, including gifts and souvenirs. Anything over this limit must be declared to customs officers on arrival.

Restricted goods, which you cannot bring into the UK without a special licence, include firearms, CB radios, animals and birds (including pets), certain plants, meat and dairy products. For more details of restrictions, see the HM Customs and Excise Web site at Ⓦ www.hmce.gov.uk.

MONEY
Currency
Pending the results of a referendum, Britain may or may not join the European Single Currency or 'euro' with the 12 nations who adopted the new currency on 1 January 2002. For the time being, the British currency is the pound sterling (£), with 100 pence (p) to a pound. One and 2p coins are copper; 5p, 10p, 20p and 50p coins are silver; the £1 coin is gold-coloured; and the £2 coin is gold- and silver-coloured. The word pence is usually abbreviated and is pronounced 'pee'.

Notes (bills) come in £1, £5, £10, £20, £50 and £100 denominations. English notes and coins are legal tender in Scotland, but you'll see rather more Scottish notes, which have the same denominations but are issued by individual banks (the Clydesdale Bank, Royal Bank of Scotland and Bank of Scotland) rather than the Royal Mint. You shouldn't have trouble changing them in shops and so on immediately south of the Scotland-England border, but elsewhere shops may not accept Scottish bank notes. All UK banks will accept Scottish bills, including £1 notes, but foreign banks will not.

Exchange Rates
The following currencies convert at these approximate rates:

country	unit		sterling
Australia	A$1	=	£0.36
Canada	C$1	=	£0.44
euro	€1	=	£0.61
Japan	¥100	=	£0.52
New Zealand	NZ$1	=	£0.29
USA	US$1	=	£0.71

Exchanging Money
Be careful using private bureaux de change; they may offer good exchange rates but frequently levy outrageous commissions and fees. Make sure that you establish the rate, the percentage commission and any fees in advance. Extra commissions for exchanging euros have been reported, so it may be better to carry cash in US dollars rather than euros.

Many TICs in the Highlands have their own bureaux de change which generally charge fair commissions (often less than high-street banks) and can exchange cash and travellers cheques in pounds, US dollars, Australian dollars, Japanese Yen and most European currencies.

There's no problem if you arrive at Inverness Airport, but regional airports such as Kirkwall (Orkney) and Sumburgh (Shetland) don't have foreign-exchange facilities; change some money in advance, or when you change planes at one of the southern Scottish airports, which all have exchange facilities and automatic teller machines (ATMs; also called cashpoints).

For an up-to-date currency converter, see the Web site at Ⓦ www.xe.net/ucc.

Cash & Cheques Nothing beats cash for convenience… or risk. Most ferry companies and places to stay and eat will accept credit cards, but ATMs and bureaux de change are fairly thin on the ground in the Highlands and islands, so it's still a good idea to travel with some local currency in cash. B&Bs, budget restaurants and cafes, and rural shops will often insist on cash, unless you can pay with a cheque, validated with a cheque-guarantee card.

Banks rarely accept foreign coins, although some airport foreign exchanges will. Try to use up your change before leaving the country, or place it in a charity box at the airport when you leave.

Travellers Cheques American Express (Amex) or Thomas Cook travellers cheques are widely accepted and have efficient replacement policies. Keep a record of the cheque numbers (and those of the cheques you've cashed) somewhere separate from the cheques themselves.

Although cheques are available in various currencies, there's little point using

US$ cheques in Scotland (unless you're travelling from the USA), since you'll lose on the exchange rate when you buy the cheques and again each time you cash one. Bring pounds sterling to avoid changing currencies twice. Not all bureaux de change exchange travellers cheques, so you are probably best off going to one of the major banks such as the Royal Bank of Scotland or Bank of Scotland.

Take most cheques in large denominations, for example £100; commissions are usually charged per cheque. It's only towards the end of a stay that you may want to change a small cheque to make sure you don't get left with too much local currency.

Credit Cards, Debit Cards & ATMs You can make cash advances on your credit card from the ATMs at the Clydesdale Bank, Bank of Scotland, Royal Bank of Scotland and Lloyds TSB; most international credit cards are accepted. There are few ATMs on the islands but you can get cash advances in person over the counter, though you may have to wait for them to manually authorise the transaction. If you have any doubts about your personal identification number (PIN), it's probably best to go to a human teller – it can be a headache if an ATM swallows your card.

Charge cards such as Amex and Diners Club are less widely accepted than other cards, especially on the islands. Some Amex cards allow you to cash up to £1000 worth of personal cheques at Amex offices in any seven-day period.

Even if you have a British bank account, you may be charged a fee of around £1 each time you use an ATM at a different bank. You'll certainly be charged for getting a cash advance on a credit card. Try to minimise the number of times you use ATMs or stick to a bank affiliated to your own bank.

International Transfers You can instruct your home bank to send you a draft. Specify the city, the bank and the branch to which you want your money directed, or ask your home bank to tell you where there's a suitable one. The whole procedure will be easier if you've authorised someone back home to access your account.

Money sent by telegraphic transfer (usually at a cost of £7) should reach you within a week; by mail, allow at least two weeks. When it arrives, it will most likely be converted into local currency – you can take it as it is or buy travellers cheques.

You can also transfer money by either Moneygram or Thomas Cook, which has several branches in the Highlands. American travellers can also use Western Union (☎ 0800 833833).

Security

The Highlands and islands are by far the safest place in the British Isles when it comes to theft, but security in hostels can be fairly relaxed and a small minority of travellers choose to fund their travels at the expense of others. Most hostels and hotels offer a safe where you can put valuable items such as money-belts, wallets and so on. It's always a good idea to keep a stash of about £50 apart from the rest of your cash in case of an emergency.

Costs

As with the rest of the British Isles, Scotland can be expensive. Fortunately backpacker accommodation is widely available, so budget travellers will be able to keep their costs down, particularly if you don't mind self-catering. In remote parts of the region, where supplies depend on ferries, you can pay a big mark-up on most items, so it may be worth bringing supplies from the mainland (this also applies when visiting offshore islands from mainland Orkney or mainland Shetland).

Travelling with a car is likely to increase your costs exponentially. Ferries between the islands charge universally high fares for cars, and petrol is considerably more pricey than in Europe, Australia or the USA. In fact, petrol is more expensive here than it is in southern England (figure on at least £15 per day). You'll pay an additional mark-up at petrol stations on the outlying islands to cover the import cost. Taking a car is a costly option, but it will save you time.

Another cost to watch out for is pub meals. Most pubs offer an inexpensive 'bar-meal' menu (with dishes from £5 to £8) and a much pricier restaurant menu (with dishes from £11 to £15). A lot of dishes appear on both menus, so ask for the bar menu if you're watching your budget.

Some typical high-season (July and August) costs are listed below:

Hostel bed	£6 to £12 per person
B&B	£16 to £25 per person
Mid-range hotel	£45 per person
Pub meals	£5 to £9
Restaurant meal	£8 to £16
Gourmet bistro	£15 to £28
Loaf of bread	40p to 80p
Pint of beer	£2.20
Bottle of wine	£4 (in supermarket)
Bottle of quality wine	£15 (in restaurant)
Car hire	from £20 per day
1L petrol	82p
Local phone call	20p
Newspaper	30p

If you stay in hostels, eat pub meals or self cater and use public transport, you can get by on £25 per day. Add on ferry trips and admission frees to attractions, plus the odd B&B and a few pints of beer, and £50 may be more realistic. Expect to spend at least £60 per day with a hire car, B&B accommodation and restaurant meals.

Tipping & Bargaining

In general, if you eat in a Scottish restaurant you should leave a tip of at least 10% unless the service was unsatisfactory. Waiting staff are often paid derisory wages on the assumption that the money will be supplemented by tips. If the bill already includes a service charge of 10% to 15%, you needn't add a further tip.

Taxi drivers expect to be tipped (about 10%), though it's less usual to tip minicab drivers. Bargaining is virtually unheard of, even at markets, although it's fine to ask if there are discounts for students, young people or youth-hostel members. Some 'negotiation' is also OK if you're buying an expensive item such as a car or motorcycle.

Taxes & Refunds

Value Added Tax (VAT) is a 17.5% sales tax that is levied on all goods and services except fresh food and books. Restaurant prices must by law include VAT. Non-EU citizens can sometimes claim a refund on VAT paid on certain goods providing they leave the EU within three months of making the purchase. The VAT-rebate rules for EU residents only apply if you're subsequently planning to leave the EU for a year so it's not really worth the effort.

On request, participating shops give you a special form/invoice; they'll need to see your passport. This form must be presented with the goods and receipt to customs when you depart (VAT-free goods can't be posted or shipped home). After customs has certified the form, it should be returned to the shop for a refund less an administration fee.

Several companies offer a centralised refunding service to shops. Participating shops carry a sign in their window. You can avoid bank charges for cashing a sterling cheque by using a credit card for purchases and asking to have your VAT refund credited to your card account. Cash refunds are sometimes available at major airports.

POST & COMMUNICATIONS
Post

Most post offices open 9am to 5.30pm weekdays and 9am to 12.30pm Saturday, but rural post offices may only open Monday to Friday. On the smaller islands, the village shop usually doubles as the post office and may only open a few hours a day.

Mail sent within the UK can go either first or second class; first-class mail is faster (normally next-day delivery) and more expensive (27p up to 60g, 41p up to 100g) than 2nd-class mail (19/33p). Airmail postcards/letters (40g to 60g) to European countries cost 37/65p; to South Africa, the USA and Canada 40p/£1.35; and Australia and New Zealand 40p/£1.49. An airmail letter generally takes five days to get to the USA or Canada and around a week to Australia or New Zealand.

If you don't have a permanent address, mail can be sent to poste restante in the town or city where you're staying. Amex offices also hold card-holders' mail free.

Telephone

Although British Telecom (BT) is still the largest telephone operator, with the most public phone booths, there are also several competing companies.

You'll see two types of phone booth: one takes money (and doesn't give change), while the other uses prepaid phonecards and credit cards. Some phones accept coins and cards. Most of the traditional red phone-boxes in the Highlands and islands are out of service and are often used as impromptu greenhouses by local residents!

All phones come with reasonably clear instructions in several languages. If you're likely to be making several calls (especially international) buy a BT phonecard. Ranging in value from £2 to £20, they're widely available from various retailers, including post offices and newsagents.

Some codes worth knowing are:

☎ 0345   local call rate
☎ 0800   toll-free call
☎ 0845   local call rate
☎ 0870   national call rate
☎ 0891   premium rate

Local & National Calls Local calls are charged by time; national calls are charged by time and distance. Daytime rates are from 8am to 6pm, Monday to Friday; cheap rates are from 6pm to 8am, Monday to Friday, and from midnight Friday to midnight Sunday.

For directory enquiries call ☎ 192 (11p per minute from public telephones but 40p per call for up to two searches from a private phone). To get the operator call ☎ 100.

The *Yellow Pages* business directory (with maps) is online at Ⓦ www.yell.com. The *Yellow Pages* also offers a Talking Pages business search service on ☎ 0800 600 900.

International Calls Dial ☎ 155 for the international operator or ☎ 153 for international directory enquiries. Direct dialling is

cheaper, though the costs can quickly mount up in a payphone; to get an international line (for international direct dialling) dial ☎ 00, then the country code, area code (dropping the first zero) and number. You can also use the Home Country Direct service to make reverse-charge or credit-card calls via an operator in your home country.

For most countries (including Europe, USA and Canada) it's cheaper to phone overseas between 8pm and 8am Monday to Friday and at weekends; for Australia and New Zealand, however, it's cheapest from 2.30pm to 7.30pm and from midnight to 7am daily.

There is a wide range of local and international phonecards available; shop around for the cheapest call deals.

eKno Communication Service Lonely Planet's eKno Communication Card is aimed specifically at independent travellers and provides budget international calls, a range of messaging services, free email and travel information. For local calls, you're usually better off with a local card. You can join online at Ⓦ www.ekno.lonelyplanet.com, or by phone from the UK by dialling ☎ 0800 169 8646. Once you've joined, to use eKno from the UK dial ☎ 0800 376 2366.

Check the eKno Web site for joining and access numbers from other countries and updates on super budget local access numbers and new features.

Mobile Phones The UK uses the GSM 900 network, which covers the rest of Europe, Australia and New Zealand, but isn't compatible with the North American GSM 1900 or the totally different system in Japan (though some North Americans have GSM 1900/900 phones that do work in Scotland). If you have a GSM phone, check with your service provider about using it in the UK; it's normally possible to set up a roaming service that routes your calls through a local network at local rates.

If your phone isn't 'SIM-locked' (ie, locked into a particular network), you may be able to buy a starter pack for a local prepaid mobile service and put the SIM card

Trawlers moored off Skye's striking coast with the Cuillin Ridge, a rock-climber's dream, behind

A beefy Highland hair-raiser

Gearrannan Blackhouse Village, Isle of Lewis

Shell out for freshly caught crab in the Orkneys.

BETHUNE CARMICHAEL

Castle Urquhart, a prime site for monster-spotting, stands boldy on the banks of Loch Ness.

GARETH McCORMACK

Look out for nimble red deer in the Great Glen.

BETHUNE CARMICHAEL

Haggis, neeps and tatties: the hearty Scots dish

provided in your existing phone; cards with credits for the pre-paid networks are widely available in shops and newsagents. It may be possible to rent a mobile phone from some TICs though you'll have to use whatever number you're given.

The international phone-hire companies Mobell (☎ 0800 243524, W www.mobell .com) and Cellhire (☎ 01904 610610, W www.cellhire.net) rent out phones from £2 to £4 per day and can deliver to anywhere in the UK.

Fax, Email & Internet Access

Most hotels have fax machines that guests can use and larger ones have business centres with fax, printing, email and Internet access. Cybercafes are few and far between in the region but most backpacker hostels offer Internet access to their customers. Alternatively, there are Internet facilities in many public libraries. Most places charge a slightly steep £4 to £7 per hour. In the islands there are a few restaurants, TICs and shops with Internet facilities.

DIGITAL RESOURCES
Web Sites

There are plenty of sites of interest to cyber-travellers. Web sites are given throughout the book where appropriate.

The best place to start your Web explorations is at the Lonely Planet Web site at W www.lonelyplanet.com, which offers speedy links to numerous sites of interest. Another fine site is W www.scotland-info .co.uk, which includes extensive online resources for the Highlands and islands. For massive link archives to Web sites on Scottish or Scotland-related topics, surf W www.scotsmart.com or W www.scotland online.com.

A good commercial genealogy service is W www.scottish-roots.co.uk. Australasians of Scottish descent may want to check out the Web site for the magazine *Scots*, which is online at W www.scots heritage.com.au.

For details of the official tourist authority Web sites see Tourist Offices earlier in the chapter.

BOOKS
Lonely Planet

If you're planning to visit other parts of Scotland, check out Lonely Planet's *Britain*, *Scotland* and *Edinburgh* guides. Walking and cycling routes in the region are covered by Lonely Planet's *Walking in Scotland*, *Walking in Britain* and *Cycling Britain* guides.

Guidebooks

The highly recommended *Touring Guide to Scotland* (2001), published by the Scottish Tourist Board, details over 1500 tourist attractions and is well worth £4.99.

People of a literary bent might like to look at the *Oxford Literary Guide to Great Britain and Ireland*, which details the writers who have immortalised the towns and villages. An excellent series of books published by the Royal Commission on the Ancient and Historic Monuments of Scotland covers all the major historic sites in *Argyll & the Western Isles*, *The Highlands*, *Shetland* and *Orkney*.

There are numerous local guidebooks, the most useful being mentioned in the text. See the Activities chapter for details of cycling and walking guidebooks.

For guides on accommodation and food see those sections later in the chapter.

Novels & Poetry

Perhaps the most important writer in the Highlands and islands was Edinburgh-born Sir Walter Scott (1771–1832), who almost single-handedly created many of the region's legends through books such as *The Pirate*, set in Shetland.

Along with Scott, Robert Louis Stevenson (1850–94) ranks as Scotland's best-known novelist. Born in Edinburgh into a family of famous lighthouse engineers, Stevenson lived briefly on Unst in Shetland and on Mull, inspiring his famous *Treasure Island*, loosely based on Unst, and *Kidnapped*, set on Erraid off the Mull coast.

The modern author Alan Warner has set several of his dark novels in the Highlands, including *Morven Callar*, a sort of *Trainspotting* for the Highlands, and his latest work *The Man Who Walks*, about two drifters on the trail of a stash of missing money that leads them to Culloden Moor.

Although he has no real Highland connection, Robert Burns (1759–96) was inspired by the region and is beloved from Berwick to Shetland; he's responsible for such fine poems as *Tam o'Shanter*, *Auld Lang Syne* and the inimitable *Address to a Haggis*.

Travel

Although James Boswell was from Edinburgh, he is responsible for introducing the English to the culture and history of the Highlands and islands, through his *Journey to the Hebrides*, a fascinating account of his expedition to Skye, Coll and Mull with the English lexicographer Dr Samuel Johnson, who compiled the first dictionary of the English language.

David Duff edited *Queen Victoria's Highland Journals*, a first-hand account of the British queen's secret rambling in the Highlands. Sir Walter Scott wrote an entertaining description of his tour of Scottish lighthouses with Robert Stevenson in *Voyage of the Pharos*.

A little outdated but still readable is John Hillaby's *Journey Through Britain*, which describes a two-month walk from Land's End to John o'Groats in 1968 and is great for measuring the changes that have taken place since then. Naturalist Mike Tomkies wrote an evocative series of books, including *A Last Wild Place*, about his experiences living in a remote West Highland cottage in the 1980s.

Nick Danziger's *Danziger's Britain* (1997) has some painfully true descriptions of life for the marginalised in the Highlands. Jim Crumley's *Gulf of Blue Air – A Highland Journey* is a good modern travelogue with a literary bent.

History & Politics

Scotland – A Concise History, by Magnus Linklater and Fitzroy Maclean, is a recommended introduction and is noted for its superb illustrations, but for detailed popular history you can't beat Professor TC Smout's excellent *A History of the Scottish People*

1560–1830 and *A Century of the Scottish People 1830–1950*. *The Scottish Nation*, by TM Devine, covers everything from 1700 to 2000. The very latest history of Scotland is Magnus Magnusson's well-informed *Scotland: The Story of a Nation* – it should be well informed: Magnusson was the presenter of *Mastermind*, the TV quiz show!

If you were wondering what happened to the Stewart dynasty, *The Forgotten Monarchy of Scotland* gives a fairly outrageous history of the royal line-up to the present day. It's written by the self-styled Prince Michael of Albany, who claims descent from Bonnie Prince Charlie. To flesh out some of the great figures of Scottish history, there are many well-written biographies, including Fitzroy Maclean's *Bonnie Prince Charlie*.

Highland History For an illuminating, entertaining and honest account of 19th-century life, take a look at *Hundred Years in the Highlands*, by Osgood Mackenzie.

Various titles cover the Highland Clearances from every perspective from evil-English to colluding-clans. John Prebble's account, *The Highland Clearances*, is strong on facts and low on sentimentality, as are his excellent *Culloden* (for a gripping dissection of the Highlands' most famous battle based on contemporary reports from both sides) and *Glencoe*. For more ancient history, Historic Scotland (HS) publishes *Picts, Gaels & Scots*, *Celtic Scotland*, *Viking Scotland* and *Medieval Scotland*.

Island History There are some fine books about the unusual history of Orkney, covering everything from Norse rule to the clearances. The definitive Norse text is the *Orkneyinga Saga*, written in the 12th century, which dramatically tells the story of the Orkney earls; several translations are available. Gerald Bowman's *The Man Who Bought a Navy* is an entertaining account of the raising of the German fleet from Scapa Flow. *No Ordinary Journey*, by Ian Bunyan et a,l is an account of the fascinating Arctic explorations of John Rae of Stromness. For an overview of Orcadian history, read Olaf Cuthbert's *Low's History of Orkney*.

The Shetland Bus and *We Die Alone*, by David Howarth, are two evocative histories of the secret role of Shetland during WWII. For a good introduction to Shetland history, HS publishes *Ancient Shetland*. The glossy coffee-table book *Shetland – Land of the Ocean* by postcard photographer Colin Baxter captures the drama of these rugged isles.

Some good books specifically about the Hebrides include Jim Wilkie's *Megagama*, a moving account of the departure of several hundred Lewis crofters to Montreal in 1923. *Survival of the Unfittest*, by Robert Mathieson, also covers the harsh conditions suffered by crofters in the clearances. Tom Steel's *Life & Death of St Kilda* is a good intro to the history of this remote isle, as is *St Kilda: Island on the Edge of the World*, by Charles Maclean. An interesting historical travelogue is *Expeditions to the Hebrides*, written by naturalist George Clayton Atkinson in 1831.

Nature

With some beautiful photographs, *Wild Scotland*, by James McCarthy, is an informative guide to Scotland's natural heritage and conservation. Magnus Linklater and Colin Prior's *Highland Wilderness*, with some fine mountain photos, is also worth checking out. The Collins pocket guides *Scottish Wild Flowers* and *Scottish Birds* are extremely useful companions for any naturalist. Bird-watchers may also be interested in *Where to Watch Birds in Scotland*, by Michael Madders & Julia Welstead.

FILMS

The Highlands and islands have been the setting for many popular and classic films. Earlier ones include Alfred Hitchcock's *The 39 Steps* (1935), the classic comedy *Whisky Galore!* (1949), *Ring of Bright Water* (1969) and *Kidnapped* (1972). The cult horror film *The Wicker Man* (1973) was filmed in and around the Isle of Skye, while parts of the WWII spy epic *Eye of the Needle* (1981) were filmed around Oban, and the popular *Local Hero* (1983) was also filmed in the western Highlands.

Highlander (1986), starring Sean Connery and Christopher Lambert, a swords-and-sorcery epic that cuts from 16th-century Scotland to modern New York, was filmed around Fort William and in Glen Coe, Glen Uig and Eilean Donan. *Rob Roy*, the 1995 rendition of the outlaw's tale, featured some dodgy Scottish accents from Liam Neeson and Jessica Lange, plus plenty of rather better Highland locations.

When it was released in 1996, Mel Gibson's Oscar-winning *Braveheart* sent a surge of Scottish nationalist spirit around the world, but notwithstanding the rather fanciful storyline, the film's credentials weren't as true blue as it first appeared. Part of *Braveheart* was filmed around Fort William, but most of it was shot in Ireland (which had been wooing Hollywood film-makers with tax breaks).

The same year saw the release of *Loch Ness*, a romantic Hollywood comedy, set against the backdrop of the monster myth and filmed around Eilean Donan and Loch Ness. The challenging *Breaking the Waves* (1996), a tragic love story about the wife of a crippled oil worker, was filmed in Skye and Mallaig in 1996.

The excellent *Mrs Brown*, starring Billy Connolly and Judi Dench, was partly filmed in the Highlands in 1997. The 1999 blockbuster *Entrapment* with Sean Connery was filmed partly in Mull, while the 1999 Bond film *The World is Not Enough* was partly set in Eilean Donan castle. Parts of the 2001 spying flick *Enigma* were filmed in Argyll. Mel Gibson is currently working on a new film, *The Bothy*, about an FBI agent pursuing a serial killer through the Highlands.

NEWSPAPERS & MAGAZINES

The Scots have a fine newspaper tradition dating back to the mid-17th century. The best of the Scotland-wide dailies are the *Scotsman* and the popular Labour tabloid, the *Daily Record*. The main broadsheet for the Highlands is the daily *Press & Journal*, which has a sprinkle of nationwide and world news amongst the Highland stories.

There are also some interesting regional papers, which feature lots of 'cow survives

150ft fall down cliff' stories and give a good window onto daily life in the far north. In the Highlands, try the weekly *Oban Times* or *West Highland Free Press*. The weekly *Shetland Times* has local events listings among the parochial articles on sheep and fishing. Also weekly, the *Orcadian* has the lowdown on events in the Orkneys.

Most papers sold in England and Wales are available in Scotland. Some of them are supposedly designed specifically for Scottish readership, but differences from English editions are usually marginal.

The monthly *Scots Magazine*, with articles on all aspects of Scottish life, has been in circulation since 1739.

You can also buy many foreign papers and magazines, especially in Inverness. These include *Time*, the *International Herald Tribune*, and *Newsweek*.

RADIO & TV

Most radio and all TV stations are linked to the UK-wide networks, but there are specific broadcasts for the region.

Radio

Radio reception in the Highlands is diabolical but you can usually tune into BBC Radio Scotland (AM 810kHz, FM 92–95MHz), which provides a mix of music, drama, news and sport from a Scottish viewpoint. As well as hourly news, Radio Scotland has a two-hour afternoon show of Scottish music. It also oversees regional stations in Aberdeen, the Highlands, Orkney and Shetland and a Gaelic-language channel, Radio nan Gaidheal.

Reception is better on the islands and you can usually pick up some of the mainland UK BBC stations. Radio 1 (FM 97.6–99.8MHz) is the main youth music station; Radio 2 (FM 88–90.2MHz) has music for older listeners; Radio 3 (FM 90.2–92MHz) plays classical music and opera; Radio 4 (FM 92.4–94.6MHz) offers a fine mix of news, current affairs, drama and comedy; Radio Five Live (AM 693 and 909kHz) intersperses sport with current affairs. For more details on BBC radio, visit the BBC Web site at Ⓦ www.bbc.co.uk/radio.

There are numerous independent radio stations throughout Scotland; wherever you go there'll be a local commercial station offering local news alongside the music. Radio frequencies and programmes are published in the daily press.

TV

Britain still turns out some of the best quality TV programmes in the world. BBC1 and BBC2 are publicly funded by an annual TV licence and don't carry advertising. BBC Scotland produces a wide range of programmes specifically for a Scottish audience, including news and drama, and Gaelic programmes from the BBC studio in Lewis. ITV and Channels 4 and 5 are commercial stations and do carry adverts, though far less than in Australia or the USA.

There are two Scottish-based commercial TV broadcasters. Scottish Television (STV) covers southern Scotland and some of the western Highlands and Grampian TV transmits to the Highlands from Perth to the Western Isles and Shetland. Both include Gaelic-language programmes.

These channels are up against competition from Rupert Murdoch's satellite TV company, BSkyB, and assorted cable channels. Cable churns out mostly missable rubbish but BSkyB is gradually monopolising sports coverage with pay-per-view screenings of many of the most popular events.

VIDEO SYSTEMS

With many tourist attractions selling videos as souvenirs it's worth bearing in mind that Britain, like much of Europe, uses the Phase Alternative Line (PAL) system which isn't compatible with NTSC or SECAM unless converted at great expense. DVD movies are now available quite cheaply in the UK and are very transportable; bear in mind that UK DVDs are Zone 2, which may not be compatible with your home DVD player.

PHOTOGRAPHY & VIDEO
Film & Equipment

Both print and slide film are widely available; if there's no specialist photographic shop around, Boots, the chemist chain, is the likeliest stockist. Thirty-six exposure print films cost from £4.50, excluding processing. Thirty-six exposure slide films cost from £4.99 excluding processing to £6.99 including processing. A three-pack of 90-minute Hi-8 video cassettes costs around £15; a 60-minute Mini DV cassette costs around £10.

Most Highland towns have several shops where you can get print films processed in as little as one hour for around £5 for a 36-exposure film. On the islands, film processing is only available in Kirkwall, Stromness, Stornoway and Lerwick.

Technical Tips
With dull, overcast conditions common, high-speed film (ISO 200, or ISO 400) is useful. When the magical golden light emerges from under the storm-clouds, you can get away with ISO 100 film, but overcast or grey skies will produce better results on ISO 400 film. In summer, the best times of day for photography are usually early in the morning and late in the afternoon when the glare of the sun has passed. Water and snow both produce large amounts of glare; a polarising filter will cut out of some of the excess light. See Lonely Planet's *Travel Photography* for more tips.

Restrictions
Many tourist attractions charge for taking photos or prohibit photography altogether. The use of flash is frequently forbidden to protect delicate pictures and fabrics. Video cameras are often disallowed because of the inconvenience they cause to other visitors.

TIME
Scotland follows Greenwich Mean Time (GMT/UTC) in winter and British Summer Time (BST) in summer. BST is GMT/UTC plus one hour – the clocks go forward at 2am on the last Sunday in March, and back again at 2am on the last Sunday in October.

When it's noon in Inverness in summer, it's 4am in Los Angeles, 7am in New York, 1pm in Paris (and the rest of Europe), 1pm in Johannesburg, 8pm in Tokyo, 9pm in Sydney and 11pm in Auckland.

Most public transport timetables use the 24-hour clock.

ELECTRICITY
In Scotland, as in the rest of Britain, electricity is supplied at 240V, 50Hz AC. Plugs have three square pins and adaptors are necessary for non-British appliances; these are widely available in electrical stores in towns and cities. North American appliances, which run on 110V, will also need a transformer if they don't have one built in.

WEIGHTS & MEASURES
Despite dogged resistance from much of the population, Britain has officially moved to the metric system, though no-one seems to have told the Highways Agency or the nation's publicans. Road distances are still quoted in miles, not kilometres, and draught beer is still sold by the pint (568ml). Scottish pubs have reluctantly dropped the traditional *dram* measure for spirits (equivalent to a quarter gill in old terms), replacing it with the Europe-wide measure of 25ml or 35ml. Petrol is sold by the litre but milk can still be bought in pints.

This book uses miles to indicate distance but the heights of mountains are given in metres, as is often the usage on the road.

For conversion tables, see the inside back cover.

LAUNDRY
Most high streets have a laundrette, usually a disheartening place to spend much time. The average cost for a single wash and dry will be about £2.50. Soap powder is usually available for around 50p. A service wash, where someone does it for you, costs about £2 more. Almost all hostels and camp sites have self-service laundry facilities, while B&Bs and hotels often offer laundry services for guests.

TOILETS
Although many city-centre facilities can be grim (graffitied or rendered vandal-proof in solid stainless steel), those at main railway stations, bus terminals, supermarkets, community centres and petrol stations are

generally good, usually with facilities for the disabled and children.

Some disabled toilets can only be opened with a special key which can be obtained from some tourist offices or by sending a cheque or postal order for £2.50 to RADAR (see Disabled Travellers later in this chapter), together with a brief description of your disability.

HEALTH

Travel health largely depends on predeparture preparations, day-to-day health care while travelling and how you handle any medical problem or emergency that may develop. In reality, few travellers experience anything worse than an upset stomach.

Tap water is always safe in the Highlands and islands unless there's a sign to the contrary (eg, on trains). Don't drink straight from a stream – you can never be certain there are no people or cattle upstream.

If you require a particular medication take an adequate supply, as it may not be available from chemists in the region. Take part of the packaging showing the generic name, rather than the brand, which will make getting replacements easier. It's a good idea to have a legible prescription or letter from your doctor to show that you legally use the medication to avoid any problems.

No jabs are required for Scotland, though it's recommended that everyone keeps up-to-date with diphtheria, tetanus and polio vaccinations.

Medical Services

Medical treatment under the UK's National Health Service (NHS) is free to citizens of EU countries, and to citizens of countries that have a reciprocal agreement with the UK (check with your own health service before you leave). Emergency ambulance transport and initial treatment in a hospital Accident and Emergency (A&E) department is free to everyone.

Travel insurance (see that section earlier in the chapter) however, is advisable as it offers greater flexibility over where and how you're treated and covers expenses for an ambulance and repatriation that won't be picked up by the NHS. Regardless of nationality, anyone will receive free emergency treatment if it's a simple matter such as bandaging a cut.

Hospitals There are well-equipped, modern hospitals at Inverness, Fort William, Oban, Thurso, Portree (Skye), Kirkwall (Orkney), Lerwick (Shetland), Stornoway (Lewis) and on Mull, Arran, Islay and Benbecula.

Not all hospitals have an A&E department; look out for red signs with an 'H', followed by 'A&E'.

Chemists (Pharmacies) Chemists generally open 9.30am to 5.30pm Monday to Saturday and can advise on minor ailments. Chemists should also have a notice in the window advising where you'll find the nearest late-night branch. Few doctors surgeries or chemists are open on Sunday except for emergencies.

Medical Problems & Treatment

Bites & Stings Bee and wasp stings are usually painful rather than dangerous. However, in people who are allergic to them severe breathing difficulties may occur and urgent medical care required. Calamine lotion or Stingose spray will give relief, and ice packs will reduce the pain and swelling.

Midges – small blood-sucking flies – are a major problem in the Highlands and islands during summer. Bring mosquito repellent, some antihistamine tablets and a head net.

Always check all over your body if you've been walking through a potentially tick-infested area as ticks can cause skin infections and other more serious diseases. To remove a tick, press down around the tick's head with tweezers, grab the head and gently pull upwards.

The chances of getting bitten by an adder, Britain's only venomous snake, are extremely remote. However, in the event of a bite, the standard rules apply: the bitten area should be wrapped tightly and immobilised with a splint, and the victim should be taken immediately to hospital, where antivenom can be administered.

Sunburn Even when there's cloud cover, it's possible to get sunburned quickly in the Highlands and islands, particularly at altitude or if you're on water, snow or ice. Use 15+ sunscreen, wear a hat and cover up with a long-sleeved shirt and trousers.

Heat Exhaustion Dehydration or salt deficiency can cause heat exhaustion. In hot conditions and if you're exerting yourself make sure you get sufficient nonalcoholic liquids. Salt deficiency is characterised by fatigue, lethargy, headaches, giddiness and muscle cramps. Vomiting or diarrhoea can rapidly deplete your liquid and salt levels.

Hypothermia This can occur when the body loses heat faster than it can produce it, resulting in the body's core temperature falling. It's surprisingly easy to progress from very cold to dangerously cold through a combination of wind, wet clothing, fatigue and hunger, even if the air temperature is above freezing.

Walkers should always be prepared for difficult conditions. It's best to dress in layers and a hat is important since a lot of heat is lost through the head. A strong, waterproof outer layer is essential. Carry basic supplies, including food that contains simple sugars to generate heat quickly.

Symptoms of hypothermia are exhaustion, numb skin (particularly toes and fingers), shivering, slurred speech, irrational or violent behaviour, lethargy, stumbling, dizzy spells, muscle cramps and violent bursts of energy.

To treat mild hypothermia, get the person out of the wind and rain, remove wet clothing and replace it with dry, warm clothing. Give them hot liquids – not alcohol – and some high-calorie, easily digestible food. Do not rub victims; instead, allow them to slowly warm themselves. This should be enough to treat the early stages of hypothermia and prevent the onset of critical serious hypothermia.

HIV & AIDS Infection with the human immunodeficiency virus (HIV) may lead to acquired immune deficiency syndrome (AIDS), which is fatal. Any exposure to blood, blood products or body fluids may put the individual at risk. The disease is often transmitted through sexual contact or dirty needles – vaccinations, acupuncture, tattooing and body piercing can be potentially as dangerous as intravenous drug use. HIV/AIDS can also be spread through infected blood transfusions but in Scotland these are screened and safe.

WOMEN TRAVELLERS
During the research of this book, there were attacks on women in several Highland towns, so caution is advised. In general women are unlikely to have any problems if they avoid walking alone at night in larger towns in the Highlands.

For the most part, women can go out to pubs and bars without drawing unwelcome attention, though some hostels arrange group trips to *ceilidhs* and pubs for those who prefer safety in numbers.

Condoms are usually available in women's toilets in bars. Otherwise chemists and most service stations stock them. Tampons are available in most shops.

The contraceptive pill is available only on prescription but the 'morning-after' pill (effective for up to 72 hours after unprotected sexual intercourse) can be bought over the counter in chemists. Family planning associations are listed in phone books.

Organisations
For general advice on health issues, contraception and pregnancy, visit a Well Woman clinic. Ask at local libraries or doctor's surgeries for the details or contact the head office at Well Woman Services (☎ 0131-343 1282), 18 Dean Terrace, Stockbridge EH4 1NL.

GAY & LESBIAN TRAVELLERS
Although many Scots are fairly tolerant of homosexuality, hostility may be encountered and overt displays of affection aren't wise if conducted away from acknowledged 'gay' venues or districts. The age of homosexual consent in the UK is now 16.

Two Web sites that contain useful information are ⓦ www.gayscotland.com, which includes details for Inverness, and W www.pridescotland.org. The monthly magazine *Scotsgay* (W www.scotsgay.com) keeps gays, lesbians and bisexuals informed about gay-scene issues. Inverness has a few gay-friendly venues, most notably Sleepers (see Entertainment under Inverness in The Great Glen & the Western Highlands chapter), but there really is no scene elsewhere in the region and many rural folk may have fairly outmoded views on homosexuality.

The main information source for Scotland is the LGBT Centre (☎ 0141-221 7203, e lgbt.glasgow@gglc.org.uk), 11 Dixon St, Glasgow, G1 4AL, but other useful resources include the Lothian Gay & Lesbian Switchboard (☎ 0131-556 4049, e mail@lgls.org) or the Lesbian Line (☎ 0131-557 0751).

DISABLED TRAVELLERS

For many disabled travellers, the Highlands and islands are a mix of user-friendliness and unfriendliness. Few new buildings are inaccessible to wheelchair users, so large, new hotels and modern tourist attractions are usually fine. However, most B&Bs and guesthouses are in hard-to-adapt older buildings. Newer buses sometimes have steps that lower for easier access, as do trains, but it's always wise to check before setting out. Disabled passengers may have to board ferries via passenger ramps as there are rarely lifts between the car decks and passenger decks.

Tourist attractions sometimes reserve parking spaces near the entrance for disabled drivers. Many nature reserves have wheelchair-friendly paths, as do most of the famous stone circles and prehistoric ruins, but few castles, brochs or regional museums have disabled facilities.

Many ticket offices, banks and so on are fitted with hearing loops to assist the hearing impaired. A few tourist attractions have Braille guides or scented gardens for the visually impaired.

Information & Organisations

Get in touch with your national support organisation (preferably the travel officer, if there is one) before leaving home. These often have complete libraries devoted to

travel, and can put you in touch with travel agents who specialise in tours for people with specific needs.

The STB produces a guide, *Accessible Scotland*, for disabled travellers and many TICs have leaflets with accessibility details for their area. For more information, including specialist tour operators, contact Disability Scotland (☎ 0131-229 8632, W www.disabilityscotland.org.uk), Princes House, 5 Shandwick Place, Edinburgh, EH2 4RG. Also useful is Capability Scotland (☎ 0131-313 5510, W www.capability-scotland.org.uk), 11 Ellersly Rd, Edinburgh EH12 6HY.

The Royal Association for Disability and Rehabilitation (RADAR) publishes a guide on travelling in the UK that gives a good overview of facilities. Contact RADAR (☎ 020-7250 3222, W www.radar.org.uk), Information Dept, 12 City Forum, 250 City Rd, London EC1V 8AF.

The Holiday Care Service (☎ 01293-774535, W www.holidaycare.org.uk), 2nd Floor, Imperial Buildings, Victoria Rd, Horley, Surrey RH6 7PZ, also publishes a guide (£7.50) to accessible accommodation and travel in Britain and can offer general advice.

Rail companies offer a Disabled Persons' Railcard for £14 per year, offering a third off most fares.

For information on any aspect of local and national transport for disabled travellers contact the Disabled Transport Information line on ☎ 0845 758 5641.

SENIOR TRAVELLERS

With an ageing population of its own, Scotland is fairly well set up for senior visitors. Discounts are available on public transport and admission fees to many tourist attractions, provided you can show proof of age. You may need to get a special pass for some discounts; the Senior Citizens Railcard, available from staffed railway stations, is for people of 60 and over, and gives a 33% discount on all rail fares. The minimum qualifying age for most senior discounts is generally 60 to 65 for men, 55 to 65 for women.

In your home country, your age may entitle you to special travel packages and discounts (on car hire, for instance) through organisations and travel agents that cater to senior travellers. Start hunting at your local senior citizens advice bureau.

TRAVEL WITH CHILDREN

Most visitor attractions in the Highlands and islands make some effort to appeal to children, though this varies from reduced admission fees to a full range of interactive displays to keep the little ones amused. Children under a certain age can often stay free with their parents in hotels, but be prepared for hotels and B&Bs that won't accept children. Modern, purpose-built hotels usually provide cots, though it might be an idea to bring a travel cot if you're self-catering or staying in B&Bs.

Admission fees to almost all museums and other attractions are usually half the adult rate for children, and similar discounts apply on public transport. Bear in mind that pubs usually won't allow children in after about 7pm, if they allow children at all.

See Lonely Planet's *Travel with Children* for more information.

USEFUL ORGANISATIONS

Membership of Historic Scotland (HS) and the National Trust for Scotland (NTS) is worth considering, especially if you are going to be in the region for a while. Both are nonprofit organisations dedicated to the preservation of the environment, and both care for hundreds of spectacular sites.

Historic Scotland

Historic Scotland (HS; ☎ 0131-668 8800, Ⓦ www.historic-scotland.net), Longmore House, Salisbury Place, Edinburgh, EH9 1SH, manages more than 330 historic sites, including top attractions such as Skara Brae and Jarlshof. A year's membership costs £30/23 for adult/senior and student, giving free admission to HS sites and half-price admission to English Heritage properties in England, and Cadw properties in Wales. It also offers short-term 'Explorer' membership costing £12/17/22 for three/seven/14 days. In this book, the initials HS indicate an Historic Scotland property.

National Trust for Scotland

The National Trust for Scotland (NTS; ☎ 0131-243 9555, Ⓦ www.nts.org.uk), 28 Charlotte Square, Edinburgh EH2 4ET, is separate from the National Trust (NT) in England, Wales and Northern Ireland, although there are reciprocal membership agreements. The NTS cares for 100 properties and 183,350 acres of countryside.

A year's NTS membership costs £28 (£12/19 under-26s/seniors) and offers free access to all NTS and NT properties. In this book, the letters NTS indicate a National Trust for Scotland property.

DANGERS & ANNOYANCES
Crime

With few big cities, the Highlands and islands have significantly less crime than the rest of Scotland, though you should take precautions such as not carrying your wallet in your back pocket nor walking around with an open bag in larger towns. It should go without saying that you shouldn't leave valuables lying around in your room, even in hotels. Bored teenagers across the region have a reputation for vandalism of parked cars; park in a well-lit area in plain view, make sure no bags or valuables are visible inside the car and always make sure doors are locked and windows are closed.

You can let your guard down on the smaller islands, as crime is almost unheard of in these tiny communities, and few residents bother to lock their doors. However, it's worth making a mental note to start being a bit more cautious when you get back to the mainland!

If the worst happens, report thefts to the police (☎ 999) and ask for a statement, or your travel insurance won't pay out; thefts from cars may be excluded.

Midges & Clegs

The most painful problems facing visitors to the Highlands and islands are midges and clegs. The midge is a tiny blood-sucking fly only 2mm long, which is related to the mosquito. Midges are at their worst during the twilight hours, and on still, overcast days. They proliferate from late May to mid-September, but especially mid-June to mid-August – which unfortunately coincides with the main tourist season.

Cover yourself up, particularly in the evening, wear light-coloured clothing (midges are attracted to dark colours) and, most importantly, use a reliable insect repellent containing DEET or DMP.

The cleg, or horse fly, is about 13mm in length and slate grey in colour. A master of stealth, it loves to land unnoticed on necks or ankles, and can give a painful bite. It can even bite through hair or light clothing. Unlike midges, they are most active on warm, sunny days, and are most common in July and August.

Military Jets
One of the most annoying and frightening aspects of touring the Highlands is the sudden appearance and sound of military jets. It's something you never get used to.

Racial Discrimination
In general, tolerance prevails and visitors are unlikely to have problems associated with their skin colour. Visitors from south of the border may find that the anti-English ribbing can grate a little, particularly around international sporting events; in the absence of a Scottish victory, the defeat of England is usually seen as a cause for celebration.

EMERGENCIES
Dial ☎ 999 or ☎ 112 (both free) for police, ambulance, fire brigade, mountain rescue or coastguard.

The Rape and Abuse Line can be contacted toll-free every evening at 0808 800 0123 (calls are answered by women).

LEGAL MATTERS
The 1707 Act of Union preserved the Scottish legal system as separate from the law in England and Wales. If you are detained and/or arrested, you have the right to inform a solicitor and one other person, though you have no right to actually see the solicitor or make a telephone call. If you don't know a solicitor, the police will inform the duty solicitor for you.

Drugs are a problem in rural communities and police come down hard on offenders; possession of a small amount of cannabis is an offence punishable by a fine, but larger amounts may be seen as intent to supply, and along with hard drugs can carry a punishment of up to 14 years in prison. Police have the right to search anyone they suspect of possessing drugs.

When driving, you're allowed to have a maximum blood-alcohol level of 35mg/100ml, but the safest approach is not to drink at all. Parking restrictions are rigorously enforced and penalties – typically £30 per offence – far exceed the crime. Speed limits are also ruthlessly enforced. Speeding and parking infringements usually incur a fine for which you're usually allowed 30 days to pay. See Road Rules under Car & Motorcycle in the Getting Around chapter for more details.

BUSINESS HOURS
Offices generally open 9am to 5pm on weekdays. Shops may open longer hours, and most open 9am to 5pm on Saturday. In the Highlands and islands, most shops are closed on a Sunday. Big chain supermarkets such as Co-op, Spar or Safeway may stay open until 8pm Monday to Saturday. In country towns, some shops have an early closing day – usually Tuesday, Wednesday or Thursday afternoon.

Post offices open 9am to 5.30pm weekdays (10am on Wednesday) and 9am to 12.30pm Saturday. Bank hours vary, but are generally 9.30am to 4pm weekdays and 9.30am to 12.30pm Saturday.

Church Regulations
In some parts of the Highlands and the Western Isles, the Free Church of Scotland and the Free Presbyterian Church observe the Sabbath strictly and all pubs, shops and restaurants are closed on Sundays.

PUBLIC HOLIDAYS & SPECIAL EVENTS
Public Holidays
Although bank holidays are general public holidays in the rest of the UK, in Scotland

they only apply to banks and some other commercial offices.

The following days are public holidays in Scotland:

New Year's Day	1 January
New Year Bank Holiday	2 January
Easter Monday	2nd Monday in April
Good Friday	Friday before Easter Sunday
May Day Holiday	1st Monday in May
Victoria Day	3rd Monday in May
Autumn Bank Holiday	3rd Monday in September
Christmas Day	25 December
Boxing Day	26 December

Special Events

Countless diverse events are held around the country all year. Even small villages have weekly markets, and many still re-enact traditional customs and ceremonies, some dating back hundreds of years.

The STB publishes a comprehensive list, *Events in Scotland*, twice a year. HS (see Useful Organisations earlier in the chapter) also publishes an annual list of events at its sites, as does the SNH.

The Traditional Music & Song Association (☎ 0131-667 5587, fax 662 9153, e e.cowie@tmsa.demon.co.uk) publishes an excellent annual listing of music, dance and cultural festivals around Scotland.

The following are the cream of the Highland and island festivals:

December/January

Hogmanay Celebrations to greet New Year, including street parties in most towns

The Ba' Two teams chase each other and a ball until one team reaches its goal, New Year's Day, Kirkwall, Orkney

Up Helly Aa Re-enactment of a Viking fire festival, last Tuesday in January, Lerwick, Shetland

Burns Night Suppers all over the country celebrating Robbie Burns, 25 January

April

Shetland Folk Festival (W www.sffs.shetland.co.uk) Held in late April and early May, a festival showcasing the magnificent folk music of Shetland, Lerwick

May

Spirit of Speyside Whisky Festival (W www.spiritofspeyside.com) Four days of distillery tours, tasting, food, art and outdoor activities

Orkney Folk Festival (W www.orkneyfolkfestival.com) Concerts, ceilidhs, workshops, Orkney

June

St Magnus Festival (W www.stmagnusfestival.com) A huge celebration of music and the arts, Kirkwall, Orkney

Arran Folk Festival (W www.arranfolkfestival.org) A week-long festival of folk

Islay Festival (W www.ileach.co.uk/festival) A traditional music and whisky extravaganza

July

Hebridean Celtic Festival The Western Isles' biggest music event, Stornoway, Lewis

Feis Bharraidh A lively and popular festival of Gaelic music, song and dance, Barra

August

Mull of Kintyre Music Festival (W www.mokmf.com) A popular celebration of Scottish and Irish music, Mull

Argyllshire Gathering One of the Highland Games' most important events, Oban

Highland Games Highland spectaculars are held at Glenfinnan, Helmsdale, Nairn and Strathpeffer

Nairn International Jazz Festival A well-attended jazz festival, Nairn

September

Shetland Storytelling Festival Showcasing the islands' rich oral tradition, Lerwick, Shetland

Orkney Blues Festival (W www.orkneyblues.com) A celebration of blues and jazz, Stromness & Kirkwall, Orkney

Northlands Festival Ceilidhs, concerts and performances, Wick, Thurso

Islay Jazz Festival (W www.ileach.co.uk/jazz) An international line-up of jazz and blues, Islay

October

Royal National Mod (W www.the-mod.co.uk) A largely competitive Gaelic music festival, various locations in the Highlands and islands

Fiddle & Accordion Festival A highlight of the folk-music calendar, attended by fiddlers and accordion players from across the globe

Tall Tales for Short Days An interesting festival of traditional tales, Orkney

COURSES

With the remarkable revival of Scottish Gaelic since the 1980s, a number of courses in the language and culture are available, including:

Cothrom na Fèinne (☎ 01599-566240) Balmacara Mains, Kyle IV40 8DN. Residential courses take place during the first week of the month, May to October. Individually tailored weekends are available November to April (£35 to £45).

Sabhal Mór Ostaig (☎ 01471-844240, W www .smo.uhi.ac.uk) Sleat, Isle of Skye, IV44 8RQ. Five-day courses with information on Gaelic language song, piping and fiddle are available here from £120 per week.

There are also several companies offering photography holidays/courses to the region, typically charging £500 to £600 per week, including accommodation, meals and transport to prime photographic locations:

Highland Wildshots (☎ 01540 651352, W www .wildshots.co.uk) Ballintean, Glenfeshie, Kingussie PH21 1NX. Seven-day courses, in various Highland locations, are available at Highland Wildshots.

Scottish Highland Landscapes (☎ 01877 382 613, W www.viewfinders.net) 18 Trossachs Rd, Aberfoyle FK8 3SW. This place offers specialist courses on Glen Coe, the Trossachs, Skye and other locations.

Skye Picture House (☎ 01471 822531, W www .skyeinfocus.co.uk) Ard Dorch, Broadford, Skye IV49 9AJ. The Picture House offers courses specialising in nature and landscapes.

WORK

Low-paid seasonal work is available in the tourist industry, usually in restaurants and pubs, though some travellers manage to land work on the big hunting and fishing estates. Hostel noticeboards sometimes advertise casual work and hostels themselves regularly employ travellers to staff the reception, clean up and so on. Without skills, though, it's difficult to find a job that pays well enough to save money. Whatever your skills, it's worth registering with a number of temporary agencies.

EU citizens don't need a work permit. The Working Holidaymaker scheme, for Commonwealth citizens aged 17 to 27 inclusive, allows visits of up to two years but arrangements must be made in advance through a British embassy. Commonwealth citizens with a UK-born parent may be eligible for a Certificate of Entitlement to the Right of Abode, which entitles them to live and work in the UK. Check with your local British embassy or consulate.

Commonwealth citizens with a UK-born grandparent, or a grandparent born before 31 March 1922 in what's now the Republic of Ireland, could qualify for a UK Ancestry-Employment Certificate, allowing them to work full time for up to four years in the UK.

Visiting full-time US students aged 18 and over can get a six-month work permit through the Council on International Educational Exchange (☎ 212-822 2600, W www .ciee.org), 205 East 42nd St, New York, NY 10017. The British Universities North America Club (BUNAC; ☎ 203-264 0901, W www.bunac.org), PO Box 430, Southbury, CT 06488, can also help organise a permit and find work.

ACCOMMODATION

This will almost certainly be your single greatest expense. Even camping can be expensive at some official sites. For budget travel, the two main options are hostels and cheaper bed and breakfasts (B&Bs). Mid-range B&Bs are often in beautiful old buildings and many rooms have private bathrooms. Guesthouses and small hotels are more likely to have private bathrooms. If money's no object, there are some superb hotels, the most interesting in converted castles and mansions.

TICs usually offer an accommodation booking service (£3, local and national), and a 10% refundable deposit is also required for most bookings. The service is worth using in July and August, but isn't necessary otherwise. Regional tourist boards publish reliable (if not comprehensive) accommodation lists that include STB-approved and -graded camp sites, hostels, self-catering accommodation, guesthouses, B&Bs and hotels. STB gradings give a fairly accurate assessment of the level and quality of facilities, but bear in mind that all these places have paid a membership fee to be included in the scheme and may pass this expense on to their guests.

Single rooms are in short supply and many accommodation suppliers are reluctant to let a double room to one person without charging a supplement, even when it's quiet.

Camping

Free wild camping is usually acceptable in unenclosed land, well away from houses and roads; try and seek permission. If it ever gets passed, the draconian Land Reform Act may make wild camping illegal.

Commercial camp sites are geared to caravans and vary widely in quality. A tent site costs from £4 to £12.

Bothies, Barns & Bunkhouses

Bothies are simple shelters, often in remote places. They're not locked, there's no charge, and you can't book. Take your own cooking equipment, sleeping bag and mat. Users should stay one night only, and leave it as they find it.

A camping barn – usually a converted farm building – is where walkers can stay for around £5 per night. Take your own cooking equipment, sleeping bag and mat. Bunkhouses, a grade or two up from camping barns, have stoves for heating and cooking and may supply utensils. They may also have mattresses but you'll need a sleeping bag. Most charge from £8.

The Shetland Islands tourism board has created a number of *böds* (converted croft homes with bunks and washing and cooking facilities), often in remote and dramatic locations. Beds cost £5 but you will need to book with the TIC in Lerwick, who will give you the keys. Visit W www.camping-bods.com for more details.

Hostels

If you're travelling on a budget, the numerous hostels offer cheap accommodation and are great centres for meeting fellow travellers. Hostels have self-catering facilities and some provide cheap meals. From May to September and on public holidays, hostels can be booked-out, sometimes by large antisocial groups. Book as far in advance as possible.

Scottish Youth Hostel Association (SYHA) The SYHA (☎ 01786-891400, fax 891333, W www.shya.org.uk), 7 Glebe Crescent, Stirling, FK8 2JA, has a network of good and reasonably priced hostels. It produces a handbook (£1.50) giving details on over 56 hostels in the region, including transport links.

Rates in the region are generally around £9/8 per adult/child. Throughout this book, higher hostel prices for seniors are given first, followed by the reduced price for children. Prices vary by season and are higher in summer; the SYHA Web site has full details. Nonmembers typically pay £1.50 more than members, though this can count towards membership. For bookings, call the central reservation service on ☎ 0870 155 3255 or e reservations@syha.org.uk. During the off-season, groups can hire out entire hostels – see W www.rentahostel.com.

At many SYHA hostels, you're usually locked out between 10.30am and 5pm, and the front door is locked at 11pm. Note that many hostels are closed during winter.

Independent & Student Hostels There are also numerous independent hostels, which operate outside the youth hostel system and are usually a touch more homely and comfortable. Almost all have cooking and laundry facilities, hot showers and bunks, with nightly rates typically starting at around £10. The small blue *Independent Hostel Guide*, available from most TICs, lists 71 independent hostels in the region. You can also get the guide by sending an A5 stamped, addressed envelope to Pete Thomas, Croft Bunkhouse & Bothies, 7 Portnalong, Isle of Skye, IV47 8SL. Many of these hostels are also listed on the Highland Hostels Web site at W www.highland-hostels.co.uk.

In the Western Isles, the Gatliff Hebridean Hostels Trust (GHHT; W www .gatliff.org.uk), 30 Francis St, Stornoway, Isle of Lewis HS1 2ND, is responsible for a number of splendid hostels in traditional blackhouses (thatched drystone crofters' cottages) spread across the islands. All have been modernised with hot showers, good kitchens and comfortable bunkrooms, and occupy splendid locations near the coast. See the Skye & the Western Isles chapter for details of GHHT hostels.

B&Bs, Guesthouses & Hotels

B&Bs provide the cheapest private accommodation. At the bottom end (£14 to £20 per person) you get a bedroom in a private house, a shared bathroom and an enormous cooked breakfast. Small B&Bs may only have one room to let. More upmarket B&Bs have private bathrooms and TVs in each room and typically charge upwards of £20.

Guesthouses, often large converted houses with half a dozen rooms, are an extension of the B&B concept. They range from £20 to £35 per person per night, depending on the quality of the food and accommodation, and differ little from mid-range hotels in terms of facilities, though few guesthouses have their own restaurants.

In the Highlands and islands, the word 'hotel' usually refers to a pub. Most have rooms upstairs and offer inexpensive B&B. Rates vary from £18 to £45, depending on the quality of the rooms; most rooms have a TV and tea- and coffee-making facilities, and you'll have a choice of shared or private bathrooms. In general, pub rooms are a bit more expensive than a comparatively comfortable B&B or guesthouse. You can invariably get a meal and drink downstairs, but hotels can be noisy and aren't always ideal for lone women travellers.

At the other end of the scale, there are some wonderfully luxurious places, including country-house hotels in superb settings, and castles complete with crenulated battlements, grand staircases and the obligatory rows of stags' heads. For these you can pay from £60 to well over £100 per person. The *Which? Hotel Guide* (£15.99) covering Britain lists many of the finest hotels.

There are also a small number of purpose-built modern hotels in places such as Inverness, Lerwick, Stornoway and Kirkwall, which mainly cater to business travellers and charge from £45 per person for comfortable but rather characterless rooms with private bathrooms, TV and telephones.

Short-term Rental

There's plenty of self-catering accommodation and staying in a house in the city or cottage in the country gives you an opportunity to get a feel for a region and a community. The minimum stay is usually one week in the summer, three days or less at other times. Details are in the accommodation guides available from TICs. Alternatively, obtain the STB's *Scotland: Self-Catering* (£5.99). Rental prices for a two-bedroom cottage range from £100 to £350.

FOOD

Scotland's chefs have an enviable range of fresh meat, seafood and vegetables at their disposal and the country as a whole has moved on leaps and bounds in its quest to become an internationally recognised gourmet centre. However, in rural areas, the menu may be as limited as steak and chips, haddock and chips, pie and chips or scampi and chips.

Where tourists gather, there are likely to be a few more choices – macaroni cheese, lasagne, chilli con carne and hot-pots (stews with meat and potatoes) crop up on most menus. Many of the larger towns in the Highlands and islands also have Indian or Chinese restaurants, which can provide some welcome variety from the ubiquitous chips. Gourmet bistros and trendy upmarket seafood restaurants are popping up in many popular tourist centres, and most mid-range and top-end hotels serve up fine Scottish food.

When you can find it, well-prepared Scottish food can be marvellous – the beef from Aberdeen Angus and Highland cattle is some of the finest in the world, Scottish salmon is legendary, local queenies (scallops) are magnificently fat and juicy, and Scottish lamb is another genuine delight. Uniquely Scottish dishes to look out for are haggis (see the boxed text 'Address to a Haggis' later in the chapter) and beef olive (actually a rolled steak filled with haggis or stuffing).

There's a strong meat-eating tradition, and vegetarians are usually restricted to pasta, pizza and curries. Vegans are barely catered for at all. There are a handful of vegetarian places to stay and eat though, many of them listed on the Web site at **W** www.highlandveggies.org.

At the bottom end of the price scale, you can eat cheaply at fish and chip shops (which also serve pies, deep-fried haggis and even deep-fried Mars bars!) and tearooms (which serve healthier fare such as sandwiches). There are also plenty of Indian and Chinese takeaways.

Lunch is served from noon to 2.30pm, dinner from 6pm or 7pm to 8pm or 9pm; it's almost impossible to get a meal outside of these times. Scotland is notorious for places that will not serve you if you arrive five seconds after 'kitchen closing time'.

Some of the best places to eat are members of the Taste of Scotland scheme, but they have to pay substantial fees for inclusion. The annual *Taste of Scotland Guide* (£8.99) is worth buying to track down these restaurants and hotels.

Scottish Breakfast

Surprisingly few Scots eat porridge and even fewer eat it in the traditional way as a savoury dish with salt and milk. These days, a Scottish breakfast, as served by B&Bs, will usually entail a glass of fruit juice and a bowl of cereal or muesli, followed by a cooked breakfast which may include bacon, sausage, black pudding (a type of sausage made from dried blood), grilled tomato, grilled mushrooms, fried bread or tattie (potato) scones (if you're lucky) and an egg or two.

More upmarket hotels may offer porridge followed by kippers (smoked herrings). As well as toast, there may be oatcakes (oatmeal biscuits) to spread your marmalade upon.

Snacks

As well as ordinary scones (similar to American biscuits), Scottish bakeries usually offer cheese, tattie and girdle scones. *Bere Bannocks* are a cross between scones and pancakes. Savoury pies include the *bridie* (a pie filled with meat, potatoes, onions and sometimes other vegetables) and the Scotch pie (minced meat in a plain round pastry casing – best eaten hot). A *toastie* is a toasted sandwich.

Dundee cake, a rich fruit cake topped with almonds, is highly recommended. Black bun is another type of fruit cake, eaten over Hogmanay (New Year's Eve).

Soups

Scotch broth, made with mutton stock, barley, lentils and peas, is highly nutritious and very tasty, while cock-a-leekie is a hearty soup made with chicken and leeks. Fish-lovers should hunt down *partan bree*, a satisfying crab soup, and delicious *cullen skink*, made from smoked haddock and potatoes. Warming vegetable soups include leek and potato soup, and lentil soup (which is traditionally made using ham stock – vegetarians beware!).

Address to a Haggis

Scotland's oft-ridiculed national dish has been unfavourably described as a sheep served in its own stomach. While this is true to the rather visceral ingredients – chopped lungs, heart and liver mixed with oatmeal and boiled in a sheep's stomach – haggis can taste surprisingly good, particularly if served the traditional way with tatties and neeps (mashed potatoes and turnips), with a generous dollop of butter and a sprinkling of black pepper.

Although it's eaten year-round, haggis is central to the celebrations of 25 January, in honour of Scotland's national poet, Robert Burns. Scots worldwide unite on Burns Night to revel in their Scottishness. A piper announces the arrival of the haggis and the Burns' poem *Address to a Haggis* is recited to this 'Great chieftan o' the puddin-race'. The bulging stomach is then lanced with a *dirk* (dagger) to reveal the steaming offal within.

Vegetarians (and quite a few carnivores, no doubt) will be relieved to know that veggie haggis is available in some restaurants in Scotland.

Meat & Game

Steak eaters will enjoy a thick fillet of world-famous Aberdeen Angus beef; Highland cattle also produce marvellously flavoursome beef. Venison, from the red deer, is leaner and appears on many menus. Both may be served with a wine-based or creamy whisky sauce. Mince (minced beef cooked with onion) and tatties is traditional Scottish home cooking and it's very filling.

Gamebirds such as pheasant and grouse, traditionally roasted and served with game chips and fried breadcrumbs, are also available. They're definitely worth trying, but watch your teeth on the shot, which isn't always removed before cooking.

Then there's haggis, Scotland's much-maligned national dish...

Fish & Seafood

Scottish salmon is famous worldwide but there is a big difference between farmed salmon and the leaner, more expensive, wild fish. Much farmed salmon is intensively produced for supermarket shelves, and connoisseurs will be faced with the tricky ethical question of whether or not to eat the tastier, but increasingly threatened, wild salmon. Smoked salmon is traditionally dressed with a squeeze of lemon juice and eaten with fresh brown bread and butter. Trout, the salmon's smaller cousin, is delicious fried in oatmeal.

As an alternative to kippers (smoked herrings) you may be offered Arbroath smokies (lightly smoked fresh haddock), traditionally eaten cold. Herring fillets fried in oatmeal are good, if you don't mind picking out a few bones. Salted pickled herring are very traditional in the Highlands, but are definitely an acquired taste. Mackerel paté and smoked or peppered mackerel (both served cold) are also popular.

While you don't see much in the way of shellfish elsewhere in the UK, lobsters, crabs, langoustines and queenies are everywhere in Orkney, Shetland and the Western Isles. Creeling (fishing for lobster and crabs with baited 'pots') is a major source of employment in the islands and you can often buy fresh seafood straight from the fisher-

men. You'll see lobster and scallops on the menu at many island pubs, and at prices you would only dream of in the south.

Cheese

The Scottish cheese industry is growing but cheddar is still its main output. Among the more accessible varieties is Orkney cheddar, which takes a distinctive flavour from the local organic milk. There are also several speciality cheese-makers on the islands of Arran, Bute, Gigha, Islay, Mull and Orkney. Perhaps the most interesting is Brodick Blue, a ewes' milk blue cheese made on Arran. There are also some small-scale producers of Highland smoked cheese in Caithness. Scottish oatcakes make the perfect accompaniment for cheese.

Puddings

Traditional Scottish puddings are irresistibly creamy, calorie-enriched concoctions. *Cranachan* is whipped cream flavoured with whisky, and mixed with toasted oatmeal and raspberries. *Atholl brose* is a mixture of cream, whisky and honey flavoured with oatmeal. *Clootie dumpling* is a deliciously rich steamed pudding filled with currants and raisins.

DRINKS
Nonalcoholic Drinks

In terms of consumption, coffee has recently overtaken tea as Scotland's most popular beverage. In the last five or six years the tide of gurgling espresso machines has spread across the Highlands and islands, dispensing cappuccinos and lattes to a caffeine-craving public. Fortunately for non-coffee drinkers, a dogged hardcore of old-style tearooms survive where you can still get a decent pot of orange pekoe to wash down your shortbread with.

Despite having some of the purest tap water in the world, Scotland has been quick to jump aboard the bottled water bandwagon, with several brands of Scottish mineral water (notably Highland Spring) available in shops, bars and restaurants.

And then there's Irn-Bru (affectionately known as 'Scotland's other national drink'), a frighteningly chemical-tasting soft drink that locals often mix with spirits, and use as a hangover cure the next morning.

Alcoholic Drinks

The legal minimum age for buying alcoholic drinks in Scotland is 18 and pubs and off-licences (liquor stores) can ask you for ID.

Wine, beer and spirits for home consumption are sold in supermarkets and neighbourhood off-licences, but in an emergency, you may be able to buy drinks to take away from bars. Opening hours for off-licences are generally 10am to 10pm Monday to Saturday and 12.30pm to 8pm on Sunday.

Most restaurants are licensed to sell alcoholic drinks, but BYO (Bring Your Own) restaurants are quite common in the region. Restaurants routinely overcharge for wine, so you can save a lot of money by buying your wine at an off-licence and taking it with you to a BYO restaurant, which usually charges £1 or £2 corkage.

Whisky Scotch whisky (always spelt without an 'e' – whiskey *with* an 'e' is Irish or American) is Scotland's best-known product and biggest export. The spirit has been distilled in Scotland since at least the 15th century and is now probably even more popular overseas than it is in Scotland. Much of the snobbery about single-malt whisky has been cultivated by Scottish expats living abroad; in the Highlands and islands, most people are happy to drink the cheaper blended whiskies as chasers and save the single malts for special occasions. See the boxed text 'How To Be a Malt Whisky Buff' later for details on how to bluff your way in single-malt circles.

Whisky is traditionally mixed only with water or served on the rocks (over ice), but whisky-mac (whisky with ginger wine) is another acceptable mixer. After a long walk in the rain there's nothing better to warm you up. As well as whiskies, there are also several whisky-based liqueurs, such as Drambuie, which are extremely sweet and are definitely an acquired taste.

At a bar, older Scots may order a 'half' or 'nip' of whisky as a chaser to a pint or half-pint of beer (a 'hauf and a hauf'). Only tourists ask for 'Scotch' – what else would you be served in Scotland? The standard measure in pubs is either 25mL or 35mL.

Beer The Highlands are dominated by the Tennent's brewery chain, which produces a range of fairly ordinary lagers ('beer' to New Worlders) and bitters (flat, slightly bitter beers, served at cellar temperature). Beers are usually served in pints (from £1.50 to £2.50), but you can also ask for a 'half' (a half pint), though halves are slightly frowned upon by male drinkers. Potency can vary from 3.2% to 8.5%.

Until comparatively recently, Tennent's and the other big breweries – Youngers, McEwans and Scottish & Newcastle – had the local beer market sewn up, but thanks to the efforts of the Campaign for Real Ale (CAMRA), the once threatened traditional beers are on the up and up.

The best ales are hand-pumped from the cask, as opposed to being carbonated and drawn under pressure, and have subtle flavours that a cold, chemical lager can't match. Most popular is what the Scots call 'heavy', a dark beer similar to English bitter. 'Light' beers, which resemble some of the European blond beers, are also available. Most Scottish brews are graded in shillings so you can tell their strength, the usual range being 60 to 80 shillings (written 80/-).

One of the tastiest heavy beers is Belhaven Best, brewed in East Lothian, but Caledonian 80/- and Maclays 80/- are also worth a try. For something darker, Orkney Breweries' Dark Island is midway between a bitter and a stout and was recently voted the best beer in Scotland. Other offerings from Orkney Breweries include Raven Ale, Red McGregor and the aptly named Skullsplitter, which is 8.5% alcohol by volume.

The Shetland Islands boast their own Valhalla Brewery, which produces mostly heavy beers, including White Wife. On the Isle of Skye, Skye Breweries make the suitably rustic Red Cuillin and the heavier Black Cuillin, while the Black Isle Brewery north of Inverness produces several very palatable organic beers.

How to Be a Malt Whisky Buff

'Love makes the world go round? Not at all! Whisky makes it go round twice as fast.'
— From *Whisky Galore*, by Compton Mackenzie (1883–1972)

Whisky-tasting today is almost as popular as wine-tasting in the yuppie heyday of the late 1980s. Being able to tell your Ardbeg from your Edradour is *de rigeur* among the whisky-nosing set, so here are some pointers to help you impress your friends.

What's the difference between malt and grain whiskies? Malts are distilled from malted barley – that is, barley that has been soaked in water, then allowed to germinate for around 10 days until the starch has turned into sugar – while grain whiskies are distilled from other cereals, usually wheat, corn or unmalted barley.

So what is a single malt? A single malt is a whisky that has been distilled from malted barley and is the product of a single distillery. A pure (vatted) malt is a mixture of single malts from several distilleries, and a blended whisky is a mixture of various grain whiskies (about 60%) and malt whiskies (about 40%) from many different distilleries.

Why are single malts more desirable than blends? A single malt, like a fine wine, somehow captures the essence of the place where it was made and matured – a combination of the water, the barley, the peat smoke, the oak barrels in which it was aged, and (in the case of certain coastal distilleries) the sea air and salt spray. Each distillation varies from the one before, like different vintages from the same vineyard.

How should a single malt be drunk? Either neat, or preferably with a little water added. To appreciate the aroma and flavour to the utmost, a measure of malt whisky should be cut (diluted) with one-third to two-thirds as much spring water (still, bottled spring water will do). Ice, tap water and (God forbid) mixers are for philistines. Would you add lemonade or ice to a glass of Chablis?

Give me some tasting tips! Order a Lagavulin (Islay) and a Glenfiddich (Speyside). Cut each one with half as much again of still, bottled spring water.

Taking each one in turn, hold the glass up to the light to check the colour; stick your nose in the glass and take two or three short, sharp sniffs.

For the Lagavulin you should be thinking: amber colour, peat-smoke, iodine, seaweed. For the Glenfiddich: pale, white-wine colour, malt, pear drops, acetone, citrus. Then taste them. Then try some others. Either you'll be hooked, or you'll never touch whisky again.

Brewed in the region since around 2000 BC, heather ale (made from fermented heather flowers) is another fine Highland beverage – the award-winning Fraoch Heather Ale is brewed in Glasgow but is widely available in the southern Highlands.

Wine For centuries people made wine from wild flowers, fruit and tree sap, but the government closed down this cottage industry in the 18th century. You can still find fruit wines at the last Highland winery at Moniack Castle, near Beauly.

Good international wines are widely available on the mainland (less so on the islands) and are reasonably priced, except in pubs and restaurants. In supermarkets, you can buy an ordinary but drinkable bottle for £5.

ENTERTAINMENT

Scotland has a reputation as a centre of culture, but little 'high culture' – theatre, opera and classical music – makes it up to the Highlands and islands. Fortunately, this is more than made up for by a vibrant tradition of folk dance, traditional music and ancient performing arts such as storytelling. Pubs have regular *ceilidhs* (traditional dances) and live bands, particularly at weekends, and you may stumble across informal folk jams in lounge bars throughout the Highlands.

Cinemas are restricted to big cities such as Inverness, Thurso and Kirkwall and mainly screen blockbusters, though the films shown are often several months behind the rest of the UK. Lerwick in Shetland has a touring cinema that comes to town every few weeks.

ASA ANDERSON

Have some reel fun at a traditional Scottish ceilidh.

Pubs

The local pub is the place to go for a drink and is an integral part of the life of rural Scotland. In smaller villages, the pub usually doubles as a hotel, restaurant and venue for live music and ceilidhs, and locals congregate each evening for the ritual consumption of pints of 'heavy' or 'light' beer, interspersed with chasers of whisky. Pubs traditionally have two bars, a larger 'saloon bar' and a smaller, cosier 'lounge bar'. Thus far, the region has escaped most of the shortsighted 'theming' that has destroyed the character of so many pubs across the UK.

Whisky is the focus rather than beer in Scottish pubs, so the selection of draught beers is often much more limited than elsewhere in the UK. Fans of real ale will be glad to hear that more and more small breweries are opening in the Highlands and islands, adding some colourful regional brews to the ubiquitous Tennant's lagers and bitters.

In general you'll get a warm reception at most country pubs, particularly if you have some Scottish family connection. However, it's not unknown for whisky to sour tempers in the larger towns in the Highlands and fights are not uncommon.

Pubs mainly open 11am to 11pm or later Monday to Saturday, and from 12.30pm on Sunday. Many pubs have a late licence at weekends, but there's a fairly informal attitude to the Westminster-imposed licensing laws throughout the week and drinks are often served until publicans decide they want to go to bed. The bell for last orders, or 'time', usually rings about 15 minutes before closing time. Infuriatingly, many pubs in the region close from 2.30pm to 5pm and may be completely closed in winter.

Ceilidhs

The traditional Scottish dance has evolved into something of a tourist spectacle, but there are still places in the region where *ceilidhs* are staged for the benefit of locals rather than visitors. Having a good time is the name of the game and there's usually a 'caller' to lead the dancers through their paces. Music is provided by bagpipes, fiddles and other traditional instruments.

If you fancy trying an eightsome reel, ask at the local TIC for details of local ceilidhs. It's not as difficult as it looks and most Scots will extend a warm welcome to visitors who are prepared to give it a go.

The tourist version can still be entertaining, and many tourist centres hold a *ceilidh* or Highland show, featuring Scottish song and dance, most nights during the summer.

SPECTATOR SPORTS

Most Scotsmen are sports mad and watch matches with fierce, competitive dedication, identifying closely with teams and individuals that compete both locally and internationally. The most popular games are football (soccer), rugby union, shinty, lawn bowls, curling and golf, the last two of which the Scots claim to have invented.

Football

Also known as soccer to distinguish it from rugby football, this is Scotland's largest spectator sport. The Scottish Football League is the main national competition and has a number of divisions. The best clubs, mainly from southern Scotland, form the Scottish Premier League.

The two most successful teams, the Catholic-backed Celtic and the Protestant-backed Rangers, are both from Glasgow but have hundreds of supporters across the Highlands and islands. Together, the teams are known as the 'Old Firm' and sectarian loyalties amongst fans are strong; it's probably best to wait until other people say who they support before backing either team.

Similarly, the Scottish-English rivalry reaches fever pitch around international sporting events such as the soccer World Cup, held every four years, and set to take place next in Japan in 2002. The Scottish national team failed to qualify, but Scottish supporters will often rally behind any team playing *against* England.

Highland teams play in the Highland League and include 2001 champions Cove Rangers, Wick, Brora and Fort William, plus current division leaders Fraserburgh. There's also a far smaller league on Lewis and Harris.

The domestic football season lasts from August to May and most matches are played on Saturday or Sunday afternoons, or Tuesday or Wednesday evenings.

Rugby Union

Rugby union football is administered by the Scottish Rugby Union based at Murrayfield in Edinburgh, where international games are played. Each year, starting in January, Scotland takes part in the Six Nations Rugby Union Championship. The most important fixture is the clash against England for the Calcutta Cup, when Scottish national pride comes to the boil.

At club level, the season runs from September to May, but most of the teams come from the south of the country. Teams from the region include Isle of Arran, RAF Lossiemouth RFC and Loch Lomond.

Golf

Although games that involve hitting a ball with a stick have been played in Europe since Roman times, it was the Scottish version that caught on. Apparently dating from the 15th century, golf was popularised by the Scottish monarchy, and today St Andrews in Fife is home to the Royal and Ancient Club (the recognised authority on the rules) and the famous Old Course. There are many highly regarded courses throughout the Highlands and islands; probably the best course is the Championship course at Royal Dornoch, ranked 9th in the country.

Shinty

Shinty (*camanachd* in Gaelic) is an amateur ball-and-stick sport similar to Ireland's hurling. The name is said to come from the cry of the players and it's fast, very physical and played most of the year. It's administered by the Camanachd Association (W www.shinty.com) and the Camanachd Cup is the most prized trophy. The final, a great Gaelic get-together, draws a large crowd and is televised on STV.

Curling

Scotland is the home of curling and the gold medal won by the Scottish women's team at the 2002 Winter Olympics is seen as proof that they're the best at it. Curling involves propelling circular polished granite 'stones' over ice in a kind of sliding rather than rolling version of bowls. Competitors brush smooth the ice in front of the moving stone to bring it as close as possible to the centre of a target. A team is made up of four players and one reserve, and almost all games are played indoors. The Royal Caledonian Curling Club (W www.rccc.org.uk) in Edinburgh is the governing body.

SHOPPING

Making things to sell to tourists is big business in Scotland, and almost every visitor attraction seems to have been designed expressly to funnel you through the gift shop. Among the tourist kitsch are some good-value, high-quality goods, but check labelling thoroughly as many 'Scottish' products are made in other countries.

Tartan, Tweed & Other Fabrics

Scottish textiles, particularly tartans, are popular, and tartan travelling rugs, scarves and ties all make inexpensive, lightweight souvenirs. There are said to be over 2000 designs, some officially recognised as clan tartans, though this tradition mainly dates back to the Victorian era. Blankets start at around £15, while woollen scarves and tartan ties cost from £10. One of the kitsch tartan souvenirs that still has some mileage is the *Tam O'Shanter*, a traditional baggy hat, that comes with or without fake red hair.

The traditional Highland dress is the 4m-to 5m-long plaid, which was banned for many years after the 1745 Jacobite rebellions. The kilt is a 19th-century romanticisation, but it's still extremely popular. The genuine article will set you back as much as a well-made suit but faux souvenir kilts cost around £20 to £30. A tailor-made kilt in your clan tartan will cost from £350 to £400, plus at least £40 for the obligatory *sporran* (purse). Ornate dress sporrans for formal occasions can cost up to £1000. Full kilts are traditionally worn only by men, while women wear kilted or tartan skirts.

The Scottish islands are best associated with the rough woollen cloth known as tweed. The finest tweed – Harris tweed – is world famous and there are various places on this Hebridean island where you can watch your cloth being woven – see Harris in the Skye & The Western Isles chapter for more information. Typically, a jacket will cost around £110, a hat or cap £16 to £30. Sheepskin rugs and jackets are also popular.

Knitwear

Scottish knitwear can be great value and is sold throughout the region. Shetland is strongly associated with high-quality woollens and the designs feature distinctive Scandanavian elements, particularly the famous

Fair Isle patterns, which are only produced on that island. At knitwear factory shops on mainland Shetland, you can buy genuine Shetland sweaters for as little as £20, though you'll pay at least £45 for a genuine Fair Isle.

Orkney also produces fine wool, including sweaters, scarves and wool-covered cushions inspired by the natural environment of the Orkneys. The Isle of Arran is also famous for its sweaters, though these coarse, warm, woolknits are very similar to those found in Wales and Cornwall.

Jewellery & Glassware

Silver brooches set with cairngorms (yellow- or wine-coloured gems traditionally found in the mountains of the same name) or amethyst, are popular, though you'll have to pick through the tacky costume jewellery to find the more attractive pieces. Designs are frequently based on traditional Celtic pin broaches. In Skye, Orkney and Shetland, there are several excellent jewellers who create modern gold and silver jewellery inspired by ancient Celtic and Viking designs. Caithness glass, produced in Wick, is another good souvenir.

Food & Drink

Sweet, butter-rich Scottish shortbread makes a good gift. The biggest manufacturer, Walkers, is famous for baking such prodigious quantities of the stuff that the Speyside town of Aberlour smells of nothing else. Heather honey can give you a reminder of Scotland when your visit is over.

If you haven't far to go, smoked salmon or any other smoked product (venison, mussels and so on) are worth buying, but few countries outside the EU allow the import of meat products.

If you're leaving the EU, you're better off buying duty-free souvenir bottles of whisky at the airport rather than in souvenir shops, unless it's a rare brand. If you go on a distillery tour, you may be given around a £3 discount to buy a bottle there, but otherwise, prices are usually lower in the big chain supermarkets. Miniature bottles of the famous single malts make good presents.

Getting There & Away

Just getting to the Highlands and islands can be an exhausting journey in itself, and it's worth spending time planning the most efficient and/or economical way of getting there, as it can make a difference to how much you enjoy your trip.

Many people begin their Highland travels in Inverness, and a cheap way of reaching it is by bus from within the UK. The trip, though, can be exhausting and the savings not always huge, especially compared with budget air fares.

From the rest of the world you will probably have to fly into London or another European hub and catch a connecting flight to Inverness or another Highland airport (see the Getting Around chapter for more details). Generally speaking, though, it'll be far more cost-effective to catch a flight to Glasgow or Edinburgh and then get a train or bus from there.

When making an assessment, don't forget the hidden expenses – getting to and from airports, departure taxes, and food and

Warning

The information in this chapter is particularly vulnerable to change. Prices for international travel are volatile, routes are introduced and cancelled, schedules change, special deals come and go, and rules and visa requirements are amended. You should check directly with the airline or a travel agent to make sure you understand how a fare (and ticket you may buy) works and be aware of the security requirements for international travel.

The upshot of this is that you should get opinions, quotes and advice from as many airlines and travel agents as possible before you part with your hard-earned cash. The details given in this chapter should be regarded as pointers and are not a substitute for your own careful, up-to-date research.

drink consumed en route – and weigh up the inconvenience against the potential savings.

AIR

As virtually no international carriers fly into Highland airports, this chapter includes information on reaching airports such as Edinburgh, Glasgow, Aberdeen and Inverness.

Airports & Airlines

The international airports visitors to the Highlands may use are:

Aberdeen
☎ 01224-722331, Ⓦ www.baa.co.uk
Dundee
☎ 01382-643242
Inverness
☎ 01667-464000, Ⓦ www.hial.co.uk
Sumburgh
☎ 01950-460224, Ⓦ www.hial.co.uk

For many, though, travel by plane will finish at one of the larger international airports:

Edinburgh
☎ 0131-333 1000, Ⓦ www.baa.co.uk
Glasgow International
☎ 0800 844844, Ⓦ www.baa.co.uk
Glasgow Prestwick
☎ 01292-479822 Ⓦ www.glasgow.pwk.com

There are frequent direct flights to Scotland from other parts of the UK and Ireland, Europe and North America, and a limited number of services from Africa, the Middle East and Asia.

The main nonbudget airlines serving Scotland are:

British Airways (BA)
☎ 0845 773 3377, Ⓦ www.britishairways.co.uk
British Midland
☎ 0870 607 0555, Ⓦ www.flybmi.com
KLM UK
☎ 0870 507 4074, Ⓦ www.klmuk.com

Other international airlines that fly into Scotland are:

Aer Lingus
☎ 0845 973 7747, W www.aerlingus.com
Air Canada
☎ 0870 524 7226, W www.aircanada.ca
Air France
☎ 0845 084 5111, W www.airfrance.com
American Airlines
☎ 0345 789789, W www.aa.com
Atlantic Airways
☎ 0141-887 1808, W www.atlantic.fo
Braathens
☎ 0191-214 0991, W www.braathens.no
British European
☎ 0870 567 6676, W www.british-european.com
Continental Airlines
☎ 0800 776464, W www.continental.com
Lufthansa
☎ 0845 773 7747, W www.lufthansa.com
Scandinavian Airlines (SAS)
☎ 0845 6072 772, W www.scandinavian.net
ScotAirways
☎ 0870 606 0707, W www.scotairways.co.uk

There are also discount, no-frills airlines whose flights do not appear on the computerised reservations systems used by travel agents. To get their fares you have to check their Web sites (which often offer extra discounts for tickets bought online) or call their reservations numbers. Flying midweek and booking several months in advance can often mean massive savings, with promotional fares from London to Edinburgh or Glasgow as low as £20 return (though don't forget to take into account the cost of reaching the airport in London or, if you're flying into distant airports such as Glasgow's Prestwick, the time and cost of getting to your destination city).

easyJet (☎ 0870 600 0000, W www.easyjet.com) A feisty carrier with bright orange aircraft, easyJet has direct flights into Aberdeen and Inverness from London Luton. It also flies from Amsterdam, Belfast and London to Glasgow and Edinburgh.

Go (☎ 0845 605 4321, W www.go-fly.com) Originally a BA spin-off but now independent, Go flies into Edinburgh and Glasgow from London Stansted, Bristol, Dublin and Belfast.

Ryanair (☎ 0870 156 9569, W www.ryan air.com) An Ireland-based airline, Ryanair flies direct to Glasgow Prestwick from London Stansted, Dublin, Brussels Charleroi, Paris Beauvais and Frankfurt Hahn, and from Dublin to Edinburgh and Glasgow.

Buying Tickets

Generally, there's nothing to be gained by buying a ticket direct from the airline. Discounted tickets are released to selected travel agents and specialist discount agencies, and these are usually the cheapest deals going.

One exception to this rule is the expanding number of no-frills carriers mentioned earlier, which only sell direct to travellers. Unlike the 'full-service' airlines, no-frills carriers, who make most of their sales online, often make one-way tickets available at half the return fare, meaning it's easy to put together an 'open-jaw' ticket where you fly to one place and leave from another.

Many travel agencies also have excellent Web sites, and the Internet is a quick and easy way to compare prices. Online ticket sales, through travel agents such as W www .travelocity.co.uk, work well if you are doing a simple one-way or return trip on specified dates. However, online fare generators are no substitute for a travel agent who knows about special deals and has strategies for avoiding layovers.

You may find the cheapest flights are advertised by obscure agencies. Most such firms are honest and solvent but there are some rogue fly-by-night outfits around. Paying by credit card generally offers protection, as most card issuers provide refunds if you can prove you didn't get what you paid for. Similar protection can be obtained by buying a ticket from a bonded agent, such as one covered by the Air Travel Organiser's Licence (ATOL) scheme in the UK. Agents who only accept cash should hand over the tickets straight away and not tell you to 'come back tomorrow'.

Many travellers change routes halfway through their trips, so think carefully before you buy a ticket that is not easily refunded or is extremely difficult to change.

Student Fares Full-time students and those aged under 26 (under 30 in some countries) have access to better deals than other travellers. You have to show a document proving your date of birth or a valid International Student Identity Card (ISIC) when buying your ticket.

Air Travel Glossary

Alliances Many of the world's leading airlines are now intimately involved with each other, sharing everything from reservations systems and check-in to aircraft and frequent-flyer schemes. Opponents say that alliances restrict competition. Whatever the arguments, there is no doubt that big alliances are the way of the future.

Courier Fares Businesses often need to send urgent documents or freight securely and quickly. Courier companies hire people to accompany the package through customs and, in return, offer a discount ticket which is sometimes a bargain. However, you may have to surrender all your baggage allowance and take only carry-on luggage.

Fares Airlines traditionally offer 1st-class (coded F), business-class (coded J) and economy-lass (coded Y) tickets. These days there are so many promotional and discounted fares available that few passengers pay full fare.

Lost Tickets If you lose your airline ticket, an airline will usually treat it like a travellers cheque and, after enquiries, issue you with another one. Legally, however, an airline is entitled to treat it like cash and if you lose it then it's gone forever. Take very good care of your tickets.

Onward Tickets An entry requirement for many countries is that you have a ticket out of the country. If you're unsure of your next move, the easiest solution is to buy the cheapest onward ticket to a neighbouring country or a ticket from a reliable airline that can later be refunded if you do not use it.

Open-Jaw Tickets These are return tickets where you fly out to one place but return from another. If available, this can save you backtracking to your arrival point.

Overbooking Since every flight has some passengers who fail to show up, airlines often book more passengers than they have seats. Usually excess passengers make up for the no-shows, but occasionally somebody gets 'bumped' onto the next available flight. Guess who it is most likely to be? The passengers who check in late. If you do get 'bumped', you are normally offered some form of compensation.

Reconfirmation Some airlines require you to reconfirm your flight at least 72 hours prior to departure. Check your travel documents to see if this is the case.

Restrictions Discounted tickets often have various restrictions on them – such as needing to be paid for in advance and incurring a penalty to be altered or cancelled. Others are restrictions on the minimum and maximum period you must be away.

Round-the-World Tickets RTW tickets give you a limited period (usually a year) in which to circumnavigate the globe. You can go anywhere the carrying airlines go, as long as you don't backtrack. The number of stopovers or total number of separate flights is decided before you set off and they usually cost a bit more than a basic return flight.

Ticketless Travel Airlines are gradually waking up to the realisation that paper tickets are unnecessary encumbrances. On simple one-way or return trips, reservations details can be held on computer and the passenger merely shows ID to claim their seat.

Transferred Tickets Airline tickets cannot be transferred from one person to another. Travellers sometimes try to sell the return half of their ticket, but officials can ask you to prove that you are the person named on the ticket. On an international flight, tickets are compared with passports.

Travellers with Specific Needs

If warned early enough, airlines can generally make special arrangements, such as wheelchair assistance at airports. 'Skycots', baby food and nappies should be provided by the airline if requested in advance. Children aged between two and 12 can usually occupy a seat for half to two-thirds of the full fare, and do get a baggage allowance.

The disability-friendly Web site **W** www .everybody.co.uk has an airline directory that provides details on facilities offered by various airlines.

Departure Tax

All UK domestic flights and those from Scotland to destinations within the EU carry a £10 departure tax. For flights to other destinations abroad the tax is £20. This is usually included in the price of your ticket.

England & Wales

There are more than a hundred flights a day between London and Edinburgh and Glasgow, and several daily to Inverness; to get to more isolated local airports you'll need to change at one of these (see the Getting Around chapter for more information on airlines flying out of these airports).

BA has flights to Glasgow and Edinburgh from London, Bristol, Birmingham, Cardiff, Manchester, Plymouth and Southampton, and to Inverness from London. British Midland flies from London Heathrow to Aberdeen, Edinburgh and Glasgow and to Edinburgh from Leeds/Bradford and Manchester. KLM UK and Go fly to Edinburgh from London Stansted, and easyJet flies from London's Luton airport to Edinburgh, Glasgow, Inverness and Aberdeen. British European (under the name Jersey European) flies from London City and Birmingham to Edinburgh; from Birmingham, Exeter, Guernsey and Jersey to Glasgow; and from London City to Aberdeen. ScotAirways flies from London City to Edinburgh, Glasgow and Dundee.

Prices can vary enormously. A standard economy return ticket from London to Edinburgh or Glasgow costs around £265 from British Midland, while Go, easyJet and Jersey European, offer return flights, travelling mid-week or on Saturday and booking about a month in advance, from as little as £20.

For students or travellers aged under 26, popular travel agencies in the UK include STA Travel (**☎** 020-7361 6262, **W** www.sta travel.co.uk), 86 Old Brompton Rd, London SW7; and Flightbookers (**☎** 020-7757 2000, **W** www.ebookers.com), 177–8 Tottenham Court Rd. STA has branches UK-wide and sells tickets to all travellers, though it caters especially to young people and students.

Ireland

Aer Lingus has daily flights from Dublin to Edinburgh and Glasgow. BA flies direct from Dublin to Edinburgh, from Belfast and Londonderry to Glasgow, and from Belfast to Aberdeen and Edinburgh; the lowest return fares start at around €70. Go and easyJet have direct flights from Belfast to Edinburgh and Glasgow; return fares start at €30. Ryanair flies from Dublin to Glasgow Prestwick and Edinburgh, and has flights from as little as €40 return, subject to conditions.

Continental Europe

The major airlines operate several direct flights a day into Edinburgh from Amsterdam, Brussels, Frankfurt and Paris, plus one or two daily from Copenhagen, Düsseldorf and Munich. In addition, it's possible to reach Edinburgh via London Stansted from various European cities using Go and easyJet, including Athens, Barcelona, Copenhagen, Geneva, Madrid, Munich, Naples, Nice, Prague, Reykjavik, Rome, Venice and Zürich.

The best fare from continental Europe is with easyJet, which offers direct flights from Amsterdam to Edinburgh from around £55 return. Flying from Munich to Edinburgh via London Stansted with Go costs from £190. Expect to pay around the equivalent of £150 on nondiscount European airlines for return tickets to Edinburgh or Glasgow.

Across Europe many travel agencies have ties with STA Travel, where cheap tickets can be purchased. Outlets in major cities include: STA Travel in Berlin (**☎** 030-311 0950, **W** www.statravel.de), Goethesttrasse

73, 10625 Berlin; Voyage Wasteels in Paris (☎ 08 03 88 70 04, fax 01 43 25 46 25, W www.wasteels.fr), 11 rue Dupuytren, 756006 Paris; and Passaggi in Rome (☎ 06-474 0923, fax 482 7436), Stazione Termini FS, Galleria di Tesla, Rome.

Nouvelles Frontiéres (☎ 02-547 44 44, W www.nouvelles-frontieres.be) at 2 blvd Maurice Lemmonier, 1000 Brussels, is also a recommended agency.

The student travel agency MyTravel Reiswinkel (☎ 020-692 7788, W www.my travel.nl – Dutch only), Linnaeusstraat 28, Amsterdam, offers reliable and reasonably low fares. Compare its prices with what's on offer in the discount flight centres along Rokin before deciding. Another recommended agency in Amsterdam is Malibu Travel (☎ 020-638 6059, fax 638 2271, W www.etn.nl/malibu), Prinsengracht 230.

Scandinavia

Icelandair (☎ 020-7874 1000, W www.ice landair.com) has daily flights between Reykjavik and Glasgow, while British Midland flies from Edinburgh to Copenhagen. Aberdeen has flight connections with the Faroe Islands (Atlantic Airways), Stavanger (British Midland, SAS and Braathens) in Norway, and Esbjerg (British Midland) in Denmark. A return flight from Stavanger to Aberdeen costs from around Nkr1700; from Reykjavik to Glasgow costs from Ikr30,000.

The USA

The majority of transatlantic flights to the UK still arrive at London, and the few that once made the journey from the east coast of America to Scotland mostly ceased after the 11 September terrorist attacks in the US; Continental Airlines and American Airlines, both flying from New York to Edinburgh and Glasgow, are the exceptions. Flight time is around 7½ hours, and return fares start from around US$650. Ask your travel agent though, because there's a good chance other direct services from the US to Scotland will have resumed by the time you read this.

Rather than fly via London, it's worth considering flying via Iceland. Icelandair has direct flights from New York, Boston, Baltimore/Washington, Minneapolis and Orlando (from October to March) to Reykjavik, where you can connect with a flight to Glasgow. Fares start at around US$530.

Discount travel agents in the USA are known as consolidators (though you won't see a sign on the door saying 'Consolidator'). San Francisco is the ticket consolidator capital of America, although some good deals can be found in Los Angeles, New York and other big cities. Consolidators can be found through the *Yellow Pages* or the major daily newspapers. The *New York Times*, the *Los Angeles Times*, the *Chicago Tribune* and the *Examiner* (San Francisco) all produce weekly travel sections in which you will find travel agency ads. Ticket Planet (W www.ticketplanet.com) is a leading ticket consolidator in the USA and is recommended.

Council Travel (☎ 800-226-8624, W www .ciee.org), America's largest student travel organisation, has 60 offices in the USA; its head office is at 205 E 42 St, New York, NY 10017.

STA Travel (☎ 800-777-0112, W www .statravel.com) has offices in Boston, Chicago, Miami, New York, Philadelphia, San Francisco and other major cities.

Canada

The charter operator Air Transat has one direct flight a week from Toronto to Edinburgh, while between them Air Canada and Air Transat (☎ 1866-847-1112, W www .airtransat.com) have two to four flights a day to Glasgow. There are also two flights a week from Calgary and one week from Vancouver to Glasgow. Return fares from Toronto start at around C$550.

Canadian discount air-ticket sellers are also known as consolidators and their fares tend to be about 10% higher than those sold in the USA. The *Globe & Mail*, *Toronto Star*, *Montreal Gazette* and *Vancouver Sun* carry travel agents ads and are a good place to look for cheap fares.

Travel CUTS (☎ 800-667-2887, W www .travelcuts.com) is Canada's national student travel agency and has offices in all major cities.

Australia

Expect to pay from A$1800 in the low season to A$2450 in the high season for a return ticket to London. Adding a connecting flight from London to Edinburgh, Glasgow or Aberdeen should only add around A$100 to the cost of the ticket.

Cheap flights from Australia to Europe generally go via Southeast Asian capitals, involving stopovers at Kuala Lumpur, Bangkok or Singapore. If a long stopover between connections is necessary, transit accommodation is sometimes included in the price of the ticket. If it's at your own expense, it may be worth considering a more expensive ticket.

Two well-known agents are Flight Centre and STA Travel. Flight Centre (☎ 131 600 Australia-wide, W www.flightcentre .com.au) has dozens of offices throughout Australia. STA Travel (☎ 03-9349 2411, W www.statravel.com.au) has offices in all major cities and on university campuses. Call ☎ 131 776 Australia-wide for your nearest branch.

New Zealand

Depending on which airline you choose, you may fly across Asia, with possible stopovers in India, Bangkok or Singapore, or across the USA, with possible stopovers in Honolulu, Australia or one of the Pacific Islands.

Prices are similar to those from Australia (from around NZ$2600 Auckland to London) but the trip is even longer – two 12-hour flights minimum.

Flight Centre (☎ 09-309 6171) has many branches throughout the country. STA Travel (☎ 09-309 0458, W www.sta.travel .com.nz) has offices in Auckland, Hamilton, Palmerston North, Wellington, Christchurch and Dunedin.

Asia

There are no direct flights from any of the major cities to Scotland. Travelling via London, a return flight from Hong Kong to Edinburgh will cost from around HK$7500, and from Tokyo around ¥140,000.

Although most Asian countries are now offering competitive air-fare deals, Bangkok, Singapore and Hong Kong are still the best places to shop around for discount tickets. Hong Kong's travel market can be unpredictable but some excellent bargains are available if you're lucky. STA has offices in Hong Kong, Thailand and Japan; check its Web site at W www.statravel.com for details.

BUS

Long-distance buses (coaches) are usually the cheapest method of getting to Scotland from other parts of the UK. The main operators are National Express (☎ 0870 580 8080, W www.gobycoach.com), and its subsidiary Scottish Citylink (☎ 0870 550 5050, W www.citylink.co.uk), with numerous regular services from London and other departure points in England, Wales and Northern Ireland.

Fares on the main routes are competitive, with many smaller operators undercutting Scottish Citylink/National Express. The cheapest London to Glasgow or Edinburgh coach is the daily overnight service with Silver Choice Travel (☎ 0141-333 1400, W www.silverchoicetravel.co.uk). It charges £24 for an Apex return, which must be bought at least seven days in advance, and is not valid for travel on Friday or Sunday; its standard return fare is £32, and journey time is nine hours. The return fare with Scottish Citylink is £36 but its services are more frequent. For details on passes and discounts see the Getting Around chapter.

Scottish Citylink runs a daily bus service from Edinburgh to various destinations in Ireland, including Belfast (£42 return, 7½ hours) and Dublin (£52 return, 10½ hours) via Glasgow and the high-speed ferry link between Stranraer and Belfast.

TRAIN

Travelling to Scotland by train is usually faster and more comfortable, but much more expensive, than taking the bus. Taking into account check-ins and the travel time between city centre and airport, the train offers a competitive alternative to air travel on the London-Edinburgh route. You can get timetable and fare information for all UK trains from the National Rail Enquiry Service (☎ 0845 748 4950).

Rest of the UK

GNER operates a fast and frequent rail service between London King's Cross and Edinburgh (four hours), with around 20 departures a day between 7am and 7pm. A standard return costs around £85 but prices can drop to £30 with special offers. The Virgin Trains service between London Euston and Glasgow, calling at Birmingham, Crewe and Preston, is slower at 5½ hours but it often has special promotional fares for as low as £20.

The Caledonian Sleeper service, connecting Edinburgh, Glasgow, Stirling, Perth, Dundee, Aberdeen, Fort William and Inverness with London Euston is operated by ScotRail and runs nightly (after 11pm) from Sunday to Friday. A standard return (sharing a two-bunk compartment) from London to Edinburgh or Glasgow costs £119, and a 1st-class return (single-bunk compartment) costs £165; the seven-day advance purchase Apex fare is £89. You also have the option of travelling on the sleeper in a 1st-class coach with a reclining seat, rather than a bunk; this costs £35/65 for an Apex/standard return. The journey lasts about 7½ hours.

ScotRail offers various 'Rail and Sail' deals between Edinburgh and Glasgow and Belfast via the ferry crossings at Stranraer and Troon. Off-peak returns cost from £45, and the journey time is about five hours.

Continental Europe

You can travel from Paris or Brussels to Scotland by train using the Eurostar (☎ 0870 518 6186 in the UK, ☎ 08 36 35 35 39 in France, Ⓦ www.eurostar.com) as far as London Waterloo station, but then you'll have to take the Underground from Waterloo to King's Cross or Euston stations to connect with the Edinburgh or Glasgow train. The total journey time from Paris is about eight hours, and the standard return fare from Paris to London is around £500; flying is usually faster and cheaper.

Buying Tickets

If the Byzantine Empire had designed a railway system, it could not have come up with anything more impenetrably complex than the labyrinthine structure created by the privatisation of British Rail in the mid-1990s.

Rail services are provided by 25 different train operating companies (TOCs), while the rails themselves, along with the stations and signalling systems, are owned and operated by a completely separate organisation.

There's a bewildering range of ticket types with various restrictions attached, depending on when you book and when you're travelling. You can check timetables and fares with the National Rail Enquiry Service (☎ 0845 748 4950), who will then give you the phone number of one of the TOCs.

ScotRail operates most train services within Scotland, as well as the Caledonian Sleeper service to London; you can book tickets by credit card on ☎ 0845 755 0033, or book online at Ⓦ www.scotrail.co.uk. GNER (☎ 0845 722 5225, Ⓦ www.gner .co.uk) operates the main, east-coast London King's Cross to Edinburgh route, and Virgin Trains (☎ 0845 722 2333, Ⓦ www .virgintrains.co.uk) runs services from London Euston, Wales and north, central, south and southwest England to Glasgow and Edinburgh.

Rail Passes

Unfortunately, Eurail passes are not recognised in Britain and their local equivalents aren't recognised in the rest of Europe. See the Getting Around chapter for details of passes valid for train travel in Scotland.

The BritRail pass, which includes travel in Scotland, must be purchased outside Britain. There are many variations available, but the most useful for a visit to Britain that takes in Scotland is probably the BritRail Flexipass. It provides unlimited train travel on a certain number of days within a specified 60-day period. Prices for adult 1st class/over-60s 1st class/standard class are:

4 days	US$350/300/235
8 days	US$510/435/340
15 days	US$770/655/515

Youth passes are valid for those aged between 15 and 25 (standard class only) and cost US$185/240/360 for 4/8/15 days.

CAR & MOTORCYCLE

See the Getting Around chapter for details of driving conditions and information on renting and buying vehicles.

Drivers of vehicles registered in other EU countries will find bringing a car or motorcycle into the UK fairly straightforward. The vehicle must have registration papers and a nationality plate, and the driver must have insurance. Although the International Insurance Certificate (Green Card) is not compulsory, it still provides excellent proof that you are covered.

BOAT
Northern Ireland

From Northern Ireland, the main car ferry links to Scotland are the Belfast-Stranraer, Larne-Cairnryan and Belfast-Troon crossings, operated by Stena Line (☎ 028 90 747 747 from Northern Ireland, ⓦ www.stena line.com), P&O Irish Sea (☎ 0870 242 4777, ⓦ www.poirishsea.com) and SeaCat (☎ 0870 552 3523, ⓦ www.steam-packet .com) respectively. There are standard and high-speed ferries on the Stranraer and Cairnryan routes, high-speed only on the Troon crossing.

Fares vary widely depending on the season, and there are special deals worth looking out for. A one-way Apex fare on the slow ferry from Belfast to Stranraer costs around £125 for a car and two people. One-way Apex fares on the high-speed catamaran between Belfast and Troon start at £96 for a car and two passengers. One-way fares for foot passengers start at around £17.

The Larne-Cairnryan high-speed catamaran is the fastest crossing – one hour compared with 2½ hours for the Troon-Belfast route or the Larne-Cairnryan slow ferry. The drive from Cairnryan or Stranraer to Glasgow or Edinburgh is 85 miles or 132 miles respectively. From Troon to Glasgow is just 35 miles.

The car ferry service between Ballycastle (Northern Ireland) and Campbeltown (Argyll), which was launched in 1997, ceased operation in 2000. It may resume in early 2003; go to ⓦ www.campbeltownferry.com to find out more details.

Continental Europe

In spring 2002, Superfast Ferries started a roll-on roll-off car ferry between Rosyth, 12 miles northwest of Edinburgh, and a port in Zeebrugge in Belgium. One crossing a day was planned and the journey time was expected to be 16 hours. Superfast's sales agent in the UK is Viamare Travel (☎ 020-7431 4560, fax 7431 5456, ⓦ www.super fastscotland.com), Graphic House, 2 Sumatra Rd, London NW6 1PU.

Scandinavia

From late May to early September the Smyril Line (its UK agent is P&O Scottish Ferries, ☎ 01224-572615, ⓦ www.smyril-line.com) operates its weekly 'North Atlantic Link' car ferry between Shetland (Lerwick), the Faroe Islands (Torshavn), Iceland (Seydisfjordur), Norway (Bergen) and Denmark (Hantsholm). The boat is ideal for cyclists on the North Sea Cycle Route and leaves from Lerwick on Monday for Bergen, and on Wednesday for Torshavn and Seydisfjordur. A one-way ticket from Aberdeen to Bergen via Lerwick on P&O Scottish Ferries and Smyril Line costs from £95/115 per person for a couchette plus £112/130 for a car up to 5m.

The Aberdeen-Lerwick crossing takes 14 hours, Lerwick to Bergen 13½ hours, Lerwick to Torshavn 13 hours, and Torshavn to Seydisfjordur 15 hours.

ORGANISED TOURS

Hundreds of companies around the world offer package tours of the region. Ask a travel agent or contact the Scottish Tourist Board or British Tourist Authority (see Tourist Offices in the Facts for the Visitor chapter). Three good tour operators are:

Ancestral Journeys (☎ 01383-720522, ⓔ ances tralconnections@compuserve.com), 105 St Margaret St, Dunfermline KY12 7PH. Ancestral Journeys will research your Scottish ancestry and organise a personalised tour, accompanied by a professional genealogist and historian, that combines sightseeing with visiting the places where your ancestors lived. Prices start at US$1850 per person for a week, including 10 hours of genealogical research.

Footprints (W www.footprints-scotland.co.uk), Moffat, Dumfriesshire DG10 9BN. These personalised tours explore Scotland's prehistoric past in the company of an archaeological expert. Highlights include visits to Pictish symbol stones, Iron-Age forts and stone circles. Three-day tours cost from £360 per person.

Taste of Scotland (☎ 01592-260101, fax 261333, e admin@robertthebruce.com) 9 Nicol St, Kirkcaldy KY1 1NY. This exceedingly posh lot offers bespoke luxury tours, staying in top hotels, eating at the best restaurants and travelling in a grand Rolls-Royce with a qualified guide and driver.

Getting Around

Public transport in the Highlands and islands is generally very efficient: buses, trains and ferries mostly run on time. However, it can be a slow and difficult process reaching the more remote areas, especially in the north and the Western Isles.

Public transport is also very expensive, particularly compared to the rest of Europe, though there are several discount tickets that can save a huge amount of money, especially if they're bought well in advance.

Buses are usually the cheapest way to get around, but are also usually the slowest, and on main routes you're often confined to major roads that screen you from the small towns and landscapes, which make touring around the region such an incredible experience. Travelling on postbuses can be very entertaining, though they're often less reliable than normal bus services.

To really get off the well-travelled road it might be necessary to hire a car, but if you're really thorough with your planning it's possible to use a combination of trains, ferries, buses, bicycles and your feet to reach every corner of the region.

Traveline (☎ 0870 608 2608, W www .traveline.org.uk) provides timetable information for all public transport services in Scotland; it doesn't provide any information on fares, nor book tickets for you, but it will give you the telephone number of the relevant operator to call.

AIR

Besides Scotland's major international airports in Edinburgh, Glasgow and Aberdeen, there's an array of minor airports in the Highlands and islands (see the individual chapters for details), many little more than a gravel strip. Internal flights should be booked as far ahead as possible, because – with so few flights and such small planes (eight-seaters are common for many services) – flights fill up fast. And, last but not least, be prepared for cancellations due to erratic weather at any time of the year.

Domestic Air Services

Most domestic air services are lifelines for remote island communities, or are geared to business needs and are very expensive – a flight from Edinburgh to the Shetland Islands can cost up to £250!

You might feel it's worth flying to Barra in the Outer Hebrides just to experience landing on a beach – one of the few airports in the world where flight schedules are dictated by tide times! Otherwise, flying is a pricey way to cover relatively short distances, and only worth considering if you're short of time and want to visit the outer reaches of the region, in particular the Western Isles, Orkney and Shetland.

Scotland's main domestic operators are British Regional Airlines (BRAL; W www .british-regional.com) and Loganair, who both fly under the franchise of British Airways (BA; ☎ 0845 773 3377), with flights from Edinburgh to Kirkwall, Sumburgh, Stornoway and Wick; from Glasgow to Barra, Benbecula, Campbeltown, Inverness, Islay, Kirkwall, Sumburgh, Stornoway and Tiree; and from Aberdeen and Inverness to Kirkwall and Sumburgh. Loganair operates inter-island flights in the Orkney and Shetland Islands and Western Isles.

Highland Airways (☎ 01851-701282, W www.highlandairways.co.uk) runs a service between Inverness and Stornoway (Monday to Saturday), and also flies to other destinations in the region. Their new Island Hopper service operates between Inverness, Stornoway and Benbecula.

Apex Fares & Air Passes

Most airlines offer a range of tickets including full fare (flexible but very expensive), Apex (which must be booked at least 14 days in advance) and special deals on some services. There are also youth fares for under-25s but Apex and special-offer fares tend to be cheaper.

Return fares from Glasgow/Inverness to Kirkwall in the Orkney Islands with BA costs from £167/117. A return flight from Edinburgh to Sumburgh in the Shetland Islands costs from £135; flights between the Orkney and Shetland Islands cost from £90 return. Flights from Inverness to Stornoway with Highland Airways costs £130 return.

BA/BRAL has a Highland Rover air pass for around £200 that allows travel on direct flights within Scotland and between Scotland and Northern Ireland, and allows you to take any five flights within seven days; there are some flights you can't take though, so ask BA or your travel agent for more details.

Domestic Departure Tax

There's a £10 airport departure tax added to the price of domestic flight tickets – find out whether this is included in the price you're quoted.

BUS

The Highlands and islands have one major bus player: Scottish Citylink (☎ 0870 550 5050, W www.citylink.co.uk), a subsidiary of National Express. It's supplemented by numerous smaller regional operators. Long-distance express buses are usually referred to as coaches.

Some regions operate telephone enquiry travel lines that try to explain the fast-changing situation with timetables; these numbers have been provided in the regional chapters. Before planning a journey off the main routes it's advisable to phone Traveline (see the introduction to this chapter) for the latest timetable information.

Bus Passes & Discounts

There's a range of discount and flexible tickets on offer including:

Scottish Citylink Smart Cards Scottish Citylink's discount cards give up to 30% off standard adult fares on coach services. Cards cost £6 per year and are available for full-time students, under-25s and those aged over 50. You'll need a passport-size photo and proof of age/student status – an ISIC card is accepted as proof of the latter. These cards also offer a discount on National Express services throughout Britain.

Scottish Citylink Explorer Pass The Explorer Pass can be bought in the UK by both UK and overseas citizens, and provides unlimited travel on all Citylink services within Scotland for three consecutive days (£35), any five days out of 10 consecutive days (£55), or any eight days out of 16 (£85). It also gives discounts on various regional bus services and on Caledonian MacBrayne (CalMac) and P&O Scottish Ferries. It is not valid on National Express coaches.

Citylink also offers discounts to holders of the Euro<26 card and the Young Scot card, which provide discounts all over Scotland and Europe.

Backpackers Buses Haggis Backpackers (☎ 0131-557 9393, W www.haggisadven tures.com), 60 High St, Edinburgh, runs a bus service on a circuit between hostels in Edinburgh, Pitlochry, Inverness, Loch Ness, Carbisdale Castle, Ullapool, Isle of Skye, Fort William, Glencoe, Oban and Stirling (although there's no obligation to stay in the hostels). You can start your tour at any point, and hop on and off the bus wherever and whenever you like, booking up to 24 hours in advance. There's no fixed time for completing the circuit, but you can only cover each section of the route once. Tickets cost £69/55 in summer/winter.

Macbackpackers (☎ 0131-558 9900, W www.macbackpackers.com), 105 High St, Edinburgh, runs a similar jump-on jump-off service, with daily departures and a fare of £55. Their seven-day 'Grand Tour of Scotland' is good value at £129, as is their three-day 'Highland Romp' for £55 and three-day Isle of Skye tour for £65.

The SYHA (☎ 0870 155 3255, W www .syha.org.uk) sells an Explore Scotland bus pass, which can be used on Citylink services. It costs £165/250 for five/eight days and includes seven nights in SYHA hostels.

Postbus Many rural regions can only be reached by Royal Mail postbuses – minibuses, or sometimes just four-seater cars, driven by postal workers delivering and collecting mail. They follow circuitous routes through some of the most beautiful areas of Scotland, and are particularly useful for walkers – there are no official stops, and you can hail a postbus anywhere on its route. Fares are typically £2 to £5 for a one-way journey. For more details contact Royal Mail Customer Service (☎ 0845 774 0740, or ☎ 01752-387112 from outside the UK) or check the online routes and timetable information at W www.postbus.royalmail .com/postbus. Regional postbus telephone numbers are listed throughout the book.

TRAIN
Scotland's rail network stretches to all the major cities and towns, but in the Highlands there are a lot of large, blank areas on the map – you'll need to switch to the bus or hire a car to explore these.

The West Highland Railway from Glasgow to Fort William and Mallaig, and the Kyle Line from Inverness to Kyle of Lochalsh, are two of the world's great scenic train journeys. Bicycles are carried free on all ScotRail trains, but space is limited. Reservations are compulsory on certain routes, including the West Highland and Kyle Railway lines, and are recommended on many others.

Rail Passes
ScotRail offers a range of good-value passes for train travel in Scotland. You can buy them from BritRail outlets in the USA, Canada and Europe; the British Travel Centre at 12 Regent St, London; train stations throughout Britain; certain UK travel agents (eg, Thomas Cook); and ScotRail telesales (☎ 0845 755 0033).

The Freedom of Scotland Travelpass gives unlimited travel on all ScotRail trains and CalMac ferries, and on certain Scottish

The West Highland Railway

The West Highland Railway runs between Glasgow and Mallaig, through some of the wildest and most spectacular mountain scenery in Scotland's Highlands and islands.

Stations such as Arrochar & Tarbet, Crianlarich, Bridge of Orchy and Spean Bridge allow you to set off on an endless array of wonderful mountain walks, direct from the platform. There are several opportunities for circular walks, or you can get off at one station, have yourself a jolly tramp, then jump on another train from another station. From Fort William Station it's only a few miles' walk to Britain's highest peak, Ben Nevis.

Possibly the most intriguing place to get off the train is at Corrour, which at 408m, is Britain's highest and most remote station. The station lies in the middle of Rannoch Moor, which was so soft and boggy that the line here had to be laid on a platform of earth, ashes and brushwood. It's a tribute to the railway's Victorian engineers that it has remained in place for over a century and nobody has ever managed (or wanted) to build a road up here. Film buffs will already know that Corrour is where Renton, Sick Boy, Spud and Tommy got back to nature in the film *Trainspotting*. Unlike them, however, you won't be disappointed: from Corrour you can reach lonely peaks or wind your way through remote valleys that are out of reach to mere motorists.

Beyond Fort William the train runs through more glorious scenery and past awe-inspiring Glenfinnan to Mallaig, from where it's a short ferry ride to the Isle of Skye, with a branch line from Mallaig to Oban, gateway port for the Outer Hebrides.

For a walker this railway is an absolute gift and for any Highland visitor, a ride is a must. From May to September there are four trains daily (three Sunday) in each direction. There are two or three trains daily from Glasgow to Fort William (£19, 3¾ hours), and one to five trains between Fort William and Mallaig (£7.50, 1½ hours).

For more details phone National Rail Enquiries (☎ 0845 748 4950) or ScotRail reservations (☎ 0845 755 0033). For more ideas on where to go once you've alighted, get the *Walks from the West Highland Railway* by Chris & John Harvey.

Citylink coach services (routes not covered by rail). It's available for four days' travel out of eight (£79/69 in high/low season) or eight days' travel out of 15 (£99/89). High season is from mid-May to mid-September. Holders of Railcards (see Railcards later in this section) get a 33% discount – if you're eligible, a Railcard will more than pay for itself when you buy a Travelpass.

The Highland Rover pass gives free train travel in the Highlands from Glasgow to Oban, Fort William and Mallaig, and from Inverness to Kyle of Lochalsh, Aviemore, Aberdeen and Thurso; it also gives free travel on Scottish Citylink coaches from Oban/Fort William to Inverness, and a discount on CalMac ferries to Mull and the Isle of Skye. It is only available for four days' travel out of eight (£49/39).

Railcards

A range of discount Railcards, which give 33% off standard adult fares, is available for travel on all train services in the UK. There are cards for full-time students (studying in the UK), those aged 16 to 25, families (up to four adults and four children) and those aged 60 or over, costing £18 (£20 for the Family Railcard) for one year. You'll need a passport-size photo and proof of age/student status – an ISIC card is accepted as proof of the latter. Pick up a Railcard application form from main train stations, or get one from ScotRail telesales.

Tickets

ScotRail (☎ 0845 755 0033 for ticket sales and reservations, ☒ www.scotrail.co.uk) operates most train services in the Highlands. Reservations are recommended for intercity trips, especially on Fridays and public holidays; for shorter journeys, just buy a ticket at the station before you go.

There are two classes of train travel: first and standard. First class costs 30% to 50% more than standard and, except on very crowded trains, isn't worth the extra.

Under-fives travel free; those aged five to 15 pay half-price for most tickets.

There's a bewildering variety of ticket types on offer, including:

Single – valid for a one-way journey at any time on the particular day specified

Day Return – valid for a return journey at any time on the particular day specified

Cheap Day Return – valid for a return journey on the day specified on the ticket, but there are time restrictions (you're not usually allowed to travel on a train that leaves before 9.15am)

Open Return – for outward travel on a stated day and return on any day within a month

Apex – one of the cheapest return fares; standard class only; reservations compulsory and you must travel on the booked services; you must book at least 48 hours in advance, but seats are limited so book early (up to eight weeks in advance)

SuperSaver – the cheapest ticket where advance purchase isn't necessary; can't be used on Friday after 2.30pm, Saturday in July and August or on bank holidays, or the day after a bank holiday before 2.30pm; the return journey must be within one calendar month

Saver – higher priced than the SuperSaver, but can be used any day and there are fewer time restrictions

SuperAdvance – similarly priced to the SuperSaver but with fewer time/day restrictions; however, tickets must be bought before 2pm on the day before travel and both the outward and return journey times must be specified; limited availability so book early

CAR & MOTORCYCLE

Travelling by private car or motorcycle enables you to get to remote places, and to travel quickly, independently and flexibly. Unfortunately, the price you pay for independence is isolation: someone travelling on public transport might end up *seeing* more of Scotland than you, and someone cycling or walking definitely will, even though they'll get to fewer places.

Roads in the region are generally good and often extremely deserted. Main roads (designated 'A') are dual or single carriageways and are sometimes clogged with slow-moving trucks or caravans; the A9 from Perth to Inverness is notoriously busy.

Life on the road is more relaxed and interesting on the secondary (designated 'B') and minor (undesignated) roads. These wind through the countryside from village to village. You can't travel fast, but you won't want to. Roads are only single track in many, if not most, Highland and island areas.

Road Distances (in miles)

	Aberdeen	Dundee	Edinburgh	Fort William	Glasgow	Inverness	Kyle of Lochalsh	Mallaig	Oban	Scrabster	Stranraer	Ullapool
Aberdeen	---											
Dundee	70	---										
Edinburgh	129	62	---									
Fort William	165	121	146	---								
Glasgow	145	84	42	104	---							
Inverness	105	131	155	66	166	---						
Kyle of Lochalsh	188	177	206	76	181	82	---					
Mallaig	189	161	180	44	150	106	34	---				
Oban	180	118	123	45	94	110	120	85	---			
Scrabster	218	250	279	185	286	119	214	238	230	---		
Stranraer	233	171	120	184	80	250	265	232	178	374	---	
Ullapool	150	189	215	90	225	60	88	166	161	125	158	---

Petrol costs around 80p per litre and diesel is only a few pence cheaper. Petrol prices tend to rise as you get farther from main population centres. In remote areas petrol stations are few and far between and sometimes closed Sunday, so be careful not to run out.

Road Rules

A foreign driving licence is valid in Britain for up to 12 months from the time of your last entry into the country. If you're bringing a car from Europe make sure that you have the car registration documents with you and that you're adequately insured.

Vehicles are driven on the left side of the road; front-seat belts are compulsory and if belts are fitted in the back seat they must be worn; the speed limit is 30mph in built-up areas, 60mph on single carriageways and 70mph on dual carriageways; you give way to your right at roundabouts (traffic already on the roundabout has right of way); and motorcyclists must wear helmets.

Rental

Car rental is relatively expensive and often you'll be better off making arrangements in your home country for a fly/drive deal. The international rental companies, found at Scotland's major airports, charge from around £150 per week for a small car (Ford Fiesta, Peugeot 106), though the longer you hire the car the cheaper the day rate will become; rates offered by local companies such as Arnold Clark (☎ 0131-228 4747) in Edinburgh, start at around £18/90 per day/ week. See the regional chapters for details of local car-hire companies. Also remember that all TICs keep lists of local car-hire firms.

The reservations numbers for the main international companies are:

Avis	☎ 0870 606 0100
Budget	☎ 0845 606 6669
Europcar	☎ 0870 607 5000
Hertz	☎ 0870 844 8844
Holiday Autos	☎ 0870 300 400
National	☎ 0870 365 365
Thrifty Car Rental	☎ 0870 066 0514

If you're going to hire a car for longer than four weeks, it may be worth checking out the long-term rental deals offered by Avis. The online car-hire service, Easycar.com, with an office near Glasgow Airport, also

A One-Track Mind

Many Highland and island roads are single track with passing places. These are indicated by a diamond-shaped signpost you'll need to look out for, though they're generally well marked. Never, *ever* park in passing places – it's illegal for very good reasons, and more than a few people have been killed or badly injured parking in passing places they thought were safe.

One of the major causes of crashes in the region is drivers not letting fast drivers behind them past; it can get a bit tedious letting such lunatics through at passing places, but it's always better than having them bear down on you for miles – or, even worse, trying to force their way past you on some lethal corner.

Generally though drivers here are unfailingly polite and not particularly aggressive, though their unhurried pace can be a little frustrating. The main hazard on single-track roads is suicidal sheep wandering onto the road (be particularly wary of lambs in spring), and the distracting beauty of the landscape.

offers good deals but, as with all rental firms, check the small print carefully.

To rent a car, drivers must usually be aged between 23 and 65 with at least one year's experience.

If you're visiting the Western Isles, Orkney or Shetland, it will often prove cheaper to hire a car on the islands, rather than paying to take a rental car across on the ferry.

Purchase
It's possible to buy a reasonable car or camper van in the UK for around £1000 to £2000. Vehicles require a Ministry of Transport (MOT) safety certificate (the certificate itself is usually referred to simply as an MOT) issued by licensed garages and valid for one year; full third-party insurance – shop around but expect to pay at least £300; registration – a standard form signed by the buyer and seller, with a section to be sent to the MOT; and a tax disc (£160 for one year,

£88 for six months; £105/57.75 for vehicles with engines less than 1549cc), available from main post offices on presentation of a valid MOT certificate, insurance and registration documents. Cars that are over 25 years old are tax exempt.

You are strongly recommended to buy a vehicle with valid MOT and tax as they remain with the car through a change of ownership; third-party insurance goes with the driver rather than the car and so you'll still have to arrange this (and beware of letting others drive the car). For further information about registering, licensing, insuring and testing your vehicle, contact a post office or Vehicle Registration Office for leaflet V100.

Motorcycle Touring
The region is ideal for motorcycle touring, with lots of good-quality winding roads and stunning scenery to stimulate the senses. Just make sure your wet-weather gear is up to scratch. Crash helmets are compulsory.

The Auto-Cycle Union (ACU; ☎ 01788-566400, fax 573585, ⓔ admin@acu.org.uk, ⓦ www.acu.org.uk), ACU House, Wood St, Rugby, Warwickshire CV21 2YX, publishes a useful booklet about motorcycle touring in Britain.

Motoring Organisations
It's worth joining a British motoring organisation if you've got your own wheels, though if you've got a rental car breakdown cover will usually be included. The two largest in the UK, both offering 24-hour assistance, are the Automobile Association (AA; ☎ 0800 917 0992, ⓦ www.theaa.com) and the Royal Automobile Club (RAC; ☎ 0800 550550, ⓦ www.rac.co.uk); one year's membership starts at £39 and £34 respectively. If you're a member of a motoring organisation back home, check to see if it has a reciprocal arrangement with a British organisation.

WALKING & CYCLING
Walking and cycling are extremely popular and definitely the most rewarding ways to explore the Highlands and islands. See the Activities chapter for further information.

HITCHING

Hitching is never entirely safe in any country and we don't recommend it; travellers who decide to hitch are taking a small but potentially serious risk. However, many people hitch, and the advice that follows should help to make their journeys as fast and safe as possible.

Hitching is reasonably easy in the Highlands and islands – village life makes it an acceptable way of getting around and there's a good chance you'll meet some real characters (and the odd creep) if you're hitching for an extended period. In the remote areas your main problem won't be getting drivers to stop, but waiting for them to appear in the first place! However, when they do appear, particularly on islands where public transport is infrequent, hitching is so much a part of getting around that local drivers may stop and offer you a lift without you even asking.

It's against the law to hitch on motorways or the immediate slip roads; make a sign and use approach roads, nearby roundabouts or service stations.

BOAT

The main car-ferry operators to Scotland's larger islands are CalMac and P&O, but there are many other car and passenger-only ferries serving smaller islands and making short sea crossings. Taking a car on a ferry – particularly to far-flung islands – can be devastatingly expensive; you might save some money hiring a car once you arrive on the island.

CalMac (☎ 0870 565 0000, W www.cal mac.co.uk) is the principal ferry operator on the west coast, with services from Oban to the islands of Barra, South Uist, Coll, Tiree, Lismore, Mull and Colonsay, from Ullapool to the Western Isles and Outer Hebrides, and from Mallaig to Skye.

CalMac's Island Rover ticket is great value and gives unlimited travel on its ferries; it costs £43/63 per person for eight/15 days, plus £210/315 for a car, or £105/158 for a motorcycle. Bikes can be taken free on Rover tickets; otherwise they cost £1 to £2 per journey. There are also 26 Hopscotch routes that enable visitors to plan which

A Way With The Ferries

God owns the world
And all that it contains
Except the western isles
They belong to MacBrayne.
— **local saying**

If you're touring the isles, you'll spend some time on the ferry service started in 1852 by David MacBrayne and his two now-long-forgotten partners, the Hutcheson brothers. And, just like locals, you too will come to resent the extortionate fares charged by this most Scottish of shipping lines.

'Twas not always thus; once there was competition among the Hebridean ferry services. But David MacBrayne's son, David Jr, did all he could to quash his competitors and, after a series of mergers in the 1970s, Caledonian MacBrayne (CalMac) has a virtual monopoly on the Hebrides and around.

Expensive though their ferries are, especially if you're lugging your car around with you, it must be said that CalMac runs a tight ship, so to speak. Their ferries are beautifully maintained and rarely late, and staff are generally very professional (even the gruff ones herding you on board).

The 1948 nationalisation of Scottish railways and transport saw the company come under the control of the government (in whose hands it remains today, though competitive tendering is in its early stages). Reborn in 1973 as the amalgamation of the David MacBrayne Ltd and the Caledonian Steam Packet Company, CalMac has 28 ships serving 23 isles, though there are only seven larger 'ro-ro' (roll-on, roll-off) ferries where cars go below deck and exit on the opposite side to which they entered the boat.

Average speeds for larger ferries is around 18 or 19 knots, although they can sometimes travel as fast as 21 knots.

islands to visit; check out the CalMac Web site for more details.

P&O Scottish Ferries (☎ 01224-572615, fax 574411, W www.posf.co.uk) has ferries from Aberdeen and Scrabster (near Thurso) to Orkney, from Orkney to Shetland and from Aberdeen to Shetland. Pentland Ferries (☎ 01856-831226, W www.pentlandferries .com) has a shorter (one hour) crossing from Caithness to St Margaret's Hope in Orkney Islands. John o'Groats Ferries (☎ 01955-611353) runs a summer only service (May to September) from John o'Groats to Burwick at the southern tip of Orkney.

See the relevant chapters for full details of local ferry services and fares.

ORGANISED TOURS

Since travel is so easy to organise in Scotland, there's little need to consider a tour. Still, if your time is limited and you prefer to travel in a group, there are some interesting possibilities.

Road

Rabbie's Trail Burners (☎ 0131-226 3133, fax 225 7028, W www.rabbies.com), 207 High St, Edinburgh, offers one- to five-day tours of the region in 16-seat mini-coaches. The three-day tour takes in Glencoe, Lochaber, Kintail, the Isle of Skye and Loch Ness, and costs £95/75 in high/low season.

Scotsell (☎ 0141-772 5928, W www .scotsell.com), 2d Churchill Way, Bishopbriggs, Glasgow, can organise self-drive car-touring holidays to the islands. A seven-night tour of the Outer Hebrides, using your own vehicle, costs from £433 per person, including hotel accommodation and ferry tickets. Car rental is available at extra cost.

Mountain Innovations (☎/fax 01479-831331, W www.scotmountain.co.uk), Fraoch Lodge, Deshar Rd, Boat of Garten, organises good-value activity holidays in the region, including walking, mountain biking, kayaking, skiing and horse riding. Packages include car hire, accommodation, food and guides. A five-day 'Highland Experience' tour that takes in the Cairngorms, Speyside, Loch Ness, Torridon, Glen Nevis and Glen Coe costs from £156 per person.

Backpackers Tours

Several companies – including Haggis Backpackers and Macbackpackers (see the Bus section earlier in this chapter) and Going Forth (☎ 0131-478 6500, W www .goingforth.com), 9 South St Andrew St – run three- to seven-day guided tours of the Highlands and islands year-round, taking in the main attractions such as Glencoe, Eilean Donan Castle, the Isle of Skye and Loch Ness. Prices range from £55 to £230, including hostel accommodation and various visits and activities.

Rail

The Royal Scotsman (☎ 0131-555 1021, W www.royalscotsman.com) is a luxury train, complete with opulent, wood-panelled sleeping cabins (16 twin and four single) and dining cars, hauled by a diesel locomotive, that makes three- and five-day tours of the Highlands from April to October. Rates, including on-train accommodation, gourmet meals and fine wines, start at £1390 per person.

ScotRail ShortBreaks (☎ 0870 161 0161) offers two-night trips to the Highlands, costing from £89 per person including accommodation, and a week-long tour of the region for £455, including rail, coach and ferry travel and accommodation.

Cruises

There are many companies offering cruises and yacht charters around Scotland's alluring west coast – acknowledged as one of the most spectacular cruise areas in the world.

Top of the range is Hebridean Island Cruises (☎ 01756-704704, fax 704794, W www.hebridean.co.uk), offering four- to 14-night luxury cruises aboard the Hebridean Princess, departing from Oban. A four-night Taste of the Hebrides tour costs from £885 per person.

Douglas Lindsay (☎ 01631-770246, fax 770246, W www.corryvreckan.co.uk) runs cruises aboard the beautiful 20m yacht *Corryvreckan*, based at Oban. The yacht has five double guest cabins, and rates include delicious gourmet meals. You don't need any sailing experience, but you can lend a hand sailing and steering if you want to. Prices are from £495 to £525 per person per week, all inclusive.

Argyll & the Southern Hebrides

Argyll can come as a shock to first-time visitors who thought they'd have to go farther north to experience the 'real' Highlands.

This stunning region – made up of terrain as diverse as the seaside resort of Rothesay on the Isle of Bute to the wind-battered Kintyre peninsula in the south, the rugged southern Hebrides in the west to the postcard-perfect harbour of Oban in the north – has long been defined as little more than the dividing point between the lowlands and the Highlands. But this once inaccessible region is so much more than just a divide.

Island life is Argyll's central drawcard, with remote places such as Islay, Jura and Colonsay and the very isolated Coll and Tiree often eerily picturesque, peaceful and solitary. More populous isles, such as Mull, are a joy to explore. And the jewel in the southern Hebridean crown is the tiny island of Iona, basking in the glory of its awe-inspiring beauty and historical importance.

The region's history is as torrid as it is fascinating; once a part of the Irish Celts' kingdom of Dàl Riata during the 4th and 5th centuries (Argyll is derived from *aragaidheal*, meaning 'boundary of the Gaels'), the region has been governed by tyrants and scoundrels, as well as more generous types; rulers have ranged from Norse invaders to Robert the Bruce to the all-powerful Mac-Donalds, lords of the Isles, to the Campbell clan, who still own massive chunks of land. And the contribution made to Western civilisation by St Columba cannot be overstated.

INFORMATION

Most of the region covered in this chapter is looked after by the ludicrously named Argyll, the Isles, Loch Lomond, Stirling & Trossachs Tourist Board, whose Web site can be found at Ⓦ www.scottish.heart lands.org. The exception is the Isle of Arran, covered by the Ayrshire & Arran Tourist Board (Ⓦ www.ayrshire-arran.com).

An invaluable guide to the archaeological heritage of the area is *Argyll & the Western*

Highlights

- Cycle the beautiful Isle of Arran, 'Scotland in miniature'
- Drink your way around Islay's evocative whisky distilleries
- Take in the soaring views from McCaig's Tower atop Oban
- Spend a night in front of the fire at the Mishnish Hotel in picturesque Tobermory on Mull
- Feel the enchanting tranquillity of tiny Iona, and visit the awesome natural phenomenon of Staffa
- Hire a wet suit and hit the waves for some world-class windsurfing in isolated Tiree

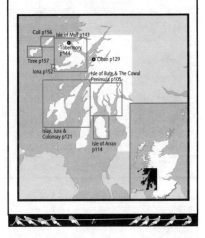

Isles (£3), published by the Royal Commission on the Ancient and Historical Monuments of Scotland.

The following Ordnance Survey (OS) Landranger maps cover Argyll and the Southern Hebrides:

Landranger 46: Coll & Tiree
Landranger 47: Tobermory & North Mull
Landranger 48: Iona & West Mull, Ulva

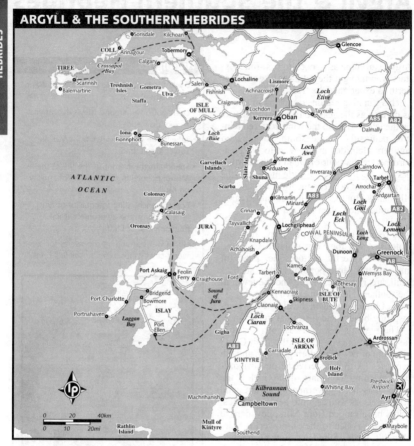

ARGYLL & THE SOUTHERN HEBRIDES

Landranger 50: Glen Orchy & Loch Etive
Landranger 55: Lochgilphead & Loch Awe
Landranger 60: Islay
Landranger 61: Jura & Colonsay
Landranger 62: North Kintyre & Tarbert
Landranger 63: Firth of Clyde, Greenock &
  Rothesay
Landranger 68: South Kintyre & Campbeltown
Landranger 69: Isle of Arran

GETTING AROUND

Argyll's public transport is mostly limited to
buses, and in remote areas they can be frustratingly infrequent. The main companies in
the region are Oban & District (☎ 01631-

562856) and Scottish Citylink (☎ 0870 5050
50). Glasgow trains (☎ 0345 484 950) pass
through northern Argyll en route to Oban.

The joy of the region is the Caledonian
MacBrayne ferry service (CalMac; ☎ 0870
565 0000, W www.calmac.co.uk) that plies
its trade on Argyll's waters and beyond.
There are few more wonderful ways of travelling than these ferries and, though they
can be devastatingly expensive (especially
if you're taking a car on board), you'll
never forget pulling into enchanting ports
such as Port Askaig (Islay), Scalasaig
(Colonsay) or Oban.

Southern Argyll & the Isle of Bute

Southern Argyll, just over an hour's drive from Glasgow, is one of the most touristy parts of the region. However, it's still possible to find tranquillity off the beaten track.

ISLE OF BUTE
☎ 01700 ● pop 7354

A short ferry ride from Colintraive on the Cowal peninsula is Bute, a top holiday destination for Glaswegians. Overrun with holiday-makers in summer – more than a million people visit each year, most on day-trips – it can be hard (though not impossible) to find sanctuary on this lush isle, just 15 miles long by 3 miles wide.

Rothesay

With lovely period mansions lining its wide cove, Rothesay, on Bute's east coast, must once have been an extremely pretty Victorian town. These days it has a slightly faded feel to it, though the jovial seaside ambience lingers on.

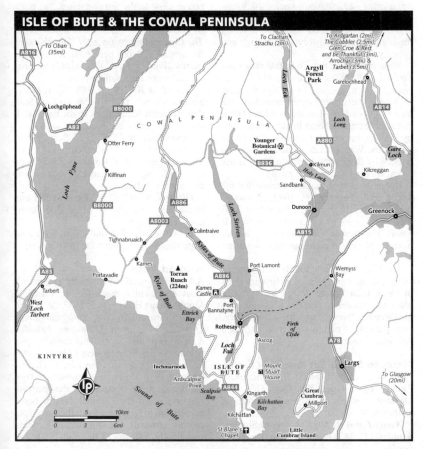

ISLE OF BUTE & THE COWAL PENINSULA

Information The friendly TIC (☎ 502151) on Victoria St, at the Isle of Bute Discovery Centre, has lists of accommodation options and makes bookings for a £2 fee. There's no youth hostel on the island, though there's an oversupply of cheap B&Bs so you should be able to get something decent for not much more than the cost a hostel.

In late July there's a popular folk festival (☎ 831614), and there's a jazz festival (☎ 502800) during the first weekend in May.

Things to See It's worth making a brief stop at **Bute Museum** *(☎ 505067, Stuart St; adult/child £1.20/70p; open 10.30am-4.30pm Mon-Sat & 2.30pm-4.30pm Sun Apr-Sept)*, which has a good collection covering the island's natural history, archaeology and geology.

More interesting though is **Rothesay Castle** *(☎ 502691, King St; adult/child £2/75p; closed Thur afternoon, Fri & Sun morning in winter, otherwise open standard HS hours)*. Owned by Historic Scotland (HS), this sizable ruin was built in the 12th century by Vikings, before falling into British hands during the Wars of Independence, and then retaken by Robert the Bruce in 1311. It has an exceptional water-filled moat.

Botanists should make a beeline for the **Ascog Hall Fernery** *(☎ 504555, Ascog; adult/child £2.50/free; open 10am-5pm Wed-Sun mid-Apr–mid-Oct)*, south towards Mt Stuart. This sunken Victorian fernery has all manner of sub-tropical species blooming away inside.

The Victorian **public toilets** on the promenade are the most palatial in Britain. Built in 1899, their ornate design incorporates glass-sided cisterns, ceramic tiles and marbled alcoves. 'Never,' says the tourist office, 'was the call of nature answered with such splendour.' Indeed.

Places to Stay & Eat *Roseland Caravan Park (☎ 504529, Canada Hill, Rothesay)* Pitches £6-8. Open Mar-Oct. This is a pleasant, well-equipped site just north of Rothesay.

Ascog Farm (☎ 503372, Ascog) Singles/doubles £17/34. On the southern edge of town, towards Mt Stuart, 250-year-old Ascog Farm's simple rooms are great value.

There's a huge selection of B&Bs on the Rothesay waterfront, and though many look less than charming, there are several gems among the dross.

Ardyne Hotel (☎ 502052, 38 Mt Stuart Rd) Singles/doubles £30/55. A comfortable hotel on the waterfront, Ardyne has spectacular views, nifty rooms and an extended Scottish menu (three-course dinner £16.50, or £14.50 for residents).

Cannon House (☎ 502819, Battery Place) Singles/doubles £32/60. This Georgian townhouse, close to the ferry terminal, has plush rooms and friendly owners. It's surrounded by cheaper guesthouses, the best of which is *The Commodore (☎/fax 502178)* with rooms for around £20 per person. If it's full, the nearby *Bayview Hotel (☎ 505411)* also has decent rooms for a similar price.

The Black Bull (☎ 502366, Albert Place) Snacks & meals £1.50-11.50, no food Sunday. Rothesay locals flock to the Black Bull for its top-quality bar food.

Kettledrum (☎ 505324, 32 East Princes St) Mains £4.75-7.75. Kettledrum is by far the least repellent of Rothesay's moribund cafes, offering cheaper snacks such as soup and a roll (£1.25).

Oliver's (☎ 503241, 22 Victoria St) Pasta mains £6. This cheery place does tasty, good-value meals.

If you're after fish and chips, *West End Cafe (Gallowgate)* does the town's best.

Around Bute

A few miles south of Rothesay is Britain's most spectacular mock-Gothic mansion, **Mount Stuart House** *(☎ 503877, Mt Stuart, ⓦ www.mountstuart.com; adult/child/family £6.50/2.50/15; open 11am-5pm Fri-Mon & Wed May–mid-Sept)*. This amazing pile belongs to the 7th marquess of Bute, and is reason enough to visit the island. The extraordinary building was constructed by the decadent 3rd marquess in the late 19th century, when the original family home burned down; left to rot from the early 20th century onwards, the dilapidated building was finally restored in the mid-1980s and thrown open to the public in the mid-1990s. It has a magnificent marble interior, a chapel and a distinctly unusual horoscope room.

It's worth spending an entire day here, not only for the house, but also for exploring the 300 acres of glorious **landscaped gardens**, from where there are vistas over the Firth of Clyde.

On the southern peninsula you'll find the impressive 12th-century ruins of **St Blane's Chapel**, with a 10th-century tombstone in the graveyard.

Kilchattan Bay, a splendid bay 2 miles south of Mt Stuart, has golden sands and is ideal for a stroll. From here there's a marked 5-mile round-circuit walk down to the isle's southern tip and then back via St Blane's.

On the west coast, there's a fine beach at **Scalpsie Bay**, or you can spot seals at nearby **Ardscalpsie Point**.

Places to Stay & Eat If you want to stay in Mt Stuart then pretty *New Farm (☎ 831646)* is a homely option, with rooms for around £25 per person.

St Blane's Hotel (☎/fax 831224, Kilchattan Bay) B&B £23-28.50 per person. This popular place to stay and eat (meals £2.95 to £5.50) is in an unusual building with a pleasant shorefront location at Kilchattan Bay.

Getting There & Around

Frequent CalMac ferries ply the waters between Wemyss Bay and Rothesay (passenger/car £3.25/13.15, 35 minutes). Another ferry crosses the short stretch of water between Rhubodach in the north of the island and Colintraive (passenger/car £1/6.60, five minutes).

The Stagecoach Western service around Bute is reliable, though limited on Sunday. Buses link with ferries at Rothesay and run roughly hourly (except Tuesday and Thursday) to Mount Stuart House (£2.50 return).

Cycling on Bute is a joy – the roads are well surfaced and fairly quiet. Bike rental is available from the Mountain Bike Centre (☎ 503554) at 22 East Prince St, Rothesay, for £6/10 per half-/full day (a £10 deposit is required).

COWAL PENINSULA

Surrounded by Loch Fyne and Loch Long, the Cowal peninsula reaches southwards into the Firth of Clyde, and has an extensive network of forests, and mountains reaching almost 800m high.

It can get busy, but the braying masses usually head for Dunoon, leaving places of great natural beauty, such as Argyll Forest Park, to more inquisitive types.

Argyll Forest Park

Stretching from Loch Lomond's western shores down to Holy Loch near Dunoon, the Argyll Forest Park is huge and provides the best scenery on the Cowal peninsula, including the rugged **Arrochar Alps**, the highest of which is Ben Arthur (also known as The Cobbler) at 870m. More approachable for the novice walker are the smaller mountains south of Glen Croe between Loch Goil and Loch Long. Though known as **Argyll's Bowling Green**, it's not very flat – it's merely a corruption of the Gaelic *baile na greine*, which translates as 'sunny hamlet'.

Ardgartan's **Argyll Forest Visitor Centre** *(☎ 01369-840666)* opens 10am to 5pm daily April to September. It can give advice on walking and cycling in the area and help with accommodation.

Arrochar

☎ 01301 ● pop 635

Arrochar, across the isthmus and the place those poor Vikings began their long haul, is the gateway to Cowal; it's an unexciting village, but has a great setting with Loch Long stretching out before it, and **The Cobbler** and other sharp peaks towering overhead.

The **Arrochar Caves** are a mile north of Succoth. Follow the track past the houses and into the forest. Bear left on a rough path and head uphill to the caves; take a torch, but don't venture too far in or you might not get back out again.

Arrochar has several hotels and shops, plus a bank and post office.

Places to Stay & Eat *Ardgartan Camping (☎ 702293)* Pitches £3-4. Open late Mar–mid-Oct. Ardgartan's well-maintained

Forest Enterprise camp site is just past Arrochar.

Loch Long Youth Hostel (☎ 702362) B&B £12.25. Closed Dec. This SYHA hostel occupies a top position on the loch.

The Village Inn (☎ 702279) Rooms around £25. The Village Inn's small but well-loved rooms are decked out handsomely, and there's a fantastic bar downstairs.

Lochside Guest House (☎ 702467, e lochsidegh@aol.com, Main St) B&B £18 per person. For spectacular views of The Cobbler, and sumptuous evening meals catering to vegetarians (£10), try Lochside.

The *Pit Stop Diner* has fish and chips (£3.20) and cheap burgers (from £1.80), while the *Arrochar Hotel (☎ 702484)* does bar meals for £4 to £5.95.

Getting There & Around Scottish Citylink (☎ 0870 550 5050) buses from Glasgow call at Arrochar and Ardgartan three times daily (£5.30, 1¼ hours); they continue to Inveraray and Campbeltown. ScotRail (☎ 0845 748 4950) runs two to five trains daily from Glasgow to Arrochar & Tarbet station (£7.30, 1¼ hours), and on to Oban and Fort William.

Hire bikes from South Peak (☎ 702288), in Glen Croe, for £8/11.50 per half-/full day.

Ardgartan to Dunoon

From Ardgartan, the A83 climbs until it reaches the top of Glen Croe, where there's a pretty and logically named stretch of flat land called **Rest & Be Thankful**. From here the photo opportunities are innumerable, as the madly snapping hordes in summer will attest. The road up this hill was built in 1774 as a military route, and in the early days of motoring became famous as *the* place in Scotland to test out your smart new horseless carriage.

On the other side of the pass, the A83 continues to **Cairndow** where you'll find the lovely *Stagecoach Inn (☎ 01499-600286)*, which has a wonderful beer garden and does B&B for £25 per person. Farther on you'll find Clachan or you can go left to Dunoon; the A813 takes you through the wildly named (and none too

wild) Clachan Strachu, after which you'll reach the picturesque and extremely narrow Loch Eck.

From here it's just a short drive to Benmore's finely named **Younger Botanical Gardens** *(☎ 01369-706261; adult/child £3.50/1.50; open 9.30am-6pm Mar-Oct)*. These charming woodlands are the sister garden of Edinburgh's Royal Botanic Gardens, and given over to the cultivation of over 250 species of rhododendrons. Waymarked walks lead to a central area where you'll find a huge display of Himalayan and other Asian plants.

Dunoon
☎ 01369 ● pop 11,320

Once a favourite holiday destination for all of southern Scotland, Dunoon is a relatively deserted place these days; the US navy's nuclear submarine base on nearby Holy Loch closed in 1992, leaving behind endemic high unemployment.

However, Dunoon is still by far Cowal's largest town and, while there's not much to see, it's a practical little place. There are banks with ATMs on Argyll St, which runs parallel with the shore, and a large Safeway supermarket on John St, just off Argyll St. The TIC (☎ 703785), 7 Alexandra Parade, opens 10am to 5pm Monday to Saturday year-round.

The only real sight in town is the **Castle House Museum** *(☎ 701422, Castle Hill; adult/child £2/free; open 10am-4pm Mon-Sat June-Oct)*, standing with the remains of Dunoon Castle on the lump of rock sitting atop the town. It tells the colourful story of this once glorious castle that changed hands regularly between battling English and Scottish forces in the 15th century.

Dunoon comes alive each August during the annual **Cowal Highland Gathering** *(☎ 703206, W www.cowalgathering.com)*, featuring over 150 pipe bands.

Places to Stay & Eat There are ample B&Bs and guesthouses to choose from, mostly along Argyll St.

Pitcairlie House (☎ 704122, Alexandra Parade) B&B £16-20. This cheap and cheery

B&B, 10 minutes' walk north of the CalMac ferry terminal, has clean, simple rooms, all with shared bathrooms.

The Enmore (☎ 702230, Marine Parade, W www.enmorehotel.com) Singles/doubles £35/69. If you're not in town to rough it, stay at the plush, vine-covered Enmore with its garden by the sea and great rooms (some with four-poster beds). They also do delectable but pricey evening meals (mains from £11).

Chatters (☎ 706402, 58 John St) Mains £5.75-14.50. Closed Sun. Chatters does fine seafood dishes from Loch Fyne and serves local beef to perfection. For cheaper nosh, try the *Argyll Hotel* (☎ 702059, Argyll St) opposite the pier; bar meals cost around £6.

There's a *fish and chip shop* (portions cost around £3.10) on Church St, plus a few cheap eateries and a *Safeway supermarket* on Argyll St.

Getting There & Around Dunoon is served by two frequent ferries from Gourock. The CalMac sailing is best if you want to arrive in the town centre.

Stagecoach Western (☎ 707701) runs several times a week to Rothesay and Tighnabruaich; three buses daily except Sunday run to Inverary. On Saturday, a postbus (☎ 01246-546329) goes to Colintraive and there's a once or twice daily service to Tighnabruaich (except Sunday).

Highland Stores (☎ 702007), 156 Argyll St, charges £13 per day for bike hire.

Tighnabruaich
☎ 01700 ● pop 196
Tighnabruaich sits at the end of the awe-inspiring drive along the A8003 and, with its access to superb sailing in the **Kyles of Bute** (the straight separating Bute from the Cowal peninsula), draws streams of visitors during summer.

It's a thriving town, with a bank (no ATM), two shops (the Spar has an ATM) and post office.

There's a **sailing school** (☎ 811396) for the ambitious, or alternatively you can catch one of several boat trips leaving from the pier in summer.

Places to Stay & Eat You'll find no better B&B in Tighnabruaich than the comfortable *Ferguslie* (☎ 811414) on the seafront. Singles/doubles cost £18/34 and it opens April to September.

Royal Hotel (☎ 811239, e info@royal hotel.org.uk) B&B £40 per person. The plush rooms at this three-level seafront hotel have wonderful views and the downstairs bar does great seafood and game dishes. Brasserie meals cost between £5.45 and £20.95, and a three-course set dinner costs £26.95.

Burnside Cafe (☎ 811739) Mains from £5.50. For basic fare try the Burnside, which does good sandwiches and pasta.

Getting There & Away Stagecoach Western (☎ 502076) runs several times a week from Tighnabruaich and Kames to Rothesay, with connections at Auchenbreck for Dunoon. There's also a postbus (☎ 01246-546329) to Dunoon Monday to Saturday.

Kames
A few miles from Tighnabruaich is Kames, a cheaper but nonetheless bonny destination where you'll find the sprawling *Kames Hotel* (☎ 01700-811489), which does B&B from £20 and great bar meals from £5. It also has great views over the Kyles of Bute.

Colintraive
On the opposite side of Loch Riddon is tiny Colintraive – meaning 'Strait of Swimming' – where you'll find the slip, for ferries to Bute, and the charming family-run *Colintraive Hotel* (☎ 01700-841207), which has tidy rooms for around £35 per person and top nosh.

Cowal's West Coast
If the crowds around the Kyles get too heavy, retreat round to the peninsula's deserted west coast. At Kilfinan you'll see little else but the *Kilfinan Hotel* (☎ 0170-82120), a luxurious place overlooking Loch Fyne, with swish rooms from £40 per person and an award-winning seafood restaurant. It's closed in February.

A few miles farther north on the B8000 is **Otter Ferry**, once linked to Lochgilphead via a ferry. 'Otter' comes from the Gaelic for gravel, *an oitir* – there's a gravel bank jutting out into Loch Fyne. Overlooking it is the wonderful *Oystercatcher (☎ 01700-821229)*, an oyster bar and pub you'd be crazy not to stop at, especially if the sun is shining.

KINTYRE PENINSULA

At 40 miles long and just 8 miles wide, the Kintyre peninsula is almost an island; only a narrow isthmus connects it to the wooded hills of Knapdale at Tarbert. In 1098, so the story goes, Viking Magnus Barefoot of Norway emphasised this point: having signed a treaty with the Scottish king Malcolm Canmore granting Magnus rule of any land he was able to circumnavigate, he had his men drag their longship across the isthmus (as King Haakon's forces also did centuries later) to validate his claim on Kintyre.

Put on the map by Paul McCartney's schmaltzy folk tune 'Mull of Kintyre', this lonely peninsula has long deserved a better tribute to its beauty. Virtually deserted after a nasty potato famine in the 17th century decimated the local population, the region has since made a slow recovery, but remains one of the least populous parts of Scotland.

Kintyre's gentle east coast is as isolated as it is alluring. The agonisingly slow single-track B842 traverses the coastline from Campbeltown to Claonaig before turning into the B8001 to Skipness. In contrast, the weather-battered west coast sees constant Atlantic waves smashing into its shores, making for some desolate scenery. Nonetheless, you'll find it a place of lonesome beauty.

Tarbert
☎ 01880 ● pop 1500

Tarbert, the gateway to Kintyre, is an attractive fishing village sitting in a sheltered harbour at the end of East Loch Tarbert. A substantial herring port in the 19th century, the fishing industry here has been in decline for decades.

Tarbert's TIC (☎ 820429) on Harbour St opens May to October. There's a *Co-op supermarket* and two banks near the head of the harbour.

Things to See & Do The **An Tairbeart Arts Centre** *(☎ 821116, Campbeltown Rd; admission free; open 10am-5pm daily)* is at the southern edge of the village and has galleries of crafts and contemporary arts, as well as displays about local natural history and the environment. On the centre's mile-long woodland trail, you may see various wild birds, including peregrine falcons, hen harriers and owls.

The crumbling, ivy-covered ruins of **Tarbert Castle** *(admission free; open year-round)* built by Robert the Bruce in the 1300s, overlook the harbour – there's a sign-posted footpath beside the Ann R Thomas Gallery on Harbour St. At the rear of the castle are several marked **walking trails** winding up into the hills above town, where there are dramatic views across Loch Fyne.

There's a 9-mile marked **forest walk** through the remote hills from Tarbert to Skipness (four to five hours); pick up a free map from the TIC.

Special Events Tarbert is a lively place, and never more so than during the annual **Scottish Series Yacht Race**, Tarbert's main drawcard and Britain's second-largest yacht race. It docks here over five days around the last weekend in May, during which the harbour is crammed with hundreds of yachts.

The **Tarbert Seafood Festival** is held during the first weekend in July, and the **Tarbert Music Festival** *(☎ 820343)* over the third weekend in September.

Places to Stay & Eat There are plenty of B&Bs and hotels, but book ahead when the Scottish Series is on.

West Loch Tarbert Holiday Park (☎ 820873, Escart Bay) Pitches £5-7.50. Open Apr-Oct. This elevated site overlooking West Loch Tarbert is 2 miles southwest of Tarbert on the road to Campbeltown.

Mrs Marshall (☎ 820413, Pier Rd) B&B £20 per person. For simple B&B, Mrs Marshall's is a good, no-nonsense place with harbour views.

West Loch Hotel (☎ 820283, on the A83 overlooking West Loch Tarbert) Singles/doubles £33/56. In an 18th-century coaching inn, this cosy place has open fires, well-kept rooms and stunning views over the loch.

Columba Hotel *(☎/fax 820808, East Pier Rd)* B&B from £36 per person. The peaceful, Victorian-era Columba is 10 minutes' walk from the village centre along the southern side of the harbour. Rooms are lovingly cared for, and there's a gym and sauna downstairs. The restaurant serves top Scottish cuisine; three-course dinners cost £20.50, and bar meals cost between £5.25 and £8.50.

Stonefield Castle *(☎ 820836)* Dinner & B&B £66 per person. If you're out to spoil yourself, this is the place for you: a Victorian mansion set in 60 acres of outstanding woodland overlooking Loch Fyne, on the A83 about 2 miles north of Tarbert. Rooms are luxurious, as is the food, made with local seafood and produce.

The Anchorage *(☎ 820881, Harbour St)* Mains £11.95-15.95. Open for dinner daily, closed Sun & Mon Nov-Mar. It isn't cheap but the tiny Anchorage does mouthwatering local seafood, game and meat dishes with a Mediterranean flavour. It gets busy so book ahead.

Victoria Hotel *(☎ 820236, Barmore Rd)* Meals served noon-2pm & 6pm-9.30pm. The bright yellow Vic, overlooking the head of the harbour, is a lively pub that's popular with yachties. It has excellent bar meals but less than excellent accommodation; B&B costs £29 per person.

Cá Dora Cafe on Harbour St serves inexpensive grub and good ice cream. The *An Tairbeart Arts Centre* also has a cafe, serving vegetarian and vegan meals and snacks.

Getting There & Away Tarbert is served by the four daily Citylink buses linking Campbeltown with Glasgow and Oban.

CalMac runs a small car ferry from Tarbert to Portavadie on the Cowal peninsula (passenger/car/bicycle £2.70/12.65/1, 20 minutes, hourly); it runs daily from Easter to September.

Ferries for Islay, Colonsay and Oban leave from the Kennacraig ferry terminal on West Loch Tarbert, 5 miles south of Tarbert.

Skipness
☎ 01880 ● pop 100

The main draws of tiny Skipness are its stunning views across to Arran, and the Skipness Seafood Cabin. You'll also find a post office and general store.

The 13th-century **Skipness Castle** *(admission free; open year-round)* and 16th-century towerhouse, with their magnificent vistas over Skipness Bay, are in excellent condition and far more impressive than Robert the Bruce's Tarbert castle.

Less than 300m from the castle is **St Brendan's Chapel**, with some remarkable tombstones in one of Scotland's most charming graveyards. Among the 200-odd graves and the crumbling chapel, are three protected graves with intriguing iconography carved into them.

Places to Stay & Eat *Skipness Estate (☎ 760207)* Doubles £120. For a romantic break try this pad with affable owners. It's part of the Wolsey Lodge group (**W** www.wolsey-lodges.co.uk) so you'll need to book in advance. The price includes B&B and dinner with wine.

Skipness Seafood Cabin *(☎ 760207)* Mains £3-7.95. Open 11am-6pm daily late May-Sept. Sit and sup on oysters, mussels and other seafoods while wallowing in the remarkable views over Kilbrannan Sound and Skipness Castle. The cabin is attached to Skipness Estate.

Getting There & Away Henderson Hiring *(☎ 820220)* runs three buses daily between Tarbert and Skipness (35 minutes).

At Claonaig, 2 miles west of Skipness, there's a daily car ferry to Lochranza on the Isle of Arran (passenger/car/bicycle £4/18.05/1, 30 minutes, seven to nine daily).

Carradale
☎ 01583 ● pop 200

The village of Carradale, with its gorgeous harbour, is the east coast's 'major' town. It has a general store and post office, as well as the interesting **Network Carradale Heritage Centre** *(☎ 01586-431296; admission free; open 10am-5pm Mon-Sat & 1pm-4pm*

Sun July-Aug, 10am-5pm Tues-Sat & 1pm-4pm Sun Apr-June & Sept-Oct), which traces the history of herring fishing in the area, as well as farming and forestry.

There are several interesting ruins in the area including a **vitrified fort** on the eastern point of Carradale Bay dating back more than 2000 years to the Iron Age. There are also some good marked **walks** off the B842. The best is 3 miles' long and begins in the Port Na Storm car park on the B879, just before town, and climbs to the summit of **Cnoc-nan Gabhor** with its amazing views across Kilbrannan Sound and down Kintyre.

Places to Stay *Carradale Bay Caravan Park (☎ 431665)* Pitches £10. Open Easter-early Oct. This caravan park is well located on Carradale Bay's broad, sandy beach.

Carradale Hotel (☎/fax 431223) Singles £25-40, doubles £50-70. The comfortable Carradale Hotel offers fine cooking, a golf course, sauna and beautiful views over to Arran. There's also a great bar.

Mains Farm (☎ 431216) B&B £17 per person. Try this pad for Carradale's no-frills option.

Saddell Abbey

Five miles south of Carradale is Saddell Abbey, founded by Somerled, lord of the Isles, in 1160. Little but the skeleton of the castle remains, though the graveyard is worth wandering through.

Tayinloan

Tidy Tayinloan, near the Gigha ferry pier, has a decent hotel and pub, a general store and not much more.

If you feel like staying here rather than on Gigha, the *Tayinloan Inn (☎ 01583-441233)* has great food and decent rooms for around £25 per person.

Isle of Gigha

☎ 01583 ● pop 120

'God's Island' goes the Norse translation of 'Gigha' (pronounced **gee**-a, with a hard 'g'), and it isn't hard to see why if you spend time walking its glorious white sandy beaches. Protected from harsh winds by Islay and kept warm by the Gulf Stream flowing round it, Gigha is decidedly warmer than the rest of Kintyre.

Sold countless times over the centuries, since being given away by King David II in 1344, the low-lying island (only 6 miles by 1 mile) was most recently put on the market in mid-2001 for £3.85m and was purchased by a community cooperative of islanders, backed by the Scottish Executive and National Lottery.

Besides making the newspapers whenever it's up for auction, Gigha is also famous for its subtropical **Achamore Gardens** *(☎ 505254, Achamore House; admission by donation; open 9am-dusk daily)*. The gardens were built by Lord Horlicks (of sleepy-drinks infamy) in the 1950s. Achamore House is 10 minutes' walk south of the ferry.

Gigha cheese is sold in many parts of Argyll and is recommended, though not cheap.

Camping isn't allowed anywhere on the island, and there's no hostel.

The McSporran family run the general store, the post office and *Post Office House (☎ 505251)*, at the top of the hill above the ferry slip, which has B&B for £20 per person. Self-catering cottages are also available – go to the Web site at ⓦ www.isle-of-gigha.co.uk for details.

Gigha Hotel (☎ 505254, ⓔ hotel@isle-of-gigha.co.uk) 4-course dinner £25. Gigha's only hotel, 100m south of the post office, has a good restaurant and lively bar. If you want to stay, singles/doubles cost £51/90.

CalMac runs a daily ferry from Tayinloan (passenger/car/bicycle £4.75/17.90/2, 20 minutes, hourly, six on Sunday) and you must buy a return ticket.

There are island walks, a nine-hole golf course and, best of all, cycling. Rent **bikes** from the post office or Gigha Hotel (£5/10 for a half-/full day).

Glenbarr Abbey

Six miles south of Tayinloan is **Glenbarr Abbey** *(☎ 01583-421247; adult/child £2.50/2; open 10am-5.30pm Wed-Mon Easter-Oct)*. A tour of this 18th-century house can be intriguingly depressing, with the laird himself taking you on an entertaining tour of the Macalister clan's slowly dimming glory. You'll have ample chance to wonder at his mind-numbingly large collection of thimbles, china and clothes, and even a pair of gloves (allegedly) worn by Mary Queen of Scots. There's a good *tearoom* attached, selling all manner of tourist paraphernalia and Macalister propaganda (along with tea).

Between Glenbarr and Campbeltown are some glorious **sandy beaches** which, if the weather decides to go crazy and get warm on you, are even possible to swim at, as the surf vans parked along the A83 will attest.

Campbeltown
☎ 01586 ● pop 6000

With its grim, grey and dishevelled houses, Campbeltown seems like a mining town plucked from the coalfields of central Scotland and dumped incongruously in the wilds of Argyll.

Once a thriving fishing port and whisky-making centre, industrial decline and the closure of the former air-force base at Machrihanish saw the town slip into decline; it's now a low-key holiday resort that feels a very long way from, well, anywhere.

The TIC (☎ 552056), open year-round, is beside the harbour, and there are plenty of shops and banks in the nearby town centre.

Things to See At production's peak in the late 19th century, over two million gallons of whisky were shipped out of Campbeltown each year from the area's 32 distilleries. Most closed down in the 1920s, and today only the **Springbank Distillery** (☎ 552085; tours by appointment) survives. Its main claim to fame is that it's the only Scottish distillery that still distils, matures and bottles all its whisky on the one site.

Many aspects of local life are covered in-depth at the **Campbeltown Heritage Centre** (☎ 551068, Big Kiln; adult/child £2/1.25; open 11am-5pm Mon-Sat & 2pm-5pm Sun Apr-Oct). The **Campbeltown Museum** (☎ 552367, Hall St; admission free; open 10am-1pm & 2pm-5pm Tues & Thur-Sat, 5.30pm-7.30pm Wed) has displays on geology, culture and archaeology, though the building itself is the most interesing bit.

The Art Deco **Wee Picture House** (☎ 553657, 26 Hall St), opened in 1913, is Scotland's oldest purpose-built cinema; new-release movies are shown nightly, except Friday which is, of course, bingo night.

One of the most unusual sights in Argyll is an eerie **cave painting** of the Crucifixion by local artist Archibald MacKinnon, painted in 1887. The cave is on the southern side of the island of Davaar, at the mouth of Campbeltown Loch, 2 miles east of town. You can walk to the island at low water across a shingle bar called **The Dhorlinn** (allow at least 1½ hours for the return trip); make sure you're not caught by rising waters (check tide times with the TIC).

The **Mull of Kintyre Music Festival** (☎ 551053, W www.mokmf.com), held over three days in late August, is a popular event featuring traditional Scottish and Irish music; pub gigs are free.

Places to Stay & Eat There are plenty of B&Bs in town, including the quiet and friendly *Eagle Lodge* (☎ 551359, 56 High St), which charges £15 per person for its simple rooms.

Ardshiel Hotel (☎ 552133, fax 551422, Kilkerran Rd) Singles £30-40, doubles £60-70. The family-run Ardshiel, near the ferry terminal, has comfortable rooms and a great garden restaurant. Mains cost from £5.25.

For bar meals you can't beat the *White Hart Hotel* (☎ 552440, Main St), while the *Dhorlinn Cafe (Longrow)* does good fish and chips.

Getting There & Away British Airways (BA) flies twice every weekday from Glasgow to Machrihanish airport, 4 miles west of Campbeltown (£76, 40 minutes).

Scottish Citylink runs three buses daily (two on Sunday) from Campbeltown to Glasgow (£11.80, 4½ hours) via Tayinloan, Kennacraig, Tarbert, Lochgilphead (£5.70, 1¾ hours) and Inveraray (£7.60, 2½ hours).

In early 2002 it was unclear whether the ferry from Campbeltown to Ballycastle in Northern Ireland would run; go to the Web site at W www.campbeltownferry.com to find out if the service will resume.

Machrihanish

Six miles west of Campbeltown on the B843, Machrihanish is home to some unspoiled beaches and an excellent 18-hole golf course with, according to Jack Nicklaus, 'the world's greatest opening hole'.

There's a *camp site* (☎ 01586-810366) nearby at East Trodigal with sites for £5 from March to September, or the cheap and cheery *Kilgour House* (☎ 01586-810233) in town has quaint rooms for £20 per person.

Mull of Kintyre & Southend

Follow the narrow, winding B842 for 18 miles and you'll reach the very Mull of Kintyre eulogised by Paul McCartney, who still owns a farmhouse in the area.

There isn't a lot to be seen in this storm-wracked, desolate place, though on a clear day you can see easily over to Ireland, just 12 miles away. If you're in need of exercise, the walk from the **lighthouse** (built by Robert Louis Stevenson's grandfather, and the closest spot in Scotland to Ireland), at the Mull's tip, to Machrihanish a good 10 miles away is highly recommended. The drive from Southend to the lighthouse can be torturously slow.

There isn't really anywhere worth staying in bleak Southend, and it doesn't have much to offer except the remains of **Dunaverty Castle**. Here, in 1648, over 300 Royalists who had surrendered were slaughtered by the earl of Argyll's crazed Covenanters.

Half a mile west of Southend is **High Keil**, where St Columba is said to have first set foot on Scotland. Nearby are a pair of **footprints** carved into the rock that zealots say are the saint's.

Isle of Arran

☎ 01770 • pop 4500

'Scotland in miniature' is the catch-cry that tourist-office brochures ram down your throat, and the annoying part is that it's so true: alluring Arran really *is* Scotland's very own Mini-Me.

Arran (Gaelic for 'Peaked Island') is divided down its centre by a faultline that sees steep mountains and long deep glens in the island's north reminiscent of the Highlands, and lush, rolling moorland and scattered farms in the south similar to southern Scotland. It even has a long, straight valley dividing north from south, a minor version of the mainland's Great Glen.

Scotland's most southerly island, Arran is easily accessible from Glasgow and Ayrshire, just one hour's ferry ride from Ardrossan. And though extremely popular, the 20-mile-long island seems big enough to absorb all-comers: the bucket-and-spade brigade fills the southern resorts, cyclists take to the island's circular road, and hikers are irresistibly drawn to its rugged mountains, including Goatfell.

Arran's other drawcards are golf – the tiny isle has a ridiculously disproportionate seven golf courses – and geology, drawing secondary-school and university field trips from all over Britain to study the island's unique rock formations.

ISLE OF ARRAN

ORIENTATION & INFORMATION

The ferry from Ardrossan docks at Brodick, the island's main town. To the south, Lamlash is the capital and, like nearby Whiting Bay, a popular seaside resort. From the village of Lochranza in the north there's a ferry link to Claonaig on the Kintyre peninsula.

Near Brodick pier, the helpful TIC (☎ 302140) opens 9am to 7.30pm (10am to 5pm Sunday) daily June to September, and 9am to 5pm Monday to Saturday the rest of the year. Tourist information is also available on the ferry from Ardrossan at peak times. There's a laundry by the Collins Good Food Shop (next to the River Cloy). The hospital (☎ 600777) is in Lamlash.

The Pier Tearoom (☎ 830217), Lochranza, offers Internet access. For online information about Arran, go to the Web site at W www.ayrshire-arran.com or W www.arrantourism.com.

The week-long **Arran Folk Festival** (☎ 302623, W www.arranfolkfestival.org) takes place in early June. There are also local village festivals from June to September.

As for cheese, Torrylinn Creamery just east of Lagg in the south is renowned for its Arran Dunlop Cheddar, which you can buy all over the island.

BRODICK

Most visitors' first sight of Arran is of the slightly dreary town of Brodick. Its population of 1000 is stretched along grand Brodick Bay. The town, by far the island's most bustling, has several hotels and B&Bs, gift shops, a Co-op supermarket and two banks with the island's only ATMs.

Brodick Castle and Gardens (☎ 302202; castle & park adult/child £6/4.50, gardens only £2.50/1.70; castle open 11am-4.30pm daily Apr-Oct, park open 9.30am-sunset year-round), 2½ miles north of Brodick, is one of Arran's must-sees. Parts of this ancient seat of the dukes of Hamilton, now in the hands of the National Trust for Scotland (NTS), date from the late 13th century. It's an interesting stately home, with a more lived-in feel than some NTS properties, and has a notable restaurant with home-cooked meals for under £7. The Victorian kitchen and scullery, with its weird and wonderful copper pots and peculiar kitchen devices, is compelling. The grounds, now a country park with various trails among the rhododendrons, are even better and have an attractive walled garden dating from 1710.

Take the main road 1½ miles north to the small **Arran Heritage Museum** (☎ 302636; adult/child £2.25/1; open 10.30am-4.30pm daily Apr-Oct). This is no blockbuster exhibition but there's still some worthwhile entertainment to be had in its late-19th-century-style furnished cottage, old 'smiddy's' (blacksmith's) workshop, and local archaeology and geology exhibits.

Stagecoach Western (☎ 302000; half-/full-day tours adult £7.50/5, child £5/3) runs full-day tours from late May to September, departing Brodick pier at 11am daily. Half-day tours run in July and early August, departing Brodick pier at 1.45pm weekdays.

Around Brodick

As you go around Brodick Bay, look out for **seals**, often seen on the rocks around Merkland Point. Two types live in these waters, the Atlantic grey and the common seal. They're easy to tell apart: the common seal has a dog-like face, the Atlantic grey seal has a Roman nose.

The coastal road continues to the pretty village of **Corrie**, where there's a shop and hotel. One of the tracks up Goatfell starts here. *Corrie Village Shop* (☎ 810209) sells wonderful Marvin Elliot sculptures.

After **Sannox**, with its sandy beach and great mountain views, the road cuts inland.

Places to Stay

Camping wild (i.e, in the wilderness, not in the camping-it-up sense) isn't allowed anywhere on Arran without the landowner's permission, but there are several camp sites (open April to October). Midges can be a major pain.

Glen Rosa Farm (☎ 302380) £2.50 per person. Open Apr-Oct. Glen Rosa Farm, 2 miles from Brodick heading inland on the B880 (the String Road), doesn't have showers but it's still a smashing setting.

Glenfloral *(☎/fax 302707, Shore Rd)* B&B £17 per person with shared bathroom. Vegetarians are also catered for in this pleasant seafront guesthouse with views across to Brodick Castle.

Tigh-na-Mara *(☎ 302538, fax 302546, The Seafront)* B&B £18-23.50 per person. Only two of the nine rooms are en suite but there are great views.

Belvedere *(☎ 302397, fax 302088, Alma Rd)* Dinner & B&B £20-25 per person. All of the rooms at the cheerful Belvedere are en suite, and at £22 including a four-course dinner (with wine), it's a bargain.

Glen Cloy Farm Guesthouse *(☎ 302351, Glen Cloy Rd)* B&B £22 per person. Close to Brodick Castle, this charming old stone farmhouse has lovely rooms, a roaring fire in its cosy drawing room and wonderful owners. Breakfast is excellent.

Kilmichael Country House Hotel *(☎ 302219, fax 302068, Glen Cloy)* Singles £75, doubles £120-150. The island's best hotel is also its oldest building, with a glass window dating from 1650. It's a tastefully decorated hideaway, a mile outside Brodick, with eight rooms and a fine restaurant (four-course dinner £29.50).

Corrie Hotel *(☎ 810273, Corrie)* Singles/doubles £21/42, en-suite rooms £26/52. The charming folk at this hotel and bar have simple, good-value rooms. The lively bar does great meals for around £6, and their beer garden is open in July and August.

Blackrock Guest House *(☎ 810282, Corrie)* B&B £18-25 per person. This white-washed seafront guesthouse, half a mile north of the Corrie Hotel, has spotless rooms (most are en suite), all with views to Bute.

Pirate's Cove *(☎ 302438, Corrie Shore)* B&B £18-20 per person. Friendly Pirate's Cove, a mile before Corrie coming from Brodick, has two fetching rooms, both overlooking the garden and sea. They also do traditional Scottish meals from £7.50.

Places to Eat

Arran has wonderful fresh seafood and a surprising array of healthy eating options.

Stalkers Eating House *(☎ 302579, Main St)* Mains around £6. In Brodick, try this place on the waterfront. It does good-value meals, including steak pie (£6.15) and jacket potatoes (from £1.65), and there are nifty puddings such as treacle sponge.

Brodick Bar *(☎ 302169, Alma Rd)* Mains £6-8. By the post office, the affable folk here do great meals. Soup and a roll costs £2.25.

Creelers Seafood Restaurant *(☎ 302810, Duchess Court)* Mains £7-16. Open Tues-Sun. This award-winning restaurant is 1½ miles north of Brodick, by the Arran Heritage Museum. There's an imaginative menu, outside seating and a shop selling seafood and smoked foods.

Stock up on local cheeses from the shop opposite, or have a snack in the pleasant ***Home Farm Kitchen*** *(☎ 302731, Duchess Court)*, with home-baked fare and baked potatoes from £2.95 including salad.

For scrumptious pizza (£2) and takeaway fish and chips (£3.50), try the ***Ferry Fry*** *(The Pier)* by the TIC.

Stock up on supplies at the ***Co-op supermarket*** on Shore Rd in Brodick.

LOCHRANZA

This picturesque village on a small bay at the north of the island was once a bustling herring fishing port. These days it's far more tranquil, and definitely one of Arran's highlights.

On a promontory on the bay stand the ruins of 13th-century **Lochranza Castle** *(admission free)*, said to be the inspiration for the castle in *The Black Island*, Hergé's Tintin adventure. Sadly for historians and travel writers, no known battles raged around the castle; it was used mostly as a hunting lodge for much of its early life. From April to September, the key to the castle is available from Lochranza Stores.

Distilling whisky is not new to Arran. Centuries ago, Irish monks brought whisky to Kintyre and Arran. It appears to be making a comeback, because in Lochranza is Scotland's newest distillery, **Isle of Arran Distillers** *(☎ 830264; tours adult/child £3.50/free; open 10am-4.30pm daily)*. It began distilling its single-malt in 1995. There's an excellent ***restaurant*** and ***cafe***, open 10am to 5pm daily except Monday;

the restaurant has sumptuous meat and seafood mains for £12 to £17. There's also a posh store selling interesting publications and positively *flogging* whisky shot glasses.

Lochranza also has a yearly boat race, fiddlers' rallies and other music events from June to August.

From late March to late October, there's a direct ferry link from Lochranza to Claonaig on the Kintyre peninsula.

Around Lochranza

Just outside Lochranza, on the left-hand side of the road, observant folk will notice an inscription 'A Sailor's Grave', the burial spot of a sailor who in 1854 died of the plague at sea; villagers refused to allow his body to be buried in the cemetery, so friends smuggled his body ashore and buried him here.

Two miles beyond Lochranza you'll find the small village of **Catacol**, notable for the neat row of whitewashed cottages known as the Twelve Apostles, built by the isle's duke of Hamilton to house people cleared from land set aside for sheep and deer.

The sunset from here is wonderful from April to August.

Places to Stay & Eat

Lochranza Golf (☎ 830273, e office@ lochgolf.demon.co.uk, Lochranza) Pitches from £6. This site is idyllically situated below the Cock of Arran and alongside Lochranza golf course.

Lochranza Youth Hostel (☎/fax 830631, Lochranza) Beds from £8.50/5. Open Mar-Oct. Certainly the best hostel on Arran, if not in the Highlands, the exceptionally helpful owners keep this SYHA hostel spotlessly clean. The building was once Arran's finest hotel, built by the duke of Hamilton.

Castlekirk (☎ 830202, Lochranza) B&B £19 per person. In a converted 19th-century church directly opposite the castle, Castlekirk has two comfortable rooms and an in-house art gallery.

Croftbank Cottage (☎ 830201, Lochranza) B&B £16-18 per person. Open Feb-Nov. Next to the post office, Croftbank is a wee B&B; its two rooms are basic but cosy enough.

Lochranza Hotel (☎/fax 830223, Lochranza) en-suite singles/doubles from £30/50. While the bar is the focus of the wonderful Lochranza Hotel – you'll meet all the affable locals here – it also has comfortable rooms, most with great views of the harbour. The beer garden out front is delightful if the sun's shining. Bar meals (£6 to £12) and three-course set menus (£15) are available, and its daily specials are a treat.

Apple Lodge (☎/fax 830229, Lochranza) Doubles £60-72. Tidy Apple Lodge, once the village manse, is Lochranza's top place to lay your weary bones. It has three luxurious double rooms and a well-manicured garden and does superb meals (three-course dinner £19).

Catacol Bay Hotel (☎ 830231, Catacol) Bar mains £5.50-8, all-you-can-eat buffet £7.50. One of Arran's highlights is the Sunday afternoon buffet here. At other times it serves wonderful food, and is Arran's top place to sink a pint or seven. It's 2 miles from Lochranza, on the waterfront, and has a great beer garden if it's sunny. In summer, there are ceilidhs (Tuesday) and live music (once a week). Not to be missed.

THE WEST COAST

On the western side of the island are the eerie **Machrie Moor Standing Stones**, nine upright sandstone slabs erected 6000 years ago, and the most impressive of the *six* stone circles on the island. To get to them, walk the 1½-mile track from the coastal road, starting from the HS sign just north of Machrie village.

Past these stones you'll come across the ruins of Moss Farm; nearby is **Fingal's Cauldron**, two circles of granite boulders where the giant Fingal allegedly tied up his dog while using the stones as a cooking stove. There's another group of circles at **Auchagallon**, surrounding a Bronze Age burial cairn.

The nearby *tearooms* attached to Mach rie Golf Club are good for snacks.

Blackwaterfoot is the west coast's largest village, and has a shop, post office and two hotels. From here you can walk, via Drumadoon Farm, to **King's Cave** – Arran is one of several islands in Argyll claiming this was *the* cave where Robert the Bruce watched a spider trying to spin its web (see the Facts about Scotland's Highlands & Islands chapter).

Places to Stay & Eat

Kinloch Hotel (☎ 860444, fax 860447, Blackwaterfoot) B&B £42-49 per person. With 44 bedrooms, this is Arran's biggest hotel. Architecturally it's disastrous but it does have great leisure facilities (handy on a wet day), including a swimming pool (£2.25 for non-residents), sauna, solarium, squash court and gym. Bar meals are available for £6 to £14.50; dinner costs £17.50.

Morvern House (☎ 860254, Blackwaterfoot) Singles/doubles from £17/34. This ex-bank manager's house looks like an ex-bank manager: slightly grim. But inside it's a treat, with clean, simple rooms and friendly owners. It's next to the post office.

SOUTHERN ARRAN

The landscape in the southern part of the island is much gentler, and is particularly lovely around **Lagg**. Walk from Lagg post office to **Torrylinn Cairn** (10 minutes each way), a chambered tomb over 4000 years old, where at least eight bodies were found. By the roadside at Kilmory, you can visit the **Torrylinn Creamery** *(☎ 870240; admission free; open 10am-4pm Sun-Fri)*. There are displays about cheese-making, and you can buy Arran Dunlop cheese.

By the roadside at East Bennan there's **Southbank Farm Park** *(☎ 820221; adult/child £2.50/2; open 10am-5pm Tues, Thur & Sun Easter-Sept)*, with various Scottish farmyard beasties to marvel at. **Kildonan** has pleasant sandy beaches, two hotels, a camp site and an ivy-clad ruined castle.

In popular but charmless **Whiting Bay**, you'll find small sandy beaches, an SYHA hostel, a village shop, post office and craft shops. There are lots of hotels and most serve meals. Check out the pubs for live music.

Places to Stay & Eat

Kildonan Hotel (☎ 820207, Kildonan) £4 per person, plus 50p per pitch. Down by the sea, the camping at Kildonan Hotel includes the use of facilities. Standard meals are also available for between £5 and £11 or, if you're feeling more Epicurean, get the lobster salad (£10.50), caught by the proprietor.

Kildonan Hotel Bunkhouse (☎ 820207, Kildonan) Dorm beds £8. This bunkhouse, right at the southern tip of Arran, now has a kitchen, but bring your own sleeping bag.

Whiting Bay Youth Hostel (☎/fax 700339, Shore Rd, Whiting Bay) Beds from £8.25/7. Open Apr-Oct. Located in a rather austere-looking building on the seafront, this SYHA hostel has excellent facilities.

Breadalbane Hotel (☎/fax 820284, Kildonan) B&B £20-27.50 per person. Flats £100-250 per week. The simple rooms in this friendly hotel all have great sea views. There are also holiday flats sleeping four to six; rates depend on the season, though outside high season they may let flats for less than a week. The hotel also does great home-made bar food at affordable prices (mains cost £4 to £10.95).

Lagg Inn (☎ 870255, fax 870250, Lagg) B&B £25-49 per person. Romantic Lagg Inn, in an 18th-century coach house, boasts a super location; some rooms are en suite and one has a four-poster bed. Food includes seafood, game and Arran lamb; main courses cost £6 to £11 and a two-/three-course dinner will set you back £16/19.

Swan's Guest House (☎ 700729, ⊜ row allanbb@aol.com, School Rd) Singles/doubles £23/40. This gorgeous B&B has a great garden with sea views, Internet access and an open fire in the residents' lounge.

Argentine House (☎ 700662, Shore Rd) B&B from £30 per person. Their flyer says 'Swiss owners – need we say more?', and they needn't. An immaculate, superbly hospitable place to stay, right on the waterfront.

Burlington Hotel (☎ 700255, fax 700232, Shore Rd) 2-/3-course dinners £15/18. This Edwardian pub has notable rooms (B&B singles/doubles £30/55; room only £20/40) but more important is the mouthwatering organic food in its fine restaurant.

Glenisle Hotel (☎ 600559, Shore Rd, Lamlash) Lunch mains £5.25-6, 2-course dinners £14. The Glenisle Hotel dishes up good food that, they assure us, 'hasn't been cooked in a microwave'!

Drift Inn (☎ *600656, Shore Rd, Lamlash*) Most mains £5.45-6.60. Enjoy your pub grub in the fine beer garden here.

Coffee Pot (☎ *700382, Golf Course Rd, Whiting Bay*) Meals and snacks £1.90-5.50. Coffee pots from around the world have found their final resting place at this charming cafe. There's a great selection of home-baked fare and cheap snacks.

HOLY ISLAND & LAMLASH

Just north of Whiting Bay is **Holy Island**, owned by a Tibetan Buddhist group and used as a retreat. Day visits to the island are allowed and the ferry (☎ 600998) operates from early May to early September and runs from Lamlash (£8, 15 minutes, four daily). There's a good walk to the top of the hill (314m), a two- to three-hour return trip. Note that no dogs, alcohol or fires are allowed on the island.

The peaceful channel running between the Holy Island and **Lamlash** has been the temporary home to some powerful ships in its time. In 1263, King Haakon of Norway anchored his huge fleet in the bay while preparing to fight Scottish king Alexander III, in an attempt to maintain Norwegian power over the Scots. In the ensuing battle, at Largs on the mainland, the Norwegians were defeated and returned to Lamlash to lick their wounds before sailing home. King Haakon fell ill and died by the time they'd reached Shetland. Centuries later, the Royal Navy anchored in the bay during both WWI and WWII.

Lamlash has hotels, restaurants, cafes, grocery stores and a post office.

WALKING AROUND ARRAN

The best walk on the island is Goatfell; see the Activities chapter for details. The northern coast also provides fine routes between North Sannox and Lochranza. There are some impressive cliffs, the site of a landslip, isolated cottages, remains of early coal mining and salt harvesting, and a fairly easygoing walk around the **Cock of Arran** – a prominent block of sandstone, not named after a rooster but from the Lowland Scots word meaning 'cap' or 'headwear'.

On a good day the views across the Sound of Bute to the mainland, the Isle of Bute and part of the Kintyre peninsula are fantastic. There's also a good chance of seeing common seals and a variety of birds.

Another good walk begins from the high point of the road between Sannox and Lochranza; from here you can head southwards (avoiding the forestry) and walk up a pleasant ridge to Caisteal Abhail (859m). Don't be tempted to follow the eastern ridge to Ceum na Caillich (Witch's Step) – it involves moderate rock climbing! Instead go southwards to Cir Mhór (798m), scramble over its pointed summit, continue down its eastern ridge to a pass, then descend steeply into Glen Sannox. Only attempt this route in good weather and allow six hours. For both routes, carry OS map No 69 and a compass. There's deer stalking on Caisteal Abhail from late August to late October; ask locally for advice.

Moderate walks include the two-hour Glen Sannox trail, which goes from the village of Sannox up the burn. From Whiting Bay Youth Hostel there are easy one-hour walks through the forest to the **Giants Graves** and **Glenashdale Falls**. Keep an eye out for golden eagles, peregrine falcons, hawks, harriers and kestrels – they all hunt in this region. Also look out for barn and tawny owls.

For more coverage obtain the invaluable *Walking in the Isle of Arran* by Paddy Dillon, which details 41 day walks on the island. The Forest Enterprise's *Guide to Forest Walks on the Isle of Arran*, available from the TIC, concentrates on southern Arran.

Guided Walks

The Countryside Rangers at Brodick Country Park (☎ 01770-302462) lead summer walks, ranging from afternoon wildlife strolls through the low-level forests to Goatfell and other peaks.

CYCLING AROUND ARRAN

With few serious hills, a 50-mile circuit on the coastal road is very popular with cyclists; if this is just a touch too long for you, the 40-mile route from Brodick to

Lochranza, clockwise via Whiting Bay and Lagg, is excellent.

Traffic isn't too bad, except in high season, and even then it's mostly concentrated in western towns such as Brodick, Lamlash and Whiting Bay. There are some moderate climbs to ride up, particularly in the east and south, and great coastal views – benches have been thoughtfully placed at scenic points along the road.

GOLF

Green fees range from £8.50 at Lochranza, where you might spot (and perhaps hit) a deer, to £18 at Brodick. The TIC in Brodick has details and all courses hire out clubs.

GETTING THERE & AWAY

CalMac (☎ 01294-463470) runs a daily car ferry between Ardrossan and Brodick (passenger £4.40 one-way, £25.50/31.50 off-peak/peak for a car, 55 minutes, four to six daily) and from late March to late October runs services between Claonaig and Lochranza (£4, £18.05/21.55 off-peak/peak for a car, 30 minutes, seven to nine daily). From late October to late March, the car ferry sails from Lochranza to Portavadie (Cowal) and Tarbert (Kintyre).

If you're visiting several islands, get a CalMac Hopscotch fare; see the Getting Around chapter for more information.

GETTING AROUND

Arran's efficient bus services are operated by Stagecoach Western (☎ 302000) and Royal Mail (☎ 01246-546329), which operates a postbus. Four to six buses daily leave from Brodick Pier to Lochranza (£1.65, 45 minutes). Buses for Blackwaterfoot run via Lochranza, the String Rd, or Whiting Bay (£1.65, 30 minutes or one hour 10 minutes respectively, at least five daily). At least four buses run daily from Brodick to Lamlash and Whiting Bay (£1.60, 30 minutes). A Daycard costs £3.

There are several places in Brodick to rent bikes, including Mini Golf Cycle Hire (☎ 302272) on Shore Rd, with bikes from only £4.50 per day. Blackwaterfoot Garage (☎ 860277) does bike hire for £7 per day.

Whiting Bay Hires (☎ 01770 820210) hires out 18-speed mountain bikes for £9 per day.

For a taxi, phone ☎ 302274 in Brodick or ☎ 600903 in Lamlash.

Islay

☎ 01496 • pop 3700

The most southerly island of the Hebrides archipelago, green, barren Islay (pronounced **eye**-la) is renowned for its smoky, single-malt whiskies. And with seven distilleries all running guided tours and pumping out thousands of gallons each year, a visit to the isle will give you ample chance to taste it.

The political centre of the Hebrides during Medieval times, **Finlaggan** was the seat of the MacDonalds, lords of the Isles. But most of the settlements to be found on the isle today date from the 19th century, when whisky distilling really got going.

Besides whisky, this island's other main draw is birdlife; with more than 250 recorded species of bird, twitchers come here in droves.

If birds aren't your thing, there's a wild coastline and immaculate beaches to wander on. You'll probably see no-one because, as famous though its whisky might be, compared to more touristy isles such as Mull or Skye, this place is deserted.

ORIENTATION & INFORMATION

Eight ferries a week dock at the hamlet of Port Askaig, a picturesque harbour across from Jura. It has a grocery store, an atmospheric but overpriced hotel and pub and, nearby, two distilleries.

Around 10 ferries dock each week at much larger Port Ellen in the south. Though it's in a beautiful location, Port Ellen has a rundown feel to it that's sure to make you hurry on, perhaps to its three distilleries, all along a dead-end road heading out to Ardtalla.

Islay Airport is near Kintra, which is 4 miles from Port Ellen.

Bowmore is the island's capital, on the west coast overlooking Laggan Bay. It also has the island's only TIC (☎ 810254), located in The Square. The distillery, aptly named Bowmore, is the island's oldest.

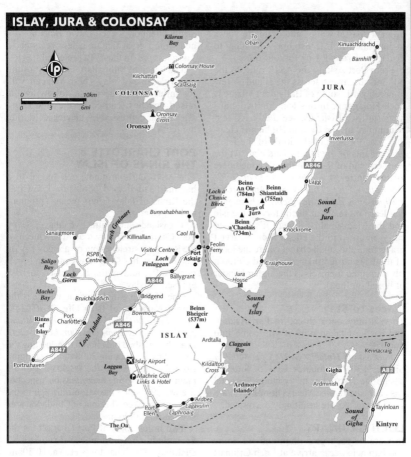

ISLAY, JURA & COLONSAY

At pretty Port Charlotte, across Loch Indaal from Bowmore, there's a post office, shop, SYHA hostel, wildlife centre and museum, and – hurrah – a distillery.

Port Ellen's MacTaggart Community Cybercafe (☎ 01496-302693, e mcc@cheap net.co.uk), Mansfield Place, opens 11am to 10pm weekdays and noon to 9pm at weekends. Access costs from £1 per 20 minutes.

The hospital is in Bowmore (☎ 810219).

PORT ASKAIG & AROUND

Little more than a ferry dock and car park at the foot of a steep hill, Port Askaig is still a charming place, especially with the rickety old *Port Askaig Hotel* overlooking it. Wander around the corner to the **lifeboat station** for better views of Jura.

The nearby **Caol Ila Distillery** (☎ *840207*), founded in 1846, has stunning views of Jura from its stillhouse, and there are tours of Caol Ila (pronounced coal-eela; £3.50 including tasting) Monday to Friday year-round; ring ahead to book.

At the top of the hill above Port Askaig and north on a single-track side road is the **Bunnahabhainn Distillery** (☎ *840646*), in a secluded bay. From Bunnahabhainn (pronounced **boo**-na-ha-ven) there are magnificent coastal walks, and dramatic views to Jura and Mull. It also opens Monday to Friday year-round; ring for tour times.

From Port Askaig the A846 runs up the hill and southwest across the island. A few hundred yards south of Ballygrant village is **Loch Finlaggan**. In this loch, on two crannogs (artificial islands; see the boxed text 'Crannogs' in The Central Highlands chapter), was the seat of the lords of the Isles, descendants of the MacDonald clan. At the northern end of the loch there's a mediocre **visitor centre** (☎ 840644; adult/chilD £2/ free; open Tues, Thur & Sun Apr & Oct, 2.30pm-5pm daily May-Sept), where you can learn more about the history of the isle and the MacDonalds; though it's better to carry on down to the **Eilean Mor**, a carved gravestone and small chapel where the lords of the Isles buried their wives and children (they granted themselves the higher honour of burial on Iona).

Places to Stay
There's only once choice in Port Askaig, and it's best taken only if you come into port late.

Port Askaig Hotel (☎ 840245, fax 840295) Singles £30-42, doubles £36-45. Situated beside the ferry slip, this picturesque hotel has adequate rooms. Meals (from £4.95) are good but drinks are insultingly overpriced.

LOCH GRUINART
In October each year, thousands of white and barnacle geese arrive at Loch Gruinart nature reserve to escape the harsh winters of their native Greenland.

North of Port Charlotte at **Aoradh** (pronounced **oo**-rig), at the base of Loch Gruinart, there's an **RSPB information centre** (☎ 850505; admission free; open 10am-5pm daily, to 4pm Nov-Mar) that's a must for wildlife buffs. Two- to three-hour guided walks are available (£2 per person, £1 for RSPB members) at 10am every Thursday and at 6pm on Tuesday in August; ring ahead to confirm.

The birds have caused havoc with farmers (who now receive government compensation for the damage they cause) and attract much media attention – even David Bellamy visited with a great fanfare a few years back. The geese are (in theory) a protected species.

The beach at **Killinallan**, northeast of the reserve, is one of Islay's best. You can walk for miles along the coast, following the **raised beaches** (caused by the land rising after being depressed by glacier ice during the Ice Age).

PORT CHARLOTTE & THE RINNS OF ISLAY
The A846 curls around Loch Indaal to a hammerhead-shaped peninsula known as the Rinns of Islay (rinns means 'promontory' in Gaelic).

The island's most attractive village, sleepy Port Charlotte, is known as 'The Queen of the Rinns'. It stretches out on a sandy bay on Loch Indaal, has some lively pubs and first-rate B&Bs, and is the best place to base yourself in Islay.

One of the highlights of the village is the quirky **Museum of Islay Life** (☎ 850358, Main St; adult/child £2/1.50; open 10am-5pm Mon-Sat & 2pm-5pm Sun, Easter-Oct), in a whitewashed old church overlooking the bay. It has a whopping 2000 items – ranging from the hilarious to the fascinating to the plain dull – covering every feasible aspect of life on Islay since the Mesolithic age to the present. The Wee Museum of Childhood area is great for children.

Two miles north of Port Charlotte is the **Bruichladdich** (pronounced **broo**-laddie) **Distillery**, which has tours (£3) at 10.30am, 11.30am and 2.30pm Monday to Saturday year-round.

At the far southwestern tip of the Rinns is **Portnahaven**, a pretty fishing village that's been here since the early 1800s, with whitewashed cottages and wonderful beaches. The world's first commercially viable, wave-powered electricity-generating station has been built on the sea cliffs, which are open to the Atlantic swell, a mile north of the village. The 500kW plant – known as 'Limpet' (land-installed, marine-powered energy transformer) – provides enough electricity to supply 200 island homes.

The beaches north of here are beautiful, but the best are at the stunning **Machir Bay** and **Saligo**. Backed by huge white sand dunes, both look good but swimming is forbidden due to the deadly undercurrent.

Places to Stay & Eat
Islay Youth Hostel (☎ 850385, Main St) Beds £9/7.75. Open Mar-late Sept. Your host might be a bit on the gruff side but he sure does look after this excellent SYHA hostel by the waterfront.

Mrs Brown (☎ 850495) £20 per person. In the old distillery directly opposite the youth hostel, Mrs Brown makes her own marmalade, cooks a great breakfast and keeps her B&B tidy. It's a top place to stay.

Port Charlotte Hotel (☎ 850360, fax 850361, Main St) B&B singles/doubles £59/95. It isn't cheap, but this four-star hotel is well maintained and superbly romantic. Built in 1829, there's 10 perfect ensuite rooms, all with great views. Tasty three-course dinners cost around £22.

Abbotsford (☎ 850587) B&B £20 per person. Near the Bruichladdich distillery, a few miles north, you'll find this charming pad overlooking the loch. Its owners really look after their guests.

Lochindaal Hotel (☎ 850364) Mains £4-8. Inside Lochindaal's twee whitewashed exterior lies a serious drinking den. They also do good lunches, including the special of fish and chips plus a pint for £3.75.

Croft Kitchen (☎ 850230) Mains £4.50-12. Last orders 8.30pm. Overlooking Loch Indaal and specialising in seafood, the Croft Kitchen does great lunches and dinners, and scrumptious sweets.

BOWMORE
On the other side of Loch Indaal is the village of Bowmore, the island's capital. Ten miles from Port Askaig and Port Ellen, it has a TIC (☎ 810254), two banks with ATMs, a post office and plenty of shops. There are washing machines at MacTaggart Leisure Centre (£3/1.50 to wash/dry).

The distinctive **Round Church** (1767), at the top of Main St, was built to ensure the devil had no corners to hide in.

On the shores of Loch Indaal, the **Bowmore Distillery** *(☎ 810441, School St; adult/child £2/1; tours 10.30am & 2pm Mon-Fri year-round, plus 10.30am, 11.30am, 2pm & 3pm Mon-Fri in summer)*, in operation since 1779, has a friendly visitor centre and offers regular guided tours. The admission charge, redeemable against purchases, includes a dram.

If you've had enough of whisky, wildlife and walking, head for Bowmore's **MacTaggart Leisure Centre** *(☎ 810767, Schoolmore St; adult/child £2.20/1.40; open 10.30am-8pm Mon-Fri, 10.30am-5.30pm Sat-Sun)*. Locals are very proud of the centre, with its pool, sauna and gym.

Places to Stay & Eat
There are several B&Bs in town for £18 to £20 per person, including *Lambeth House (☎ 810597, Jamieson St)* and *Meadowside (☎ 810497, Birch Drive)*.

Harbour Inn (☎ 810330, The Square) Singles/doubles £40/75. The rather posh Harbour Inn has plush rooms and a top-notch restaurant serving local fare. It serves breakfast 9.30am to noon, and you should know that it won the 1998 World Porridge Championships. Lunch mains cost £4 to £10, and dinner costs between £11 and £17

Lochside Hotel (☎ 810244, e ask@loch sidehotel.co.uk, 19 Shore St) Singles/doubles £39.50/79. The Lochside's bar has around 400 malts on offer, including a 29-year-old Black Bowmore for £1.50 per 35ml! It runs speciality malt-whisky weekends from £125 per person, including whisky tours and three nights dinner and B&B.

Bridgend Hotel (☎ 810212, fax 810960, Bridgend) B&B singles/doubles £40/48. Though this village at the Port Charlotte turn-off is usually just passed through, the Bridgend Hotel is a comfortable place to spend a night if you arrive on a late ferry. The bar does great food.

PORT ELLEN
Port Ellen gets more ferry landings than Port Askaig, but it's also a much uglier introduction to the isle. It has a grocery store, pub, hotel and bank (no ATM, closed

Wednesday and afternoons except Thursday), but there's nought to see in the town.

The coast stretching northeastwards from Port Ellen, though, is one of Islay's loveliest parts. There are three whisky distilleries in close succession – **Laphroaig** (pronounced la-**froyg**) (☎ *302418*), **Lagavulin** (☎ *302400*) and **Ardbeg** (☎ *302244*) – all of which offer tours by appointment.

Islay was an early focus for Christianity. The exceptional late-8th-century **Kildalton Cross**, at the roofless **Kildalton Chapel**, 8 miles northeast of Port Ellen, is one of the few fully intact Celtic high crosses outside Iona. There are carvings of a biblical scene on one side of the 2.1m-high cross and animals on the other. There are several extraordinary grave slabs at the chapel, some carved with swords and crosses – symbols of the enigmatic Knights Templar.

A few miles north is **Claggain Bay**, a sandy white beach that sits below Beinn Bheigeir, the isle's highest rise at 537m.

At **Kintra** (pronounced **kin**-traw), 4 miles from Port Ellen, there's a top restaurant and hostel.

The **Ardmore Islands**, off the southeastern corner of Islay near Kildalton, are a wildlife haven and home to the second largest colony of common seals in Europe.

Three miles northwest of Port Ellen is the **Machrie Golf Links & Hotel** (☎ *302310, fax 302404*, **W** *www.machrie.com*), Islay's only course. Designed in 1891 by famed designer Willie Campbell, it hosted the 1901 British Open, which then had the world's largest prize, set at £100. Rounds cost around £20.

Southwest of Port Ellen, a road goes to the peninsula of **The Oa**, a wild area with spectacular, isolated coastline and an impressive headland. You'll come across a monument to two US ships wrecked off the coast here in 1918 during a terrible storm.

Places to Stay & Eat

There's a couple of decent places to stay in Port Ellen, including *Mrs McGillivray's* (☎ *302420*), who charges £18 per person for a night in her simple cottage.

Trout Fly Guest House (☎ *302204, 8 Charlotte St*) Singles/doubles £18.50/30.

Like most things in Port Ellen, this three-room guest house looks dismal from the outside. But inside, the Trout Fly is a great place to lay your rod for a night.

MacTaggart Community CyberCafe (☎ *302693, Mansfield Place*) Meals £2.20-4.40. Open 11am-10pm Mon-Sat, noon-9pm Sun, food served till 5.30pm. Port Ellen's Internet cafe does snacks to eat in or take away, as well as tea and cakes.

Kintra Farm (☎ *302051, Kintra Farm*) Dorms £9, plus £2.50 for bedding. B&B £18 per person. Pitches £7. Open Apr-Sept. Four miles north of Port Ellen, this hostel on Kintra Beach has 23 beds. It also does farmhouse B&B, has tent pitches and rents out attractive cottages by the week (£300 to £400). In summer, the *Granary Restaurant* attached to Kintra Farm serves snacks and meals for £4 to £7.

Glenmachrie Farmhouse (☎ *302560*, **e** *glenmachrie@lineone.net*) B&B £30 per person. Although being located next to an airport isn't usually a pointer to top quality, Glenmachrie is an exception. The farmhouse has five en-suite rooms.

The *Old Kiln Cafe* at Ardbeg distillery serves good soup, sandwiches and home-made fare.

SPECIAL EVENTS

The **Islay Festival** (**W** *www.ileach.co.uk/festival*), held at the end of May, is a celebration of traditional Scottish music and includes the **Islay Whisky Festival** (**W** *www.islaywhiskyfestival.com*). Events include ceilidhs, pipe bands, distillery tours and whisky tastings. Both festivals are promoted by Distillery Destinations (☎ *01414-290762*, **W** www.whisky-tours.com).

The annual three-day **Islay Jazz Festival**, promoted by Assembly Direct (☎ *01315-534000*, **W** www.ileach.co.uk/jazz), takes place over the second weekend in September and sees a varied line-up of international talent playing at venues across the island.

GETTING THERE & AWAY

CalMac (☎ *302209*) runs ferries from Kennacraig in West Loch Tarbert to Port Ellen (passenger/car £7.05/37.50, 2¼ hours) and Port Askaig (same fare, two hours). They operate daily, except Wednesday when there's only a ferry to Port Askaig, and on Sunday when there's only a ferry to Port Ellen. On Wednesday in summer, the ferry continues from Port Askaig to Colonsay (£3.55/18.75, 1¼ hours) and returns in the evening, allowing six hours ashore.

British Airways (BA) Express flies from Glasgow to Islay twice on weekdays and once on Saturday (from £95 return, 40 minutes).

GETTING AROUND

A bus service operates between Ardbeg, Port Ellen, Bowmore, Port Charlotte, Portnahaven and Port Askaig. There's only one bus on Sunday. Get a copy of the bus timetable from the TIC.

Taxis are available in both Bowmore (☎ 810449) and Port Ellen (☎ 302155).

Hire bikes in Bowmore, at the post office near the church at the top of Main St, for £10 a day, or from Port Charlotte Bike Hire (☎ 850488) opposite Port Charlotte Hotel, for the same price.

Jura

☎ 01496 • pop 200

Magnificently wild Jura is an incredible place to walk. Which is fortunate, because there's little else to do here, other than poke around Craighouse, the island's only village, and perhaps make a pilgrimage to Barnhill, the house where George Orwell wrote *1984*.

Walkers will be rewarded with superb vistas to or from the Paps of Jura, so called because of their resemblance to some particularly remarkable breasts (especially since there's three of them) and, if walking in the island's north, spectacular views of the Corryvreckan tidal race, a truly world-class natural phenomenon.

With a human population of 200 and a red-deer population of 5000, this is an aptly named island, Jura being derived from the Norse 'dyr-ey' – Deer Island.

In a Spin

The Gulf of Corryvreckan – the 1000m-wide channel between the northern end of Jura and the Island of Scarba – is home to one of the three most notorious tidal whirlpools in the world (the others are the Maelstrom in Norway's Lofoten Islands, and the Old Sow in New Brunswick, Canada).

The tide does not just rise and fall twice a day here; it flows – dragged around the earth by the gravitational attraction of the moon. On the west coast of Scotland, the rising tide (known as the flood tide) flows northwards. As the flood moves up the Sound of Jura, to the east of the island, it is forced into a narrowing bottleneck jammed with islands and builds up to a greater height than the open sea to the west of Jura. As a result, millions of gallons of sea water pour westwards through the Gulf of Corryvreckan at speeds of up to 8 knots – an average sailing yacht is going fast at 6 knots.

The Corryvreckan whirlpool forms where this incredible mass of moving water hits an underwater pinnacle, which rises from the 200m-deep seabed to within just 38m of the surface, and swirls over and around it. The turbulent waters create a magnificent spectacle, with white-capped breakers, bulging boils and numerous miniature maelstroms whirling around the main vortex.

Corryvreckan is at its most violent when a flooding spring tide, flowing westwards through the gulf, meets a westerly gale blowing in from the Atlantic. In these conditions, standing waves of up to 5m high can form and dangerously rough seas extend more than 3 miles west of Corryvreckan, a phenomenon known as the Great Race.

You can see the whirlpool by making the long hike to the northern end of Jura, or by taking a boat trip from Easdale (see The Slate Islands section later in the chapter).

THINGS TO SEE

Such 'sights' as there are on Jura are in or around the village of **Craighouse**, where you'll find **The Isle of Jura Distillery**

George's Animal Farm

George Orwell first stepped onto Jura's shores in 1945 as a tourist. Less than a year later, he was living at a remote farmhouse called Barnhill at the isolated far north of the island.

Determined to escape being 'constantly smothered by journalism', Orwell came to Jura to recover from the death of his first wife, and 'to write another book'. That book was *1984* (working title: *The Last Man in Europe*), and it would be his last.

Having escaped London and the telephone that rang for him incessantly in his job at the *Observer*, Orwell was determined to write. He finished *1984* in 1948 (he cunningly named his book by simply reversing the last two digits), having spent countless nights alone in his bedroom furiously banging away at a typewriter balanced on his knees.

He was also determined to turn the remote farmhouse (even today the road to Barnhill remains untarred) into a dairy farm. It was a dream he would never realise; suffering from tuberculosis even before his arrival on Jura, Orwell's condition worsened steadily until he was forced to head for a London sanatorium. He died in January 1950.

(☎ 820240; admission free; open by appointment only). Craighouse, the island's only village, is also graced by a shop (Jura Stores).

Two miles before Craighouse (coming from the ferry) is **Jura House** *(☎ 820315; £2; open 9am-5pm daily)*, with its beautiful gardens filled with wildflowers and native Australian trees and plants.

WALKING AROUND JURA

The wildness of Jura's uplands is matched only on the island of Rum, and on Harris in the Western Isles. Much of the island is managed for deer stalking, so the best time to visit is from early May to early July.

The Scottish Mountaineering Club's guide *The Islands of Scotland including Skye* by DJ Fabian, GE Little & DN Williams covers the mountains, with a section on path walks.

Look out for adders – the island is infested with these dangerous snakes, but they are quite shy and should move away as you approach. If they don't and you do get bitten, seek medical help as soon as possible.

The Paps of Jura

Climbing the Paps is a tough hill walk requiring good navigational skills; it takes around eight hours (though the record for the Paps of Jura fell race is just three hours). The three conical peaks – Beinn a' Chaolais (734m), Beinn an Oir (784m) and Beinn Shiantaich (755m) – dominate the island and are visible from far away. The 12-mile circuit of their summits provides a fairly energetic and outstandingly scenic day.

A convenient place to start is by the bridge over the Corran River, about 3 miles north of Craighouse.

The West Coast

It's possible to follow the west coast from Feolin Ferry all the way to the northern tip of Jura, but it's a gruelling endurance test and only suitable for a fit, well-equipped and experienced party. It's about 40 miles one-way and takes at least five days, so you'll have to camp. You're likely to encounter: raised beaches; unbridged rivers; wildlife, including wild goats; tussocks; caves with rooms, ladders and beds; and a range of other experiences. There's little chance of encountering any other humans. You'll never forget Jura afterwards.

PLACES TO STAY & EAT

Accommodation on Jura is limited, so book ahead.

There's a small *camp site* in the field adjoining the Jura Hotel (see overleaf), with showers (£1) and a launderette, for £5 per person. There are also *bunkhouses* at Knockrome *(☎ 820332)*, 3½ miles north of Craighouse, and Kinuachdrachd *(☎ 07899-912116)*, in the far north of the island, but these are geared mainly to groups rather than individual travellers.

Gwen Boardman *(☎ 820379, 7 Woodside, Craighouse)* and *Liz Mack* *(☎ 820332, Knockrome)* offer B&B for £18 per person.

Ivy Cottage (☎ *820322, Inverlussa)* B&B £15-20 per person. This delightful cottage, with one double and one single room, overlooks the bay at Inverlussa, 17 miles north of Craighouse. You can also get a three-course dinner here for £12.

Jura Hotel (☎ *820243,* e *jurahotel@ aol.com, Craighouse)* Rooms £33-49 per person. The family-run, 18-room Jura Hotel is a great place to stay, though you wouldn't guess it from the outside. It's also a fantastic (and the *only*) place to drink on Jura. Try to get the rooms at the front for the views. They also offer a three-course dinner for £16.95.

Antlers Tearoom (☎ *820395, Craighouse)* serves tea, coffee and snacks.

GETTING THERE & AROUND
Jura is reached via Islay. A small car ferry shuttles between Port Askaig and Feolin (passenger/car £1.80/10, five minutes), roughly hourly from Monday to Saturday and less often on Sunday; if the weather is really wild the ferry may not run.

Charles MacLean (☎ 820314 or ☎ 820221) runs an infrequent bus service five or six days a week between Feolin and Craighouse. One or two of the runs go as far as Inverlussa, where the road ends in the island's north.

Colonsay & Oronsay

☎ 01951 ● pop 106

When people dream of Scottish islands, Colonsay is the sort of paradise they have in mind: lush green fields bordered by a rocky coastline and treacherous cliffs. Add to this tempting sandy beaches backed by machair and woodland, all combined with remote ports and villages and Colonsay becomes the perfect destination to spend a few days unwinding and exploring.

ORIENTATION & INFORMATION
The ferry docks at Scalasaig, the main village, where you'll find a grocery store and post office, restaurant, telephones and the Isle of Colonsay Hotel. There is no TIC and

no banks or ATMs on the island. For a doctor call ☎ 200328.

THINGS TO SEE & DO
By the pier at Scalasaig, the old CalMac ferry waiting room is now a small **Heritage Centre**, open when the ferry docks.

Inland, 2 miles to the north at Kiloran, is the lovely **Colonsay House**, which dates from 1772. The house is off-limits, but the picturesque **gardens** *(admission free)* are worth strolling through. The garden uses the land's natural contours and rivers well, and is famous for its outstanding collection of hybrid rhododendrons and unusual trees. The formal walled garden around the mansion, which has a terrace *cafe*, opens Wednesday and Friday, Easter to September.

Half a mile farther north is the stunning **Kiloran Bay**, the island's most attractive beach and described in tourist paraphernalia as 'the most beautiful in the Hebrides', which may not be an exaggeration, with crisp waves crashing in from the Atlantic.

There are **standing stones** dotted around the island, at Garvard in the south and at Kilchattan on the west coast, where you'll find the beautifully named **Final's Limpet Hammers**. Near the hotel in Scalasaig, you'll also find an Iron-Age fort known as **Dub Eibhinn**.

Keep an eye out for the dizzying array of **wildlife** on the isle: choughs, one of the UK's rarest birds, live here, as well as corncrakes, merlins, falcons and golden eagles.

Just below the south coast of Colonsay is tiny **Oronsay**, with a population of eight humans and innumerable goats. The tidal island can be reached on foot at low tide, across mud flats known as 'The Strand'. It's about a two-hour round journey to walk from there to the ruins of an **Augustinian priory** dating from the 14th century. Don't miss the spectacular late-15th-century stone **Oronsay Cross** at the entrance, and a large collection of 15th- and 16th-century carved tombstones in the Prior's House. You have about three hours for the entire journey (but check with locals to be absolutely sure of tide times – they can sometimes be as short as two hours or as long as four). There is nowhere to stay on Oronsay, but you can eat at the excellent **Barn Cafe**, open daily except Saturday in summer.

Legend has it that St Columba made his first landfall on Oronsay after leaving his native Ireland plagued with guilt. Climbing to the top of Ben Oronsay, he found he could still see the hills of Ireland; fearful of homesickness and his resolve to never again set foot there weakening, he sailed on, eventually finding Iona.

Boat trips (☎ 200320, ℮ byrne@colonsay .org.uk), costing £15 per person, are available from Kevin and Christa Byrne.

PLACES TO STAY & EAT

If you're planning on staying on the island, you must book ahead: there are few places to stay and camping isn't allowed.

Backpackers Lodge (☎ 200312) Beds £8.50-10. This hostel, in a former gamekeeper's house, is 30 minutes' walk from the ferry, in the middle of the island near Loch Fada. It has a fully equipped kitchen and hires out bikes for £5 per day.

Seaview (☎/fax 200315) B&B £23 per person. The Lawson's run a mean B&B at their peaceful farmhouse is in Kilchattan, near the rugged west coast of the island. They also do dinner (£16) and packed lunches (£3.50).

Isle of Colonsay Chalets (☎ 200320, ℮ chalets@colonsay.org.uk) Singles/doubles £25/40. These comfortable modern chalets are 10 minutes' walk from the Scalasaig ferry pier. Check availability online at Ⓦ www.colonsay.org.uk/newother/lodges .html.

Isle of Colonsay Hotel (☎ 200316, ℮ colonsay.hotel@pipemedia.co.uk) Dinner B&B £69-80 per person, including bike hire. The plush Isle of Colonsay has eight well-appointed rooms, and does a choice dinner (£4 to £6) of locally caught seafood. Attached to the hotel is **Virago's**, a decent bookshop that also does snacks and coffee.

The Pantry (☎ 200325) tearoom, just up from the ferry pier, does tasty home cooking, plus snacks and ice creams throughout summer, and on days the ferry is in port the rest of the year.

GETTING THERE & AROUND

CalMac ferries sail to Colonsay from Oban on Sunday, Wednesday and Friday (passenger/car £10.10/48.50, two hours), and on Wednesday only in summer from Islay's Port Askaig (passenger/car £3.55/18.75, 1¼ hours) and Kennacraig on the Kintyre peninsula (passenger/car £10.10/48.50, 3½ hours).

From April to September, if you're staying near Kennacraig or on Mull and a few days on Colonsay is too much peace and quiet to cope with, on Wednesdays you can do a daytrip on the ferry from Port Askaig that will leave you on Colonsay for about five hours.

Bicycle hire is available from A McConnel (☎ 200355). On Tuesday, Wednesday and Saturday, there's a postbus service (☎ 01463-256200) around the island – it also goes to Oronsay, with times dependent on the tides.

Northern Argyll

OBAN

☎ 01631 ● pop 8517

Beautiful Oban is the hub of the southern Hebrides and northern Argyll, and is a good place to use as a base for exploring this part of Scotland.

Overrun by visitors in summer, Oban is a large town by Highland standards, although you can easily get around on foot (even if the hills overlooking the town require effort).

The island of Kerrera, picturesquely situated a few hundred metres away across the bay, provides the town with a wonderful natural shelter and has made this the most important ferry town on the west coast.

Orientation

The bus, train and ferry terminals are conveniently grouped by the harbour on the bay's southern edge. Argyll Square is one block east of the train station, and George St runs northwards along the promenade to North Pier. From here, Corran Esplanade runs around the northern edge of the bay.

The TIC sells maps and guidebooks, or else try WHSmith on George St.

The mysterious 6000-year-old Machrie Moor standing stones, Isle of Arran

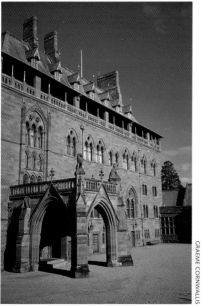

Mock-Gothic Mount Stuart House, Isle of Bute

Blooms of pink sea thrift carpet the coast.

Carved pillars at Iona Abbey, founded in 1200

BRYN THOMAS

GRAEME CORNWALLIS

A replica of a curious Iron Age crannog at Kenmore, Loch Tay

NICOLA WELLS

The West Highland Way

Hexagonal basalt pillars around Fingal's Cave, Staffa

NICOLA WELLS

Follow the path of St Columba and anchor yourself in picturesque Iona, off the Isle of Mull.

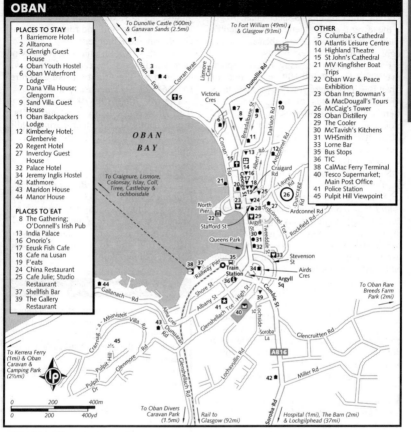

OBAN

PLACES TO STAY
1 Barriemore Hotel
2 Alltarona
3 Glenrigh Guest House
4 Oban Youth Hostel
6 Oban Waterfront Lodge
7 Dana Villa House; Glengorm
9 Sand Villa Guest House
11 Oban Backpackers Lodge
12 Kimberley Hotel; Glenbervie
20 Regent Hotel
27 Invercloy Guest House
32 Palace Hotel
34 Jeremy Inglis Hostel
42 Kathmore
43 Maridon House
44 Manor House

PLACES TO EAT
8 The Gathering; O'Donnell's Irish Pub
13 India Palace
17 Onorio's
17 Eeusk Fish Cafe
18 Cafe na Lusan
19 F'eats
24 China Restaurant
25 Cafe Julie; Studio Restaurant
37 Shellfish Bar
39 The Gallery Restaurant

OTHER
5 Columba's Cathedral
10 Atlantis Leisure Centre
14 Highland Theatre
15 St John's Cathedral
21 MV Kingfisher Boat Trips
22 Oban War & Peace Exhibition
23 Oban Inn; Bowman's & MacDougall's Tours
26 McCaig's Tower
28 Oban Distillery
29 The Cooler
30 McTavish's Kitchens
31 WHSmith
33 Lorne Bar
35 Bus Stops
36 TIC
38 CalMac Ferry Terminal
40 Tesco Supermarket; Main Post Office
41 Police Station
45 Pulpit Hill Viewpoint

Information

Oban TIC (☎ 563122, e info@oban.org.uk) is in an old church on Argyll Square and opens 9am to 9pm Monday to Saturday plus 9am to 7pm Sunday, July and August; and 9am to 5.30pm Monday to Saturday plus 9am to 5pm Sunday, May, June and September. It's closed on Sunday the rest of the year.

The post office is in the Tesco supermarket on Lochside St.

For Web access, there are machines at Oban Youth Hostel (50p per five minutes) or at Cafe na Lusan (☎ 567268) at 9 Craigard Rd. The cafe opens 11am to 4pm Monday, 11am to 9pm Tuesday to Friday and 10am to 9pm on Saturday and charges £1/3.50 per 15/60 minutes.

Argyll & the Isles Hospital (☎ 567500) is located at the southern end of Oban, just off Soroba Rd.

Things to See

Crowning the hill above town is the rather odd **McCaig's Tower** *(admission free; open year-round)*, built at the end of the 19th century. Intended to be an art gallery, it was never completed and now looks like a version of Rome's Colosseum. From the top there are impressive views across the bay to Kerrera, and Oban looks spectacular. To get to the tower take the steep climb up 'Jacob's Ladder' from Argyll St and then follow the signs. See the boxed text below.

Even better are the staggeringly impressive views from **Pulpit Hill**, to the south of Oban Bay. From here you can see mountains and isles hundreds of miles away, and there's a bronze marker with pointers for mountains and isles and their distances from Oban. It's a hell of a slog up by foot, but well worth the effort, especially for the amazing sunsets.

Since 1793, **Oban Distillery** *(☎ 572004, Stafford St; tours adult/child aged 8-16 £3.50/free; 5 tours per day Mon-Fri year-round & also Sat Easter-Oct)* has been producing single-malt whisky in the centre of the town. Even if you don't join a tour, it's worth visiting the distillery for the small exhibition in the foyer. Children aged under eight are not admitted.

If the weather's poor, while away some time at the **Oban War & Peace Exhibition** *(North Pier; admission free; open daily, except Sun Apr-Dec)*. It's mostly war memorabilia and details of military exercises in the area, but if the gents running the show don't make you nostalgic for times past, nothing will.

The **Oban Rare Breeds Farm Park** *(☎ 770608, New Barran Farm, Glencruitten; adult/child £5/3.50; open 10am-5.30pm late Mar-Oct, extended hours mid-June–Aug)* is 2 miles east of the town centre. The 30-acre park keeps rare breeds of farm animals once common throughout Britain, and others never common – there's llama, alpaca, Vietnamese pot-bellied pigs, as well as more pedestrian creatures.

Activities

Wander 20 minutes along the coastal road from Oban Youth Hostel and you'll come to the picturesque ruins of **Dunollie Castle**, built by the MacDougalls of Lorn in the 13th century, and unsuccessfully besieged for a year during the 1715 Jacobite rebellion. You can continue along this road to the beach at **Ganavan Sands**, 2½ miles from Oban.

A TIC leaflet lists local bike rides. They include a 7-mile **Gallanach circular tour**, a 16-mile route to Seil and routes to Connel, Glenlonan and Kilmore.

Or if driving rain and gale force winds keep you indoors, instead of the pub, why not head for the **Atlantis Leisure Centre's** *(☎ 5668000, Dalriach Rd)* pool.

The **MV Kingfisher** *(☎ 563138; £7.50; trips 10am & 2pm daily Apr-Sept)* has boat trips to spot seals and other marine wildlife from Corran Esplanade, 200m north of North Pier.

Organised Tours

From April to October, *Bowman's & Mac-Dougall's Tours (☎ 563221, 3 Stafford St)* offers a 'Three Isles' day-trip from Oban to Mull, Iona and Staffa (adult/child £32/17, 10 hours, Sun-Thur). A shorter day-trip visits Mull and Iona only (adult/child £21/12, 8 hours, daily).

A Towering Folly

Though described in tourist-office literature as 'important', it's difficult to work out just what this stone folly is doing here.

Built atop the soaring Battery Hill, the circular tower – 'The Crown of Oban' – was the brainchild of Oban banker John McCaig, who conceived of the project as a means of employment for local stonemasons who were finding few sources of regular employment in winter.

Begun in 1895, the tower took four years to build. McCaig visited Rome in the 1880s, and it's thought perhaps he was inspired by the Colosseum.

Originally, a 29m tower was planned, with museum, gallery and church attached. McCaig abandoned these ideas, though in his will he instructed the tower be embellished with bronze statues of the McCaig family. He died in 1902 and, perhaps in the interest of good taste, the executors of the will conveniently managed to avoid commissioning the statues.

Gordon Grant Tours (☎ 562842), opposite the train station on Railway Pier, also offers combined coach and boat excursions to Mull, Iona and Staffa from March to October.

Special Events

When **West Highland Yachting Week** *(☎ 563309,* W *www.whyw.co.uk)* hits town in late July and early August, Oban's harbour and bars get jammed with thirsty sailors.

The **Argyllshire Gathering** *(☎ 562671)* is held annually in late August and is one of the Highland Games' most important events. The games are held at Mossfield Park on the eastern edge of town.

Places to Stay

Oban is choked with places to stay so, except perhaps in July or August, you'll have no trouble finding a good-value place. If you visit in high season, it's worth the £1 booking fee you'll pay the TIC to find you somewhere.

Camping *Oban Divers Caravan Park (☎/fax 562755, Glenshellach Rd)* Pitches £6.50-8. Open Mar-Oct. The nearest camp site to the train station, this place is 1½ miles south of town in Glenshellach, and has excellent facilities.

Oban Caravan & Camping Park (☎ 562425, fax 566624, Gallanachmore Farm) Pitches £8-9. Open Apr–mid-Oct. This site has a great hill-top location overlooking Kerrera, 2½ miles south of Oban.

Ganavan Sands Caravan Park (☎ 562179, Ganavan Rd) Pitches/beds £4/8.50. Open Apr-Oct. Beside a sandy beach, 2 miles north of the town, Ganavan Sands has pitches and a six-bed bunkhouse.

Hostels *Oban Backpackers Lodge (☎ 562107,* e *oban@scotlands-top-hostels .com, Breadalbane St)* Beds £11. This friendly place has a communal kitchen and grungy bar with pool tables. Rooms are rough around the edges but the party atmosphere means you'll be too drunk to notice. Breakfast costs an additional £1.50.

Oban Youth Hostel (☎ 562025, Corran Esplanade) Beds £12.25/10.75. Oban's first-rate SYHA hostel is in a refurbished stone building with stunning ocean views. For groups, there's the 'chalet-style' Oban Lodge. Prices drop to £9.50/6.50 from November to March and increase by £1 in July and August.

Jeremy Inglis Hostel (☎ 565065, fax 565933, 21 Airds Crescent) Dorm beds £6.50, singles £11-12, doubles £13-15. Jeremy has been here for years, doing cheap B&B; it's a simple place to stay near the ferry terminal and train station.

Oban Waterfront Lodge (☎ 566040, fax 566940, 1 Victoria Crescent) Beds £10-20. On the waterfront with great views across Oban bay, this place has big comfy beds and friendly, helpful staff.

B&Bs *Dana Villa House (☎/fax 564063, Dunollie Rd)* B&B £20 per person. This end of Dunollie Rd has nothing but B&Bs, and this is the best. The owner is a bit gruff, but she runs a mean B&B, with spotlessly clean (if decidedly chintzy) rooms. If it's full, try *Glengorm (☎ 565361)* a few doors down, which has similar rooms and prices.

Sand Villa Guest House (☎ 562803, Breadalbane St) B&B £15-20 per person. Breadalbane St is similarly packed with places to stay, and 15-room Sand Villa is one of the cheapest and most efficient.

Invercloy Guest House (☎ 562058, Ardconnel Terrace) B&B £18-22 per person. High above town, this quiet street is yet another heaving with B&Bs. The tastefully decked out Invercloy has panoramic views over the bay, and superb rooms.

Maridon House (☎ 562670, e *maridon hse@aol.com, Dunuaran Rd)* B&B singles/doubles £20/38. On the southern side of town near the ferry terminal, Maridon House's owners are as friendly as their building is blue (and it's quite blue). There are eight charming rooms, all en suite.

Back on the northern side of town, Corran Esplanade has slightly more expensive guesthouses and small hotels; if you can afford above £20 per night per person, look here before anywhere else as this is Oban's most romantic stretch, with views to Kerrera and a footpath on which to promenade.

Alltavona (☎ 565067, W *www.alltavona .co.uk)* B&B from £25 per person. This lovely Victorian villa has a great garden out back, sea views out front and excellent bedrooms (all en suite).

Glenrigh Guest House (☎/fax 562991) Singles/doubles £25/46. This guesthouse, in a gorgeous sandstone terrace, does particularly good B&B.

Barriemore Hotel (☎/fax 566356) B&B £23 per person. Closed Dec-early Mar. The sturdy, old, bluestone Barriemore is the last in this strip on the Esplanade but definitely not least, with its magnificent views and great breakfasts.

You'll find plenty more less enticing B&Bs along Soroba Rd and Glencruitten Rd. Friendly *Kathmore (☎ 562104, Soroba Rd)* is one of the better ones, with B&B for £15 to £22.50 per person; they also do decent food.

Hotels *Kimberley Hotel (☎ 571115,* W *www.kimberley-hotel.com, 13 Dalriach Rd)* Singles/doubles £70/130. Oban's grandest boutique hotel, the classy Kimberley has spectacular views and beautifully decked-out rooms. The 19th-century home is at the top of steep Dalriach Rd.

There are also several cheaper – but still classy – guesthouses nearby on Dalriach Rd; the best is *Glenbervie (☎ 564770)*, with rooms from £22 per person.

Regent Hotel (☎ 562341, fax 565816, Corran Esplanade) Singles/doubles from £35/60. On the waterfront near the town centre, the Art Deco Regent has comfortable, if faded, rooms, a decent restaurant and a remarkably grim bar downstairs.

Manor House (☎ 562087, fax 563053, Gallanach Rd) Doubles £64-120. Around the bay, where the rich folk dwell, is stylish Manor House, Oban's top hotel. Built in 1780, the building originally belonged to the duke of Argyll, and later served time as Oban's first bank.

Places to Eat
Oban has no shortage of eateries, though there's a distinct lack of quality. Besides what's listed here, you'll find few other culinary delights.

Manor House (see Places to Stay) Mains £12-16. If you're far too poor to stay at Manor House but rich enough to afford their glorious French or Scottish cuisine you'll never regret it. It opens for lunch and dinner daily March to October, and Monday to Saturday November to February.

Studio Restaurant (☎ 562030, Craigard Rd) Mains £10-16. Open 5pm-10pm daily. This snug place, up the hill off George St, continues to deserve its reputation earned by its superb a la carte menu. It's often packed so book ahead. The set three-course dinner is a bargain at £13.50 (£11.50 before 6.30pm).

Eeusk Fish Cafe (☎ 565666, 104 George St) Mains £9-15. Open noon-3pm & 6pm-10pm daily. It isn't cheap, but the seafood at this semi-classy bistro – in a converted bank – is superb.

China Restaurant (☎ 563575, 39 Stafford St) Mains £7-9.50. Open noon-2pm & 5pm-10.30pm daily. Opposite the Oban Distillery, the enigmatically named China Restaurant cooks good Chinese meals (table service and takeaways are both available).

India Palace (☎ 566400, 146 George St) 3-course lunch £4.95, dinner mains £5-8. Open noon-2pm & 5pm-midnight daily. Oban's best tandoori has an all-you-can-eat buffet for £8.95 every night.

The Gallery Restaurant (☎ 564641, Argyll Square) Mains £4-6. Open 11am-10pm Mon-Sat. This first-class cafe, near Tesco, does simple light lunches and tantalising Scottish fare at night.

Cafe na Lusan (☎ 567268, 9 Craigard Rd) Snacks £1.90-5, mains £5.95-7.50. Open 11am-4pm Mon, 11am-9pm Tues-Fri & 10am-9pm Sat. This chilled-out cafe does sumptuous veggie meals and great coffee. Internet access is available for £3 per hour.

The Gathering (☎ 565421, Breadalbane St) Bar meals £4-5. Served 5pm-11pm. This place is a touch too touristy but as it's been here since 1882 and bar meals (avoid the restaurant) are cheap we felt compelled to include it.

Onorio's (☎ 565477, George St) Open 5pm-10pm daily Apr-Oct. If you're after great takeaway fish and chips (from £4), Onorio's does the best in town.

F'eats (☎ 565422, 1 John St) Sandwiches £2.70-3.95. The pannini (£3.20) at this perfect sandwich joint are spectacularly good.

Cafe Julie (☎ 565952, 37 Stafford St) Sandwiches £2.10-3.20. Open 10.30am-5pm Mon-Sat & noon-4pm Sun Apr-Oct. Nip into Julie's (opposite the distillery) for coffee and cake, tea and a scone, or some delicious Luca's ice cream.

Shellfish Bar (Railway Pier) Sandwiches £2.20-2.50. Open 9am-6pm daily. Oban's renowned seafood stall has fresh or cooked fish and seafood to take away – try a prawn sandwich (£2.50) or oysters (45p each).

Self-caterers will revel in the glory of Oban's huge *Tesco*, the largest supermarket in the area (there's a big Safeway in Fort William).

Entertainment

Let's state the obvious: Oban ain't no Ibiza (thankfully), and most of the town's pubs are, at best, mildly terrifying places to drink. In fact, Oban mostly has places at which to get drunk rather than to drink. But there are exceptions.

Oban Inn (☎ 562484, Stafford St) The lively Oban Inn, overlooking the harbour by the North Pier, is exceptionally good. Its traditional bar (with wood panelling, brass, and stained glass), its wide range of single-malt whiskies and its great bar food make it worthy of all but the most grotesquely hip of visitor.

O'Donnells Irish Pub (☎ 656421, Breadalbane St) Open 2pm-1am Sun-Thur, 2pm-2am Fri & Sat. This Irish bar, opposite Oban Backpackers and downstairs from The Gathering restaurant, has Celtic music most nights and severely sloshed patrons every night.

McTavish's Kitchens (☎ 563064, 34 George St) Adult/child £4/2 show only. Open noon-2pm & 6pm-10pm daily. Shows 8.30pm-10pm May-Sept. The epitome of the kilts-and-tartan tourist market though it may be, there's still something mildly charming (perhaps too mild for some) about the Scottish show and dance put on by McTavish's each night. The food – standard fare such as haddock and chips (£7) or hamburgers (£6) – is unremarkable but affordable. The show only costs £2/1 if dining.

Lorne Bar (Stevenson St) Open noon-2am Thur-Sat. The renovated Lorne Bar plays host to Oban's skateboarding and scooter-riding community, as well as a few Generation Xers abandoned in Oban by their much cooler mates who moved to Glasgow long ago. When visiting Oban, said mates demand to be taken to the *Cooler (☎ 565078, 60 George St)*, a slick wine bar below Mondo restaurant, which aspires in its promotional material to 'Big City' bar status. It opens 10pm till the wee hours Thursday to Saturday.

If all this boozin' sounds too hectic for you, go see a flick at the *Highland Theatre (☎ 562444, 140 George St)*, which has two screens showing new releases.

Getting There & Away

Bus Scottish Citylink runs two to four buses daily to Oban from Glasgow (£11.20, three hours) and Edinburgh (£14.10, 4½ hours) via Inveraray. Four buses daily (except Sunday) follow the coast northwards via Appin to Fort William (£7, 1½ hours), with connections to Inverness.

Train Oban is at the end of a scenic route that branches off the West Highland Railway at Crianlarich. There are up to three trains daily from Glasgow to Oban (£15.50, three hours).

The train's useless for getting from Oban to other parts of Scotland. To reach Fort William, for instance, requires a trip via Crianlarich – get the bus instead.

Ferry The joy of Oban is its CalMac ferries. There are services to Mull (£6.10 return, five to seven daily), Colonsay (£17.20 return, three times per week), Coll and Tiree (£19.35 return, daily except Thursday and Sunday), Barra and South Uist (£32, five sailings per week) and Lismore (£4.10 return two to four daily, except Sunday).

Getting Around

Oban & District (☎ 562856) is the local bus company and has services up to McCaig's Tower and Ganavan Sands beach.

There's a taxi rank outside the train station. Otherwise call Oban Taxis (☎ 0800 123 444) or Kennedy's (☎ 564172).

Hazelbank Motors (☎ 566476, W www .obancarhire.co.uk), Lynn Rd, rents out small cars from £35/195 per day/week.

Rent bikes from Oban Cycles (☎ 566996), Craigard Rd, for £10 per day, or Hazelbank Motors for £14/60 per day/week.

KERRERA
☎ 01631

The easiest way to escape the hordes descending on Oban in summer is by ferrying to captivating Kerrera. The island provides perfect shelter from the harsh southwesterly winds that would otherwise batter Oban and, though Kerrera rises to less than a hundred metres, it has stunning views to Mull and back to Oban.

The isle has some of the area's best **walks**, including a 6-mile circuit (two to three hours) of the island, where you'll have the chance to spot wildlife such as Soay sheep, wild goats, otters, golden eagles, peregrine falcons, seals and porpoises.

Without leaving the shore in Oban you will be able to make out **Hutcheson's Monument** at the northern end of Kerrera; it's a memorial to David Hutcheson, founder of the steamer company he handed down to son-in-law David MacBrayne, and whose name the ferry service still bears.

The Bunk House (see Places to Stay & Eat later) overlooks **Gylen Castle**, built in the 16th century by the MacDougall clan and burned to the ground a century later. From the castle, you can look down the Firth of Lorne.

History buffs won't need to be told that near the ferry terminal at Horseshoe Bay is where Alexander II died in 1249, after being injured fighting Vikings in the first Battle of Largs.

Places to Stay & Eat
Kerrera Bunk House & Tea Garden (☎ 570223, e kerrerabunkhouse@talk21 .com) Dorm beds £8-10. On the island's southwestern corner, this attractive place in a converted 18th-century stable building does accommodation and simple meals. It

is advisable to book ahead, especially in winter. There are no shops on the island, though the Bunk House keeps basic supplies. The owners will pick up your luggage at the ferry if you're planning to walk around the island.

Ardentrive Farm Hostel (☎ 567180) Beds £8. Open year-round. A working farm at the northern end of the island, just south of the yacht marina, this place has basic accommodation. Book ahead before setting out.

Getting There & Away
The passenger-only ferry from Gallanach, 2½ miles south of Oban, is run by Duncan MacEachan (☎ 01631-563665) on request April to September (£3/1.50 return, bicycles 50p, five minutes, first ferry leaves at 8.40am, final service 6pm). Other months, or if there's a storm a brewin', you'll need to ring ahead. To request the ferry at Gallanach, simply turn the white timetable at the ferry slip over so it shows black; this will bring the ferry hurtling towards you. Turn it back to white before the ferry arrives.

LISMORE
☎ 01631 ● pop 150

It's only 4 miles to Lismore but, stepping off the ferry from Oban, it feels an age away. This quiet, fertile island (its name in Celtic means 'Great Garden') is about 9½ miles long and just over a mile wide, with a road running along almost its full length. With its gentle undulations and wonderful views over to Morven and Mull, it's a dream for cyclists and walkers.

There are a few scattered communities and two ferry terminals, one halfway up the east coast, at **Achnacroish**, the other at the island's northernmost point. Lismore Stores is the main shop and post office, north of Achnacroish, towards Clachan.

Lismore's main historical claim to fame comes in the tale of the battle between St Columba of Iona fame, and St Moluag, another proselytiser of the 12th century, to be the first to reach Lismore, and thereby win the rights to found the isle's first monastery. Moluag, in his religious fervour, was neck-and-neck with Columba right up until just before they reached the shores; to ensure he touched the isle first, Moluag pulled out his trusty knife and cut off a finger, which he threw onto Lismore, thus claiming possession.

Things to See & Do

Near the village of **Clachan**, in the north, stand the remains of the **Cathedral of St Moluag**. Though little of the church has been well preserved, it's still an interesting site. Nearby are the ruins of 13th-century **Castle Coeffin**, with a great coastal location. One mile away, on the isle's eastern side, is the 2000-year-old **Broch of Tirefour**, a circular tower built in AD 100 to provide refuge from Roman invaders. It has double stone walls reaching 3m in height.

Lismore's best **walk** runs from Kilcheran, in the south, up to the top of **Barr Mór** (127m), then southwestwards along the ridge to the southern end of the island, returning to Kilcheran by track. The round trip is about 6 miles; allow three to four hours to appreciate the fantastic views of surrounding mountains.

Places to Stay & Eat

The Schoolhouse (☎ 760262) B&B £20 per person. This B&B, just north of Clachan, is one of a few scattered around the island.

Self-catering options can be found online at W www.isleoflismore.com.

Getting There & Around

CalMac (☎ 566688) ferries depart Oban for Achnacroish two to four times daily, Monday to Saturday (passenger/car £2.45/21, 50 minutes). Argyll and Bute Council (☎ 01546-604695) sails from Port Appin to the isle's northern point eight to 12 times daily; the ferry takes passengers and bikes only (£1/free, 10 minutes).

The island postbus (☎ 01246-546329) does several runs Monday to Saturday, but only calls at the island's northern point at 12.40pm.

Lismore is great for cycling; contact Island Bike Hire (☎ 760213) to hire bikes from the ferry terminal at the northern point for £6/10 per half-/full day.

Rock Chick

At Lismore's southern tip is Lady's Rock, which becomes totally submerged at high tide. It takes its name from a plot hatched in 1523 by Lachlan Maclean of Duart Castle, just across the water on Mull, to dispose of his wife, Catherine.

Having failed to produce an heir for him, Lachlan rowed Catherine out to this rock at low tide and abandoned her in the hope she would drown when high tide came.

Rescued by a passing boat, Catherine – sister to the chief of the powerful Campbell clan – returned to her family, who some months later killed Lachlan in retribution.

NORTH OF OBAN
Connel

Four miles from Oban, Connel has a store, several places to stay and a rather average position, it must be said, on this stunning loch. The town's main (and only) attraction is to be found where Loch Etive exits to the sea under the Connel bridge, where there's an underwater rock ledge; at certain times of the tide, this causes **The Falls of Lora**.

Dunstaffnage Castle

Two miles west of Connel and easily reached by bus from Oban is Dunstaffnage Castle *(☎ 01631-562465; adult/child £2/1.50p; open 9.30am-6.30pm daily Apr-Sept & 9.30am-4.30pm Sat-Wed Oct-Mar)*. Built on a rock plinth around 1260, the castle was captured by Robert the Bruce during the Wars of Independence in 1309, and remained in the hands of his supporters until 1471 when it was captured by the Campbell clan; it was eventually destroyed by fire in the early 19th century. The nearby ruins of the 13th-century chapel are slightly creepy, as is the trip through the housing estate to get to the castle – but it's well worth the journey.

Oban Sea Life Centre

Sea lovers and those travelling with kids should stop at the Sea Life Centre *(☎ 01631-70386; adult/child £6.50/5.50; open 9am-*

6pm daily mid-Feb–mid-Nov), on the A828, just south of Barcaldine Castle. Local fish and sealife swim in well-presented tanks, and there are excellent displays, some interactive, explaining the ocean around this area of Scotland. The seals, fed hourly, will enchant youngsters. The centre also claims that fish and seals are returned to the sea at the end of each season.

You can get to the centre by Oban & District buses from Oban.

Port Appin

Fans of Robert Louis Stevenson's *Kidnapped* ought stop in Port Appin as the book is based on the 'Appin Murder' of 1752, when Colin Campbell was shot by a Stewart clan member.

There's no particular site for the murder, so a much better reason to stop is for a holiday snap of majestic **Castle Stalker**, which stands on its own island with a backdrop of highly photogenic soaring mountains. Built in the 16th century by the Stewarts of Appin, it fell into the claws of the Campbell clan after the 1745 rebellion.

Continue on from the castle to get to the Lismore ferry at Port Appin (adult/child £1/50p, 10 minutes, hourly in summer, every two hours in winter). Next to the pier is the ***Pierhouse Hotel*** (☎ 01631-730302), an upmarket pad with stunning views of Morvern and Lismore. Singles/doubles cost £45/80 and it does great seafood at lunchtime; mains are pricey at £14 to £18.

THE SLATE ISLANDS

The islands of Seil, Easdale and Luing are known as The Slate Islands because, from the 1600s on, they were responsible for much of Europe's roofing slate. Quarrying has long since gone, leaving behind ugly blemishes on the landscape that the environment will take centuries to even partially recover from. At the same time, there are still some worthwhile places to visit here.

Seil & Easdale

☎ 01852 ● pop 506

The small island of Seil, 10 miles south of Oban, is best known for its connection to the

mainland – the so-called **Bridge Over the Atlantic**, designed by Thomas Telford and opened in 1793. The bridge, formally known as the Clachan Bridge, has a high single-stone arch spanning the narrowest part of the tidal Clachan Sound, allowing small boats to pass underneath.

On the west coast, 4 miles from the Clachan bridge, is the pretty village of **Ellanbeich** (confusingly, it's also known as Easdale – the name of the small island across a narrow channel from the village), which seems at first glance to be entirely made of slate. There's a post office and grocery store here, as well as a vast array of quaint white-washed cottages. The village was built for slate quarrying, but the industry collapsed in 1881 when the sea flooded the main quarry pit, which can still be seen.

Coach tours flock to the **Highland Arts Studio** (☎ 300273; open 9am-9pm daily Apr-Sept, 10am-6pm daily Oct-Mar), a crafts shop and shrine to the eccentric output of the late 'poet, artist and composer' C John Taylor. Try to keep a straight face.

Separated from Ellanbeich by a 364m channel is the small Island of **Easdale**, which has old slate-workers' cottages and the interesting **Easdale Folk Museum** (☎ 300370; adult/child £2/50p; open 10.30am-5.30pm daily Apr-Oct), with displays about the slate industry and life on the islands in the 18th and 19th centuries. Climb Easdale's one hill (which soars to an awesome 38m) for a great view of the surrounding area.

Organised Tours *Sea.fari* (☎ 300003, Easdale Harbour) 2hr whirlpool trips adult/child £22/16.50; 15min Easdale Island trips £4.50/3. This company runs exciting boat trips in speedy semirigid inflatable boats to the spectacular Corryvreckan whirlpool (see the boxed text 'In a Spin' earlier in the chapter) and the remote Garvellach Islands.

Places to Stay & Eat There are a few B&Bs on Seil, and a smattering of hotels.

Inshaig Park Hotel (☎/fax 300256) B&B singles/doubles £43/70. Dinner & B&B £58/100. This grand Victorian pile, just outside Ellanbeich, used to be the foreman's house overlooking the slate yards and has been a hotel for decades. The current owners do a great job keeping the luxurious bedrooms spotless, and there are good sea views.

Tigh na Truish (☎ 300242, Nr the Bridge Over the Atlantic) Meals £5-8. Open noon-2pm & 6pm-8.30pm daily. At this little inn – the 'House of the Trousers' is the translation from Gaelic – islanders were forced to swap kilts for trousers before entering the bar in order to conform to the 1745 ban on Highland dress. These days the pub offers simple rooms with self-catering facilities (doubles cost £45). However, this place is more about booze and good grub. There's also a bar packed with character and a great beer garden.

In Ellanbeich village, the *Seafood & Oyster Bar (☎ 300121)* is a delightful whitewashed restaurant serving cheap seafood – £10 will get you a decent platter. Book ahead in summer.

Getting There & Around Oban & District (☎ 01631-562856) runs buses at least twice daily, except Sunday, from Oban to Ellanbeich and on to North Cuan for the ferry to Luing (see the Luing section for details).

Argyll and Bute Council (☎ 01631-562125) operates the daily passenger-only ferry service from Ellanbeich to Easdale (passenger/bicycle £1/free, five minutes). Most runs are on request; to call the boat to Ellanbeich pier, sound the hooter during daylight, or switch on the light at night.

Luing
☎ 01852 ● pop 180
Rugged Luing (pronounced ling), 6 miles' long and 1½ miles' wide, is separated from Seil by the narrow Cuan Sound. There are two quiet villages, Cullipool in the north, 2 miles from the ferry, which has a well-stocked shop and post office, and Toberonochy in the east. Little happens on Luing, besides cattle breeding (there's a well-known breed named after the island). But it's flat and ideal for cycling, or you can visit both villages, the fort, the ruined chapel and the scenic west coast on a pleasant 8-mile circular walk.

There are two **Iron-Age forts** on the isle, the best being Dun Leccamore, about a mile north of Toberonochy.

In Toberonochy are the ruins of the late-medieval **Kilchatton Church** and an unusual graveyard with slate gravestones.

Getting There & Around The small car ferry (☎ 01631-562125) from Cuan (on Seil) to Luing runs daily, roughly twice an hour (passenger/car/bicycle £1/5.20/free, five minutes).

There's a Monday to Saturday postbus (☎ 01463-256200) service around Luing, connecting to Ellanbeich on Seil.

Isle of Luing Bike Hire (☎ 314256) in Cullipool rents bikes for £6/10 per half-/full day; book your bike the day before.

ARDUAINE
The prettiest spot to stop on the A816 road from Oban to Lochgilphead is definitely **Arduaine Gardens** *(☎ 01852-200366; adult/concession £3/2; open 9.30am-sunset daily)*. About halfway between the two towns, these charming 20-acre gardens are set in an amazing point on Loch Melfort, with beautiful views over to the Slate Islands and Jura. Arduaine, meaning 'high green place', was begun in 1897 and passed through various hands until acquired by the NTS in 1992.

The best time of year to visit is in May and June, when the rhododendrons are out in full bloom, but at any time of year this place is thriving.

The gardens were built by James Campbell, who also built the stunning *Loch Melfort Hotel (☎ 01852-200233, W www.loch-melfort.co.uk)*, with its awesomely romantic views over the loch, and an excellent bar and restaurant. It has plush singles/doubles for £55/80, most with a view. It's a wonderful place to stop for lunch or a drink, especially on a fine day when you can sit on the lawn overlooking the bay.

KILMARTIN GLEN
Six miles north of Lochgilphead is Kilmartin Glen, an area filled with Bronze-Age and Neolithic cairns, 3m-high standing stones, sculptured stones, and ruined castles

and forts, making this *the* most important prehistoric site on mainland Scotland. Most remarkable among these impressive sites is the **linear cemetery**, a row of burial cairns that stretch off into the distance for more than 2 miles.

So impressive is the list of sites it's hard to describe in the space allowed; far better is a visit to **Kilmartin House** *(☎ 01546-510278, adult/child £4.50/3.50, open 10am-5.30pm daily)*. This interpretative centre, housed in the old manse by the church in the nearby village of Kilmartin, helps to explain the vast array of sites in Kilmartin Glen, via displays and audiovisual programmes.

Next door to the church are the **Kilmartin Crosses**, which date from around AD 1000.

A few miles south of Kilmartin village is **Móine Mhór** (Great Moss), a nature reserve home to a stunning range of bird and plant life, and also one of the last wild raised peatbogs left in Britain. Inside the flat expanse of Móine Mhór is the Iron-Age hill fort of **Dunadd** *(admission free)*, located on a rocky outcrop that dominates the area. This is one of Scotland's most important Celtic sites and was capital of the Scottish kingdom of Dàl Riata in AD 500; by tradition this was where Scottish kings were inaugurated, and carved into the summit are a footprint and bowl believed to have been used in the ceremony.

If you want to stay and explore Kilmartin Glen or Dunadd more, the best places are the **Kilmartin Hotel** *(☎ 01546-510250, Kilmartin Village)*, which has comfortable rooms for £30 per person and also does fantastic bar meals, or **Tibertich** *(☎01546-810281, e bar bara@tibertich.com)*, a farm in the hills north of Kilmartin Glen, which does B&B for just £17 per person.

LOCHGILPHEAD
☎ 01546 ● pop 2600

This sleepy town at the head of Loch Gilp is the administrative capital for the Argyll & Bute area and, besides that dazzling claim to fame, has little else going for it.

A planned town, it's laid out on wide, open streets lacking in charm. It is, however, a useful base for exploring the region and has a few decent places to stay and eat, and to buy supplies.

The TIC (☎ 602344), Lochnell St, opens April to October. On Argyll St, there's a post office and chemist, and two banks with ATMs on Poltalloch St.

If the weather's miserable and swimming is your thing, try the Mid-Argyll Swimming Pool (☎ 606676) on the A816 to Oban.

Places to Stay & Eat *Lochgilphead Caravan Park (☎ 602003, Bank Park)* Pitches £7.50. Open Apr-Oct. A short walk west of the town centre, this camp site also rents out bikes for around £10 per day – useful for getting to Dunadd and around Kilmartin.

Argyll Hotel (☎ 602221, e argyllhotel@ btclick.com, 69 Lochnell St) Singles/doubles £20/38. The whitewashed old Argyll, refurbished in early 2001, has spotless, quiet rooms on its second floor, and a steak-house restaurant (meals cost £6) and lively bar, with beer garden, downstairs. It's the best place to stay in town.

Stag's Head Hotel (☎ 602496, Argyll St) Singles/doubles £30/45. Mains £4.50-7. If the Argyll is full, this is another option, though a bit rougher around the edges. The restaurant downstairs though does a surprisingly international menu, from Thai vegetables to chicken Kiev.

Empire Travel Lodge (☎ 602381, Union St) B&B £22-24 per person. This comfortable, nine-room lodge in a converted cinema has basic rooms and does a mean fry-up each morning.

Foodwise, there are a few options; on Argyll St is *Cockles*, a fish shop with a well-equipped deli with all manner of delectables. A few doors down is *The Stables* cafe that does hearty soups (£3) and sandwiches (£2.30 to £4). Round the corner on Lochnell St are the *Taj Mahal* Indian restaurant *(☎ 606296)*, which does mains for £5 to £8, and a Chinese takeaway.

The *Spar* and *Co-op supermarkets* are on Argyll St.

Getting There & Away There are three daily Citylink buses from Glasgow to Lochgilphead (£7.65, 2½ hours), continuing to Campbeltown. There's also a daily (except Sunday) bus to Oban (£3.50, 1½ hours).

CRINAN CANAL
☎ 01546

The scenic Crinan Canal runs 9 miles from Ardrishaig, 2 miles south of Lochgilphead, to Crinan, 7 miles northwest of Lochgilphead. Completed in 1801, the canal allows seagoing vessels – mostly yachts these days – to take a short cut from the Firth of Clyde and Loch Fyne to the west coast of Scotland, avoiding the long passage around the Mull of Kintyre. You can easily walk or cycle the full length of the canal towpath in a day.

At the northwestern end of the canal *Gemini Cruises* (☎ 830238, Ⓦ www .gemini-crinan.co.uk, Kilmahuaig) runs two-hour trips (adult/child £12/7.50) to the Gulf of Corryvreckan. They also ferry groups to northern Jura (£40 for up to 12 passengers and bicycles, 30 minutes).

KNAPDALE

Running southwards from Crinan Canal down to Loch Tarbert and Kintyre is Knapdale, with its gently rolling hills and three distinct 'fingers' jutting into the Sound of Jura. There are plenty of walking trails here and more head-spinning views, this time to Jura in the west and Cowal in the east.

The **Knapdale Forest**, planted during the 1920s Depression, is dotted with tiny lochs and walking trails. The easiest trail starts from the B8025 near the town of **Bellanoch**. The same road leads through the picture-postcard town of **Tayvallich**, where you might choose to stop at the harbour-side *Tayvallich Inn* (☎ 01546-870282) for some of their delectable seafood, before continuing down to the medieval **Keils Chapel** and **Cross**.

Across Loch Sween from here is **Castle Sween**, a sprawled ruin surrounded by a grim caravan park, and a few miles south is the 13th-century **Kilmory Knap Chapel**. Carved stones inside the chapel are protected by a glass roof. Nearby is the impressive 15th-century **MacMillan's Cross**, a 3m-high carving that depicts the crucifixion on one side and a hunting scene on the other.

On the isolated southern tip of the third 'finger' of Knapdale is **Kilberry**. The main attraction here, besides the carved Kilberry Stones, is the *Kilberry Inn* (☎ 01880-770223, Ⓦ www.kilberryinn.com), offering achingly good seafood and an achingly quiet atmosphere. Singles/doubles cost £39/67.

INVERARAY
☎ 01499 ● pop 704

Like Lochgilphead, Inveraray is a planned town; where they differ is that Inveraray is a picturesque place that seems to have a life of its own, even though it's overrun by tourism. Set on the northern shores of Loch Fyne, Inveraray has splendid views over to Argyll Forest Park and the Cowal peninsula.

The town was built by the duke of Argyll in the 1700s in order to create a buffer zone between his gracious new Inveraray Castle and what he evidently saw as the filthy underlings in his employment. Elegant Inveraray is one of the earliest and best-preserved planned towns in Scotland.

There's not much more to the town than Main St that runs through it. The helpful TIC (☎ 302063), just off Main St on the street running along the loch, opens year-round. There's a Spar shop and two banks with ATMs, as well as a chemist.

Inveraray Castle

On the edge of the town, Inveraray Castle (☎ 302203; adult/child £5.50/4.50; open 10am-6pm Mon-Sat & 1pm-6pm Sun July & Aug, closed Fri Apr-June & Sept-Oct) has been the seat of the dukes of Argyll (the chiefs of the Campbell clan) since the 15th century. Today it resembles the Walt Disney ideal of castledom (if somewhat faded and jaded).

The current neo-Gothic castle, dating from 1745, includes whimsical turrets and fake battlements, as well as a magnificent armoury hall, which has walls patterned with an extensive collection of more than 1000 pole arms, dirks, muskets and Lochaber axes.

And if you think your family is complicated, visit the intriguing room dedicated to the excruciatingly violent family history of the Campbell clan.

There is also a wonderful garden, the highlight of which is a hill-top folly.

Inveraray Jail

The Georgian jail and courthouse (☎ 302381, Church Square; adult/child £4.90/2.40; open 9.30am-6pm daily Apr-Oct, 10am-5pm daily Nov-Ma) in the centre of town was the county courthouse and jail for Argyll from 1820 until the 1930s. It's now been converted into an entertaining tourist attraction. You sit in on a trial, try out a cell while chatty warders in 19th-century costume accost you, and discover the meaning of 'picking oakum'. The last admission is one hour before closing.

Inveraray Maritime Museum

The **Arctic Penguin** (☎ 302213, The Pier; adult/child £3/1.50; open 10am-6pm daily Apr-Sept, 10am-5pm daily Oct-Mar), a three-masted schooner built in 1911 and one of the world's last iron sailing ships, now serves as a 'unique maritime experience'. There are displays on the maritime history of the Clyde, piracy and the Highland Clearances, as well as archive videos to watch and activities for children.

Parish Church

These days Inveraray's town church is unexceptional, except in its role as an eye-catching roundabout. But things weren't always so simple. The church was originally two-in-one, built in 1802 with a wall splitting it down the middle, dividing the Gaelic- and English-speaking patrons. But by the 1950s, with few Gaelic speakers left, that portion of the church was turned into a hall.

Places to Stay & Eat

Argyll Caravan Park (☎ 01499-302285) Pitches £8. Open Apr-Sept. In a former navy base, this camp site on the A83 has good facilities.

Inveraray Youth Hostel (☎ 302454, Dalmally Rd) Beds £8.50/7.25. Open Apr-Sept. In a grey, miserable modern bungalow on the left just through the arched entrance to Dalmally Rd, is this clean and well-run SYHA hostel.

The Old Rectory (☎ 302280, Main Rd) B&B £17.50 per person. In a pretty row of terraces on the waterfront (just before you reach the centre of town on the road from Lochgilphead), the Old Rectory has comfortable, neat rooms and helpful owners.

Claonairigh House (☎ 302160, Bridge of Douglas) B&B £16-24 per person. Set in a grand house dating from 1745, this B&B has three hectares of garden on the bank of a salmon river (fishing available). It's 4 miles south of town on the A83.

Argyll Hotel (☎ 302466, W www.the-argyll-hotel.co.uk, Front St) B&B £55-67 per person. Dinner & B&B £75-89 per person. A touch expensive, the plush four-star Argyll with its loch views still has the weight of history on its side. Among past guests are Boswell and Johnson, Dorothy Wordsworth, and Robert Burns, who wrote of the hotel 'There's nathing here but Highland pride/And Highland scab and hunger/If Providence has sent me here/Twas surely in anger'.

George Hotel (☎ 302111, Main St East) Bar meals £4.75-6.25. This whitewashed pub is a cosy place for a meal, with peat fires, stone walls and excessively low ceilings. They do mostly pastas, steaks and stews. Their accommodation is also decent, if basic; B&B costs £20 to £30 per person.

Loch Fyne Oyster Bar (☎ 600236, Clachan, Cairndow) Mains £7.25-19.95. Open 9am-9pm daily. The best place to eat in the area – perhaps in Argyll – is the Loch Fyne Oyster Bar, 6 miles north of Inveraray on the A83. The menu includes local mussels and oysters, and there's a good range of fresh and smoked fish and shellfish. The neighbouring shop sells packaged seafood to take away.

The Coffee House (☎ 302132, 1 Quay Close) Mains £3-6. Near the pier and maritime museum, this place does good baked potatoes (£3), as well as simple pasta dishes.

Fernpoint Hotel (☎ 302170, Nr the pier) Mains £5.50-7. Though the B&B (from £23 per person) doesn't much bear thinking about, the food does and, if it can be eaten in the fantastic beer garden overlooking Loch Fyne, all the better.

Getting There & Away

There are five daily Citylink buses (four on Sunday) to Inveraray from Glasgow (£6.90,

1¾ hours). Three of these continue on to Campbeltown and Lochgilphead (£7.60, 2½ hours); others continue to Oban (£4.90, 1¼ hours).

LOCH AWE & AROUND

Loch Awe, with rolling forested hills at its southern end and spectacular mountains at its north, is beautiful: its brooding, black waters stretch over 24 miles, though it's little more than a mile wide. The lake is made all the more haunting by soaring **Ben Cruachan** (1126m) in the north, and the gentle **Inverliever Forest** in the south.

At its northern end, there are also islands you can visit: **Inishail** has a ruined church and **Fraoch Eilean** a broken-down castle. For details of boat hire, contact Oban TIC (☎ 01631-563122).

The might of the water flowing out of Loch Awe, through the Pass of Brander to Loch Etive and the sea, caused construction of the Awe Barrage electricity generator and, if you're fascinated by all things electrical, you can take a tour of **Cruachan Power Station** (☎ 01866-822618; adult/ child £3/1.50; open 9.30am-5pm daily Apr-Nov) by the A85 on the northern shore. Electric buses take you more than half a mile inside Ben Cruachan, allowing you to see the pump-storage hydroelectric scheme in action.

Nearby is the strategically situated and much-photographed **Kilchurn Castle** (admission free; closed winter). Built in 1440, the castle is situated on a tiny peninsula guarding the northern tip of the loch. Long held by the Campbell clan, it was enlarged in 1693 to garrison government troops during the Jacobite uprising; it was then abandoned in the 1750s after a fire ran through most of it. Nowadays it's a shell, although a very picturesque one. It's accessible by foot up a rough track from the A85, or you can take a tour on the *Flower of Scotland* steamboat, run by the **Loch Awe Steam Packet Company** (☎ 01866-200440). They sail hourly from Lochawe village pier to the castle, between 10am and 4pm daily from April to November (adult/child £4/3 return, 40 minutes).

If you want to run your own boat tour, trek across to the loch's western side to the village of Dalavich, 15 miles southwest of Taynuilt, to find **Lochaweside Marine** (☎ 01866-844209), who rent out boats from £32 per day including fuel, as well as fishing rods and permits from £11 per day.

If this all sounds too hectic, **St Conan's Kirk**, a mile south of Lochawe village on the A85, is a contemplative, if somewhat bizarre place that shouldn't be missed if you're passing. The original church, begun in 1881 and finished in 1886, was a tiny affair. But when eccentric architect Walter Campbell got his hands on it, he turned it into a heady mix of Norman mini-grandeur and Saxon strangeness. He began transforming the existing church in 1907 and, upon his death in 1914, his sister Helen carried out the remaining plans. The best parts of the church are definitely the views over Loch Awe through its clouded glass, and the cloisters in the northwestern corner of the church.

Dalmally (pop 300), near the loch's northern end, is popular with anglers, and has a train station, post office, shop and the **Glenorchy Lodge Hotel** (see Places to Stay & Eat later in the section for details).

Glen Orchy

Not far from Dalmally, take the tiny B8074 road and follow beautiful Glen Orchy to the Bridge of Orchy and Loch Tulla, where there are lots of Munros to spot or bag. (Alternatively, follow the grim A85 to Tyndrum if you're in a hurry.) The A82 Glasgow–Fort William road passes the eastern side of Loch Tulla, but go around to Black Mount on the western side and you'll have perfect silence in which to ponder the remnants of the ancient Caledonian pine forest.

Pass of Brander

Loch Awe escapes to the sea through the narrow Pass of Brander ('brander', loosely translated from Gaelic, means 'ambush'), where Robert the Bruce defeated the MacDougall clan. At its narrowest point, so the tale goes, an elderly woman once held back an entire army equipped with nothing but a scythe and fiery attitude.

Places to Stay & Eat

Loch Awe has a scarcity of cheap B&Bs.

Loch Awe Hotel (☎ *01838-200261, fax 200379*) Singles/doubles from £33/60. Open Feb-Dec. This Scottish baronial pile sits on the busy A85 with perfect views over Kilchurn Castle. Its Travelodge-esque rooms would seem more at home in a Denver motel, but they're comfortable enough.

Tower of Glenstrae (☎ *01838-200285*) B&B from £30 per person. This impeccably well-maintained late-19th-century house, a few hundred metres from the Loch Awe Hotel, is much more romantic, and has an almost identical view of Kilchurn Castle. The rooms are furnished handsomely.

Ardnaiseig Hotel (☎ *01838-83333,* W *www.ardnaiseig-hotel.com, 3 miles east of Kilchrenan*) Singles/doubles £65/130. The ultimate in luxury and romance for this part of the world, the Ardnaiseig sits opulently on the tranquil shores of Loch Awe just waiting for film-location scouts to discover it.

Glenorchy Lodge Hotel (☎ *01838-200312, Dalmally*) Singles/doubles from £30/50. This hotel in Dalmally was built as a hunting lodge. It does decent counter bar meals for £5.

Bridge of Orchy Hotel (☎ *01838-400208, fax 400313, Bridge of Orchy*) Singles/doubles from £25/40. Bunkhouse beds from £9. About 13 miles from the north of Loch Awe on the A82, this hotel has beautifully decked-out rooms and a large bunkhouse (without a kitchen).

Back in Lochawe village is the **Tight Line** (☎ *01838-200215*), which does reasonable bar meals for £3.95 to £5.50.

Getting There & Around

Trains from Glasgow to Oban stop at Dalmally and Lochawe village, while trains from Glasgow to Fort William stop at Bridge of Orchy. Scottish Citylink buses from Glasgow to Oban go via Dalmally, Lochawe village and Cruachan Power Station. Bridge of Orchy is served by the Glasgow to Fort William Citylink bus.

A postbus (☎ 01246-546329) operates in the area Monday to Saturday.

LOCH ETIVE

One of Scotland's most exquisite sea lochs, Loch Etive extends for 17 miles from Connel to Kinlochetive and is flanked by some impressive mountains, including **Ben Cruachan** (1126m) and **Ben Starav** (1078m).

Taynuilt

☎ 01866 ● pop 700

A couple of miles west of the Pass of Brander is Taynuilt, near the shores of Loch Etive. Its main attraction is the **Bonawe Iron Furnace** (☎ *822432; adult/child £2.30/1.75; open 9.30am-6.30pm daily Apr-Sept, irregular hours Oct-Nov*). Founded in 1753 by a group of Cumbrian ironmasters, at the peak of production in the mid-1800s, it produced more than 600 tonnes of pig iron per year. It's the best-preserved charcoal-burning ironworks in Scotland, and has an excellent exhibition.

Near the Bonawe Heritage Centre, is the pier that **Loch Etive Cruises** (☎ *822430*) sails from. They go to the head of the loch and back one to three times daily from April to October. There are 1½-hour and three-hour cruises (£5 and £8 respectively); you may see eagles, otters, seals and deer.

On the southern side of the village is a road known as the Glen Lonan Rd; about 2 miles along this road are Barguillean's **Angus Gardens**, an exquisite, peaceful garden dedicated to the memory of journalist Angus McDonald, killed while reporting on the Cyprus conflict in 1956.

The best place to stay is the **Taynuilt Hotel** (☎ *822437*), which does B&B for around £20 per person. Taynuilt has a few of grocery shops and the **Robin's Nest** tearoom for snacks and lunches.

Scottish Citylink buses and trains to and from Oban stop in Taynuilt.

Isle of Mull

Second only to Skye in the popularity stakes, Mull is second to none in rainfall. Virtually no visit to this fascinating isle is complete without a good soaking or two, whenever you're here.

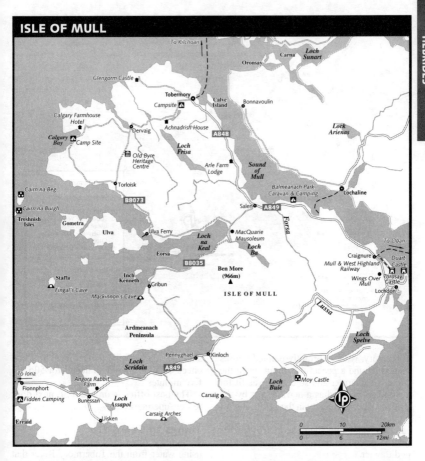

ISLE OF MULL

To Kilchoan

Loch Carna *Loch Sunart*

Oronsay

Glengorm Castle

Tobermory
Campsite

Calve Island

Bonnavoulin

Calgary Farmhouse Hotel

Dervaig

Achnadrish House

Loch Arienas

Calgary Bay Camp Site

A848

Old Byre Heritage Centre

Loch Frisa

Arle Farm Lodge

Sound of Mull

Cairn na Beg

Torloisk

Balmeanach Park Caravan & Camping

Lochaline

B8073

Salen A849

Treshnish Isles

Cairn na Burgh

Gometra

Ulva

Ulva Ferry

MacQuarie Mausoleum

Forsa

To Oban

Eorsa

Loch na Keal

Loch Ba

Craignure

Duart Castle

Staffa

Inch Kenneth

Gribun

B8035

Ben More (966m) ▲

Mull & West Highland Railway

Wings Over Mull

Torosay Castle

Fingal's Cave

Mackinnon's Cave

ISLE OF MULL

Lochdon

Ardmeanach Peninsula

Lussa

Loch Spelve

To Iona

Pennyghael Kinloch

Loch Scridain A849

Loch Buie

Moy Castle

Fionnphort

Angora Rabbit Farm

Fidden Camping

Bunessan

Loch Assapol

Carsaig

Erraid

Uisken

Carsaig Arches

0 ———— 10 ———— 20km
0 ———— 6 ———— 12mi

Funnily enough, it isn't the weather that keeps visitors returning, it's the variety of the place: hospitable locals, spectacular mountains, tranquil beaches, unique castles and some of the prettiest Hebridean villages.

ORIENTATION & INFORMATION

Almost two-thirds of Mull's population live in the ultra-pretty northern capital, Tobermory. Most visitors arrive at Craignure, on the island's southeast coast, where ferries from Oban stop. Fionnphort is at the far western tip of the Ross of Mull, where Iona ferries depart.

You'll find TICs at Tobermory and Craignure. There's a bank with an ATM at Tobermory. Every town has a foodstore and post office, though Tobermory's Co-op supermarket is the best place for provisions.

The hospital (☎ 01680-300392) is centrally located at Salen. For a doctor in Tobermory or Bunessan call ☎ 01688-302013 or ☎ 01681-700261 respectively.

TOBERMORY

☎ 01688 ● pop 840

Set on a sheltered bay surrounded by steep hills, there are few prettier ports than

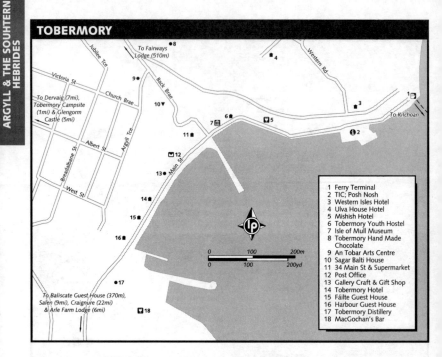

TOBERMORY

To Fairways Lodge (510m)

Jubilee Tce

Victoria St

To Dervaig (7mi), Tobermory Campsite (1mi) & Glengorm Castle (5mi)

Church Brae

Back Brae

Western Rd

To Kilchoan

Albert St

Breadalbane St

Argyll Tce

Main St

West St

To Baliscate Guest House (370m), Salen (9mi), Craignure (22mi) & Arle Farm Lodge (6mi)

1   Ferry Terminal
2   TIC; Posh Nosh
3   Western Isles Hotel
4   Ulva House Hotel
5   Mishish Hotel
6   Tobermory Youth Hostel
7   Isle of Mull Museum
8   Tobermory Hand Made Chocolate
9   An Tobar Arts Centre
10 Sagar Balti House
11 34 Main St & Supermarket
12 Post Office
13 Gallery Craft & Gift Shop
14 Tobermory Hotel
15 Fáilte Guest House
16 Harbour Guest House
17 Tobermory Distillery
18 MacGochan's Bar

0   100   200m
0   100   200yd

Tobermory, with its brightly painted houses ranged around a peaceful harbour; even the name is a charmer and so cute it was fit for a womble. Planned as a herring port by the British Fisheries Society in the 1700s, it wasn't destined to become a thriving hub of fish-catching, and nowadays scores of yachts littered around the harbour far outnumber the odd trawler.

Unless you're a car nut, stay away from Mull at all costs during mid-October when the **Mull Car Rally** is on; up to 3000 rev-heads flood the island, many roads are closed and finding somewhere to stay can be difficult. Much more peaceful is the traditional Scottish music festival, held each Easter; the crowds are more your pipe-and-fiddle-loving-music-intelligentsia types, but the island gets just as full.

Information

The helpful TIC (☎ 302182), beside the ferry terminal, opens 10am to 5pm (later in summer) daily April to October. You can check email at the youth hostel for 50p per five minutes.

The post office is on Main St, next door to the supermarket.

Things to See & Do

The smoky Tobermory Single Malt is made using water from the Tobermory River that comes thundering down the hill at the harbour's southern end. A tour of the **Tobermory Distillery** (☎ 302645, Main St; adult/child £2.50/1; open 10.30am-4pm Mon-Fri Easter-Oct, tours every 30 mins) will let you in on the secrets of this lovely liquid and includes a dram.

If chocolate's more your thing, **Tobermory Hand Made Chocolate** (☎ 302526, Main St on Back Brae corner; open 9.30am-5pm Mon-Sat & noon-4pm Sun) is where to go for your cocoa fix. In summer they run children's workshops at 11am on Tuesday and Thursday.

The **Hebridean Whale & Dolphin Trust's Marine Discovery Centre** *(☎ 302620, 28 Main St; admission free; open 10am-5pm Mon-Fri & 11am-4pm Sun Apr-Oct, 11am-5pm Mon-Fri Nov-Mar)* has videos and interactive exhibits on dolphin and whale biology and ecology.

Based in a renovated Victorian school overlooking Tobermory Bay is **An Tobar Arts Centre** *(☎ 302211, fax 302218, Argyll Terrace; open 10am-6pm Mon-Sat & 1-4pm Sun Apr-Oct, 10am-4pm Tues-Sat Nov-Mar)*, which has a regular programme of art exhibitions, music and workshops. It also has – wait for it – divine views.

If you've spent countless sleepless nights wondering how a croft fireplace works, you'll find solace at the quaint **Isle of Mull Museum** *(☎ 01688 302208; adult/child £1/50p; open 10am-4pm Mon-Fri & 10am-1pm Sat Easter-Oct)*. Its cluttered displays on the isle's geology and history since AD 1000 make it an ideal place to while away a few rainy hours. It has an interesting section on the Tobermory Galleon.

Finally, if you're after something for the folks back home, you'll do no better than the *Gallery Craft & Gift Shop (☎ 302114)* in an old church on the harbour. There's some tourist tack here, but you'll also find wonderful local arts and crafts.

Places to Stay

Accommodation in Tobermory fills up quicky, especially in summer, so it is advisable to book ahead.

Tobermory Campsite (☎ 302525, ⓔ angus .williams@icscotland.net, Newdale, Dervaig Rd) Adult/child £3.50/2 per night. Open Mar-Oct. This peaceful, riverside site is a mile west of town on the Dervaig road.

Tobermory Youth Hostel (☎ 302481, Main St) Beds £8.75/7.50. Open Mar-Oct. On the waterfront, this SYHA hostel has institutional rooms matched in cleanliness only by the excellent kitchen.

Arle Farm Lodge (☎ 01680-300343, Arle Farm, Aros) Dorm beds £11. This modern, well-appointed place, 6 miles south of Tobermory on the road to Craignure, has 26 hostel-style beds.

34 Main St (☎ 302530) Singles/doubles £10/20. This no-nonsense place (without a sign outside) doesn't do breakfast and has tiny rooms, but, even so, why can't there be more like it? Clean, functional and cheap, it's constantly full over summer.

Harbour Guest House (☎ 302209, 59 Main St) B&B £20 per person. Simple, comfortable rooms, kindly owners and fair prices make this a good place to stay.

Fáilte Guest House (☎/fax 302495, Main St) B&B £20 per person. A simple, unspectacular B&B on the waterfront with pleasant rooms and friendly owners.

Baliscate Guest House (☎ 302048, ⓦ www.baliscate.com) B&B £23 per person. Up the *steep* hill at the harbour's southern end, Baliscate is set well back from the road at the end of a glorious rambling garden. Rooms are none too stylish but they're comfortable, and the breakfast is delicious.

Tobermory Hotel (☎ 302091, ⓔ tobhotel @tinyworld.co.uk, Main St) Singles/doubles £45/80. The swish rooms of this charming hotel on the waterfront are perfect, and their restaurant, the Water's Edge, is possibly Mull's best. Oozing class is an understatement.

Western Isles Hotel (☎ 302012, fax 302297 ⓔ wihotel@aol.com) Singles £41-180, doubles £82-190. One of Mull's top hotels, this grand Victorian pile commands the heights above the harbour. Rooms are luxurious and the flash conservatory bar has panoramic views.

Ulva House Hotel (☎/fax 302044, ⓔ info@ulvahousehotel.co.uk, Western Rd) Dinner B&B £47.50-54.50 per person. The snug, six-room Ulva House overlooks the harbour from above the ferry terminal. The food is top notch, and there are log fires to warm your weary feet by after a hard day's hiking.

Fairways Lodge (☎/fax 302238, ⓔ derek _mcadam@msn.com, Erray Rd) B&B £28 per person. The hotel's spectacular views and nine-hole course make it golfer heaven; green fees are cheaper for guests, who also enjoy comfy rooms.

Glengorm Castle (☎ 302321) B&B from £50 per person. Glengorm is an impressive, rambling castle overlooking the Atlantic that's about 5 miles northwest of Tobermory.

Places to Eat

Sagar Balti House (☎ 302422, Back Brae) Mains £7-12. Open noon-2pm and 5pm-11.30pm daily. Kashmir has come to Tobermory, and we should be grateful. This delectable eatery serves meals with style, and while it ain't cheap, portions are generous and the staff are ultra-professional.

Mishnish Hotel (☎ 302009, Main St) Mains £4.50-12.50. You can't miss the virulently yellow facade of the 'Mish', favoured hang-out for yachties and local poets. It serves good bar meals, has a pool table and there's often live music and sometimes a disco. Local pubs don't come better than this in Scotland.

Posh Nosh (Above the TIC at the CalMac ferry terminal) Mains £3-6. Open 10am-11pm daily. Posh it ain't, and nosh it is (though only just). With its array of the usual fried food, this posh nosh may well clog your arteries, but the wonderful views from up here combined with the friendly staff will probably increase longevity.

For truly posh nosh, try *Pisces* seafood restaurant at the Western Isles Hotel or the *Water's Edge* at the Tobermory Hotel (see earlier); expect to pay around £20 per head plus wine.

For self-caterers, there's a decent-size *Co-op supermarket* on Main St.

Entertainment

A trip to Tobermory isn't complete without a whisky in front of the fire at the *Mishnish* (see earlier). Feel neglected if at least one poet doesn't try to sell you a book of his work.

MacGochan's (☎ 302350, Ledaig) Open 11am-midnight Sun-Thurs, 11am-2am Fri & Sat. The seedy vibe at this modern, waterfront bar feels more like Utah than Scotland, but there's good live music at weekends and, let's face it, beer is beer. On sunny days, their outside tables facing onto the harbour are wonderful, and the food (served noon to 10pm daily) is decent. Mains cost £4 to £6; the burgers (£4) are great.

NORTH MULL
Dervaig
☎ 01688

From Tobermory the road hairpin-bends its way steeply through the undulating terrain until, after 8 miles, you make a dramatic arrival at hills overlooking Dervaig, a charming village filled with stone whitewashed houses. The town's name means 'The Little Grove' and, when built in 1799, originally consisted of just 26 of these beautiful cottages (it hasn't grown much since).

Dervaig has a post office and small general store in the main street.

Dervaig's top drawcard is the **Mull Little Theatre** *(☎ 400245; adult/child around £12/7; shows begin 8.30pm Apr-Sept)*. With just 43 seats, it's Scotland's smallest theatre, but stages first-rate productions.

One mile south of Dervaig (take the Torloisk turn-off) you'll find the interesting **Old Byre Heritage Centre** *(☎ 400229; adult/child £3/2; open 10.30am-6.30pm daily Easter-Oct)*. Displays range from six cases of stuffed birds and a 40cm model of a midge, to Plasticine models of life on Mull and Iona from the Stone Age to the present. The centre's *tearoom* serves inexpensive snacks, including delicious soup and 'clootie dumpling' with cream.

Places to Stay & Eat *Glenbellart House (☎ 400282, Main St)* B&B singles/doubles £18/36. The affable owners and well-cared for rooms make this cottage (one of Dervaig's original buildings) charming.

Bellachroy Hotel (☎ 400314, Main St) B&B £28 per person. Comfortable rooms and excellent meals make this, Mull's oldest hotel, an ideal base in the area. Mains (£5 to £8) are your standard pub fare – haddock and chips, and the like – but done very well. There's a cosy pub, with live music Friday nights. You can also hire bikes for around £12 per day.

Achnadrish House (☎ 400388, [e] achnadrish@hotmail.com, Dervaig Rd) B&B £22-30 per person. This luxurious, romantic B&B, situated 2 miles out of Dervaig on the road to Tobermory, dates from 1695 and was once a shooting lodge for a much larger estate. The place is an absolute bargain and is run by a retired marketing chieftain for a multinational hotel chain, who spoils his guests.

There is the small *Coffee & Books cafe*, opposite the Bellachroy Hotel.

Calgary
☎ 01688

The white sands of Calgary bay are one of the gems of Mull. Designated an area of 'outstanding natural beauty' by the Scottish Scenic Trust, the beach is flanked by cliffs and has stunning views out to Coll and Tiree. The bay is about 4 miles west of Dervaig.

At the southern end of the bay is a very basic *camp site* charging £4 per person.

*The Calgary Farmhouse Hotel (☎/fax 400256, e farmhouse@virgin.net) £36 per person. The well-appointed rooms of this B&B are set around a courtyard, which has a stone-arched tearoom and gallery with works by local artists. It's a short stroll to Calgary Bay. There are also two self-catering apartments (sleeping two to four persons) for £360 per week. Their restaurant, the *Dovecote*, opens for dinner (mains from £12), and has delectable local meats and fish.

Salen
☎ 01680

Halfway between Tobermory and Craignure on the A849 is Salen – a small, practical town that can serve as a useful base for the area.

There's a few B&Bs in town. *Duntulum (☎ 300513)* is on the main road and is a nice enough place with comfortable rooms, all with bathrooms, for £18 per person. Directly across the road is *Aros View (☎ 300 372)*, which also has adequate rooms for around £20 per person.

The *Salen Hotel (☎ 300324, fax 300599)*, is more expensive, with singles/doubles from £21/52. Rooms are plain and functional, though the dining room has good views over the Sound of Mull.

The *Coffee Pot* next door to the town store does good snacks and a mean cup of tea.

Three miles southwest of Salen is the **Macquarie Mausoleum**, home to the remains of the 'Father of Australia', Lachlan Macquarie (1762–1864), successor to the unpopular William Bligh as governor general of Australia. Macquarie, notable for his humanitarian policies towards convicts and public works programmes, was a Scot and his tomb is maintained, on behalf of Australia's National Trust, by the National Trust for Scotland.

Five miles from Salen, on the A849 just before the Fishnish-Lochaline ferry turn-off, is *Balmeanach Park Caravan & Camping (☎ 300342)*, which has pitches for £8 per person, and a *cafe* doing great tuna sandwiches (£2.95) and home-made cakes.

ULVA

Ulva, meaning 'Wolf's Island' in Norse, is a peaceful place to escape the crowds thronging Mull in the summer. In the winter it's a bleak, romantically desolate place, which might be just what you're looking for.

Ulva lies just off Mull's west coast and is linked by a bridge to the even more remote **Island of Gometra**.

Once Scotland's main centre for – wait for it – kelp gathering, the island once had a population approaching 1000; kelp was an essential ingredient in soap production. Today the population has fallen to around 50, with many removed from the area in the clearances, in 1850. You can still see many of the derelict crofts used by farmers of decades long past.

A short walk north of the ferry landing is **Sheila's Cottage Heritage Centre** (☎ 500241; adult/child £4/2; open 9am-5pm Mon-Fri Easter-Oct, also 9am-5pm Sun June-Aug), a reconstruction of a traditional crofter's cottage, with displays about the island's history. The price includes the ferry.

The Boathouse tearoom, beside the ferry landing, serves locally harvested oysters with Guinness, as well as soup, toasties and filled rolls. Upstairs, an interpretative centre has information on walks and natural history.

There's no accommodation on the island, but you can camp; contact the **island caretaker** (☎ 01688-500264, e ulva@zetnet .co.uk) for permission.

The two-minute ferry crossing (☎ 500226; £4/2 including admission to the Heritage Centre) runs on demand during Heritage-Centre opening hours. At other times, phone to make arrangements.

STAFFA

This uninhabited island is one of Scotland's – and perhaps the world's – truly awesome natural phenomenons. Immense hexagonal basalt pillars loom out of the sea to form a series of cathedralesque caverns, the most notable of which is the stunning **Fingal's Cave**, which pushes up out of the sea like a grand pipe organ. When composer Felix Mendelssohn visited the cave, the sound of waves crashing inside made such an impact on him that he composed his *Hebridean Overture*; this led to a series of other visitors – Turner who painted it, Wordsworth who eulogised it, and Queen Victoria, who brought the masses in her wake.

You can land on the island and walk into the cave via a causeway if the sea is calm, but if it's rough, it's still worth making the journey – this place is that impressive, and some of the caves, such as **Boat Cave**, can't be reached on foot. Staffa also has a sizable puffin colony, north of the landing place.

Organised Tours

In summer, *Gordon Grant Marine* (☎ 700388) runs 2½-hour boat trips twice daily to Staffa from Fionnphort and Iona (adult/child £12.50/6.50). Tours on the *MV Iolaire* (☎ 700358) are similar and cost £12.50/5.

Turus Mara (☎ 0800 085 8786) runs 3½-hour boat trips to Staffa from Ulva Ferry in central Mull (£14.50/8). It also runs 10-hour day-trips (£24/12.50) to Staffa by bus and boat from Oban via Mull. More expensive tours take in Iona and the Treshnish Isles.

THE TRESHNISH ISLES

Two miles northwest of Staffa lie the Treshnish Isles, a memorable archipelago of deserted, volcanic islands. None is more than a mile long, and two of them – **Cairn na Beg** and **Cairn na Burgh** – are home to the remains of ruined castles.

The two main islands are **Lunga** and the curiously shaped **Dutchman's Cap**. You can land on Lunga and visit the shag, puffin and guillemot colonies on the west coast at **Harp Rock**. You can *camp* here, though you'll need to bring food and drinking water.

Gordon Grant Marine (☎ 700388) sails to Staffa and the Treshnish Isles from Fionnphort and Iona on Tuesday, Wednesday, Thursday and Saturday mid-May to July (£25/12.50, six hours). Turus Mara (☎ 0800 085 8786) sails from Ulva Ferry to the Treshnish Isles and Staffa daily except Friday May to September (£33/17, six hours).

BEN MORE & THE ARDMEANACH PENINSULA

At 966m, **Ben More** is Mull's tallest mountain and, with the exception of Skye's Cuillin Ridge, the only Munro not on the mainland. See Walking Around Mull later for details of climbing Ben More ('Big Mountain').

Surrounding it is dramatic landscape that feeds down into the Ardmeanach Peninsula. The B8035 road around the peninsula has fantastic views over to **Inch Kenneth**, which lies a few hundred metres off the coast.

Inch Kenneth was where Unity Mitford, infamous supporter of Hitler and the Nazis, saw out her final years. Living in Germany from 1934 to 1939, Mitford was brought home by her parents after shooting herself in the head with a gun given to her by Hitler; she'd done so soon after Britain had declared war on Germany. Her suicide attempt was successful, in a way: the bullet lodged in her brain and she died 12 years later of a brain abscess it had caused. Her life was later satirically chronicled by her sister Nancy in her book *Love in a Cold Climate*.

When passing through **Gribun**, where the houses fit tightly between the ocean and the spectacular cliffs above, spare a thought for the newlywed couple who on the day of their marriage, in the 1950s, were crushed to death when a boulder falling from these cliffs crashed through their roof.

If you're properly equipped and the weather is fine, strike out from the car and explore the peninsula on foot; its highlight is **Mackinnon's Cave**, at 182m long and 30m high one of the biggest in Scotland. If the tide is rising, *do not* – repeat, *do not* – enter the cave. Visitors have been drowned in the past (though they were allegedly the victims of the evil spirits who live here, not rising waters).

CENTRAL MULL
Craignure
If passing through Craignure, chances are you're getting on or off the 40-minute ferry service to Oban.

Though the village is not much more than a few cottages dotted along the waterfront, there's a TIC (☎ 01680-812377), opposite the quay, open 9am to 5pm Monday to Saturday and 10.30am to 5pm Sunday (it closes later in summer).

In the village, there's the ***Craignure Inn*** *(☎ 01680-812305)*, on the main road just south of the pier. Its four rooms are all cosy enough and singles/doubles cost £29/55. The bar does standard fare for £7 to £11.

In the village of Lochdon, 3 miles south of the ferry terminal, is the ***Old Mill Cottage*** *(☎/fax 01680-812442)*, an old corn mill lovingly transformed into a great B&B (£25 per person). The full Scottish breakfast is delicious.

Torosay Castle
Torosay Castle *(☎ 01680-812421; adult/child £4.50/1.50, gardens only £3.50/1; house open 10.30am-5.30pm daily Easter–mid-Oct, gardens open 10.30am-dusk daily Easter–mid-Oct)* is a rambling Victorian pile in the Scottish baronial style with a delightfully informal manner. 'Take your time but not our spoons', advises the sign, then you're left to wander at will or look through impressive family scrapbooks.

The castle is striking, but its real glory is its wonderful garden, with its statue walk and lush lawns with good views. In fine weather the superb downstairs ***tearoom*** spreads onto the lawns, doing soup (£2.75) and filled rolls (from £2).

Connecting Torosay Castle to Craignure 1½ miles away is the narrow-gauge **Mull & West Highland Railway** *(☎ 01680-812494; adult/child £2.50/1.50 one-way; open Apr–Oct)*. Proudly billed as the only island rail-

way in Scotland, this miniature steam train leaves from near Craignure (just past Sheiling Camping) and chugs along for a scenic 20-minute journey.

Duart Castle
We apologise for these stairs. They were built in 1360 to enable one man wielding a sword in his right hand to defend the entrance to the upper keep.
— a sign on Duart Castle's skinny stairwell

A 30-minute walk around the bay from Torosay Castle is dramatic Duart Castle *(☎ 01680-812309; adult/child £3.80/1.90; open 10.30am-6pm May–mid-Oct)*, a formidable fortress on this picturesque peninsula that juts out into Duart Bay and the Firth of Lorn, dominating the Sound of Mull. The seat of the Maclean clan, this is one of the oldest inhabited castles in Scotland – the central keep was built in 1360. In 1911, Sir Fitzroy Maclean bought and restored the castle. It's now complete with damp dungeons, vast halls and bathrooms equipped with ancient fittings. The real highlight of this place is the stunning views from the rooftop over the Sound of Mull and Loch Linne; they're unmissable on a clear day, when you can see Ben Nevis and beyond.

There's a wonderful *cafe* attached, where there's a dizzying array of scrumptious cakes (£1.20), home-made soups (£1.90), and Internet access for £1.50 per 15 minutes.

Wings Over Mull
Rounding off this mix of attractions is the outstanding Wings Over Mull *(☎ 812594; adult/child £4.50/1.50; open 10.30am-5.30pm daily Apr-Oct, flying displays start at noon)*. Located off the main road midway between Torosay and Duart castles, it's home to a collection of birds of prey from around the world. The trained birds give flying demonstrations, and can be viewed (in cages, mind you) up close when not in the air. Children will love it.

Lochbuie
A couple of miles past Duart and Torosay castles is the turn-off to Lochbuie, a remote,

peaceful beach 6 miles off the A849. Here you'll find the 15th-century ruins of **Moy Castle** that once belonged to the Maclean clan. Nearby is a **prehistoric stone circle**, a rarity in this region and certainly the only on Mull.

One of Mull's best walks is from here to the Carsaig Arches; see Walking Around Mull later in the section for details

ROSS OF MULL

Most zip through the Ross of Mull en route to Iona, but if you've got time there are several beautiful stops that might be as memorable as anything you see in Scotland.

Pennyghael

There are two hotels in Pennyghael, and little else, but it makes a good base.

Pennyghael Hotel (☎ 704288, fax 704205) Singles £30-50, doubles £65-72. Open Mar-Oct. This delightful hotel beside Loch Scridain has six well-maintained rooms, all with views over the loch and to Ben More, and a choice restaurant.

The Kinloch Hotel (☎ 01681-704204, e kinloch@ukgateway.net) B&B £34 per person. Open Easter-Oct. The Kinloch has simple rooms and friendly owners, and does bar lunches and dinners until 11pm daily. The views over Loch Scridain are stunning.

Surprisingly, the **Angora Rabbit Farm** *(☎ 700507; adult/child £2/1.50; open 11am -5pm Sun-Fri Apr-Sept)* just east of Bunessan is excellent. The owners are a touch miserable, and seem to derive far more pleasure from their bunnies than pesky visitors, but the rabbits are impossibly cute and fluffy. The daily clipping of the rabbits is at noon and spinning of their wool at 3pm. At the time of writing the farm's future was uncertain so ring ahead if you're keen.

Bunessan
☎ 01681

Bunessan is a charmless village, though there are some B&Bs here and a reasonable supermarket for supplies. There's also a police station (☎ 700222).

The village is home to the **Ross of Mull Historical Centre** *(☎ 700659; admission £1;*

open 10am-4.30pm Mon-Fri Apr-Oct, by arrangement Nov-Mar), which covers local history, geology, archaeology, genealogy and wildlife.

The Argyll Arms (☎ 700240, e argyll arms@isleofmull.co.uk) is grim outside, but its six rooms at £28 per person (B&B) are pleasant enough; some have views over Loch Scridain, though this is the loch's most dismal vantage point. We can recommend its bar meals (£4 to £10) whole-heartedly though; their occasional karaoke nights are good fun too, according to locals.

Uisken, a mile south of Bunessan, has a delightful beach with ruined crofts scattered along the foreshore.

Fionnphort
☎ 01681

At the Ross of Mull's western end is Fionnphort (pronounced **finn**-a-fort). It would be an utterly charming village, with its blend of pink granite rocks, white sandy beaches and vivid turquoise seas stretched out along the main road, were it not for the tawdry CalMac ferry terminal at the road's end; but it's a necessary evil, as Iona is what draws visitors through here.

The village's main attraction is the **St Columba Centre** *(☎ 700660; admission free; open 10am-6pm Mon-Sat & 11am-6pm Sun Apr-Oct)*. It has displays about the life of St Columba, the Celts, and the history of Iona. There's free long-term car parking here, for those staying on Iona more than a few hours (or if you'd rather not pay for foreshore parking).

Places to Stay If you're camping, the nearest site is *Fidden Camping (☎ 700427)*, a pretty but very basic site by the sea and behind a farmhouse in nearby Fidden, about a mile south of town.

There's a decent range of B&Bs, all dotted along the main road leading down to the Iona ferry slip.

Seaview (☎ 700235, e john@seaview mull.co.uk) Singles/doubles £22/40. This quaint granite building on the waterfront, at the top of the rise, looks onto the ocean. Its four rooms are nice, if a bit twee.

***Staffa House** (☎/fax 700677)* Singles/doubles £25/40. Slightly closer to the ferry terminal, Staffa House is surrounded by gardens and filled with antiques. There are three lovely rooms, and a conservatory in which to munch on breakfast while pondering some sterling views of Iona.

***Shore House** (☎ 700631,* e *i.slade@ zetnet.co.uk)* Singles/doubles £22/36. Right next to the ferry slip, this picturesque, whitewashed cottage overlooks both the Sound of Iona and the CalMac terminal. Rooms are small but serviceable.

***The Keel Row** (☎ 700458)* Open noon-midnight Mon-Sat, noon-4pm then 6-11pm Sun in summer, shorter hours in winter. This seriously cosy pub does a great lunch and dinner, with tasty burgers (£3.20) and nachos (£4). You can thaw out by the peat fire too.

The ***Ferry Shop**, Fionnphort's general store, is well stocked with supplies, and has a good range of magazines and even a decent bookshop. There are some local crafts too, as well as general tourist tat.

WALKING AROUND MULL
Ben More
The highest peak on the island, Ben More (966m) has spectacular views to the surrounding islands when the weather is clear.

A trail leads up the mountain from Loch na Keal, by the bridge on the B8035 over the Abhainn na h-Uamha, the river 8 miles southwest of Salen. There's good wild camping by the roadside here (ask permission first). Return the same way, or continue down the narrow ridge to the eastern top, A'Chioch, then descend to the road via Gleann na Beinn Fhada. The glen can be rather wet and there's not much of a path. Allow five to six hours for the round trip. Take care with your bearings, as the magnetic rock can play havoc with compasses.

Carsaig Arches
One of the best walks on Mull is along the coast west of Carsaig Bay to the Carsaig Arches at Malcolm's Point. There's a good path below the cliffs all the way from Carsaig, but it becomes a bit exposed near the arches – the route climbs then traverses a steep slope above a vertical drop into the sea. You'll see spectacular rock formations on the way, including one that looks like a giant slice of Christmas cake. The Nun's Pass is a gap in the cliffs, through which some nuns from Iona fled after the Reformation. The arches are two sea-cut rock formations. One, nicknamed 'the keyhole', is a free-standing rock stack; the other, 'the tunnel', is a huge natural arch. Allow three to four hours walking time plus at least an hour at the arches.

GETTING THERE & AROUND
The isle is well served by ferries. At least five ferries sail from Oban to Craignure every day (passenger/car £3.55/24, 40 minutes). For sailings to/from Kilchoan see The Great Glen & the Western Highlands chapter. From Lochaline to Fishnish, there's at least eight sailings per day (passenger/car £2.15/9.65, 15 minutes).

Most of the island can be reached via bus, with RN Carmichael (☎ 01688-302220) running regular services from Tobermory to Salen. Bowman's (☎ 01680-812313) takes care of the Tobermory–Craignure run with daily services year-round, and Highland Coaches (☎ 01680-812510) runs from Craignure to Fionnphort daily. TICs in Oban, Tobermory and Craignure stock the free *Mull Area Transport Guide*.

In Tobermory, Brown's Hardware Shop (☎ 01688-302020, fax 302454) at 21 Main St rents out bicycles for £8/13 per half-/full day. The gruelling cycle from Tobermory to Dervaig is highly recommended. In Salen, On Yer Bike (☎ 01680-300501) has bikes from £8 per day.

Iona

☎ 01681 • pop 175

The religious pilgrimage to beautiful Iona has these days been somewhat usurped by the tourist frenzy of day-trippers from Mull, who can make this tiny isle uncomfortably full; the island gets almost 200,000 visitors per year, a figure that's always rising.

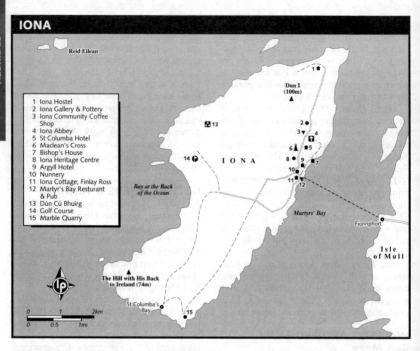

IONA

Reid Eilean

Dun I
(100m) ▲

1 Iona Hostel
2 Iona Gallery & Pottery
3 Iona Community Coffee Shop
4 Iona Abbey
5 St Columba Hotel
6 Maclean's Cross
7 Bishop's House
8 Iona Heritage Centre
9 Argyll Hotel
10 Nunnery
11 Iona Cottage; Finlay Ross
12 Martyr's Bay Resturant & Pub
13 Dún Cú Bhuirg
14 Golf Course
15 Marble Quarry

I O N A

Bay at the Back of the Ocean

Martyrs' Bay

Fionnphort

Isle of Mull

The Hill with His Back to Ireland (74m) ▲

St Columba's Bay

0   1   2km
0   0.5   1mi

Manage to stay overnight, though, and it's almost certain you too will harbour thoughts of a return to its impossibly turquoise waters, dazzling beaches and coves, and monumentally sacred sites. It's a very special place.

HISTORY

Pilgrims have landed on Iona for 14 centuries, since St Columba and his 12 disciples called the island home in AD 563. Known as the 'Cradle of Christianity', this was a centre of learning and artistic activity, especially during the Dark Ages when Iona at its zenith saw the creation of *The Book of Kells* (which now resides in Trinity College, Dublin).

In AD 794, Vikings came to Iona and within four decades extinguished the light of learning the island had become (the pinnacle of the Vikings' achievements was the slaughter of 68 monks in Martyrs' Bay).

By 1144, the Celtic Church was being suppressed by King David I, and within 50 years, Iona had become part of the mainstream church, with the establishment of the Augustinian Order of the Black Nuns, and the Benedictine monastery.

Then, in the 16th century, the Reformation saw Dunfermline overshadow Iona's power, and the island was ransacked, and all but three of its 360 Celtic crosses were destroyed.

Iona was again decimated in the potato famine in 1847, losing 98 islanders – more than a fifth of the population. Things had regrouped by the end of the century though, with holiday-makers and honeymooners beginning to spend time on the isle.

In 1899 the island's owner, the 8th duke of Argyll, gave Iona Abbey to the Church of Scotland, and repair work took place over the next two decades. In 1938, the Iona Community was formed and began to rebuild the monastery.

Today, almost the entire island is owned by the NTS, though the Iona Community still plays a big part in the upkeep of the monastery and abbey.

ORIENTATION & INFORMATION

Just 3 miles long and a mile wide, you can easily walk Iona in an afternoon. The ferry lands at the only village on the island, Baile Mór ('big village'), where there's a Spar shop and post office. There is no tourist information on the island; the nearest is the St Columba Centre in Fionnphort.

BAILE MÓR

Up the hill in front of the ferry slip are the picturesque ruins of the **nunnery**, with their tranquil cloistered garden. One of the best-preserved remains of a typical medieval nunnery, it was founded around AD 1200 by Reginald, son of Somerled the ruler of the Isles. It belonged to the Augustinian Order and was known as 'The Black Church', after the nuns' robes.

The nunnery was occupied until the 16th-century Reformation, when it passed into the hands of the Macleans of Duart, who allowed it to fall into disrepair.

Nearby, in the former manse built by Thomas Telford (of Caledonian Canal fame) is the well-maintained **Iona Heritage Centre** (☎ 700576; admission £1.50; open 10.30am-4.30pm Mon-Sat Apr-Oct). It has displays covering crofting, fishing, the island's lighthouses and history. There's soup, teas and cakes available in the centre's *coffee shop*.

Opposite the Heritage Centre stands **Maclean's Cross**, an intricately carved high cross, made in the 15th century – at its foot there's an armed horseman, presumably the Maclean chief who commissioned the cross. It stands in its original location, close to the former junction of three medieval streets linking the boat jetty, nunnery and abbey.

IONA ABBEY

Founded in 1200, the first abbey was tiny, and there was certainly no cloister. Over the next 200 years, various additions were made, especially from 1450, when 50 years was spent building the southern transept, which collapsed 300 years later. By 1899, the ruins were given to the Church of Scotland. Restoration commenced in 1902, and most buildings here were rebuilt or restored by 1910.

St Oran's Chapel, built in 1220 and located by the front gate, survives mostly untouched. It's quite plain except for an impressive Norman doorway.

Surrounding it is Iona's sacred burial ground, **Reilig Odhráin** (Oran's Cemetery), which contains the graves of 48 Scottish kings, including Macbeth's pal Duncan, eight Norwegian kings, and four Irish. The stones standing today though are mostly the graves of esteemed Highlanders. One recent plot belongs to former Labour-party leader John Smith.

On the **Road of the Dead**, which leads from the abbey to St Oran's Chapel, stands **St Martin's Cross**, the best example of a high cross left on the island; hundreds like it were once dotted everywhere around Iona. This one dates from about AD 800 and, with its huge arm span of 2.2m, is the largest in the British Isles. Composed of several huge stone pieces fitted together, its

St Columba

If you're a hagiographer (someone who studies saints), you'll already know about St Columba (*Colum Cille* in Gaelic). Born in County Donegal in AD 521, Columba was a descendant of a legendary 4th-century Irish king, Niall of the Nine Hostages.

Carefully groomed for the priesthood, Columba founded monasteries all over Ireland until, at age 40, he involved his clan in the bloody Battle of Cooldrevny, where many lost their lives.

As penance for his role in their deaths, he vowed to never again set foot on his beloved Ireland; instead he would gain as many souls for Christ as those he had lost at Cooldrevny.

Twelve disciples followed him, and in May 563 Columba set out in a small boat made of wickerwork and covered with hides (a *curaich*). Days later, they landed at Iona, and here Columba's work really began.

His 32 remaining years were spent preaching the Christian faith to northern Scotland, with remarkable success.

sections are carved with Celtic serpent-and-boss and spiral ornaments on one side, and with depictions of the Virgin and Child and Abraham sacrificing Isaac.

There's a reproduction of **St John's Cross** nearby; the original of this equally impressive cross is in the **Infirmary Museum** on the abbey's far left-hand side as you enter. Many other gravestones from Reilig Odhráin are in there too.

To the left of the abbey's main entrance is **St Columba's Shrine**, a steep-roofed little building where the saint was almost certainly entombed.

Make sure to pick up a map of the abbey *(HS; ☎ 700512; suggested donation £2; open year-round)* from the little hut at the gate as you come in.

Across the road from the abbey is the exquisite **Iona Gallery & Pottery** in a beautiful stone cottage. From here you can buy pottery and other local crafts.

WALKING AROUND IONA

Iona is a novice walker's dream: not only is it compact but the variety of landscape makes it ideal for those finding their feet. If you get lost, just walk in one direction for 20 minutes and you'll come to something!

The island's best walk is to the **Bay at the Back of the Ocean**, once the favourite walk of Labour's John Smith. It's a leisurely 2-mile plod along a quiet back road to one of Scotland's most sublime beaches. Nearby are the remains (admittedly not many) of Dún Cú Bhuirg, a small fort that's Iona's only Iron-Age monument.

More ambitious (though not much) walkers will head south for **St Columba's Bay** – also known as Port na Curaich ('harbour of the skin-covered boat'), because this is where St Columba is said to have first landed. The **cairns** you can see here were piled up by monks as a penance for their sins. Just northwest of the bay is a long-disused **marble quarry**, built in 1693 and last used in 1914; much of the abbey came from here.

The island's highest hill is **Dun I**, which rises to the dizzying height of 100m. From here there are stunning views to Mull, which are enchanting at dusk.

PLACES TO STAY
Hostels

Iona has only one hostel, and there's no camping on the island.

Iona Hostel (☎ 700642, e info@iona hostel.co.uk, at the far northern end of the island) Beds £12, sheets £1.50. This shiny new 21-bed hostel, opened in 2001, has stunning views to Staffa and the Treshnish Isles. Rooms are clean and functional, and the cosy, well-equipped lounge/kitchen area has an open fire and, best of all, duck eggs on sale for 15p each. To get there, turn right off the ferry and follow the road for 1½ miles until it ends.

B&Bs

There are few B&Bs on Iona, so it's essential to ring ahead, or be sure you can get back to Mull for the night. There is sometimes a list on the noticeboard just inside the cloisters at the abbey listing houses offering B&B.

Iona Cottage (☎ 700579) B&B £20-24 per person. This beautiful whitewashed cottage with blue trim, directly in front of the ferry slip, has some of the friendliest, helpful owners in the land. The views across to Fionnphort are stunning, and breakfast is a wonder to behold. The stylish rooms have futon beds.

Bishop's House (☎ 700800, fax 700801) B&B £24-31 per person. Open Mar-Oct. This intimidating old church quarters has spartan, comfortable rooms and great views over the Sound of Iona.

Finlay Ross (☎ 700357, Nr ferry slip) B&B £20 per person. At first glance, things are a bit grim at this place run by the general store. It's opposite the Martyrs' Bay pub (on your left as you get off the ferry), in a modern, drab single-story building. Inside, however, things are cheerier and you can fill up on a great breakfast.

Hotels

Argyll Hotel (☎ 700334, e reception@ argyllhoteliona.co.uk) Singles £43-46, doubles £44-96. The Argyll's quaint old rooms are cosy enough, but it's the roaring fire in the lounge room, the views from the sun-room out front, and the delightful staff that make this an enchanting place. There are also excellent dinner and B&B deals.

St Columba Hotel (☎ 700304, e colum ba@btconnect.com) Singles/doubles £38/75. Just down the road from the abbey, this well-situated but charmless modern building has stunning views to Mull, friendly staff and pleasant, functional rooms that make up for it slightly, as does the good food.

PLACES TO EAT

Argyll Hotel Bar lunches £4-6, 4-course dinner £19.50. Lunch 12.30pm-2pm, dinner 7pm-8.30pm. The island's top place to eat, the Argyll does mouth-watering meals made from fresh local produce. Prices are very reasonable, and if you stick to one or two courses, the damage won't be too different to a meal anywhere else on Iona.

Martyrs' Bay Restaurant (☎ 700382, directly on left from ferry) Mains £6-9. It might look a bit depressed, but inside this 1960s building lies great food, loads of quality alcohol and friendly bar staff. The fish and chips (£7) is a standout, and the views from the bar are incredible.

The cakes and soups at the *Iona Community Coffee Shop* (opposite the Abbey) are scrumptious; it opens noon to 4.30pm Monday to Saturday.

GETTING THERE & AROUND

The Fionnphort ferry (£3.30 return, five minutes) runs frequently between 8.15am and 6.15am daily. There are also various boat trips available from Oban to Iona – see Activities in the Oban section earlier.

Finlay Ross general store (☎ 700357) rents out bicycles for around £10 per day.

Coll & Tiree

Certainly the most isolated of the southern Hebrides, these two windswept isles seem at first sight barren and miserable, but they are as fertile and green as any in the region.

Because there are no mountains on these two low-lying isles, there's an outstanding record of sunshine – the clouds have no-

where to get stuck. That's the good news. The bad news is that it's often *very* windy; wind has formed sand dunes up to 30m high on the west coast.

COLL
☎ 01879 ● pop 172

This windswept, treeless island, 12 miles long and 3 miles wide, is shaped like, well, a fish. Surrounded by white sandy beaches and blue waters, isolated Coll is the perfect place for navel gazing. Of course, some places offer *too much* room to navel gaze; Dr Johnson, stuck indoors here for five days as punishing weather halted his and Boswell's journey to Skye, observed that he wanted 'to be on the mainland and go on with existence. This is a waste of life'.

The ferry lands near **Arinagour**, Coll's only village. Here you'll find Coll Stores, the Corner Shop and a post office.

Things to See & Do

If you're here to wander beaches, the best are on the western side and on the southern tip at **Crossapol Bay**, a huge expanse surrounded by towering sand dunes.

Nearby is the medieval **Breachacha Castle**, a restored tower built in the 15th century and now used as a school by Project Trust volunteers. The broken-down old mansion nearby (confusingly, also known as Breachacha) was the 'mere tradesman's box' where Dr Johnson and Boswell were stranded those five days in 1772.

At **Calgary Point** close by there's an **RSPB reserve** (☎ 230301) with a free information centre (open year-round); listen for the corncrakes walking on the machair.

It's worth making the effort to get up **Ben Houg**, the island's highest spot at a soaring 113m. It's a 2-mile trip from Arinagour, and the views are good. On the east coast you can stroll the gentle 3 miles up to quiet Sorisdale; there isn't much here except untouched wilderness and blue ocean.

Places to Stay & Eat

Garden House Camping (☎ 230374, Uig) Pitches £5 per person. Open May-Sept. Situated 4½ miles south of Arinagour, near

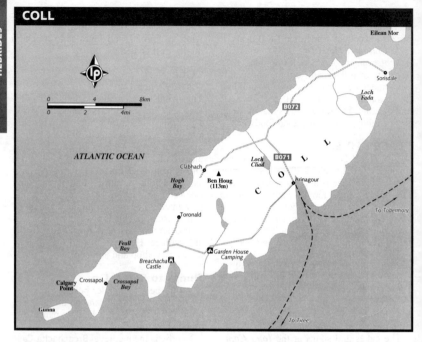

COLL

Eilean Mor

Sorisdale

Loch Fada

B072

ATLANTIC OCEAN

Clabhach

Loch Cliad

B071

COLL

Hogh Bay

Ben Houg (113m)

C

Arinagour

To Tobermory

Toronald

Feall Bay

Garden House Camping

Breachacha Castle

Calgary Point

Crossapol

Crossapol Bay

Gunna

To Tiree

0 — 4 — 8km
0 — 2 — 4mi

Breachachadh Castle, this is a basic site with toilets and cold water.

B&Bs include *Taigh Solas* (*☎/fax 230333*) in Arinagour, charging £18 to £22 per person, and *Achamore* (*☎ 230430*), 1½ miles north of Arinagour, for £20 per person.

Coll Hotel (*☎ 230334*, **W** *www.coll hotel.freeserve.co.uk, Arinagour*) B&B £25 per person, dinner & B&B £45. The island's only watering hole, the jolly old Coll has simple, tidy rooms and a great restaurant serving top-notch seafood.

For light meals and snacks, try the *Corner Cafe* in Arinagour, or the *Lochside*, also in Arinagour and open April to September.

TIREE
☎ 01879 ● pop 750

Tiree claims, far more triumphantly than Coll it seems, to be Scotland's sunniest place. While that's certainly true, the winds can howl through here just as bitingly as they do on Coll. Tiree is also so flat that it's

nicknamed 'The Isle Below the Sea'; a plus for those averse to cycling up hill.

But Tiree has turned this into an advantage by becoming Scotland's windsurfing capital, known to many (only half laughingly) as the 'Hawaii of the North', and the isle hosts the Wave Classic each October. With its long, sandy white beaches the Atlantic breakers roll in with monotonous regularity, as do the strong winds.

The ferry arrives at **Gott Bay**, towards the eastern end of the island. There's a bank (no ATM), post office and *Co-op supermarket* in Scarinish, the main village, a half-mile south of the ferry pier. There's another shop at Crossapol, just south of the airport, which is in the centre of the island. For the island's doctor, call ☎ 220323.

Five miles from Scarinish, hidden among the rocks on Vaul Bay, are the remains of **Dun Mor**, a Pictish Broch constructed in around AD 100. A farther 2 miles to the west is the **Ringing Stone**, a massive glacial

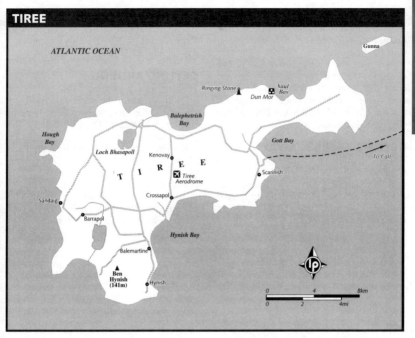

TIREE

ATLANTIC OCEAN

Gunna

Ringing Stone
Vaul Bay
Dun Mor

Balephetrish Bay

Hough Bay

Loch Bhasapoll   Kenovay   Gott Bay

T I R E E   To Coll
Tiree Aerodrome   Scarinish

Sandaig   Crossapol

Barrapol

Hynish Bay

Balemartine

Ben Hynish (141m)   Hynish

0   4   8km
0   2   4mi

boulder adorned with Bronze-Age cup marks that ring when struck. Island lore has it that should the stone ever be broken, Tiree will instantly plummet below the waves.

If genuine island history and genealogy are more your thing, head straight for **An Iodhlann** (☎ 220793), next to the shop in Scarinish. It has an interesting exhibit on island life. Better is the **Island Life Museum** (admission free; open 2pm-4pm Mon-Fri June-Sept) at Sandaig, in the island's far west; it's in a terrace of thatched buildings with a reconstruction of a 19th-century crofter's home. There is also a history of the island clearances on Tiree that saw the population fall from 4,500 in 1830 to less than half that 50 years later.

The **Skerryvore Lighthouse Museum** (admission free; open daylight hours) is at Hynish, near the southern tip of the island. The signal tower, pier and cottages, built using granite from the Ross of Mull, were used as a base for the construction in 1843 of the remote Skerryvore Lighthouse 10 miles to the southwest.

For the island's best views, walk up **Ben Hynish** (141m), at the island's southerly tip.

If you want to perfect your windsurfing, **Wild Diamond Windsurfing** (☎ 220399, W www.tireewindsurfing.com) runs courses at Loch Bhasapoll in Tiree's northwest; a five-hour beginner's course costs £40.

Places to Stay & Eat

Accommodation on the island isn't cheap. There's a basic *camp site* near the Co-op in Scarinish; if you want to camp elsewhere, ask permission from landowners.

Kirkapol House (☎/fax 220729, Gott Bay) B&B from £25 per person. The best place on the island, Kirkapol House is a converted 19th-century church overlooking enchanting Gott Bay.

Scarinish Hotel (☎ 220308, fax 220410, Scarinish) Singles/doubles £25/46. Overlooking the harbour in Scarinish, this is

Tiree's largest hotel with six simple rooms. A better option is the similarly priced *Tiree Lodge* (*☎ 220368, fax 220994*), with a great Gott Bay location.

Foodwise, the island's top option is *The Glassary* (*☎ 220684*) in Sandaig on the west coast. This tastefully decked-out place also does first-rate B&B from £28 per night. If that's too much of a hike, the *Tiree Lodge* does good bar meals.

GETTING THERE & AWAY

The CalMac ferry runs from Oban to Coll (3 hours, daily) and Tiree (4½ hours), except Thursday and Sunday (passenger/car £11.40/65, 2¾ hours). The same ferry runs between Coll and Tiree (£2.90/16.65, 55 mins) on the same days.

If the ferry's far too proletarian for you, British Airways (BA) flies from Glasgow to Tiree Airport (☎ 220309) daily except Sunday (around £100 return).

GETTING AROUND

The best way to get around Coll is walking or riding (unless the wind howls). Hire mountain bikes in Arinagour from Tammie Hedderwick (☎ 230382), Coll Pottery, for £8 per day.

On Tiree, you can hire cars from the Tiree Motor Company (☎ 220469) or McLeannan Motors (☎ 220555). For a taxi call ☎ 220344.

Rent bikes from Mr MacLean (☎ 220428) in Kenovay, just north of the airport. The postbus (☎ 220301) does daily runs (except Sunday), including an airport service.

The Central Highlands

Long, narrow lochs, purple moors, rocky mountains and bubbling burns all run through the central Highlands, a mishmash of several regions and the transitional area between the lowlands and the north. Northern Perthshire, the Trossachs, Loch Lomond and brooding Rannoch Moor make up this richly varied part of Scotland, once a stronghold of several warring clans. These days it's a peaceful place with a middle-of-nowhere atmosphere – so much so there's a village in it called Dull.

HISTORY
In the region's heart is the area of Breadalbane, stretching from Aberfeldy to Tyndrum, which literally means 'Scotland's uplands'. There's evidence of an early-Celtic settlement here and, according to legend, St Fillan, a healing monk, lived in the area with a wolf who befriended him.

Clans farmed the area up until the mid-18th century. Following the 1746 Battle of Culloden, in which many clansmen fought for the Jacobites, government troops burned clan villages and destroyed crops. After the Highland Clearances, rich landowners who were keen on field sports, built shooting lodges, developed grouse moors and bred deer in place of sheep.

Forestry was another important industry from the 17th to the 19th centuries, and logs were transported on the Rivers Tay and Tummel. Today the rivers are used in the production of hydroelectricity.

ORIENTATION & INFORMATION
The region begins just 20 miles north of Glasgow at Loch Lomond, which straddles the Highland line. Tourists have been visiting the Trossachs (the lochs and hills just east of Loch Lomond) for over 150 years – Queen Victoria among them.

Both Dunkeld and Pitlochry, to the north, are appealing though touristy places that are useful if you're doing some walking, as frequent buses and trains service them.

Highlights

- Hire a canoe and row the bonny waters of Loch Lomond
- Wander the pristine pine-covered hills and soaring peaks of the Trossachs
- Climb Ben Lawers near Killin for dazzling views of the Atlantic
- Get back to the Iron Age in a crannog at Kenmore on Loch Tay
- Listen to Britain's only private army piping at sprawling Blair Castle
- Walk wild, bleak and beautiful Rannoch Moor – if the weather lets you

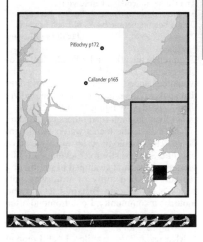

Pitlochry p172

Callander p165

And Rannoch Moor is a place you'll never forget if you elect to do some trekking across its soggy, romantic plains.

The following Ordnance Survey (OS) Landranger map sheets cover the Central Highlands:

Landranger 42: Glen Garry & Loch Rannoch
Landranger 43: Braemar & Blair Atholl
Landranger 51: Loch Tay & Glen Dochart
Landranger 52: Pitlochry to Crieff
Landranger 56: Loch Lomond & Inveraray
Landranger 57: Stirling & the Trossachs

GETTING AROUND

There are few parts of the central Highlands that are particularly difficult to reach by public transport, especially since so many buses and trains travel north from the transport hubs of Dundee, Perth or Glasgow to Inverness, Fort William or Oban.

By car it's also easily accessible as the huge A9 cuts a vast swathe through the region travelling up to Inverness.

Loch Lomond & The Trossachs

LOCH LOMOND

I'll take the low road,
And you'll take the high road,
And I'll be in Scotland before you.
But me and my true love will never meet again,
On the bonnie, bonnie banks of Loch Lomond.

Jacobite folk song

Captured in the aftermath of Culloden, Jacobite prisoner Donald MacDonnell knew he would be hanged, and penned this little ditty that spoke of his return to Loch Lomond via the low road – swinging from the gallows – rather than the high road others would take.

These days, the loch's waters would not be so readily eulogised by even the most patriotic Scot. Vastly overdeveloped on its western shores and swamped in summer by the self-satisfied army of waterway hotheads that make up Britain's jet ski and motorboat community, Loch Lomond often seems to be drowning under the weight of its own past glory.

Measuring 27½ sq miles, Loch Lomond is the largest lake in mainland Britain, and is in parts still quite eye-catching. But its proximity to Glasgow – just 20 miles northwest – mean that it's beauty can be hard to appreciate, what with all those other pleasure-seekers looking for it too.

History

Formed during the Ice Age by the gouging action of south-flowing glaciers, Loch Lomond from the 5th century onwards lay at the junction of the three ancient Scottish kingdoms of Strathclyde, Dàl Riata and Pictland. Some of the 37 islands in the loch made perfect retreats for early Christians. The missionary St Mirrin spent some time on Inchmurrin, the largest island, which is named after him.

Orientation & Information

The loch is 22 miles long and up to 5 miles wide. The A82 is a major route north and sticks to the western shore, where you'll see an uninterrupted string of holiday homes, caravan parks and marina developments. The main thoroughfare on the eastern shore is the West Highland Way walking trail, which can be reached by road from Drymen and Aberfoyle. As Loch Lomond crosses the Highland line, its character changes quite obviously as you move from south to north, with the most dramatic scenery in the north. The highest mountain in the area is Ben Lomond, on the eastern shore.

There are TICs at: Balloch (☎ 01389-753533), Balloch Rd, open April to October; Drymen (☎ 01360-660068), in the library on the square, open May to September; and Tarbet (☎ 01301-702260), at the A82/A83 junction, open April to October.

Activities

Walking The big walk around here is the West Highland Way (see the Activities chapter for details) and from Rowardennan you can tackle Ben Lomond.

Ben Lomond Standing guard over Loch Lomond is Ben Lomond, at 973m Scotland's most southerly Munro. It's thought the name Lomond comes from an old Scots word *llumon*, or the Gaelic *laom*, meaning a 'beacon' or 'light'.

The six-hour route starts at the car park by the Rowardennan Hotel. You can return via the popular Ptarmigan Route (731m) – so named because of the ptarmigan, a chicken-size bird found in the area that blends in perfectly with its surroundings (so you probably won't see it!).

The TIC (☎ 01360-660068), in Drymen public library, stocks information on walks in the area and opens daily from late May

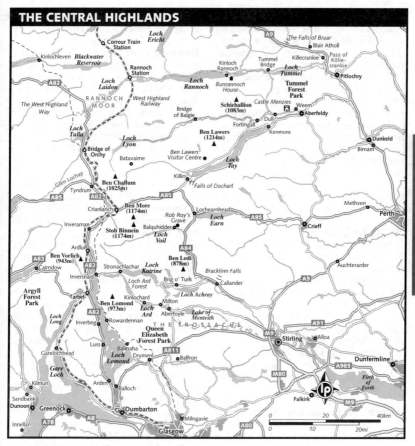

THE CENTRAL HIGHLANDS

to late September. There is also a TIC at the Rowardennan car park.

If you haven't done much walking, National Trust for Scotland rangers (☎ 01360-870224) lead hikes up Ben Lomond. The Loch Lomond Park rangers (☎ 01389-757295) also occasionally lead walks in the summer.

Cycling The main cycle route in the area is the Glasgow to Killin Cycle Way, which reaches the loch at Balloch. Most of the route is set back to the east of the loch, through the Queen Elizabeth Forest Park.

Along the western shore, the A82 is very busy in summer, but there are short sections of the old road beside it that are quieter.

Boat Trips The main centre for boat trips is Balloch.

Sweeney's Cruises (☎ 01389-752376, Balloch Harbour; 1hr trips adult/child £4.90/2.50, 2½hr trips £7.50/3.50) operate one-hour cruises around the loch, departing on the hour from 10.30am until 3.30pm in summer. They also run 2½-hour trips to the rather twee village of Luss on the loch's western shores, departing at 2.30pm and allowing 30 minutes ashore. There's also a good evening cruise (£6.50) departing at 7.30pm. **Mullen's Cruises** (☎ *01389-751481*) run similar cruises also departing from Balloch pier.

Operating from Tarbet, **Cruise Loch Lomond** (☎ *01301-702356*) goes to Inversnaid, to the cave allegedly used as a hideout by both Rob Roy and Robert the Bruce.

MacFarlane & Son (☎ *01360-870214*) do the loch's mail run, but from Monday to Saturday you can go with them to the loch's inhabited islands for a small fee, as well as Inchcailloch – the 'Isle of the Old Woman', that for centuries, from AD 912 onwards, was a burial ground for the clans living around the loch; it's now a nature reserve.

Places to Stay
Camping *Lomond Woods* (☎ *01389-755000, fax 755563, Tullichewan, Balloch)* Pitches £7. This is the best camping and caravan park in the area.

Forestry Commission Cashel Camp Site (☎ *01360-870234, Rowardennan)* Pitches £7.50. Open late Mar-Oct. This popular camp site is on the eastern shore, 3 miles north of Balmaha and also has a cafe.

Backpacker's Camp Site (☎ *01301-704244, Ardlui)* Pitches £5. Near the station in Ardlui is this tiny backpacker's camp site with basic facilities.

Hostels *Loch Lomond Youth Hostel* (☎ *01389-850226, fax 850623, Arden)* Dorm beds £11.75. Open Mar-Oct. The SYHA is justifiably proud of this turreted mansion, certainly one of Scotland's most impressive hostels. Set in beautiful grounds, it's 2 miles north of Balloch and you'll need to book ahead in summer. And yes, it is haunted.

Rowardennan Youth Hostel (☎ *01360-870259, fax 870256, Rowardennan)* Dorm beds £6-9. Open Mar-Oct. Halfway up the eastern shore of the loch, this SYHA hostel is right on the West Highland Way, and also an activity centre. It makes the perfect base for walking the Way or climbing Ben Lomond.

Beinn Ghlas Farm Wigwams (☎/fax *01301-704281, Inverarnan)* Beds £9. If you've always dreamed of getting back to

your Native Indian roots, where better to do it than the banks of Loch Lomond?

B&Bs & Hotels Numerous B&Bs are clustered around Balloch, Luss, Inverbeg and Tarbet and tend to be rather expensive; if you're headed somewhere – anywhere – else, go there if possible. Otherwise, there are a few places that should ease the melancholy the area prompts in most travellers.

Kinnoul House (☎ *01389-721116, Drymen Rd, Balloch)* B&B £19 per person. This pretty Victorian home is run by hospitable owners and has comfortable rooms that verge on being classy. Their 'hearty Scottish breakfast' is just that.

Drover's Inn (☎ *01301-704234,* e *the droversinn@aol.com, Inverarnan)* B&B from £23. The Drover's Inn, at the northern end of the loch, is a pub you shouldn't miss. It has smoke-blackened walls, a grand hall filled with moth-eaten stuffed animals and wee drams served by kilt-clad barmen. It's a great place to get down to some serious brain-cell destruction. Accommodation varies from basic rooms with shared bathroom in the old building to plush en-suite rooms in an annexe. Bar snacks and meals cost between £1.95 and £11.25.

Ardlui Hotel (☎ *01301-704243, fax 704268,* w *www.ardlui.co.uk)* Singles/doubles from £40/60. The Ardlui, at the head of Loch Lomond, is a finely decorated, rambling loch-side house. It is also very relaxed, has great views and does tasty bar meals (£5.95 to £14.50).

Inverbeg Inn (☎ *01436-860678, fax 860686, Inverbeg)* Singles/doubles from £45/76. This charming inn ain't cheap but it is one of the gems of the loch, with its views to Ben Lomond and delectable Scottish food that's served all day every day (bar meals cost £6.50 to £8.50 and the three-course restaurant dinner costs £20 to £25).

Places to Eat
You'll not go hungry around Loch Lomond; the upside of the tourist numbers is that demand for a decent meal is high.

Stagger Inn (☎ *01301-704274, Inverarnan)* Mains £4.25-13.95, 3-course dinner

£19.50. Across the road from the Drover's Inn, the cheery Stagger Inn serves good food.

Rowardennan Hotel (☎ *01360-870273, Rowardennan*) Bar meals £5.95-13.95. Daily specials are available at this hotel near the Rowardennan Youth Hostel.

Princess Rose (☎ *01389-755873, Luss Rd, Balloch*) Mains around £6-9. Balloch's only Chinese restaurant, the Princess Rose does takeaways as well as table service.

In Luss, there's a decent **coffee shop** that does home-baked fare and snacks.

Getting There & Away
Scottish Citylink (☎ 0870 550 5050) runs regular daily buses from Glasgow to Balloch (£3.60, 40 minutes), but the bus stops are at lay-bys nearly a mile from the town centre; the buses then continue up the A82 to Luss (55 minutes) and Tarbet (65 minutes). Most of the buses go to Ardlui (£7.40, 1¼ hours) and, north of the loch, Crianlarich.

There are two railway lines from Glasgow. One serves Balloch twice an hour (£3.20, 35 minutes); the other is the West Highland Railway to Oban and Fort William (two to five daily), which follows the loch from Tarbet to Ardlui.

TARBET
There's nothing much to see in Tarbet ('isthmus' in Gaelic), on the loch's western shore, but this is where King Haakon, in 1263, had his entire Viking fleet of around 100 galley ships pull their boats out of the water and drag them across the isthmus to Loch Lomond. From here, they sailed through Loch Lomond to the Firth of Clyde then down to Largs, where they were duly annihilated by Alexander III's superior forces.

THE TROSSACHS
Strictly speaking, the narrow glen between **Loch Katrine** and **Loch Achray** is the Trossachs, but the label is used to describe the area around the southern border of the Highlands. With a richly diverse landscape – from pine-covered slopes to dramatically rising mountains – this is a wild area that's well worth walking if you have time.

The main population centres are Aberfoyle and Callander, and as all the tourist literature repeatedly informs you, this is Rob Roy country. Liam Neeson was only the most recent of Rob Roy's popularists – Sir Walter Scott's historical *Rob Roy* flooded the region with tourists in the 19th century, and Loch Katrine was the inspiration for Scott's *Lady of the Lake*; since the early 20th century, the SS *Sir Walter Scott* has cruised the loch's waters, and you can

THE CENTRAL HIGHLANDS

Rob Roy

Robert MacGregor (1671–1734) was given the nickname Roy from the Gaelic ruadh, meaning 'red', thanks to his shock of red hair. Born into the MacGregor clan, already notorious for violent lawlessness and rebellion, he was a cattle trader who made occasional raids to the lowlands to rustle livestock. He owned much of the land around Inversnaid and had effectively become head of the clan soon after the age of 30.

In 1711, his business was bankrupted when his head drover absconded with his annual profits, and he was subsequently betrayed and outlawed by the duke of Montrose, a former ally. His home was burned and his family evicted, and he took to the hills to begin a campaign of revenge against the duke. Tales of his generosity to the poor and daring escapes from the clutches of the law earned him a reputation as a Scottish Robin Hood, and legends and romantic stories have since ensured him a place among the characters of popular Scottish history. Hollywood's recent *Rob Roy* (largely shot in Glen Nevis) is a contemporary addition to the legend.

There's not much of real interest about Rob Roy to actually go and see. The cave, for instance, where he is supposed to have hidden from the duke's men is north of Inversnaid and can be visited from the West Highland Way, but there seems little reason really, since so much about him – including this cave – can be attributed more to mythology than to hard fact.

get onboard these days for a 100-minute cruise for £6/2.50 per adult/child.

Aberfoyle
☎ 01877 ● pop 600

Known as the southern gateway to the Trossachs, Aberfoyle is on the Queen Elizabeth Forest Park's eastern edge. The village makes a good base for walks and cycle rides in the area but can overflow with tourists in summer.

The TIC (☎ 382352), Main St, opens April to October.

About half a mile north of Aberfoyle, on the A821, is the **Queen Elizabeth Forest Park Visitors Centre** *(☎ 382258; admission free, car parking £1; open 10am-6pm Mar-Christmas)*, which has audiovisual displays, exhibitions and information about walking and cycling routes in and around the park.

Three miles east is one of Scotland's two lakes, **Lake of Menteith**. A ferry runs from Port of Menteith village (on the lake) to the substantial ruins of **Inchmahome Priory** *(☎ 385294, Inchmahome Island; adult/child £3.30/1.20, including ferry; open 9.30am-5.15pm daily Apr-Sept)*, where Mary Queen of Scots was kept safe as a child, during Henry VIII's 'Rough Wooing'.

You can rent boats from **Lake of Menteith Fishing** *(☎ 385664)* from April to October, or rent bicycles from **Trossachs Cycle Hire** *(☎ 382614)* at The Trossachs Holiday Park for £7.50/12 per half-/full day.

Places to Stay & Eat *Cobleland Campsite (☎ 382392, Cobleland)* Pitches around £4. Camp at this site, 2 miles south of Aberfoyle, off the A81.

Old Coach House Inn (☎ 382822, Main St, Aberfoyle) B&B from £19 per person. The rooms here are fairly simple, though it's mostly a pub and eatery; the specials (around £5) are good.

Lake Hotel (☎ 385258, Lake of Menteith) B&B from £35 per person. The Lake is the top place to stay in the area and has spectacular views over Inchmahome Island from its restaurant, as well as plush rooms.

Eilean Gorm (☎ 387212, Kinlochard) B&B/dinner & B&B £20/30 per person.

Four miles west of Aberfoyle on the B829 is the tiny village of Kinlochard, on Loch Ard, where you'll find this spacious family cottage.

Forth Inn (☎ 382372, fax 382488, Main St, Aberfoyle) Bar meals £4.95-5.95. In the middle of the village, the Forth Inn does passable bar meals all day. They also do not-so-hot B&B from £28 per person if everything else is full.

Covenanters Inn (☎ 382347, fax 382785, Aberfoyle) B&B £30-35 per person, dinner £13-15 extra. The friendly Covenanters Inn has a great location on a hillock just south of the River Forth, only a short walk from Main St. Bar meals are also available and there's regular live music.

For cheaper coffee and snacks, try the *Coffee Shop (Main St, Aberfoyle)*, with baked potatoes (£2.50) and a range of meals, or the *Scottish Wool Centre coffee shop*.

Getting There & Away First Edinburgh has up to four daily buses from Stirling (£3.40) and up to five connecting services per day from Glasgow (£4.60) via Balfron.

A postbus service (☎ 01246-546329) operates twice on weekday afternoons from Aberfoyle to Callander via Port of Menteith (30 minutes). Another postbus does a round trip, Monday to Saturday, from Aberfoyle to Inversnaid on Loch Lomond, giving access to the West Highland Way. The Trossachs Trundler (☎ 01786-442707) has a day ticket for Aberfoyle, Callander, Port of Menteith and Stirling costing £8/5 per adult/child.

Callander
☎ 01877 ● pop 3000

At the eastern end of the Trossachs, Callander makes no bones about its hunt for the tourist dollar, as the array of tartan and shortbread shops reveal. But there's something you've got to respect about their unashamed pandering to the traveller's every need – they've been doing it since Queen Victoria came and took a look 150 years ago.

Callander has two post offices, one off the western end of the main street, the other about half a mile to the east. The police station is at the end of Church St. You'll find two banks near the visitor centre and the Health Clinic (☎ 331001) is at 4 Bracklinn Rd. There's a swimming pool (£2/1) and a climbing wall (£3/2) in the McLaren Community Leisure Centre (☎ 330000).

Cycle Hire Callander (☎ 331052), next to the visitor centre, rents mountain bikes for £6/10 per half-/full day.

At the friendly **Rob Roy & Trossachs Visitor Centre** (☎ 330342, Ancaster Square; admission free, adult/child £3.25/2.25 for audiovisual show; open 10am-4.15pm daily Mar-Dec), in a refurbished church, you can learn where Hollywood and Liam lied to you in the telling of the Rob Roy tale. Or, if that's all a bit serious for you, just try on some of the old Highland costumes that are on hand for comedy photo opportunities.

The centre also contains the helpful TIC. It opens 10am to 5pm daily year-round (11am to 4pm at weekends during January and February).

Walking The impressive Bracklinn Falls are reached by track and footpath from Bracklinn Rd (30 minutes each way from the car park). Also off Bracklinn Rd, a woodland trail leads up to Callander Crags, with great views over the surrounding area; a round trip takes 1½ hours.

Places to Stay & Eat As you'd expect, Callander is a hotbed of activity on the B&B front, and there are camping and hostel options too.

Keltie Bridge Caravan Park (☎ 330606, fax 330075) Pitches from £6. Open Apr-Oct. This camp site, at the eastern end of Callander and just off the A84, has basic facilities.

Trossachs Backpackers (☎/fax 331200, ℮ mark@scottish-hostel.co.uk, Invertrossachs Rd) Dorm beds £10. The Trossachs Backpackers is about 1 mile along Invertrossachs Rd, which runs on the southern side of the river draining Loch Vennachar. There are 30 comfy beds, all in dorms, and bike rental is available for £10 per day.

Linley Guest House (☎ 330087, 139 Main St) B&B from £17 per person. This no-nonsense two-level cottage on busy Main St is well priced and very friendly.

Arden House (☎/fax 330235, Bracklinn Rd) B&B £25-30 per person. Arden House, just north of Main St, is a rather grand

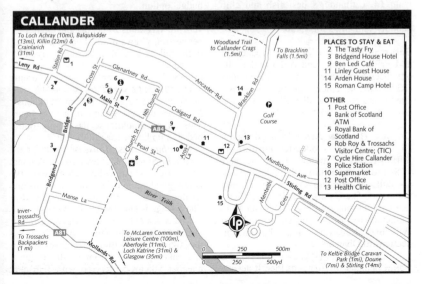

CALLANDER

To Loch Achray (10mi), Balquhidder (13mi), Killin (22mi) & Crainlarich (31mi)

Leny Rd

Station Rd

Cross St

Glenartney Rd

Main St

Bridge St

Bridgend

Nth Church St

Craigard Rd

Church St

Pearl St

A84

La

Manse La

Invertrossachs Rd

River Teith

Ancaster Rd

Woodland Trail to Callander Crags (1.5mi)

To Bracklinn Falls (1.5mi)

Bracklinn Rd

Golf Course

Murdiston Ave

Menteith Cres

Stirling Rd

To Trossachs Backpackers (1mi)

A81

Mollands Rd

To McLaren Community Leisure Centre (100m), Aberfoyle (11mi), Loch Katrine (31mi) & Glasgow (35mi)

To Keltie Bridge Caravan Park (1mi), Doune (7mi) & Stirling (14mi)

0   250   500m
0   250   500yd

PLACES TO STAY & EAT
2 The Tasty Fry
3 Bridgend House Hotel
9 Ben Ledi Café
11 Linley Guest House
14 Arden House
15 Roman Camp Hotel

OTHER
1 Post Office
4 Bank of Scotland ATM
5 Royal Bank of Scotland
6 Rob Roy & Trossachs Visitor Centre; (TIC)
7 Cycle Hire Callander
8 Police Station
10 Supermarket
12 Post Office
13 Health Clinic

THE CENTRAL HIGHLANDS

Victorian home with beautiful rooms. If you ever saw the BBC's *Doctor Finlay's Casebook* (there must be a few of you out there), stay here: parts were filmed in this house.

Bridgend House Hotel (☎ 330130, fax 331512, Bridgend) B&B from £25 per person. The mock-Tudor Bridgend House, across the river and by the A81 Mollands Rd, serves good Scottish-style bar meals (£4.95 to £13.45) and has four reasonable rooms with attached bathrooms.

Roman Camp Hotel (☎ 330003, fax 331533, W www.roman-camp.co.uk, Off Main St) Singles/doubles £75/120. In a former hunting lodge dating from 1625 and set in 20 acres of stunning woodland, there is absolutely no need to snigger at the name of this luxurious hotel. It has a renowned a la carte restaurant (mains from £20; reservations required) and a tiny chapel if something about Callander's kitsch inspires you and your beloved to get hitched.

Along Main St, there's a *Co-op supermarket* and lots of places offering meals and snacks for under £5. Most of the restaurants are over priced and lack quality.

The *Ben Ledi Café* (☎ 331212, Main St) is an exception, with basic healthy mains from £4. Callander's best fish and chip shop, *The Tasty Fry (6 Main St)*, does good haddock and chips for £3.50.

Entertainment On Monday, Wednesday and Friday in July and August, the TIC organises Scottish evenings, with fiddlers (£3.50/3). The cinema at the TIC shows classic and recent Scottish films on Thursday in summer (£2/1.50).

Getting There & Away First Edinburgh (☎ 01324-613777) operates buses from Stirling (£2.90, 45 minutes, hourly Monday to Saturday) and Killin (£3.40, 45 minutes, six daily Monday to Friday, three daily Saturday). There's also a twice daily Scottish Citylink bus (☎ 0870 550 5050) from Callander to Edinburgh (£8.10) and Fort William (£11.80) via Crianlarich, with connections to Oban and Skye.

A postbus service (☎ 01246-546329) runs from Callander to Trossachs Pier. It departs at 9.15am Monday to Saturday, and links with the 11am weekday (except Wednesday) sailing of the SS *Sir Walter Scott* on Loch Katrine. On weekday afternoons, the postbus runs from Callander to Aberfoyle (one hour) and returns via Port of Menteith.

The Trossachs Trundler calls at Callander and reaches the pier on Loch Katrine 26 minutes later.

CRIANLARICH & TYNDRUM
☎ 01838 ● total pop 350

Little more than service junctions on the A82 road, these villages are in the middle of great walking country on the West Highland Way.

At Crianlarich, there's a train station. The Mace supermarket, on Station Rd, is home to Crianlarich's post office. Tyndrum, just 5 miles along the road, is blessed with two train stations and a useful new TIC (☎ 400246), open daily April to November.

Places to Stay & Eat
Crianlarich Youth Hostel (☎ 300260, Station Rd) Dorm beds £9.25. Open mid-Feb–Oct. This well-equipped SYHA hostel, located near Crianlarich Station, is the best budget option.

Auchtertyre Farm (☎ 400251, fax 400248) Wigwams £9 per person. Pitches £3 per person. Wigwams must be on the comeback trail as this place, with 16 five-bed heated wigwams, shows. It is located off the A82 between Crianlarich and Tyndrum.

Pine Trees Leisure Park (☎ 400243, Tyndrum) Pitches £3.50 per person, bunkhouse £8.50 per person. Swimming £2 per hour. This simple bunkhouse has comfy dorm beds but no kitchen facilities.

Craigbank Guest House (☎ 300279, Crianlarich) Singles/doubles £20/36. Among Crianlarich's inexplicably expensive B&Bs is this good-value exception. Its rooms are small but clean, and the owners are friendly. The cottage is situated by the A85.

Rod & Reel (☎ 300271, Crianlarich) Bar meals £5.10-11.20. The Rod & Reel, by the A85 towards Killin, also serves snacks and baked potatoes (from £3.70). It has a cheaper takeaway service with fish and chips (£3.10) and burgers (£2.85). Packed lunches for hungry walkers cost £2.75.

West Highlander Restaurant (☎ 400314, Tyndrum) Breakfast from £2.75. Mains £4.25-6.50. The West Highlander does decent food, with soup and a roll for £1.95. It's attached to Pine Trees Leisure Park.

Self-caterers can stock-up at *Brodie's,* Tyndrum's grocer's and post office, or at *The Mace* in Crianlarich.

Getting There & Away

Scottish Citylink runs several buses daily from both villages to Glasgow, Oban, Fort William and Skye.

A postbus service (☎ 01246-546329) links Crianlarich, Tyndrum and Killin twice on each weekday (with connections to Callander) and once on Saturday. On Saturday, the postbus makes a return trip to Callander (1½ hours).

ScotRail (☎ 0845 748 4950) runs train services from both villages to Fort William, Oban and Glasgow. Journey times and fares from Crianlarich are 1¾ hours (£12.50), one hour (£7.40), and 1¾ hours (£11.40), respectively.

BALQUHIDDER

Ten miles north of Callander, off a small side road, is the tiny village of Balquhidder, notable only as the burial place of Rob Roy. A visit to his simple gravestone, in the graveyard behind the church ruins, is one of the main Rob Roy shrines for those following his martyrdom trail. Red Rob's wife and two sons are also buried here.

LOCHEARNHEAD

Three miles north of the Balquhidder turn-off is Lochearnhead, at Loch Earn's western tip. Watersports enthusiasts, especially beginners, flock to the loch to try their hand at a spot of Canadian canoeing, kayaking or windsurfing. **Loch Earn Watersports** *(☎ 830 330)* rents out equipment for all three pursuits for around £12 per day, and can give basic lessons if you've never done any of them before. They also organise waterskiing, though it can be expensive unless you managed to pack your own speedboat.

If you want to stay in town, the *Earknowe (☎ 01567-830238, Lochside)* does B&B for around £18 per person. The plusher *Clachan Cottage Hotel (☎ 01567-830247),* just down the road, does B&B from £28 per person.

Loch Tay & Around

Past Lochearnhead, getting onto the A827 you'll come to pretty Glen Dochart, which leads down to Loch Tay, loomed over by the mighty Breadalbane mountains on the northern shore; among this range is Ben Lawers (1214m), Perthshire's highest Munro and Scotland's ninth-tallest peak.

At the loch's western end is the village of Killin, and at the eastern end is Kenmore, with its Scottish Crannog Centre, and Aberfeldy. The nearby village of Fortingall claims not only to be the burial place of Pontius Pilate, but to also have Europe's oldest living thing – an ancient yew tree.

KILLIN

☎ 01567 ● pop 700

With the frothy Falls of Dochart tumbling through town, this place is, at first glance, a real charmer; once you've been here for a few minutes, you realise there's not much to do in this touristy village but stare at the gushing water – and for the best views you have to stand on a narrow bridge with cars hurtling past you. Still, this is a good base for walks in the spectacular Breadalbane mountains and the surrounding glens.

Information

The TIC (☎ 820254) is in the Breadalbane Folklore Centre, by the River Dochart. It opens 10am to 5pm daily March to October (longer hours June to September).

Killin hosts a folk festival (☎ 820224) in mid-June, with free session bands in pubs.

The Outdoor Centre (☎ 820652), Main St, sells and hires all sorts of equipment, including canoes (£30 per day) and mountain bikes (£11/15 per half-/full day).

The village has a post office and Bank of Scotland ATM, both on Main St. There's a

THE CENTRAL HIGHLANDS

laundrette near the supermarket (£2 to wash, £1 to dry).

Things to See
Tourists are drawn to the pretty **Falls of Dochart** in the village centre. The MacNab clan **burial ground** lies on an island in the river, crossed by the main road and just downstream from the falls; ask the TIC for the gate key.

The **Breadalbane Folklore Centre** (☎ 820254; adult/child £2/1.50; open 10am-5pm Mar-Oct, 9.30am-6.30pm July & Aug) is in an old water mill overlooking the falls. St Fillan, a 7th-century missionary, preached on this site and his sacred healing stones are kept in the centre. There are also well-written and badly organised displays about clan history, including the MacGregors and MacNabs.

One mile from Killin on the Glen Lochay road, **Moirlanich Longhouse** (☎ 820988, Glen Lochay; adult/child £1.50/1; open 2pm-5pm Wed & Sun May-Sept), owned by the National Trust for Scotland (NTS), is a well-restored example of a mid-19th-century byre.

Walking & Cycling
Glen Lochay runs westwards from Killin into the hills of Mamlorn. You can take a mountain bike for 11 miles up the glen to just beyond Batavaime. The scenery is impressive and the hills aren't too difficult.

On a sunny day it's possible to walk over the top of Ben Challum (1025m) and descend to Crianlarich, but it's very hard work. The passes on either side of this hill provide low-level alternatives. Allow two days from Killin to Crianlarich; wild camping is possible in upper Glen Lochay from 20 October to 12 August, if you're discreet.

For details on climbing Ben Lawers see Walking in the Activities chapter.

Places to Stay & Eat
Shieling Accommodation (☎/fax 820334, Aberfeldy Rd). Pitches £3.50 Apr-Oct, chalets from £150 to £550 per week year-round. For lovely woodland camping and luxurious wooden chalets try Shieling just outside Killin.

Killin Youth Hostel (☎ 820546, Lochay Rd) Dorm beds from £8.75/6. Open Mar-Oct & winter weekends. This well-equipped SYHA hostel is at the northern end of the village in a large traditional building.

Fairview House (☎ 820667, Main St) Singles/doubles £22/40. This old villa has comfortable, simply furnished rooms. You can get dinner for an extra £14.

Riverview (☎ 820241) B&B £15 per person. Over the bridge from the Falls of Dochart Inn, this old stone cottage has simple, affordable rooms and a kindly owner.

Falls of Dochart Inn (☎ 820270) Rooms £20-25 per person. This whitewashed hotel overlooking the wild falls has neat rooms, all with attached bath. It's also a great place for a meal or drink, with good bistro meals (£4.95 to £10.75).

Craigbuie Guest House (☎ 820419, Main St) Singles/doubles £24/40. This guesthouse, in a sturdy stone cottage, borders on chintzy but ends up being charming.

Killin Hotel (☎ 820296, e killinhotel@ btinternet.com) Singles/doubles £35/58. The slightly posh Killin is on a breathtaking spot by Loch Tay. It was once a grand old building and still has pleasant rooms.

Coach House (☎ 820349, Lochay Rd) Mains from £3.50. The Coach House serves great pub food, including curry and chilli dishes. Scottish folk bands play here in summer. If you want to stay, rooms cost from £18 per person.

Shutters (☎ 820314) Closed Thur. This little eatery has flash meals such as gammon and pineapple (£6.65) and delicious haddock and chips (£6.25).

Tarmachan Teashop (☎ 820387, Main St) The Tarmachan Teashop does snacks, sandwiches and salads from £1.50 to £4.

In the car park at the village hall, there's a van selling chicken and chips, burgers and so on. There are **Costcutter** and **Co-op supermarkets** on Main St.

Getting There & Away
First Edinburgh runs buses Monday to Saturday from Stirling (£4.75, 1¾ hours, six daily Monday to Friday, three on Saturday) via Callander. There is a postbus

(☎ 01246-546329) between Killin and Callander on Saturday (one hour). A postbus runs along the south Loch Tay road, to Ardtalnaig, then back to Killin (Monday to Saturday). A postbus service also runs from Aberfeldy to Killin Monday to Saturday (three hours to Killin, 1¾ hours to Aberfeldy).

KENMORE
☎ 01887

The village of Kenmore is at the eastern outlet of Loch Tay, 6 miles west of Aberfeldy. The short main street is dominated by a church with a clock tower and a spectacular archway, the entrance to privately owned Taymouth Castle.

A quarter of a mile along the south Loch Tay road from the village is the **Scottish Crannog Centre** *(☎ 01887-830583, adult/child £3.50/2.50; open 10am-4.30pm daily Mar-Nov)*, one of the area's highlights. It has a reconstruction of a wonderfully atmospheric Iron-Age crannog, and you're taken on a one-hour tour that includes demonstrations of how the Scots who lived in these homes got by, and how they built these impressive structures. You can try on a skin tunic while watching videos and displays explaining the history of crannogs and the lives of the people here 2600 years before you.

There's camping at **Kenmore Camping & Caravan** *(☎ 830226)*, with pitches from £6.

Kenmore Hotel *(☎ 01887-830205, fax 830262, The Square)* B&B singles £45-50, doubles £70-80, double suites £110. The Kenmore claims, like a plethora of other places round the country, to be Scotland's oldest inn; it dates from 1572. Look out for the Burns poem on the wall, written here in 1787. Top-floor rooms, such as 'The Square', also have great character. In the bar, filled baguettes start at £3.50 and mains cost £5.95 to £15.95.

If you want to get out on the water, just near the Crannog Centre is **Croft-na-Caber** *(☎ 830588)*, a fantastic watersports centre. They run courses in windsurfing, sailing, rafting, hiking, jet biking, clay-pigeon shooting and sports shooting. You can also hire canoes and kayaks (£20 per day). You

Crannogs

Usually built in a loch for defensive purposes, a crannog (from the Gaelic word *crann*, meaning 'tree') consists of an artificial rock island with timber posts and struts supporting a hut above high-water level.

Crannogs were used on many lochs, including Lochs Awe, Earn and Tay, from prehistoric times till the 18th century. Some crannogs had curious underwater causeways that zigzagged or had traps, making night-time assaults without a boat extremely difficult.

can hire **bikes** from here, or from **Perthshire Bikes** *(☎ 830291)* in town.

The Aberfeldy-Killin postbus passes through Kenmore once daily, except Sunday.

FORTINGALL

Northwest of Kenmore is Fortingall, one of the region's prettiest villages; its 19th-century thatched cottages make for a tranquil, picturesque setting. Designed by James Marjoribanks McLaren (Charles Rennie Mackintosh's teacher), the village's main fame claim comes inside the impressive town **church** *(admission free; open 10am-4pm daily Easter-Sept)*. In the churchyard, there's a 3000-year-old yew tree. Locals make the bold claim that this is the oldest living thing in Europe; certainly the beautiful tree was already ancient when the Romans camped on the meadows by the River Lyon.

Rather harder to prove is the claim Pontius Pilate is buried here. A gravestone in the churchyard bears the initials 'PP', which is hardly conclusive proof. He was the son of a Roman officer stationed here, though, so it's conceivable.

Fendoch *(☎ 01887-830322,* **e** *fendoch@eidosnet.co.uk)* Singles/doubles £18/34. Fendoch is Fortingall's snuggest B&B. All of the rooms have bathrooms and they also serve evening meals (£8 to £12).

Fortingall Hotel *(☎/fax 01887-830367)* B&B £25-35 per person. Part of the hotel dates from 1300; there are some great rooms

THE CENTRAL HIGHLANDS

on the first floor, especially room eight. The bar meals (from £6) are excellent; try the local venison braised in red wine and juniper berries (£7.50).

Around Fortingall

If you're driving, take a detour up **Glen Lyon**, one of Scotland's most wonderful glens, with the stunning River Lyon flowing through it. The long single-track road ensures few visitors penetrate its remote upper reaches, where capercaillie live in patches of Scots pine forest. Just 3 miles upstream from Fortingall, opposite Chesthill, there's a **Roman bridge** crossing the Allt Dà-ghob, where there's a waterfall. You can see the bridge from the Glen Lyon road.

Perhaps the best site around Fortingall, though, is the village of **Dull**, 4 miles away, off the B846. There's absolutely nothing to see or do in Dull, which is the whole point.

The postbus (☎ 01246-546329) from Aberfeldy to Glenlyon runs via Fortingall once daily, except Sunday.

ABERFELDY

☎ 01887 ● pop 1956

Slightly shabby Aberfeldy stands on the easternmost point of Loch Tay, with the unique distinction of sitting at the exact geographic centre of Scotland. Not much happens in Aberfeldy, though the town square around the TIC can get a touch raucous at the weekend, with local teenagers riding their skateboards and occasionally drinking a cider or two.

The TIC (☎ 820276), in an old church on the square, opens year-round. Two banks have ATMs and you can check your email at the TIC for a pricey £7 per hour.

The cottage hospital (☎ 820314) is on Old Crieff Rd.

Things to See

The B846 to Tummel Bridge crosses the River Tay in Aberfeldy by a fine **bridge**; construction was begun in 1733 by General Wade as part of his Pacification of the Highlands project. Nearby stands the **Black Watch** monument, which commemorates the first muster in 1740.

The **Aberfeldy Water Mill** (☎ 820803, Mill St; adult/child £2.50/1; open 10am-4.30pm Mon-Sat & noon-4.30pm Sun Easter–mid-Oct) was built in 1825 and restored in 1983. Stone-ground oatmeal is produced by water power and two stones, each weighing 1½ tonnes.

Castle Menzies (☎ 820982; adult/child £3/2; open 10.30am-5pm Mon-Sat & 2pm-5pm Sun Apr–mid-Oct, last admission 4.30pm), 1½ miles west of town by the B846 in the wonderfully named town of Weem, is the impressively restored 16th-century seat of the chief of the Menzies clan, a 'Z-plan' castle. There's a small clan museum and a *tearoom*.

Places to Stay & Eat

Aberfeldy Caravan Park (☎ 820662, Dunkeld Rd) Pitches £8-9.75. Open Apr-Oct. This charmless park is located on the eastern side of town.

Dunollie House (☎ 820298, Taybridge Drive) Dorm beds £7.50-13. This simple hostel is at the western end of town, by the A827 and the river.

Tighnabruaich (☎ 820456, fax 829254, Taybridge Terrace) Singles/doubles £18/35. A homely Victorian place, Tighnabruaich has three sunny rooms with a shared bathroom. The owner does great home baking

Tigh'n Eilean Guest House (☎/fax 820109, Taybridge Drive) Singles/doubles £18/38. This is another fine and superbly decorated Victorian house with good food, en-suite rooms and a wonderful lounge with an open fire. They do dinner for £13 extra.

Breadalbane Arms Hotel (☎ 820634, Bank St) B&B £25 per person. An abundance of plywood and good cheer make this a comfortable if unremarkable place to bed down for the night. The bar food is cheap and cheery, with steaks (£7) and scampi (£5) as inexpensive as you'll find.

Khanam Tandoori (☎ 829200, 48 Dunkeld St) Mains £5.95-12.95. If you've been craving a truly delicious curry, don't come here. But Khanam does do acceptable tandoori dishes that should tide you over.

Black Watch Inn (☎ 820699, Bank St) Mains from £3.75. At the Black Watch you can enjoy a good home-cooked meal in the bar or the quieter lounge.

On A Roll (☎ *829154, Dunkeld St*) is a wonderful no-nonsense cafe and bakery, with cheap baguettes, pastries and soups. There's a *fish and chip shop* next door.

There's a well-stocked *Co-op supermarket* in The Square for self-caterers.

Getting There & Away

Stagecoach runs buses from Aberfeldy to Pitlochry (£2.10, 45 minutes), Dunkeld (£3, 1¼ hours) and Perth (£3, around 1¾ hours) up to 10 times daily (Monday to Saturday). Strathtay Scottish has a twice-daily service (schooldays only) between Aberfeldy and Blairgowrie (£3, 1¼ hours), via Dunkeld (£2.15, 40 minutes). A postbus (☎ 01246-546329) goes to Killin (three hours) via Kenmore, and another goes to the top of Glen Lyon, at Lubreoch, via Fortingall (both once daily except Sunday). Elizabeth Yule Transport (☎ 01796-472290) operates from Aberfeldy to Kinloch Rannoch (£2.40, one hour 10 minutes, once daily) on schooldays.

The central bus stop is on Chapel St.

Pitlochry to Rannoch Moor

PITLOCHRY

☎ 01796 ● pop 2439

Filled though it is with tacky tourist shops, the Victorian Pitlochry somehow maintains its charm as an attractive Highland town. Set on the River Tummel and overlooked by towering Ben Vrackie, it makes a useful base for exploring the area; there are good transport connections if you don't have your own wheels.

The TIC (☎ 472215), 22 Atholl Rd, opens 10am to 5pm Monday to Saturday, with longer opening hours in summer. You'll find an ATM at the Royal Bank of Scotland, Atholl Rd, by the post office.

Things to See

Pitlochry has two whisky distilleries. Bell's **Blair Athol Distillery** (☎ *482003, Perth Rd;*

admission £3, includes voucher redeemable against purchases; open 9am-5pm Mon-Sat & noon-5pm Sun Easter-Sept, otherwise reduced hours Mon-Fri only) is at the southern end of the town. **Edradour** (☎ *472095, By A924; admission free; open 9.30am-5pm Mon-Sat & noon-5pm Sun Mar-Oct, phone to confirm winter times)* is nestled in rolling hills 2½ miles east of town on the A924. It's Scotland's smallest distillery.

When the power station was built on the River Tummel, a fish ladder was constructed to allow salmon to swim up to their spawning grounds. It's in the **Scottish & Southern Energy Visitor Centre** (☎ *473152; adult/child £2/1; open 10am-5.30pm daily Mar-Oct*), where there are high-tech interactive displays on hydroelectric power and a salmon video. Admission to the observation chamber for the fish ladder is free. May and June are the best months to watch the fish.

Places to Stay

Pitlochry is positively packed with places to stay, though anything central is a bit pricey.

Pitlochry Youth Hostel (☎ *472308, Knockard Rd*) Dorm beds £8/6. Open year-round. In a sturdy old mansion, the pebble-dash exterior of this SYHA hostel is less than dazzling, but it does have great views over the town centre, a cosy lounge and clean kitchen. Laundry facilities are available, as is Internet access (50p per five minutes).

Pitlochry Backpackers (☎ *470044, fax 470055, 134 Atholl Rd*) £11 per person. Open Mar-Oct. If the SYHA hostel is full, try this place: it has neat dorm rooms and also offers fairly average doubles or twins.

Dundarave House (☎ *473109, Strathview Terrace*). B&B £22 per person. This towering 19th-century B&B has panoramic views of the Tummel, and rooms that, though badly decorated, are exceptionally clean and have extremely comfortable beds. The breakfast is excellent.

There are plenty of places to stay along Atholl Rd.

Carra Beag Guest House (☎ *472835, Toberargan Rd*) B&B £17 per person. A semi-grand old building set back from Atholl Rd, behind the tourist office, this place has plush

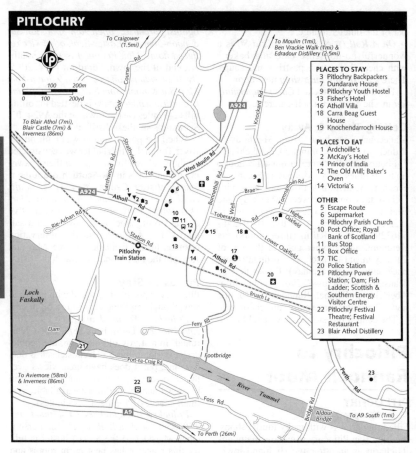

PITLOCHRY

To Craigower
(1.5mi)

To Moulin (1mi),
Ben Vrackie Walk (1mi) &
Edradour Distillery (2.5mi)

0   100   200m
0   100   200yd

To Blair Atholl (7mi),
Blair Castle (7mi) &
Inverness (86mi)

To Aviemore (58mi)
& Inverness (86mi)

To Perth (26mi)

To A9 South (1mi)

Loch
Faskally

Dam

Pitlochry
Train Station

River   Tummel

Footbridge

Ferry Rd

Port-na-Craig Rd

Foss Rd

Aldour
Bridge

Golf Course Rd
Larchwood Rd
Strathview
Rie-Achan Rd
Station Rd
Atholl Rd
West Moulin Rd
Bonnethill Rd
Tce
Brae
Well
Toberargan Rd
Higher Oakfield
Lower Oakfield
Tommafuigan Rd
Knockard Rd
Atholl Rd
Bruach La
Perth Rd
Bridge Rd

PLACES TO STAY
3 Pitlochry Backpackers
7 Dundarave House
9 Pitlochry Youth Hostel
13 Fisher's Hotel
16 Atholl Villa
18 Carra Beag Guest
    House
19 Knochendarroch House

PLACES TO EAT
1 Ardchoille's
2 McKay's Hotel
4 Prince of India
12 The Old Mill; Baker's
    Oven
14 Victoria's

OTHER
5 Escape Route
6 Supermarket
8 Pitlochry Parish Church
10 Post Office; Royal
    Bank of Scotland
11 Bus Stop
15 Box Office
17 TIC
20 Police Station
21 Pitlochry Power
    Station; Dam; Fish
    Ladder; Scottish &
    Southern Energy
    Visitor Centre
22 Pitlochry Festival
    Theatre; Festival
    Restaurant
23 Blair Athol Distillery

THE CENTRAL HIGHLANDS

if slightly faded rooms and a similarly elegant dining room. The owners aren't particularly helpful but it's good value.

Atholl Villa (☎ 473820, 29 Atholl Rd) B&B singles/doubles £28/45. It might be on the main road but that doesn't stop this pad being one of the top places to stay in town. There's a charming garden and breakfast room attached.

Knockendarroch House (☎ 473473, fax 474068, Higher Oakfield) B&B £48-63 per person. Knockendarroch is one of Pitlochry's finest hotels. Flash Scottish dinners are included in the price, and are also available to nonresidents for £21; you'll need to book in advance though.

Fisher's Hotel (☎ 472000, Atholl Rd) B&B £25 per person off-peak rising to £45 at peak times. This sumptuous hotel, with B&B rates to match, is in a grand old heritage building. Rooms are unremarkable but extremely tidy. It also has an a la carte restaurant.

Places to Eat

Festival Restaurant (☎ 484626, Foss Rd) 2-/3-course set dinner £18/21. You'll have to book if you want to get a table here during summer. The excellent set dinner, featuring Scottish dishes, is good value.

The Old Mill (☎ 747020, Mill Lane) Mains £6-12. By a gorge running down to the River Tummel, the Old Mill is a splendid place to sit outside in summer (inside it's a bit soulless and modern). The food here is wonderful and their salmon fillet (£8.95) is a treat. The fish and chips (£7) and steaks (£11) are also good.

McKay's Hotel (☎ 473888, 138 Atholl Rd) Mains around £5-8. Bar meals at McKay's Hotel include beef and Guinness pie (£6.95).

Victoria's (☎ 472670, 45 Atholl Rd) This comfortable eatery, occupying a pleasant corner spot does delicious coffee and generally has a pasta special (£7).

Prince of India (☎ 472275, Station Rd) Mains £5-9. This place does great tandoori dishes, offers a 10% discount on takeaways and has a £6.95 lunch special.

On Atholl Rd, try the hot pies for 57p at the *Baker's Oven*, or *Ardchoille's* takeaway fish and chips. There's a *Co-op supermarket (West Moulin Rd)* for self-caterers.

Entertainment

The well-known *Pitlochry Festival Theatre (☎ 472680, Foss Rd)* stages a different play six nights out of seven during its season from May to mid-October; tickets cost £4 to £25. There's a box office in the centre of town, on Bonnethill Rd.

Getting There & Away

Scottish Citylink runs buses to Inverness (£8.10, two hours), Aviemore (£6.40, 1¼ hours), Perth (£5, 40 minutes), Edinburgh (£8, two hours) and Glasgow (£8, 2¼ hours).

Stagecoach runs daily buses to Aberfeldy (£2, 30 minutes, three to seven daily), Blair Atholl (£1.30, 25 minutes, once daily on weekdays) and Dunkeld (£1.90, 25 minutes, up to 12 daily except Sunday). There's also a Monday to Saturday postbus service (☎ 472386) to Blair Atholl (£2.30, 45 minutes). Buses stop on Atholl Rd.

Pitlochry is on the main rail line from Perth to Inverness. There are seven trains a day from Perth (£8.20, 30 minutes), fewer on Sunday.

Getting Around

Escape Route (☎ 473859), 8 West Moulin Rd, hires bikes for £9/15 per half-/full day, and also does repairs.

For a taxi, call Elizabeth Yule Transport on ☎ 472290.

AROUND PITLOCHRY

Four miles north of town, the A9 travels through the **Pass of Killiecrankie**, a magnificent wooded gorge that was the setting for the 1870's Battle of Killiecrankie, where English forces were defeated by the 'Viscount Bonnie Dundee', Graham of Claverhouse. There's an NTS **visitors centre** *(☎ 473233; admission free; open Mar-Oct)*.

If you want to spoil yourself, at the top of the pass is the *Killiecrankie Hotel (☎ 01796-473220)*, which does luxurious B&B for around £40 per person.

Dunkeld & Birnam

☎ 01350 ● pop 1050

Ten miles south of Pitlochry, Dunkeld is an attractive village bordering the Highlands with great walks surrounding it. Dunkeld TIC (☎ 727688), The Cross, opens April to December.

The main reason for coming through here is to see **Dunkeld Cathedral** *(☎ 01316-686800, High St; admission free; open standard Historic Scotland hours Apr-Sept)*, one of Scotland's most beautifully sited cathedrals. Half of it is still in use as a church, the rest is in ruins. The oldest part of the original church is the choir, completed in 1350. The 15th-century tower is also still standing. The cathedral was damaged during the Reformation and burned during the Battle of Dunkeld (1689).

On High and Cathedral Sts is a collection of 20 artisans' houses restored by the NTS. Across the bridge is **Birnam**, made famous by Macbeth, but there's not much left of Birnam Wood.

Good local walks include the **Hermitage Woodland Walk**, starting from a car park by the A9, a mile west of Dunkeld. The well-marked trail follows the River Braan to the **Black Linn Falls**, where the duke of Atholl built a folly, Ossian's Hall, in 1758.

THE CENTRAL HIGHLANDS

In Caputh, 5 miles east of Dunkeld, you'll find *Wester Caputh Independent Hostel* (☎/fax 01738-710617) with dorm beds for £10. It's a lively 18-bed hostel by the A984 Coupar Angus road and they offer free pick-up from Birnam or Dunkeld. Guests frequently attend traditional music sessions in Dunkeld at *MacLean's Real Music Bar* (☎ 727340, Tay Terrace).

Getting There & Away Scottish Citylink buses between Glasgow/Edinburgh and Inverness stop at the train station (by Birnam) two or three times daily. Birnam to Perth or Pitlochry takes 20 minutes (£4.30 and £4, respectively). Trains to Inverness (£15.80, two hours) or Perth (£4.50, 18 minutes) run three to eight times daily.

Stagecoach buses from Perth to Pitlochry and Aberfeldy all stop in Dunkeld. Strathtay Scottish (☎ 01382-228345) has a service (twice-daily Monday to Friday) from Blairgowrie to Aberfeldy, via Dunkeld.

BLAIR ATHOLL
☎ 01796

One of Scotland's top tourist attractions, **Blair Castle** (☎ 481207, Blair Atholl; adult/child/family £6.25/4/18, grounds only £2/1/5; open 10am-6pm daily Apr-Oct, last admission 5pm) is the seat of the duke of Atholl, though the sprawling castle and its 70,000 acres are managed by a charitable trust. This turreted, whitewashed baronial behemoth is set beneath forested slopes above the River Garry.

The castle's original tower was built in 1269 but the castle has undergone significant remodelling since, especially after being besieged by Jacobite forces in 1746 who inflicted much damage trying to wrest control from Butcher Cumberland's Hanoverian forces. It was the last castle in Britain to be subject to siege.

Thirty rooms are open to the public, and are packed with paintings, arms and armour, china, lace and embroidery, presenting a wonderful picture of upper-class Highland life from the 16th century onwards. The impressive ballroom has a wooden roof and the walls are covered in antlers.

As an added bonus, visitors here may see soldiers from Britain's only private army, the Atholl Highlanders – established by Queen Victoria in 1844 and with a force of around 60 – who each day play their bagpipes in front of the castle.

The castle is 7 miles north of Pitlochry, and a mile from Blair Atholl village. There's a *restaurant* and a giftshop on site.

The only other thing of interest in Blair Atholl village is the **Atholl Country Collection** (☎ 481232; adult/child £2/1; open 1.30pm-5pm daily June-Oct, 10am-5pm July–mid-Sept) mostly because it has a stuffed highland *coo* (cow), though there are several other interesting displays too.

Hire bikes from **Atholl Mountain Bikes** (☎ 473553) for £8/12 per half-/full day.

Elizabeth Yule Transport (☎ 01796-472290) runs a service four or five times daily except Sunday between Pitlochry and Blair Atholl (£1.30, 20 minutes). Some buses go straight to the castle. There's also a train station but not all trains stop here.

Four miles west of Blair Atholl, where the B8079 meets the A9 to Inverness, is the mildly terrifying **House of Bruar** shopping centre. Designed along lines of an American 'discount centre' (though with more class), it's a mecca for all cliches Scottish: sporrans, tartan throws and golf balls are sold by the truckload, although there's no discount on any of it – its prices are worth stopping for only if you're in need of a laugh, because they're hilariously high. We shouldn't be too harsh though, because there's a posh food section selling a dizzying array of magnificent produce – smoked salmon, caviar, exquisite jams and so on.

Behind the centre is a good walk to the **Falls of Bruar**, where you can watch the River Bruar roll down through rocky drops.

LOCH RANNOCH & RANNOCH MOOR

West of Pitlochry, the B8019 travels out as far as Rannoch Station, and along the way is some spectacular scenery. A visit in autumn is highly recommended as the birch trees are at their finest. In winter, **Tummel Bridge** is often one of the coldest places in Scotland.

At the eastern end of Loch Tummel, **Queen's View Visitor Centre** (☎ *01796-473123, Strathtummel; £1 parking charge; open 10am-6pm daily Apr-Oct*) has a magnificent outlook towards the popular peak of Schiehallion (1083m). The near-perfect shape of this hill allowed physicists to use its gravitational attraction on a pendulum to estimate the gravitational constant, G, and hence calculate the mass of the Earth.

Kinloch Rannoch is a pleasant village, though driving in past the burned-down old hotel it can seem decidedly creepy. There's a grocery shop and post office here. It's the last place to stock on supplies if you're hiking, and a good base for local walks or a cycle trip around Loch Rannoch. There's an interesting clan trail around the loch, with roadside notice boards about local clans. Beyond the western end of the loch, you enter bleak Rannoch Moor, which extends all the way to Glen Coe. The rivers and lochs on the moor are wonderful for fishing.

Rannoch Moor

From Rannoch Station, the moor begins and civilisation finishes for a while. Barren, bleak, desolate and inhospitable: all describe the wild expanse of Rannoch Moor; the largest in Britain, stretching over 50 sq miles.

A triangular plateau of blanket bog, the moor is framed by mountains and has a base of grey granite about 400 million years old. The moor owes its present form to the last glacial period, when it served as a gathering area for ice. Since then the area's exposure and high rainfall have ensured the poorly drained ground has become covered in bog and lochans. The moor holds so much water some say it's possible to swim across in summer and to skate across in winter.

The impression that the walker receives when skirting the moor is highly dependent on the season and weather conditions. On a calm day, with the blue sky reflected in the lochans, and curlew, golden plover and snipe darting among the tussocks, the sense of open space is inspiring. In poor weather, especially if low cloud, driving wind and rain conspire, less endearing descriptions of the moor can be much appreciated.

Places to Stay & Eat

Glenrannoch House (☎ *01882-632307, Kinloch Rannoch*) En-suite singles/doubles £22/44, add £15 for dinner. This simple B&B also does great vegetarian food.

Bunrannoch House (☎/fax *01882-632407, Kinloch Rannoch*) B&B/Dinner & B&B £22/38 per person. Perhaps this former hunting lodge seems slightly spooky because the owners let you know it's built on a medieval settlement. There are open fires, excellent views and spacious rooms, all en suite. It's about 1 mile south of Kinloch Rannoch town.

Loch Rannoch Hotel (☎ *01882-632201, fax 632203*) B&B £60 per person. On the loch, just through Kinloch Rannoch, you'll find this plush hotel, part of a luxurious time-share resort. Rooms are immaculate and there's a swimming pool and gym.

Moor of Rannoch Hotel (☎ *01882-633238*) B&B £35 per person. For fabulous food try this hotel and eatery in Rannoch Station.

For those walking on from Rannoch Station there's the wonderful *Corrour Station Bunkhouse* (☎ *01397-732236*), by the West Highland Railway Station, which has 12 bunk beds for £8 per night each, and a small *cafe* attached. The *Loch Ossian Hostel* (☎ *01397-732207*) is 1 mile from Corrour Station (408m). It's a rustic SYHA hostel and charges just £7 per night in dorms.

Getting There & Away

On schooldays only, Elizabeth Yule Transport (☎ 01796-472290) operates from Kinloch Rannoch to Aberfeldy (£2.40, 70 minutes, once daily in each direction). The Kinloch Rannoch to Pitlochry service runs one to three times daily, except Sunday (£2.40, 50 minutes).

The Pitlochry to Rannoch Station postbus (☎ 01246-546329) has a once daily service (except Sunday and public holidays) via Kinloch Rannoch and both sides of the loch.

ScotRail runs trains from Rannoch Station, north to Fort William and Mallaig, and south to Glasgow.

THE CENTRAL HIGHLANDS

Strathspey, the Cairngorms & the Angus Glens

Stuck between the magnificent Cairngorms and the mighty Monadhliath mountains, the wide valley of the River Spey – Strathspey – has long been one of Scotland's most touristy areas. In its lower reaches, visitors come for the salmon fishing and whisky drinking, while its upper waters are the domain of mountain-bikers, hikers, skiers and snowboarders.

Aviemore, the tawdry village where ski bunnies gather in midwinter, is the region's main resort. To the east is the sizable Georgian town of Grantown-on-Spey, where bird spotters congregate en-masse in order to twitch themselves an osprey, Britain's rarest bird. Farther north still is Speyside and the malt whisky triangle. Back down south is quiet Kingussie, where anglers come to do their thing in the River Spey.

The following Ordnance Survey (OS) maps cover the Strathspey, the Cairngorms and Angus Glens:

Landranger 35: Kingussie & Monadhliath Mountains
Landranger 36: Grantown, Aviemore & Cairngorms
Landranger 43: Braemar & Blair Atholl
Landranger 44: Ballater & Glen Clova

Aviemore & the Cairngorms

The ski-slope-dotted Cairngorms are Britain's second-highest mountain range and soar above forests of regenerating native Caledonian pine in the upper reaches of Strathspey. Nature-lovers will find paradise in these native woodlands, which are home to rare species such as pine martens, wildcats and red squirrels. Scotland's only herd of wild reindeer survive here too.

Highlights

- Hike up to the stunning Cairngorm plateau for mind-bending views
- Fish for Britain's tastiest salmon on the River Spey
- Hire a mountain bike in Braemar and ride to the dramatic Linn of Dee at Inverey
- Take a wee dram or two on the whisky triangle around Dufftown
- Ski Scotland's biggest and best ski runs at Glenshee
- Spend a night at picturesque Kirkton of Glenisla at the enchanting Glen Isla Hotel

Aviemore p178

AVIEMORE
☎ 01479 ● pop 2500

A nominee for *Unlimited* magazine's 2001 'Most Dismal Place in Scotland' awards, Aviemore is far from picturesque. In 1960, this was a sleepy Highland village of 200 inhabitants; today it looks like a down-market resort in the Rockies that can't live up to its swanky aspirations. Fortunately,

STRATHSPEY, THE CAIRNGORMS & THE ANGUS GLENS

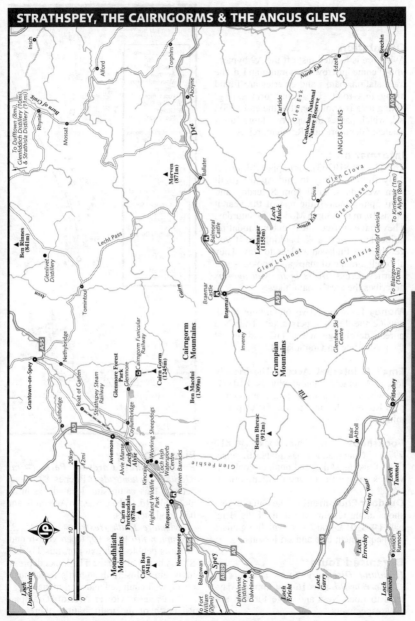

visitors can avoid the kitsch that reigns through summer by heading for the hills.

Orientation

Aviemore is located just off the A9 bypass; you'll come into town on Grampian Rd; the train station, banks and eateries are found along this road. The Cairngorm skiing/hiking area is 8 miles east at the end of Ski Rd, which passes through two large forest estates: Glenmore and Rothiemurchus.

Information

The TIC (☎ 810363), Grampian Rd, opens daily from mid-July to mid-August (until 7pm weekdays, until 6pm Saturday and until 5pm Sunday); the rest of the year it opens 10am to 5.30pm Monday to Saturday. They have a free local accommodation guide, but charge a £3 booking fee if you get them to find you a place to stay. They also sell a range of maps and books.

Ernest Cross' *Walks in the Cairngorms* describes the area's main hikes.

Money There are ATMs on Grampian Rd, outside the Tesco supermarket. There's a bureau de change at the TIC and one at the post office on Grampian Rd.

Email & Internet Access The friendly folk at Aviemore Photographic (☎ 810371, W www.aviemorephotographic.com), Grampian Rd, offer Internet access for £1 per 10 minutes.

Bookshops James Thin Books (☎ 810 797), 87 Grampian Rd, has a fantastic selection of hiking, skiing and outdoor books, as well as general fiction and nonfiction titles.

Outdoor Equipment Of the outdoor-gear shops along Grampian Rd, try Ellis Brigham (☎ 810175), at No 9, which organises both equipment hire and ski lessons.

Organised Tours

Highland Discovery Tours (☎ 811478, 27 Corrour Rd) runs 16-seat minibus daytrips to Loch Ness and Skye for £18 and £29 respectively.

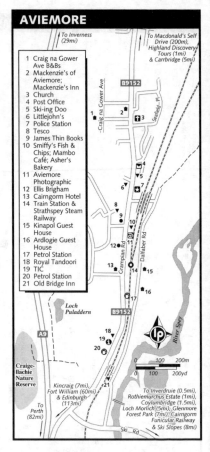

AVIEMORE

1 Craig na Gower Ave B&Bs
2 Mackenzie's of Aviemore; Mackenzie's Inn
3 Church
4 Post Office
5 Ski-ing Doo
6 Littlejohn's
7 Police Station
8 Tesco
9 James Thin Books
10 Smiffy's Fish & Chips; Mambo Café; Asher's Bakery
11 Aviemore Photographic
12 Ellis Brigham
13 Cairngorm Hotel
14 Train Station & Strathspey Steam Railway
15 Kinapol Guest House
16 Ardlogie Guest House
17 Petrol Station
18 Royal Tandoori
19 TIC
20 Petrol Station
21 Old Bridge Inn

Places to Stay

Rothiemurchus Caravan Park (☎/fax 812800, Coylumbridge) Pitches £3.50 per person. This camp site, located 1½ miles along Ski Rd, is the closest to Aviemore and has good facilities.

Aviemore Youth Hostel (☎ 810345, 25 Grampian Rd) Beds £9. Open year-round. With its pebble-dash exterior, this 114-bed SYHA hostel above the TIC looks depressingly glum. Inside though it's fastidiously clean, well equipped and well managed.

On Craig na Gower Ave, off Grampian Rd north of the train station, there's an enclave of B&Bs offering year-round accommodation, including:

Karn House (☎ 810849, Craig na Gower Ave) B&B £18 per person. This modern house might look like the B&B from hell but inside it's a satisfactory place to stay, with comfortable, well-kept rooms and friendly owners.

Eriskay (☎ 810717, Craig na Gower Ave) B&B £20 per person. Everything's grey on the outside but spectacularly floral inside at this B&B.

Dunroamin (☎ 810698, Craig na Gower Ave) Singles/doubles £20/32. This no-nonsense, cheap B&B has tidy rooms and helpful owners.

On Dalfaber Rd are two larger guesthouses:

Kinapol Guest House (☎/fax 810513, e kinapol@aol.com, Dalfaber Rd) B&B from £16 per person. This place has three rather genteel and surprisingly affordable rooms.

Ardlogie Guest House (☎/fax 810747, Dalfaber Rd) B&B doubles £36-40 (no singles). The highfalutin Ardlogie has five immaculate en-suite rooms.

Grampian Rd is positively resplendent with affordable places, as well as some pricier ones:

Cairngorm Hotel (☎ 810233, e reception@cairngorm.com) Singles/doubles £25/50. The towering Cairngorm looks beyond the average traveller's means at first glance, with its lovely lawn and prime position, but its dark, characterful rooms (all en suite) are eminently affordable.

Mackenzie's Inn (☎ 810672, fax 810595) En-suite doubles £36-50. Mackenzie's, in a traditional villa that has been modernised and extended, is brimming with bonhomie and has eight well-equipped doubles.

On Ski Rd there are some great places to stay:

Corrour House Hotel (☎ 810220, fax 811500, Inverdruie) En-suite rooms £30-40 per person. Dinner £12-20 per person. Closed Nov. This Victorian country home is a real charmer, with soaring views of the Lairig Ghru Pass and wonderful evening meals.

Mrs Bruce (☎ 810230, Dell Mhor) Singles/doubles £16/32. This wee B&B is great value and Mrs B keeps things ship-shape. It's just beyond Inverdruie on Dell Mhor.

Hilton Coylumbridge (☎ 811811, fax 811309, Coylumbridge) Singles £55-110, doubles £70-130. The Hilton Coylumbridge is perhaps the finest of the resort hotels; it's got your standard bland four-star hotel rooms but there's a top-notch indoor swimming pool and gym, and it has a handy location near the Caledonian Pine Centre in Coylumbridge village.

Places to Eat

As with places to stay, there's an array of eateries in town but, sadly, few are particularly good.

Old Bridge Inn (☎ 811137, 23 Dalfaber Rd) Mains £8.95-14.50. The Old Bridge Inn, near the youth hostel, is as laid-back a place as you'll find in Scotland, and does tasty dishes such as stewed venison (£6).

Smiffy's Fish & Chips (Grampian Rd) Smiffy's, near the station, does takeaways and a reasonable fry-up, with cod and chips for £2.40.

Royal Tandoori (☎ 811199, 43 Grampian Rd) Mains £5.50-10. Near the TIC, the Royal Tandoori has five vegetarian choices as well as typical Indian dishes. There's a 10% discount for takeaways.

Littlejohn's (☎ 811633, 113 Grampian Rd) Mains from £4.25. This branch of Littlejohn's, opposite the police station, serves steaks, pizzas, burgers, ribs, potato skins, burritos and so on. It's dependable fare, if nothing else.

Ski-ing Doo (☎ 810392, 9 Grampian Rd) Steaks up to £13. Ski-ing Doo, across the road from Littlejohn's, serves a range of steaks, including 10oz sirloins (£11.99) and 16oz T-bones (£12.99).

Mambo Café (☎ 452776, off Grampian Rd) Mains £4-7. This garish place fails early in the cool stakes by being inside Aviemore Mall, but with its international menu and jetsetting snowboard- and skate-fraternity customers, it's at least trying. They do make a superior coffee.

STRATHSPEY, THE CAIRNGORMS & THE ANGUS GLENS

Asher's Bakery (☎ 453206, Grampian Rd) Churning out delicious pork pies since 1877, Asher's Bakery is the place in town for snacks and sweet treats.

There's a small *cafe* along Ski Rd in Glenmore Forest Park. The *snack bar* and *restaurant* at the ski resort day lodge in Coire Cas serves snacks, meals and drinks until 4.30pm or 5pm in winter and until 11pm in July and August.

If you're self-catering, there's a *Tesco supermarket (☎ 887400, Grampian Rd)*, or for smoked trout, venison, paté and other such delicacies visit *Rothiemurchus Larder (☎ 810858, Rothiemurchus Estate Visitor Centre)*, 1 mile along Ski Rd.

Entertainment

Mackenzie's Inn (☎ 810672, 125 Grampian Rd) The occasional live-music gigs here are usually free but when the huge acts hit town they may charge £2.

Cairngorm Hotel (☎ 810233, Grampian Rd) The Cairngorm also hosts occasional bands and weekend disco-type affairs, which don't much bear thinking about in summer but attract a fairly discerning crowd in winter.

Getting There & Away

Bus Scottish Citylink (☎ 0870 550 5050) connects Aviemore with Inverness (£4.70, 45 minutes), Kincraig (£2.50, 10 minutes), Kingussie (£3.60, 18 minutes), Newtonmore (£4.20, 25 minutes), Dalwhinnie (£5.30, 40 minutes), Pitlochry (£6.40, 1¼ hours), Perth (£9, two hours), Glasgow (£12.50, 3¼ hours) and Edinburgh (£12.50, 3¼ hours). For Aberdeen, change at Inverness.

There's a daily overnight bus service to London's Victoria coach station (12 hours); call National Express (☎ 0870 550 5050).

Highland Country Buses (☎ 811211) runs two buses daily (June to September) from Aviemore to Fort William (£6.30) via Kingussie, Newtonmore and Laggan. There are also various weekday or schoolday runs from Aviemore to Kingussie (£3.20).

Buses stop on Grampian Rd; buy tickets at the TIC.

Train There are direct train services to London (from £63.60, 10½ hours), Glasgow/Edinburgh (£28.70, three hours) and Inverness (£9.30, 40 minutes, four to nine daily). For details phone ☎ 0845 748 4950.

Strathspey Steam Railway (☎ 810725) operates five daily services mid-April to October between Aviemore train station (the station is just east of the main train station), Boat of Garten and Nethybridge.

Getting Around

Highland Country Buses (☎ 811211) links Aviemore and Cairngorm seven times daily from June to September and from late October to April (£2.50). Buses run twice hourly (except Sunday) between Aviemore and Coylumbridge.

You can rent cars from MacDonald's Self Drive (☎ 811444), 13 Muirton Rd, from £34 per day. The company will deliver and collect from your hotel.

Several places in central Aviemore rent mountain bikes; most charge £9 to £14 per day. You can also hire bikes in Rothiemurchus Estate and Glenmore Forest Park.

AROUND AVIEMORE

There's little of interest in Aviemore; the real fun is to be had in the surrounding mountain areas.

Craigellachie Nature Reserve

Just across the A9 from Aviemore, this nature reserve at the foot of the Monadhliath Mountains makes a great place for day hikes over steep hills and through natural birch forest.

Look out for birds and other wildlife that shelter here, including finches, jackdaws and peregrine falcons (which nest from April to July). You may even spot a capercaillie.

Rothiemurchus Estate
☎ 01479

The Rothiemurchus Estate **visitors centre** *(☎ 810858, Ski Rd; admission free; open 9am-5pm daily)* is 1 mile from Aviemore along Ski Rd. It publishes a free *Visitor Guide and Footpath Map*, detailing the 50 miles of footpaths and trails through the estate, which takes in the villages of Inverdruie and Coylumbridge and extends from near Aviemore to the Cairngorm tops.

It's owned by a single family who manage the extensive Caledonian pine forest and facilities for visitors, who can also opt for ranger-guided walks, clay-pigeon shooting instruction, Land Rover tours and fishing for rainbow trout at the estate's fish farm or in the Spey.

Glenmore Forest Park
☎ 01479

Surrounding beautiful Loch Morlich, 7 miles from Aviemore, the Glenmore Forest Park – around 2000 hectares of pine and spruce – has a sandy beach and a popular **watersports centre** *(☎ 861221, Glenmore; prices vary; open daily May-Oct)* offering canoeing, windsurfing, sailing and fishing.

If travelling with kids, the **Cairngorm Reindeer Centre** *(☎ 861228; adult/child £5/3)*, by Glenmore village on the lake's east shore, is a must. You're allowed to feed the reindeer on tours with the ranger.

The **Glenmore Visitor Centre** *(☎ 861220; near the loch; open daily)* is run by Forest Enterprise and sells the excellent *Glenmore Forest Guide Map*, which details local walks (£1.50).

Places to Stay *Glenmore Camping & Caravan Park (☎ 861271, Glenmore)* Pitches £5. Open Jan-Oct. The Forestry Commission's well-organised camp site is 5 miles from Rothiemurchus, near Loch Morlich.

Loch Morlich Youth Hostel (☎ 861238, Glenmore) Beds from £9.25. Open year-round. This clean and well-run SYHA hostel has a great location in Glenmore Forest Park, 7 miles from Aviemore. It's popular so book ahead.

Cairngorm Funicular Railway

Much to the dismay of environmentalists, who waged a gallant battle to stop the huge ecological damage this attraction may still do, you can now get straight to the good views atop the Cairngorm plateau via the **funicular** *(☎ 861261, Cairngorm; adult/child £7.50/5; open 10am-5pm daily May-Nov, late closing July & Aug)*.

It starts from the car park at the end of Ski Rd and climbs to the 1085m level, where you'll find Britain's highest *cafe* (serving Scottish food), with a free mountain exhibition. For environmental and safety reasons, you're not allowed out of the top station – part of the downside of this wonder of 'convenience' – and you must return with the funicular to the car park.

Activities
Walking There are dozens of challenging walks in this area with no less than 49 Munros and four of Britain's eight mountains higher than 1333m. We only have room for two of the best here, but the Glenmore Visitor Centre (see above) can provide information on most walks in the region.

The challenge was taken out of reaching the **Cairngorm plateau** when the funicular opened in 2002, but hiking from the car park at the end of Ski Rd to the summit of **Cairn Gorm** (1245m) takes only about two hours one-way and is a far better way of seeing the mountain. From the plateau, you can continue south to climb **Ben Macdui** (Britain's second highest peak at 1309m), but this can take eight to 10 hours return from the car park and it's a serious proposition for most.

The 24-mile **Lairig Ghru** tramp – generally regarded as the finest mountain pass in Britain – traverses several massive peaks before winding down to Braemar. The walk can be done in a (long) day, travelling from Aviemore over the Lairig Ghru Pass to Braemar, but if you're not doing the full route, it's still worth taking the six-hour return hike up to the pass and back to Aviemore. The walk starts at Sugar Bowl car park, on the northeastern side of Ski Rd about 2 miles south of Glenmore.

Wherever you walk, the Cairngorms should be taken seriously – this is not the place to go for a casual stroll. The weather is notoriously fickle with low cloud, mist, strong wind, sleet and snow likely at any time – so always be prepared for the worst, even in midsummer.

STRATHSPEY, THE CAIRNGORMS & THE ANGUS GLENS

Skiing Aviemore isn't Aspen or Val d'Isère, but with 28 runs and 20 miles of piste, it's one of Britain's biggest ski areas. The season lasts from January until the snow melts, which may be as late as May.

The ski area is 9 miles southeast of Aviemore, near Glenmore Forest Park. The ski tows and funicular start at the main Coire Cas car park, connected to the more distant Coire na Ciste car park by a free shuttle bus. A Cairngorm Day Ticket for lifts costs £21 for adults and £12 for under-16s. Ski or snowboard rental costs £14.50 per day. The Cairngorm Combi (£32/21 per adult/child per day) includes equipment hire and lift tickets. The TIC distributes the free *Cairngorm Piste Map & Ride Guide*.

If there's an abundance of snow, there are several good **cross-country** routes around Loch Morlich and through the Rothiemurchus Estate, though recent years have seen few good covers at either.

During the season the TIC displays relevant avalanche warnings. For reports on snow conditions, go to W www.cairngorm mountain.com or W www.born2ski.com, or tune into Cairngorm Radio Ski FM on 96.6.

Fishing When winter's over fisher folk flood the region, both on the Spey and in most of the lochs. Rothiemurchus Estate has trout fishing in its stocked loch in Inverdruie; hire rods there. Outdoor shops in Aviemore, and all around the region, sell fishing permits for £15 for stocked lochs and £22 for fishing on the Spey, or you can rent them for £7 and £11 per day respectively.

LOCH ALVIE
☎ 01479

If you're in a car, a far better alternative to staying in Aviemore is to travel 4 miles southwest of town on the B9152 to Loch Alvie, where you'll find *Alvie Manse (☎ 810 248)*, one of the loveliest and most affordable (£22 per person) B&Bs in the area. Its impressive, huge conker tree in the front yard and its romantic rooms (especially the yellow room) will have you hooked. The B&B also rents fishing rods for those who want to dangle their bait in Loch Alvie, where pike fishing is all the rage (though you'll need to arrange a licence with them first).

Next door to Alvie Manse is the equally attractive **Alvie chapel**, which is shrouded in a gory mystery. In the late 19th century, excavations revealed 150 bodies laid head to head beneath the chapel and all brandishing weapons. No-one knows when the corpses were buried there or how they died, though it's thought they were victims of a local clan battle.

KINCRAIG
☎ 01540

Six miles southwest of Aviemore is the hamlet of Kincraig and, though there's not much more than a few shops and a fairly drab hotel here, it is a good Cairngorm base. The *Suie Hotel (☎ 651344)*, in a charming old stone building, is in need of some tender lovin' care but it does decent B&B for £23 or dorm beds for £13.

Just outside the village is the Royal Zoological Society of Scotland's **Highland Wildlife Park** *(☎ 651270; adult/child £6.50/ 4.35; open 10am-6pm daily Apr-May & Sept-Nov, 10am-7pm daily June-Aug, 10am-4pm daily Dec-Mar; last admission*

PATRICK WATSON

Mooch around the Highland Wildlife Park in Kincraig.

two hours before closing). There's a drive-through safari park offering most people their best opportunity to come face-to-face with an elusive wolf, wildcat or a furiously displaying male capercaillie; less unusual animals include Highland cattle, sheep and deer. Visitors without cars can be driven around by staff (at no extra cost), and there are also several woodland walks attached.

Also near Kincraig is Loch Insh, formed as the Spey widens. Here you'll find the **Loch Insh Watersports Centre** *(☎ 651272)* that offers two-hour beginners lessons (around £20) in everything from canoeing, windsurfing and sailing to archery and fishing. And if you don't need lessons, you can hire equipment for these activities, and lots more too – this is a seriously well-equipped place. Heck, there's even *B&B* accommodation from £18.50 per person in comfortable en-suite rooms. The food here is good, especially after 6.30pm when the lochside cafe metamorphoses into a *restaurant*.

Running off the loch is Glen Feshie, which extends eastwards into the Cairngorms. It's a quiet glen with lots of pine woods and heathery hills soaring up to their bald summits. The excellent *Glen Feshie Hostel (☎ 651323,* e *glenfeshiehostel@ totalise.co.uk)* has 14 dorm beds costing £8. It's popular with hikers, and the overnight charge includes linen and a steaming bowl of porridge to start the day.

Anyone with kids – actually, just plain anyone really – should visit the **Working Sheepdogs** *(☎ 651310)* at Leault Farm, off the Loch Insh road. Here you can see up to eight exceedingly lovable sheepdogs manoeuvring sheep and, oddly, ducks through obstacle courses. There's also a chance to feed lambs and cuddle some collie pups.

KINGUSSIE
☎ 01540 • pop 1461

Built around a charming main street, the tranquil Speyside town of Kingussie (pronounced **king**-yewsie) is home to a section of Scotland's finest folk museum, the Highland Folk Museum (the other section is in nearby Newtonmore), and is a wonderful place to base yourself in the area.

Much recent tourism to the area has been due to the BBC setting its recent TV series *Monarch of the Glen* in the never-never land of Glenbogle, and much of the village footage is shot in Kingussie.

The TIC (☎ 661297), Duke St, is in the Highland Folk Museum entrance, and opens 9.30am to 4.30pm Monday to Saturday April to October (longer hours in summer).

Things to See
The fascinating **Highland Folk Museum** *(☎ 661307, Duke St; £3; combined admission with Newtonmore £5; open 9.30am-5.30pm Mon-Sat Apr-Oct)* is split into two great parts: in Kingussie, the focus is on the everyday domestic items that were part of the traditional Highland way of life; the kitchenware, clothing, furniture and the social life of villagers. See Newtonmore & Around later in this chapter for details of the Newtonmore site.

Kingussie's other big attraction is **Ruthven Barracks** *(admission free; open at all times).* Built in 1719 on the site of an earlier 13th-century castle, the barracks, 1 mile south of Kingussie across the A9, were one of four fortresses constructed after the first Jacobite rebellion of 1715 as part of a Hanoverian scheme to control the Highlands. Given the long-range views, the location is perfect. The barracks were last occupied by Jacobite troops awaiting the return of Bonnie Prince Charlie after the Battle of Culloden. Learning of his defeat and subsequent flight, they destroyed the barracks before taking to the glens.

Walking
The Monadhliath Mountains, northwest of Kingussie, attract fewer hikers than the nearby Cairngorms, and make an ideal destination for walkers seeking peace and solitude. However, during the deer-stalking season (August to October), you'll need to check with the TIC before setting out.

The recommended six-hour circular walk to the 878m summit of Carn an Fhreiceadain, above Kingussie, begins north of the village. It continues to Pitmain Lodge and along the River Allt Mór before climbing to the cairn

STRATHSPEY, THE CAIRNGORMS & THE ANGUS GLENS

on the summit. You can then follow the ridge east to the twin summits of Beinn Bhreac (913m) before returning to Kingussie via a more easterly track.

Places to Stay & Eat

There's camping alongside *Kingussie Golf Club* (☎ 661600, Gynack Rd) for £6 per pitch.

Lairds Bothy (☎ 661334, fax 662063, 68 High St) Beds £9. This hostel lies behind the Tipsy Laird pub and has four family rooms sleeping up to six, and several eight-bed dorms.

Avondale House (☎ 661731, Newtonmore Rd) B&B £19 per person. This Edwardian home offers luxurious rooms for the price, and there's a scrumptious breakfast as well.

Arden House (☎ 661369, Newtonmore Rd) B&B from £18 per person. Arden is an imposing two-level Victorian number with well-groomed rooms and a charming garden.

Homewood Lodge (☎ 661507, Newtonmore Rd) Singles/doubles £20/30. In an old stone building with a pretty garden, friendly Homewood Lodge does four-star B&B and dinner for £10 extra. It's on the western outskirts of town.

Osprey Hotel (☎/fax 661510, Ruthven Rd) Singles/doubles from £26/50. The Osprey is a comfortable Victorian townhouse, with pleasant rooms, but its speciality is its delicious food; a four-course table d'hôte dinner will set you back £22.

The Cross (☎ 661166, fax 661080, Tweed Mill Brae, Ardbroilach Rd) Dinner & B&B £95-115 per person. Dinner £37.50 for nonresidents. Closed Tues & Dec-Mar. If you're feeling flush, visit The Cross, one of the best hotel restaurants in the Highlands. It's in a converted water mill.

Tipsy Laird (☎ 661334, High St) Mains £6.50-9.95. The jovial staff at the Tipsy Laird dole out enormous pub meals that taste as if a happy chef had a part in their making.

La Cafetiére (☎ 661020, 54 High St) The most promising of the High St cafes, it does speciality coffees from 90p, soup and a roll for £1.50 and toasties from £2.20.

Getting There & Away

Kingussie is on the Edinburgh/Glasgow to Inverness rail and bus routes; all trains stop here but only some Citylink buses. Highland Country Buses (☎ 01479-811211) run a twice-daily service (June to September) between Aviemore, Kingussie, Newtonmore and Fort William. For rail information phone ☎ 0845 748 4950.

NEWTONMORE & AROUND
☎ 01540 ● pop 1172

It's hard to imagine a more relaxed place than Newtonmore, which is strung out along one main street. The only time it ever hit the news was during the severe winter of 1995–96 when the Braeriach Hotel's boiler exploded, causing extensive damage.

In the main street, you'll find hostels and hotels, the post office, an ATM, a TIC and a Co-op supermarket. The TIC (☎ 673253), at Ralia, 1½ miles south of Newtonmore along the A9, opens daily Easter to October.

At the Newtonmore branch of the wonderful **Highland Folk Museum** (see Kingussie earlier in this chapter for details), 3 miles west of Kingussie, whole buildings have been painstakingly reconstructed according to the technology available to villagers, and using the much-forgotten skills they would have used. There's a water-powered sawmill, a joiner's workshop, a school, and on-site demonstrations include woodcarving, spinning and peat-fire baking. There's also a traditional thatch-roofed Isle of Lewis blackhouse and a 19th-century corrugated iron shed for smoking salmon.

If you're stuck for further entertainment options, there's always the **Clan MacPherson Museum** (☎ 673332, Main St; admission free; open 10am-5pm Mon-Sat & 2.30pm-5.30pm Sun May-Sept), which tells the rollicking tale of the MacPhersons and the Badenoch district.

Ten miles south is Scotland's highest distillery at **Dalwhinnie** (☎ 672219; admission including tasting £3, redeemable on purchase; open 9.30am-4.30pm Mon-Fri Mar-Dec, plus 9.30am-4.30pm Sat June-Oct & 12.30pm-4.30pm Sun July & Aug), where you can watch distillers do their thing.

The gorgeous hamlet of **Laggan**, 9 miles west of Newtonmore, was used as the village of Glenbogle in *Monarch of the Glen* and offers visitors a charming church, and a community store serving decent coffee and selling top-notch souvenir tea towels.

Places to Stay & Eat

Newtonmore Independent Hostel (☎/fax 673360, e pete@highlandhostel.co.uk) £9.50. Opposite the Craig Mhor Hotel, this hostel's clean and warm rooms make it a wonderful place to kip down for a night. The dining room looks out onto a picturesque garden. Ring ahead for weekend bookings, as this place gets busy.

Strathspey Mountain Hostel (☎ 673694, e strathspey@newtonmore.com) Dorms £10. A simple, well-cared-for hostel catering mostly for walkers and mountain bikers. This place has a good kitchen and dining area with an open fire.

There are a few average looking B&Bs on the main street if you're desperate.

The cosy *Glen Hotel (☎ 673203)* does great bar meals for £4.50 to £10.

The Pantry (☎ 673783, Main St) Snacks £2-5. If you're just passing through for breakfast or lunch, you'll do no better than The Pantry and its £3.75 breakfast or £3 quiche lunch.

Bands play on weekends occasionally at the *Mains Hotel (☎ 673206, Main St)*, but there's a cheery atmosphere every night.

Getting There & Away

From Kingussie, the A86 to Fort William leaves the A9 and follows a route through Newtonmore skirting Loch Laggan and Loch Moy, providing fine views of Ben Nevis.

A postbus (☎ 01246-546329) runs daily, except Sunday, between Newtonmore, Kinlochlaggan and Ardverikie House (also used in *Monarch of the Glen*).

Highland Country Buses (☎ 01479-811211) runs a twice-daily service (June to September) between Aviemore, Kingussie, Newtonmore and Fort William.

Only four or five trains and six or seven Citylink buses between Inverness and Edinburgh/Glasgow stop in Newtonmore.

BOAT OF GARTEN

☎ 01479 ● pop 571

Eight miles northeast of Aviemore, Boat of Garten is known as the 'Osprey Village', as these rare birds of prey nest at the RSPB's **Loch Garten Osprey Centre** *(☎ 831694, Grianan, Tulloch, Nethybridge; admission £2.50/50p; open 10am-6pm daily Apr-Aug)* in Abernethy Forest, 2 miles east of the village.

The best way of reaching Boat of Garten is on the Strathspey Steam Railway (see Getting There & Away under Aviemore earlier in this chapter).

There's a general store and post office here, plus a few places to stay.

Loch Garten Lodges (☎ 831769) Pitches £4-9. You can stick up a tent at this caravan park or rent a cottage for £200 to £370 per week year-round.

Fraoch Lodge (☎/fax 831331, Deshar Rd) Beds £7.50-12. Open year-round. You must bring your own sleeping bag to this independent hostel if you want one of the cheaper beds. Breakfast, dinner and transport to/from the hostel can be arranged in advance.

Heathbank (☎ 831234, Boat of Garten) B&B £38 per person. The Rennie Mackintosh-inspired conservatory fits oddly with the rest of this prim Victorian B&B, but it's a great place to stay. Some rooms have four-poster beds and there's a cosy fire to toast yourself in front of.

Boat Hotel (☎ 831258, fax 831414, Boat of Garten) Bar meals £6.95-12.95, 3-course dinner £29.50. The Boat's rooms (B&B from £22.50 per person.) are decent but it's the cheap eats you come here for – dishes as exquisite as pan-fried Scottish salmon with grape risotto cost just £8.

CARRBRIDGE

☎ 01479 ● pop 543

Established as a skiing village before Aviemore, this pretty place is another good option if you're hitting the slopes.

The **Landmark Highland Heritage & Adventure Park** *(☎ 841613; adult/child £5.95/4.20; open 10am-6pm daily Apr–mid-July, 10am-7pm daily mid-July–Aug, 10am-5pm* *daily Sept-Mar)*, set in a forest of Scots pines, offers a few novel and worthwhile concepts, such as the raised Treetop Trail that allows you to view red squirrels, crossbills and crested tits, and the steam-powered sawmill.

You'll find the ultimate **humpback bridge** in the centre of the village. Built in 1717, it now looks decidedly unsafe but remains impressive, especially with the thundering rapids below.

Places to Stay & Eat
Carrbridge Bunkhouse (☎/fax 841250) Beds £6.50-7.50. About half a mile out of town on the left if you're heading west on the A938 to Inverness, this cosy hostel has 18 beds in dorms and, most importantly, a sauna.

Dalrachney Lodge (☎ 841252) Singles/doubles £35/54, dinner & B&B £45/80. The Dalrachney, in a former hunting lodge, is the poshest place to stay in town and does tasty lunches and dinners.

Cairn Hotel (☎ 841212) Singles/doubles £26/44. Bar meals £4.50-4.95. This white-washed tavern has a few comfy rooms and does decent evening meals.

Carrbridge also has a *Spar supermarket* and an inexpensive *coffee shop*.

Getting There & Away
Highland Country Buses (☎ 01479-811211) runs several services daily (except Sunday) from Inverness to Carrbridge (£3.15, 45 minutes) and onwards to Grantown-on-Spey (£2.05, 17 minutes).

NETHYBRIDGE
☎ 01479 • pop 675

There's nought to do in Nethybridge but sit and soak up its clean air and good-livin' atmosphere.

There's year-round hostel accommodation at *Nethy House (☎/fax 821370)*, where dorm beds cost £6 to £9.50. Or, if you fancy a night in a former police station, try *Aspen Lodge (☎ 821042, fax 821131)*, with B&B singles/doubles from £25/39.

The Strathspey Steam Railway (see Getting There & Away under Aviemore earlier

in this chapter) finishes here, though it's being extended to Grantown-on-Spey.

Highland Country Buses (☎ 01479-811211) runs four times daily Monday to Friday from Grantown-on-Spey to Nethybridge; two buses continue to Inverness.

GRANTOWN-ON-SPEY
☎ 01479 • pop 3241

This genteel Georgian town (usually referred to as just Grantown) is situated amid an angler's paradise on the Spey and attracts older tourists by the coach-load in summer.

Most hotels can kit you up for a day of fishing or put you in touch with someone who can. Otherwise, the TIC (☎ 872773) at 54 High St, open daily March to October, will point you in the right direction. Other amenities include a bank, ATMs, food shops and post office. Perhaps the town's most shocking aspect, if you've been in small Highland towns for a few weeks, is its lonely set of traffic lights.

Places to Stay
Grantown's accommodation reflects its senior clientele, with plenty of comfortable upmarket hotels. However, there are some budget options too.

Grantown-on-Spey Caravan Park (☎ 872474, Seafield Ave) Pitches from £5. Half a mile from the town centre, this camp site opens April to October; there also are caravans to rent for £150 to £250 per week.

Speyside Backpackers (☎/fax 873514, 16 The Square) Dorm beds £9.50-11. This average hostel – the only one in town – is also known as the Stop-Over. Breakfast (£3.50) and double rooms (£15 per person) are also available.

Bank House (☎ 873256, 1 The Square) B&B £15-20 per person. The Bank of Scotland has moved out and this basic B&B has moved in. The main thing recommending it is the price; it's a fairly laid-back affair.

Rossmor (☎/fax 872201, Woodlands Terrace) B&B £25 per person. This grey-stone Victorian terrace has elegantly furnished rooms and friendly owners.

Garth Hotel (☎ 872836, Main St) B&B £29.50 per person. Mains from £4. This sprawling hotel, on your right as you enter town from Nairn, has generously sized, well-kept rooms. More importantly it does good food: its two-course lunch (soup and a roast, Monday to Saturday only) for £4.95 is a winner, as is its fabulous beer garden if it's sunny.

Places to Eat

On the High St, you'll find huge portions of fish and chips (£2.60) at the **Royal Fish Bar**. Also on High St, the **Coffee House & Ice Cream Parlour** does soup and snacks and Neapolitan *gelati* that's raved about all over town. The **Golden Grantown** *(☎ 873421, 58 High St)* is responsible for Grantown's Chinese takeaway needs; it's two doors along from the TIC.

JJ's Restaurant *(☎ 870100, Main St)* Mains £5-9. This wee restaurant, with its cosy atmosphere and kind staff, is deservedly packed with locals on weekends. It has a varied menu offering everything from chicken fajitas (£5.75) to braised lamb shanks (£6).

Culdearn House *(☎ 872106, fax 873641, Woodlands Terrace)* 4-course dinner £25. Treat yourself to a posh Scottish menu here; bookings are essential.

Ben Mhor Hotel *(☎ 872056, High St)* Mains £4.15-8.95. This hotel, opposite the TIC, has a simply decorated but ultra-friendly restaurant downstairs dishing up inexpensive and average food – but it's served with such charm you forgive them. The rainbow trout (£7) is the one standout dish.

The liveliest bar in town (and that's not saying much) is the **Claymore** *(10 Main St)*, where the staff are great fun and there's the occasional band.

Getting There & Away

Highland Country Buses (☎ 01479-811211) has six to nine buses daily, except Sunday, from Aviemore (£3.70, 35 minutes). To/from Inverness via Carrbridge, buses run two or three times daily, except Sunday (£4.20, one hour). Also, work is continuing to extend the Strathspey Steam Railway to Grantown-on-Spey.

Speyside & the Whisky Triangle

One of Scotland's loveliest valleys, Speyside is synonymous with whisky, concentrated as it is with more malt-whisky distilleries than any other part of Scotland. Famous brands include Glenfiddich and Glenlivet, but there are plenty of other, less-well-known but equally excellent distillers pumping out huge quantities each year.

DUFFTOWN

☎ 01340 ● pop 1700

Founded in 1817 by the modest 4th earl of Fife, James Duff, Dufftown is a good place to start the Malt Whisky Trail. There are seven distilleries in the area and although some haven't been working for decades they still sell copious amounts of whisky; as the local saying goes 'Rome may be built on seven hills, but Dufftown's built on seven stills'.

The TIC (☎ 820501), in the clocktower in the square, opens 10am to 1pm and 2pm to 6pm Monday to Saturday and 1pm to 6pm Sunday Easter to October.

Stagecoach Bluebird bus No 10 links Dufftown to Elgin (£3.25, 50 minutes), Huntly, Aberdeen and Inverness.

At the northern edge of town there's the **Glenfiddich Distillery Visitors Centre** (see the boxed text 'The Malt Whisky Trail' overleaf). Nearby is 13th-century **Balvenie Castle** *(owned by Historic Scotland, HS; ☎ 820121; adult/child £1.50/50p; open 9.30am-6.30pm daily Apr-Sept)*, built by Alexander 'the Black' Comyn. It was transformed into a stately home after 1550 and Mary Queen of Scots visited in 1562. Note the moat and external latrine chutes.

Places to Stay & Eat

For a central B&B, try **Davaar** *(☎ 820464, 17 Church St)* just across the street from the TIC, or **Morven** *(☎ 820507)* on Main Square. Both have simple, good-value rooms for around £18 per person.

Commercial Hotel *(☎ 820313, 4 Church St)* B&B £17 per person. At the Commercial

Hotel there are *ceilidhs* at 8.30pm on Thursday from June to September and whisky-tasting sessions at 8pm on Tuesday.

Fife Arms Hotel (☎ 820220, fax 821137, 2 The Square) Bar snacks from £1.40, mains from £5. Lunch noon-2.30pm, dinner 6pm-8pm. The bar meals menu at the Fife Arms includes locally farmed ostrich steaks. Accommodation is also available for around £25 for singles and £40 for doubles.

A Taste of Speyside (☎ 820860, 10 Balvenie St) Mains £9.90-11.90. Open 12.30pm-9pm Mon-Sat. Downhill from the TIC, this upmarket eating place prepares traditional Scottish dishes using fresh local produce.

TOMINTOUL
☎ 01807 ● pop 320

Perched at 345m, Tomintoul (pronounced **tom**-in-towel) is the highest village in Scotland. Not much more than a single road, Tomintoul was built in the 18th century by the local laird who wanted to keep a watchful eye on villagers; today it's a tourist town, serving The Lecht ski scene in winter. Tomintoul also marks the end of the Speyside Way (see the Activities chapter for details), so both skiers and walkers are found here year-round.

There's a TIC (☎ 580285) on The Square, open Easter to October.

The Malt Whisky Trail

Speyside is home to the 70-mile-long Malt Whisky Trail, a well-signposted romp around the area's distilleries. Unless you're intent on getting to know your whiskies, it's best just to visit a couple. All offer tastings at the end of their tours, and the price of entry for most is redeemable on purchases in the store at the end of the tour.

Glenfiddich Distillery Visitors Centre *(☎ 01340-820373; admission free; open 9.30am-4.30pm Mon-Sat, noon-4.30pm Sun Easter–mid-Oct, 9.30am-4.30pm Mon-Fri mid-Oct–Easter)* Visitors are guided through the process of distilling, and can even see whisky being bottled. There's no admission charge, so your free dram really is free.

Strathisla *(☎ 01542-783044, in Keith 10 miles northeast of Dufftown; £4, of which £2 is redeemable with purchases; open 9.30am-6pm Mon-Sat, 12.30pm-6pm Sun Feb-Nov)* The oldest distillery in the region, Strathisla occupies a beautiful position next to the River Isla. This whisky is blended into the better known (and slightly cheaper) Chivas Regal.

Speyside Cooperage *(☎ 01340-871108, near Craigellachie; admission £2.50; open 9.30am-4.30pm Mon-Sat Jun-Sep, 9.30am-4.30pm Mon-Fri Oct-May)*. This is a place for genuine whisky-lovers to admire the fascinating craft of producing the oak casks, which are used by many distilleries in Scotland.

Glen Grant *(☎ 01542-783318, Rothes on the A941; admission £3, of which £2 is redeemable with purchases; open 10am-4pm Mon-Sat Mar-Oct, 11am-5pm daily Jun-Sep)* There's no production going on here at the moment, but it's a charming place to stop and wander through the Victorian gardens and orchards, set next to a gorgeous burn.

Cardhu *(☎ 01340-810498, on the B9102 at Knockando; admission £2 redeemable with purchases in store; open 10am-4pm Mon-Fri Mar-Nov, 9.30am-4.30pm Sat Apr-Sep, 11am-4pm Sun Jul-Sep)* Opened in the late 19th century, this distillery produces a full-bodied, peaty whisky.

Dallas Dhu *(☎ 01309-676548, near Forres off the A940; admission £3; open daily 10am-6pm Apr-Sep, 10am-4pm Mon-Wed & Sat, 9.30am-noon Thur, 2pm-4.30pm Sun Oct-Mar)* No longer churning out whisky, you can still wander around this atmospheric Victorian distillery and inspect the equipment while listening to your audioguide.

Glenlivet *(☎ 01542-783220; £2.50 redeemable with purchases; open 10am-4pm Mon-Sat Apr-Oct)* Though whisky had been produced long before, this distillery 9 miles north of Tomintoul was the first licensed in the region, being granted permission by parliament in 1824. Since then it's become one of the big names in world whisky and is now owned by Seagram's, the world's largest alcohol producer.

STRATHSPEY, THE CAIRNGORMS & THE ANGUS GLENS

Tomintoul Museum & Visitor Centre
(☎ 673701, The Square; admission free; open 10am-4pm Mon-Sat June-Sept, 10am-4pm Mon-Fri May & Oct) has displays on local history. **Glenlivet Estate** (☎ 580283, Main St) has an information centre distributing free walking and cycling maps.

You can pick up a spur of the **Speyside Way** (see the Activities chapter for details of the walk) footpath that runs from Tomintoul to Ballindalloch, 15 miles to the north.

Infrequent buses connect Tomintoul with Aberlour (on schooldays, with a connection to Elgin), Elgin (Thursday only, 1¼ hours) and Keith via Dufftown (Tuesday only, 1¼ hours). For details phone Roberts of Rothiemay on ☎ 01466-711213.

Places to Stay & Eat
The basic but friendly SYHA **Tomintoul Youth Hostel** (☎ 580282, Main St) has dorm beds for £6.75/6; it's open mid-May to late October. Alternatively, the slightly better **Tomintoul Bunkhouse** (☎ 01343-548105, The Square) charges £8 for beds and opens year-round.

The Glenavon Hotel (☎ 580218, fax 580733, The Square) is a more comfortable option, with B&B for £15 to £26 per person.

There are various places to eat, including the **Clockhouse** on The Square. Two shops sell groceries (including the post office).

Deeside

Rising in the Cairngorms, the River Dee flows eastwards towards Aberdeen, and the valley through which it flows is known as Deeside – or, more commonly, as Royal Deeside due to its connections with the royal family, who've been holidaying at Balmoral since the days of Queen Victoria in the 1850s.

Thankfully this royal link has saved Deeside from the mass development that has so spoiled nearby regions, and there's an air of proud opulence in the villages that line the A93. It's also a wonderful area for fishing, hiking, mountain biking and canoeing.

BALLATER
☎ 01339 ● pop 1260
Ballater is desperately pleased with its royal connection; it supplies nearby Balmoral Castle with its provisions – hence the many shops sporting 'By Royal Appointment' crests. But if you can forgive the royal toadying, Ballater's a bonny place, even though accommodation is fairly expensive and budget travellers are better advised to head for Braemar.

The TIC (☎ 755306), Station Square, opens from Easter to October. There's a supermarket and a bank with an ATM on Bridge St.

The village is set around a pretty **parish church** and central square with a clocktower dating from 1798. There isn't really much to see, though there are a few pleasant **walks** in the hills around town. The woodland walk up **Craigendarroch** (400m) takes just over an hour, but it's quite steep. **Morven** (871m) is a more serious prospect, taking around six hours, but there are good views from the top.

The best walk in the area goes to the summit of **Lochnagar** (1155m) from Spittal of Glenmuick car park. It's not a difficult route, but care should be taken on the summit plateau – there are huge cliffs on the northern side.

If you need to get any outdoor gear, the staff at **Lochnagar Leisure** (☎ 756008, Station Square) are a helpful bunch. Bike and fishing-equipment hire are available from **Wheels & Reels** (☎ 755864, 2 Braemar Rd); bicycles cost £10 per day or £50 per week.

Places to Stay & Eat
There's no hostel in town, but if you're camping, the town **camp site** (☎ 755727) has a reasonable location by the river, and pitches from £6.

Easily the best of the affordable B&Bs in town is **Inverdeen House** (☎ 755759, e info@inverdeen.com, 11 Bridge Square), a snug two-level cottage by the Alexandra Hotel. In high/low season B&B costs £25/22 per person.

Glenaden Hotel (☎ 755488, 6 Church Square) B&B from £18 per person. This slightly grim drinking emporium behind the church actually has decent accommodation, and great food; its chicken curry (£4.50) is delectable.

The snooty B&Bs on Braemar Rd should be avoided by anyone not sporting a blue rinse and driving a late-model estate; an exception to this rule is the wonderful *Auld Kirk Hotel & Restaurant (☎ 755762, e auldkirkhotel@aol.com, Braemar Rd)*, a charming old church that has been turned into a fairly luxurious B&B. Accommodation costs around £40 per person and there's also a top-notch menu.

Alexandra Hotel (☎ 755376, 12 Bridge Square) B&B £24-30 per person. Although this place does B&B you're more likely to want to come here for a relaxing ale or two.

Green Inn (☎ 755501, e green.inn@ next.org.uk, 9 Victoria Rd) 2-/3-course dinner £28/32. This magnificent inn is probably the best place to stay and eat in town. Its dazzling a la carte menu isn't cheap but the quality of food is second to none. You can do dinner and B&B from £60 per person, including an equally wonderful breakfast.

Station Restaurant (☎ 755805, Station Square) Mains from £2. This place is a much cheaper alternative, with home-baked fare from £1.80 and inexpensive burgers for around £2. xNearby the *Silver Teapot (8 Bridge St)* does wonderful soups (£1.65) and sandwiches (£1.50 to £2.70).

La Mangiatoria (☎ 755999, Tullich Rd) Mains £5-10. Open 5pm-10pm weekdays, noon-10pm weekend. If you've been desperate for decent Italian food, this is probably the only place in the region you'll get your fix. The huge pizzas (£5 to £7) are delicious, as is the *pasta primavera* (£6.40).

Getting There & Away

Stagecoach Bluebird buses run almost every hour from Aberdeen (1¾ hours); every two hours on Sunday. The service continues to Braemar.

BALMORAL CASTLE
☎ 01339

Eight miles west of Ballater, Balmoral *(☎ 742334; adult/child £4.50/1; open 10am-*

5pm daily mid-Apr–end July) was built for the area's all-powerful Gordon family, but bought by Queen Victoria in 1852; she and husband Prince Albert had originally sought out a residence much farther north, but were advised by doctors that Albert's delicate constitution might not withstand the harsh climates.

The grounds and an exhibition of paintings, artwork and royal tartans in the ballroom are open, but the rest of the castle is closed to the prying eyes of the public. On the edge of the estate is **Crathie Church**, which the Royals visit when they're here; crowds desperate for a glimpse of royal flesh gather by the TIC car park on Sunday morning and wait for Liz and Phil (if they're in residence) to drive past on their way to morning worship.

The castle is beside the A93 and can be reached on the Aberdeen-Braemar bus (see the following Braemar section).

BRAEMAR
☎ 01339 ● pop 410

Lying at the base of the Cairngorm massif, Braemar is the final town along the River Dee. Because it is picturesquely situated on booming waters rushing into the Dee, it can be a touristy bus-'em-in-bus-'em-out town in summer.

But it's also a vigorous outdoors kind of place year-round, with wonderful walking opportunities in summer and skiing at Glenshee in winter. However, it can get chilly in winter months: Britain's coldest temperature of -29°C was recorded here. During spells of severe cold, hungry deer wander the streets looking for a bite to eat.

There's a helpful TIC (☎ 741600), The Mews, Mar Rd, open year-round. It has lots of useful information on walks in the area. There's a bank with an ATM at the junction in the centre.

Things to See

Just north of the village, turreted **Braemar Castle** *(☎ 741219; adult/child £3/1; open 10am-6pm daily July & Aug, 10am-6pm Sat-Thur Apr-June & Sep-Oct)* dates from 1628 and is worth a visit. This L-shaped

Braemar Gathering

There are gatherings in many Highland villages, but the biggest and best known is Braemar's.

Taking place on a well-tended 12-acre site near the town centre, the gathering is held on the first Saturday of each September and includes events such as Highland dancing, pipers, tug-of-war, a hill race up Morrone, caber tossing, hammer and stone throwing, and the long jump.

These types of events took place informally in the Highlands for many centuries as tests of skill and strength, but were formalised around 1820 due to rising pseudo-Highland romanticism caused by the likes of King George IV and Sir Walter Scott. Queen Victoria attended the Braemar Gathering in 1848, starting the tradition of royal patronage that continues to this day.

Organised by the Braemar Royal Highland Society since 1817, it's the town's major event each year, and there's absolutely no guarantee you'll get a ticket if you just turn up. It is best to buy tickets early; they go on sale on 1 February from the Bookings Secretary, BRHS, Coilacriech, Ballater AB35 5UH. They cost from £6 for admission to the field and £10 to £12 for the uncovered stand, to £18.50 for the grandstand.

fortress was a government garrison after the 1745 Jacobite rebellion, and has impressive vaulted ceilings and a particularly nasty pit prison. Its big attraction is the world's largest cairngorm (a semi-precious variety of quartz); the yellow, brown and grey slab of rock weighs a monumental 52lb.

The **Braemar Highland Heritage Centre** (☎ 741944, Mar Rd; admission free; open 9am-6pm daily May-Sept, 9am-5pm Mon-Fri, 10am-5pm Sat & Sun), by the TIC, tells the story of the area with displays and video (in several languages).

The town's only Internet access is at the youth hostel (50p per five minutes).

Walking & Cycling

For outdoor or ski gear try the well-stocked **Braemar Mountain Sports** (☎ 741496, Invercauld Rd), which opens daily. It also rents bikes for £10/15 per half-/full day.

An easy walk from Braemar is up **Creag Choinnich** (538m), a hill to the east of town, above the A93. There are route markers and the walk takes about 1½ hours. For a longer walk (three hours) and superb views of the Cairngorms – especially in autumn when the colours are extraordinary – climb **Morrone** (859m), the mountain southwest of Braemar.

Places to Stay & Eat

Because of the crowds that flood this town, there's a variety of cheap B&Bs and hostels.

Braemar Youth Hostel (☎ 741659, 21 Glenshee Rd) Dorm beds £9.25. Open year-round. This huge SYHA hostel is in an imposing old four-storey stone mansion surrounded by a slightly spooky pine forest, on its own block of land off the A93 going south to Blairgowrie. The kitchen and lounge facilities are excellent.

Rucksacks (☎ 741517, 15 Mar Rd) Beds £8.50 per person. This delightful hostel, behind the newsagent/chemist, is a cheery, sociable place to stay. It has 26 bunk beds in three separate dorms, plus a chalet sleeping up to 10 and one twin bedroom.

Braemar Lodge (☎/fax 741627, Glenshee Rd) B&B from £20 per person. Dinner & B&B from £40. The top B&B in town, this restored Victorian shooting lodge on the outskirts of the village is now a wonderful place to stay and eat; the chef is renowned right round Deeside as a culinary wonder and his fried duck (£13) and roasts (£8) are specialities. There's also a well-designed and spotlessly clean *bunkhouse* at the back of the lodge. It's a simple but classy set-up with 12 beds in three areas separated by simple walls. There's no kitchen.

Schiehallion House (☎ 741679, 10 Glenshee Rd) B&B £19-21 per person. Nearby is this immaculate B&B, whose combination of striped wallpaper and floral everything else might just send you crazy if you're a loosely hinged type; should you

STRATHSPEY, THE CAIRNGORMS & THE ANGUS GLENS

survive the night, the delightful owners will serve you a tasty cooked breakfast.

Other good B&Bs nearby include *Craiglea* (☎ 741641, Hillside Dr) with B&B for £17 to £19 per person and *Wilderbank* (☎ 741651, Kindrochit Dr) with B&B for £18.50 to £20 per person.

Callater Lodge Hotel (☎ 741275, e maria@hotel-braemar.co.uk, 9 Glenshee Rd) B&B £24-29 per person. This impressive, free-standing stone cottage has charming rooms and helpful owners; it's popular so book ahead.

Fife Arms Hotel (☎ 741644, Mar Rd) B&B from £30 per person. This huge place has slightly characterless rooms, but its main attraction is its great bar meals (£4.95 to £9.95) in front of a roaring log fire in winter. There's a daily carvery and always a roast lunch special for around £6. This is also where the town's nightlife happens – the bar is a great place to drink; there's a pool table and live music every Friday and Saturday night.

Gordon's Restaurant (☎ 741247, 20 Mar Rd) Mains £5-7. This traditional tearoom does Scottish fare as well as the occasional curry night to keep the locals on edge.

Cheaper alternatives include the *Braemar Takeaway* (14 Invercauld Rd) with fish and chips for £3.10.

There's an *Alldays supermarket* next door to Gordon's Restaurant.

Getting There & Away

The drive from Perth to Braemar is idyllic but public transport is limited to one daily bus, operated by Stagecoach Bluebird (bus No 200), which departs Perth at 4.45pm (£6, 2¼ hours). From Aberdeen to Braemar (£6, 2¼ hours), there are several Stagecoach Bluebird buses.

INVEREY
☎ 01339

Five miles west of Braemar at the end of the road is the tiny settlement of Inverey and the lovely **Linn of Dee**, where the Dee plunges through a dramatic gorge.

Numerous mountain walks (see the Activities section earlier in this chapter) start from here, including the adventurous **Lairig Ghru** route. The Cairngorm peaks of Cairn Gorm and Ben Macdui are actually on or just this side of the regional border.

You also find the excellent SYHA *Inverey Youth Hostel* (☎ 741969) here. It opens mid-May to early October and dorm beds cost £6.50.

There's an afternoon postbus (daily except Sunday) from Braemar to Inverey hostel and the Linn of Dee.

GLENSHEE SKI CENTRE
☎ 01339

Halfway between Braemar and Blairgowrie is the Glenshee Ski Centre. At the crest of the magnificent Cairnwell Pass (733m) – Britain's highest road pass – Glenshee is the largest skiing area in the country, with 32 pistes and a reasonable amount of cross-country skiing. If you are driving here from Braemar you can marvel at the impressive views.

The chairlift at the **Glenshee Ski Centre** (☎ 741320, e glenshee@sol.co.uk, w www .ski-glenshee.co.uk), on the border of Perthshire and Aberdeenshire, can whisk you up to 920m, near the top of The Cairnwell (933m). It opens daily in winter, whenever there's enough snow, and a one-day lift pass and ski hire costs from £26; two-hour class instruction costs £12.

Five miles south on the A93 is the **Spittal of Glenshee** village, where you'll find the *Spittal of Glenshee Hotel* (☎ 885215). It has B&B/bunkhouse accommodation (including breakfast) for £28/13.50 per person.

Dalmunzie House Hotel (☎ 885224, fax 885225) Singles/doubles from £42/80. This grand hotel is set in a 6500-acre estate, 1½ miles off the main road. It does exquisite restaurant meals for around £20 extra.

BLAIRGOWRIE & AROUND
☎ 01250 ● pop 8500

This busy town is the pseudo-capital of the area, and has an industrious centre. There isn't much of interest to keep you here, though it's a great place to stop for a bite to eat. The TIC (☎ 872960), at 26 Wellmeadow on the central square, has good

Get a piste of the action: skiing and snowboarding in Aviemore

Climber atop Beinn Mheadhoin

Rambling over the rugged terrain at Buachaille Etive Mór, Glencoe

Purple haze: the spine-tingling views across the Mamores from Ben Nevis

PAT YALE

GRAEME CORNWALLIS

GARETH McCORMACK

GARETH McCORMACK

Edzell's Dalhousie Arch (1889) straddles High St.

The call of the wild in the Grampians

Dee-lightful Linn of Dee gushes through Inverey.

Eilean Donan Castle looms over Loch Duich.

The bonny walled garden at Edzell Castle

information on the surrounding areas. On Allan St, just off Wellmeadow, there are two banks with ATMs.

The **Keathbank Mill & Heraldry Centre** (☎ 872025, Balmoral Rd; adult/child £4/2; open 10.30am-5pm daily Easter-Sept), off the A93 Braemar road, is well worth a look. You'll see Scotland's largest working waterwheel, a steam engine dating from 1862, two model railways, a heraldry museum and woodcarving displays.

If you need to hire bicycles, **Scottish Cycling Holidays** (☎ 876100, 87 Perth St) does mountain bikes and hybrids from £45/10 per week/day.

If you're absolutely desperate for a sight to tick off your list, 3 miles south of Blairgowrie is the **Meikleour beech hedge**, planted in 1746 and, at 30m, the world's highest hedge.

About 5 miles east of Blairgowrie on the A926 to Kirriemuir is the attractive village of **Alyth**. Ask the TIC for the *Walk Old Alyth* leaflets; there are many old buildings to see, including church ruins dating from 1296.

Places to Stay & Eat
Dunmore (☎ 874451, Newton St) Singles/doubles £18/34. This neat pad has four double rooms with shared bathroom.

Angus Hotel (☎ 872455, fax 375615, 46 Wellmeadow) B&B £40 per person. The Angus' motto is 'No stay is long enough', but we'd have to say one night is just about perfect; the comfortable, well-appointed rooms are fine, though it's on the busiest corner in town and not a particularly gracious one at that. The bar food (£4.50 to £8.95), however, is excellent and its £80 weekend dinner, B&B and Sunday lunch deal is a real bargain.

Cargill's Bistro (☎ 876735, Lower Mill St) Mains £5.50-14.95. In a pleasant riverside area, Cargill's Bistro also does great snacks, such as soup and a roll for £1.75.

There are several supermarkets, including *Somerfield*, by Wellmeadow.

Alyth has some good places to stay, the best of which is *Drumnacree House (☎/fax 01828-632194, St Ninian's Rd)*, with singles/doubles from £45/80. There's also

a good restaurant attached, serving traditional Scottish fare (mains £4.80 to £13.90).

Blackbird Inn (☎ 01828-632293, Nr Alyth) Meals £3.25-3.75. The Blackbird Inn, by the A926 just west of Alyth, dates from 1869 and serves home-made bar meals.

Getting There & Away
Strathtay Scottish (☎ 01382 228 054) operates a service from Perth to Blairgowrie (£2.20, 50 minutes, six or seven daily, except Sunday). There's also a bus from Blairgowrie to Dundee (£2.40, 50 minutes, six to eight daily, except Sunday).

The only service from Blairgowrie to the Glenshee area is the postbus (☎ 872766) to Spittal of Glenshee (no Sunday service).

The Angus Glens

In the far southeast of the Highlands lie the Angus Glens, a series of five alluring glens – Isla, Prosen, Clova, Lethnot and Esk – running roughly parallel to each other. Rising from the rich farming land along the Strathmore plain, all five are exceptionally peaceful, and offer some easy hiking over grand rolling hills and dales. Filled with tourists (especially Clova and Esk) in the height of summer, these places are almost deserted in spring and autumn and you're likely to have the whole area to yourself. In winter, they're virtually impenetrable, even on cross-country skis.

There's a limited postbus service, but getting around the glens properly is really only possible with your own transport.

KIRRIEMUIR
☎ 01575 ● pop 5306
The gateway to Glens Isla, Prosen and Clova, Kirriemuir is an attractive conservation town, with narrow winding streets that evoke a great feeling of times past. It is flooded with hunters in the stalking season but it makes a good base for exploring the Angus Glens.

The TIC (☎ 574097), Cumberland Close, opens 10am to 5pm Monday to Saturday April to September.

Things to See

Owned by the National Trust for Scotland (NTS), **Barrie's Birthplace** (☎ *572646, 9 Brechin Rd; adult/child £2.50/1.80; open 10am-5.30pm Mon-Sat & from 1.30pm Sun May-Oct)* is a two-storey house where the author of *Peter Pan*, JM Barrie, was born in 1860. His work is eulogised, and there's a variety of newspaper clippings and photos of the great man, as well as his writing desk.

By the town square you'll find **The Tolbooth**, dating from 1604, and previously used as a jail. The **Aviation Museum** (☎ *573233, Bellies Brae; donations welcome; open 10am-5pm)* has a large collection of WWII relics.

Places to Stay & Eat

Airlie Arms Hotel (☎ *572847, fax 573055,* @ *info@airliearms-hotel.co.uk, St Malcolm's Wynd)* Singles/doubles £28.50/56. Once a medieval monastery, this inn is a great place to eat even if all that history and all the men with guns (hunters love this place) make it a slightly spooky place to stay. Rooms are tidy and well cared for though and the staff are a chatty bunch. The bar is definitely the best in town.

Cheaper B&B is available at *Crepto* (☎ *572746, Kinnordy Place)* and *Woodlands* (☎ *572582, 2 Lisden Gardens)*, both with basic rooms from £22 per person.

The *Kirrie Food Bazaar (Reform St)* does cheap takeaways for around £1 to £1.80, and the Chinese restaurant *Tin On (30 Roods)* does chicken chow mein for £3.80. There's a large *Tesco* supermarket across the street.

GLEN ISLA
☎ 01575

Running roughly parallel with Glen Shee, this glen lies on the beautiful (but torturously slow) B951 and B954 roads, which have several scattered communities along it. At the foot of the glen, by Bridge of Craigisla, is the pleasant waterfall of **Reekie Linn** ('smoking fall').

Five miles north is Kirkton of Glenisla, where you'll find the wonderful *Glen Isla Hotel* (☎ *582223,* @ *glenislahotel@col*

.co.uk), a cosy 17th-century inn that has romantic log fires in its bar, magnificently plush bedrooms, and professional, friendly owners. Rooms cost from £27 per person and it's a special place to stay.

The wild and mountainous upper reaches of Glen Isla also include the **Caenlochan National Nature Reserve**, which can be reached from several trails near here; ask at the hotel for more information.

A postbus (☎ 0845 774 0740) operates from Blairgowrie to Auchavan Monday to Saturday.

GLEN PROSEN

Near the foot of the glen, 5 miles north of Kirriemuir, is the tiny village of Dykehead. From here Glens Prosen and Clova divide; tranquil Glen Prosen goes deep into the Grampians and, compared to Glen Clova, has relatively few walkers scurrying over its hills.

From Glenprosen Lodge, at the top of the glen, the **Kilbo Path** leads over a pass between Mayar (928m) and Driesh (947m), descending to *Glendoll Youth Hostel* (see Glen Clova below) at the end of the Glen Clova public road.

The Kirriemuir to Glen Prosen postbus (☎ 0845 774 0740) runs once daily, except Sunday.

GLEN CLOVA
☎ 01575

This long and lush glen, by far the most touristy of the five glens, stretches north from Kirriemuir and is dominated by craggy mountains at its head. Look out for the **waterwheel** by the Clova Hotel, and picturesque **Cortachy Castle** in the lower part of the glen, where Charles II stayed in the 17th century.

There are some great hikes in the glen, including the four-hour **Loch Brandy** circuit from the hotel, and the six-hour walk to **Mayar** and **Driesh** from Glendoll Youth Hostel.

You can also walk **Jock's Road** from the hostel to Braemar (five to seven hours), but this route climbs above 900m and is not an easy option.

There's a *camp site* (☎ *550233)* with basic facilities (April to September) by the bridge at Acharn (near the end of the road). Pitches costs £3.

Glendoll Youth Hostel (☎ *550236)* Beds £8.25. Open Apr–mid-Sept. Located at the end of the Glen Clova public road, this SYHA hostel is in a good position for exploring the surrounding hills.

Clova Hotel (☎ *550350, fax 550292)* B&B £35-39 per person. Bunkhouse bed £9.50. This hotel, 3½ miles down the road from the hostel, is popular with climbers and has regular ceilidhs in summer. There's also a year-round 30-bed bunkhouse with a fully fitted kitchen.

The Kirriemuir to Glen Clova postbus (☎ 0845 774 0740) runs services twice on weekdays and once on Saturday. The 8.30am departure from Kirriemuir goes to the hostel, but the 3.05pm departure from Kirriemuir (not Saturday) only goes as far as Clova Hotel.

GLEN ESK
☎ 01356

The road runs a scenic 13 miles from the village of Edzell to the head of beautiful Glen Esk, the most easterly Angus Glen. Three miles before you get to the end of the road, though, is the excellent **Glenesk Folk Museum** (☎ *670254; adult/child £2/1; open noon-6pm daily June-Oct, noon-6pm Sat-Mon Easter-May)*. In an old shooting lodge known as The Retreat, the extensive local folk history collection is insightful. There's also a *tearoom* attached.

GLEN LETHNOT
☎ 01356

To reach these two final glens, you must first travel east to the large town of **Brechin**, 14 miles east of Kirriemuir. At Glen Lethnot, the least touristy of the Angus Glens, there are two extraordinary Iron-Age hill forts, the **Brown and White Caterthuns**.

At Bridgend, 4 miles west of Edzell, is *The Post House* (☎ *660277)*, with B&B for £14 per person and dinner for £6 extra.

EDZELL
☎ 01356

A planned village at the foot of Glen Esk and 6 miles north of Brechin, Edzell has an arched stone gateway known as the **Dalhousie Arch**. One mile to the west is **Edzell Castle** (HS; ☎ 648631; adult/child £2.80/1; open 9.30am-6.30pm daily Apr-Sept, 9.30am-4.30pm Mon-Wed & Sat, 9.30am-1pm Thur & 2pm-4.30pm Sun Oct-Mar)*, a 16th-century L-plan towerhouse. It has a splendid garden, and even though the castle is roofless, it is definitely worth a visit.

Inchcape (☎ *647266, High St)* B&B £18 per person. Inchcape is the village's best B&B, offering comfortable en-suite rooms in an attractive Victorian house.

Glenesk Hotel (☎ *648319, fax 647333, High St)* Singles/doubles £58/95. The Glenesk is a plush hotel adjoining the town's golf course, and boasting a pool, spa and sauna.

Strathtay Scottish runs two to six buses daily from Brechin to Edzell (20 minutes). There's no public transport from Edzell into the glen, so you'll need your own wheels.

STRATHSPEY, THE CAIRNGORMS & THE ANGUS GLENS

The Great Glen & the Western Highlands

Best known as home to Loch Ness and its unconfirmed monster, the Great Glen – which comprises the four lochs stretching from Inverness in the north down to Fort William in the south – is one of the world's major geological fault lines, formed when the glaciers of the last Ice Age slid 50 miles southwards.

This remarkable and often incomprehensibly beautiful region has long been an important communication route – General George Wade built a military route along the southern side of Loch Ness in the early 18th century to quash the Jacobite rebellion, and in 1822 the Great Glen's four lochs were linked when the Caledonian Canal created a waterway spanning the breadth of Scotland. The modern A82 road was completed in 1933, and immediately filled each summer with Nessie-spotters.

Nearby are the spectacular western Highlands, taking in scenery as diverse as the soaring Glen Shiel mountains, picturesque Plockton, the bleak splendour of Ardgour and the isolated Morvern peninsula. Geologists will find nirvana among the shattered rock formations of isolated Ardnamurchan, while history buffs will enter paradise amid the stunning glory of Glenfinnan, where Bonnie Prince Charlie began his rebellion. Clan groupies will be enraptured by Lochaber, stretching from Loch Leven to Moidart in the west, and was the base for the well-known Macdonald and Cameron families. Meanwhile, beach-lovers can wallow in white sandy beaches and crystal-clear turquoise waters along the magnificent Road to the Isles from Fort William to Mallaig.

The following Ordnance Survey (OS) Landranger maps cover the Great Glen:

Landranger 25: Glen Carron & Glen Affric
Landranger 26: Inverness & Loch Ness, Strathglass

Highlights

- Climb towering Ben Nevis for Scotland's most staggering views
- Walk the shores of atmospheric Glen Coe, site of the Glen Coe massacre that changed Scotland forever
- Pack your watercolours and join the painters on the waterfront in pretty Plockton
- Picture Bonnie Prince Charlie rowing ashore at breathtaking Glenfinnan to start the 1745 uprising
- Wander the azure beaches between Arisaig and Morar on the exhilarating Road to the Isles
- Spot dolphins from the isolated Ardnamurchan lighthouse

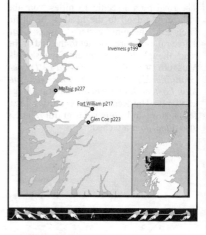

Landranger 27: Nairn & Forres, River Findhorn
Landranger 33: Loch Alsh, Glen Shiel & Loch Hourn
Landranger 34: Fort Augustus, Glen Albyn & Glen Roy

THE GREAT GLEN & THE WESTERN HIGHLANDS

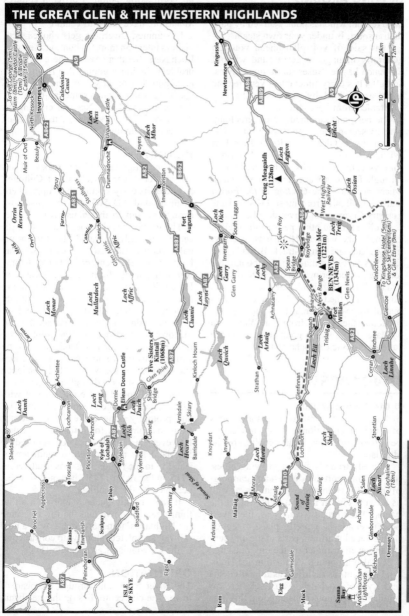

GETTING AROUND

The best way to get around this often isolated region, which is poorly served by public transport, is under your own steam.

That said, if you plan ahead you can generally manage to get around without too much hassle. Buses run to most towns, and all TICs carry timetables. Very remote areas are served by postbuses; pick up timetables from post offices.

The best, and admittedly most gruelling, way of seeing the region is by bike. The 80-mile Great Glen Cycle Route from Fort William to Inverness, via Fort Augustus, follows canal towpaths and gravel tracks through forests to avoid the busy roads, where possible. The *Cycling in the Forest* leaflet, available from most TICs and the Forestry Commission, gives details.

Cycling around other parts of the region, especially the western Highlands, is a joy: many roads are single-track B-roads that few cars take. On main roads, though, the tour buses thundering past can be terrifying.

The West Highland Railway (see the boxed text in the Getting Around chapter) is one of the world's great train journeys, in particular the section from Fort William to Mallaig. There's also great scenery on the Inverness–Kyle of Lochalsh train.

Inverness

☎ 01463 ● pop 42,300

Still drunk on the awesome cultural kudos of official recognition as a city in December 2000, Inverness is the 'capital' of the Highlands.

One of Britain's fastest growing cities, it's the transport hub and main jumping-off point for Highland explorations, as well as a lively city in its own right. Set on the banks of the broad River Ness, the Inverness riverside is a pretty place – though things get a bit grim in parts of the city centre and even grimmer on the city outskirts.

It's also a popular destination for Highland residents as far afield as John o'Groats and Kyle of Lochalsh, who flock here for regular conspicuous consumption; this is as far north as the colonies of retail empires such as Sainsburys, Dixons and Virgin Megastore have dared to venture.

In summer, Inverness gets choked with visitors intent on monster-hunting at nearby Loch Ness. In other seasons, there's never a problem finding a good-value room and a great pub. Whenever you're here, it's worth spending some time promenading along the picturesque River Ness, or cruising on the Moray Firth in search of its flocks of bottlenose dolphins.

HISTORY

Like every Highland village, truck stop and bus shelter, Inverness claims St Columba as one of its early visitors; he stopped here in or around AD 565, pausing just long enough to convert the Pictish King Brude.

Things didn't really hot up until the 12th century, when King David I built the original Inverness Castle (the present one was built in the 19th century by Oliver Cromwell using stones from Macbeth's castle at Dingwall) to command lucrative sea trading routes. Inverness soon became rich with its brisk trade in fur, fish, timber and wool.

Riches didn't give peace a chance though; the town's importance as a trade route made it a prime target for Highland clans. In the 13th century it would also become a key staging post in the War of Independence between the Scots and English armies.

The next round of trouble arrived with Mary Queen of Scots, who came in 1562 and promptly hanged the town governor from the ramparts for refusing her entry. However, she quickly became fascinated by Highland life and brought a modicum of stability to the region; this was shattered in 1715 and again in 1745 when the town was occupied by the Jacobites.

It wasn't until Queen Victoria's era that things calmed down and the town became the Highlands' transport centre, with a new railway completed, along with construction of the Caledonian Canal, in the 1800s.

ORIENTATION

The River Ness runs through the heart of town. The city centre lies on the east bank,

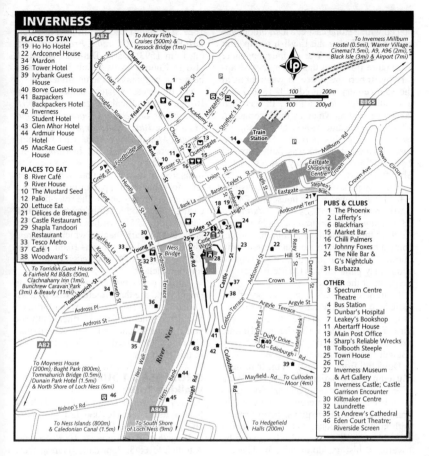

INVERNESS

PLACES TO STAY
19 Ho Ho Hostel
22 Ardconnel House
34 Mardon
36 Tower Hotel
39 Ivybank Guest House
40 Borve Guest House
41 Bazpackers Backpackers Hotel
42 Inverness Student Hotel
43 Glen Mhor Hotel
44 Ardmuir House Hotel
45 MacRae Guest House

PLACES TO EAT
8 River Café
9 River House
10 The Mustard Seed
12 Palio
20 Lettuce Eat
21 Délices de Bretagne
23 Castle Restaurant
29 Shapla Tandoori Restaurant
33 Tesco Metro
37 Café 1
38 Woodward's

PUBS & CLUBS
1 The Phoenix
2 Lafferty's
6 Blackfriars
15 Market Bar
16 Chilli Palmers
24 The Nile Bar & G's Nightclub
31 Barbazza

OTHER
3 Spectrum Centre Theatre
4 Bus Station
5 Dunbar's Hospital
7 Leakey's Bookshop
11 Abertarff House
13 Main Post Office
14 Sharp's Reliable Wrecks
18 Tolbooth Steeple
25 Town House
26 TIC
27 Inverness Museum & Art Gallery
28 Inverness Castle; Castle Garrison Encounter
30 Kiltmaker Centre
32 Laundrette
35 St Andrew's Cathedral
46 Eden Court Theatre; Riverside Screen

To Moray Firth Cruises (500m) & Kessock Bridge (1mi)

To Inverness Millburn Hostel (0.5mi), Warner Village Cinema (1.5mi), A9, A96 (2mi), Black Isle (3mi) & Airport (7mi)

To Torridon Guest House & Fairfield Rd B&Bs, Clachnaharry Inn (1mi), Bunchrew Caravan Park (3mi) & Beauly (11mi)

To Moyness House (200m), Bught Park (800m), Tomnahurich Bridge (0.5mi), Dunain Park Hotel (1.5mi) & North Shore of Loch Ness (6mi)

To Ness Islands (800m) & Caledonian Canal (1.5m)

To South Shore of Loch Ness (9mi)

To Hedgefield Halls (200m)

To Culloden Moor (4mi)

Train Station

Eastgate Shopping Centre

---

at the foot of the castle hill. The bus and train stations are just north of the centre.

INFORMATION

The TIC (☎ 234353, [e] inverness@host .co.uk), on Castle Wynd, has a ferry office, accommodation-booking service, bureau de change and also sells tickets for tours. You can check your email here (£2 per 20 minutes). It opens 9am to 8pm Monday to Saturday, and 9.30am to 5pm on Sunday.

The main post office on Queensgate opens 9am to 5.30pm weekdays and 9am to 6pm on Saturday.

If you need your brain expanded with a second-hand book or two, head for Leakey's (☎ 239947), Greyfriars Hall, Church St; it opens 10am to 5.30pm Monday to Saturday and there's also a good cafe.

The launderette on Young St, open 8am to 8pm weekdays and 8am to 6pm Saturday, charges £3/1.40 to wash/dry a load.

THINGS TO SEE

The baronial turrets of **Inverness Castle** dominate the city from their vantage point high above the River Ness. In the 11th century, a timber castle stood to the east of the present site; in the 12th century it was replaced with a stone castle. Much blood was spilled here during the English occupation of the castle in the War of Independence; even more flowed in the subsequent recapture by Robert the Bruce. It was rebuilt in the 15th century, repaired in 1718 and dramatically expanded in 1725. It was then taken over and blown up by the Jacobites in 1746 (who became expert at blowing up castles during this period). The present rose-coloured structure was built between 1837 and 1847, and today serves as the Sheriff's Court.

The only part of the castle open to visitors is the Drum Tower, which houses the **Castle Garrison Encounter** (☎ 243363; adult/child £3/2; open 10.30am-5.30pm daily Easter-Nov). In this interactive exhibition, you become a new recruit in the Hanoverian army during the Jacobite uprising, and a troop of actors play parts such as Quartermaster and Sergeant of the Guard.

In front of the castle is a statue of the Skye heroine **Flora MacDonald**, whose bird-dropping-splattered visage stares towards far-off Skye, where she helped Bonnie Prince Charlie flee after he was defeated by 'Butcher' Cumberland.

Downhill from the castle is the **Inverness Museum & Art Gallery** (☎ 237114, Castle Wynd; admission free; open 9am-5pm Mon-Sat). It has mildly entertaining wildlife dioramas, geological displays, period rooms with historic weapons, Pictish stones and a missable art gallery. If you're fascinated by Inverness' history, don't miss it. The entrance is immediately uphill from the TIC.

Nearby stands the ornate Gothic-style **Town House** where in 1921 Prime Minister Lloyd George held the first-ever emergency Cabinet meeting outside London, to discuss the Irish crisis. There's not much to see, though the huge stone **Mercat Cross** is a worthwhile diversion. Over the road, on the corner of Bridge and Church streets, is **Tolbooth Steeple**, built in 1791 and drastically repaired after an earthquake hit in 1814.

Thanks to Inverness' violent history, few buildings of real historical significance survive, and much of the city dates from the

completion of the Caledonian Canal in 1822. The oldest building in town is **Abertarff House** (Cnr Church & Fraser Sts), dating from 1593; nearby **Dunbar's Hospital**, also in Church St, was built in 1668 as a home for beggars and the destitute.

On Inverness' western bank near Ness Bridge is the **Kiltmaker Centre** (☎ 222781, 4 Huntly St; admission £2; open 9am-10pm Mon-Sat & 10am-5pm Sun May-Sept, 9am-5.30pm Mon-Sat Nov-Apr). After watching kiltmakers in action and learning every detail of tartan construction, you can be measured up for a kilt in your very own pattern, for which you'll pay through the nose.

Nearby, directly across the river from the castle, is neo-Gothic **St Andrew's Cathedral**, dating from 1866. Farther along the river is the **Eden Court Theatre**, which hosts regular art exhibitions. It opens 10am until late most days; go to **W** www.eden-court.co.uk for more details.

A mile or so farther south, adjacent to Bught Park, are the attractive **Ness Islands**, joined to both river banks by footbridges. Wander another half-mile farther south and you'll come to one end of the Caledonian Canal (see the boxed text 'Canal Plus' later in this chapter).

ORGANISED TOURS
Walking Tours
Guided city walks (adult/child £4/2) leave from outside the TIC and last 1¼ hours; check with the TIC for details.

Davy the Ghost Tours (☎ 07730-831069) Adult/child £6/3. 7pm daily. During these 1¼-hour tours, visitors are treated to tales of Inverness' horrific past, including murders, ghosts, witches, torture and hangings. Led by an '18th-century ghost' dressed in authentic period costume, tours depart from the blackboard outside the TIC.

Bus & Taxi Tours
Over Easter and from May to September, **Guide Friday** (☎ 224000) runs hop-on hop-off bus tours of Inverness and the Culloden battlefield (see under Around Inverness later). An all-day ticket for the Culloden tour (1 hour 20 minutes) costs adult/child

Moray Firth Dolphins

The Moray Firth supports a tiny population of bottlenose dolphins, probably the most intelligent of sea creatures (remember, they were second in intellect only to mice in Douglas Adams' *The Hitchhiker's Guide to the Galaxy*). In summer, this is the species' most northerly breeding ground, and there's a decent chance of spotting them frolicking in the waters from the shore. Herds of up to 40 dolphins have been sighted here.

The number one vantage point is Chanonry Point, on the Black Isle across the water from Fort George; next best is Kessock Bridge, north of Inverness.

£7.50/2.50; for the city only (30 minutes) it costs £5.50/2.50.

Guide Friday also offers bus tours to Loch Ness and Urquhart Castle that include admission to the Official Loch Ness Exhibition Centre and a half-hour cruise on the loch from Drumnadrochit. Tickets cost adult/child £14.50/6.50 and the tours, which last three hours, depart from the TIC at 10.30am and 2.30pm daily.

From June to early September, ***John o'-Groats Ferries*** (☎ 01955-611353) operates daily tours (13½ hours) by bus and passenger ferry from Inverness to Orkney for adult/child £44/22.

Highland Taxi Tours (☎ 220222) has a range of day-trips to places as far afield as Skye and Deeside. Tours include three-hour trips to Fort George and Culloden (£40), and four-hour tours of Loch Ness (£50); fares are per car (up to four passengers).

Cruises

From Tomnahurich Bridge, a mile south of town, the ***Jacobite Queen*** (☎ 233999) departs for 3½-hour cruises on Loch Ness for adult/child £10/8. A one-way trip to Urquhart Castle, including admission, costs £10.50/8.50.

Moray Firth Cruises (☎ 717900) offers 1½-hour wildlife cruises (adult/child £10/7.50) to look for dolphins, seals and bird

life. Boats depart from 10.30am to 4.50pm daily, March to October (until 6pm in July and August). Sightings aren't guaranteed but it's still fun, especially on fine days. Follow the signs to Shore St Quay from the far end of Chapel St. A shuttle bus leaves from the TIC 15 minutes before sailings.

PLACES TO STAY

Inverness has a dizzying array of hostels, B&Bs and hotels, and generally finding a place to stay is easy. Still, at the height of summer it's worth booking ahead. The TIC charges £1.50 for bookings.

Camping

There's a basic, centrally located camp site near in Bught Park, and a nicer site a few miles west of town.

Bught Camping Park (☎ 236920, fax 712850, Bught Park) Pitches £4.30, plus £2 per car. Open Apr-Sept. Inverness' major camp site has top-notch facilities; it's 1 mile southwest of the city centre near Tomnahurich Bridge.

Bunchrew Caravan Park (☎ 237802) Tent & 2 people £5. Open Apr-Oct. This attractive, grassy site among trees is on the shore of the Beauly Firth, 3 miles west of the city centre. It's popular with families and midges so come prepared.

Hostels & Halls of Residence

Inverness Millburn Hostel (☎ 231771, Victoria Drive) Beds £11.75 including continental breakfast; add £2/1 in July/Aug. Inverness' flashy 166-bed SYHA hostel is a 10-minute walk northeast of the city centre. In a former school hall of residence, many claim it's Scotland's best hostel. Booking is essential, especially during Easter, July and August.

Bazpackers Hostel (☎ 717663, 4 Culduthel Rd) Dorm beds £10, twins & doubles £14 per person. This friendly 31-bed place just past the castle has a wood-burning stove, a small garden and great views over the river.

Inverness Student Hotel (☎ 236556, 8 Culduthel Rd) Beds £10. This bustling, 57-bed hostel is part of the MacBackpacker chain and has great views.

THE GREAT GLEN & THE WESTERN HIGHLANDS

Ho Ho Hostel (☎ 221225, 23a High St)
Dorm beds £8.90-9.90, twin room £12 per
person, including breakfast. The 70-bed Ho
Ho occupies a fine, ragged-round-the-edges
Victorian building that once housed the
stately Highlands Club; if only those refined gents could see the joint now. Enter
through an alley between High St and
Baron Taylor's St.

Hedgefield (☎ 713430, 23 Culduthel Rd)
Family & twin rooms £11 per person. Open
July & Aug only. Lovely Hedgefield – Inverness College's student residence – is a
big old mansion in country-house grounds,
just 10 minutes' walk south of the castle.
Booking is recommended; call between
9am and 5pm Monday to Friday.

B&Bs

B&Bs and guesthouses swamp Old Edinburgh Rd and Ardconnel St, south of the
city centre.

Borve Guest House (☎/fax 234728, 9
Old Edinburgh Rd), an old stone cottage
with nifty red trim and run by the person-
able van Horriks, offers B&B for £25 to
£35 per person. **Ardconnel House** (☎/fax
240455, 21 Ardconnel St) does B&B for
£20 to £35 per person, has cosy rooms and
serves great breakfast. **Park Hill Guest
House** (☎ 223300, 17 Ardconnel St), a few
doors down, has dinky rooms of a similar
standard for £20 per person.

Ivybank Guest House (☎/fax 232796,
e ivybank@talk21.com, 28 Old Edinburgh
Rd) B&B doubles & twins £20-27.50 per
person. Open fireplaces, plush rooms and
enthusiastic owners make this charming
Georgian guesthouse a good choice. Rooms
are spacious and well cared for.

Across the river a few streets east are
Kenneth St and adjoining Fairfield Rd,
where you'll find many reasonable B&Bs
charging £15 to £22, including **Mardon**
(☎ 231005, 37 Kenneth St), **Torridon Guest
House** (☎/fax 236449, 59 Kenneth St),
Strome Lodge (☎ 221553, 41 Fairfield Rd)
and **Amulree** (☎ 224822, 40 Fairfield Rd).

The better B&Bs along Ness Bank on the
River Ness are worth forking out the extra
pounds for.

MacRae Guest House (☎/fax 243658, 24
Ness Bank) Singles/doubles £35/52. This
three-storey Victorian stone house is one of
the riverfront's prettiest B&Bs. The rooms
are well maintained.

Ardmuir House Hotel (☎/fax 231151, 16
Ness Bank) B&B £35 per person. Classy
Ardmuir, in a three-storey Georgian house,
has kind owners and oh-so-tasteful rooms
with views over the river, from which to
watch the seething masses promenading
below.

Hotels

The best hotels are sprinkled either side
of the River Ness, along Ness Bank or
opposite on Ardross Terrace.

Brae Ness Hotel (☎ 712266, W www
.braenesshotel.co.uk, 17 Ness Bank) Singles/
doubles from £37/60. Open Apr-Oct. The
best choice in town, the Brae Ness oozes
class and charm. Its 10 rooms fill up early so
book ahead.

Glen Mhor Hotel (☎ 234308, fax 713170,
W www.glen-mhor.com, 9-12 Ness Bank)
Singles £49-69, doubles £70-118. Overlooking the river with towering elegance is
the four-storey Glen Mhor. The slightly
chintzy rooms are comfortable, staff are
affable and the traditional Scottish meals (£9
to £14) at their two classy **restaurants** eminently edible.

Tower Hotel (☎ 232765, fax 232970, 4
Ardross Terrace) Singles £36-48, doubles
£56-72. Recognisable by its Addams Family
tower, this hotel has a great setting overlooking the river and St Andrew's Cathedral.

Moyness House (☎/fax 233836, 6 Bruce
Gardens) B&B £31-35 per person. This
attractive seven-room Victorian villa is west
of the river in a quiet area close to the Eden
Court Theatre, just off the A82. Rooms are
spotless and the breakfast's exceptional.

Dunain Park Hotel (☎ 230512, fax
224532, e info@dunainparkhotel.co.uk,
Dunain Park) Doubles £69-99 per person.
This luxury hotel, on the A82 (Fort William
Rd) 1 mile southwest of Inverness, is the
place to spoil yourself. A country mansion
set in beautiful wooded grounds, it's a five-
minute stroll from the Caledonian Canal

and River Ness. The more expensive of the 12 rooms have Victorian four-poster beds, and the hotel restaurant serves exceptional French cuisine (£11 to £16).

PLACES TO EAT

The *Inverness Museum* has a small coffee shop, but the healthy *River Café* (☎ 714884, 10 Bank St) is a nicer place for your tea and scones (£1.75), plus there's a restaurant upstairs with more filling fare such as casseroles and lasagne (£5.50 to £6.50).

Lettuce Eat (☎ 715064, 7 Lombard St) Sandwiches £1.20-2.50. Open 8.30am-4pm Mon-Sat. This is a good place for cheap sandwiches, baguettes, salads and the like.

Castle Restaurant (☎ 230925, 41 Castle St) Mains £4-8. Close to the TIC, the Castle is a top-notch greasy spoon that prides itself on plentiful portions and low prices.

Shapla Tandoori Restaurant (☎ 241919, 2 Castle Rd) 3-course lunch £5.95. Mains £4.55-8.95. Open noon-2.30pm & 6pm-11pm daily. The Shapla, upstairs overlooking the river, dishes up average curries.

Inverness has an increasing number of top-end eateries.

Café 1 (☎ 226200, 75 Castle St) Mains £7.50-14.50. Open for lunch noon-2pm & dinner 6pm-9pm Mon-Sat. Long Inverness' grooviest place to be spotted, Café 1 is known for its 'modern Scottish' and innovative preparation of local meats and seafood. There are also excellent vegetarian options.

Woodward's (☎ 709809, 99 Castle St) Mains £6.85-10.25. Open 5.30pm-late daily. Set in a renovated old house, this place dishes up swanky 'Scottish fusion' cuisine – try the seared salmon fillet in a Thai green curry sauce with mussels (£10.25).

The Mustard Seed (☎ 220220, 16 Fraser St) Mains £6.45-11.65. Open 11am-10pm daily. This cheerfully yellow bistro has decent vegetarian choices and does a two-course lunch (noon to 3pm) for £4.95.

River House (☎ 222033, 1 Greig St) 2-/3-course dinner £22.95/26.95. Open 6.30pm-10.30pm Mon-Wed, 12.15pm-10.30pm Thur-Sat. The River House is an elegant eatery of the polished-wood, crisp-linen variety. It serves pedantically prepared beef,

seafood venison, lamb and duck. There are a couple of vegetarian choices too.

Other places worth a visit include the *très français* **Délices de Bretagne** (☎ 712422, 6 Stephen's Brae), at the eastern end of the High St, which does supreme coffee and Breton *galettes* (pancakes; £2.40-5.30). **Palio** (☎ 711950, 26 Queensgate) is a stylish Italian restaurant with pizzas for £4 to £6 and a two-course lunch for £4.95.

For a real splurge, try the restaurants at the **Glen Mhor Hotel** for classy Scottish fare or the **Dunain Park Hotel** for magnificent French (see Places to Stay earlier); expect to pay around £30 per head at both.

The **Tesco Metro supermarket** on King St opens 8.30am to 8pm Monday to Saturday (to 9pm Thursday and Friday) and 9am to 6pm on Sunday.

ENTERTAINMENT
Pubs & Clubs

There's a good online guide to Inverness' pubs, clubs and events at [W] www.ness web.co.uk.

The Phoenix (☎ 233685, 108 Academy St) Open 11am-midnight Mon-Sat & 12.30pm-11pm Sun. Meals noon-3pm & 6pm-9pm daily. This is the best of the city centre's traditional pubs, with a horseshoe bar, comfortable family-friendly lounge and great pub grub. Real ales on tap include the rich and fruity Orkney Dark Island.

Blackfriars (☎ 233881, 93-5 Academy St) Open 11am-midnight Mon-Sat & 12.30pm-11pm Sun. Food served noon-3pm & 6pm-9pm daily. Near the Phoenix, Blackfriars is a friendly place with good bar meals from £4.95 and live music most nights.

Lafferty's (☎ 712270, Academy St) Open 11am-midnight Mon-Sat & 12.30pm-11pm Sun. A big, bustling Irish pub, Lafferty's beams with out sport on its big-screen TV and has karaoke on Friday nights.

Johnny Foxes (☎ 236577, 26 Bank St) Open 11am-midnight Mon-Sat & 12.30pm-11pm Sun. Overlooking the river, Johnny Foxes is another boisterous Irish theme bar, that's far less awful than most of its type. Food is served all day and there's live music every night.

Sleepers (☎ 231926, Station Square) Open 11am-11pm Mon-Thur, 11am-1am Fri, 11am-12.30am Sat noon-11pm Sun. This is the best gay-friendly bar in Inverness.

Barbazza (☎ 243342, 5-9 Young St) Open 11.30am-1am Mon-Thur, 11.30am-1.30am Fri & Sat, 12.30pm-11pm Sun. Cool Barbazza has the highest pierced-belly-button count in Inverness. It serves great booze-absorbing grub such as burgers and nachos. There are regular DJs, and drink promos on Wednesday and Sunday.

The Nile Bar & G's Nightclub (☎ 233322, 9-21 Castle St) Open 9.30pm-1.30am Wed-Mon; last admission midnight Fri, 11.15pm Sat, 10.30pm Sun, 12.30am Mon, Wed & Thur. The Nile's theme is all things Egypt. The bar feeds into G's Nightclub, in the same building, where you'll find cheap drinks on Monday (student night) and Thursday. There's a cover charge (£3 to £5) every night except Sunday.

The small and cosy *Market Bar*, upstairs in the Old Market Inn (tucked up an alley behind the Victorian Market off Church St), is an old-fashioned boozer, with live folk music most evenings. *Chilli Palmers (73 Queensgate)* is a modern cafe-bar, and a laid-back place to relax and chat.

Just over 1 mile northwest of the centre, on the A862 towards Beauly, the *Clachnaharry Inn (☎ 239806, 17-19 High St, Clachnaharry)* is a delightful old coaching inn with tempting real ale and good food.

Music & Theatre

Inverness' main cultural venue is the *Eden Court Theatre (☎ 221718 or 234234 W www.eden-court.co.uk, Ness Walk)*, on the west bank of the river. It has a busy programme of drama, dance and music, and an excellent cinema (see Cinema later) – pick up a listing from the foyer or check its Web site. There's also a good bar and restaurant.

During the summer, the *Spectrum Centre Theatre (☎ 0800 015 8001, 1 Margaret St)* stages 'Scottish Showtime', an evening of traditional Scottish music, song and dance. Doors open at 8pm Monday to Thursday mid-June to mid-July, and 8pm Monday to Friday mid-July to mid-September.

Cinema

Riverside Screen (☎ 221718, Bishop's Rd), in the Eden Court Theatre complex, is Inverness' art-house cinema, showing recent films and old classics. Tickets cost adult/child £4.50/3.

There's a multiplex cinema, the seven-screen *Warner Village (☎ 711147, Eastfield Way)*, way out on the eastern edge of town, just south of the A96 road to Nairn.

GETTING THERE & AWAY
Air

Flights from Inverness go to Glasgow, Edinburgh, Stornoway, Orkney, London and Amsterdam; see the Getting There & Away chapter for details.

Bus

For Inverness bus station, phone ☎ 233371. Scottish Citylink (☎ 0870 550 5050) connects with lots of major centres in England, including London (£28, 13 hours) via Perth and Glasgow. There are numerous buses to Glasgow (£14, 3½ hours) and Edinburgh (£14, four hours) via Perth. Buses to Aberdeen (£10, three hours) are run by Stagecoach Bluebird (☎ 01463-239292).

In summer, there are two or three Citylink buses daily to Ullapool (£6, 1½ hours) via Dingwall and Strathpeffer, connecting with the CalMac ferry to Stornoway on the Isle of Lewis (not Sunday).

There are three to five daily Citylink services to Thurso and Scrabster (£10, three hours) via Dornoch, Helmsdale and Wick, connecting twice a day (not Sunday) with the ferry to Orkney. There are also regular daily services along Loch Ness to Fort William (£7.40, two hours).

Citylink/Skye-Ways (☎ 01599-534328) runs three buses a day (two Sunday) from Inverness to Kyle of Lochalsh and Portree, on Skye (£12.40, three hours).

It's possible to head northwestwards via Lairg. Stagecoach Inverness (☎ 239292) operates a service to Lairg Monday to Saturday (and Sunday in summer). There are also connections to Durness Monday to Saturday in Summer. There's also a postbus service (☎ 01246-546329), operating

Monday to Saturday, which travels the Lairg-Tongue-Durness route.

Train
The standard one-way fare from London to Inverness costs £90.50 and the journey takes eight hours. There are direct trains from Aberdeen (£17.80, 2¼ hours), Edinburgh (£30.60, four hours) and Glasgow (£29.90, four hours).

The 82-mile ride from Inverness to Kyle of Lochalsh (£14.70, 2½ hours) offers one of the greatest scenic journeys in Britain; there are three trains daily Monday to Saturday. Trains to Thurso (£12.50, 3½ hours) have the same frequency.

Car
The TIC has a handy Car Hire leaflet. The big boys charge from around £35 per day, or you could try Sharp's Reliable Wrecks (☎ 236694) 1st Floor, Highland Rail House, Station Square, for cheaper cars and vans from £24 per day.

GETTING AROUND
Inverness Airport (☎ 232471) is at Dalcross, 8 miles east of town on the A96 to Nairn. Bus No 11 from Inverness' main post office runs there every hour Monday to Saturday (☎ 222244; £2.50, 20 minutes). A taxi costs £10; call Central Taxis (☎ 222222).

Bus
Stagecoach Inverness (☎ 239292) and Highland Country/Rapsons (☎ 222244) operate to places around Inverness, including Nairn, Forres, the Culloden battlefield, Dingwall, Beauly and Lairg.

A Stagecoach Inverness Day Rover Highland ticket costs £6.50/3.25, while a Highland Country/Rapsons Day Rover ticket costs £9/4.50. The return fare to Culloden/Cawdor with Highland Country/Rapsons is £2.10/2.50.

Bicycle
There are some great cycling opportunities out of Inverness, and several rental outlets, including Wilder Ness (ask at Bazpackers Hostel), charging £7.50/10 per half-/full

day, and the accommodation desk in the train station, which charges £12 per day.

AROUND INVERNESS
Stretching east of Inverness, along the Moray Firth, are undulating heather-covered hills, pristine farmlands and some of Scotland's most momentous historical sites, including Culloden where contemporary Scotland's future was decided. Nearby is the pretty village of Cawdor, with its 14th-century castle that was certainly not where the gruesome events detailed in Shakespeare's *Macbeth* took place; that doesn't stop the tourists piling in though. Also nearby is the seaside town of Nairn. In the more mountainous western part of the district are several wild and beautiful glens, with plenty of wildlife to look out for. Autumn is the best time to visit, with the forest colours at their very best.

Culloden
Six miles east of Inverness is the windswept Culloden Moor. On 16 April 1746, this field played host to the gruesome Battle of Culloden, the last major battle fought on British soil. The horrors meted out by Hanoverian troops on this field were substantial. Having chased Bonnie Prince Charlie and his army all the way from Derby – just 127 miles north of London – they slaughtered over 1500 Jacobites in a 68-minute rout that earned the duke of Cumberland the label 'Butcher' Cumberland. His English redcoats, who outnumbered the Jacobites by only one-third but who were equipped with a far more modern and lethal arsenal, lost just 50 men.

The sombre 49-hectare moor where the conflict took place has scarcely changed in the 250 years since. The 15-minute audiovisual presentation on the battle that is presented by the **National Trust for Scotland (NTS) Visitor Centre** (*☎ 01463-790607; adult/child £4/3; open 9am-5.30pm daily Apr-Oct, 10am-4pm daily Nov-Mar*) gives a good idea of whereabouts on the moor the bloody conflict happened. Guided tours of the battlefield (adult/child £3/2) depart at 10.30am, noon, 1.30pm and 3pm daily.

Clearly signposted 1½ miles east of Culloden, the **Clava Cairns** are a picturesque group of cairns and stone circles dating from the late Neolithic period (around 4000 to 2000 BC). There's a superb railway viaduct nearby.

The Highland Country/Rapsons bus No 12 from Inverness' main post office leaves regularly for Culloden from Monday to Saturday (return £2.10). You can also catch the Guide Friday tour bus (see Organised Tours under Inverness earlier in this chapter), leaving Bridge St, Inverness from April to September (first bus 10.30am).

Fort George
☎ 01667

Eleven miles northeast of Inverness, off the A96, is the magnificent and virtually unaltered 18th-century artillery fortification of Fort George *(owned by Historic Scotland, HS; ☎ 462777; adult/child £4/1.50; open 9.30am-6.30pm daily Apr-Sept, 9.30am-4.30pm Mon-Sat & 2pm-4.30pm Sun Oct-Mar)*. One of the best of its kind in Europe, this Hanoverian fort stands majestically on a bank jutting into the Moray Firth. Completed in 1769 as a base for George II's army, it has a mile-plus walk around the ramparts offering sweeping views out to sea and back to the Great Glen.

Within the fort is the **Regimental Museum of the Highlanders**, which tells the rollicking tale of the current Queen Lizzie's very own band of merry men. On display are relics from the regiment's battles over recent centuries, from Napoleonic swords and daggers to guns and gas masks from the Gulf War.

Highland Bus No 11 runs from Inverness' main post office to Fort George (nine daily Monday to Saturday).

Nairn
☎ 01667 ● pop 11,220

Genteel Nairn, a seaside resort beside a sandy beach stretching 5 miles to the Culbin Forest, sports pleasant beachfront paths overlooked by Victorian mansions, and not much else. Promoted as 'The Brighton of the North', it's a pretty enough place but there's little to do except enjoy traditional Scottish relaxation, taking in the bracing air and getting in a round of golf should it take your fancy.

The compact centre has the usual array of shops selling fish and chips and ice cream, as well as a supermarket, banks and post office. The TIC (☎ 452763), 62 King St, opens 10am to 6pm Monday to Friday, 10am to 5pm Saturday and 1.30pm to 4pm Sunday, April to October. There's also a swimming pool, on Marine Rd.

The most pleasant part of Nairn is the old fishing village of Fishertown, down by the harbour. **Nairn Museum** *(☎ 458531, Viewfield House; adult/child £1/50p; open 10am-4.30pm Mon-Sat May-Sept)*, a few minutes' walk from the TIC, has displays on the history of Fishertown, as well as on local archaeology, geology and natural history.

Nairn's **Champions Links** *(☎ 462787)*, just east of the town, has hosted some big tournaments, most recently the 1999 Walker Cup, and is the best golf course in the region. The steep fees can be as high as £25 per round.

Special Events Every August the Nairn Highland Games *(admission free)* is a major event held on the Links. The Nairn International Jazz Festival is also held on the Links in August. Contact the TIC for details of both.

Places to Stay & Eat Nairn doesn't have a hostel, but there's camping at *Spindrift Caravan Park (☎ 453992, Little Kildrummie)*, 2 miles southwest of town on the B9090 towards Cawdor; pitches cost £4.50 to £8.50. There are rooms for £16 per person at *Braighe (☎ 453285, Albert St)*, or rural *Brightmony Farm House (☎ 455550)* in Auldearn, 2 miles east of town.

Bracadale House (☎ 452547, Albert St) B&B from £22 per person. This well-kept Victorian home has pleasant, tidy gardens to match, and serves a great breakfast.

Ascot House (☎ 455855, 7 Cawdor St) Rooms from £22 per person. This cottage has a fancy garden and attractive rooms.

Havelock House Hotel (☎ 455500, fax 45550, W www.havelockhousehotel.co.uk, Crescent Rd) Singles £20-30, doubles

Enchanting Cawdor Castle, home to the Thanes of Cawdor

£30-50. This house was built by the Emir of Jaipur as his summer residence after he was exiled from India in 1857; it's grandeur has now faded but it's still good fun. Plus you can still get a good curry in the *restaurant* for just £5.95.

The Links Hotel (☎ 453321, 1 Seabank Rd) B&B from £53 per person. Mains £7-11. Adjacent to the golf course and with fabulous sea views and plush rooms, The Links wins the Swishest Joint In Town award. It serves excellent bar meals in its attractive conservatory.

Clifton House (☎ 453119, Viewfield St) B&B £50 per person. If you're after something more unique, try Clifton House, with classy rooms piled to the rafters with antiques and artworks.

Friar Tucks (30 Harbour St) is the best place for a fish supper, while *Asher's Bakery* (2 Bridge St) is recommended for cakes and snacks.

Getting There & Around Stagecoach Bluebird (☎ 01463-239292) runs buses hourly (less frequently on Sunday) from Inverness to Aberdeen via Nairn.

Nairn lies on the Inverness-Aberdeen railway line; there are five to seven trains daily from Inverness (£3.30, 20 minutes).

Bike hire is available at The Bike Shop (☎ 455416), 178 Harbour St.

Cawdor Castle
☎ 01667

For over six centuries this castle (☎ 404615; adult/child £5.60/3; open 10am-5pm daily May-Oct), 5 miles southwest of Nairn, has

been home to the Thanes of Cawdor, and each summer they politely push off, giving tourists the run of the place. Though its name is often linked with Macbeth's castle in Shakespeare's play, it's unlikely Duncan really met his grizzly end here, as the central tower dates from the 14th century (the wings are 17th-century additions) and Macbeth died in 1057. Still, it's an impressive place, its most appealing aspect being the stunning gardens, complete with a hedge maze and putting green.

Cawdor Tavern (☎ 404777) Mains £5-8. This pretty pub in the village serves top-notch food, and if you're a whisky drinker you're spoilt for choice as it stocks over 100 varieties.

Highland Country/Rapsons bus No 12 leaves regularly from Inverness' main post office for Cawdor, Monday to Saturday. Buses also run regularly from Nairn.

Brodie Castle
☎ 01309

Last but not least among the region's castles comes Brodie (NTS; ☎ 641371; adult/child £5/free; open 11am-5.30pm Mon-Sat & 1.30pm-5.30pm Sun Apr-Sept), set in 70 hectares of delightful parkland 8 miles east of Nairn. Although the Brodies have lived here since 1160, the present structure dates from the 16th century. You can look around several rooms, some of which have wildly extravagant ceilings, and see the large collection of paintings and furniture. Don't miss the huge Victorian kitchen just beyond the small cafe. There are also woodland walks and an observation hide by the pond.

Stagecoach Bluebird bus No 10 runs half-hourly from Inverness to Elgin and Aberdeen via Culloden, Nairn and Brodie.

Loch Ness to Spean Bridge

The A82 stretches along the side of the Loch Ness with stunning views and access to some great loch-side towns.

THE GREAT GLEN & THE WESTERN HIGHLANDS

Marketing the Monster

Ever since the 6th century, when that maniacal monk St Columba claimed to have seen a heinous beast in the dark, bitterly cold waters of Loch Ness, visitors have been straining their eyes for a glimpse of Nessie.

Movies, starring such legends of the silver screen as Ted Danson, have been made about the beastie, and millions have been spent hunting it over the 20th century – by everyone from whacko Texan billionaires to Oxford PhDs, with everything from giant eels to the bones of plesiosaurs pulled victoriously from the loch and claimed as the true Nessie.

For a while Nessie created quite an industry in elaborate hoaxes, the best coming in 1960 when 31 hotel guests were amazed at the sight of two huge humps sailing through the water; this later turned out to be industrious Edinburgh University students who had planned the prank months in advance.

Nessie has also created quite an industry in tourist tat, which reaches fever pitch in Drumnadrochit where two Loch Ness Monster centres sit next door to each other. The two wage such a ferocious battle for customers that it has on occasion led to fisticuffs between the employees (all of which is well documented in the *Oban Times*, which revels in reporting the madness of those crazy 'northerners').

Though more scientific research in recent decades has actually yielded enigmatic results, making it difficult to dismiss Nessie as a complete myth, the Monster of the Loch can probably be put down to one factor: too much whisky.

LOCH NESS

Impressive as Loch Ness is, with its rugged hills climbing steeply from the loch's dark, 330m-deep waters, most visitors here are interested in one thing: Nessie-spotting.

Stretching 24 miles across the Great Glen fault dividing Highland Scotland from Inverness to Fort William, the loch holds more water than all the lakes in England and Wales combined and is Britain's largest body of fresh water. The A82 running along the western side of the loch is choked with buses and hire-car traffic in summer, while on the southeastern shore the more tranquil, picturesque B862 is quiet (and agonisingly slow) year-round. A complete circuit of the loch covers about 70 miles – travel anticlockwise for the best views.

DRUMNADROCHIT

☎ 01456 ● pop 600

Exploitation of poor old Nessie peaks at Drumnadrochit, where two Monster exhibitions compete for your dosh. The village has an ATM and supermarket (open daily until 10pm).

The villages of Milton, Lewiston and Strone almost touch Drumnadrochit, while **Urquhart Castle** lies immediately south.

The prominent **Official Loch Ness Exhibition Centre** (☎ 450573; adult/child £5.95/ 3.50; open 9am-8pm daily July & Aug, 9am-6pm daily June & Sept, 9am-5.30pm daily Oct, 9.30am-5pm daily Easter-May, 10am-3.30pm daily Nov-Easter) is the better of the two Nessie-theme centres, featuring a 40-minute audiovisual presentation and displays of equipment used in various underwater monster hunts.

Next door, the **Original Loch Ness Monster Centre** (☎ 450342; adult/child £3.50/ 2.75; open 9am-8pm daily July & Aug, 10am-5.30pm daily Apr-June, Sept & Oct, 10am-4pm daily Nov-Mar) barely rates a mention, with its dreary 30-minute Loch Ness video, though it does have a rather mindblowing range of souvenirs.

Much better than visiting either centre is to head out on the loch. One-hour monster-hunting **cruises** from Drumnadrochit aboard the **Nessie Hunter** (☎ 450395; adult/child £8/5) come complete with sonar and underwater cameras; boats run from 10.30am to 5pm daily, April to October. Or you can do some pony trekking along the shores of the loch, through the **Highland Riding Centre** (☎ 450220; from £20 per person) near Urquhart Castle.

Urquhart Castle

Rising from the southern banks of Urquhart Bay, this historic castle *(HS; ☎ 450551; adult/child £3.80/1.20; open 9.30am-6.30pm daily Apr-Sept, 9.30am-4.30pm Mon-Sat & 2pm-4.30pm Sun Oct-Mar)* is one of Scotland's best known. Half a mile south of Drumnadrochit, the stunning castle has provided the foreground for countless snaps of Loch Ness.

Its history has been equally dramatic. Built to guard Loch Ness' southern shores, the castle was taken and lost by Edward I, held for David II against Edward III and fought over by every army passing this way. Repeatedly sacked, damaged and rebuilt over the centuries, the unfortunate inhabitants of the Loch Ness and the surrounding area. were also frequently pillaged and robbed in the process.

Destruction and reconstruction followed so regularly that it's hard to trace the full story of the castle's development. By the 1600s, it had become redundant, superseded by more palatial residences and more powerful fortresses at Fort William and Inverness. It was blown up in 1692 to prevent Jacobites using it, and its remains perch dramatically on the edge of the loch, approached by a steep path from the car park.

The five-storey towerhouse is the most impressive remaining fragment and offers striking loch views.

Places to Stay & Eat

Borlum Farm Camping (☎ 450220) Pitches £3-4 per person. This camp site, half a mile southeast of Drumnadrochit, is the nearest to the village.

Loch Ness Backpackers Lodge (☎ 450807, e hostel@lochness-backpackers.com, Coiltie Farmhouse, East Lewiston) Beds £9.50. This smart hostel lies within easy walking distance of both Drumnadrochit and Urquhart Castle.

Drumnadrochit also boasts numerous B&Bs charging £16 to £20 per person, though single rooms are in short supply.

Gillyflowers (☎/fax 450641) B&B doubles £14-21 per person. The affable owners of this tidy B&B (in their modern home

that's attached to a renovated 18th-century farmhouse) are knowledgeable about the local area. Breakfast takes place around a large communal table where you'll meet the other guests. Rooms, all named after Scottish isles, are simply furnished and comfy.

Oakdale (☎ 450678) B&B £25 per person. Run by the owners of Fiddler's Cafe Bar (see below) across the road, this impeccably tidy cottage has cosy rooms you'll enjoy settling into for the night, though the house's vicinity to the noisy A82 might put you off.

Drumbuie Farm (☎ 450634) B&B £18-22 per person. Dinner £12. Welcoming and comfortable Drumbuie Farm is on the right as you enter Drumnadrochit from Inverness.

Drumnadrochit Hotel (☎ 450202) B&B £17.50-40 per person. The hotel's pricey restaurant, *Hunters,* does top-notch sirloin (£14) and tuna steaks (£13). However, the decent rooms in this hideous 1980s chalet, next to the Official Loch Ness Exhibition Centre, should be your last choice in town.

Near the Drumnadrochit village green are the *Glen Cafe Bar (☎ 450282)* with cheap pasta meals, and the more expensive but excellent *Fiddler's Cafe Bar (☎ 450678)* which, with its traditional Scottish fare (whisky salmon salad £11.95) and non-GM food policy, is usually full in summer.

Getting There & Away

Scottish Citylink (☎ 0870 550 5050) runs five or six buses daily between Fort William (1½ hours) and Inverness (30 minutes) via Drumnadrochit and Urquhart Castle. July to September, there are four additional daily services between Inverness and Urquhart Castle (one way £4.50).

CANNICH & GLEN AFFRIC

The A831 road from Drumnadrochit goes to **Cannich**, at the start of the only road to Loch Affric. The village was established to house forestry workers in the 1950s. There's a small shop, open daily, with a post office, booze and a good range of supplies.

Cannich Caravan & Camping Park (☎ 01456-415201), located off the road from Drumnadrochit, has pitches for £6.50

for two people, or six-berth vans for £30. *Cannich Hostel* (☎ 01456-415244), open March to October, is an SYHA hostel with beds for £8.25. *Comar Lodge* (☎ 01456-415251), just west of the village, is a comfortable B&B in a listed building (built in 1740). All rooms are en suite and cost £18 per person.

Foodwise, the old-style *Glen Affric Hotel* (☎ 01456-415214) specialises in local game, while the cheaper and cheerier *Slaters Arms* (☎ 01456-415215) has bar meals including good vegetarian choices.

Beautiful **Glen Affric** might just be the brightest star in the Highland Glens' constellation. With the dramatic River Affric running through the gorge, and the Caledonian woodland that fills the area, there are few more striking places in Scotland.

The area also has one of the few youth hostels in Britain you can't drive to. With Loch Cluanie and Glen Shiel to the south and remote Loch Mullardoch and Glen Cannich to the north, the SYHA's **Glen Affric Hostel** is centred in a magnificent, road-free area extending north to Strathcarron in Wester Ross. The hostel doesn't have a telephone, so contact central reservations (☎ 0870 155 3255); it's best to book at least a week ahead, if possible. Open from mid-March to late October, beds cost £7.75 and you'll need a sheet (blankets are provided) or sleeping bag. For its isolated location, amenities are luxurious – running water and hot showers, electricity (thanks to a wind turbine) and gas for cooking. You'll need all your own food, a bag to carry out your rubbish, and footwear for indoors. You can also *camp* for free nearby.

The most popular hike in the area is the overnight walk from Glen Affric to Shiel Bridge (about 25 miles). While it's not extremely difficult, you need to have done some hiking before and be *very* well prepared with wet-weather gear, food and stout hiking boots. You'll need OS Landranger maps Nos 25 and 33 (listed at the start of this chapter). You can stay at the Glen Affric Hostel on the way.

It's also possible to experience much of the beauty and remoteness of Loch Affric

on a day walk around the loch, starting and finishing at the Loch Affric car park.

Getting There & Away
Highland Country/Rapsons (☎ 01463-222244) runs buses Monday to Saturday to Cannich from Inverness, via Drumnadrochit. Ross's Minibuses (☎ 01463-761250) has a more limited service between Inverness and Cannich via Beauly.

INVERMORISTON
The pretty village of Invermoriston has a series of marked trails through the nearby woods, and not much else besides the first-rate *Glenmoriston Arms* (☎ 01320-351206), which does bar lunches and a vast assortment of whiskies and ales.

Loch Ness Caravan and Camping (☎ 01320-351207) Pitches £5 per person. This camp site is on the banks of the loch at East Point, 1 mile south of Invermoriston.

Loch Ness Hostel (☎ 01320-351274) Beds from £9. Open Mar-Oct. About 3 miles north is the area's friendly SYHA hostel, with an excellent lounge room and kitchen.

FORT AUGUSTUS
☎ 01320 ● pop 600
This historic village sits on the southern tip of Loch Ness and was created as a barrack town after the Jacobite rebellions of 1715 and 1719.

As part of his plan to pacify the Highlands, General Wade built a fort at the point where the River Tarff joined Loch Ness, and 250 miles worth of roads and around 40 bridges in the area, which also boosted trade. These roads were of little benefit when, in 1745, Bonnie Prince Charlie's forces arrived and within two days overran the town and took control of the barracks.

These days, Fort Augustus is overrun by tourists, but somehow it still manages to convey a slightly medieval ambience. It's also busy with boats coming and going from the Caledonian Canal, one end of which emerges here.

The TIC (☎ 366367), in the village car park by the petrol station, opens Easter to October. There's an ATM and a bureau de change (in the post office) beside the canal. You can access the Internet for £1.50 per 15 minutes at Neuk Café (see Places to Stay & Eat later).

Things to See & Do

In 1876, the fort built by General Wade was taken over by Benedictine monks, who transformed it into Fort Augustus Abbey. The abbey closed in 1998, but in 2001 the **Abbey Cloisters & Gardens** *(adult/child £3/2; open 10am-5pm daily)* opened to the public. You can visit the monks' burial ground and relish the great views along Loch Ness.

Boats using the **Caledonian Canal** are raised and lowered 12m by five locks, the water level in each lock changing by 2.4m. It's a pretty sight, reminiscent of another time, and some serious promenading goes on up the canal steps in summer, as people wander up to enjoy the fine views over Loch Ness from the promontory between the canal and the River Oich.

If you're looking out to Loch Ness, keep your eyes peeled for tiny **Cherry Island**, on the northern side of Fort Augustus. For centuries, this was thought to be Loch Ness's only island. In 1908 a monk from Fort Augustus Abbey borrowed diving equipment from canal engineers to explore the island. Purely by accident, he discovered it was not an island, but the remnants of a crannog, a Bronze Age lake home (see the boxed text 'Crannogs' in The Central Highlands chapter).

The **Clansman Centre** *(☎ 366444; adult/child/family £3.50/2.50/8; open 10am-6pm Apr-Sept)* is staffed by local enthusiasts, clad in clan tartan and sporrans, who take you through an enjoyable presentation on clan life in the 17th century and, if you're lucky, gleefully swing the odd sword or axe. The **Caledonian Canal Heritage Centre** *(☎ 366493; admission free; open 10am-5pm daily)*, beside the lowest lock, has some interesting photos and displays on the canal's history.

Cruises on Loch Ness on the **Royal Scot** *(☎ 366277)* operate hourly between 10am and 7pm daily, April to October. The 50-minute trip costs adult/child £6/3.

Places to Stay & Eat

Fort Augustus Caravan & Camping Park (☎ 366618). Pitches £4/2.50 per adult/child. This camp site is just south of the village, on the western side of the road to Fort William.

Morag's Lodge (☎ 366289, Bunnoich Brae) Beds £10.50. Morag's, next to the petrol station, is a bit grim but it's the only backpacker accommodation in the area.

There are a few B&Bs in town charging £15 to £20 per person, including *Appin (☎ 366541, Inverness Rd)*, *Greystone's (☎ 366736, Station Rd)* and *Kettle House (☎ 366408, Golf Course Rd)*.

Bank House (☎ 366755, Station Rd) B&B £20 per person. This pad, in a gracious two-story building with a classy garden and rooms overlooking the canal, must be one of the few B&Bs in Scotland that share their premises with a sizable Bank of Scotland.

Caledonian House (☎ 366256, Station Rd) Rooms from £30 per person. This friendly, quasi-grand place overlooks the abbey.

Neuk Café (☎ 366208) Mains £3-6. Open 9am-9pm summer, 9am-6pm rest of year. Neuk in Gaelic means 'small cosy corner', and that's exactly what this bright, airy cafe overlooking the canal is. Comfortable wooden tables, a fantastic window for people-watching, good coffee and tasty, cheap food make it Fort Augustus' best place to eat. It also provides Internet access.

The Bothy (☎ 366710, Station Rd) Mains £5-8. This place has a top local reputation and serves excellent haddock and chips (£6). Originally built as a workshop for canal construction workers, it still has a roaring fire to sip your dram in front of.

The *Scots Kitchen (☎ 366361)*, opposite the village car park, is a decent cafe with snacks and some mains such as steak and ale pie (£5.95).

Lock Inn (☎ 366302) Open 11am-11pm Mon-Sat & noon-11pm Sun. This popular bar by the canal, near the A82, has the mandatory 100 whiskies and is the best place in town for a drinking binge. The *Gilliegorm* restaurant inside dishes up memorable haggis (£3.50), plus seafood and tasty burgers from £5.

Getting There & Around

Scottish Citylink (☎ 0870 550 5050) runs five or six buses daily between Inverness and Fort William, via Fort Augustus. The trip to either town takes an hour and costs £6.

You can hire bikes from Scottish Voyageurs (☎ 366666) on the A82 near the canal.

INVERGARRY & AROUND

For 33 miles, between Fort Augustus and Fort William, the A82 provides access to some of the forested glens and narrow lochs of the Lochaber region.

The sleepy village of Invergarry stands where the A82 branches out to meet the A87 to Kyle of Lochalsh. The area surrounding it, particularly through Glen Garry, is worth exploring. Just off the A87 is the turn-off for **Loch Garry**, and for 20 stunning miles you can drive along this road to **Kinloch Hourn**, a sea loch on the western coast.

Loch Lochy Hostel (☎ 01809-501239) Beds £8.25. This SYHA hostel, a mile or so south of Invergarry in South Laggan, is a well-cared-for place with friendly staff.

Invergarry Hotel (☎ 01809-501206) Rooms from £25 per person. In the village, this pretty Victorian coaching inn on the western side of Loch Oich has comfortable rooms and a fabulous restaurant.

Ardgarry Farm (☎ 01809-501226) Dinner & B&B £21. In a peaceful location just west of the village, this well-appointed place offers great value.

Faichemard Farm Campsite (☎ 01809-501314) Car, tent & 2 adults £6. Oodles of thought has gone into the excellent facilities at this camp site near Ardgarry Farm.

Tomdoun Hotel (☎ 01809-5112440) Dinner & B&B from £39. Open for lunch (bar meals) & dinner. This renowned hotel, on the minor road through Glen Garry, dates from the 1890s and remains as sparkling clean as the day it was built.

Skiary Guest House (☎ 01809-511214) Rooms £70 per person. Open Apr-Oct. If achieving a Zen state of complete tranquillity is your main ambition, you'll find nowhere better than this ultra-remote guesthouse on the shores of Loch Hourn, a mile

from its head. Every room has breathtaking views taking in the loch and surrounding hills, including three Munros, and the price includes a luxury breakfast, packed lunch and scrumptious dinner. You are collected by boat (the only way in or out) from Kinloch Hourn, where there is parking for cars. Skiary also has space for helicopter access.

ACHNACARRY & LOCH ARKAIG

The B8004 between Banavie and Gairlochy follows the western side of the Great Glen, with wondrous views of Ben Nevis (literally 'Mount Heaven'). From Gairlochy, the B8005 turns northwards and follows the shore of Loch Lochy to the **Clan Cameron Museum** (☎ 01397-712480, Achnacarry; adult/child £3/free; open 11am-5pm daily July & Aug, 1pm-5pm daily Easter, June, Sept & Oct), which displays the history of the clan and gives a great insight into the Jacobite rebellions and events of 1745. Just to the west lies lovely Loch Arkaig. By the road, at the mouth of Gleann Cia-aig, there's a series of spectacular waterfalls.

SPEAN BRIDGE & ROYBRIDGE
☎ 01397

Spean Bridge derives its name from Thomas Telford's bridge over the River Spean. There's a busy TIC (☎ 712576) here, which opens 10am to 6pm Monday to Friday, 10am to 5pm Saturday year-round (in summer it also opens on Sunday and longer hours Monday to Saturday). There is also a **monument** to the British Army's elite commando troops who trained in the Lochaber region from 1942 until the end of WWII. Scott Sutherland's bronze memorial statue depicting three proud commandos sits high on a stone plinth, overlooking the A82 and the fantastic views beyond.

The best accommodation in Glen Spean is *Smiddy House* (☎ 712335, fax 712043), with B&B for £20 per person. It's next door to the old village blacksmith's workshop, and the bistro menu includes ample vegetarian choices and other mains from £7.

From Spean Bridge, **Glen Spean** extends southwest to northeast for around 25 miles along the River Spean and through to the head of Loch Laggan (where much of the BBC show *Monarch of the Glen* was shot). Along its southern side two groups of sprawling, high mountains are separated by beautiful Loch Treig. On the glen's opposite side, above Loch Laggan, is a smaller cluster of peaks dominated by awesome Creag Meagaidh (1128m), moulded by two million years of advancing and retreating glaciers and ice sheets.

A few miles on from Spean Bridge is Roybridge, the only other village for some distance; it has a shop and post office. More importantly, this is where you'll find the road to **Glen Roy**, noted for its intriguing 'parallel roads' – ancient terraced shorelines formed by the waters of an ice-dammed glacial lake during the last Ice Age. Whenever the dam burst, or otherwise allowed water to spill out, the level dropped and formed a new terrace.

There are plenty of serious walks in the area, but if that kind of furious activity isn't your thing, the best place to view the terraces is 3 miles up Glen Roy from Spean Bridge – drive, cycle or walk up the road.

In Roybridge, the independent *Roybridge Inn Hostel* (☎ 712236) has a bar and beds for £9.

Àite Cruinnichidh (☎ 712315, e info@ highland-bunkhouses.co.uk) Beds £8-12. This converted barn, 2 miles east of Roybridge, provides 24 dorm beds and an en-suite family room that sleeps up to six (£24 for the room). There's a great kitchen, a sauna, and a living room with stunning views over the Monessie Gorge (indicated by the huge sign put there for the trains that chug past the car park). The lovely owners are very knowledgeable about the area. Phone ahead for a free pick-up from Roybridge train station.

If it's full, 3 miles farther east is the *Station Lodge Bunkhouse* (☎ 732333), in an original station building dating from 1894. Beds cost £10, including linen, and there's a kitchen.

Getting There & Away

Highland Country/Rapsons (☎ 01463-222244) has bus services from Fort William

to Achnacarry, Spean Bridge and Roybridge. Scottish Citylink buses connect Fort William with Spean Bridge, Invergarry, Skye and Inverness. The railway from Fort William to Glasgow has stops at Spean Bridge and Roybridge.

The Road to Skye

The beautiful stretch of the A87 running between Invermoriston and Kyle of Lochalsh is, by itself, worth the cost of a ticket to Scotland, especially if you're a hiker and tackling Glen Shiel, or you're headed for the picturesque village of Plockton or to see Scotland's most photographed castle, the wonderful Eilean Donan.

Things are rather flat until you hit striking **Loch Cluanie**, from which point the A87 gets ever more dramatic: the seemingly impenetrable walls of Glen Shiel grow higher and more spectacular, and the mountains that tower above you reach up to 1166m.

There's some of the world's best hiking all along Glen Shiel, but remember that the weather can be truly wild, and none of the routes along the way should be attempted without proper maps, gear and supplies. The views on top of peaks such as the Five Sisters are truly remarkable and it's worth waiting for a clear day.

That said, there's an army of people walking the **South Glen Shiel Ridge**, one of Scotland's great walks. It begins near the *Cluanie Inn* (☎ 01320-340238, fax 340293, w www.cluanie.co.uk), a class Highland lodge and favourite with walkers and rock-climbers. B&B costs from £25 to £50 per person, bar meals cost around £8, or you can try the freshly prepared haggis (£5.95). There's even a Jacuzzi and sauna here, and a TIC at reception that can fill you in on hiking in the area.

From the inn you can walk several mountain ridges, bagging Munros to your heart's content (though check locally about the deer-stalking, which runs from August to October). There's a low-level route through to Glen Affric Hostel (see Cannich & Glen Affric earlier in this chapter), which takes three hours, but it gets very wet at certain times of year.

Closer to **Loch Duich**, to the north of the A87, are the unmistakable **Five Sisters of Kintail** (1068m), towering above the road.

SHIEL BRIDGE
☎ 01599

There's little to do in Shiel Bridge, but it has good eating and sleeping options.

Shiel Bridge Campsite (☎ 511211) Pitches £4/7 for 1/2 people. Enquire at the Five Sisters Restaurant (see below) for this well-equipped site.

Kintail Lodge (☎ 511275, fax 511226) Dorm beds £10, singles/doubles £40 per person June-Aug, from £30 at other times. Bar meals £7-12.50. Spectacularly located on the loch at the foot of the Five Sisters, the Kintail Lodge has plush, slightly faded rooms, plus a bunkhouse with a kitchen. Meals include local venison and salmon.

Ratagan Hostel (☎ 511243, Ratagan) Beds from £9.25/6. Open Feb-Oct. This particularly good SYHA hostel is located near Loch Duich, a mile or so from Shiel Bridge.

Five Sisters Restaurant (☎ 511307) Mains £5.95-7.50. The BP petrol station is a jack of all trades at Shiel Bridge; besides selling petrol and groceries, it also runs the decent Five Sisters Restaurant, with several vegetarian dishes.

GLENELG & AROUND
At Shiel Bridge, a narrow side road goes to Ratagan, then continues to the village of Glenelg on the Sound of Sleat, where there's a ferry to Skye. The road has some spellbinding views. Leaving Shiel Bridge, the road climbs sharply to the top of **Ratagan Pass**, where the view of the Five Sisters is truly remarkable. Then you plummet into Glen More and Glenelg, the main village on this lonely peninsula.

An attractive village with whitewashed cottages overlooking the bay across to Skye, Glenelg has only one place worth staying in town: the cosy *Glenelg Inn (☎ 01599-522273, fax 522283)*, in some former stables. Dinner and B&B costs from £50 per person, and bar meals £7 to £10.

The wacky kilt-clad proprietor is a gem, and the accommodation's excellence is surpassed only by its delicious meals.

You can continue past Glenelg to the two ruined Iron-Age brochs, **Dun Telve** and **Dun Troddan**. Dun Telve still rises to a height of 10m, making it the second best-preserved broch in Scotland, after Mousa in Shetland.

From Glenelg round to the road-end at Arnisdale, the scenery becomes spectacular again, with great views across Loch Hourn to Knoydart. The Scottish author Gavin Maxwell (1914–69) wrote his autobiographical book *Ring of Bright Water* (1960) while living at Sandaig, on the coast just south of Glenelg.

Getting There & Away
Just before you come to Glenelg from Shiel Bridge, the road forks; at the end of the right fork you'll find the Glenelg-Kylerhea ferry, which takes five minutes to reach Skye. The tiny eight-car ferry runs from mid-April to early October, and is far and away the most romantic way of reaching Skye, especially if there's fog. See Kylerhea in the Skye chapter for details. For details of the open-boat service between Arnisdale and Barrisdale (in Knoydart), see The Knoydart Peninsula section later in this chapter.

There's a postbus (☎ 01246-546329) operating once daily, except Sunday, from Kyle to Arnisdale via Shiel Bridge and Glenelg.

EILEAN DONAN CASTLE
Strategically and, more importantly these days, photogenically sited at the confluence of Lochs Duich, Long and Alsh, Eilean Donan Castle (☎ 01599-555202, **W** www .eileandonancastle.com; adult/child £3.95/ 3.20; open 10am-6pm daily mid-Mar–Nov) is the most recognisable of Scottish castles, having appeared in thousands of calendars, millions of postcards and at least two successful films (the Bond flick *The World is Not Enough* and *Highlander*).

On an offshore islet and magically linked to the mainland with a stone-arched bridge, the first castle here was built in 1230 by Alexander II to protect the region from Vikings; it was ruined in 1719 after Spanish

Jacobite forces were defeated at the Battle of Glenshiel, and rebuilt between 1912 and 1932. The reconstruction isn't completely accurate inside, but from the outside, this evocative place is the castle you *always knew* you'd one day see in Scotland.

There's an excellent exhibition, history display panels, spiral staircases, vaulted ceilings, tower bedrooms, impressive interiors (furniture from the 1650s) and a recreation of the kitchen as it was in 1932. There's also a good cafe and gift shop overlooking the entrance to the castle.

DORNIE
☎ 01599 ● pop 256

This quiet village just across the road from Eilean Donan has a general store, post office and little else, though it's a good base for exploring the area and has several reasonable places to stay and eat.

Dornie Bunkhouse (☎ 555264, Carndubh) Beds £9, including breakfast. This tiny four-bed hostel offers simple accommodation, half a mile along the eastern side of Loch Long.

Rockhouse (☎ 555387) Beds from £10. Directly opposite the castle sits this clean, well-run hostel in a modern bungalow.

Dornie Hotel (☎ 555205, fax 555429, Francis St) Singles £25-35, doubles £50-70. Bar meals £7-17. The whitewashed Dornie Hotel has good rooms with plush beds, and excellent bar meals.

Scottish Citylink (☎ 0870 550 5050) buses (£12.45, five daily) from Fort William and Inverness to Portree stop opposite the castle and by the bridge at Dornie.

KYLE OF LOCHALSH
☎ 01599 ● pop 1000

Before the controversial Skye Bridge opened in 1995, Kyle of Lochalsh (usually just called Kyle) was the main jumping-off point for trips to Skye. Now Kyle's many B&B owners have to watch their trade whizz past without stopping, which isn't necessarily a bad thing as there's not much to hold travellers here.

The TIC (☎ 534276), beside the main seafront car park, opens April to October

and stocks information on Skye. In the village, you'll find two supermarkets, two banks (with ATMs), a post office and a swimming pool (admission £2.20).

Organised Tours
Sea Probe Atlantis (☎ 0800 980 4846) is a glass-bottomed boat sailing four times daily from the old ferry quay near the traffic lights in Kyle. Cruises last from 30 minutes to 2½ hours and cost from adult/child £6.50/3.50. Depending on the tour, you may see a WWII shipwreck, kelp forests, seals or other marine life.

Places to Stay & Eat
Cuchulainn's (☎ 534492, Station Rd) Beds £9.50. Attached to the rear of Kyle's main pub, Cuchulainn's dorm accommodation is surprisingly peaceful and well kept.

Lochalsh Hotel (☎ 534202). B&B from £35 per person. If faded grandeur is your thing, stay at this place by the pier with its stunning views. It has sizable, tidy rooms and wonderful bar meals (from £7).

Seagreen Restaurant & Bookshop (☎ 534388, Plockton Rd) Mains £5-10. Locals claim the Seagreen is Scotland's best vegetarian eatery, which probably isn't true but it is excellent; we recommend their broccoli, wild mushroom and local cheese quiche (£4.45). It also does seafood, and at 75p to 95p each their baked oysters are a delectable bargain, as is the oak-smoked seafood platter (£7.25). It's 1 mile north of Kyle, on the road to Plockton.

Head for *Gateway Café (☎ 534030, Station Rd)* for Kyle's best fish and chips (£3.45).

Getting There & Away
Kyle can be reached by bus (two hours, three daily Monday to Saturday) and train (1½ hours, three daily Monday to Saturday, two on Sunday) from Inverness (see Getting There & Away under Inverness earlier), and by direct Scottish Citylink buses from Glasgow (£17.50, 5½ hours). Citylink buses continue to Kyleakin (£1.60, 10 minutes) and on to Portree (£7.40, one hour) and Uig (£7.90, 1½ hours); from Uig there are ferries to Tarbert on South Harris and Lochmaddy on

North Uist. Highland Country/Rapsons run buses to/from Kyleakin twice an hour.

PLOCKTON
☎ 01599 ● pop 428

Utterly picturesque is the best description we can give of Plockton. It's composed of a long row of whitewashed cottages ranged along a wooded bay, which is hit by a unique light that, at dusk on a sunny afternoon, will make you chuckle with glee.

It is a highly gentrified place, which got its 15 minutes of fame when BBC TV and Robert Carlyle visited in the early 1990s to film the quirky *Hamish Macbeth* series. Fan trips have dwindled, but there's still a steady stream of tourists, and in summer you might find it fairly busy. Any other time of the year, though, this idyllic town is one of the premier places to stay in Scotland.

Plockton has a grocery shop, and Internet access (£3 per 15 minutes) at the post office in Cooper St, open 10am to 1pm weekdays except Wednesday.

That wonderful light draws painters to the village in droves, and you can find some of the best work in the *Studio Craft Shop* on the corner of the seafront and the road leading out of town.

Organised Tours
Calum's Seal Trips (☎ 544306) last for one hour and cost adult/child £5/3. You're guaranteed a free ride if you don't spot a seal, though there's little chance of that as there are swarms of them just outside the harbour. The friendly captain, a native of the area, gives a wonderful commentary.

Sea Trek Marine (☎ 544356) operates similar tours, with hourly departures through the day; it also offers guided hill walks.

Places to Stay & Eat
Plockton Station Bunkhouse (☎ 544235, e gill@ecosse.net) Beds £8.50-10. Open year-round. This comfortable place is situated in the former station building, a little way up the hill from the waterfront.

The Shieling (☎ 544282) B&B from £18 per person. On a tiny headland overlooking the harbour, the comfortable Shieling is in a modern building next to Plockton's only thatched cottage

Plockton Hotel (☎ 544274, fax 544475, W www.plocktonhotel.co.uk, 41 Harbour St) B&B from £30 per person. Mains from £5.25. Overlooking the harbour, this jet-black hotel is a wonderful place to stay, with spotless, well-appointed rooms and a picturesque beer garden overlooking the bay. The award-winning seafood is a treat and the breakfast spread is superb.

Plockton Inn (☎ 544222, Innes St) B&B from £30. Equally good is the Plockton Inn, which has top seafood and well-positioned boozing benches out the front.

Haven Hotel (☎ 544223, Innes St) B&B £38-41 per person. 4-course meals £25. Cosiest of all is the swish Haven, with plush bedrooms and renowned seafood.

Off The Rails (☎ 544423, W www.off-the-rails.co.uk, Plockton Station) Meals around £6-13. Good home-made food is served up here; for dinner try the delicious 'whisky haggis and clapshot' (£5.95).

Getting There & Away
The train from Kyle of Lochalsh (15 minutes) is the simplest way here, or there's a Scottish Citylink bus (30 minutes) from Kyle. If you're driving, on the A890 keep a lookout for the sign for Stromeferry and turn off a few miles before the village.

Fort William & Glen Coe

FORT WILLIAM
☎ 01397 ● pop 10,774

Set amid one of Scotland's most magnificent landscapes, beside Loch Linnhe and metres from Ben Nevis, Fort William could have been one of the prettiest towns on the planet. Instead, a drab motorway runs along the loch, fast-food outlets and supermarkets are your first glimpse of the town if you're coming from the north, and the centre has its back to the loch and the lovely hills of Ardgour – enough to make you want to kneecap a town planner.

Despair not though, because, once the gloom of the waterfront is behind you, you'll find this a heartwarming place to spend a day or two, or to use as a base to explore the surrounding Lochaber area. The pedestrianised High St and the friendliness of Fort William's wonderful community make this a great town worth visiting; there's even talk of moving the motorway to the other side of town, though this rumour surfaces once or twice every decade.

As a major tourist centre, it's easily accessed by bus and rail – the stunning West Highland Railway runs through here. Magical Glen Nevis begins near the northern end of the town and extends south and east below the slopes of Ben Nevis. 'The Ben', Britain's highest mountain at 1343m and neighbouring ranges are a magnet for hikers and climbers. The glen is also popular with film-makers – parts of *Braveheart*, *Highlander* and *Rob Roy* were filmed here.

For full details on climbing Ben Nevis see Walking in the Activities chapter.

Orientation & Information

The town meanders along the edge of deep Loch Linnhe for around 3 miles and the centre, with its small selection of shops, takeaways and pubs, is easy to get around

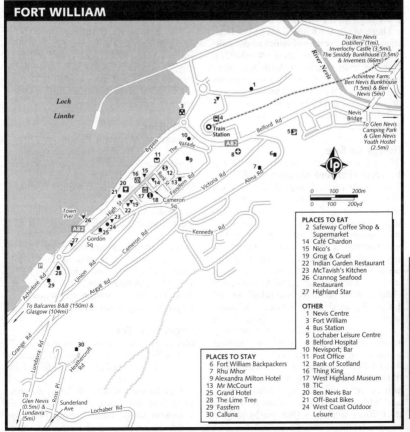

FORT WILLIAM

PLACES TO EAT
2 Safeway Coffee Shop & Supermarket
14 Café Chardon
15 Nico's
19 Grog & Gruel
22 Indian Garden Restaurant
23 McTavish's Kitchen
26 Crannog Seafood Restaurant
27 Highland Star

OTHER
1 Nevis Centre
3 Fort William
4 Bus Station
5 Lochaber Leisure Centre
8 Belford Hospital
10 Nevisport; Bar
11 Post Office
12 Bank of Scotland
16 Thing King
17 West Highland Museum
18 TIC
20 Ben Nevis Bar
21 Off-Beat Bikes
24 West Coast Outdoor Leisure

PLACES TO STAY
6 Fort William Backpackers
7 Rhu Mhor
9 Alexandra Milton Hotel
13 Mr McCourt
25 Grand Hotel
28 The Lime Tree
29 Fassfern
30 Calluna

THE GREAT GLEN & THE WESTERN HIGHLANDS

on foot (though some B&Bs are farther away).

The TIC (☎ 703781, **e** fortwilliam@ host.co.uk) in Cameron Square has an good range of books and maps, and helpful staff. It opens 10am to 6pm Monday to Friday and 10am to 5pm Saturday year-round (in summer it also opens on Sunday and has longer hours Monday to Saturday). For local walks, get a copy of the handy *Best Walks Around Fort William* (£1.99), which incorporates maps and basic information on 15 routes. More information is available from the Glen Nevis (Ionad Nibheis) Visitor Centre; see Glen Nevis later for details.

The best place in the town centre to check your email is Thing King (☎ 703651) in the High St; it charges from £3 per hour.

There are banks with ATMs in the High St, as well as several well-stocked outdoor-equipment shops. Nevisport (☎ 704921), near the train station at Airds Crossing, has a great range of books and maps for mountaineers. West Coast Outdoor Leisure (☎ 705777) is at 102 High St.

Belford Hospital (☎ 702481) is opposite the train station in Belford Rd.

Things to See
Of the few real sights in town, the best is the **West Highland Museum** *(☎ 702169, Cameron Square; adult/child £2/1.50; open 10am-5pm Mon-Sat June-Sept & 2pm-5pm Sun July & Aug, 10am-4pm Mon-Sat Oct-May)*. Next to the TIC, the museum looks rather dowdy outside but inside it's packed with fascinating displays on Highland history, geology, archaeology, crofting and clans. Of particular interest is the secret portrait (an anamorphosis) of Bonnie Prince Charlie. After the Jacobite rebellions all things Highland were banned, including pictures of the exiled leader. Seen on its own, the picture looks like a smear of paint, but placed next to a curved mirror it reflects a credible likeness of the prince.

A Highland highlight, the **Jacobite Steam Train** *(☎ 01524-732100, **W** www.westcoast railway.co.uk)* runs along the West Highland Railway from Fort William to Mallaig at 10.20am weekdays (and on Sunday in

August, 1½ hours) from mid-June to late September, returning at 2.10pm. The journey, with awe-inspiring and often surreal views, takes you across the historic Glenfinnan Viaduct and looks down wonderful Loch Shiel (for both see The Southwest Peninsulas later in this chapter). A 2nd-class day return costs adult/child £22/12.50.

There's little left of the original **fort** from which Fort William takes its name; an idiot town planner of an earlier age pulled it down in 1889 to make way for the railway. The first fort (which stretched as far as the present-day Safeway's front door, as the plaque in the supermarket's entrance attests) was built in 1654 to control the Highlands, but the surviving ruins are of the structure built in 1690.

The **Ben Nevis Distillery** *(☎ 702476, Lochy Bridge; tour & tasting £2; open 9am-7.30pm Mon-Fri & 10am-4pm Sat July & Aug, 9am-5pm Mon-Fri Sept-June)* has a visitors centre and sales outlet. It is a no-frills kind of place and only worth a visit if you're a hardened distillery fan.

Activities
Snowgoose Mountain Centre *(☎ 772467, fax 772411, **W** www.highland-mountain-guides.co.uk, Station Rd, Corpach)*, attached to The Smiddy Bunkhouse (see Places to Stay later in this section) 4 miles northwest in Corpach, organises a range of activities; beginners courses in rock climbing and mountaineering/kayaking/sailing cost £35/25/30 per day.

The **Lochaber Leisure Centre** *(☎ 704359, Belford Rd)* has a swimming pool (adult/child £2.20/1.20), climbing wall (£2.50) and gym. The **Nevis Centre** *(☎ 700707, An Aird)*, near the bus station, has snooker and 10-pin bowling (from £2.50).

Organised Tours
Glengarry Mini Tours (☎ 01809-501297) does half- or full-day tours around Lochaber and Glen Coe, starting at £7.50 for a four-hour afternoon tour.

Seal Island Cruises (☎ 703919), operating from the Town Pier where there's a booking kiosk, runs 1½-hour boat trips (adult/child £6/3) on the loch. There are four trips daily, plus an evening cruise (£14, with a buffet) at 7pm on summer weekdays.

Places to Stay

Even though Fort William has countless accommodation options, be sure to book ahead (for hostels too) in summer.

Camping *Glen Nevis Camping Park (☎ 702191, fax 703904, Glen Nevis)* 1 person £4.30-6.30, 2 people £5-7.30, car £1.70-3.30. Open mid-Mar–Oct. The best camping option is up scenic Glen Nevis, 3 miles from town and near Glen Nevis Youth Hostel.

Hostels *Fort William Backpackers (☎ 700711, e fortwilliam@scotlands-top-hostels.com, Alma Rd)* Beds from £10. Open year-round. A popular hostel, it's just a short walk from the bus and train stations.

Glen Nevis Youth Hostel (☎ 702336, Glen Nevis) Beds from £9/6. Open year-round. Beside the start of one of the paths up Ben Nevis, 3 miles from Fort William, is this bland and institutional 40-bed SYHA hostel.

Ben Nevis Bunkhouse (☎ 702240, e achinee.accom@glennevis.com, Glen Nevis) Beds £9.50. Open year-round. A better option is the bunkhouse at Achintee Farm, over the river from the Glen Nevis Visitor Centre. There's a cafe with occasional live music and Internet access.

Calluna (☎ 700451, fax 700489, e mountain@guide.u-net.com, Heathercroft Rd) Beds £10. This great little bunkhouse, run by local mountain guide Alan Kimber, can be difficult to find; ring for directions or a free pick-up from town.

The Smiddy Bunkhouse (see Activities earlier) Beds £6-10. This hostel with 26 comfy beds is in Corpach, 4 miles along the A830 road heading to Mallaig and northwest of Fort William.

B&Bs & Hotels There's a staggering choice of B&Bs on and near Achintore Rd, which runs southwards along the loch, and a few B&Bs on Alma and Fassifern Rds, close to the train and bus stations.

The Lime Tree (☎ 701806, e info@lime treestudio.co.uk, Achintore Rd) Singles/doubles £20/32, en-suite doubles £40. The unique Lime Tree B&B, run by friendly owners David & Charlotte, is an 'art gallery with rooms', as the sign out front says. All its stylish, comfortable rooms are decorated with David's high-quality paintings, drawings and watercolours of Highland landscapes. The Studio Gallery downstairs sells some of his work. And if that isn't enough to convince you, their breakfast is easily the best in town, if not Scotland.

Fassfern (☎ 704298, Achintore Rd) B&B £20 per person. If The Lime Tree is full, a good alternative is Fassfern next door. Its hotel-standard rooms, all with spotless bathrooms, are reasonably priced and it also cooks a mean breakfast.

Balcarres (☎ 702377, Seafield Gardens) B&B from £20 per person. This well-run B&B has welcoming owners, and its four en-suite rooms are all decked out with classy furnishings. It also has great loch views.

Rhu Mhor (☎ 712213, Alma Rd) This B&B, with tidy rooms, is part of a two-storey stone terrace.

Mr McCourt (☎ 703756, 6 Caberfeidh, Fassifern Rd) Singles/doubles £20/36. Mr M's may look a touch bleak on the outside but his three rooms, all en suite, are comfy enough and well maintained.

There are several more upmarket options in and around town.

Alexandra Milton Hotel (☎ 702241, The Parade) Singles/doubles £39/69. Don't let the snooty staff put you off this traditional hotel with 97 refined rooms. On the downside, the views over the ugliest shops on the High St are unfortunate.

Grand Hotel (☎/fax 702928, Gordon Square) Singles £25-42.50, doubles £44-65. Though it no longer looks so grand, the Grand does good food and its rooms vary from functionally fine to downright decent.

Inverlochy Castle (☎ 702177, fax 702953, w www.inverlochy.co.uk, Tor lundy) Singles £180-255, doubles £250-480. Set in 200 hectares of grounds 3 miles north of Fort William, Inverlochy Castle is an opulent Victorian creation (completed in

THE GREAT GLEN & THE WESTERN HIGHLANDS

1865) that has everything you might expect in a castle: open battlements, stags' heads, log fires and a sweeping staircase. It also caters for weddings.

Places to Eat

Fort William is no culinary hot spot, but there are several decent options in town. For those on a tight budget, the **Safeway Coffee Shop** (☎ 700333) sells good-value light meals, such as filled jacket potatoes (from £2) and an all-day breakfast (£2 to £3). It opens 8am to 8pm Monday to Saturday, and 9am to 6pm Sunday.

Nico's (37 High St) is tops for fish and chips, while **Café Chardon** (☎ 702116, 28 High St), upstairs in P Maclennan's store, serves soup (£1.95), filled ciabatta sandwiches (£3.55) and quiche (£2.55). **McTavish's Kitchen** (☎ 702406, 100 High St) serves up unremarkable but affordable Scottish fare (mains around £6), and there's a self-service cafe downstairs.

Indian Garden Restaurant (☎ 705011, 88 High St) Mains around £9, 2-course weekday lunches £5.95. This place is jumping on Monday nights, when it does an £8.50 all-you-can-eat buffet. At other times it can be deathly quiet, and not particularly cheap, but the quality of dishes is generally excellent. It also does takeaway.

Highland Star (☎ 703905, 155 High St) Mains from £6. The town's only Chinese restaurant, this place does good a takeaway (from £5.30).

Grog & Gruel (☎ 705078, 66 High St) Mains £5.60-11.95. Food doesn't strike you as something the Grog & Gruel is likely to do well, as its main role is as the town's best drinking den, but the Tex-Mex-orientated menu here is great, with enchiladas, burritos and fajitas, as is their more regular fare such as burgers, steaks and pasta.

Crannog Seafood Restaurant (☎ 705589, Town Pier) Mains £11.50-15.50. The town's only true gourmet restaurant also has the best location, in a converted bait shop on the pier. Diners have an uninterrupted view over Loch Linnhe, and ample chance to sample seafood as good as any they'll eat in the region.

Entertainment

McTavish's Kitchen (see Places to Eat) Adult/child £4/2 show only, £2/1 if dining. 3-course dinner £10.25. Open noon-2pm & 6pm-10pm daily. Shows from 8pm daily. With dancing, a live band and a piper to top it off, the shows at McTavish's Kitchen *can* be fun.

Ben Nevis Bar (☎ 702295, 105 High St) A popular Thursday and Friday night music venue, this bar is a good place for a drink or inexpensive meal (mains £3.50 to £5.95).

Nevisport Bar (☎ 704921, Airds Crossing) Downstairs at the Nevisport complex, the Nevisport Bar beckons walkers and climbers and, on the second Saturday of each month, blues, folk and jazz fans with its free performances.

The **Grog & Gruel** (see Places to Eat) is the most chilled-out pub in town for a quiet ale and a chat.

Getting There & Away

Bus Fort William's bus station is next to the train station, in the car park adjoining the Safeway supermarket

Scottish Citylink (☎ 0870 550 5050) runs four buses daily to Glasgow (£11.80, three hours) and twice daily to Edinburgh (£16.50, 3¾ hours), both via Glencoe village and Crianlarich. There are three buses daily to/from Kyle of Lochalsh (£10.70, two hours), and two to four on weekdays to/from Oban (£6.90, 1½ hours). Five or six buses run daily to/from Inverness (£7.40, two hours).

Shiel Buses/Scottish Citylink runs one bus a day Monday to Saturday to/from Mallaig (£4, 1¼ hours), via Glenfinnan (£2, 35 minutes).

Highland Country/Rapsons (☎ 702373) runs six daily bus services to Kinlochleven (£2.65, 50 minutes) via Glencoe village (£2.05, 40 minutes). June to September, two buses daily run to Cairngorm via Laggan, Newtonmore and Aviemore.

Train The most spectacular part of the West Highland Railway runs from Fort William to Mallaig (see the boxed text 'The West Highland Railway' in the Getting Around chapter) and you'd be a fool not to take it.

There's no direct rail link between Oban and Fort William; use Citylink buses to avoid the long detour inland to Crianlarich.

Car For car hire it's worth trying Nevis Garage (☎ 702432, W www.nevis-garage .co.uk), Ardgour Rd, Caol, or ask at the TIC for their Car Hire leaflet.

Walking Fort William lies at the end of the 95-mile West Highland Way (see the Activities chapter) from Glasgow.

Getting Around
From June to September, Highland Country/ Rapsons (☎ 702473) does the 10-minute run from the bus station to Glen Nevis Youth Hostel (£1.10); buses leave hourly (every two hours in the evening) from 8.25am to 10.10pm Monday to Saturday, with a reduced service on Sunday. Buses to Corpach (85p, 15 minutes) run as frequently as four per hour.

Taxis wait in the High St opposite McTavish's Garrison Restaurant, or you can call ☎ 702545 or 773030.

For bicycle rental, try Off-Beat Bikes (☎ 704008), 117 High St, which has mountain bikes for £8.50/12.50 per half/full day.

AROUND FORT WILLIAM
Nevis Range
The **Nevis Range Ski Station** (☎ 01397-705825), 6 miles north of Fort William, just off the A82, skirts the upper slopes of Aonach Mór (1221m).

The 1½-mile gondola ride to the 655m-high station at the top operates from Boxing Day to early November, and costs adult/child £6.90/4.25 return (15 minutes each way).

During the ski season, passes for the lift from the top station of the gondola cost adult/child £20/11.50 per day. A four-hour ski lesson costs £17.75 and one day's ski/snowboard hire costs £14/17.50.

The *Snowgoose Restaurant* at the top of the station serves hearty, inexpensive meals (£4.50 to £8), but more important are the breathtaking views from its deck. There are walking routes from the restaurant and through nearby **Leanachan Forest**.

A new downhill mountain-bike trail (for experienced riders only; open mid-May to mid-September) runs from the Snowgoose Restaurant to the base station; bikes are carried on a rack on the gondola. A one-way trip costs adult/child £9.25/6.75 and a one-day pass costs £15/11.50. You can hire bikes for £17.50/35 for a one-way trip/full day.

Glen Nevis
South of Fort William is serious walking country. **Glen Nevis (Ionad Nibheis) Visitor Centre** *(admission free; open 9pm-6pm Apr-Oct, 9am-5pm Nov-Mar)*, 1½ miles southwest of Fort William, up the road to Glen Nevis, has information on walks in the area.

One of the area's best walks is the simple 3-mile hike through one end of Glen Nevis, through the gorge at the eastern end to Steall Meadows, with a 100m-high waterfall. Drive to the car park at the very end of the Glen Nevis road, from where a marked trail leads up and over a few riverside cliffs and rises until you emerge below **Steall Falls**. You can try crossing the wire bridge to get really close to the falls, but only fit adults should attempt it, unless you want a dunking in the freezing waters below.

GLEN COE
Breathtakingly spectacular Glen Coe is perhaps Scotland's most famous and atmospheric glen, and also one of its most accessible. It's known as the 'glen of weeping', not because of the huge rainfall levels but because it was the scene of the infamous massacre that stands in such stark contrast to its beauty. Charles Dickens called this hauntingly beautiful place 'bleak and wild and mighty in its loneliness', and these days its grandeur is a magnet for tourists, walkers and mountaineers alike.

Be warned, however: police have reported an alarming increase in the number of thefts from parking areas in the Lochaber and Glen Coe area. Police notices are posted at several of the most popular access spots, but the general advice if you are leaving a car is to ensure you hide all belongings and take valuables such as cameras and wallets with you.

The Glen Coe Massacre

In February 1692, an event so gruesome and cruel it's still difficult to imagine took place in the homes of this tiny Highland village. It was to prove a defining moment in the Jacobite movement, causing many who were undecided or who had supported the status quo to question the tyrannical rule of the English.

In 1691 King William III demanded that all Scottish clan chiefs sign an oath of allegiance to the crown by 1 January the following year. Failure to sign, the king decreed, meant death.

Maclain, the chief of the MacDonalds of Glencoe village, went to Fort William to sign the oath on behalf of his village, only to discover signatures were being collected farther south in Inveraray. The mistake meant he didn't give his signature until 6 January, but Maclain nonetheless left Inveraray with the impression his allegiance had been accepted.

The Secretary of State for Scotland, Sir John Dalrymple, declared the MacDonalds should be punished as an example to other Highland clans, some of whom had not even bothered to take the oath. He dispatched to the glen a company of 120 soldiers, mainly of the Campbell clan, who had a decade-old grudge against the MacDonalds.

It was a long-standing Highland tradition for clans to provide hospitality to passing travellers and, as the regiment's leader was related to Maclain by marriage, the troops were billeted in MacDonald homes. For 12 days they enjoyed room and board from the villagers.

In an extraordinary act of betrayal, the Campbell men rose at 5am on the morning of 13 February and revealed to their hosts the orders they had received from Sir Dalrymple two weeks earlier: to exterminate all MacDonald men under the age of 70.

A handful of Campbells alerted the MacDonalds to their intended fate and allowed them to flee, while others simply shot or stabbed their hosts, killing Maclain and 37 other men, women and children. Some died before they knew what was happening; and some 300 others fled into the snow and perished from hunger and exposure.

The ruthless brutality of the incident caused a public uproar, and the very lords in London who'd approved the massacre instantly distanced themselves from Dalrymple, who lost his job.

Signal Rock, where the order was given to begin the massacre, is on the north bank of the River Coe, 200m west of the Clachaig Inn; members of the MacDonald clan still gather here on 13 February each year.

GLENCOE VILLAGE
☎ 01855 ● pop 360

Standing by Loch Leven at the glen's entrance, there's little to see in this flat, slightly glum village apart from the thatched **Glencoe Folk Museum** (☎ 811664; adult/child £2/free; open 10am-5.30pm Mon-Sat mid-May–Sept), which has collections ranging from costumes and military memorabilia to domestic items and dairy equipment.

There's a post office, and **McCubbin's Store** is useful if you're low on provisions.

Glen Coe Visitor Centre (NTS; ☎ 811307, Inverigan; open 9.30am-5.30pm daily May-Aug, 9.30am-5.30pm Mon-Fri, 10am-3pm Sat & closed Sun Sept-Apr), by the A82

about a mile south of the village, opened in spring 2002. Exhibitions include interactive displays about the massacre, local natural history, the NTS and its work in the glen, and the development of mountaineering.

Places to Stay & Eat

There's a good range of accommodation and eating options in the glen. Glencoe village's main street has a few average B&Bs, with rooms starting at £15 per person.

Invercoe Caravans (☎/fax 811210) Pitches £9-14. Chalets & cottages £200-510 per week. Here you can camp, or rent a chalet or cottage by the week. The view down Loch Leven is stunning.

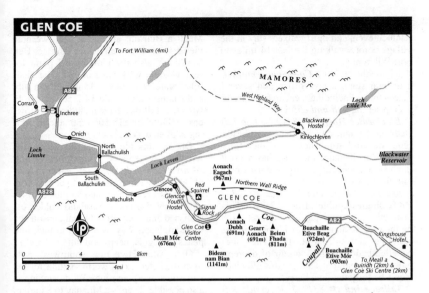

GLEN COE

Glencoe Youth Hostel (☎ *811219*) Beds from adult/child £8.50/5. Open year-round. Two miles from the village on the old Glencoe road, this SYHA hostel is a touch institutional but it's well cared for and has plenty of information about walks in the area. It's popular with climbers, so book ahead.

Leacantuim Farm Bunkhouse (☎ *811256*) Beds £6.50-7.50. This simple bunkhouse, near the SYHA hostel, is a good alternative if the hostel's full. It also runs **Red Squirrel Campsite**, farther along the Glencoe road, charging campers £4 each.

Clachaig Inn (☎ *811252*) B&B from £22 per person. Bar mains £5.75-13.95. Climbers clamour to stay at this classic Highland pub, 2½ miles southeast of the village. The ice axe door handle is decidedly quirky, as is the sign at reception: 'No Hawkers or Campbells'. The inn has good food and live Scottish, Irish and blues music several times a week, plus from January to March slide lectures on mountain topics are held fortnightly (admission from £5).

Getting There & Around

Highland Country/Rapsons (☎ 01397-702373) runs up to seven buses daily,

except Sunday, from Fort William to Glencoe village (35 minutes). Scottish Citylink buses run four times daily to Glasgow (£10.30, 2½ hours) and Fort William (£3.40).

You can hire bicycles at **Glencoe Mountain Bikes**, at the rear of the Clachaig Inn.

KINLOCHLEVEN
☎ 01855 ● pop 1100

Hemmed in by high mountains at the head of the beautiful fjord-like Loch Leven, Kinlochleven sits 7 miles east of Glencoe village. An aluminium factory which once supported the village closed in 2001, hitting the local economy hard, but plans to turn Kinlochleven into Scotland's premier mountaineering centre have gathered momentum, and a multimillion-pound redevelopment scheme will include Scotland's first artificial ice-climbing wall.

But Kinlochleven hasn't left heavy metal behind altogether – the surprisingly good Aluminium Story is told at the excellent **Kinlochleven Visitor Centre** (☎ *831663, Linnhe Rd; admission free; open 10am-1pm & 2pm-5pm Mon-Fri year-round, plus 6pm-8pm Tues Apr-Oct*), by the factory.

The **West Highland Way** passes through Kinlochleven, and most walkers stay in the village before walking the last 14 miles to Fort William.

Kinlochleven has a *Co-op supermarket*, a general store, a post office and several places to eat, including a cheap *bakery* and a shop selling *fish and chips*.

Blackwater Hostel (☎ 831253, Lab Rd) Beds £10, pitches £4.50. This wonderful, renovated old stone house by the River Leven is well maintained and has a great kitchen and lounge; it also organises bike hire for £6/10 per half-/full day.

Mamore Lodge Hotel (☎/fax 831213) B&B singles/doubles from £21/40. This distinctly wacky old hunting lodge sits high on the hillside above Kinlochleven and has stunning views from its bar. The pine-panelled bedrooms have an air of decrepitude about them, but a stay in this old place won't be forgotten in a hurry.

Tailrace Inn (☎ 831777, Riverside Rd) Snacks from £1.70, bar meals from £4.75. There's music in the bar and occasional *c*, so only come here if like it loud.

MacDonald Hotel (☎ 831539, fax 831416, Fort William Rd) En-suite B&B £28-34 per person. This place has great views over the loch and serves a hearty breakfast. Rooms are plain but comfortable. Bar meals are also available for £5 to £11.

Getting There & Away
Highland Country/Rapsons buses (☎ 01397-702373) run from Fort William/Glencoe village to Kinlochleven 10 times a day Monday to Saturday, and three on Sunday (£2.65/£1.05, 50/15 minutes).

GLENCOE SKI CENTRE & GLEN ETIVE
Follow the A82 southeast for about 9 miles and you'll pass the magnificent mountain **Buachaille Etive Mór** ('The Great Shepherd of Etive') on your right. Soon after you'll reach the car park and base station for the **Glencoe Ski Centre** (☎ *01855-851226*, W *www.ski-glencoe.co.uk),* where commercial skiing in Scotland began in 1956, on the White Corries ski run.

The **chair lift** climbs the 833m rise up to Meall a Buiridh, and there are awesome views over Rannoch Moor and to Ben Nevis; it's also the jumping-off point for several good walks in summer. The chair lift operates 9.30am to 4.15pm daily in July and August (adult/child £4/2.50 return). In winter, a full-day pass including ski tows costs adult/child £18.50/10.50, and the skiing is often decent.

On the opposite side of the A82 is the wonderfully isolated *Kingshouse Hotel (☎/fax 01855-851259),* where superb views of Buachaille Etive Mhor are to be had from the bar and restaurant, and singles/doubles cost £23.50/54. This is Scotland's oldest established inn, and attracts walkers on the West Highland Way, who stop to tuck into plates of haggis, neeps and tatties (£5.95).

Quiet **Glen Etive** runs southwestwards from the hotel and is worth visiting for the fantastic scenery en route. Wild camping is also possible. There's a Monday to Saturday postbus run (☎ 01246-546329) from Fort William to Glen Etive via Kingshouse Hotel.

The Southwest Peninsulas

Southwest of Fort William lies Scotland's Empty Quarter, a remote and unrelentingly rugged landscape of wild mountains, lonely coastlines and few roads.

ROAD TO THE ISLES
Known as the Road to the Isles, the A830 traverses a dramatic 46 miles filled with unique history, dramatic loch and mountain scenery and gorgeous flora and fauna. The striking beauty reaches its pinnacle along the coast stretching from Arisaig to Mallaig, where machair-backed beaches give way to stunningly azure blue waters flowing out to Eigg and Rum to the west and Skye to the northwest. Details on the area can be found at W www.road-to-the-isles.org.uk.

Wander the best part of the Caledonian Canal (see the boxed text 'Canal Plus') at **Neptune's Staircase** in Banavie, 3 miles

The verdant shoreline of Loch Torridon is the perfect place to stop and unwind...

...or if your hunger for intrepid adventure lingers on, climb the Liathach ridge near Torridon.

TOM SMALLMAN

GRANT DIXON

Which way next in Sutherland? The bar perhaps...

Wish you were here! Loch Lurgainn

GRANT DIXON

Mossy birch forest, Inverpolly Nature Reserve

GRAEME CORNWALLIS

Stacks of fun at the Old Man of Stoer

Canal Plus

Over twenty years in the making, the Caledonian Canal was the first to carry ships from one side of Britain to the other. Designed by Thomas Telford and completed in 1822 at a cost of £900,000 – a staggering sum then – the canal links the east and west coasts of Scotland, via lochs Linnhe, Lochy, Oich and Ness.

Once used by thousands of cargo ships each year, with the advent of speedier means of transport the canal now sees only pleasure and fishing crafts through its sturdy gates. Neptune's Staircase is the best place to check out the canal; Fort Augustus is next best.

north of Fort William. Here you'll see what Telford called Neptune's Staircase: eight lock gates spaced out over 460m and gradually climbing the 19m height difference between sea-level and the canal. It's great fun watching boats manoeuvring through the locks.

Glenfinnan
☎ 01397

From Fort William, the 9-mile drive along flat Loch Eil brings you to the awe-inspiring Glenfinnan, where Bonnie Prince Charlie was rowed to shore on 19 August 1745, ready to reclaim his father's place on the throne of England. The top-notch NTS Visitor Centre (☎ 722250; adult/child £1.50/1; open 9.30am-6pm daily May-Aug, 10am-5pm daily Apr, Sept & Oct) recounts the story of the prince and the 1745 rising that ended 14 months later, when he fled to France. The highlight of the centre are the headsets that tell the story of the rebellion and the Prince's failure. There's something very special about listening to the tale while staring out the window to the towering monument and down the beautiful loch, where this most remarkable episode in British history began. There's a first-rate *cafe* attached to the centre serving home-cooked goodies.

You can climb the monument when the weather's good; ask at the centre if the entrance isn't staffed.

Just behind the visitor centre is the Glenfinnan Viaduct, one of the most spectacular sections of the West Highland Railway from Fort William; for details see Things to See & Do under Fort William earlier in this chapter.

Half a mile farther on is Glenfinnan Station, where you'll find a rather humourless Station Museum (☎ 722295; adult/child 50/25p; open 9.30am-4.30pm daily June-Sept), with relics from the opening of the Glenfinnan section of the railway line in 1901 until today . Attached is a *bunkhouse* and *restaurant* (see Places to Stay & Eat).

Loch Shiel Cruises (☎ 722235) sails on Loch Shiel four to six times weekly from April to October; cruises vary from one to six hours and cost from £5 to £15. Departures are from the Glenfinnan House Hotel.

And, finally, the Glenfinnan Highland Games (☎ 722324) are held on a Saturday in mid-August; phone for details.

Places to Stay & Eat *Sleeping Car Bunkhouse* (☎ 722295, Glenfinnan Railway Station) Beds £10 per person. An old carriage has been turned into a tiny 10-bed bunkhouse with good sleeping facilities for backpackers. It also takes group bookings.

Railway Carriage Restaurant (☎ 722300, Glenfinnan Railway Station) Meals £5-10. Open 9.30am-11pm Fri-Sun May-Sept. Next to the bunkhouse, this is a fantastic place for a sandwich or coffee during the day, or a more substantial meal in the evening.

Prince's House Hotel (☎ 722246, W www.glenfinnan.co.uk) Singles/doubles £35/70. We can't be sure if Bonnie Prince Charlie stayed at the historic Prince's House Hotel in 1745, but since it dates from 1658 their marketing blurb alludes to it. Regardless, the hotel has good accommodation and a great bar; prior to 1980, when the bar was refurbished, there was a hatch in the floor through which locals could fish while enjoying a pint. Bar mains cost £7 to £15.

Arisaig & Morar
☎ 01687

The road continues on from Glenfinnan through rising hills and alongside Loch Eilt, until coming to Lochailort and the

THE GREAT GLEN & THE WESTERN HIGHLANDS

Bonnie Prince Charlie

Born in Italy in 1720, Bonnie Prince Charlie was the grandson of the exiled James VII, who was King of England for three years from 1685 before being forced to flee for fear of a revolt: James' Catholic faith was unpopular with many powerful English families.

Raised in a 'court in exile' in Italy, the prince had a romantic sense of his own destiny as the rightful ruler of England. It led him, in 1744, to travel to Paris in great secrecy for preparations for a French invasion of England. However, the fleet of ships that was to attack England was all but destroyed in a storm before they could sail, and before they could be repaired or rebuilt, French interest in the invasion waned. But not Bonnie Prince Charlie's.

In July 1745, without the support or knowledge of France's Louis XV, the prince set sail for Scotland with two ships laden with military stores and several hundred men. Eighteen days later, they landed in Scotland, first on the island of Eriskay, then on the mainland near Arisaig, and then finally reached Glenfinnan on 19 August 1745.

Here at this most enchanting of spots, the prince was met by close to 1000 Highland clansmen. The Prince's flag was raised by the duke of Atholl and His Majesty King James VIII, the prince's father, who was proclaimed King of England and Ireland, with Bonnie Prince Charles as his regent.

The Hanoverians, though, had a pure hatred for the prince, and the pan-European Catholic empire that he stood for – let it not be forgotten that the prince's full name was Charles Edward Louis John Casamir Sylvester Severino Mariah Stewart. The Hanoverian's bitter loathing of this papal connection would see a disastrous end for the Jacobite cause just eight months later at the Battle of Culloden.

A861 turn-off to Ardgour, Ardnamurchan & Morvern (see The Morvern & Ardnamurchan Peninsulas later in this chapter). If you want to stay here, the *Lochailort Inn* (☎ *01687-470208*), open March to late September, does simple B&B singles/doubles from £30/60 and good-value meals (mains from 4.50).

You're better off continuing to **Arisaig**, a beachside village where you'll find a post office and a **Spar shop**, and a ferry to the Small Isles. The **Land, Sea & Islands Heritage Centre** *(adult/child £1.50/1; open 10am-4pm daily Apr-Oct)* has exhibits covering local culture and natural history.

Arisaig was the birthplace of Long John Silver, who helped build the nearby lighthouse at Barrahead, which was designed by Robert Louis Stevenson's father; the builder must have had an impression on the young Robert, who later immortalised him in *Treasure Island*.

From Arisaig you can take the tiny road westwards to the **Rhue Peninsula** for some seal-spotting.

Between Arisaig and Morar, the road winds around some of the most remarkable beaches in Scotland, if not Europe; most beautiful is the **Back of Keppoch**, with its gloriously clear, blue waters, flowery machair, white sand and views to Skye.

The beauty continues until you reach **Morar**, where scenes from the 1984 film *Local Hero* were shot. The village lies at the outlet of 330m-deep Loch Morar, Britain's deepest body of fresh water and said to contain Morag, who is in need of some serious monster PR if she is ever to catch up with Nessie in the fame stakes.

Places to Stay & Eat There are three decent choices in Arisaig, and just one option in Morar. You'll also find a number of camp sites scattered north along the coast; most are open only in summer. *Camusdarach* (☎ *01687-450221, Morar*) is a relaxed site just outside Morar that opens March to September and charges £9 per tent.

Kinloid Farm (☎ *01687-450366, Arisaig*) B&B £24 per person. Open Mar-Oct. This is a simple B&B half a mile north of town.

Arisaig Hotel (☎ *01687-450210,* W *www.arisaighotel.co.uk, Arisaig*) B&B from £28 per person. Bar meals from £4. Most of the rooms in this slightly dishevelled Jacobean-era hotel overlook the bay.

The Old Library (☎ *01687-450651, Arisaig)* Singles £40-48, doubles £68-96. This is the best place to stay town, with great views, kindly staff and spotless rooms. The restaurant serves snacks (from £2.10), lunches and dinners (£6 to £10.50).

Morar Hotel (☎ *01687-462346, Morar)* Rooms from £30 per person. This is an atmospheric drinking den with average rooms.

Mallaig
☎ 01687 ● pop 900

It's a bit of a shock to reach the shabby fishing village of Mallaig after the pure unspoilt beaches between Arisaig and Morar. But this busy port is well situated, and the hustle-bustle of the waterfront – with huge ferries, fishing boats and sailing boats all jumbled together – and the lively pub life make it a wonderful stopover between Fort William and Skye or the Small Isles.

The TIC (☎ 462170), Main St, opens 9.30am to 5.30pm Monday to Friday, and 10am to 2.30pm on Saturday.

For medical services, call the doctor on ☎ 462202.

The main tourist attraction is **Mallaig Marine World** (☎ *462292; adult/child £2.75/1.50; open 9am-9pm Mon-Sat & 10am-6pm Sun June-Sept, 9am-5.30pm Mon-Sat & 10am-5pm Sun Oct, Apr & May, 9am-5.30pm Mon-Sat Nov-Mar)*, an aquarium which keeps local aquatic species. Many are surprisingly colourful and you can touch the skates and rays.

The **Mallaig Heritage Centre** (☎ *462085, Station Rd; adult/child £1.80/90p; open 1pm-4pm Mon-Fri)* looks at the region's archaeology and history, including some rather disturbing details on the 19th-century Clearance of Knoydart, and information on steam trains and the fishing industry.

For details of sea-fishing trips and seal-watching tours on the **MV Grimsay Isle**, ring ☎ 462652. In summer, the **Jacobite Steam Train** runs from Fort William to Mallaig (see Things to See & Do under Fort William earlier in this chapter); ask at Mallaig train station for details.

Places to Stay & Eat Mallaig has some great places to stay, and the nosh ain't bad either.

Sheena's Backpacker's Lodge (☎ *462764, fax 462708, Harbour View)* Beds £10. This slightly grungy 12-bed hostel has a happy atmosphere, a first-rate kitchen and lounge, and also the *Tea Garden* cafe downstairs.

Seaview (☎ *462059, Station Rd)* B&B £16 per person. There are lovely views over the harbour from this decent B&B with comfy rooms and helpful owners. If it's full, the *Anchorage* (☎ *462454, Station Rd)* nearby has similar rooms for £18 per person.

Marine Hotel (☎ *462217, fax 462821, Station Rd)* Mains £6-12. The Marine serves great meals, including good vegetarian options, and its modern rooms (singles/doubles £30/56) are comfortable enough.

Cabin Seafood Restaurant (☎ *462207, Main St)* Mains £5-10. At this local cafe everyone knows they'll get dependable fish, attentive service and great harbour views.

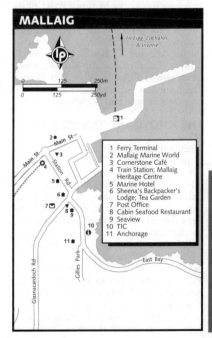

MALLAIG

To Eigg, Lochalsh & Inverie

0 125 250m
0 125 250yd

1 Ferry Terminal
2 Mallaig Marine World
3 Cornerstone Café
4 Train Station; Mallaig Heritage Centre
5 Marine Hotel
6 Sheena's Backpacker's Lodge; Tea Garden
7 Post Office
8 Cabin Seafood Restaurant
9 Seaview
10 TIC
11 Anchorage

Main St
Station Rd
Glasnacardoch Rd
Gillies Park
East Bay

THE GREAT GLEN & THE WESTERN HIGHLANDS

Cornerstone Café (☎ *462306, Main St*) Snacks £3-5, mains from £5. The Cornerstone, at the harbour, does tasty fish and chips (£4) and outstanding mussels (£6).

Getting There & Away Shiel Buses/Scottish Citylink (☎ 01967-431272) operates one bus a day Monday to Saturday to/from Fort William (£4, 1¼ hours), via Glenfinnan (£3, 35 minutes).

The West Highland Railway links Fort William with Mallaig (£22/12.50, 1½ hours) one to five times daily, with connections on to Glasgow.

Ferries run from Mallaig to the Small Isles and Skye year-round (Skye ferries now take vehicles year-round). From July to early September, a car ferry runs between Mallaig and Castlebay (Barra) and Lochboisdale (South Uist). Arisaig Marine's MV *Shearwater* (☎ 450224) connects Arisaig to Rum, Eigg and Muck. For details, see the Skye & The Western Isles chapter.

A ferry service run by Bruce Watt Cruises (☎ 462320) has two return trips from Mallaig to Inverie on the Knoydart peninsula (one-way/day return £5/7) on Monday, Wednesday and Friday at 10.15am and 2.15pm (the afternoon trip also includes a quick visit to Tarbet in upper Loch Nevis). There are also Tuesday and Thursday sailings from June to mid-September.

THE KNOYDART PENINSULA
☎ 01687

Stuck solidly between heaven and hell – actually, the lochs of Nevis ('heaven') and Hourn ('hell') – the Knoydart Peninsula is now a wilderness region thanks to depopulation in the 19th-century Highland Clearances. As a result, walkers can tramp for days through wild country without seeing another rucksack.

With just 60 inhabitants, **Inverie** is the peninsula's only population centre, and the only village in Scotland without access to the road system. For local tracks, you can hire bikes from **The Pier House** (☎ *462347*), where there's also a post office.

A favoured two-day hiking route from here leads to **Kinloch Hourn** via Barrisdale;

on the way you can stop at Barrisdale to climb the dramatic 1020m peak **Ladhar Bheinn** (pronounced **lar**-ven), which affords some of the west coast's finest views – though this will add a day to your journey.

Places to Stay & Eat
There are very few places to stay in Knoydart, so ring ahead.

Knoydart Hostel (☎ *462242, fax 462272, Inverie*) Beds £7.50. This no-frills hostel is near Inverie House, half a mile east from the ferry landing.

Shieling Hostel (☎*/fax 462669*) Beds £15. Open year-round. The atmospheric Shieling Hostel, ¾ mile west from the pier, has got comfortable dorms and a wood-burning stove in its sitting room.

Barrisdale Bothy (☎ *01599-522302, Barrisdale*) Sleeping-bag space £2.50. This very basic hostel in Barrisdale has sleeping platforms without mattresses. You can also camp outside.

Pier House (☎ *462347, Inverie*) £20 per person. This plain B&B has hospitable owners, though there's not much more than that to recommend it; rooms are clean but not very homely.

The Old Forge (☎ *462267, Inverie*) 2-course meals from £10. This pub in Inverie, by the pier, also sells bread and milk.

Getting There & Away
For ferry information see Mallaig earlier. Len Morrison (☎ 01599-522352), Croftfoot, Arnsdale, runs a fair-weather open boat from Arnsdale to Barrisdale (and other places), by arrangement. Mr Morrison can take up to five passengers for £13 plus £3 per person each way.

Postbuses (☎ 01246-546329) link Invergarry and Kinloch Hourn Monday, Wednesday and Friday. They arrive/depart from Kinloch Hourn at around 1pm, but you should confirm in advance. The bus can only take two or three people with luggage.

THE MORVERN & ARDNAMURCHAN PENINSULAS
Separated from Lochaber and Glen Coe by Loch Linnhe, this area has a tiny population,

a result of its turbulent history. In the Highland Clearances, entire villages were evicted by zealous landlords who preferred sheep to tenants, undermining the Gaelic culture and pushing families off the land.

The name Ardgour means 'height of the goats', but there is also an abundance of many other creatures in this region, including deer, pine martens, wildcats and eagles. The Morvern peninsula consists of huge, bleak hills, while the Ardnamurchan peninsula, to the west, is a wild place that is often hit by furious Atlantic gales.

For hikers, although the peaks are not particularly high (there are no Munros), the terrain can be serious and the added remoteness means getting into difficulties can have grave consequences. There are numerous possibilities for low-level walks in this area, both among the long, lonely glens and along stretches of the Atlantic coastline. For more information on the entire region, go to W www.ardnamurchan.com, or you can send £3.75 to the Ardnamurchan Tourist Association for a copy of their excellent book *30 Walks Around Ardnamurchan*.

Getting There & Around

The region can be reached most easily via the five-minute ferry crossing from Corran, 9 miles south of Fort William, to Ardgour (cars £4.70, pedestrians and bicycles free), There are crossings every 10 minutes from 7.30am to 7.30pm (to 8.30pm in summer). The road journey, on the A830 through Glenfinnan and then a slower drive through the Moidart area, is frustratingly long.

Shiel Buses (☎ 01967-431272) has one a day Monday to Saturday between Fort William and Kilchoan (£6) via Corran (£1.25), Strontian (£2.50) and Acharacle (£4). It also runs buses from Fort William to Acharacle via Lochailort (£4.25) and Glenuig (£3.50), once or twice a day Monday to Saturday.

Postbuses (☎ 01246-546329) run regularly round the peninsula, but their schedules may be less than convenient; you're better off in a car or on a bike if the weather is decent.

Ferries run from Tobermory to Kilchoan (see under Kilchoan later for details).

Acharacle
☎ 01967

In the 19th century, this sleepy village seemed destined for greatness as the western sea outlet of the Caledonian Canal. Sadly for the good folk of Acharacle, the proposed extension via Glenfinnan and Loch Shiel never happened.

The main reason to visit this crofting community is to see the picturesque roofless ruin of 13th-century **Castle Tioram**, whose name (pronounced cheerum) means 'dry land'. The castle, 2½ miles north of Acharacle, sits in Loch Moidart on an island connected to the mainland by a narrow strand that becomes submerged at high tide. It served as the headquarters for the MacDonalds of Clanranald, but was severely damaged by the Jacobites after the failed rebellion of 1715, in the hope of discouraging a takeover by Hanoverian troops. Today it's surrounded by signs saying 'Keep Clear – Falling Walls', though there are plans to restore it.

The village has a small shop, a post office within *Mave's Pantry* (☎ 431220) – where you can get a good quick sandwich or snack (mains £2 to £5) – a tearoom and the jovial *Stacks of Snacks* takeaway.

Loch Shiel Hotel (☎ 431224, Acharacle) Singles/doubles £37.50/65. Bar meals £4.50-8.25. Sitting in a picturesque spot overlooking the loch, this place has 10 plush rooms and a cosy restaurant where you can eat delectable Scottish 'fayre' such as smoked venison (£8.25) and fresh scallops (£7). On a warm day, the wonderful beer garden is the region's premier spot for a drink.

Clanranald Hotel (☎ 431202, Mingarry) B&B £20 per person. Bar meals around £6. Famed for its Highland bonhomie, the affable Clanranald is slightly tattered round the edges and has pretty basic rooms, but it's nice enough and serves good meals in the homely bar. The hotel is in Mingarry, 3 miles north of Acharacle.

Salen
☎ 01967

The last village before the slow drive to Ardnamurchan or Lochaline, Salen sits at the head of constricted Salen Bay and has a shop and an outdoors store, **Druimbeg Supplies** (☎ 431444), which sells hiking and fishing equipment.

Salen Inn (☎/fax 431661) Bar meals £5-12.50. Though it looks hideous from the outside, things improve somewhat inside; the inn serves up decent meals, including seafood, venison and other game dishes.

Nearby, **Sunart Crafts** (☎ 431648) on the A861 does coffee and snacks, and is the village purveyor of high-quality local arts and crafts. Sit outside and be dazzled by the views to Loch Sunart.

Resipole Caravan Park (☎ 431235) Pitches from £7. In summer you can also get good meals at this camp site, 2 miles east of Salen on Loch Sunart.

Strontian
☎ 01967

This little town's greatest claim to fame is lending its name to the element strontium (a radioactive shield), discovered in ore from nearby lead mines in 1790. Strontian has an attractive setting on Loch Sunart, but in town things get a bit dire as most buildings are soulless and blandly modern, and some parts are quite run down. There's a post office, snack bar, supermarket and, next door, a TIC (☎ 402381) open April to October. The **Ariundle Nature Reserve**, 2 miles north of town, offers a pleasant nature trail through the glen.

Glenview Caravan Park (☎ 402123) Camping £3.50 per person. Half a mile behind the TIC, this caravan park has basic facilities.

Kinloch House (☎ 402138) B&B £20 per person. This modern house a few hundred metres to the east of town has comfortable rooms, helpful owners and stunning views over the loch.

Carm Cottage (☎ 402268) Singles/doubles £20/34. Next door to Kinloch House, this equally unremarkable place has cheerful rooms, pleasant owners and a loch vista.

Strontian Hotel (☎ 402029, fax 402314) Singles/doubles £25/40 (add £10 in summer). Bar meals £4-9.50. Overlooking the upper reaches of Loch Sunart, this whitewashed hotel was built in 1808; bits of it feel like they haven't been renovated since, although all the rooms are comfortable and well kept.

Lochaline
☎ 01967

Although the Morvern peninsula's eastern coast has been ruined by the Glensanda Superquarry, the inland A831 road to Lochaline passes through some alluring hillscapes.

Most visitors are simply passing through on their way from the Mull ferry (from Fishnish), which docks at Lochaline. Lochaline offers supplies, a post office and an interesting art gallery.

Lochaline Hotel (☎ 421657, fax 421350) B&B singles/doubles £23/35. Bar meals £5-11. The Lochaline Hotel serves reasonable bar food and has good rooms, small though they are. It's half a mile from the ferry pier.

Glenborrodale
☎ 01972

The most westerly point on the British mainland, the rugged Ardnamurchan peninsula is reached via the torturously slow, single-track B8007. The unspoiled scenery begins with rolling woodlands, but the trees quickly vanish and the terrain becomes wild, rocky and barren; virtually no-one lives here bar the odd family dotted here or there, eking out a living on small crofts. Volcanoes and glaciers are the geological foundation of these hills, streams and woods, and they play host to otters, deer, wildcats and eagles.

The first village of any note is **Glenborrodale**, and only because of its castle, which you can't visit but which was most recently owned by Jesse Boot, founder of the chain of chemists.

Just to the castle's west is the wonderful **Ardnamurchan Natural History Centre** (☎ 500209; adult/child £2.50/1.50; open 10.30am-5.30pm Mon-Sat & noon-5.30pm Sun Easter-Oct). Devised by local photographer Michael MacGregor, it brings you face-to-face with the flora and fauna of the Ardnamurchan peninsula. The Living Building is designed to attract local wildlife and you'll have a decent chance of observing pine martens, eel-like butterfish and bird life. Snacks are available in the *tearoom*. The bus that runs between Fort William and Kilchoan stops here. Sadly, at the time of writing there was some uncertainty over the centre's future; it's advisable to call ahead and check.

If you're interested in going on a cruise from Glenborrodale, contact Anne or Andy at **Ardnamurchan Charters** (☎ 500208); they run regular trips to Tobermory (adult/child £17.50/12.50), stopping for five hours. They also run trips to Staffa on request (adult/child £30/20) but you'll need to ring a couple of days in advance.

Kilchoan
☎ 01972

There's not much to this scattered crofting village besides a pub and a few B&Bs. It's only historic feature is the fortified tower of ruined Mingary Castle down by the slip for the Tobermory ferry.

The TIC (☎ 510222) in the new community centre has information on the geology of Ardnamurchan and can also find you a place to stay. It opens 10am to 5.30pm Monday to Saturday and 11am to 3pm Sunday Easter to October. You'll find provisions at the incongruously named *Ferry Stores*, in the village, a mile from the pier.

Kilchoan House Hotel (☎/fax 510200) B&B/pitches £25/6 per person. Open Mar-Oct. The hotel offers B&B in simple, no-fuss bedrooms, or you can camp here.

Meall Mo Chridhe (☎ 510238) Singles/doubles £35/60, dinner & B&B £65/98. This charming, two-storey former manse was built in the 1790s and has been restored to perfection. It serves tasty dinners and upstairs there are great views over to Mull.

Sonachan Hotel (☎ 510211) B&B £25 per person. A mile on from Kilchoan is this

cosy B&B, where the friendly owners also do good bar meals starting from £4.

Getting There & Away There's a direct bus from Corran ferry to Kilchoan at 12.30pm on weekdays, year-round; it takes about two hours to reach Kilchoan and returns almost immediately. The car ferry to Tobermory leaves from Kilchoan seven times a day Monday to Saturday, Easter to October, and on Sunday from June to August only (35 minutes; car/passenger £18.05/3.40). The rest of the year there's only a passenger ferry to Tobermory.

Ardnamurchan Lighthouse

After Kilchoan, the B8007 continues out to Ardnamurchan Lighthouse at rocky, wind-battered Ardnamurchan Point. The imposing 36m-high lighthouse, on the westernmost point of the British mainland, dates from 1849. There's also a great **visitor centre** (☎ 01972-510210; adult/child/family £2.50/1.50/7; open 10am-5pm daily Apr-Oct) that has a hotch-potch of badly organised but wonderfully written and designed information on Ardnamurchan and the region's history, and a surprisingly engrossing history of lighthouses. *Stables Cafe* is attached, and does light meals; a delectable soup and roll costs £1.80.

If you're here on a still day (they are possible, though not likely) head straight for the observation point at the foghorn: spotting Minke whales is not unknown, and dolphin sightings are common.

A mile north of Ardnamurchan Point is stunning **Sanna Bay**, with its pure white sands and amazing views over to Eigg and Muck. Sanna is famed geologically for its rare 'ring-dyke' system, a huge natural rock formation that is the crater of a long-extinct volcano, which encircles the nearby town of Achnaha.

Skye & the Western Isles

The islands off western Scotland offer some of the best scenery in Europe, from beautiful white-gold beaches to craggy mountain peaks and rolling moorlands. The best time to visit is from spring to early summer, when the weather's at its best, the midges haven't hatched, and a pleasing freshness pervades the air. After the midges arrive, walks in the isles can be torture. Winter brings its own set of problems; brutal storms sweep in from the Atlantic and air and ferry services can often be disrupted for days at a time.

The Small Isles are reached from Mallaig, south of Kyle of Lochalsh. Each is different – Muck is flat and sandy, Eigg is hilly with one rocky peak, Rum (Rhum) has a high mountain ridge, and Canna has an interesting history and a great view of the Cuillin Ridge (Isle of Skye).

Skye is great for walking and there are also historic castles to explore, lots of wildlife and an attractive capital, Portree. However, the island positively swarms with visitors during summer.

Scenery in the wild Western Isles includes bleak moors and stone circles on Lewis, wonderful beaches and towering mountains on Harris, and the maze of lochs and moorland on North and South Uist. Far out in the Atlantic is St Kilda, a desperately remote group with rocky stacks, ruined settlements and a huge population of wild birds.

These islands were one of the first areas to be dominated by the Vikings in the 8th century, but were later populated by Gaelic-speaking clans from the mainland who established small feudal kingdoms throughout the isles, before they were suppressed by James V. These days, Gaelic is experiencing a huge revival and there's even a Gaelic college on Skye. In Lewis and Harris, the Free Presbyterian church still has a strong influence and the Sabbath is strictly observed.

Most islands are still occupied by traditional crofting communities and there are few glitzy 'visitor attractions'. The islands' rich archaeological heritage also remains

Highlights

- Try to spot the magnificent white-tailed sea eagle on the nature-reserve island of Rum
- Hike among the jagged peaks of the spectacular Black Cuillin on Skye
- Trip out to haunted castles and the curious Quiraing peaks on Skye's Trotternish peninsula
- Surf the wild west coast of Harris, Britain's best and most reliable surfing
- Ponder the meaning of the mysterious Calanais Standing Stones on Lewis
- Walk the beaches on sea-drowned South Uist

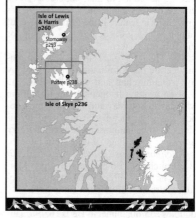

largely untapped, with the exception of the spectacular stone circle at Calanais, on Lewis, which is second only to Stonehenge.

The islands are still one of the least-visited parts of Scotland, with the exception of Skye, which is effectively part of the mainland and has seen a vast upsurge in tourism in the last 10 years.

ACTIVITIES

There's plenty to do in the islands, from hill-walking and bird-watching to surfing and scuba diving. With the exception of Skye and Stornoway on Lewis, the infrastructure for tourism is fairly undeveloped, so you'll need to bring your own equipment for many activities.

There are lots of great walks, from easy coastal rambles to scrambling on the rugged Cuillin Ridge (Skye); see Rock Climbing in the Activities chapter for details.

The fantastic beaches along the exposed west coast of Lewis and Harris offer some excellent waves for surfers; see Activities in The Western Isles section for more information.

Bird-watchers congregate on the moorland RSPB reserves at Balranald on North Uist and Druidibeg on South Uist, which are easily accessible by public transport. By far the best bird-watching in the area is on the islands of Pabbay and Mingulay or on St Kilda, 41 miles west of North Uist.

Other popular activities include scuba diving, golf and angling – pick up a copy of the *Wild Fishing in the Western Isles* brochure published by the Western Isles Tourist Board (WITB) for listings of the main fishing estates. The brown-trout season runs from March to October, while salmon and sea trout are fished from February to October. Note that Sunday fishing is prohibited on most islands.

Small Isles

The Small Isles consist of Muck, Eigg, Rum and Canna, lying between the Ardnamurchan peninsula and the Isle of Skye. These diverse islands are reached by ferry from Arisaig or Mallaig.

The Ordnance Survey (OS) Landranger map No 39 covers the Small Isles.

GETTING THERE & AWAY
The main ferry operator here is Caledonian MacBrayne (CalMac; ☎ 01687-462403) which sails daily, except Sunday (for religious reasons).

There are services from Mallaig to Rum (Monday, Wednesday, Friday and Saturday), Eigg (daily except Wednesday and

Sunday), Muck (Tuesday, Thursday, Friday and Saturday) and Canna (Monday, Wednesday, Friday and Saturday) as well as linking services between the islands; for Rum, Muck and Eigg you have to transfer to a lighter boat to reach the shore. One-way fares from Mallaig to Muck/Eigg/Rum/Canna are £7.25/4.75/7.10/8.10; bikes can be carried for £2 on any leg. From Mallaig, there are connecting rail services to Fort William and Glasgow.

Arisaig Marine (☎ 01687-450224) sails from Arisaig (May to September), with four runs per week to Eigg (£15 return) and Rum (£19 return), and one per week to Muck (£15 return). Sailing times range from one to five hours, with whale-watching en route. Child fares are about half of adult fares.

MUCK
☎ 01687 • pop 34
Muck is tiny, measuring only 2 miles by a mile, but the beaches are lovely and the flat and exceptionally fertile machair and gives way to wild flowers every spring. The name is thought to derive from the Gaelic *muc mara* meaning 'sea-pig' or porpoise, and porpoises are still regularly spotted

around Muck. There are pleasant scenic walks from the main settlement of Port Mór to the top of **Beinn Airein** (137m), which has panoramic views of the Small Isles, and you may see corncrakes.

Ferries call at **Port Mór**. The *tearoom/craft shop* (☎ 462362), situated in a blackhouse-style building, does great snacks and evening meals on request; it also sells fresh bread. Ask here for permission to camp.

Port Mhor Guesthouse (☎ 462365, Port Mór) Dinner B&B with shared bathroom £35 per person. The recommended three-course dinners here are available to non-residents for £15 (reserve by the previous evening).

EIGG
☎ 01687 • pop 78

This small but instantly recognisable island is dominated by the **Sgurr of Eigg**, a 393m-high basalt peak, which thrusts up from the wide plateau that makes up the rest of the island. Like Fingal's Cave on Staffa and the Devil's Causeway in Ireland, the Sgurr is formed from columnar pitch-stone lava and you'll pass some impressive geological formations during the easy climb along its western ridge. The islanders of Eigg made history by buying the island from

their landlord in 1997 (see the boxed text below).

A monastery was built at Kildonan, a mile north of Galmisdale, but all 53 monks were murdered by pirates in 617. At the monastery site, there are ruins of a 14th-century church and a Celtic cross slab. There are several caves around the coast including **Uamh Fraing**, where 395 Mac-Donalds were killed by MacLeods from Skye in 1577. The island was sacked in 1588 by pirates and again in 1746, this time by the government, which didn't think much of the islanders' Jacobite sympathies.

Eigg has two villages, Cleadale in the north and **Galmisdale**, where the ferries call, which has a post office, shop, and a *tearoom* (☎ 482487) offering Internet access. Visit Ⓦ www.isleofeigg.org for more information on the island.

Camping is allowed near Galmisdale (£3); there are showers and toilets at the pier.

The Glebe Barn (☎/fax 482417, Galmisdale) Open year-round. Beds £9.50, twins £22. This is the only hostel on Eigg, and they also rent out bikes.

Lageorna (☎ 482405, fax 482432, Cleadale) Dinner B&B £35 per person, including lunch. Six-bed self-catering cottages from £250 per week. This friendly

---

The Eigg Revolution

In 1997, the crofters of Eigg made history by buying their island from their landlord, ending centuries of feudal oppression. This piece of island intrigue was triggered by the arrival of Keith Schellenberg, an English millionaire and bobsleigh champion, who purchased the island in 1975. From the start, Schellenberg showed scant regard for the sensibilities of the natives. The Union Jack was raised from the top of the island and Schellenberg was regularly seen speeding around in his 1927 Rolls Royce or sailing in his yacht, dressed up as an Imperial German Admiral.

When local people resisted his attempts to turn Eigg into a crafts cooperative, Schellenberg began handing out eviction notices like they were party invitations. For the islanders, enough was enough. One dark night, Schellenberg's Rolls Royce was destroyed in a fire, in a shed without electricity, and with no witnesses. The landlord fled to England, describing the islanders as 'rotten, dangerous and totally barmy revolutionaries'.

In the subsequent auction, the islanders were able to buy the island by forming a partnership with the Highland Council and the Scottish Wildlife Trust, aided by considerable donations from the National Lottery. Since the community cooperative took over, the island population has stabilised and Eigg now has full employment, though several mainland Scottish commentators were outraged that National Lottery money was used to pay the islanders' mortgage

B&B is about 3 miles north of the ferry landing.

Kildonan House (☎ 482446) Dinner & B&B from £35 per person. This beautiful slate-roofed farmhouse is close to the harbour, overlooking Kildonan Bay.

RUM (RHUM)
☎ 01687 ● pop 30

Mountainous Rum is the largest of the Small Isles and a nature reserve, owned entirely by the Scottish Natural Heritage (SNH). Nearly everyone on the island works for SNH, and you'll have to contact the organisation's reserve office (☎ 462026) for permission if you want to visit. The island's peaks soar to over 750m and there are large populations of deer, wild goats, diminutive Rum ponies and golden and white-tailed sea eagles.

From 1888 to 1957, Rum was owned by the eccentric Bullough family, who constructed the grand turreted **Kinloch Castle** *(☎ 462037, Kinloch; adult/child £3/1.50; open for guided tours only, in conjunction with boat arrivals)* at the mouth of Loch Sresort. This extravagant seat was the first place in the Highlands to be lit by electricity and once had magnificent gardens, with 14 greenhouses, six palmhouses and imported hummingbirds, turtles and alligators! The gardens are a shade of their former glory, but it's well worth visiting the castle to see the fine furnishings.

There's also the **Bullough Mausoleum** *(admission free; open year-round)*, a folly in Glen Harris, which wouldn't look out of place in Athens. Glen Harris is a 10-mile return walk from Kinloch along an old drovers road – allow four to five hours' walking time. South of Kinloch, you can follow the main ridge from Hallival to the island's highest point, **Askival** (812m) – the route involves some scrambling and takes about six hours from Kinloch.

Kinloch is the main centre and ferries arrive here. Rum has a shop and post office.

There are two *SNH bothies* on the island, but you need to get permission from the SNH to use them (☎ 462026, fax 462805). The SNH also manages *camping* on the island at Kinloch (£3 per person).

Farmhouse Hostel (☎/fax 462037, Kinloch) Beds £8. Hostel accommodation is available for 14 people at the castle's bothy.

Kinloch Castle (☎/fax 462037, Kinloch) Hostel beds £12 (bedding £1 extra), B&B £18.50, hotel doubles £71. The hotel rooms, some with four-poster beds, at Kinloch Castle have a wonderful ambience. Bistro dinners cost £10.

CANNA & SANDAY
☎ 01687 ● pop 16

These pleasant roadless islands can easily be explored in a day. The ferry arrives at the hamlet of **A'Chill** on Canna, owned by the National Trust for Scotland (NTS), where tourists have created extensive graffiti on the rock face south of the harbour. There are no shops, but you'll find a tiny post office in a hut, a **Celtic cross**, and the remains of the 7th-century **St Columba's Chapel**. There are now two churches, surely more per head of population than anywhere else; the Protestant church has an unusual circular bell tower. Just east of the ferry pier is **An Coroghon**, a jailhouse dating from the Middle Ages. At the northeastern corner of Canna, magnetic Compass Hill (143m) contains enough iron to affect compasses in passing ships. Canna is linked to the adjacent Sanday by bridge.

Contact the NTS warden on ☎ 462466 for permission to camp. Self-catering accommodation may also be available.

Isle of Skye

pop 8847

Skye is a rugged island stretching about 50 miles from end to end and ringed by a breathtaking coastline. The scenery is unparalleled, particularly in the magnificent Cuillin Ridge, home to 12 of Scotland's 284 Munros. The peaks positively swarm with Munro baggers in summer, but in spring and autumn you can experience this dramatic scenery in relative peace and quiet. The climate is notoriously changeable – the Gaels called the island Eilean a Cheo ('Isle of Mist') – and Skye can switch from sun to rain in a flash.

Tourism is vital to the island economy, and Skye gets very crowded from May to August. Portree and Broadford are the main population centres, and there's still a glimmer of life at Kyleakin, where the ferry from the mainland used to dock. Getting around the island is fairly straightforward Monday to Friday, but transport dwindles to nothing at weekends and in winter – even more dramatically (so it seems) when it rains.

Numerous place names on Skye have Norse origins – including the name, Skye, derived from the Norse word for 'cloud'.

The Vikings were expelled from Skye in the 12th century by the Gaelic chief Somerled, whose descendants gave rise to the MacDonald clan and the lords of the Isles. The other important clan here were the MacLeods of Dunvegan, originally of Norse descent, who were arch rivals of the MacDonalds. The eccentric Dr Samuel Johnson and James Boswell toured Skye in 1773, fleshing out a lot of the characters of the time in their book *Journey to the Hebrides*.

Gaelic is still spoken by some of Skye's residents and there's a Gaelic college,

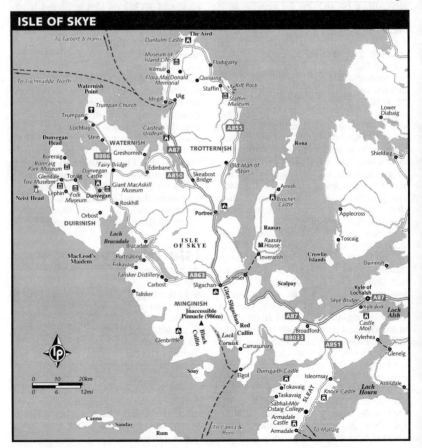

ISLE OF SKYE

Sabhal Mór Ostaig, at Teangue (An Teanga), but Skye is certainly the most developed and Anglicised of the Hebridean islands. In fact, there's some debate as to whether Skye still qualifies as an island since the building of the toll-bridge from Kyle of Lochalsh. Kyleakin and Kyle of Lochalsh both suffered an instant downturn in tourist income when the bridge opened and local residents formed a resistance movement known as SKAT (Skye & Kyle Against Tolls), which has campaigned for a reduction of the bridge tolls for years. Tailgating (following paying cars through the barriers) is still widely practised and there are regular court cases.

If you still feel like arriving by sea, there are ferries from Mallaig to Armadale and Glenelg to Kylerhea (the latter, mid-April to October only). See Kylerhea later in this section.

WALKS AROUND SKYE
Skye is one of the best places in Scotland for walking and a detailed guidebook is recommended. For the Cuillin Ridge, the best is *Black Cuillin Ridge – A Scrambler's Guide*, by SP Bull (Scottish Mountaineering Trust). Also handy are Charles Rhodes' *Selected Walks – Northern Skye* and *Selected Walks – Southern Skye*, for use with the OS Landranger maps Nos 23 and 32 (see below). Don't attempt the longer walks without proper experience and avoid long routes in winter or in bad weather. In an emergency you can call Mountain Rescue on ☎ 01478-612888.

There are numerous possible routes from easy hikes, such as the Sligachan to Camasunary walk (four hours), to the mighty traverse of the Cuillin Ridge – see that section in the Activities chapter.

OS Landranger maps that cover Skye include:

Landranger 23: North Skye, Dunvegan & Portree
Landranger 32: South Skye & Cuillin Hills

Many climbers swear by the Harvey's *Cuillin Hills* map.

ORGANISED TOURS
Several backpacker tours from Edinburgh and Inverness include Skye on their itineraries and offer a shuttle service between these cities and their affiliated hostels in Kyleakin. Try *Haggis Adventures (☎ 0131-557 9393)* or *MacBackpackers (☎ 0131-558 9900)* – day tours from Kyleakin cost around £15.

GETTING AROUND
There are several local bus companies on Skye, but the main operator is Highland Country/Rapsons (☎ 01478-612622), which covers the coastal route from Portree south to Kyleakin and across the Skye Bridge to Kyle of Lochalsh. You can buy one-/three-day bus Rover tickets for £6/15. The *Western Isles & Skye* public transport guide is widely available from TICs for £1.

PORTREE (PORT RIGH)
☎ 01478 ● pop 2500
Port Righ is Gaelic for 'King's Harbour', named after James V, who landed here in 1540 to assert his authority over the lords of the Isles. It's an attractive town, with a delightful harbour and a string of colourful harbour-side houses, looking out over a deep sea loch to the surrounding hills. Portree is the largest town on Skye and has banks with ATMs, petrol stations, a post office with foreign exchange facilities and two supermarkets. The hospital can be reached on ☎ 613200.

The TIC (☎ 612137), Bayfield Rd, opens 9am to 5pm Monday to Saturday and 10am to 4pm Sunday (late opening Monday to Saturday July to August). There's a bureau de change and you can pick up the free *Traveller's Companion* brochures, which cover all sorts of things to do across Skye.

Things to See
On the southern edge of Portree, the **Aros Experience** *(☎ 613649, Viewfield Rd; adult/ child/family £3/1/7; open 9am-6pm daily Apr-Sept, 10am-5pm Oct-Mar)* offers a lively introduction to Skye life and includes excellent live CCTV viewing of a sea-eagle's nest. There's also a good *restaurant*.

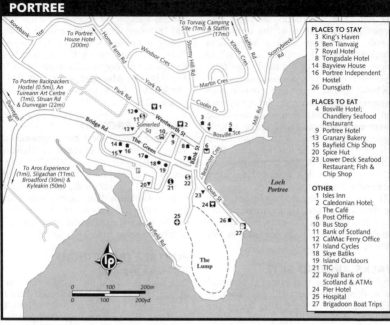

PORTREE

PLACES TO STAY
3 King's Haven
5 Ben Tianvaig
7 Royal Hotel
8 Tongadale Hotel
14 Bayview House
16 Portree Independent Hostel
26 Dunsgiath

PLACES TO EAT
4 Bosville Hotel; Chandlery Seafood Restaurant
9 Portree Hotel
13 Granary Bakery
15 Bayfield Chip Shop
20 Spice Hut
23 Lower Deck Seafood Restaurant; Fish & Chip Shop

OTHER
1 Isles Inn
2 Caledonian Hotel; The Café
6 Post Office
10 Bus Stop
11 Bank of Scotland
12 CalMac Ferry Office
17 Island Cycles
18 Skye Batiks
19 Island Outdoors
21 TIC
22 Royal Bank of Scotland & ATMs
24 Pier Hotel
25 Hospital
27 Brigadoon Boat Trips

An Tuireann Art Centre (☎ *613306,* W *www.antuireann.org.uk, Struan Rd; admission free; open 10am-5pm Mon-Sat, shorter hrs in winter),* on the Struan road (B885), hosts contemporary art exhibitions and has a stylish modernist *cafe.*

The annual **Isle of Skye Highland Games**, a one-day event, are held in Portree in early August.

Organised Tours

Brigadoon Boat Trips (☎ *613718)* runs two-hour wildlife tours three times daily out to the Sound of Raasay (adult/child £10/5). Porpoises, seals and eagles are commonly seen, and you can explore sea caves in the boat.

Places to Stay

Torvaig Camping Site (☎ *612209, Torvaig)* Pitches £7. Open Apr-Oct. This well-run site is located on the edge of town on the Staffin road.

Portree Independent Hostel (☎*/fax 613737, The Green)* Beds £9.50-10.50. This friendly and excellently located hostel is in the old post office, near Somerled Square. There's a laundry in the basement.

Portree Backpackers Hostel (☎ *613641, fax 613643, Dunvegan Rd)* Beds £9. This hostel is near the Co-op supermarket but about half a mile from Somerled Square.

Bayview House (☎ *613340, Bayfield)* Beds from £15 per person. This is a friendly place with en-suite facilities, owned by the Bayfield Chip Shop.

Ben Tianvaig (☎ *612152, 5 Bosville Terrace)* B&B £17.50-28 per person. This very comfortable guesthouse looks out over the harbour.

Kings Haven (☎*/fax 612290, Stormyhill Rd)* Doubles/twins £44-70. Uphill from the harbour, this attractive Georgian house is nicely decorated and has cosy rooms.

Dunsgiath (☎ *612851,* e *stay@dunsgiath.com, The Harbour)* B&B £17-26 per person. Dunsgiath is another recommended harbour-side B&B.

***Tongadale Hotel** (☎ 612115, fax 613376, Wentworth St)* B&B £20-25 per person. Just off Somerled Square, friendly Tongadale is a lively pub with cheap and cheerful rooms.

***Bosville Hotel** (☎ 612846, fax 613434, 9–10 Bosville Terrace)* Singles £50-65, doubles £70-100. This well-heeled hotel overlooks the harbour and has good bar meals and a fine seafood restaurant.

***Royal Hotel** (☎ 612525, fax 613198, Bank St)* Singles/doubles/twins £50/78/78. Formerly known as MacNab's Inn, the historic Royal Hotel can claim James V, Bonnie Prince Charlie and Flora MacDonald as famous guests.

Places to Eat

Several of the hotels do very good pub meals, and there are several more upmarket choices.

***The Café** (☎ 612553, Wentworth St)* Snack meals £1-4. This cafe, at the Caledonian Hotel in Wentworth St, is a good spot for lunch.

***Granary Bakery** (☎ 612873, Somerled Square)* Sandwiches, burgers & light meals £3-7. The Granary Bakery has an amazingly popular cafe, but sees huge queues of schoolchildren on schoolday lunchtimes.

There's good pub food at the ***Portree** (Somerled Square)*, ***Tongadale** (Wentworth St)* and ***Bosville** (Bosville Terrace)* hotels. Mains range from £5 to £13.

***Portree House Hotel** (☎ 613713, Home Farm Rd)*. Meals £5-8. Open 12.30pm-3.30pm and 5.30pm-10pm. Up on the hill, this restaurant has an adventurous menu with Middle Eastern dishes as well as the usual Scottish favourites.

***Chandlery Seafood Restaurant** (☎ 612846, 9–10 Bosville Terrace)* Mains £13-22, 3-course meal around £27. If lobster and langoustines are more to your taste, this restaurant at the Bosville Hotel serves the finest seafood in Portree.

***Lower Deck Seafood Restaurant** (☎ 612033, Quay St)* Mains £8-16. This is a decent fish and shellfish place, down by the harbour, with a much cheaper fish and chip shop next door.

***Spice Hut** (☎ 612681, Bayfield Rd)* Mains £6-9. Open noon-3.20pm and 5pm-late. This passable curryhouse is in an old pub, downhill from the TIC.

***An Tuireann Art Centre Café** (☎ 613306, Struan Rd)* Light meals £2-6. Open 10am-5pm Mon-Sat, shorter hrs in winter. The bright and arty cafe at this art centre caters for vegetarians and vegans.

There is a large ***Co-op supermarket** off Dunvegan Rd

Entertainment

***Caledonian Hotel** (☎ 612641, Wentworth St)* The bar here is popular with locals, with varied live music Thursday to Saturday.

***Pier Hotel** (☎ 612094, Quay St)* The Pier is a popular waterfront drinking spot.

***Isles Inn** (☎ 612129, Somerled Square)* The Isles features a Jacobean-theme bar with a flagstone floor and real fires.

Shopping

If you're planning any hill-walking, ***Island Outdoors** (☎ 611073)* on the Green, near the TIC, is a well-stocked outdoor-gear shop. ***Skye Batiks** (☎ 613331, The Green)* sells a wide selection of Celtic-inspired batiks, featuring designs taken from Pictish stones and ancient manuscripts.

Getting There & Away

Somerled Square is the Portree bus stop. Scottish Citylink (☎ 0870 550 5050) runs a Glasgow–Fort William–Kyle–Kyleakin–Portree–Uig route, three times daily in summer, taking three hours from Fort William to Portree (£14.50). It also runs the Inverness to Portree service twice daily (£12.40, 3¼ hours), with transfers to Uig. Postbuses operate to Dunvegan Monday to Saturday .

Highland Country/Rapsons has four buses from Portree to Kyle of Lochalsh Monday to Friday, and one on Saturday, all via Sligachan, Broadford and Kyleakin. Several other services cover the route as far as Broadford or Kyleakin.

CalMac has an office (☎ 612075) on Park Rd, near the Council Offices.

Getting Around

Cars can be hired from Portree Coachworks (☎ 612688), Broom Place, Portree Industrial Estate for around £35 per day.

Island Cycles (☎ 613121), The Green, rents out bikes for £10 per day.

TROTTERNISH PENINSULA
☎ 01470

North of Portree, the Trotternish peninsula has the most dramatic coastal scenery in Skye, with numerous columnar dolerite formations such as **Kilt Rock** and a series of bizarre rock formations inland, formed by a vast prehistoric landslide. The most famous landmark is the rocky spike of the **Old Man of Storr**, a free-standing pinnacle six miles north of Portree, which attracts hordes of photographers and rock-climbers.

Farther north near **Staffin** (Stamhain), are the spectacular peaks of **Quiraing**, a curious series of cliffs, rock towers and rounded turrets, like a giant stone chess set. Structures such as the **Needle** and the **Prison** are easy to spot, and tucked among the spires is the **Table**, a curious flat platform where locals used to play shinty. There are wonderful views south from here to the huge buttresses of the Trotternish Ridge. Several trails lead up to the Quiraing peaks; probably the easiest is the level path starting just west of Quiraing on the inland road from Staffin to Uig.

The whitewashed village of **Staffin** is the largest settlement on the peninsula, with a shop and an award-winning community centre, Columba 1400 (☎ 01478-611400), offering daily meals and Internet access (except Sunday). North of the centre is the little **Staffin Museum**, which has a collection of fossils and farm machinery.

Three miles north of Staffin is the tiny hamlet of **Flodigarry** (Flodaigearraidh), the one-time home Flora MacDonald.

Flora MacDonald

Skye's most famous resident was probably Highland heroine, Flora MacDonald, who helped Bonnie Prince Charlie escape his defeat at the Battle of Culloden. Flora was born in 1722 at Milton in South Uist, but after her mother's abduction by the devious Hugh MacDonald of Skye, she was reared by her brother and educated in the home of the Clanranald chiefs at Ormaclade in Benbecula. She assured her place in history by transporting Bonnie Prince Charlie, who was disguised as her Irish maidservant, from Benbecula to Skye. The little boat was fired on, but managed to land safely and Flora escorted the Prince to Portree where he gave her a gold locket containing his portrait before setting sail for Raasay. The epic escape was immortalised in the *Skye Boat Song*:

> Speed bonnie boat, like a bird on the wing,
> 'Onward' the sailor's cry.
> Carry the lad that is born to be king,
> Over the sea to Skye...

While Charles went free and eventually fled to France, Flora was not so lucky. The boatmen were waylaid on the way home and Flora was arrested and imprisoned in the Tower of London. She returned home in 1747, marrying Allan MacDonald of Skye, with whom she had nine children. Her family were quite prosperous when English lexicographer Dr Samuel Johnson stayed with her in 1773 during his journey round the Western Isles, but later poverty forced them to emigrate to North Carolina.

Unfortunately Flora's husband sided with the Redcoats during the War of Independence and was captured by rebels. The family fled to Kingsburgh on Skye, where Flora died in 1790. She was buried in Kilmuir churchyard, wrapped in the sheet in which both Bonnie Prince Charlie and Dr Johnson had slept, attended by nearly 3000 mourners, who drowned their sorrows with 300 barrels of whisky.

Right at the tip of the peninsula is **Duntulm**, home to the ruined MacDonald fortress of **Duntulm Castle**, which was deserted in 1739, reputedly because it was haunted. The most famous spirit is the gibbering phantom of Hugh MacDonald, a local noble who was imprisoned in the dungeon for trying to seize Trotternish. As punishment, he was deprived of water by his jailers and fed salted beef until he went insane, starving to death in the cells below the castle. You might also see the ghost of a nursemaid who accidentally dropped the baby of a Mac-Donald chieftain from the battlements and was executed by the grief-stricken chief.

At **Kilmuir** (Cille Mhoire) near the northern tip of the peninsula, the **Skye Museum of Island Life** (☎ 552206, Kilmuir; adult/child £1.75/75p; open 9.30am-5.30pm Mon-Sat Apr-Oct) re-creates crofting life in a series of thatched cottages overlooking marvellous scenery. Uphill from the museum in the Kilmuir Cemetery is the **grave of Flora MacDonald**; the current memorial was built in 1955 to replace the original cairn which was stripped to the ground by souvenir hunters. Also in the graveyard is a fine medieval grave-slab with a carving of a knight in chainmail, brought here from Iona.

Whitewave Outdoor Centre (☎ 542414, e info@white-wave.co.uk, Linicro) offers half-day sea-kayaking trips for £20/14 (adult/child), windsurfing for £25/18 and mountain-bike hire for £8. *B&B* (from £17.50) is also available.

Skyeways Travel (☎ 01599-534328) runs a weekday bus service from Portree to Flodigarry.

Places to Stay & Eat

Dun Flodigarry Hostel (☎/fax 552212, Flodigarry) Beds £9. This large white house gazes out to sea at the foot of the Trotternish Ridge and is well located for walks in the Quiraing.

Tigh Cilmarin (☎ 562331, Staffin) B&B from £18. This handsome white cottage is behind the Church of Scotland in Staffin.

Duntulm Castle Hotel (☎ 552213, fax 552292, Duntulm) Singles £26-36, doubles £40-72. This hotel has a fine location over-

looking the castle and serves good-value meals (from £6).

Flodigarry Country House Hotel (☎ 552 203, fax 552301, Flodigarry) Singles/doubles from £49/98. This award-winning country house hotel has luxurious rooms and a fine restaurant (bar meals £5 to £15, table d'hôte £35) in an Indian-inspired folly at the end of the house. Flora MacDonald's cottage sits in the expansive grounds.

Glenview Inn (☎ 562248, fax 562211, Culnaknock) Mains £8-17. Open Mar-Oct. The Glenview Inn, 3 miles south of Staffin at Culnaknock (Cùl nan Cnoc), serves excellent meals. It also does accommodation for between £40 and £60 per room.

UIG (UIGE)
☎ 01470 ● pop 300

Uig (pronounced **oo**-ig) is a plain, modern settlement by the jetty for the CalMac ferry to North Uist and Harris. Uphill from the jetty on the road south, you'll pass the attractive Uig Free Church and a folly built by Captain Frazer of Kilmuir. Farther south at Cuidrach, a trail marked with posts leads out to the ruined 17th-century tower of **Caisteal Uisdein**, home of the treacherous Hugh MacDonald.

At the jetty, the **Isle of Skye Brewery** (☎ 542477) sells locally brewed and bottled beers. Uig has a shop and post office, plus two hotels and some seasonal cafes down by the pier.

Uig Bay Camping & Caravan Site (☎ 542714, 10 Idrigill) Pitches from £5.50. This simple site is just along the shore from the pier.

Uig Youth Hostel (☎ 542211, Uig) Beds from £9/7.75. Open late Apr-Sept. Uig's well-equipped SYHA hostel is located on a hillside south of the town.

Orasay (☎ 542316) B&B from £16. This is a comfortable modern B&B by the jetty.

Ard na Mara (☎ 542281, fax 542289, 11 Idrigill) B&B from £18. This shore-side bungalow is opposite Orasay.

Uig Hotel (☎ 542205, fax 542308) Singles/doubles from £25/40. This respectable coaching inn has a fine position overlooking the bay.

Pub on the Pier *(☎ 542212, The Pier)* Mains £4-8. Open noon-11pm daily. As well as the usual fish and chips, the cook here can rustle up a few vegetarian dishes.

Getting There & Around

From Uig pier, CalMac has daily services to Lochmaddy on North Uist (passenger/car/ bicycle £8.50/40/2, 1¾ hours) and from Monday to Saturday to Tarbert on Harris (same prices, 1½ hours). Uig has once- or twice-daily Scottish Citylink (☎ 0870 550 5050) bus connections with Portree, Inverness, Fort William and Glasgow, connecting with the ferries.

The Orasay B&B hires out bikes for around £11 per day.

WATERNISH PENINSULA
☎ 01470

Few people make it out to the peninsula southwest of Uig, reached from the Fairy Bridge on the A850 Dunvegan road. The main village on Waternish is **Stein**, with an absurdly pretty strip of whitewashed houses on the shore and a 16th-century hotel and restaurant.

At the tip of the peninsula is the ruin of **Trumpan Church**, which was set alight by the MacDonalds of Uist in 1578, burning alive an entire congregation of MacLeods. MacLeod forces marched from Dunvegan under their famous Fairy Flag, massacring the MacDonalds as they tried to flee to their galleys. Ghostly singing is said to be heard here on the anniversary of the battle. Among the graves is the ancient **Trial Stone**, a squat stone pillar with a hole that the accused had to put their finger into while blindfolded; failure was taken as instant proof of guilt.

Dive & Sea Hebrides *(☎ 592219)* 2 boat dives £25. Just south at Lochbay, this company offers scuba dives on local wrecks and underwater caverns.

Stein Inn *(☎ 592362, Stein)* B&B £23.50-28.50 per person. This lovely 16th-century inn has good rooms, fine pub meals (£5 to £9) and an intimate and cosy bar.

Loch Bay Seafood Restaurant *(☎ 592235)* Main £10-20. This is another

fine place to sample the area's magnificent seafood.

DUNVEGAN (DÙN BHEAGAIN)
☎ 01470

On the northwest coast of Skye at the start of the pinched-off Duirinish peninsula, Dunvegan is an unremarkable village spread out along Loch Dunvegan, with a camp site, shops and a TIC (☎ 521581, **e** dunvegan@host.co.uk), open 9am to 5pm Monday to Saturday and 10am to 4pm Sunday (shorter hours in winter).

The ancient MacLeod stronghold of **Dunvegan Castle** *(☎ 521206; adult/child £5.50/3; open 10am-5.30pm daily, 11am-3.30pm in winter)* dates back to the 13th century and was visited by Johnson and Boswell in 1773. It received a major facelift in the mid-19th century and the interior is suitably regal. There are a few unusual relics of the MacLeods. The most famous exhibit is the **Fairy Flag**, which the MacLeods claim was a gift from the fairies with the power to protect the clan from harm, as it seemingly did at the Battle of Glendale in 1490 and the Spoiling of the Duke in 1578.

In summer, seal cruises run daily from the castle (adult/child £4/2.50).

Also in Dunvegan is the **Giant Angus MacAskill Museum** *(☎ 521296; adult/child £1/free; open 10am-6pm daily)*, dedicated to the stage-show giant Angus MacAskill, who was born on Berneray.

Places to Stay & Eat

Kinloch camp site *(☎ 521210, Dunvegan)* From £4 per person. This appealing site sits across the loch at the southern end of Dunvegan.

Roskhill House *(☎ 521317, fax 521761, Roskhill)* B&B from £35. Just south of Dunvegan, this B&B is housed in an immaculate white cottage.

Tables Hotel *(☎/fax 521404, Dunvegan)* Singles £28-48, doubles £52-76. This relaxed hotel is in the middle of the village and serves good food (dinner from £17).

Dunvegan Hotel *(☎ 521497, Dunvegan)* Singles/doubles from £45/65. This comfortable upmarket hotel is on the main street in Dunvegan and has a good restaurant (mains £8 to £11); look for the blue awning.

Old School House (☎ *521421, Dunvegan*) Evening mains £6-13. This fairly posh restaurant serves plenty of game and seafood.

Getting There & Away

On weekdays you can get to Dunvegan by Nicolson's Coaches (☎ 01470-532240); there are two or three buses daily – for a day-trip, you can take the 10am bus from Portree, returning from the castle at around 4.30pm. Most buses continue on to Colbost and Glendale.

There are two to three postbuses Monday to Saturday from Dunvegan to Glendale and Colbost and one service to Neist Point.

DUIRINISH PENINSULA
☎ 01470

This sparsely populated peninsula is dominated by the distinctive flat-topped peaks of Helabhal Mhor (469m) and Helabhal Bheag (488m), known locally as **MacLeod's Tables**. There are some fine walks from Orbost, including the summit of Helabhal Bheag (allow 3½ hours return) and the 5-mile trail from Orbost to **MacLeod's Maidens**, a series of pointed sea-stacks at the southern tip of the peninsula.

From Dunvegan, a tiny road cuts across to the west coast, passing through several small villages with museums and B&Bs. **Colbost**, at the head of Loch Snizort Beag, has the informal **Colbost Croft Museum** (☎ *01470-521296, Tigh na Bruaich, Colbost; adult/child £1/free; open 10am-6.30pm daily Apr-Oct*), a re-created 19th-century blackhouse croft.

Farther north at Totaig, a road loops north to **Borreraig**, the site of an ancient piping college. Here you'll find the **Borreraig Park Piping Centre** (☎ *01470-511311; adult/child £2/50p; open 9am-7pm*) with farm machinery and piping memorabilia. From the end of the road, you can walk to the impressive seacliffs at Dunvegan Head.

Across the peninsula, **Glendale** (Gleann Dàil) was the home of the Glendale Martyrs who were imprisoned for staging a dramatic

rent-strike against their MacLeod landlords in 1882. The rebellion was a pivotal event in the struggle; the crofters here became the Highlands' first owner-occupiers in 1904.

Glendale has two shops – the ***Glendale village shop*** (☎ *511275*) hires bikes for £9 per day – and a basic restaurant. The recommended **Glendale Toy Museum** (☎ *511240, Holmisdale House; adult/child £2.50/1; open 10am-6pm Mon-Sat*) is just down the road at Lephin and has plenty of interesting old toys. Continuing west, a narrow lane runs from Glendale to the gorgeously scenic **Neist Point**, a slender promontory on the west coast with a desperately exposed Stevenson lighthouse. The point is reached via a steep stairway down the cliffs.

Mrs Kernachan (☎ *511371, 4 Lephin*) B&B from £15 per person. Down the back road past the Glendale shop, this is a decent B&B.

Three Chimneys (☎ *511258, fax 511358,* ***e*** *eatandstay@threechimneys.co.uk*) 2-/3-/4-courses £25.50/33/40. This fantastic restaurant offers first-class food and wine, including lobster, scallops and local lamb. It also has excellent rooms (B&B £53 to £80), that are popular with wedding parties.

THE CUILLINS
☎ 01478

The rocky Cuillin Ridge, west of Broadford, provide spectacular walking and climbing. The peaks are divided into two obvious ridges by Glen Sligachan, which runs all the way to Camasunary on the west coast. To the north are the mighty **Black Cuillin**, named for their black rocky summits, which include many Munros. The Inaccessible Pinnacle (986m) was the only Munro not to be climbed by original Munro bagger Reverend Robertson.

South of Glen Sligachan, the Red Cuillin, crowned with red heather, are gentler but equally popular with walkers; Blà Bheinn (928m) is a popular Munro. Sligachan was the scene of a crofters rebellion in 1881, when the people of The Braes, the headland north of Loch Sligachan, refused to pay rent to the MacDonalds. There's a monument to the Battle of The Braes, where policemen from Glasgow brutally suppressed the up-rising, at Balmeanach, across from Raasay.

One of the main bases for climbers and hill-walkers is **Sligachan** (Sligeachan), mid-way between Portree and Broadford. Sligachan has a hotel, hostel and camp site, while there's a good hostel, basic camp site and a shop at Glenbrittle. Broadford is another good base for walks in the Red Cuillin, or you can take the ferry from Elgol to Loch Coruisk in the heart of the mountains.

For details on rock climbing in the Cuillin Ridge see the Activities chapter.

Places to Stay & Eat

The *camp site* at Sligachan (☎ 650333) is a popular jumping-off point for Cuillin climbers (£4 per head).

Sligachan Hotel (☎ 650204, fax 650207, Sligachan) Singles/doubles £35/40 (£50 with dinner). Bunkhouse beds £8. This excellent and welcoming hotel serves warming Scottish meals (restaurant mains £7 to £15) and caters to hill-walkers of all budgets. The bar serves real ales from the Skye Brewery and local whiskies and has live music on Saturday.

Glenbrittle
☎ 01478

Probably the most popular base for trips to the Black Cuillin is Glenbrittle (Gleann Bhreatail), tucked away on a black-stone beach at the end of the glen of the same name. From here all the Black Cuillin Munros are within a few miles' walk. The demanding ascent of Sgurr na Banachdich (965m), with sensational views of the Main Ridge, takes about five hours (round trip) from the youth hostel.

Glenbrittle Youth Hostel (☎ 640278, Glenbrittle) Beds from £9/7.75. Open Apr-Sept. In the glen, most people head for the pleasant SYHA hostel. Climbing groups often hire out the hostel in winter – call SYHA central bookings (☎ 0870 155 3255).

There's a popular *camp site (☎ 640404)* down by the sea, but the midges can be diabolical. It only costs £3.50 per person, including use of the hot shower (closed October to March).

Highland Country/Rapsons does twice-daily Monday to Saturday runs from Portree to Glenbrittle via Sligachan and Carbost from May to September. Hitching to Glenbrittle can be slow, especially late in the day, so be prepared to walk.

MINGINISH PENINSULA
☎ 01478

West of Sligachan, the A863 cuts along pretty Glen Drynoch to the peaceful Minginish peninsula, home to Skye's famous **Talisker Distillery** *(☎ 614306, Carbost; admission £4, including dram and discount voucher; open Mon-Fri year-round, plus Sat July-Sept)*. The distillery was established in 1830 and produces a robust single malt that was one of Robert Louis Stevenson's favourite tipples. There are several places to stay in the village of **Carbost**, which has a store and a post office, or farther north at **Portnalong**.

Croft Bunkhouse & Bothies (☎/fax 640254, 7 Portnalong) Beds £6.50-10. This complex of bothies is a good hostel choice; there's a variety of rooms and you can also camp (£3).

Skyewalker Independent Hostel (☎ 640250, fax 640420, Fiskavaig Rd, Portnalong) Beds £7-8.50. This hostel is at the Old School towards Fiskavaig and has good facilities including a small licensed *cafe* and a shop.

Taigh Ailean Hotel (☎ 640271, 11 Portnalong) En-suite rooms from £23. This is a pleasant small hotel that also serves meals (snacks from £2, mains £6 to £12).

Old Inn (☎ 640205, fax 640450, Carbost) Bunkhouse beds £10, hotel B&B £24.50-26.50 per person. This is a favourite with walkers and climbers and serves hearty pub meals (£5 to £11).

Tigh na Bruach (☎ 640467, Carbost Beag) Singles/doubles from £27/44. This large shorefront house is a very comfortable choice.

Over on the west coast, **Talisker** (Talasgair) is a magnificent place, with a sandy beach, sea stack and waterfall. There's a fine circular walk from Talisker to Fiskavaig (around 6 miles, two to three hours), passing a ruined broch and a series of dramatic cliffs.

Talisker House (*☎ 640245, fax 640214, Talisker*) B&B from £45 per person. Open mid-Mar–Oct. Talisker House is a magnificent whitewashed building with four-poster beds. You can also tuck into a hearty dinner for £25.

Getting There & Around

Highland Country/Rapsons operates a bus service from Portree to Portnalong and Fiskavaig on Tuesday and Thursday only during the school term, but Nicolson's Coaches (*☎ 01470-532240*) covers the same route twice daily Monday to Friday.

Carbost Mountain Bike Hire (*☎ 640247*) charges £4/8 per half-/full day.

ELGOL (EALAGHOL)

☎ 01471

About 14 miles southwest of Broadford on the isolated Strathaird peninsula, the tiny village of Elgol may well be the most scenic place on Skye. The view from the pier towards **Loch Coruisk**, in the heart of the Cuillins, is possibly the definitive Skye vista. From Elgol, you can walk along a precarious cliff-top path to Camasunary (where there's a basic bothy) continuing to Loch Coruisk and crossing the Black Cuillin to the SYHA hostel at Glenbrittle. An alternative route to Camasunary begins at Kirkibost on the Elgol road, with great views of Blà Bheinn (four hours each way).

From Elgol, there are dramatic boat trips to **Loch na Cuilce**, at the mouth of the River Scavaig. Seals, otters and porpoises are commonly seen. Many hikers use the tours as a short cut to the heart of the Cuillin Ridge. The **Bella Jane** (*☎ 0800 731 3089*) charges £13.50/6.50 per adult/child return (£10/5 one-way) and runs from April to mid-October – call ahead for sailing times. From April to October, the **Celtic Explorer** (*☎ same*) runs day tours to Canna (£35 per person) and half/full-day tours to Rum (£20/35) with an optional castle tour (£3).

Rowan Cottage (*☎/fax 866287, 9 Glasnakille*) B&B £20-25 per person. Open mid-Mar–Nov. About 2 miles east of Elgol

at Glasnakille, this delightful crofting cottage has good rooms and serves excellent home-cooked seafood.

Strathaird House (*☎ 866269, fax 866320, Kilmarie*) B&B £25-30 per person. Overlooking Kilmarie Bay, about 3 miles north of Elgol, this country house is well located for the walk to Camasunary.

A 14-seater postbus runs from Broadford to Elgol in the morning (Monday to Saturday) and afternoon (Monday to Friday), but you have to stay overnight in Elgol to do a boat trip.

BROADFORD (AN T-ATH LEATHANN)

☎ 01471 ● pop 530

Broadford, the main service centre of several scattered communities, is a fairly plain village, but it's a useful base for walks to Blà Bheinn. The route starts from the head of Loch Slapin, 7 miles west of Broadford on the road to Elgol; allow six hours return. Postbuses to Elgol provide access to the trailhead, but you can't return the same day by public transport.

Broadford itself is lacking in tourist attractions. The best thing here is the **Serpentarium** (*☎ 822209, The Old Mill, Harrapool; adult/child/family £2.50/1.50/7; open 10am-5pm Mon-Sat Easter-Oct & Sun July-Aug*) where you can see and touch all sorts of snakes, some of them illegally imported, impounded by Customs and given refuge here.

The TIC (*☎ 822361*), by the 24-hour Esso petrol station, opens Easter to October. Broadford has a **Co-op supermarket**, a bank (with ATM) and a hospital (*☎ 822137*).

Broadford Youth Hostel (*☎ 822442, Broadford*) Beds from £9.50/8.25. Open Mar-Oct. This well-equipped SYHA hostel is at the northern end of the bay, signposted from the highway.

Fossil Bothy (*☎ 822297, 13 Lower Breakish*) Beds £8. Around 2 miles east of Broadford, you'll find this intimate eight-bed hostel.

Lime Stone Cottage (*☎ 822142, 4 Lime Park*) B&B from £24. This charming stone cottage is a very cosy choice.

***Ptarmigan* (☎ 822744, Broadford)** B&B £23-30. This comfortable modern house is just south of Broadford on the waterfront.

***Claymore* (☎ 822333, Broadford)** Snacks and bar meals £2-8. Claymore, by the road to Kyle, does good bar meals.

***Failte da Rendezvous* (☎ 822001, Upper Breakish)** Mains £10-15. You'll get a great meal at this posh French/Gaelic place.

Getting There & Away
All Citylink buses to and from Portree pass through Broadford. You can hire a mountain bike from Fairwinds Cycle Hire (☎ 822270) for £7 per day, or rent a car from £30 per day from Skye Car Rental (☎ 822225) at the Sutherlands petrol station.

SLEAT
☎ 01471
The other route to Skye from the mainland is via the CalMac ferry from Mallaig to Armadale, which sits right at the southern end of Skye on the narrow Sleat peninsula. This low-lying peninsula is studded with small lochs and is home to several impressive castles, as well as the renowned Gaelic-language college of Sabhal Mór Ostaig (☎ 844373, W www.smo.uhi.ac.uk) at the turn-off to Tarskavaig. The most attractive part of the island is south of Armadale towards Aird of Sleat; the popular walk from Aird to the lighthouse at **Point of Sleat**, the most southerly point on Skye, takes two to three hours return.

On the west coast, the tiny village of **Tarskavaig** has grand views towards the Cuillins, particularly from the headland west of the village cemetery. Farther south at Tokavaig is the ruined MacDonald fortress of **Dunscaith Castle**. On the east coast near the turn-off to Tokavaig is another ruined castle, **Caisteal Camus**, said to be haunted by a Green Lady or *gruagach* (a spirit who follows the fortunes of a family).

At **Armadale Castle**, built in 1815 for the MacDonalds, there's the **Museum of the Isles** (☎ 844305, Armadale; adult/child £3.90/2.85; open 9.30am-5.30pm Apr-Oct). The museum is housed in a restored wing of the castle surrounded by wonderful gardens,

and tells the convoluted story of Scotland's most famous clan, who claim descent from the Gaelic chieftain Somerled. Genealogy research facilities are available and there's an appealing, if pricey, restaurant housed in the beautifully converted castle stables.

Armadale has a few accommodation options, a foodstore, post office, and a summertime *cafe* and *takeaway* by the pier.

Places to Stay & Eat
***Armadale Youth Hostel* (☎ 844260, Ardvasar)** Beds from £9/7.75. Open Apr-Sept. This SYHA hostel is 900m from the Armadale ferry terminal.

***Flora MacDonald Hostel* (☎ 844440, The Glebe, Kilmore)** Beds £8. About 3 miles north of Armadale at Kilmore (A'Chille Mhór), this hostel is a peaceful choice; it's down the lane opposite the Free Church of Scotland but they also pick up from the pier.

***Mrs Newman* (☎ 844218, The Old Schoolhouse, Aird of Sleat)** B&B £20-25 per person. Open Mar-Oct. This pleasant B&B is in the old school at Aird of Sleat.

***Hotel Eilean Iarmain* (☎ 833332, fax 833275, Eilean Iarmain)** En-suite singles/doubles from £67.50/90. This charming whitewashed hotel sits right by the water at Isleornsay (Eilean Iarmain), about 8 miles north of Armadale; the bar and restaurant meals (bar meals £5 to £8, five-course set dinner £31) are excellent.

Leopard Man of Skye

At a secret and remote location in southern Skye, accessible only by canoe, is the bothy home of the world's most tattooed man, Tom Leppard, aka The Leopard Man of Skye. An astonishing 99.2% of the Leopard Man's body is covered by a yellow and black leopard pattern tattoo, which took 16 months to apply and cost £5500. Now in his 60s, Tom lives as a recluse in a remote and partly ruined croft, canoeing occasionally to civilisation for supplies. The Leopard Man is sometimes spotted by kayakers, but local people have sworn to protect his privacy from prying tourists.

Getting There & Away

Ferries from Mallaig to Armadale are run by CalMac (☎ 844248); there are seven services daily Monday to Saturday (also Sunday June to August) and tickets cost £2.80/15.65/2/7.85 per passenger/car/bike/motorbike (30 minutes). In winter there's one morning and afternoon service Monday to Friday.

Highland Country/Rapsons does five runs (Monday to Saturday) to Broadford and Portree via Sligachan, connecting with most of the ferries.

You can hire a bike from the Ferry Filling Station (☎ 844249) for around £7 per day.

KYLEAKIN (CAOL ACAIN)
☎ 01599

Even more than Kyle of Lochalsh, Kyleakin has had the carpet pulled from under it by the opening of the Skye Bridge. It's a pleasant place, and it's become something of a backpacker city. There are three hostels here and even a backpackers pub.

Bright Water Visitor Centre (☎ 530040; open 9am-6pm Mon-Sat Apr-Oct), near the pier, has nature displays and offers ranger-led tours of the nature reserve at Eilean Bàn, the island between Skye and the mainland near the Skye Bridge (adult/child £8/4).

At the southern edge of the village is the picturesque ruin of **Castle Moil**, a 14th-century castle formerly occupied by the MacDonalds.

Seacruise (☎ 534760) charges adult/child £5.50/3.50 for one-hour cruises to see seals, a shipwreck and an otter sanctuary, and £10/5 for evening cruises to Eilean Donan Castle.

Kyleakin Youth Hostel (☎ 534585) Dorm beds from £10.50/9. The SYHA hostel was formerly a hotel and has good facilities, though it isn't the most intimate hostel on the block.

Skye Backpackers (☎/fax 534510, e skye@scotlands-top-hostels.com, Benmhor) Beds £10-11, doubles/twins £12.50-15. Breakfast £1.40. This busy backpackers is part of the MacBackpackers group and offers good tours and lots of communal spirit as well as comfortable rooms.

Dun Caan Independent Hostel (☎/fax 534087, e info@skyerover.co.uk, Castle View) Dorm beds £10. Near the old ferry quay, friendly Dun Caan hostel is quieter than the other hostels and also hires bikes.

Saucy Mary's (☎ 534845) Bunks £10.50, doubles/twins £12.50. This is a boozy backpackers pub with good-value meals (around £5) and the busiest nightlife on Skye.

King's Arms Hotel (☎ 534109, fax 534190) Rooms £20-35 per person. This old-fashioned place is the better of the two hotels in town.

Pier Coffee House (☎ 534641) Snacks & meals £1-5. Closed Nov-Jan. This friendly coffee shop on the waterfront is a hang-out for SKAT protesters and offers snack meals in the evening.

Crofter's Café (☎ 534134) Lunches £5-7. This bright and airy restaurant just beyond the Skye Bridge roundabout serves filling fare at reasonable prices.

Getting There & Around

Highland Country/Rapsons runs twice hourly to Kyle of Lochalsh and one to three times daily, except Sunday, to Broadford and Portree. Scottish Citylink runs to Inverness (twice daily), Fort William and Glasgow (three daily) and Broadford and Portree (five daily).

Coming by car from the mainland, the Skye Bridge costs £5.70 per car and £2.90 per motorcycle (£4.70 and £2.40 in winter).

You can hire bikes for £10 to £12 per day from the Skye Backpackers and Dun Caan hostels.

KYLERHEA (CAOL REITHE)

About 3 miles back from Kyleakin, a waterlogged road leads southwards to Kylerhea, where there's a 1½-hour nature trial to a shorefront **otter hide**, where you stand a good chance of seeing these elusive creatures. A little farther on is the jetty for the car ferry to Glenelg on the mainland.

Sea.fari (☎ 822361) runs two-hour RIB (rigid inflatable boat) trips around the area for adult/child £20/15. Longer trips to Canna, Rum and so on can be arranged (but you'll need cast-iron buttocks).

The ferry (☎ 01599-511302, 🔲 www
.skyeferry.co.uk), for six cars, operates
from 9am to 5.45pm Monday to Saturday
from mid-April to October (there are crossings till 7.45pm from mid-May to July and
Sunday services from 10am to 5.45pm mid-
May to October). Price for passenger/car/
motorcycle/bike are 70p/£6/3/30p.

RAASAY
☎ 01478 • pop 163

This long, narrow and very quiet island
nestling near Skye's eastern seaboard was
a traditional stronghold of the MacLeods,
who were at various times enemies and
allies of the MacDonalds of southern Skye.
There are scenic hills in the south of the
island, including the flat-topped hill of Dún
Caan (443m), an easy but exhilarating walk
from the ferry jetty at **Inverarish**.

Boswell and Johnson were guests at
Raasay House, a mansion of the MacLeods,
in 1773, describing their reception as akin
to emerging 'from darkness into light'. After
the last MacLeod of Raasay emigrated to
Australia in 1846, the house passed to a
string of clearance-happy landlords. The
evictions of the Raasay crofters are mov-
ingly described in verse by the famous local
poet Sorley MacLean.

At the northern end of the island, the
extraordinary ruin of **Brochel Castle** was
home to Calum Garbh MacLeod, an early-
16th-century pirate who looted passing
ships. There are several good walks around
the remote northern end of Raasay, but you
have to cover 10 miles of road on foot to get
here. Having come this far, it's worth continuing the last 1½ miles along **Calum's
Road** from Brochel to Arnish, which was
constructed by Calum MacLeod, the local
postman, over a period of 20 years.

Raasay Outdoor Centre (☎ 660266 or
660200, 🔲 freespace.virgin.net/raasay
.house, Raasay House) This popular activity centre in Raasay House offers a wide
range of outdoor pursuits for adults and
children, including rock-climbing, kayaking and wind-surfing, from £38 per day,
plus longer residential courses. The restaurant is open to nonguests and charges

around £6 for mains. You can also camp
from £4.

Raasay Youth Hostel (☎ 660240, Crea-
chan Cottage) Beds from £8.75/7.50. Open
mid-May–Aug. Raasay's SYHA hostel is
located on the hillside overlooking Skye.

Mrs MacKay (☎ 660207, fax 0870 122
7170, 6 Oskaig Park) B&B from £20 per
person. This comfortable B&B is 3 miles
north of the ferry terminal.

Isle of Raasay Hotel (☎/fax 660222,
Borodale House, Inverarish) B&B £25-30
per person. There are 12 en-suite rooms and
a kitchen provides hearty broth and other
traditional Scottish meals.

Getting There & Away
Raasay is reached by CalMac ferry from
Sconser, midway between Portree and
Broadford. In summer, the ferry operates
up to 11 times daily, Monday to Saturday
only (passenger/bicycle/car £2.30/1/9.35,
15 minutes). There's no petrol on Raasay,
but there is a traditional store and post
office at Inverarish.

The Western Isles

Also known as the Outer Hebrides (the two
names are interchangeable), these wild outlying islands are synonymous with remoteness – the name Hebrides comes from the
Norse *havbredey* meaning 'islands at the
edge of the earth'. Even today, this is one of
Europe's most isolated frontiers, home to
deeply traditional Gaelic-speaking communities. Although desolate, the landscapes
have a mournful beauty, with sweeping vistas of sky and water and dazzling beaches
untouched by human footprints. The landscape is generally flatter than the mainland,
but there are pockets of high ground offering spectacular views.

The islands have a rich and varied history, recalled by Neolithic standing stones,
Iron-Age brochs and Viking place names.
You'll see ruined traditional stone crofts
known as blackhouses (because of the soot
left on the walls by the central peat fire) all
over the islands, as well as the occasional

Wee Frees & Other Island Creeds

Religion plays a complex and important role in island life, and there is a tangible cultural split between the Protestant islands north of Benbecula and the Catholic islands to the south. Hebridean Protestants are perhaps the most fundamentalist sect in Britain, with Sunday being devoted exclusively to religious services, prayer and Bible reading. On Lewis and Harris, virtually everything closes down and social life is restricted to private homes. Until comparatively recently, even children's playgrounds were locked, with padlocks on the swings and chains wrapped around the slides. Public drinking is frowned upon at any time, and pubs are far removed from the vibrant social centres of the mainland.

The Protestants are divided into three main sects with emotionally charged histories. The Church of Scotland, the main Scottish Church, is state-recognised or 'established' and dates back to the Covenanters of the 17th century. The Free Presbyterian Church of Scotland and the Free Church of Scotland (or Wee Frees) are far more conservative and strict, permitting no ornaments, organ music or choirs. Their ministers deliver uncompromising sermons (usually in Gaelic) from central pulpits, and *precentors* lead the congregation in unaccompanied but fervent psalm singing, reminiscent of the Torah chanting of Hassidic Jewish congregations. Visitors are welcome to attend services, but smart dress (preferably a tie) is essential.

The most recent split occurred in 1988 when Lord Mackay, lord chancellor and a prominent Free Presbyterian, committed the dreadful offence of attending a friend's Catholic requiem mass. The Church elders threatened him with expulsion, so he and his supporters responded by establishing the breakaway Associated Presbyterian Church!

large whitehouse (named for the lime applied to the walls) belonging to one or other of the noble families of the Isles. Most of the contemporary villages are straggly, modern creations of unattractive (though no doubt comfortable) concrete bungalows. With the notable exception of the Calanais Standing Stones, there are few of the carefully excavated and preserved historic relics found elsewhere in Scotland.

Around 23,500 of Scotland's 80,000 Gaelic-speakers live on the islands and religion still plays a pivotal role in island life, especially in the Protestant north. The Sunday Sabbath is strictly observed; all shops and pubs remain closed and public transport grinds to a complete halt. A third of Scotland's crofts are found here, and most Hebrideans remain beholden to some absentee landlord or other. Despite the efforts of clan leaders, landlords and the Western Isles Council, unemployment is a major problem and many younger islanders leave the islands for good, contributing to the slow depopulation of the Western Isles.

Life moves very slowly here, with supplies dependent on boats and planes. Often newspapers and bread are unavailable before 10am. Bad weather can cause supplies to dry up altogether, and all modes of transport can be affected. Accommodation is in fairly short supply throughout the islands so book ahead in summer. You'll get more out of the islands if you spend a while here and soak up the peace and quiet and the slow pace of life; a whistlestop tour by car is likely to be somewhat unsatisfying.

HISTORY

The Western Isles have been occupied by humans since at least 4000 BC, when Stone-Age farmers settled the islands from mainland Britain and Europe. The most impressive legacy of Scotland's original inhabitants is the extraordinary stone circle at Calanais on Lewis. Later, Bronze-Age Beaker people and Iron-Age Celts arrived from Europe, taking over many ceremonial sites and building some fine defensive brochs.

Vikings settled in the islands by AD 850, and many clans, including the Morrisons, Nicholsons, MacAulays and MacLeods, are thought to have Norse backgrounds. The traditional island blackhouses have changed little from the Viking longhouses. The Western Isles were part of the Norse empire until 1266, when the islands were gifted to Scotland in the Treaty of Perth. The Middle Ages saw an influx of Gaelic-speaking Celts from Scotland and Ireland, and a weakening of the links to Norway, resulting in a Gaelic-speaking Celtic population with Norse and Irish blood.

The islands were later dominated by the ambitious MacDonald clan, who set themselves up as lords of the Isles, until James V reigned in the renegade Highland chieftains in the 15th century. Many islands subsequently fell under the influence of the MacLeod clan, descended from a family of Norse nobles. The isles suffered terribly in the clearances under both their own clan leaders and immigrant landlords, creating problems of depopulation and unemployment which persist to this day.

ORIENTATION & INFORMATION

Lewis and Harris are actually one island divided by a ridge of hills. The northern half of Lewis is low and flat with endless peat moors; southern Lewis and Harris are covered with impressive mountain scenery and glorious beaches. In the south, Berneray, North Uist, Benbecula, South Uist and Eriskay are joined by bridges and causeways. Mostly these low-lying islands are half-drowned by lochs and open to the sea and sky.

There are several TICs – one in every ferry port, open late for ferry arrivals up to 10pm from April to mid-October.

The main WITB office (☎ 01851-703088, **W** www.witb.co.uk), 26 Cromwell St, Stornoway HS1 2DD, produces a free brochure that lists all accommodation possibilities, from hotels to B&Bs and self-catering cottages. TICs also stock a series of excellent walking leaflets (50p to 75p each). *The Outer Hebrides Handbook & Guide* (£7.95), written by local experts, gives lots of data on the islands' history, culture, flora and fauna.

The Web site **W** www.escapetotheedge .co.uk covers the Western Isles in detail.

ACTIVITIES

The great west-coast beaches of Lewis and Harris provide top-notch surfing, particularly after Atlantic storms. The water temperature is fine in summer, but in autumn and spring you'll need a full-length wet suit and lots of stamina. Most surfers bring their own boards, but you can hire gear from **Hebridean Surf Holidays** (☎ 701869, **e** hebsurf@madasafish.com, **w** www .hebrideansurf.co.uk) in Stornoway, Lewis; it also offers tailor-made surf holidays.

There are great walks on the Western Isles; a series of excellent *Western Isles Walks* brochures (50p) covering all the islands from Barra to Lewis are available from the TICs at Tarbert and Stornoway.

OS Landranger maps that cover the Western Isles include:

Landranger 8: Stornoway & North Lewis
Landranger 13: West Lewis & North Harris
Landranger 14: Tarbert & Loch Seaforth
Landranger 18: Sound of Harris & St Kilda
Landranger 22: Benbecula & South Uist
Landranger 31: Barra, South Uist, Vatersay & Eriskay

There is good fly-fishing in the lochs and lochans dotted across the islands. Permits are usually arranged through hotels or TICs.

In May, committed long-distance runners gather for the **Hebridean Challenge**, a gruelling endurance race from Barra to the Butt of Lewis. As well as running, competitors have to swim or kayak between the islands, though mountain bikes can be used for some of the land stretches – see the Web site **W** www.hebrideanchallenge.com for more information.

A popular way of getting around the Western Isles is by cycling from Lewis in the north to Barra in the south, but you'll need at least a week for the trip. Gales can blow up out of nowhere and the islands' exposed position ensures that there's an almost continuous breeze. Cars are generally cautious around cycles, but sheep seem to believe they have the right of way in most situations.

Bikes can be hired in Stornoway (Lewis), Lochmaddy (North Uist), Howmore (South

Uist) and Castlebay (Barra). Booking is advisable and you should definitely carry a puncture-repair kit and bicycle pump.

ORGANISED TOURS

Scotia Travel (☎ 0141-305 5050) in Glasgow offers three-day/four-night packages to Lewis and Harris including accommodation, car hire and dinner, and return flights from Glasgow or Edinburgh from £299 (add £100 for connecting flights from London). Similar two-day/three-night packages to Benbecula cost from £269.

Based in Lochs in Lewis, *Albannach Guided Tours (☎ 01851-830433)* offers custom-made guided tours of Lewis and Harris, specialising in less-visited areas such as Pairc and Uig.

GETTING THERE & AWAY
Air
British Airways (BA) subsidiary British Regional Airlines/Loganair (☎ 0845 773 3377, from outside the UK ☎ 44-141 222 2222) flies to Stornoway from Glasgow, Edinburgh and Inverness (Monday to Saturday); return fares start at £126, £113 and £60 respectively; note that single fares may be more expensive than returns! The same company also has flights from Glasgow to Benbecula and Barra from Monday to Saturday – see those sections for fare details. At Barra the planes land on the beach, so the timetable depends on the tides.

Highland Airways (☎ 01851-701282) has a hopper flight from Inverness to Stornoway (£55/110 one-way/return) continuing on to Benbecula (£56/111). Stornoway to Benbecula costs £170/85; child fares are about 30% cheaper.

Bus
Regular bus services operating to Ullapool, Uig and Oban connect with the ferries and the principal operator is Scottish Citylink (☎ 0870 550 5050).

Train
Spectacular train services run as far as Oban, Mallaig and Kyle of Lochalsh from Glasgow and Edinburgh. In order to get to Ullapool for the Stornoway ferry, take the train to Inverness, then a bus to Ullapool. Phone ☎ 0845 748 4950 for rail details.

Boat
CalMac operates most routes between the isles, with regular car and passenger ferries daily, except Sunday. Rates can seem a little steep, particularly if you're travelling with a car, but the CalMac monopoly ensures that there are regular services to all the islands. For reservations and service details, contact CalMac (☎ 0870 565 0000 car reservations, ☎ 01475-650100 enquiries). Booking is essential in summer.

Car and passenger ferries run from Ullapool to Stornoway on Lewis (2¾ hours) two or three times daily, except Sunday (£13 per person, plus £62 for a car). There are one or two services daily Monday to Saturday from Uig (Skye) to Tarbert on Harris (passenger/car £8.50/40, 1¾ hours).

There are also boats from Uig to Lochmaddy on North Uist (passenger/car £8.50/40, 1¾ hours) once or twice daily except Sunday. From Mallaig there are ferries on Tuesday to Lochboisdale on South Uist (£13.85/49.50) and on Sunday to Castlebay on Barra (£13.85/49.50). There are also services from Oban to Lochboisdale daily, except Tuesday and Sunday (£18.75/67). Castlebay to Lochboisdale is £5.30/30.50. Bikes are carried for £2 on any leg.

Connecting Otternish on North Uist to Leverburgh on Harris, ferries run three or four times Monday to Saturday (£4.75/21.90). Bikes cost £1.

There are 12 different Island Hopscotch fares for set routes in the Western Isles, offering around a 10% saving (they're valid for one month). Island Rover Passes give unlimited travel on all CalMac routes for eight days (passenger/motorbike/car £43/105/210) or 15 days (£63/158/315); convenient certainly, but make sure you will use enough services to recoup the cost.

GETTING AROUND
Bus
Bus transport is extremely limited, although a bare bones service allows crofters to get to

the shops in the morning and return in the afternoon. Services are shared by a few regional bus companies; Hebridean Coaches (☎ 01870-620345), Macdonald Coaches (☎ 01870-620288) and Grenitote Travel (☎ 01876-560244) serve Benbecula and the Uists, while Harris Coaches (☎ 01859-502441), Galson Motors (☎ 01851-840269), J MacDonald (☎ 01851-612224) and Maclennan Coaches (☎ 01851-702114) cover Lewis and Harris.

There are also early morning and afternoon postbuses on Barra, South Uist, Benbecula, North Uist and Lewis. Call ☎ 0845 774 0740 or visit the Web site Ⓦ www .royalmail.com/postbus for schedules and information.

Services and operators change regularly, but TICs in the islands can provide up-to-date timetables. Visitors without their own transport should anticipate a fair amount of hitching and walking.

Car

Car hire is available in Stornoway and Arnol in Lewis, Liniclate and Balivanich in Benbecula, Leverburgh in Harris and Lochboisdale in South Uist. See these towns for details. Rates typically vary from £18 to £22 per day. Petrol stations are far apart, expensive and almost always closed on Sunday; fill up on Saturday night if you mean to do any driving on Sunday.

LEWIS (LEODHAIS)
☎ 01851 ● pop 19,634

At the northern end of the Western Isles, Lewis is dominated by peat bogs, and the smell of peat fires still hovers evocatively over the moors. The coastal fringes have small arable plots and larger areas of machair but most livestock grazes on the uncultivated peatlands.

The main town – indeed the only town in the Western Isles – is Stornoway, on the east coast, which sits on a protected bay in the lee of the Eye peninsula. There are ferries and flights from Stornoway to the mainland. From Stornoway, a network of roads fans out across the moors. The A857 cuts across the island to the west coast and the

Butt of Lewis, the island's most northerly point. Heading southwards, the A859 runs down the island to Harris, meeting the A858, which runs across the island to the Calanais Standing Stones.

Stornoway (Steornabhagh)
pop 5975

The island's only sizable town sits on a beautiful natural harbour, but the general lack of opportunities for young people has brought big-city problems to this small town. Drink and drugs are the main culprits, despite the best efforts of the Church, though visitors generally see the better side of Stornoway.

The town is dominated by the glorious Lews Castle, built by the island's less-than-glorious former landlord Sir James Matheson. The main part of Stornoway is across the bay, behind the busy Stornoway docks. The town is the Western Isles' administrative and commercial centre, and the base for the Western Isles Council (Comhairle nan Eilan), which has been pivotal in advancing Gaelic culture in the islands.

The Sabbath is very strictly observed here and Stornoway closes down almost entirely every Sunday, though you can usually find one or two hotels and restaurants open. As compensation, this is one of the best places in the isles to attend a Gaelic-language church service.

Orientation & Information The CalMac ferry from Ullapool docks close to the town centre at the obvious ferry terminal on Shell St and most places to stay are within easy reach. The main bus station is immediately in front of the ferry terminal, and it's a short walk to Point St, the main shopping street, which leads uphill from the docks.

The main Western Isles Tourist Board office (☎ 703088, Ⓔ stornowaytic@witb .ossian.net, Ⓦ www.witb.com) is just north of Point St at 26 Cromwell St. The office has a good selection of brochures, including timetables for buses on the Western Isles, and a bureau de change. The office opens 9am to 6pm Monday to Saturday and for later ferry arrivals from April to October.

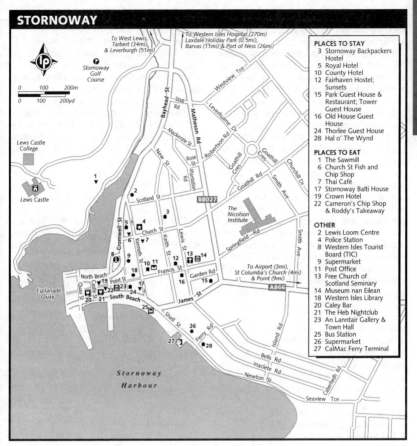

STORNOWAY

To West Lewis,
Tarbert (34mi),
& Leverburgh (51mi)

To Western Isles Hospital (270m)
Laxdale Holiday Park (0.5mi)
Barvas (11mi) & Port of Ness (26mi)

Stornoway
Golf
Course

Lews Castle
College

Lews Castle

To Airport (3mi),
St Columba's Church (4mi)
& Point (9mi)

The
Nicolson
Institute

Esplanade
Quay

North Beach

South Beach

Stornoway
Harbour

Westview Tce
Leverhulme Dr
Bayhead St
Stag Rd
Matheson Rd
Mackenzie St
New St
Rose St
Plantation Rd
Robertson Rd
Coathill Cres
Coathill Rd
Coathill Cres
Churchill Dr
Smith Ave
Springfield Rd
Smith Ave
Island Rd
Caberfeidh Rd
Scotland St
Cromwell St
Church St
Kenneth St
Keith St
Lewis St
Francis St
Point St
Garden Rd
James St
Shell St
Ferry Rd
Bells Rd
Inaclete Rd
Newton St
Seaview Tce
Quay St

B8027
A866

PLACES TO STAY
3 Stornoway Backpackers Hostel
5 Royal Hotel
10 County Hotel
12 Fairhaven Hostel; Sunsets
15 Park Guest House & Restaurant; Tower Guest House
16 Old House Guest House
24 Thorlee Guest House
28 Hal o' The Wynd

PLACES TO EAT
1 The Sawmill
6 Church St Fish and Chip Shop
7 Thai Café
17 Stornoway Balti House
19 Crown Hotel
22 Cameron's Chip Shop & Roddy's Takeaway

OTHER
2 Lewis Loom Centre
4 Police Station
8 Western Isles Tourist Board (TIC)
9 Supermarket
11 Post Office
13 Free Church of Scotland Seminary
14 Museum nan Eilean
18 Western Isles Library
20 Caley Bar
21 The Heb Nightclub
23 An Lanntair Gallery & Town Hall
25 Bus Station
26 Supermarket
27 CalMac Ferry Terminal

0   100   200m
0   100   200yd

The WITB produces a very useful Western Isles guide (free) which lists accommodation throughout the Hebrides.

The main post office is on Francis St and also has a bureau de change. The main banks all have branches with ATMs in Stornoway. The Western Isles Library or *an leabharlann* (☎ 703064) is at 19 Cromwell St and has Internet access for £1 per 15 minutes from 10am to 5pm Monday to Saturday. Baltic Books (☎ 702082), at 8 Cromwell St, has the best stock in the Outer Hebrides and sells the *Stornoway Gazette* newspaper, which comes out every Thursday.

The Western Isles Hospital (☎ 704704) is three-quarters of a mile north of the centre.

Wednesday is early closing day in Stornoway.

Things to See Museum nan Eilean (☎ 703773, Francis St; admission free; open 10am-5.30pm Mon-Sat Apr-Sept, 10am-5pm Mon-Fri, 10am-1pm Sat Oct-Mar) is uphill from the village and has a changing programme of exhibitions about the history of Lewis and Harris.

The **Lewis Loom Centre** (☎ 704500, 3 Bayhead St; admission £2.50; open 9am-

6pm Mon-Sat) in the Old Grainstore, does good 40-minute tours, with demonstrations of Harris tweed making.

There's also the **An Lanntair Arts Centre** *(☎ 703307, Town Hall, South Beach; admission free; open 10am-5.30pm Mon-Sat)* in the rather imposing Scots-Baronial Town Hall. The centre is a major sponsor of local arts, with temporary exhibitions and folk-music performances and a cosy *cafe*.

The extravagant **Lews Castle** was built in 1863 for Sir James Matheson, the notorious landlord who evicted huge numbers of crofters from Lewis during the clearances. It was later taken over by Lord Leverhulme, who donated the castle to the town when he left in 1923. The mansion is now empty, but there are wonderful walks through the densely forested grounds, which were planted for Sir James and are currently maintained by Stornoway Trust (☎ 702002).

The roofless ruin of the 14th-century **St Columba's Church** sits on the shore 4 miles east of town on the Eye peninsula and has some interesting medieval tombs, including the grave slabs of Roderick MacLeod, 7th clan chief (around 1498). Hourly buses (Monday to Saturday) to Point pass the turn-off to the church, where there's a stone monument in the from of a cairn torn asunder, a reminder of the Aignish Farm Raiders, who stormed Matheson's farm at Aignish in 1888 to protest against the clearances. At the tip of the peninsula is the Stevenson-built **Rubha an Tiumpain Lighthouse**.

On Sunday, there are interesting Gaelic-language services at the **Free Church of Scotland** seminary next to Museum nan Eilean on Francis St starting at 6.30pm. The unaccompanied psalm chanting is a haunting, moving experience.

Special Events Every July, Stornoway hosts the huge *Hebridean Celtic Festival* *(☎ 07001-878787, W www.hebceltfest.com)* in the grounds of Lews Castle, drawing musicians from all over the Celtic world.

Places to Stay *Laxdale Holiday Park* *(☎ 703234, 6 Laxdale Lane)* Pitches from £6.50. Open Apr-Oct. Bunkhouse beds

£8-9, open all year. The camp site is 1½ miles north of town, off the A857.

Fairhaven Hostel (☎/fax 705862, 17 Keith St) Bunks £10, B&B from £12.50. This friendly hostel is the best backpacker choice in town and offers surfing trips to the island's beaches. Residents can also enjoy a three-course dinner for £8.

Stornoway Backpackers Hostel (☎ 703628, 47 Keith St) Dorm beds £9, including breakfast. Stornoway's other hostel choice is a five-minute walk from the ferry and bus station.

Thorlee Guest House (☎ 703250, Cromwell St) B&B from £16.50 per person. This old-style guesthouse is right opposite the town hall.

Old House Guest House (☎ 704495, 4 Lewis St) B&B from £23. This handsome guesthouse has a pleasant walled garden and smart rooms.

Hal o' the Wynd (☎/fax 706073, 2 Newton St) B&B from £22.50-25. Just uphill from the ferry terminal, this is a decent B&B.

Park Guest House (☎ 702485, fax 703482, 30 James St) B&B £19-42 per person. The restaurant here is highly recommended (see Places to Eat) and the rooms are probably the best in town.

County Hotel (☎ 703250, 12 Francis St) Singles/doubles from £42/65. The old-fashioned County Hotel isn't a bad choice and the restaurant is open on Sunday.

Royal Hotel (☎ 702109, fax 702142, Cromwell St) Singles/doubles from £55/72. Rooms are very pleasant at this traditional hotel, which overlooks the water just north of the centre. There's also a great restaurant.

Places to Eat Self-caterers should head for the large *Safeway supermarket* on Shell St, or the *Co-op* on Cromwell St (both closed on Sunday).

There are several chip shops on Point St, including *Cameron's Chip Shop (☎ 703200)* and *Roddy's Takeaway (☎ 705114)*, which serve fish and chips for around £3.

The Sawmill (☎ 706916) Light meals under £5. This very pleasant cafe is set in the beautiful grounds of Lews Castle and has an exhibition upstairs on the history of the gardens.

Sunsets (☎ 705862, 26 Francis St) Mains £5-12. Open noon-2pm & 5pm-9pm Mon-Sat. This fine restaurant has a surf theme and serves great local seafood such as razor shells and fresh hake and megrim.

Thai Café (☎ 701811, Church St) Mains £4-6. Noon-2pm & 5pm-11pm Mon-Sat. This Thai place tones the chilli down for the locals but the food is tasty and authentic.

County Hotel (☎ 703250, 12 Francis St) Bar meals £6-8. Restaurant mains £10-15. Open 2pm-9pm daily. The bar meals here are pretty average but the restaurant serves good fare, and it's a great place to stop for a beer on Sunday.

Royal Hotel (☎ 702109, Cromwell St) Bar meals £5-8, restaurant mains £8-16 (closed Sun). The nautical-themed restaurant at this upmarket hotel serves smashing seafood; there's a similar but cheaper selection in the cosy bar next door.

Stornoway Balti House (☎ 706116, 24 South Beach St) Most mains around £7. You can eat in or takeaway at this decent curryhouse, and it's one of the few eateries open on Sunday.

Park Guest House (☎ 702485, 30 James St) Lunches £9-15, dinners £13-16. Open noon-9pm Mon-Sat. One of the best places to eat in Stornoway, this place specialises in local shellfish, game and lamb; bookings are advised.

Entertainment Stornoway is the entertainment centre of the Western Isles, but it's all fairly low-key and good-natured. Friday is the main party night (Saturday night is overshadowed by the impending Sabbath).

Caley Bar (☎ 702411, Point St) The rear bar at the Caledonian Hotel is the most popular drinking hole in Stornoway and is usually great fun at weekends.

The Heb (☎ 702289, South Beach) Stornoway's only nightclub is extremely popular and charges around £5 admission.

Shopping The craft shop at the **Lewis Loom Centre** (☎ 704500, 3 Bayhead St) sells clothing made locally from Harris tweed (closed Sunday). The definitive Lewis souvenir is a set of Lewis Chessmen, copied from the 12th-century Viking chess pieces found here in 1831; various sets are on offer in Stornoway made from wood, resin or stone.

Getting There & Away British Airways (BA) has flights from Stornoway airport to Benbecula, Inverness, Glasgow and Edinburgh.

Buses from Stornoway to Tarbert and Leverburgh are run by Harris Coaches (☎ 01859-502441) with three or four daily services (except Sunday). Galson Motors (☎ 840269) runs the service to Port of Ness six to 10 times daily, except Sunday. Maclennan Coaches (☎ 702114) runs the circular route from Stornoway to Arnol, Carloway, Cala-nais and Stornoway (or reverse) several times daily Monday to Saturday. The bus station waiting room offers luggage storage for 70p to £1 per day.

The ferry terminal is housed in an obvious building on Shell St. For details on CalMac ferries see the Getting Around chapter.

Getting Around Alex Dan's Cycle Hire (☎ 702934), 67 Kenneth St, opens 9am to 6pm Monday to Saturday and hires bikes for £8.50 per 24-hours.

Cars can be hired from £18 to £22 per day from Loch's Motor Transport (☎ 705857), 33 South Beach; Autohire (☎ 706939), 3–5 Bells Rd; Mackinnon Self Drive (☎ 702984), 18 Inaclete Rd; or Stornoway Car Hire (☎ 702659) at the airport. By a bizarre quirk of local law, sports personalities, fashion models, circus employees and pop musicians are prohibited from hiring cars on Lewis.

Tolsta (Tolstaidh)

Due north of Stornoway, a single-track road passes a string of decent sandy beaches, finishing at pretty **Tràigh Mhór**, which is framed by Tolsta Head and the rocky stack of **Casteal a Mhorair**, crowned by a 13th-century castle ruin. From here a fine, long coastal path skirts the coast to Ness, passing several ruined shieling villages (where crofting families used to summer with their livestock) and a number of rock arches and Iron-Age forts. Allow four to six hours.

Calanais (Callanish)

The construction of the magnificent **Calanais Standing Stones** began around 5000 years ago, so they're similar in age to the earliest Egyptian pyramids. Perched on an exposed hill top overlooking East Loch Roag, the 54 tall stones are arranged in the shape of a crude Celtic cross, with the remains of a chambered cairn where the arms cross. In fact the shape is coincidental – the site predates both Christianity and the Celts by several millennia. The major circle and the avenues of megaliths are thought to have been erected by ancient farmers as a lunar and solar calendar; the tomb was added much later and used for Beaker burials.

The site was deserted sometime around 1500 BC, coinciding with a dramatic worsening of the climate of Lewis. The stone circle subsequently sunk into the peat, and was largely ignored until it was excavated by Sir James Matheson in 1851. Today, Calanais is one of the most complete stone circles in Britain, and unlike Stonehenge, you can wander around the stones and appreciate the undeniable sense of antiquity and power that the stones exude.

Just south of the circle and hidden from sight, the **Calanais Visitor Centre** (☎ 621422; admission to exhibition adult/child £1.75/75p; open 10am-6pm daily Apr-Sept, 10am-4pm Wed-Sat Oct-Mar) is a tour de force of discreet design and has a good exhibition on the stones, plus a good cafe – snacks such as hoagies (filled rolls) cost from £2 – and the inevitable souvenir shop. You can camp in the field by the visitor centre with permission.

Inland from the main circle are several other stone circles which many people miss. **Calanais 2** is a short walk southeast, and features four large stones in a single circle, while **Calanais 3** farther east is a large double circle of smaller stones overlooking an area of wild moor. Coming from Stornoway you can follow the A859 south and cut across the moors on the A858.

Just north of Calanais, there's the **Stones, Sky and Sacred Landscape Exhibition** (☎ 621277, New Park; admission free; open Mon-Sat, whenever someone is around) with interesting displays including astronomical items that relate to the Calanais stones. Tours of the stones cost £20 per group per hour.

Places to Stay Mrs Morrison (☎ 621392, 27 Calanais) B&B £20. Open Mar-Sept. This B&B is housed in a cottage close to the stones.

Farther northwards at Breasclete (Breascleit), you can turn east on the back road to Stornoway, passing two excellent modern guesthouses.

Eshcol Guest House and **Loch Roag Guest House** (☎/fax 621357, 21 & 22a Breascleit) B&B £29-31. Dinner £18. These attractive guesthouses are next door to each other, have the same owner and offer cosy rooms and good dinners.

Tigh Mealros (☎ 621333, Garynahine) 2-course dinners £10-18. Open 7pm-9pm Mon-Sat. Tigh Mealros is a pleasant family-run restaurant set in an interesting sculpture garden; the food is great (the local scallops are particularly renowned).

Getting There & Away MacLennan Coaches (☎ 702114) has buses that follow a circular route from Stornoway to Calanais, Carloway, Arnol, Barvas Junction and back to Stornoway. There are four to six buses daily Monday to Saturday.

Carloway (Carlabagh)

The landscape becomes more rugged and interesting as you head north from Calanais. The village of Carloway has the dramatically located **Dun Carloway Broch** (Dun Charlabhaigh), built in the Iron Age but later taken over by the Morrison clan of Ness during its war with the MacCaulays of Uig in the 17th century. James Matheson's agents reported that there was still a 'respectable-looking family' living on the ground floor of the broch in 1870! The lower level is still intact, but the upper walls have partially collapsed, giving the broch a strange truncated appearance. There are panoramic views from the top of the surviving stairway.

Nearby, the subterranean grass-roofed **Doune Broch Centre** (☎ 643338, Carloway; admission free; open 10am-5pm Mon-Sat late May–mid-Sept) has a wonderful re-creation of the interior of a broch and exhibitions about the history of Dun Carloway and the life of the people who lived there.

Braes Hotel (☎ 643252, fax 643435, Carloway) Singles £30-35, doubles £56-70. The welcoming Braes Hotel is the closest accommodation to the broch and offers good-value rooms and meals.

Garenin (Na Gearrannan)

About a mile north of Carloway, the impressive **Gearrannan Blackhouse Village** (W www.gearrannan.com) consists of nine restored thatch-roofed blackhouses. The village was occupied from the 17th century right up until 1974 and the houses have been authentically re-created down to the peat fires and the weighted ropes that hold down the roof thatch. In the second-closest house to the entrance, the **museum** (☎ 643416, Garenin; adult/child £2/1; open 11am-5.30pm Mon-Sat Apr-Sept) is furnished as it was in 1955 and is well worth a visit. There are also occasional live re-enactments, with actors spinning wool and cutting peat.

Garenin Crofters' Hostel (Garenin) Dorm beds £6.50/5. Open all year. The wonderful thatch-roofed Gatliff Trust/SYHA hostel, in one of the blackhouses, is one of the most atmospheric hostels in Scotland (or anywhere else, for that matter).

You can arrange self-catering accommodation at four of the other *blackhouses* (☎ 643416, fax 643488), either on a nightly (£16 to £72 per night) or weekly (£90 to £368 per week) basis. The blackhouses are unique and luxurious, with attached kitchens and lounges, and are highly recommended. Cottages sleep from two to 16 people.

Blackhouse Village Cafe (☎ 643416, Garenin) Soup & snacks from £2. This pleasant cafe is next to the museum.

Carloway to Barvas

The best beaches in Lewis are tucked into small coves along the strip of coast north of Carloway, including **Dalmore** and **Dalbeg** (Dail Beag), which sits in a bay that's backed with machair and flanked by cliffs and sea stacks. The coast here has some of the most consistent surf in Europe; **Hebridean Surf Holidays** (☎ 701869) in Stornoway can provide gear and transport.

Farther north at Shawbost (Siabost), a signposted trail cuts westwards across the moor to **Norse Mill & Kiln**, a restored water-powered mill and lime kiln of a type introduced by the Vikings. In the old stone schoolhouse in Shawbost is the **Shawbost Crofting Museum** (open 9am-6pm Mon-Sat Apr-Oct), an informal collection of local memorabilia.

Eilean Fraoich camp site (☎ 710504, Shawbost) Pitches £3-7.50. Open May-Oct. This simple camp site is behind the church in Shawbost.

Airigh (☎ 710478, 1 Teachers House, Shawbost) B&B £18-26. Just south of the museum, this pleasant B&B is housed in the former teachers' cottages.

At nearby **Bragar**, the jaws of a vast blue whale form a **whalebone arch** by the roadside, with the rusting harpoon that killed the whale dangling from the centre; it was more impressive before the bones were encased in fibreglass.

Barvas (Barabhas) to Ness (Niss)

The A858 finishes at the unremarkable village of Barvas; from here the A857 heads southeast across the moors to Stornoway and northeast along the coast to Ness.

Just west of Barvas at Arnol village you'll find the **Arnol Blackhouse Museum** (☎ 710395; adult/child £2.80/1; open 9.30am-6.30pm Mon-Sat Apr-Sept, 9.30am-4.30pm Mon-Sat Oct-Mar, last admission 30 minutes before closing), owned by Historic Scotland (HS). This remarkable blackhouse croft has been left exactly as it was when the last occupant left in 1964 and has been maintained by traditional methods ever since. There's also a visitor centre with interpretative displays on the crofting tradition.

Buses from Stornoway to Ness pass through Barvas; change here for south-bound buses to Calanais.

Butt of Lewis (Rubha Robhanais)

If the local council had a penny for every time someone pulled the obvious gag at the Butt of Lewis sign, this would be the richest district in the Hebrides. Known locally as Rubha Robhanais, Lewis' northern tip is bleak and windswept, with a menacing black-towered lighthouse, pounding surf, seals and large colonies of nesting fulmars. It's a humbling spot that gives a real sense of the isolation of the isles.

Just before the turn-off to the Butt at Eoropie (Eoropaidh), **St Moluag's Church** (Teampull Mholuidh) is an austere Episcopal kirk with tiny windows, thought to date from the 12th century. The main settlement here is Ness, which has an attractive stone harbour. From Skigersta (Sgiogarstaigh), a mile south of Ness, a walking trail runs 10 miles to the beach at Tolsta. Ness also has the interesting **Ness Historical Society Museum** *(☎ 810735; £1 donation requested; open 9am-5pm Mon-Sat Easter-Oct, 10am-5pm Mon-Fri winter)* in a converted shop. The eclectic collection ranges from old radar equipment to quern stones and stone axes.

There's good hostel accommodation at South Galson, about 7 miles south of Ness.

Galson Farm Guesthouse & Bunkhouse *(☎/fax 850492, ⓔ russell@galsonfarm .freeserve.co.uk, South Galson)* B&B £31-45. Dorm beds from £8. The recommended Galson Farm is a fine old building with comfortable B&B, pleasant hostel accommodation (with kitchen, shower and so on) and good dinners, including vegetarian choices.

Eisdean *(☎ 810240, 12 Fivepenny, Ness)* B&B from £18. This decent B&B is near St Moluag's Church.

Galson Motors (☎ 840269) runs buses from Stornoway to Port of Ness and Eoropie every few hours from morning to evening (except Sunday). Change at Barvas Junction for buses south to Carloway and Calanais.

Great Bernera (Bearnaraigh)
pop 262

This rocky island is connected to Lewis by a road bridge and has an interesting **folk history museum** *(☎ 612331, Breaclet; adult/child £1.50/50p; open noon-4pm Tues-Sat May-Sept)* in the hamlet of Breaclete (not to be confused with nearby Breasclete on the Lewis mainland), with exhibits on the island's history and a *tearoom* that serves home-baked goodies.

Heading northwards, you'll reach the junction at Tobson, where there's a **memorial cairn** to the Bernera Rioters; crofters who were responsible for some of the most militant acts of civil disobedience during the Highland Clearances. The right fork (signposted 'To The Shore') leads to the glorious sandy beach at Bosta (Bostadh), where there's a restored **Iron-Age house** *(☎ 612331, Bosta; adult/child £1.50/50p; open noon-4pm Tues-Sat May-Sept)*. The roundhouse is based on some Iron-Age huts that were discovered nearby following a sandstorm in 1992. There are good views from the top of the hill out to the distant Flannan Isles (where the lighthouse keepers famously disappeared in 1900).

Kelvindale (☎ 612347, 17 Tobson) B&B £16 per person. By the shore at Tobson village, this comfortable pink house has decent rooms. It also does meals for £13.

J MacDonald (☎ 612224) runs buses four or five times daily except Sunday between Great Bernera and Stornoway. By car, you should turn off the A858 near Calanais, take the B8011 south then turn right onto the B8059 for Great Bernera.

Uig Sands & Mealista (Mealasta)

The B8011 continues southwestwards from Bernera, passing the turn-off to Cliff (Cliobh) and Kneep (Cnip), where there are beautiful wave-lashed beaches (treacherous for swimming) and Iron-Age ruins. Cliff has a basic *camp site (☎ 672265)*.

Beyond the Cliff turn-off, the B8011 passes through the steep fissure of Glen Valtos to **Timsgarry** (Timsgearraidh), over-looking the shimmering Uig Sands. Timsgarry has a pretty beach at low tide and the

Uig Heritage Centre (☎ 672481, Uig Community Centre; adult/child £1/50p; open noon-5pm Mon-Sat). The famous 12th-century walrus-ivory Lewis chess pieces were uncovered by a cow in the sand dunes here in 1831, but most of the hoard of 78 Viking chessmen ended up in the British Museum in London.

From Miavaig pier at Uig, **Seatrek** (☎ 672464) offers nature-spotting tours around the caves and stacks of the Kyles of Pabbay, with seal sighting almost guaranteed. Trips last 2½ hours and cost £15/12 per adult/child.

Baile na Cille Guest House (☎ 672242, fax 672241, Timsgarry) B&B £24-39. This splendid step-gabled house has wonderful views and serves good meals.

Bonaventure (☎ 672474, Aird Uig) B&B from £17 per person. Hostel beds £10 (£9 with own sleeping bag). Three miles north at Gallan Head, there's unusual accommodation in rambling buildings at the former RAF base. There is also a well-regarded Scottish-French restaurant, which opens noon to 2pm and 7pm to late Wednesday to Saturday (it also opens 7pm to late Tuesday) but is closed November and February. Two-/three-course lunches cost £7.95/9.95 and bookings are essential for dinner.

Continuing southwards from Uig Sands, there are excellent beaches at **Mangersta** and **Breanais** before the road peters out at the boulder-strewn beach at **Mealista**. From here there are wonderful wild walks into the surrounding hills, including the summit of Mealisval (574m).

There are several daily A MacLennan (☎ 702114) buses from Stornoway to Timsgarry, via Miavaig, supplemented by post-buses.

Lochs

South of the turn-off to Calanais, just outside Stornoway, the A859 winds across the moors to the top of Harris, passing the turn-off to Lochs, a remote area of scattered lochans and tiny crofting communities. To the south is the truly isolated **Pairc** peninsula, a desolate range of hills with some fine walking and no roads or human habitation. On the A859 is a monument to the Pairc Deer Raiders, a group of cottars (landless islanders) who raided the Pairc deer estate in 1887, killing a number of the landowner's deer.

Ravenspoint Visitors Centre (☎ 880236, fax 880213, Kershader) Bunks £8.25/7.25 adult/child. Near the start of the Lochs road at Kershader, the visitors centre includes a SYHA hostel, tearoom and shop, housed in the old village schoolhouse.

HARRIS (NA HEARADH)
☎ 01859 ● pop 1866

Actually the rugged southern tip of Lewis, Harris is the most dramatic of the Western Isles, with looming mountains, magnificent beaches and broad expanses of machair. The Gaelic name for Harris, hearadh, is derived from the Viking word for 'high island'. Most of the peaks are clustered in the north, including the rocky mass of Clisham, Harris' highest peak at 799m. The pinched-off peninsula to the south is fringed by a broad strip of machair and has some of the best beaches in Scotland. Ferries to Otternish on North Uist leave from Leverburgh at the southern end of Harris.

The boundary between Harris and Lewis was originally a clan division. The territory to the north belonged to the MacLeods of Lewis, descended from the Norse noble Torquil, while Harris belonged to the MacLeods of Harris and Skye, who were descended from Torquil's brother Tormod. Needless to say, relations between the two brothers – and subsequently the two clans – were less than amicable.

Harris is famous for Harris tweed, a high quality woollen cloth with a distinctive her-ring-bone weave. The industry still employs around 400 local weavers; Tarbert TIC has information about visits to tweed workshops. Many locals still rely on crofting and fishing, but tourism provides an income for many islanders.

Tarbert (An Tairbeart)
pop 480

Tarbert sits on the narrow isthmus between North and South Harris, overshadowed by

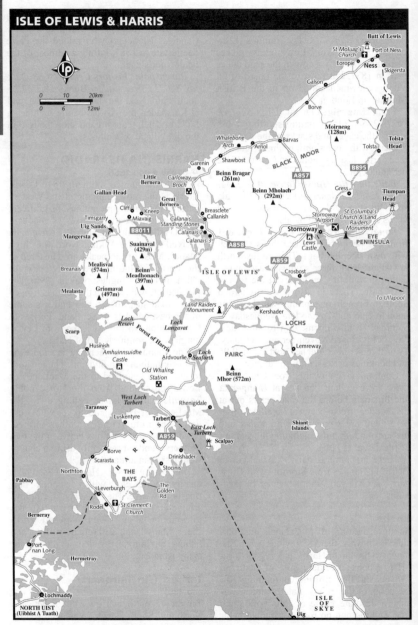

ISLE OF LEWIS & HARRIS

mountains and tucked between two very pleasant sea lochs. It's appealingly laid out along a single street leading down to the harbour.

The all-year TIC (☎ 502011), Pier Rd, is just uphill from the ferry near the main carpark; it opens 9am to 6pm Monday to Saturday and again for late ferry arrivals (9am to 5pm Monday to Friday from October to April). Tarbert has a petrol station, an ATM at the TIC and two general stores.

Firstfruits Tearoom (☎ *502439, Pier Rd*) Snacks from £2. Open Apr-Sept. This pleasant tearoom, opposite the TIC, is handy while you wait for a ferry.

Rockview Bunkhouse (☎/*fax 502626, Main St*) Dorm beds £9. There are 32 beds and rooms are warm and comfortable. Bike hire can be arranged.

Alan Cottage (☎/*fax 502146, Tarbert*) Doubles/twins £72/62. This luxurious cottage on the main road through the village is run by a hospitable couple and offers luxury and fine dining (four-course dinner £27).

Tigh na Mara (☎ *502270, Tarbert*) B&B £17-20 per person. Dinner £10. This cosy B&B, with views of the east loch, is a five-minute walk eastwards from the ferry.

Waterstein House (☎ *502358, Main St*) B&B £14 per person. Closer to the ferry terminal, Waterstein House is a bland building with four rooms.

Harris Hotel (☎ *502154, fax 502281, Tarbert*) Singles £38.50-43.50, doubles £67-77. Pub meals £6-13, set dinner £18.50. Between the east and west lochs, the old-fashioned Harris Hotel is Tarbert's best choice. The bar is a great shelter from the weather and the restaurant serves good bar meals and posh dinners of salmon and venison.

Getting There & Away Tarbert is the departure point for CalMac ferries to Uig on Skye – see that section earlier for details. For ferry information, phone CalMac on ☎ 502444.

Harris Coaches (☎ 502441) is based in Tarbert and has trips to Leverburgh (some buses run as far as Rodel) and Stornoway every few hours, daily except Sunday. There are also services to Scalpay.

Harris Tweed

The favourite fabric of the English upper-classes, Harris tweed is warm and durable and is still hand-woven by industrious islanders in their own homes. The process of making tweed dates back 2500 years; the wool is first hand-scoured and dyed with lichen and heather flowers, before being spun and woven on hand-operated looms. As a final treatment, the finished fabric is dipped in sheep urine and beaten against a table (waulked) to soften the fabric (don't worry – they wash it afterwards!).

Today there are about 400 weavers in Lewis and Harris, working with locally produced wool in their own croft-house workshops. Harris tweed still has a somewhat exclusive (some would say stuffy) image, but a number of British fashion designers, including John Galliano and Vivienne Westwood, have found radical new uses for the fabric. Real Harris Tweed will always be hand-woven in Lewis or Harris and should carry the distinctive Harris tweed 'orb' logo.

North Harris

The mountainous triangle of North Harris is bound by Loch Seaforth and Loch Resort and offers many fine opportunities for climbing and walking. It's a desperate landscape, scarred by retreating glaciers, and most of the walking is on open hillsides. **Clisham** (799m) can be reached from the high point of the Stornoway to Tarbert road; the round trip takes about four hours and offers wonderful views. Another good walk is the **Harris Walkway** from Scaladale (near Ardvourlie) to Seilibost on the west coast of Harris. This network of maintained paths covers 20 miles and a wide variety of landscapes. Tarbert is a good place to break the journey, but wild camping is another option.

Scaladale Centre (☎ *502502, Ardvourlie*) Dorms from £10. This comfortable youth centre has good communal facilities and rooms; various activities are offered.

Ardvourlie Hotel *(☎ 502307, Ardvourlie)*
Rooms £65-75 per person. Overlooking
Loch Seaforth, this fine and friendly country house has a lovely aspect and fine period
furniture in all the rooms. It also offers
dinner for £25.

A minor road branches off the A859
near Loch Maarug and heads towards the
tiny village of **Rhenigidale** (Reinigeadal).
This remote crofting community has only
recently become accessible by road and
has a secluded GHHT hostel. You can
walk here from Urgha Beag on the road
from Tarbert to Scalpay, or scramble up
the small peak of Toddun (528m) for grand
views.

Reinigeadal Crofters' Hostel *(Rhenigidale)* Beds £6.50/5. This excellent GHHT
hostel is housed in a low white croft standing above the road on the east side of the
glen.

Harris Coaches services Ardvourlie on
the way from Tarbert to Stornoway. Call
☎ 502221 to book a seat on the taxibus to
Rhenigidale from Tarbert.

Hushinish (Huisinis)

A tiny road runs along the northern shore of
West Loch Tarbert beneath the looming
peaks to the tiny village of Hushinish. Less
than a mile from the junction with the A859
are the ruins of an **old whaling station**,
one of Lord Leverhulme's failed social-
improvement projects.

Farther west, an old estate road leads
deep into the hills along Glen Meavaig, providing access to many of the surrounding
peaks. Just outside the grounds of privately
owned **Amhuinnsuidhe Castle**, the road
crosses a natural salmon ladder at the mouth
of Loch Beag.

The road ends at the tiny hamlet of
Hushinish, where there's a lovely silver-
sand beach. Just northwest of Hushinish,
the deserted island of **Scarp** was inhabited
until 1970 and was the scene of bizarre
attempts to send mail by rocket in 1934.
The first rocket exploded, but the second
actually reached its destination. A movie
about the 'rocket post' was filmed in Harris
in 2001.

Scalpay (Scalpaigh)
pop 388

East of Tarbert, a single-track road leads to
the little crofting island of Scalpay, joined
to the mainland by a new bridge. There's a
fine 3-mile walk around the headland to
Eilean Glas Lighthouse, Scotland's very
first lighthouse, built by the Stevensons
in 1788. You may pass 'lazy-beds' or *fean-
nagan* (small arable plots) on some of the
crofts.

There are a few shops and campers can
use the showers (50p) at the community
centre. **Scalpay Diving Services** *(☎ 540328)*
can arrange scuba diving in the area for
around £12.50 per dive – call for details.

Seafield *(☎ 540250, Scalpaigh)* B&B
from £17. Open Feb-Nov. This B&B in a
welcoming crofthouse is just south of the
village.

About 2 miles from Tarbert on the Scalpay road, Urgha Beag is the starting point
for the hill-walk to Maraig (4 miles) via
the Laxdale lochs. Another path heads east
to the GHHT hostel at Rhenigidale (3½
miles).

There are Harris Coaches and community
minibuses to Scalpay from Tarbert.

South Harris

The dominant landscape in South Harris is
machair, which gives way to some of the
finest beaches in Britain, sprinkled with
magnificent white-blond sand. The beaches
begin at the shimmering strands of **Luskentyre**, continuing all along the west coast to
Tràigh Scarasta. The machair on the foreshore attracts birds and becomes a riot of
wildflowers in spring. At Horgabost and
Scarasta are some large standing stones.
There are several spread-out settlements
along the 45 miles from Tarbert to Leverburgh, where the boat departs for North
Uist.

Moravia *(☎ 550262, 7 Losgaintir)* B&B
£17-20. This comfortable cottage is a short
walk from the glorious strands of Luskentyre.

Scarista House *(☎ 550238, fax 550277,
Scarasta)* B&B from £62.50 per person.
Dinner £35. This white mansion is right by

a lovely beach and offers top-class cooking; it's well worth the splurge.

Borvemore Cottage (☎ 550222, Sgarasta Mhor) Blackhouse cottage (sleeps four) £275-375 weekly, self-catering cottages £225-335 (sleep six). These self-catering cottages are in the stone stables by the beach, and in a traditional thatched blackhouse.

At **Northton** (Toabh Tuath), a road leads northeastwards across the rolling machair to the base of Chaipaval (365m), an isolated heath-topped hill linked to the rest of Harris by a low sandy spit. The peak offers wonderful views along the coast.

Seallam! *(☎ 520258, Northton; adult/child £2.50/2; open 9am-6pm Mon-Sat)* has exhibits covering local and natural history, and houses the excellent **Co Leis Thu?** genealogy centre, with extensive historical archives and a computer database, to help you hunt down your ancestors. There's also an excellent bookshop.

Nearby is the **MacGillivray Centre** with rather limited displays on local wildlife, but some of the best public toilets in Britain (there's even a sign saying so!). There are guided nature walks from here in summer at 2.30pm on Monday and Friday (adult/child £2/free).

Tetherstone Guest House (☎ 520357, 40 Northton) B&B from £25. This friendly guesthouse is on the road out to the headland at Northton.

Offshore from Luskentyre is the abandoned crofting island of **Taransay**, which was recently used as the setting for the hit TV series *Castaway*. As well as fine scenery, the island has numerous deserted crofts, lazy-beds and a ruined dun. In summer *Angus Mackay (☎ 07747-842218)* offers day-trips to Taransay from Horgabost beach (adult/child £19/18); trips leave at 9.30am Monday to Friday.

The Bays (Na Baigh)

Although the main road follows the more attractive west coast, most of the population was evicted to the deeply indented eastern seaboard during the clearances. Known as **The Bays**, this inhospitable moonscape of eroded crags and black lochans is reached by the so-called Golden Road (named by local people who didn't think so much money should be spent building it), providing an alternative route from Tarbert to Leverburgh. On your way down the coast, look out for the photogenic little stone post office at **Stocinis** where a crude path cuts over the hills to Seilibost.

Drinishader Bunkhouse (☎/fax 511255, Drinishader) Dorm beds £8. This hospitable white croft looks out over the sea about 3 miles from the Bays turn-off and has a lovely peaceful location. Bike hire is available for £8 per day.

Hillhead (☎ 511226, Scadabay) B&B from £16 per person. Farther south, this quiet B&B is run by a friendly couple who make Harris tweed.

Leverburgh

The small village of Leverburgh (An t-Ob) was a planned project of Lord Leverhulme, who hoped that the small village, then known as Obbe, would become Scotland's premier fishing port. The market for Harris fish never materialised, but Leverburgh did well out of the deal and is today a busy place, with numerous wooden houses and a small fishing industry. Ferries leave from here to Otternish on North Uist. To fish on beautiful Loch Langavat (2½ miles north of Leverburgh), call **Obbe Fishings** *(☎ 520466)*.

By the large loch in Leverburgh, the An Clachan shop has a TIC (☎ 520370), tearoom and an informal heritage exhibition. In summer, you can take wildlife cruises with *Strond Wildlife Cruises (☎ 520204)* for around £30 per hour.

Am Bothan (☎/fax 520251, Leverburgh) Dorm beds £12. This quirky hostel is housed in an obvious wooden building just off the Rodel road and is colourfully decked out inside.

Caberfeidh House (☎ 520276, Leverburgh) B&B £17-20. Dinner £10. This greystone house is close to the ferry terminal.

Sorrel Cottage (☎ 520319, 2 Glen) B&B £17-20. This friendly cottage is on the outskirts of Leverburgh on the way to Tarbert.

Anchorage Restaurant (☎ 520225, Leverburgh) Mains £5-7. Open Mar-Oct. Located right by the ferry terminal, this cosy cafe serves a good selection of fast food.

Getting There & Around CalMac ferries (☎ 502444) sails from Leverburgh to Otternish (North Uist), near the bridge to Berneray. From Monday to Saturday there are three or four daily sailings from Leverburgh to Otternish (two sailings from March to October). The fare for a passenger/car is £4.75/21.90 (one-way, one hour).

Harris Coaches (☎ 502441) has a bus that meets the ferry at Leverburgh and runs up to Tarbert and Stornoway, as well as providing local services to Scalpay and Rodel.

Leverburgh Car Hire (☎ 520460) charges around £25 a day. Sorrel Cottage hires out bikes for £8 per day.

Rodel (Roghadal)

Three miles east of Leverburgh, the village of Rodel is known for the magnificent **St Clement's Church**, built by Alexander MacLeod of Dunvegan between the 1520s and 1550s, only to be abandoned after the Reformation. The fortified construction leaves little doubt that the church was built in troubled times. The church was extensively renovated by Catherine Herbert, countess of Dunmore, in 1875.

There are several tombs inside the echoing stone hall, including the cenotaph of Alexander MacLeod, carved with hunting scenes, a *burlinn* (a traditional island longboat), a castle, and various saints, including St Clement clutching a skull. There are also interesting carved tomb-slabs featuring swords and Celtic knotwork. You can climb the tower for good coastal views. On your way out look for the carved *sheila-na-gig* – a pagan fertility symbol – on the tower.

You can climb Roineabhal (460m) from here; Lafarge Redland Aggregates recently attempted to open a vast superquarry on the peak but the project was blocked campaigns by environmentalists.

Rodel Hotel (☎ 520210, Rodel) Doubles £85-95. Self-catering apartments £400 per week. This large grey-stone hotel has been

entirely renovated and has good rooms and a posh restaurant (bar meals £5, restaurant meals £10 to £14).

There are several buses between Leverburgh and Rodel daily Monday to Friday, with connections to Tarbert.

BERNERAY (BEARNARAIGH)
☎ 01876 ● pop 140

The beaches of Berneray are unparalleled and the island has a lovely sense of peace. There's a good walk around the northern end of the island, passing a ruined 13th-century chapel and a standing stone. The island is joined to North Uist by a modern causeway and there are two grocery shops.

Gatliff Hostel (Baile) Dorm beds £6.50/5. Open year-round. This gorgeous thatch-roofed blackhouse is probably the most welcoming of the Gatliff Hostels and is just 2 miles from the causeway/ferry terminal.

Burnside Croft (☎/fax 540235, ⓔ splash mackillop@burnsidecroft.fsnet.co.uk Borve) B&B £20-26 per person. Open Feb-Nov. You'll get the finest island hospitality at this excellent B&B, run by the colourful 'Splash' MacKillop. Among other famous guests, Prince Charles stayed here and helped out on the croft. Four-course dinners cost £20 and, if you want to cycle it off, they also rent out bikes for around £15 per day.

In summer, snacks are available at *The Lobster Pot (☎ 540288, Nr the causeway)*, the tearoom attached to Ardmarree Stores.

There are Monday to Saturday postbus services (☎ 0845 774 0740), and Grenitote Travel (☎ 560244) buses, from Berneray (Gatliff Hostel) to Lochmaddy.

Ferries to Leverburgh (Harris) leave from Otternish, just across the bridge on North Uist – see the earlier South Harris section for details.

NORTH UIST (UIBHIST A TUATH)
☎ 01876 ● pop 1386

North Uist is half-drowned by lochs and has some magnificent beaches and several interesting Neolithic sites. There are several small hills with great views across to the mountains of Harris at the northern end of the island. A circular road runs around the coast, meeting the highway to Benbecula at Clachan na Luib.

Lochmaddy (Loch nam Madadh)

Tiny Lochmaddy is the largest settlement on North Uist but things are usually pretty quiet. Ferries sail from here to Uig on Skye, and there are a couple of stores, a Bank of Scotland (with ATM), a petrol station, a post office and a pub. Otters are often seen on the shore near the **Botham am Faileas,** a camera obscura near the so-called Spanish footbridge near the Outdoor Centre.

The **Taigh Chearsabhagh** *(☎ 500240,* **W** *www.taigh-chearsabhagh.org, Lochmaddy; adult/child £1/50p; open 10am-5pm Mon-Sat Feb-Dec)* contains an interesting museum and arts centre. The cafe next door offers free Internet access and does snacks.

The TIC (☎ 500321) opens 9am to 5pm Monday to Saturday April to October, and for late ferry arrivals. Check out **W** www .uistonline.com for more local information.

Uist Outdoor Centre (☎ 500480, **e** *info@uistoutdoorcentre.co.uk, Ceann Dusgaidh, Lochmaddy)* Beds £10/8 with/ without bedding. This independent hostel is comfortable and popular and is often booked-out by large parties. Outdoor activities, including scuba diving and sea kayaking, can be arranged for around £50 per day, including accommodation and meals.

Old Courthouse (☎/fax 500358, Lochmaddy) En-suite B&B £23-25. This comfy B&B is in a handsome stone building north of the pier; take the first right as you come into Lochmaddy from the pier.

Old Bank (☎ 500275, Lochmaddy) B&B from £20. This attractive B&B is in the old bank, on the corner opposite the post office.

Lochmaddy Hotel (☎ 500331, fax 500210, Lochmaddy) En-suite singles £37.50-45, doubles £70-85. Bar meals £6-13. This traditional pad has a top selection of rooms, good-value meals and attracts large numbers of anglers.

Getting There & Around CalMac ferries sail between Lochmaddy and Uig on Skye once or twice daily. For ferry information, phone CalMac on ☎ 500337.

Hebridean Coaches (☎ 01870-620345) and Macdonald Coaches (☎ 01870-620288) run at least four daily (not Sunday) services to Lochboisdale, via Benbecula. There are also regular Monday to Saturday buses to Berneray via Otternish (for the Harris ferry) with Grenitote Travel (☎ 560244).

Bike hire can be organised with Morrison's Cycle Hire (☎ 580211) for £7 per day (£2 extra for delivery). Alda's Taxis (☎ 500215) offers two-hour tours of North Uist Monday to Friday for £6 per person, taking in the main sights.

The North

The north coast is home to several sand-filled sounds; the largest separates the main island from the isle of **Vallay** (Bhalaigh), home to current laird, Lord Granville.

Straun House (☎ 560282) B&B £17-20 per person. This cosy B&B has lovely views across the strands to Vallay.

On the west coast at Scolpaig is **Scolpaig Tower,** a ruined castle on a small island in the loch. North Uist's main attraction, **Balranald Nature Reserve,** sits about 4 miles south, at the island's most westerly point. This wetland bird reserve is surrounded by fine beaches and is home to red-necked phalaropes and corncrakes as well as numerous migrant waders. The visitors centre (☎ 510372) provides leaflets and information from April to September. Peter Rabbit (yes, really) can take you on a 2½-hour guided walk in the reserve at 6.30pm on Tuesday and at 11.30am Thursday, May to August (adult/child £2.50/1).

About 2½ miles south is Bayhead (Ceann a Baigh), where you'll find **Uist Animal Visitors Centre** *(☎ 510706; adult/child £2.50/ 1.50; open noon-7pm daily)*, with Highland cattle, Scottish wildcats and Eriskay ponies.

Another 2½ miles south is **Claddach Kirkibost,** where you can check the Internet (£1 per 30 minutes) at the Claddach Kirkibost Centre (☎ 530390), open 9.30am to 5pm Monday to Friday.

The South

Heading southwards from Lochmaddy, the road passes through an area of swampy land with hundreds of tiny lochans and low heather-covered hills.

The chambered Neolithic burial tomb of **Bharpa Langass** stands on a desolate moor, 6 miles southwest of Lochmaddy. The huge cairn measures 24m in diameter and is believed to date back 5000 years. However, the inner chamber has collapsed and the cairn can no longer be entered.

Pobull Fhinn (Finn's People) is a dramatically situated stone circle of similar age accessible from a path beside Langass Lodge Hotel. A marked circular route from the hotel takes less than an hour and includes both sites.

Langass Lodge Hotel (☎ 580285, fax 580385, Locheport) 3-course bar meals £20. This fine old stone house is particularly noted for its food and sits among pine plantations. It does singles/doubles for £45/75.

On the west coast is Baleshare (Baile Sear) island, with fine beaches along the west shore; there's a friendly hostel just before the Baleshare bridge. **Clachan na Luib** village has a post office and shop, plus *Mermaid Fish Supplies (☎ 580209)* where you can buy delicious flaky smoked salmon.

Taigh mo Sheanair (☎ 580246, Claddach Baleshare) Bunks from £9, pitches £4.50 per person. This tastefully modernised crofthouse hostel is very homely.

Carinish Inn (☎ 580673, fax 580665, Carinish) En-suite singles/doubles/twins from £45/65/70. Open Mon-Sun. The modernised Carinish Inn has very good rooms and meals (from £5) and is recommended.

BENBECULA (BEINN NA FAOGHLA)
☎ 01870 ● pop 1883

Benbecula is plainer and less interesting than North Uist and most visitors put their foot down and drive straight across the island without stopping. A British army base takes up most of the west coast and jets still destroy the peace on a regular basis. The now vanished castle of Ormaclade was the ancestral seat of the Clanranald.

The main reason to visit is to take advantage of the facilities at **Balivanich** (Baile a'Mhanaich), the dormitory town for the army base, which has a hospital (☎ 603603), a post office, a bank (with ATM) and a large Spar supermarket. The Sgoil Lionacleit Leisure Centre (☎ 602211) is about 4 miles south of Balivanich, and has a swimming pool, games hall and sauna, plus an exhibition space for the Kildonan Museum, open Monday to Saturday in summer.

Places to Stay & Eat
Bàgh an T-Slige (☎ 602447, Liniclate) Pitches from £5 per person. Open Mar-Oct. You may find this camp site rather exposed.

Taigh na Cille Bunkhouse (☎ 602522, Balivanich) Dorm beds £10-11. The bunkhouse is near the little-used airport and is close to the causeway to North Uist.

Stepping Stone Restaurant (☎ 603377, Balivanich) Mains £5-9. This popular restaurant serves good food from pie, beans and chips to steamed halibut steak.

For entertainment, the *bar* at the airport is better than the dingy *Low Flyer (☎ 602426)* pub in Balivanich.

Dark Island Hotel (☎ 630030, fax 602347, Liniclate) Singles/doubles from £68/97. If you choose to stop on Benbecula, this comfortable hotel is a good choice.

Getting There & Around
There's one daily Loganair flight (except Sunday) to Glasgow, from £115 return. On weekdays, Highland Airways (☎ 01851-701282) flies to Stornoway on Lewis (£58/116 one-way/return). For bus details, see the North Uist Getting There & Away section earlier.

Maclennan Brothers Ltd (☎ 01870-602191) in Balivanich and Ask Car Hire (☎ 01870-602818) in Liniclate can both arrange car hire for under £30 per day.

SOUTH UIST (UIBHIST A DEAS)
☎ 01878 ● pop 2064

This flat and water-logged island is quite a shock after the spectacular topography of Skye or the Highlands, but the landscape has a lonely expansiveness that grows on you. The west coast is effectively a single sandy beach, backed by a splendid strip of machair. The east coast is broken by four large sea lochs, the most southerly of which contains the main settlement and ferry port, Lochboisdale. The scenery is particularly eye-catching at Polochar (Pol a'Charra).

In contrast to the northern Hebrides, many islanders on South Uist and Barra managed to retain their Catholic faith through the Reformation, despite the expulsion of Catholic priests in the 17th century. Keep an eye out for roadside shrines to Catholic saints. A number of Iron-Age wheelhouses were excavated on South Uist in the first half of the 20th century, but were subsequently filled-in by local farmers who regarded the ruins as a hazard for sheep.

The passenger ferry to Barra leaves from the island of Eriskay, joined to the tip of South Uist by Scotland's longest causeway.

Lochboisdale (Loch Baghasdail)
The rather uninspiring village of Loch boisdale has ferry links to Oban and Mallaig on the mainland and a seasonal TIC (☎ 700286), open 9am to 5pm Monday to Saturday from April to October, and for late ferry arrivals. Next door is a public toilet block with hot showers (50p). For ferry information phone CalMac on ☎ 700288. There's a branch of the Royal Bank of Scotland (no ATM), which can give cash advances on credit cards (open Monday to Friday). There are petrol stations and a decent *Co-op supermarket* 3 miles east at Daliburgh (Dalabrog), where the A856 turns north towards Benbecula.

Places to Stay & Eat *Bayview (☎ 700329, Lochboisdale)* B&B £18-20. Open Mar-Oct. This simple B&B is just around the bay from the TIC.

Brae Lea House (☎ 700497, Lasgair) En-suite B&B £25-30. This comfortable modern guesthouse is just north of the main road out of Lochboisdale, a mile west of the ferry.

Lochboisdale Hotel (☎ 700332, fax 700367, Lochboisdale) B&B £38-46.50. Bar meals £8-11. The slightly faded Lochboisdale Hotel, above the ferry terminal, caters mainly to anglers and cooks good pub food. Enquire here for angling permits and boat hire.

Past & Present Tearoom (☎ 700820) Snacks £3-5. Open daily. Right by the pier, this is a good place for a snack while you wait for the ferry.

Polochar Inn (☎ 700215, fax 700768, Polochar) En-suite singles/doubles/twins £35/55/60. Bar and restaurant meals £5-16. The Polochar Inn is a very comfortable hotel by a small beach on the way to Eriskay.

Getting There & Away Hebridean Coaches (☎ 01870-620345) does at least three daily runs (except Sunday) from Lochboisdale to Eriskay via Polochar. In the opposite direction, Hebridean and Mac-Donald Coaches (☎ 01870-620288) runs several times a day (except Sunday) to Lochmaddy on North Uist, via Howmore, Kildonan and Balivanich.

From Monday to Saturday, there are also several daily postbuses from Lochboisdale to the airport on Benbecula, and south to Eriskay.

For car hire, try Laing Motors (☎ 700267).

The North
The main road sticks close to the beach-lined west coast as it heads northwards to Benbecula. About 7 miles farther north is the excellent **Kildonan Museum** *(☎ 710343; adult/child £1.50/free; open 10am-5pm Mon-Sat & 2pm-5pm Sun Easter-Oct)* with interesting displays on the life and work of the islanders and the carved Clanranald Stone, which was stolen from its original location at Howmore in 1990 and rediscovered years later in a bedsit near Euston Station in London. The adjacent *cafe* serves basic snacks and meals from £1 to £4. Just before Kildonan, a small road leads west to Milton, the **birthplace of Flora MacDonald**; the house itself has vanished but a small cairn marks the spot.

If you leave the main road at Bornish (Bornais), a small lane passes a number of historic sites on the west coast, including an Iron-Age broch at Rubha Ardvule, a ruined 17th-century castle at Ormiclate and a dun at Loch Altabrug. There are tracks down to peaceful sections of beach all along this road.

Howmore (Tobha Mor)

Just north of Altabrug is the attractive old village of Howmore, which is home to some well-restored blackhouses and an excellent GHHT hostel. There are a few ruined medieval chapels in the vicinity of the hostel and a pretty beach just over the hill.

Tobha Mor Crofters' Hostel *(Howmore)* Dorm beds £6.50/5. The Gatliff Trust/SYHA hostel is near the church at the end of the village; there are three crofts here – the hostel is the stone-walled blackhouse in the middle.

Bicycle hire is available from Rothan Cycles (☎ 01870-620283), in the shed at the junction with the main road, for around £7 and there's a shop and petrol station just south on the main road.

Loch Druidibeg & Around

Two miles north of Howmore, the main road passes through the **Loch Druidibeg Nature Reserve**, which occupies a broad strip from the west coast all the way to Hecla (606m) on the east coast. SNH has an information office by the roadside at Stilligarry (☎ 620238), staffed Monday to Friday. The reserve is home to golden eagles, short-eared owls, greylag geese and red deer and bursts into colour every spring. There's a 5-mile self-guided trail (two hours), or a crude path from the hostel at Howmore along the northeastern ridge of **Beinn Mhor** (660m), looping back through the reserve (allow six hours).

Drimisdale House *(☎ 01870-620231, Drimisdale)* B&B £15 per person (£23 with dinner). Right by the reserve, this is a friendly and welcoming B&B.

North of the reserve, a short road leads east to **Our Lady of the Isles**, a slender white-granite statue at the base of the missile-tracking station at Rueval hill. At the **Salaar factory** *(☎ 01870-610324)*, a mile southeast of Orosay, you can buy the local delicacy of flaky smoked salmon.

Orasay Inn *(☎ 01870-610298, fax 610390, Lochcarnan)* En-suite singles/doubles from £36/60. Mains £6-17. The best place to eat in the Uists is the Orasay Inn, with excellent bar and restaurant meals, including lamb hotpots, salmon and scallops, and vegetarian dishes; rooms here are also very comfortable.

ERISKAY (EIRIOSGAIGH)

☎ 01878 ● pop 173

This tiny but beautiful island is where Bonnie Prince Charlie first set foot in Scotland, during the rebellion of 1745. The island is best known for the shipwreck of the SS *Politician*, which sank just off the coast in 1941 with a cargo of around 250,000 bottles of whisky. Local residents retrieved as much whisky as they could, embarking on a binge of dramatic proportions, which only ended when the police turned up and arrested a number of the revellers. The story was immortalised in good humour by Sir Compton Mackenzie in his book *Whisky Galore*, later turned into a film. The machair here is home to the rare sea convolvulus flowers said to have arrived as seed dropped from Bonnie Prince Charlie's pocket in 1745.

The **Catholic church** in Haunn (the northernmost settlement) uses the prow of a boat as its altar and there's a good view from **Ben Scrien** (186m). Look out for the distinctive semi-wild Eriskay ponies on the way.

The island has a grocery store, post office and pub.

Am Politician *(☎ 720246, Haunn)* Mains £5-7. Open 11am-8pm daily. The island's pub serves popular seafood meals; look for the red and white flag near the cemetery.

Getting There & Away

The passenger ferry to Barra (☎ 01878-701702) leaves from the new causeway in the south of Eriskay. There are two or three sailings Monday to Friday and one sailing on Saturday to Eoligarry/Ardveenish on Barra (passengers/bikes £5/2.50, one hour).

BARRA (BARRAIGH)

☎ 01871 ● pop 1212

Also known as the 'Island of Flowers', Barra is just 14 miles around and ideal for exploring on foot. With exceptional beaches, sculpted hills and a strong sense of community, Barra encapsulates the Western Isles experience, and the machair becomes a riot of colour in spring. Barra is the traditional home of the MacNeil clan, but the family fell on hard times and sold the island to the ruthless Gordon of Cluny in 1838, who embarked on a sadly familiar campaign of clearances. The MacNeils reacquired the island in 1937, ushering in more peaceful times. Barra still retains a strong Gaelic Catholic identity, largely due to its proximity to Ireland, and is famous for its cockles, which are still collected on Tràigh Mhor beach; also the island's runway.

The TIC (☎ 810336) in **Castlebay** (Bagh a'Chaisteil), the largest village, opens 9am to 5pm Monday to Saturday from April to October. More information on Barra is available on the island Web site at Ⓦ www .isleofbarra.com. Castlebay is attractively spread out along the coast and has a post office, a petrol station, a bank (no ATM), and Co-op and Spar supermarkets.

Barra comes to life every July during the **Feis Bharraidh**, a lively and popular festival of Gaelic music, song and dance. Accommodation during the festival should be booked well in advance.

CalMac (☎ 810306) has ferries between Castlebay and Lochboisdale (South Uist), Mallaig and Oban.

Things to See

On an islet in the bay at Castlebay, the historic **Kisimul Castle** *(HS; ☎ 810313, Castlebay; adult/child £3/1, including ferry; open 9.30am-6.30pm daily Apr-Sept)* occupies a romantic location. This classic medieval castle was built by the MacNeil clan in the 11th century, and gifted to Historic Scotland in 2000 for a nominal annual rent of £1 and a bottle of whisky. Tour prices include boat transfers from Castlebay.

The **Barra Heritage Centre** or **Dualchas** *(☎ 810413, Castlebay; adult/child £2/75p; open 11am-4pm Mon-Fri May-Sept, otherwise shorter hrs)* has Gaelic-theme displays, local art exhibitions and a tearoom. It also runs a restored **19th-century cottage** *(☎ 810413, Craigston, Borve; adult/child £2/75p; open 1pm-4pm Mon-Fri May-Sept)*, 3 miles north of Castlebay.

There are fine sandy beaches at the northern end of Barra, including the strands of **Tràigh Mhor**, where the plane from Glasgow lands. Inland is the ruin of **Cille Bharra** (St Barr's Chapel), a medieval church with some ancient grave-slabs and a cast of a Viking cross found in the grounds. The author Sir Compton MacKenzie was buried here in 1972. For dramatic views of the whole island, walk up to the top of Heaval (383m); the path starts about a mile northeast of Castlebay (allow two hours from the end of the road). Heading westwards from Castlebay, there are more nice beaches and the ruins of **MacLeod's tower**, an ancient seat of the MacLeods overlooking Loch St Clair.

Joined to the southern tip of Barra by a modern causeway, the tiny island of **Vatersay** (Bhatasaigh) has a narrow waist with fine sandy beaches on either side. At the start of the western beach (Tràigh Siar) is a monument to the *Annie Jane*, an emigrant ship en route from Liverpool to Quebec, which struck the rocks here in 1853. About 350 passengers and crew were drowned and buried at this lonely spot.

Places to Stay & Eat

***Dunard Hostel** (☎/fax 810443, Ⓔ dunard@ isleofbarrahostel.com, Castlebay)* Beds £10, twins & doubles £24-32. This friendly hostel is 150m west of the pier; sea kayak tours cost £12/18 per half-/full day.

There are just a handful of B&Bs scattered around the island and some ferries arrive late in the evening, so it's best to book ahead. Meals are available from the two hotels in town.

***Tigh-na-Mara Guest House** (☎ 810304, fax 810858, Castlebay)* B&B from £22. This attractive stone cottage is a two-minute walk from the ferry.

***Mrs Clelland** (☎ 810438, 47 Glen)* B&B from £18. Open year-round. Just half a mile from the pier, this is a decent B&B.

***Craigard Hotel** (☎ 810200, fax 810726, Castlebay)* En-suite B&B from £35. The comfortable Craigard Hotel is the prettier of the two hotels in Castlebay and serves excellent bar and restaurant meals (£6 to £12), including a catch of the day special and vegetarian dishes.

Northbay House *(☎/fax 890255, Bolna-bodach)* B&B £24-26. About four miles northeast of Castlebay, this wonderful old schoolhouse has pleasant rooms.

Kismul Galley *(☎ 810645, Castlebay)* Meals £4-7. Open daily. Kismul Galley, in the village centre, does tatties, light meals and good home-made soup.

At the northern end of the island, the ***airport tearoom*** does snacks.

Getting There & Away

British Airways (BA) Express flies to Barra from Glasgow from Monday to Saturday (from £99/138 one-way/return).

See Getting There & Away at the start of the Western Isles section for CalMac ferry details. The small passenger ferry (☎ 01878-701702) to the jetty at Eriskay operates two to four times daily Monday to Saturday, (passengers/bikes £5/2.50). This service is particularly vulnerable to the weather, so call ahead to make sure the boat is running.

Getting Around

There are several daily postbus services (☎ 0845 774 0740) around the island, connecting on to Vatersay and Eoligarry.

Barra Car Hire (☎ 810243) rents cars for around £20 per day and delivers to the ferry and airport. For bike hire, call Barra Cycle Hire (☎ 810284), which charges £8 per day.

PABBAY (PABAIDH) & MINGU-LAY (MIUGHALAIGH)

Off the southern tip of Vatersay are the now uninhabited islands of Sanday, Pabbay, Mingulay and Berneray, which were acquired by the NTS in 2001. These former crofting islands are home to large populations of seabirds and the remains of human settlements from the early 20th century.

Pabbay, roughly a mile across, was abandoned in 1912 and rises to dramatic cliffs at its southwestern tip, while Mingulay is larger, at 2 miles by a mile, and has towering cliffs, vast caves and natural arches on its western side. Boats land on the sheltered east coast, where there are remains of the last village on Mingulay, abandoned in 1908.

A trip to Mingulay, especially during the puffin season from June to early August, is highly recommended. ***George McLeod*** *(☎ 01871-810223, Castlebay, Barra)* sails to Mingulay (usually at weekends) for around £10/20 per person without/with landing, depending on weather and numbers.

ST KILDA

About 41 miles west of North Uist and exposed to the full ferocity of the Atlantic, St Kilda (Hiort) was one of the most remote settlements in Britain. A resilient group of Gaelic-speaking crofting families (known as the *hiortaich*) survived on these inhospitable volcanic stacks right up to the 1930s, when the last 36 residents were evacuated. Locals scraped a living here by keeping domesticated Soay sheep, fishing, growing a few basic crops, and climbing barefoot on the seacliffs to collect bird chicks and eggs, but the tradition of using fulmar oil on the umbilical cord of new-born babies killed about 80% of island children. Over the centuries the small genetic pool and the evolutionary pressures of barefoot climbing resulted in a genetic peculiarity – St Kildan men have unusually long big-toes.

Today, this World Heritage Site is owned by NTS and leased to SNH. There are four main islands, the largest and most dramatic being **Hirta**, with the derelict crofts and ancient chapel of the main settlement of *Am Baile* (the Village). Hirta measures only about 2 miles by a mile, but rises out of the sea with sheer cliffs on three sides and a broad scenic bay. From Conachair (430m), Britain's highest seacliff, there are splendid views of **Boreray** (384m) and the great rock towers of **Stac Lee** (172m) and **Stac an Armin** (196m). The islands are also home to Britain's largest colonies of gannets, puffins and fulmars. There never was a Saint Kilda; the name is probably a corruption of the Norse *skildir* meaning 'shields'.

Information

To find out more about St Kilda, visit online at Ⓦ www.kilda.org.uk. The island can only be visited with permission or on a tour; contact NTS for details (☎ 01631-570000).

Organised Tours

The NTS charges volunteers for doing archaeological and conservation work in and around the village ruins. Archaeology/restoration trips run from mid-May to mid-August; you have to work 36/24 hours per week, and the cost is £450/500 (including transport from Oban in a converted lifeboat, and full board in dorm accommodation). Volunteers must be fit and the minimum age is 18. There are 11 in each party, and the selection process takes place in February – for the following summer, get your application form from the NTS in November. Write to: St Kilda Work Parties, National Trust for Scotland, Lochvoil House, Dunuaran Rd, Oban, Argyll PA34 4NE.

Boat tours to St Kilda are expensive and usually only able to land on Hirta. *Guideliner Wildlife Cruises* (☎ 01631-720610, e info@guideliner.co.uk) offers excellent six-/12-day cruises through the Hebrides, stopping at St Kilda, for £550/1100 every summer. Another possibility is *Island Cruising* (☎ 01851-672381, e cuma@sol.co.uk), based in Uig, Lewis.

Getting There & Away

Apart from organised trips, the only access to St Kilda is by private boat, with permission from the NTS. Landing on all of the islands, except Hirta, is virtually impossible due to the ocean swell; even Hirta can be tough in a southerly to northeasterly wind.

The Northwest Highlands

The northwest Highlands are divided from the southern Highlands by a series of broad glens, opening to the sea at Loch Carron near Kyle of Lochalsh. The landscape to the north is wild and untamed, with rugged mountains and serene lochs reflecting the racing skies, and plenty of wide, empty, exhilarating spaces. This is one of Europe's last great wildernesses.

ORIENTATION

The most direct route from Inverness to the northwest is the A890, which cuts inland through Strathpeffer and Achnasheen, emerging at Glen Carron. The most dramatic countryside lies north of here between Ullapool and Durness, where there are dozens of Munros and *very* scenic walks. From Durness to Thurso, the landscape becomes low-lying and pastoral, turning into rolling fields at the northeastern tip of the country.

Most population centres are dotted along the coast and the exposed interior is still mostly uninhabited (in fact it's less inhabited than it used to be, due to the Highland Clearances and the efflux of Highlanders to the lowlands). The main settlements on the west coast are Ullapool and Gairloch, while Thurso is the principal town in the northeast and the gateway to Orkney.

INFORMATION

The Highlands of Scotland Tourist Board (☎ 01997-421160, ⓔ admin@host.co.uk, Ⓦ www.host.co.uk), Peffery House, Strathpeffer, Ross Shire IV14 9HA, publishes an invaluable free accommodation guide for the Highlands north of Glen Coe (including Skye and the Small Isles). There are tourist information centres (TICs) in all the major centres in the Highlands but many offices close during the low season or have shorter winter opening hours. The tourist board changes the location and opening times of its TICs from year to year – if may be worth calling ahead to check that local TICs are open before you visit.

Highlights

- Bag some of Scotland's finest Munros from the scenic village of Torridon
- Make the pretty coastal village of Ullapool your base for walks around scenic Loch Broom
- Visit the ancestral home of the notorious duke of Sutherland at magnificent Dunrobin Castle
- Hike to the remote, beautiful and supposedly haunted beach at Sandwood Bay, near Cape Wrath
- Go castle-spotting on the shore between Thurso and Wick
- Follow in the footsteps of the Picts on the Black Isle

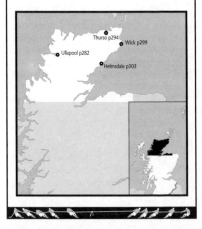

A useful guide to the archaeological heritage of the Highlands is *The Highlands* by Joanna Close-Brooks, part of the Royal Commission on the Ancient and Historical Monuments of Scotland.

The following Ordnance Survey (OS) Landranger maps cover the northwest Highlands:

Landranger 9: Cape Wrath, Durness & Scouries
Landranger 10: Strathnaver, Bettyhill & Tongue

THE NORTHWEST HIGHLANDS

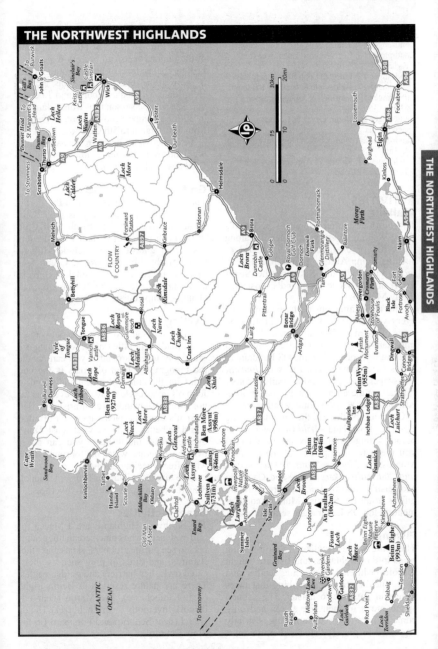

Landranger 11: Thurso & Dunbeath
Landranger 12: Thurso & Wick, John o'Groats
Landranger 15: Loch Assynt, Lochinver &
Kylesku
Landranger 16: Lairg & Loch Shin, Loch Naver
Landranger 17: Helmsdale & Stath of Kildonan
Landranger 19: Gairloch & Ullapool, Loch
Maree
Landranger 20: Beinn Dearg & Loch Broom,
Ben Wyvis
Landranger 21: Dornoch & Alness, Invergordon
& Tain
Landranger 24: Raasay & Applecross, Loch
Torridon & Plockton

ACTIVITIES
Walking
The northwest offers some of Scotland's finest walking country, whether it's along the coast, or on inland peaks and ridges such as Beinn Alligin, Liathach, An Teallach, Stac Pollaidh, Suilven (the Sugar Loaf) or Ben Hope (Scotland's most northerly Munro).

The mountains can be treacherous and every year some walkers come unstuck on some of the more difficult ascents. The most important thing to carry is a decent map, and you can't get better than the OS Landranger series (see above). The *Press & Journal* newspaper contains a useful daily weather forecast, or there's a mountain weather forecast online at W www.onlineweather.com.

Campers should read the Mountaineering Council of Scotland's *Wild Camping* leaflet before setting up in someone's paddock. If you mean to attempt any of the region's Munros, *The Munros: Scottish Mountaineering Club Hillwalkers Guide* and Cameron McNeish's *Munro Almanac* are portable guides to all the Scottish Munros, complementing the OS Landranger series of maps.

Fishing
There are some excellent salmon-fishing beats in the Highlands, and fish are caught the old-fashioned way, using feather and wire 'flies' as bait – something that takes time and patience to master. The salmon spend much of their life at sea and only come inshore to breed, so fishing is strictly regulated to preserve stocks. Permits must

be obtained from the estate-owners – usually arranged through hotels or TICs – and some of the famous beats can be very expensive. Fishing for sea trout or brown trout in lochs is more affordable. Popular spots include Helmsdale, Gairloch, Scourie and Lochinver. The salmon season runs from 1 January to 30th September; brown trout are caught from 15th March to 5th October.

Visit the Web site at W www.fishing-highland.co.uk for more info on fishing in Caithness and Sutherland.

Golf
There are some fine courses in the northwest with dramatic scenery as their main attraction. The Royal Dornoch Golf Club in Dornoch is one of Britain's finest courses. Other good courses include Muir of Ord, Strathpeffer and Brora. Green fees range from £10 to £15 at smaller clubs to a whopping £45 at the Royal Dornoch championship course.

Cycling
The Highlands are covered by a network of small roads with little traffic, so cycling is a great way to get around if you can handle the topography. John o'Groats is the end point for the epic 874-mile Land's End to John o'Groats cycle route. However, the far northwest Highlands are surprisingly flat, so if it's dramatic landscapes you're after, you'd be better off on the west coast. Don't over estimate the distance you can cover over the glens and watch out for rogue sheep when free-wheeling downhill!

Bike hire is available in Thurso, Ullapool, Rogart and Lairg, or nearby in Inverness.

Other Activities
The northwest Highlands are a Mecca for bird-watchers, who come here in huge numbers to see puffins, fulmars, skuas and other seabirds, and birds of prey such as short-eared owls, hen harriers and golden eagles. There are nature reserves at Beinn Eighe (near Kinlochewe), Isle Martin (near Ullapool), Inverpolly (near Lochinver), Handa Island (near Scourie) and Forsinard (in the Flow Country).

Thurso has good surf, but the Isle of Lewis is better (see the Skye & the Western Isles chapter). Pony trekking and deer stalking are other popular activities.

GETTING AROUND

Buses and trains run from Inverness across the Highlands to Kyle of Lochalsh and Ullapool, with bus connections all along the west coast. There are also regular bus and train connections from Inverness up the coast to Wick and Thurso. For places inland, you'll have to rely on infrequent local buses and postbuses. It's worth hiring a car in Inverness if you want to explore the Firthlands or any of the rugged interior.

With the exception of the Firthlands, the east coast is a little busy for cycling, but the northwest is wonderful cycling country; bike hire is available in Thurso and Wick.

Bus

Wick, Thurso and Ullapool can all be reached by bus from Inverness or Kyle of Lochalsh. Local bus companies provide linking services all around the coast from Kyle of Lochalsh to Inverness. Transport along the east coast is easy year-round with the regular Citylink buses, but the north and west coast can be quite a struggle from October to May.

Starting from Loch Carron, the MacLennan bus service (☎ 01520-755239) runs from Strathcarron to Torridon once daily Monday to Friday from June to September, otherwise Monday, Wednesday and Friday only; postbuses continue on to Applecross.

Westerbus (☎ 01445-712255) has a once daily (except Sunday) service between Inverness and Gairloch, via Dundonnell (Monday, Wednesday and Saturday) or Kinlochewe and Loch Maree (Tuesday, Thursday and Friday). The route via Dundonnell provides a link between Ullapool and Gairloch (via Braemore Junction). Westerbus also runs every Thursday year-round between Ullapool and Gairloch direct, and has local services to Red Point and Melvaig; postbuses also cover this last route.

There are two Scottish Citylink (☎ 08705-505050) buses daily except Sunday between

Inverness and Ullapool (£6.50, 1½ hours), via Contin, Garve and Braemore Junction, where you can change for buses south. From June to September, Tim Dearman Coaches (☎ 01349-883585) runs buses once daily except Sunday on the same route, continuing on to Durness via Lochinver, Kylesku, Scourie and Kinlochbervie.

Between June to September there are daily (except Sunday) Highland Country/Rapsons (☎ 01847-893123) buses from Durness to Thurso, via Bettyhill and Melvich, leaving Thurso at 11.30am (£7.25, 2½ hours) and returning from Durness at 3pm. At other times, services just run as far as Bettyhill. You can also connect from Durness to Inverness through Lairg, continuing southwards on the Monday to Saturday Stagecoach Inverness buses (☎ 01463-239292) or daily train services to Inverness.

Between Thurso and Wick there are daily Scottish Citylink and very regular Highland Country/Rapsons buses; the latter company also has buses to John o'Groats (from Thurso and Wick; three or four daily except Sunday) and Helmsdale (from Wick; four daily except Sunday). Citylink buses continue on from Wick to Inverness via Helmsdale, Brora, Dornoch, Tain and Evanton. The area north of Inverness is served by Highland Country/Rapsons and Stagecoach Inverness (☎ 01463-239292).

Train

There are two Highland railway lines from Inverness – up the east coast to Wick and Thurso, and west to Kyle of Lochalsh. You can use the Kyle of Lochalsh line to reach Garve (for Ben Wyvis), Invershin (for the Carbisdale youth hostel) and Strathcarron, a jumping-off point for Applecross and Torridon. The Thurso line includes stops at Beauly, Dingwall, Tain, Lairg, Golspie, Dunrobin Castle, Brora, Helmsdale, Forsinard Nature Reserve and Wick. For rail information phone ☎ 0845 748 4950 or see the Web site at W www.scotrail.co.uk.

Postbuses

Postbuses operate throughout the Highlands and charge from 40p to £4 for passengers, providing access to many smaller villages that buses don't serve. Postbuses only run Monday to Saturday but there are services year-round.

Currently, there are daily return services on the following postbus routes (most leave early in the morning, returning in the early afternoon):

Alligin to Kinlochewe, via Torridon
Applecross to Torridon, via Shieldaig
Red Point to Melvaig, via Badachro and Gairloch
Lochinver to Drumbeg, via Achmelvich and Stoer
Drumbeg to Lairg, via Lochinver, Inchnadamph, Elphin and Ledmore Junction
Scourie to Lochinver, via Kylesku
Scourie to Tarbet, via Fanagmore
Durness to Lairg, via Kinlochbervie and the Cape Wrath Hotel
Durness to Lairg, via Tongue and Altnaharra (returning via Dun Dornadilla)
Tongue to Lairg, via Altnaharra
Bettyhill to Thurso, via Melvich
Bettyhill to Tongue
Thurso to Tongue
John o'Groats to Wick
Ardgay to Strathoykel, via Carbisdale SYHA hostel
Dingwall to Strathpeffer
Shieldaig to Strathcarron, via Lochcarron

Postbus routes change frequently, so it's worth calling the Royal Mail helpline on ☎ 0845 774 0740 or checking the Royal Mail Web site for the latest situation – W www.royalmail.co.uk/postbus.

Car Hire
Renting a car is an excellent way to get around the area. Car hire is available in Wick and Thurso.

Wester Ross

Wester Ross stretches roughly from Applecross to just south of Lochinver and includes some of the Highlands' best-loved peaks, including Beinn Eighe, An Teallach, Stac Pollaidh and Suilven. It's less than 50 miles as the crow flies from Kyle of Lochalsh to Ullapool, but it's more like 150 miles along the circuitous coastal road, with fine views of beaches and bays, backed by mountains all the way.

STRATHCARRON TO ACHNASHELLACH
The scenic route, or rather the *more* scenic route, from Kyle of Lochalsh to Inverness passes along the edge of Loch Carron, turning inland at **Strathcarron** which has a train station and the inviting *Strathcarron Hotel (☎/fax 01520-722227, Strathcarron)* that offers singles/doubles for £32.50/56 and free camping. It also does good pub meals (mains from £6).

Heading up Glen Carron towards Inverness you'll come to the little village of **Achnashellach**, which has a railway station and is surrounded by woodland with some delightful **forest walks**.

Gerry's Hostel (☎ 01520-766232, Craig Achnashellach) Bunkhouse beds £9. This quiet little hostel is very homely and well located for walks in the hills.

LOCHCARRON
☎ 01520 ● pop 871
This appealing white-washed village is on the northern shore of Loch Carron, at the foot of Maol Chean Dearg (933m). Lochcarron has supermarkets, a bank (with an ATM), a post office, petrol and a golf course. The TIC (☎ 722357) opens 10am to 5pm Monday to Saturday year-round.

The village is a good base for hillwalking; Maol Chean Dearg is the most obvious objective, but the peaks around the Bealach na Ba pass on the way to Applecross are more accessible. Ask the TIC or the hotels for details of trails.

While here, it's worth visiting the **Smithy Heritage Centre** *(☎ 766229, Locharron; admission free; open 10am-5.30pm Apr-Oct)* on the main road, or **Lochcarron Weavers** *(☎ 722212, Locharron; admission free; open 9am-5pm Mon-Sat Easter-Oct)* on the way to Strome, where you can watch tartan being made (weekdays only).

At the tip of the headland south of Lochcarron are the ruins of **Strome Castle**, a

MacDonald fort that was demolished in 1601 during a siege by the rival MacKenzie's.

There are lots of places to stay in Lochcarron, including:

Old Bank House (☎ 722332, fax 722780, Main St) B&B with shared bathroom £25. This comfortable B&B is housed in the same red-sandstone building as the Bank of Scotland, near the turn-off to Strome Castle.

Rockvilla Hotel (☎ 722379, fax 722844, Main St) Singles £32-40, doubles £44-60. Bar meals £6-11. The Rockvilla is the better of Lochcarron's two hotels and the restaurant here serves up great seafood.

APPLECROSS
☎ 01520

This wonderfully remote village is surrounded by bare crags, and offers tremendous views across to the Isle of Raasay. The shortest route from Lochcarron passes over the Bealach na Ba pass (626m), a narrow slot between two 700m peaks, making for one of the most scenic drives in the Highlands. However, even light snow will close this route so you may have to take the slow coastal road via Shieldaig, which will add an extra 25 miles to the journey.

Applecross is a great base for walking and there are a number of well-signposted woodland tracks around Applecross bay. **Mountain & Sea Guides** (☎ 744393) runs a variety of adventure activities in the area, including guided mountaineering (£15 for two hours) and sea kayaking (£12 for two hours). The sound between Applecross and Raasay is a natural wind-funnel so wrap up warmly for walks. From Monday to Saturday, there's a once-daily postbus from Torridon.

Applecross has a hotel, a petrol station and a post office/shop.

Places to Stay
Applecross Hotel (☎ 744262, fax 744400, Shore St) B&B from £25 (£30 en suite) per person. This friendly little family-run hotel is the heart of the local community with some of the best pub meals (from £7 to £11) in the west and a truly welcoming bar.

Applecross Camp Site & Flower Tunnel (☎/fax 744628, winter ☎ 744284) Pitches from £9. Open Easter-Oct. Above Applecross on the Bealach na Ba road, this camp site also has a licensed pizza restaurant (pizzas £4 to £7.50) in a flower-covered conservatory.

There are several family-run B&Bs in the villages of Camusteel and Camusterrach, just south of Applecross.

Bracken Hill (☎ 744206, Camusterrach) B&B £16-20 per person. Mrs Dickens offers comfortable rooms in this house near the school in Camusterrach.

Caol Mor (☎ 744454, Camusteel) B&B from £18. Down by the shore in Camusteel, Mrs McPartlin's B&B is a good choice.

KISHORN & SHIELDAG
Over the headland, at the mouth of Loch Kishorn, **Kishorn** village has a general store and post office, plus a good seafood restaurant.

Kishorn Seafood & Snack Bar (☎ 733240, Kishorn) Dishes from £2-10. This is a great, economic place to sample the local scallops, langoustines and lobster.

The A896 continues north to **Shieldaig**, with its shorefront avenue of white-washed houses, where there's a shop, post office, and a free camp site. From here, a single-track road runs all the way round the headland to Applecross. Duncan McLennan (☎ 755239) provides a bus service between Shieldaig and the railway station at Strathcarron from Monday to Saturday (May to October only), or there's a postbus to Lochcarron and Strathcarron via Kishorn (Monday to Saturday).

Tigh an Eilean Hotel (☎ 755251, fax 755321, Shieldaig) Singles/doubles £49.50/55. The rooms at this hotel are attractive, if pricey. Bar meals are available from £6.

Rivendell Guest House (☎ 755250, Shieldaig) B&B from £16.50 per person. Just down the road, this large guesthouse is good value.

Tigh Fada (☎ 755248; 117 Doireaonar) B&B from £15. Run by Mrs Calcott, this pleasant and well-maintained B&B is set in peaceful woodland on the Applecross road.

TORRIDON
☎ 01445 ● pop 198

In the shadow of the mighty Liathach ridge (1055m), Torridon is an understandably popular base for hill-walkers. There are numerous Munros in the area, including Liathach and the multiple peaks of Beinn Eighe (972–993m) to the northeast, Beinn Alligin (922–986m) to the northwest and Maol Chean Dearg (933m) to the south. There are plenty of less energetic walks around Loch Torridon.

If Munro bagging isn't *your* bag, there is an National Trust for Scotland (NTS) **Countryside Centre** *(☎ 01445-791221, Torridon; adult/child £1.50/1; open 10am-5pm Mon-Sat & 2pm-5pm Sun May-Sept)* with nature displays and an unstaffed **Deer Museum** *(open year-round)*.

A single-track road heads west from Torridon through a landscape of knobbly crags to the village of Diabaig, which clings perilously to the hillside above a small beach. There's a remote SYHA hostel about 3 miles beyond Diabaig, on the popular walking trail to the headland at Red Point.

There are buses to Torridon daily except Sunday from Applecross and Kinlochewe, plus an early-morning postbus.

Places to Stay & Eat

Camp Site (☎ 791313) Pitches £4. This campsite has good showers and is just opposite the Countryside Centre.

Torridon Youth Hostel (☎ 01445-791284) Beds £9/7.75. Open Mar-Oct. This modern, 60-bed SYHA hostel, next to the camp site is well maintained.

Loch Torridon Country House Hotel (☎ 791242, fax 791296, e *stay@lochtorridonhotel.com)* Singles £55-90, doubles £88-260, both en suite. This spectacular hotel is one of the finest country houses in Scotland. The building – complete with its own clocktower – is wonderful, and the interior is everything you'd expect from a country-house hotel. All sorts of activities are available, including clay-pigeon shooting, sea kayaking, fishing and archery.

Ben Damph Lodge (☎ 791242, fax 791296) This hotel has good-value bar meals from around £5 (March to October).

Mrs Ross (☎ 790240, Croft No 3, Diabaig) B&B £17 per person. This crofthouse B&B is on the road down to the beach at Diabaig and has lovely views.

KINLOCHEWE
☎ 01445 ● pop 107

This pleasant wee village sits at the junction of the A896 and the A832, which runs west to Gairloch and east over the glens to Strathpeffer. There's a small outdoor supplies shop – *MORU (☎ 760322)* – plus a hotel, petrol station and shop/post office that runs a cafe in summer. There's a free camp site just north of the village.

Walkers Lodge Bunkhouse (☎ 720253, fax 720240, Achnasheen) Bunkhouse beds £10. Owned by the Ledgowan Lodge Hotel, the Walkers Lodge bunkhouse is a good base for treks; you'll need to bring your own linen or sleeping bag.

Hillhaven (☎ 760204, fax 720240, Kinlochewe) En-suite B&B £25 per person. This excellent friendly B&B is run by a couple who keep birds of prey.

Kinlochewe Hotel (☎ 760253, e *kinlochewehotel@tinyworld.co.uk, Kinlochewe)* Bunkhouse beds £8, B&B without/with bathroom £22.50/25 per person. Although ageing, this hotel is still good value, and serves OK meals from £5.

Cromasaig (☎ 760234, fax 760333, e *cromasaig@msn.com, Torridon Rd)* B&B from £20. This well set-up B&B is about a mile back towards Torridon and caters to vegetarians (dinner from £13). The trail up Beinn Eighe starts nearby.

East of Kinlochewe, the single-track A832 continues to Achnasheen, where there's a train station and useful bunkhouse.

Ledgowan Lodge Hotel (☎ 720252, fax 720240, Achnasheen) En-suite singles £35-40, doubles £62-98. Open Apr-Oct. This friendly old-fashioned hunting lodge has an aquarium and an attractively remote location. Bar meals are available for £6 to £9.

BEINN EIGHE & LOCH MAREE

This vast Scottish Natural Heritage (SNH) reserve covers 11,800 acres of high ground overlooking beautiful Loch Maree and was

Britain's first National Nature Reserve (NNR). Within the reserve are a few Munros, including the multiple peaks of Beinn Eighe (972–993m) and Sgurr Ban (989m). The lower slopes of the massifs are covered in woodland, with alpine plants such as dwarf willow and the appealingly named prostrate juniper. Golden eagles and pine martens are sometimes seen. The SNH runs the **Beinn Eighe Visitor Centre** (*☎ 01445-760258, Kinlochewe; admission free; open daily Easter-Oct*) on the shore of Loch Maree, with details on local geography, geology, ecology, and walking routes.

If you don't feel up to tackling the Munros, there are two shorter walking trails that begin about a mile beyond the visitor centre, with interpretive noticeboards about the plants and animals in the reserve; the car park for the trails is signposted 'Glas Leitir Trails'.

The A832 runs alongside **Loch Maree**, before turning back out towards the coast at Slattadale, where there are more walks and a forest information point. The views along this stretch of road are stupendous, with the wave-lapped loch in the foreground and mighty peaks, including 980m-high Slioch on the far shore. The Victoria Falls (commemorating Queen Victoria's 1877 visit) tumble down to the loch through forestry land between Slattadale and Talladale. The turn-off to the falls is marked 'Hydro Power'.

There are several places to stay along the shores of Loch Maree.

Campers (tents only) can use the free SNH *camp site* at Taagan Farm, on the A832 about 500m west of the visitor centre.

Loch Maree Hotel (*☎ 760288, fax 760241, Slattadale*) Singles/doubles from £40/70. Open Easter-Oct. This period hotel still proudly displays the coat of arms from when Queen Victoria stayed here in 1877, and offers comfortable rooms in a great location.

Slattadale House (*☎ 712334*) B&B from £22-25. This delightful B&B is located down by the shore near the forest information point at Slattadale and has lovely views across the loch.

GAIRLOCH
☎ 01445 ● pop 1061

Gairloch is actually a group of pretty villages, comprising Charlestown, Auchtercairn and Strath, clustered around the inner end of Gair Loch, though it would be nicer without all the B&B signs. Tourism has come to Gairloch in a big way and there are many places to stay spread out along the loch. The surrounding area is noted for its sandy beaches, good trout fishing and birdwatching. Hill-walkers use Gairloch as a base for the Torridon hills and the Munros of Cnoc Breac (962m) and An Cuiadh (972m).

Coming from Loch Maree, the first village you reach is Charlestown, where you'll find Gairloch harbour and a post office. Farther around the bay, beyond the cemetery and golf club, is Auchtercairn, where a road branches off to the main centre at Strath.

The TIC (*☎ 712130*), at the car park in Auchtercairn, opens 10am to 5pm Monday to Saturday Easter to October (and on Sunday from June to September). It has a bureau de change. Across the A832 is a Mace supermarket and there are shops and a post office in Strath. If you need cash, there's a bank (with an ATM) between Auchtercairn and Charlestown. For a doctor, call the Auchtercairn health centre on ☎ 712229.

Things to See

The excellent **Gairloch Heritage Museum** (*☎ 712287, Achtercairn; adult/child £2.50/50p; open 10am-5pm Mon-Sat Apr-Sept, 10am-1.30pm Mon-Sat Oct*), near the TIC, has all sorts of interesting displays on life in the West Highlands from Pictish times to the present. There's a *cafe* and *restaurant* onsite too.

By the harbour in Charlestown, the **Gairloch Marine Life Centre** (*☎ 712636, Pier Rd, Charlestown; admission free; typically open 9.30am-4pm Mon-Fri, noon-3.30pm Sat & Sun Easter-Sept*) has audiovisual and interactive displays, lots of charts and photos and knowledgeable staff.

Organised Tours

Wild Exposure Guided Walks (*☎ 741717, [W] www.wildexpo.co.uk*) £19 per day. Wild

Exposure offers guided hikes up local Munros such as Beinn Alligin.

Kerry Sea Angling (☎ *712458*) £15 per person. Based at the Kerry Chandlery by the harbour, Kerry Sea Angling offers daily fishing trips from the pier in summer; prices include bait and fishing tackle.

Gairloch Marine Cruises (☎ *712636*) Adult/child £14/12; 3 daily trips Easter-Sept. This company, based at the Marine Life Centre, organise sea cruises from The Pier, Charlestown; during the two-hour trip you may see basking sharks, porpoises and Minke whales.

Places to Stay & Eat

There are lots of places to stay in Gairloch. Call the TIC for details of self-catering options in the area.

Gairloch Holiday Park (☎ *712373, Mihol Rd, Strath)* Single/double tents £5.50/7.50. This well-maintained site is just uphill from the Millcroft Hotel in Strath.

Newton House (☎ *712007, Mihol Rd, Strath)* B&B from £12.50. Close to the camp site, this friendly independent B&B is great value.

Duisary (☎*/fax 712252, 24 Strath)* B&B £16-20. Open Apr-Oct. Run by Mrs Mac-Kenzie, Duisary is a fine B&B, but only one room is en suite.

Bains House (☎ *712472, Strath)* B&B £16-22. This attractive cottage on the main road in Strath has nice rooms.

The Old Inn (☎ *712006, fax 712445, Charlestown)* En-suite B&B from £25. This attractive old pub offers unpretentious rooms and good hearty meals (£6 to £13).

Myrtle Bank Hotel (☎ *712004, fax 712214, Low Rd)* En-suite singles/doubles £36/72. Down by the shore in Strath, this is a tidy modern hotel with decent bar meals (£7 to £11).

Millcroft Hotel (☎ *712376, fax 712091, Strath)* Singles/doubles £28/42. The Italian-run Millcroft Hotel has good en-suite rooms and one of the few Italian restaurants in the Highlands; pasta and pizzas from £5 to £9.

Mountain Lodge & Restaurant (☎ *712316)* Singles/doubles/twins £27.50/36/38. Open Mar-Oct. Right by the ocean, this place has a coffee shop (serving great coffee), a guesthouse and a shop selling new-age stuff and mountaineering books.

Getting There & Away

Bus services in the Gairloch area are run by Westerbus (☎ 712255), based at the petrol station in Charlestown. Buses run to Inverness Monday to Saturday, via Poolewe, Dundonnell and Braemore Junction, where you can pick up a Citylink bus to Ullapool (buses run via Kinlochewe on Tuesday, Thursday and Friday). There are also weekday buses and morning postbuses to Melvaig (from where you can walk to the hostel at Rubha Reidh – see the Around Gairloch section) and Red Point, via Badachro.

Around Gairloch

North of Gairloch is a rocky and exposed peninsula, dominated by the massive bulk of Cnoc Breac (962m) and An Cuiadh (972m). A single-track road runs from Strath around the headland to Melvaig and finally up to the lighthouse at Rubha Reidh, which also doubles as a splendidly remote hostel. Closer to Gairloch, there's an SYHA hostel at Carn Dearg.

Carn Dearg Youth Hostel (☎ *712219, by Gairloch)* Beds from £9.50/8.25. Open mid-May–Sept. The SYHA hostel is 3 miles west of Gairloch, on the road to Melvaig – you can get here on the Westerbus or postbus service to Melvaig.

Rua Reidh Lighthouse Hostel (☎ *771263, e ruareidh@netcomuk.co.uk, by Melvaig)* Beds £8, twins & doubles from £10 per person. At the end of the road, 13 miles from Gairloch, this excellent hostel will give you a taste of the lighthouse-keeper's life. Facilities are excellent and the food isn't bad either (dinner £9; meals should be booked in advance). Buses and postbuses run as far as Melvaig.

About 3 miles south of Gairloch, a narrow roads leads to the village of Badachro, where there's a great pub and a bunkhouse, and Red Point, where a walking trail heads southwards to Diabaig and Torridon. Two Westerbus services run from Gairloch to Red Point every weekday.

Badachro Bunkhouse (☎ *07760-3400 08/07909-946449, Badachro)* Bunks £8.50. This stone cottage offers no-frills bunkhouse accommodation.

Badachro Inn (☎ *741255, Badachro)* Meals under £8. Open lunch & dinner daily. This attractive pub on the waterfront is a great spot for a pub lunch.

POOLEWE
☎ 01445

At the head of broad Loch Ewe, the village of Poolewe is warmed by the waters of the Gulf Stream, which allowed Osgood MacKenzie to build a subtropical garden on a peninsula just north of here in 1862. Apart from the gardens, there isn't much to see, but there are nice walks in the area.

About a mile north of the village, the splendid **Inverewe Gardens** *(NTS; ☎ 781200, Poolewe; adult/child £5/4, free Oct-May; open 9.30am-sunset daily)* provide a welcome dash of colour to an otherwise bleak stretch of coast. Plants were gathered from as far afield as Australia, Chile and China and there are free guided tours at 1.30pm on weekdays (March to October) plus a pleasant garden restaurant.

There's a pretty low-level walk along the banks of the River Ewe to nearby Loch Kernsary, offering excellent views of Slioch and other lofty peaks (three hours). With a bit more time, you can head southwest along the shores of Loch Maree towards Gairloch.

Poolewe Hotel (☎ *781241, fax 781405, Poolewe)* B&B from £30 per person. This down-to-earth hotel has decent rooms and good pub meals (from £9).

Bridge Cottage Café (☎ *604644, 29 Bridge St, Poolewe)* This pleasant coffee shop serves up real coffee and cakes from Easter to October.

DUNDONNELL & AROUND
☎ 01854 ● pop 169

Between Braemore and Poolewe there is but lots of magnificent scenery with relatively few houses. The tiny hamlet of Dundonnell crouches at the foot of intimidating **An Teallach** (1062m); the summit can be reached by a path starting less than 500m southeast of the Dundonnell Hotel.

There's a small ***camp site*** just before Badcaul (pitches from £5).

Sail Mhor Croft Hostel (☎/fax *633224,* e *sailmhor@btinternet.com, Camasnagaul)* Dorm beds £9. About 1½ miles west of Dundonnell, this stone cottage is a popular base for climbers on a budget.

Dundonnell Hotel (☎ *633204, fax 633366, Dundonnell)* En-suite B&B with £60. This is a very cosy choice and there's a good restaurant (bar meals £6 to £11; three-course dinner around £28) and an extremely welcoming bar – just what you need after climbing An Teallach.

From Dundonnell, a single-track road runs cuts north and west along the Scoraig peninsula to Badrallach, a tiny village on the shores of Loch Broom.

Badrallach Bothy (☎ *633281,* e *michael .stott2@virgin.net, Croft No 9 Badrallach)* Sleeping bag space £3, pitches £3 per person, B&B £15 per person. Near the loch about 7 miles from Dundonnell, Badrallach Bothy has a range of accommodation for lovers of peace and quiet.

Just west of Dundonnell, in the middle of Gruinard Bay, is **Gruinard Island**, which became famous after being contaminated with anthrax spores as part of a biological-weapons test in WWII. After extensive treatment with formaldehyde in the 1990s, the island was declared safe.

BRAEMORE & AROUND

The A832 meets the main Inverness to Ullapool road (A835) at Braemore Junction, which is surrounded by the remains of the Braemore and Inverlael Forests. By the junction are the spectacular **Falls of Measach**, which spill 45m into the eerily deep and narrow Corrieshalloch Gorge. You can cross from on a wobbly suspension bridge, built by Sir John Fowler of Braemore.

Braemore Square (☎ *01854 655357, Loch Broom)* B&B £16-22. This charming B&B is housed in the wonderful stone gatehouse to Sir John's estate, just off the A835.

Heading southeastwards from Braemore junction, the A835 continues over wild

Dirrie More to the Glascarnoch dam, with great views of Beinn Dearg on the way. This section is sometimes closed by snow in winter.

Citylink buses operate from Inverness to Ullapool twice daily except Sunday.

ULLAPOOL
☎ 01854 ● pop 1370

This pretty fishing village is the largest settlement in Wester Ross and was named after a Viking noble; the old name, Ulla-Bolsadr means 'Ulla's farmstead'. The village was planned by the important-sounding British Society for Extending the Fisheries and Improving the Sea Coasts of the Kingdom of Great Britain, who laid out the grid pattern of streets in 1788. The land originally belonged to the McLeods and MacKenzies of Easter Ross but was ceded to the crown after the 1745 rebellion.

At the height of the herring boom, hundreds of 'dipping luggers' plied the waters around Loch Broom, but the 'silver darlings' eventually vanished from the loch after WWII. Ullapool found a new lease of life as a mackerel-fishing station, attracting dozens of Eastern Bloc factory ships until the collapse of the Soviet Union. Today there are only about 12 local boats, fishing mostly for prawns, lobsters and scallops.

Although it's a popular stop on the tourist circuit, Ullapool still has heaps of charm and is an excellent base for exploring the west coast. There are good walks in the area, plus some excellent places to stay and regular transport links to other parts of the Highlands. Ferries sail from Ullapool to Stornoway on the Isle of Lewis daily except Sunday.

Orientation & Information

You'll find most of the pubs and places to stay in Ullapool along Shore St, which runs along the waterfront, and Quay St, which runs uphill from the ferry terminal. The helpful TIC (☎ 612135, ⓔ ullapool@host.co.uk) is at 6 Argyle St, one street back from the waterfront, and opens 9am to 5.30pm Monday to Saturday and 10am to 4pm Sunday (1.30pm to 4pm Monday to Friday October to March). The TIC sells a good 'Around Lochbroom' guide (£1.50) with details of local walks and activities.

There are ATMs at the Royal Bank of Scotland on the corner of Ladysmith and Argyle Sts, and at the Bank of Scotland on

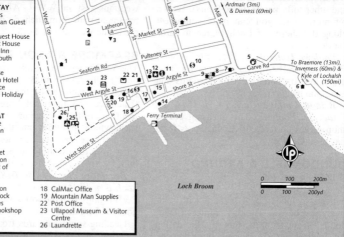

ULLAPOOL

PLACES TO STAY
1 Sea Breezes
4 Eilean Donan Guest House
6 Sheiling Guest House
7 Brae Guest House
8 Ferry Boat Inn
9 Ullapool Youth Hostel
20 West House
21 Caledonian Hotel
24 Ceilidh Place
25 Broomfield Holiday Park

PLACES TO EAT
3 Jade House
17 Seaforth Inn

OTHER
2 Supermarket
5 Petrol Station
10 Royal Bank of Scotland
11 TIC
12 Police Station
13 Ullapool Clock
14 Boat Cruises
15 Ullapool Bookshop
16 Bank of Scotland
18 CalMac Office
19 Mountain Man Supplies
22 Post Office
23 Ullapool Museum & Visitor Centre
26 Laundrette

Ardmair (3mi) & Durness (69mi)

To Braemore (13mi), Inverness (60mi) & Kyle of Lochalsh (150mi)

Ferry Terminal

Loch Broom

0   100   200m
0   100   200yd

Warning

The Esso service station on Garve Rd in Ullapool is the last petrol station in the northwest that still sells leaded petrol. If your car runs on leaded fuel, lead-replacement fuel additives are available which will allow your engine to run safely on unleaded fuel.

West Argyle St, or you can change money at some of the souvenir shops on Shore St. The post office is on West Argyle St and there's a handy laundrette at the camp site on Shore St. *The Ullapool Bookshop* (☎ 612356) opposite the Seaforth Inn on Quay St is excellent and has loads of books on Scottish topics. For outdoor equipment, try *Mountain Man Supplies* (☎ 613323), near the museum.

Things to See

The **Ullapool Museum & Visitor Centre** (☎ 612987, 7-8 West Argyle St; adult/student/child £2/1.50/free; open 9.30am-5.30pm Mon-Sat Mar-Oct, 11am-3pm Wed, Thur & Sat Nov-Feb) is in a converted Telford Parliamentary church. An audio-visual presentation, interactive exhibits and various other displays chart the history of Loch Broom and its people.

The curious and ornate **Ullapool Clock**, at the junction of Quay and Argyle Sts, was erected in 1899 in honour of Sir John Fowler of Braemore.

About 2½ miles north of Ullapool is the prehistoric settlement of **Rhue**, first inhabited during the Bronze Age. All that remains are several circles of stones in the heather, but it's a pleasant walk here from Ullapool (follow the signs for Rhue from the A835). See the boxed text 'Walking Around Loch Broom' or more walking information.

Organised Tours

The **MV *Summer Queen*** (☎ 612472) operates four-hour trips to the Summer Isles from Monday to Saturday in summer (adult/child £16/9). They land on Tanera Mhor, where there's a cafe and a post office which

issues its own stamps. There's also a daily two-hour nature cruise to Isle Martin at 2.15pm (and 11am on Sunday), for £9/5.

The **West House hostel** offers day tours of the Lochinver and Achininver area for £14.50, leaving at 9.30am.

Places to Stay

Broomfield Holiday Park (☎ 612664, fax 613151, West Lane) Hiker & tent £5, car & tent £9. Open May-Oct. There's not much shelter at this exposed site but the location is very central.

Ullapool Youth Hostel (☎ 612254, fax 613254, 22 Shore St) Dorm beds £9.75/8. Closed January. It's worth booking ahead at this well-set-up SYHA hostel. Internet access is available.

West House (☎/fax 613126, West Argyle St) Bunks £8.50, doubles £25. Open year-round. Part of the Scotpackers group, this fine independent hostel offers Internet access, bike hire and day tours by bus to Lochinver and Achiltibuie.

Sea Breezes (☎ 612148, 2 West Terrace) B&B £15-17.50. The highly recommended Sea Breezes is particularly friendly and has a great location on the waterfront.

Brae Guest House (☎ 612421, Shore St) B&B £20-25 per person. Open May-Oct. This place, right by the sea, has spic and span rooms with/without bathroom.

Eilean Donan Guest House (☎ 612524, 14 Market St) Rooms £18-24 per person. This friendly and well-managed guesthouse also has a pleasant restaurant (mains £8 to £13; closed Sunday).

Sheiling Guest House (☎ 612947, Garve Rd) B&B £23-25 per person. This very attractive house is set in a pleasant garden on the shore and has very comfortable rooms and a guest lounge.

Ceilidh Place (☎ 612103, fax 612886, 14 West Argyle St) Bunkhouse £15 per person, B&B from £45. There are excellent rooms at this large old hotel, which also serves as Ullapool's main entertainment centre, plus a comfortable bunkhouse.

Ferry Boat Inn (☎ 612366, fax 613266, Shore St) Singles/doubles from £31/58. Here you'll get pleasant hotel rooms with

Walking Around Loch Broom

Ullapool is a great base for walks. If you're just after a stroll, try the low-level track beside the Ullapool River to Loch Achall (two hours return) starting from the sign at the end of Mill St. The path is well marked and offers grand views of An Teallach (1062m) on the far side of Loch Broom. For something slightly longer, there's a pleasant hill walk along the Ullapool River to East Rhidorroch Lodge, a return trip of 16 miles (seven hours). Much more challenging is the 'Postie's Path', an eight-hour scramble through the hills several days a week. The SYHA hostel has leaflets on all these walks and the routes are also described in the Around Ullapool booklet.

Serious hill-walkers come to Ullapool to bag the nearby Munro of **Beinn Dearg** (1084m), northeast of Braemore, reached by a good path from the Inverlael forest, at the inner end of Loch Broom. Another way of approaching this rough and wild mountain is from the south, from the top of Loch Glascarnoch (no path). Both routes will take about eight hours. Make sure that you're well equipped, and remember to carry OS map No 20. The regular buses to Inverness on the A835 can be used to reach either trailhead.

Ridge-walking on the Fannichs, the rugged range south of Braemore, is relatively straightforward and many different routes are possible. The western Fannichs are best reached from the A832 Braemore-Dundonnell road at Loch a'Bhraoin. From the eastern end of the loch, a path goes southwards to a pass at 560m, giving access to Sgurr Breac (999m) to the west. From here, you can follow the ridge even farther west to another easily baggable Munro, A'Chailleach (997m). You can return to Loch a'Bhraoin via Loch Toll an Lochain; carry OS map Nos 19 and 20.

views up the loch and the downstairs pub and restaurant are both recommended.

Caledonian Hotel (☎ 612306, fax 612679, *Quay St)* En-suite rooms from £20-35. Open Mar-Oct. This big mock-Tudor hotel has passable rooms and pub meals in season.

Places to Eat

Seaforth Inn (☎ 612122, *Quay St)* Mains £5-8. Open 9am-11pm. The upstairs restaurant at the Seaforth Inn serves the best food in Ullapool, with lots of seafood including an above-average portion of fish and chips. Good-value takeaways are available from the hatch downstairs.

Ferry Boat Inn (☎ 612366, *Shore St)* Bar lunch £5-8, 2-/3-course set dinner £15.75/18.50. The excellent home-made food at the Ferry Boat Inn is served in a pleasant dining room.

Ceilidh Place (☎ 612103, *14 West Argyle St)* Mains £8.50-17. The coffee shop at the Ceilidh Place (open from 8am) is full of wooden furniture and is a lovely spot to sit down with a cup of coffee and a newspaper.

The evening restaurant is much more expensive, but there's live music most nights in summer (£5 admission to concerts).

Jade House (☎ 613202, *Latheron Lane)* Mains £4-5. Open 5-11pm daily. This takeaway serves up plenty of Chinese food, toned down to local tastes.

Self-caterers should head for the large *Safeway* supermarket on Latheron Lane.

Getting There & Away

Ullapool is 60 miles from Inverness and 150 miles from Kyle of Lochalsh. From Monday to Saturday, Citylink has two daily buses from Inverness to Ullapool (£6.50/11 one way/return, 1½ hours), connecting with the ferry to Stornoway.

Spa Coaches (☎ 01997-421311) has buses from Ullapool to Achiltibuie twice daily from Monday to Friday and once on Saturday. Spa and Highland Country/Rapsons (☎ 01847-893123) buses run to Lochinver Monday to Saturday.

Westerbus (☎ 712255) has a weekly service to Gairloch on Thursday or you can take the Inverness bus and change at Braemore Junction (Monday, Wednesday and Saturday) or Garve (Tuesday, Thursday and Friday).

CalMac runs comfortable car and passenger ferries from Ullapool to Stornoway on Lewis (2¾ hours) two or three times daily except Sunday (£13 per person, plus £62 for a car). See the Skye and the Western Isles chapter for more details.

Getting Around
Rent bikes from the SYHA and West House hostels for £10/6 per day/half-day.

NORTH OF ULLAPOOL
Although it's only 69 miles from Ullapool to Durness at the top of Sutherland, there are dozens of interesting detours.

After leaving Ullapool, the A835 touches the coast at **Ardmair**, where there's a camp site and a long pebble beach.

Ardmair Point Camping & Caravan Park (☎ 612054, Ardmair Point) Pitches £6.50-11. Set on a quiet pebble beach, this pleasant camp site offers boat trips to the private bird reserve at **Isle Martin**, an early Irish monastic centre, every Saturday (£3 per person) – call for more information.

Achiltibuie & Achininver
☎ 01854 ● pop 290
North of Ullapool, a narrow road turns off the A835 at Drumrunie, skirting around the edge of Loch Lurgainn to the peaceful villages of Achiltibuie and Achininver at the mouth of Loch Broom. The coastline here is broken by a series of pebble bays and it's a great place to get away from it all. In summer, there are boat tours to the appealing Summer Isles (from the Norse word *simmer* meaning 'boundary'), which are still used as seasonal sheep pastures by local crofters. There's a hostel at Achininver and a post office, hotel and general store in Achiltibuie.

Things to See & Do The **Hydroponicum** *(☎ 622202, Achiltibuie; adult/child £4.75/ 2.75; hourly tours 10am-5pm daily Apr-Sept noon & 2pm only Mon-Fri Oct)* grows tropical fruit, vegetables and flowers, with-

out soil, serving up some of the produce at the attached cafe. About 5 miles northwest of Achiltibuie, the **Smokehouse** *(☎ 622353, Altandhu; admission free; open 9.30am-5pm Mon-Sat Easter-Oct)* smokes and sells everything from cheese to eels and salmon – a whole side of smoked salmon costs £30 – and you can watch the smoking process.

Summer Isles Cruises *(☎ 622200)* run boat trips to the Summer Isles from Badentarbet Pier at Achiltibuie. The 3½-hour cruises costs £15/7.50 per adult/child and leave at 10.30am and 2.15pm, which includes an hour ashore on Tanera Mor.

Places to Stay & Eat *Achininver Youth Hostel (☎ 622254, Achininver)* Beds £8.75/ 7.50. Open mid-May–Sept. This spartan hostel has a satisfyingly secluded location at the south end of Achiltibuie.

Dornie House (☎ 622271, Achitilbuie) B&B from £16. About a mile north of Achiltibuie, this is a friendly B&B in a wonderfully remote location.

Summer Isles Hotel (☎ 622282, fax 622251, Achiltibuie) Singles/doubles from £69/104. Open Apr-Oct. This can be an expensive option, but the rooms and food are excellent and there's a fine wine list. Bar meals cost £7 to £12, and a five-course dinner will set you back £40.

Getting There & Away Spa Coaches (☎ 01997-421311) has buses from Ullapool pier to Achiltibuie (£2.50, one hour, twice daily Monday to Friday plus once Saturday).

Inverpolly Nature Reserve & Knockan Crag
From Drumrunie to the junction with the A837 at Ledmore, the A835 skirts the edge of the scenic Inverpolly Nature Reserve, which includes the three peaks of Cul Mor (849m), Stac Pollaidh (613m) and Cul Beag (769m). Stac Pollaidh is one of the most exciting walks in the area, with some good scrambling on its narrow sandstone crest. The trail up here begins at the car park on Loch Lurgainn, on the road from Drumrunie to Achiltibuie; allow three hours for the return trip.

On the opposite side of the A835 just south of Elphin is the geological interpretation centre of **Knockan Crag** *(SNH;* ☎ *01854-613418; open year-round)*. There are interactive displays with buttons and levers to keep children amused and a sculpture trail leading up to the geological anomaly that inspired all this – an area of bed rock where the top deposits are older than the rocks at the bottom.

From Loch Cam, just north of **Elphin**, you can walk to the distinctive peaks of Suilven (731m) and Canisp (846m) and continue on to Lochinver – see South of Lochinver later for more information.

Birchbank Lodge (☎ *01854-666215, Knockan, Elphin)* B&B £20 per person, dinner & B&B £32. Open June-Mar. This comfortable wooden lodge on a working croft has lovely views of the moors. The owner is a renowned mountain guide and can offer advice on walking and fishing in the area.

Caithness & Sutherland

The remainder of the northern Highlands is covered by these two rugged and sparsely populated districts. Caithness and Sutherland are brimful of weird and wonderful Highland landscapes. Almost all of the population live on the indented coastline; the bleak interior is almost uninhabited. Apart from Ben Hope (927m) near Tongue, there are few actual Munros, but the hill-walking is still superb.

The vast district of Sutherland accounts for an eighth of the total area of Scotland. Amazingly, this huge region was once the property of just one man, the notorious duke of Sutherland, who banished a staggering 15,000 people from their homes to make way for sheep farms. Inland is the desolate moorland of the Flow Country, while there are numerous historic relics and castles around the coast, most notably the opulent home of the Sutherlands, Dunrobin Castle.

Caithness covers just the northeastern tip of Scotland, roughly the extent of the Viking territories in the north. The land was later divided up between lowland nobles so it's culturally quite distinct from the rest of the Highlands. Caithness is renowned for the incredible variety of ancient sites that dot the hills between Melvich and Helmsdale, from Iron-Age brochs and Pictish stones to ruined medieval castles.

Most places of interest are accessible from the road that follows the coast from Lochinver to the Dornoch Firth. Banks and petrol stations are few and far between in this corner of Scotland, so check your funds and fuel before setting out.

LEDMORE TO LOCHINVER

Heading northwards from Ledmore, the Lochinver-Lairg road (A837) runs through appealing wild country to meet the Durness road (A894) at **Skiag Bridge** on the edge of glimmering Loch Assynt.

On the ridge overlooking the loch are the so-called **Bone Caves**, where archaeologists discovered the bones of bears, wolves, reindeer and lynx. It's a short scramble up the ridge from the car park at Gleann Dubh, about 1½ miles from Inchnadamph.

At the head of Loch Assynt, the village of Inchnadamph has a couple of accommodation options.

Inchadamph Lodge & Assynt Field Centre (☎ *01571-822218,* e *info@ inch-lodge.co.uk, Inchadamph)* B&B from £12.50-15 per person, hostel beds £8.50-10. This attractive old white mansion offers good-value rooms and hostel beds and can offer advice on walks in the Assynt Hills.

Inchnadamph Hotel (☎ *822202, fax 822203)* En-suite B&B £32-39 per person, without bathroom £20-25. Across the burn, this big old hotel has been recently renovated and also serves good pub meals.

Perched on an island at the edge of the loch, about 1½ miles from Inchnadamph, are the romantic ruins of **Ardvreck Castle**, a 15th-century stronghold of the MacLeods of Assynt. There are rumoured to be several ghosts at Ardvreck, including the daughter of a MacLeod chieftain who was sold in marriage to the devil by her father. Nearby are the ruins of a barrack house built by the MacKenzies in the 1720s.

Inland from Loch Assynt are the spectacularly shaped **Hills of Assynt**, a popular destination for hill-walkers. The principal attraction here is the Munro of Ben More Assynt (998m), reached by a seven-hour return trip via Gleann Dubh and the northern ridge of Conival (988m) – the Inchnadamph Lodge is an ideal base for this hike. You can start the walk from the parking area at the head of Loch Assynt or from Loch na Gainmhich, about 2 miles north of the turn-off to Lochinver. Remember to check locally regarding access during the deer-stalking season, from August to October.

LOCHINVER
☎ 01571 ● pop 639

This working fishing port is a popular tourist stop, and the surrounding countryside is spectacular. Lochinver is a good base for walks to the dramatic peaks of Suilven (731m) and Canisp (846m), two mighty ridges separated by a windswept plateau. To the north, the ridge of Quinag (808m) offers several peaks for walkers.

The TIC and award-winning visitor centre (☎ 844330, e lochinver@host.co.uk) on Main St, opens 9am to 5pm Monday to Saturday and 10am to 4pm Sunday year-round. There's an interpretive display and an exhibit of bear and lynx bones from the Bone Caves near Knockan. The TIC can organise fishing permits for Loch Assynt and the surrounding lochans. There's a grocery, a post office, a bank (with an ATM), a petrol station, and a doctor (☎ 844755).

Places to Stay & Eat
Polcraig (☎ 844429, e cathelmac@aol.com, Lochinver) B&B £20-40. This comfortable B&B is just uphill from the visitor centre.

Ardglas (☎ 844257, Inver) B&B from £16. On the road to Baddidarach, this big modern house has great views of the loch.

Culag Hotel (☎ 844270, fax 844483, Lochinver) Bar meals £6-8. Housed in a stately Victorian building near the harbour, the Culag Hotel serves decent meals.

The Albannach (☎ 844407, fax 844285, Baddidarrach) Dinner & B&B singles £87-117, doubles £165-190. If money is no ob-

ject, this plush hotel on the road to Point of Stoer is the finest place to stay in Lochinver.

Lochinver Larder & Riverside Bistro (☎ 844356, 3 Main St) Mains £5-17. Open lunch & dinner daily. This pleasant bistro in a large conservatory serves interesting Scottish food (mainly fish) to eat in or take away.

Caberfeidh Restaurant (☎ 844321, 5 Main St) Sandwiches under £4, mains £8-10. Open lunch & dinner daily. This lively place serves snacks and plenty of freshly caught fish, plus a few vegetarian options.

For cheap eats, head for the *Royal National Mission to Deep Sea Fishermen* (☎ 844456, Lochinver) near the harbour.

For details on postbuses that serve Lochinver, see the Getting Around section at the start of the chapter. From Monday to Saturday (May to September only), Tim Dearman Coaches (☎ 01349-883585) has a daily bus from Inverness to Durness via Ullapool, which stops in Lochinver (£11.50 from Inverness, three hours). The journey from Ullapool to Lochinver costs £5.50 (one hour).

South of Lochinver
From Lochinver, a narrow road leads south to Achiltibuie passing a series of bays. At Strath, there's a pleasant walk to a picnic spot in **Culag Wood**. A mile farther south at Inverkirkaig, there's a sandy bay and a great walk along a scenic burn for 2 miles to the Falls of Kirkaig. Serious hill-walkers can continue up to the saddle of Bealach Mor from where it's a long scramble up to the peak of **Suilven** (731m) and on to Canisp (846m). A boggy trail continues southwards from Bealach Mor via Loch Cam to Elphin, where you can pick up the bus to Ullapool.

Valhalla (☎ 844405, fax 844073, Inverkirkaig) B&B from £20 per person, self-catering chalets from £250 per week. This complex includes a pleasant farmhouse B&B and a series of wooden chalets.

Suilven (☎ 844358, Badnaban) B&B from £17. This modern B&B offers comfortable rooms close to Inverkirkaig.

Achlins Bookshop & Coffee Shop (☎ 844262, Inverkirkaig). Achlins is a well-stocked bookshop with a pleasant cafe; it's at the start of the trail to the Falls of Kirkaig.

THE NORTHWEST HIGHLANDS

North of Lochinver

Heading north from Lochinver, the winding B869 skirts around the edge of the Stoer peninsula, passing a series of secluded beaches and cliffs. This land was formerly part of the Assynt estate, but the crofters brought their land from the local landowner in 1993, inspiring a series of similar buy-outs throughout the Highlands. This part of Assynt is now managed by a community trust which controls the fishing rights to most lochs in the area; permits and fishing information are available from the Lochinver visitor centre.

There are good beaches between Lochinver and Stoer, including the sandy cove at **Clachtoll**, which has a camp site and a small nature and history display. There's a ruined broch on the ridge between Clachtoll beach and Stoer.

There's yet another wonderful sandy cove at **Achmelvich**, where there's a camp site and hostel.

Shore Caravan Site (*☎ 01571-844393, fax 844782, 106 Achmelvich)* Pitches £4.50-8. With the lovely Achmelvich beach on the doorstep, this is one of the better camp sites on the west coast.

Achmelvich Youth Hostel (*☎ 01571-844480, Achmelvich)* Beds £8.75/7.50. Open Apr-Sept. This SYHA hostel is about 1½ miles from the Lochinver-Drumbeg postbus route (see Getting Around at the start of the chapter), and 4 miles from Lochinver.

Stoer has a nice sandy beach and a ruined church, plus a very welcoming B&B.

Stoer Villa (*☎ 855305, Stoer)* B&B from £15. Stoer Villa is run by a friendly couple and is a good base for walks on the Stoer peninsula.

POINT OF STOER

At the tip of the peninsula is the **Point of Stoer** and the **Rhu Stoer Lighthouse** – built by Thomas Stevenson, father of the author Robert Lewis Stevenson, in 1870. From the lighthouse there's a bracing one-hour walk along the clifftop to the **Old Man of Stoer**, perhaps the best of the sea stacks – towers of rock rising from the sea – on the mainland.

It's roughly 10 miles to Point of Stoer from Lochinver, but you can continue around the peninsula to the friendly village of **Drumbeg**, which has fantastic views of Sail Garbh (808m), and on to meet the main A894 near Loch Glencoul. Drumbeg has a shop and post office and there's a nice sandy beach nearby at **Clashnessie**.

From Easter to October, the **Drumbeg Hotel** (*☎ 833236)* does bar meals (from £5).

KYLESKU & LOCH GLENCOUL
☎ 01971

Hidden from the main road on the shores of deep Loch Glencoul, Kylesku is the starting point for cruises to the waterfall of **Eas a'Chual Aluinn**, Britain's highest falls at 213m. There isn't much at Kylesku – just a few houses and a pub – but it's a good base for walks and there are several places to stay. Nearby is the architecturally interesting modern bridge over Loch a'Chàirn Bhàin, which has a huge curve in it.

The **MV Statesman** (*☎ 01571-844446)* runs twice-daily trips in summer around Loch Gencoul, taking in the falls (adult/child £10/5) from Kylesku Old Ferry Pier. It's a fine three-hour, 6-mile return trip walk to the top of the falls, starting from beside Loch na Gainmhich (OS Landranger map No 15 shows the route). You can continue to Ben More Assynt (998m) from here.

Kylesku Lodges (*☎ 502003, ℮ info@kyleskulodges.co.uk, Kylesku)* Hostel beds £10-11, chalets from £180 per week. Open year-round. This complex of wooden A-frame chalets has a grand location by the loch and there's also a basic 12-bed hostel.

Kylesku Hotel (*☎ 502231, fax 502313, Kylesku)* Mains £6-11. This allegedly haunted hotel is the only place to eat in Kylesku and serves good-value pub meals including freshly caught crustaceans. It also does singles/doubles for £35/65.

Newton Lodge (*☎/fax 502070, Unapool)* B&B from £28 per person. This attractive wooden building sits on a bluff overlooking Loch Glencoul and offers very comfortable rooms and great food (dinner £16).

For postbus details see the Getting Around section at the start of the chapter.

The Skye's the limit: rocky Black Cuillin is reflected in the waters of a small lochan.

Lazily grazing among headstones in Elgol

OIFIS A'PHUIST

AN T-ATH LEATHANN

Gaelic is spoken by half of Skye's population.

Sheep and shearful: spring trims on Skye

GRANT DIXON

Harris, originally named 'high island' by the Vikings, is renowned for its handwoven tweed.

HELEN FAIRBAIRN

Hiking around Loch Coruisk on the Isle of Skye

GRANT DIXON

An old fishing boat and lobster traps, Lewis

ANDREW MARSHALL & LEANNE WALKER

Pretty in pink: Portree's colourful harbourside cottages

SCOURIE
☎ 01971 ● pop 150

Scourie is a pretty crofting community in the middle of an excellent area for angling – the Scourie Hotel can arrange permits and boats. There's a supermarket, petrol station, post office, camp site and several B&Bs.

Just offshore of Scourie Bay is the important **Handa Island** seabird sanctuary; the reserve is run by the Scottish Wildlife Trust and has large populations of skuas, puffins and seals. There's a nice beach here and great views across to the Old Man of Stoer on the far side of Eddrachillis Bay. The **boat** *(☎ 502347; adult/child £7/3.50 return)* for Handa leaves from Tarbet Pier, 1 mile north of Scourie, Monday to Friday from April to September. If you fancy stopping the night, there's a small *camping bothy (Scottish Wildlife Trust; ☎ 01463-714746; £5 per person)* on the island. From Monday to Saturday there's an afternoon postbus from Scourie to Tarbet via Fanagmore.

Scourie Hotel (☎ 502396, fax 502423, Scourie) Bar meals £5-11. Everything at the Scourie Hotel is devoted to angling and the set-up here is very well organised; rooms are also rather good, with singles for £34 to £46, and doubles for £58 to £80.

Eddrachilles Hotel (☎ 502080, fax 502477, Badcall Bay) B&B £39-45 per person. If you want to get away from it all with a bit of style, this attractive hotel is tucked away from the road in lovely surroundings, just south of Scourie. It also does a three-course *table d'hôte* dinner for £13.

Seafood Restaurant (☎ 502251, Fanagmore) Mains from £10. Open noon-8pm Mon-Sat Easter-Oct. This informal restaurant by the pier at Fanagmore, just north of Tarbet, is a real find – the seafood is all freshly caught and prawns and lobster regularly feature on the menu.

Stock up on provisions at the Mace **supermarket**.

Just north of Tarbet at Fanagmore, **Laxford Cruises** *(☎ 502251)* offers two-hour boat tours of Handa Island at 10am, noon and 2pm Monday to Saturday from May to September (adult/child £8/4).

KINLOCHBERVIE
☎ 01971 ● pop 464

Continuing north from Scourie, the road passes through an inhospitable landscape of boulder-fields, broken up by quiet lochans and marshes. On the edge of Loch Inchard, a tiny road leads out to Kinlochbervie, which was one of Scotland's premier fish-landing ports until the mid-1990s. It's still possible to buy fish straight from the fishermen in the evenings. Kinlochbervie has a well-stocked *Mace supermarket* and a few places to stay.

Braeside (☎ 521325, Kinlochbervie) B&B £18-20 per person. On the main road through Kinlochbervie, this friendly B&B is housed in a modern bungalow.

Old School Hotel & Restaurant (☎/fax 521383, Inshegra) En-suite B&B from £29 per person. This appealing hotel is housed in an old stone schoolhouse halfway between Kinlochbervie and Rhiconich and is known for its excellent Scottish meals (from £8 to £11.50).

Kinlochbervie Hotel (☎ 521275, fax 521 438, Kinlochbervie) En-suite B&B £45-55 per person. The well-appointed Kinlochbervie Hotel is fairly popular with locals and tourists. Bar meals are available for £6 to £11.

There's a lovely beach at Oldshoremore, a crofting settlement about 2 miles northwest of Kinlochbervie. A little farther north at Balchrick, a dirt track leads across the peninsula to Sandwood Bay, which boasts one of Scotland's best and most isolated beaches, guarded at one end by the spectacular rock pinnacle Am Buachaille; it's about 2 miles to the beach from the end of the track. Alternatively, you can follow the splendidly remote trail from Cape Wrath to the north (allow eight hours) and continue on to Kinlochbervie. At the far end of the beach is the ruin of Sandwood House, a creepy place reputedly haunted by the ghost of a shipwrecked 17th-century sailor.

CAPE WRATH

From the turn-off to Kinlochbervie, the A838 strikes inland across the moors to the Kyle of Durness, a gorgeous sandy inlet

THE NORTHWEST HIGHLANDS

which changes from deep blue to pale green as the tide recedes. On the eastern side of the inlet, accessible by a passenger ferry, is the rugged headland of Cape Wrath, crowned by a lighthouse (dating from 1827). The dramatic name comes from the Norse word for turning point, rather than the sentiments of sailors shipwrecked on the rocks. The main reason to come here is to see the seabird colonies on Clo Mor Cliffs (281m), the highest sea cliffs on the mainland. You can also walk south to Sandwood Bay and on to Kinlochbervie (eight hours).

The ferry trip across the Kyle of Durness (☎ 01971-511376) leaves from Keodale Pier (the main road at the standing stone) and costs £2.40/3.80 one way/return. A connecting minibus (☎ 01971-511287) runs the 11 miles to the cape (£4.50/6.50 one way/return, 40 minutes one way). The services operate daily from May to September, and up to eight times daily in July and August (weather permitting).

Nearby **Garvie Island** is a Ministry of Defence bombing range, and Cape Wrath is usually out of bounds while the jet pilots bombard this tiny islet – call ☎ 0800 317071 to see if the cape is open.

Cape Wrath Hotel (☎ 511212, Keodale) B&B £20-36. This huge white-washed hotel stands on the hillside just off the A838, on the way to the Cape Wrath ferry. Dinner is available for an extra £15.

DURNESS
☎ 01971 ● pop 353
The spectacularly located village of Durness is tucked away between several gorgeous white-sand beaches. It's a magical spot and John Lennon spent many happy holidays here. The village has several budget places to stay and is a great base for relaxing beachfront strolls. The spread-out nature of the village also keeps down the tourist numbers.

Orientation & Information
What's known as Durness is really two villages, Durness, at the turn-off to Balnakeil, and Smoo, a mile to the east, which is partly reclaimed from the old military base. The friendly TIC (☎ 511259, ℮ durness@ host.co.uk) and visitor centre is in Durness, open 9am to 5.30pm Monday to Friday and 10am to 4pm on Sunday (from October to May, it only opens 10am to 1.30pm weekdays). There's a bureau de change here and the centre organises guided walks in summer. The attached **visitor centre** *(admission free)* has an impressive collection of whale bones collected off Balnakeil beach.

There is a *Mace supermarket* (with a post office), a petrol station, health centre (☎ 511273) and travelling bank (once a week) in Durness. Smoo has a *general store* with good baked goods.

The annual **Highland Gathering** takes place during the last weekend in July; contact the TIC for details or check the village Web site at ☒ www.durness.org.

Things to See & Do
About one mile east of Durness at Smoo (from the Viking *smjugg* meaning 'hole'), a narrow inlet runs up to the entrance of vault-like **Smoo Cave**. Centuries of erosion have opened a large blowhole in the roof and the waters of Loch Meadaidh descend in a roaring waterfall at the back of the main chamber.

In summer, a rubber boat ferries people in front of the falls to a low cavern at the back (£3/1.50), including a tour of the various limestone stalactites and stalagmites (remember, stalactites hang tight to the ceiling). It's become a tradition for people to write their names in pebbles on the grassy slopes around the geo. From June to September, *Cape Sea Tours (☎ 511284)* offers 1½-hour wildlife spotting cruises from the Smoo Cave inlet – call for more details.

Durness has several beautiful beaches, starting at **Rispond** to the east. One of the best is **Sangobeg**, but there's also a 'secret beach' just to the east that can't be seen from the road. You may see caves, seals, whales and traces of shipwrecks around the coast. Enquire at the TIC for **trout fishing** permits.

The disused radar station at **Balnakeil**, less than a mile north of Durness, has been turned into a new-age **Craft Village** *(open*

9.30am to 6pm daily in summer), with a host of artisans producing prints, ceramics and enamelware. There's an excellent bookshop and restaurant here.

At the end of the road, there's the ruined **Balnakeil Church**, dating from 1619, on the site of an 8th-century church. In the kirkyard is a mass grave containing the remains of people from the *Canton*, an immigrant ship which sank with all hands off **Faraid Head** in 1849. Also here is the grave of McMurdo, a 16th-century highwayman who is said to have murdered his victims by tossing them down the blowhole into Smoo Cave. Austere **Balnakeil Farm**, overlooking the church, incorporates parts of a former Mackay castle.

A walk north along the gorgeous beach will take you to Faraid Head, where puffin colonies can be seen in early summer. In May 2001, some tourists discovered the grave of a Viking warrior on the beach at Balnakeil – there's a display on the excavation of the tomb in the TIC at Durness.

Places to Stay & Eat

Sango Sands Oasis (☎ 511222, fax 511205, Durness) Pitches adult/child from £4.20/2.10. This pleasant camp site is right by the beach and has a camp kitchen and an attached restaurant serving fish & chips, burgers and sandwiches for under £10.

Lazy Crofter Bunkhouse (☎ 511366, e mackay@bosinternet.com, Durness) Dorm beds £9. Near the turn-off to Balnakeil, this very comfortable hostel has dorms and double rooms plus a good TV lounge; reception is at the Parkhill Hotel.

Durness Youth Hostel (☎ 511244, Smoo) Dorm beds £8.75/7.50. Open Apr-Sept. The SYHA hostel is housed in two basic cabins at Smoo, on the eastern side of the village, just before the car park for Smoo Cave.

Parkhill Hotel (☎ 511202, fax 511321, Durness) Singles/doubles from £21/39. Open Apr-Oct. This central hotel has decent rooms and pub meals.

Durness also has several B&Bs, including:

Corrie Lochan (☎ 511336, Durness) B&B £18-20. This attractive B&B is one of several comfortable modern places on the main road west of Durness.

Puffin Cottage (☎/fax 511208, Durine) Doubles £17-21 per person. Open Apr-Sept. Puffin Cottage is a particularly good B&B near the turn-off to Balnakeil.

Smoo Falls (☎ 511228, Smoo) Doubles from £16 per person. Open Mar-Oct. Run by Mrs Conlon, this friendly B&B is across the road from Smoo Cave and is the best choice.

Loch Croispol Bookshop & Restaurant (☎ 5112777, 17c Balnakeil Craft Village) Lunch & snacks £2-5, 2-/3-course dinner

---

Durness Riots

In 1841, the duke of Sutherland sent one of his factors (estate managers) to clear the villages of Ceannabeinne and Sangobeg near Durness, triggering one of the most famous uprisings of the Clearances. The cowardly sheriff's officer chose to deliver the eviction notice while the men were away cutting grass, but the village women forced him to burn the eviction notice. Humiliated, the official fled to Durness and requested the support of 14 special constables, who agreed to meet the Durness crofters at the Durine Inn.

Some 50 crofters attended the meeting – not to refuse the eviction, incredibly, but to humbly request that it be postponed until after the Sabbath – but all their entreaties were ignored. Outraged, the crofters seized and disarmed the constables and pursued the officials through the inn, capturing them and frog-marching them to the parish boundary. Shortly after the riots, another sheriff was sent to inform the villagers that troops from the 53rd Regiment would be called in from Edinburgh to remove them from their homes.

There was a flurry of interest in the case by the newspapers in Edinburgh, leading to a judicial enquiry, which found the duke's threats to be unlawful. However, the judges found nothing legally wrong with the eviction, and the crofters were ordered to leave their homes in 1842. The riot did have one positive effect; the castigated duke decided to spare the crofters of neighbouring Balnakeil.

£9.50/12.50. This well-stocked bookshop also has a welcoming licensed restaurant serving good Scottish food.

DURNESS TO THURSO

It's 80 winding and often spectacular coastal miles from Durness to Thurso, passing Ben Hope (927m), Scotland's most northerly Munro.

Durness to Tongue

From Durness it's 37 miles to Tongue via the modern causeway across the Kyle of Tongue, or longer if you take the scenic old road around the head of the kyle.

East of Durness, the A838 skirts the edge of the curiously named Loch Eriboll, Britain's deepest sea inlet, which was an anchorage for Russian convoys during WWII. British servicemen stationed here used to call it 'Loch 'Orrible', but it's a lovely spot. *Port-Na-Con Guest House (☎/fax 511367, Loch Eriboll)* Singles/doubles from £27/38. This fantastically located house sites right on the lochshore and has its own stone harbour. Set three-course dinners are available for £12.75.

On the far side of Loch Eriboll are the **Ardneackie Lime Kilns**, built in the 1870s on a small island linked to the shore by a sandy spit. Over the headland at Loch Hope is the turn-off for the scenic B873 (see the following section). *Craggan Hotel (☎/fax 01847-601278, Melness)* Mains £6-16. The atmospheric Craggan Hotel does great bar meals, with an adventurous menu. There are four ensuite rooms (B&B from £17.50 per person).

Loch Hope to Bettyhill via the Inland Road

From the mouth of Loch Hope, a winding and incredibly scenic single-track road (the B873) cuts inland along Glen Strathmore beneath the menacing profile of **Ben Hope** (927m), meeting the Tongue to Lairg road at Altnaharra. About 10 miles east of the turn-off is **Dun Dornaigil** (aka Dun Dornadilla), a well-preserved broch on the banks of a fast-flowing burn. If you'd like to bag Ben Hope, it's a three- to four-hour

return trip along the saddle and up to the seemingly inaccessible summit; the easiest trail begins about 2 miles before the broch, near a large barn.

Just beyond **Altnaharra**, with its pretty stone bridge, the B873 passes ruined **Grummore Broch** on the shore of Loch Naver, home to a handful of stunted trees. At Syre, another tiny road heads east through the bleak Flow Country to meet the A897 to Helmsdale, passing **Rosal Township**, a 200-year-old crofting village abandoned during the clearances; a series of informative panels tells the tragic story.

Tongue

☎ 01847 ● pop 445

Tongue (from the Norse *tunga* meaning 'narrow peninsula') was first settled by Vikings in the 8th century, but passed to the Mackay clan after the defeat of the Norsemen at Largs. There are great views from the 14th-century Mackay fortress of **Varrich Castle** on the edge of the Kyle, including the peaks of An Caisteal (764m) and Ben Hope (927m). Tongue later became part of the estate of Sutherland, with sadly predictable consequences during the clearances. The village has a shop and post office, a petrol station and a bank.

Tongue Youth Hostel (☎ 611301, Tongue) Dorm beds from £9.25/8. Open Apr-Sept. Down by the causeway, the SYHA hostel has a spectacular location looking up and down the Kyle of Tongue.

Tigh-Nan-Ubhal (☎ 611281) B&B from £18 per person, flats from £160 per week. This nice stone house at the main junction in Tongue also has several holiday flats.

Inchverry (☎ 611312) B&B from £12.50 per person. On the back road around the kyle, this lovely stone croft offers great value and lovely views to the south.

Ben Loyal Hotel (☎ 611216, fax 611212, Tongue) Singles/doubles from £30/50. This excellent and friendly hotel, just off the main road serves fine meals (from £8) and the rooms come highly recommended.

Just beyond Tongue, the A836 cuts inland to Lairg, but if you've got time, it's worth taking the scenic B873, which starts about

10 miles west of Tongue at Loch Hope. About 2 miles north of Tongue, the Watch Hill viewpoint overlooks the wonderful golden-sand beach at Coldbackie.

Mrs MacIntosh (☎ 611251, 77 Dalcharn) Singles/doubles £15/26. Just east of Coldbackie, this pleasant B&B also offers dinner for an extra £7.

There's a Monday to Saturday postbus from Tongue to Thurso, or you can pick up one of the Highland Country/Rapsons buses from Durness to Thurso.

Bettyhill (Am Blaran Odhar)
☎ 01641 • pop 553

This innocent-sounding crofting community takes its name from Elizabeth, countess of Sutherland, who kicked the entire tenant population of Strathnaver off their land, resettling them on this exposed strip of coast. There are some delightful sandy beaches at both **Farr Bay** and **Torrisdale Bay**.

Bettyhill TIC (☎ 521342) opens Easter to October. There's also a shop and post office. The **Strathnaver Museum** *(☎ 521418, Farr Bay; adult/child £1.90/50p; open 10am-1pm & 2pm-5pm Mon-Sat Apr-Oct)*, in the old church by the TIC, tells the sad story of the Strathnaver Clearances and there's an intricate 8th-century Pictish cross-slab in the graveyard.

Dunveaden (☎ 521273, Bettyhill) B&B £16-18 per person, pitches £7, caravans £9. This friendly B&B also runs the camp site across the road.

Bettyhill Hotel (☎/fax 521352, Bettyhill) B&B from £15 per person, dinner & B&B £21. This simple, friendly hotel has a mixture of rooms with/without bathroom. Bar meals are available from £5.

From Bettyhill the B871 turns south for Helmsdale, through **Strathnaver**, where the clearances took place. There's a **Clearance Village** with interpretive panels at Achinlochy; follow the signs from the Naver bridge. Nearby are the ruins of several large chambered cairns.

Melvich

This small village sits on a sandy bay at the end of the A897, which runs southwards

through the so-called Flow Country – an area of desolate rolling heathland – to Helmsdale on the east coast. From **Strathy Point**, about 2 miles northwest of Melvich, there are lovely views of the coast in both directions.

Halladale Inn (☎/fax 01641-531282, Melvich) Pitches from £6. Bar meals from £5. This extended stone pub has decent pub food and a good camp site.

Melvich Hotel (☎ 01641-531206, Melvich) Singles £25-40, doubles £40-60. This homely white-washed pub is close to the beach and serves a variety of meals (£6 to £13), including venison and shellfish.

The Flow Country

From Melvich, the A897 runs south along Strath Halladale, passing through the exposed moorland of the Flow Country (from the Viking *floi* meaning 'marshy ground'). This region comprises 13% of the world's blanket bogs and is home to numerous rare Highland plants and animals. The flat, sparse heathland also provides a perfect hunting ground for birds of prey, including owls, harriers, merlins and golden eagles.

Today the RSPB owns 20, 743 acres of peatland around **Forsinard Station**, which is protected as a bird reserve. There's a visitor centre (☎ 01641 571225) with details on walks in the reserve, open 9am to 6pm daily April to October. The most popular walk is the Dubh Lochan trail (1 mile), which passes several lochans (small inland lochs) with plentiful birdlife. There are also guided walks from the centre (call for details).

Trains from Inverness to Thurso stop right by the visitor centre at Forsinard (£12 from Inverness).

Dounreay Nuclear Power Station

On the coast about 5 miles west of Thurso, Reay village is best known for the controversial **Dounreay Nuclear-Waste Reprocessing Plant**, which closed in 1996 after a series of radiation leaks. The **visitor centre** *(☎ 01847-802572, Dounreay; admission free; open 10am-4pm daily May-Oct)* tells the 'official' story of the Dounreay experimental reactor and its decommissioning;

environmental groups paint a slightly less rosy picture – see Ecology & Environment in the Facts about Scotland's Highlands and Islands chapter.

About 3 miles east of Reay are the 5000-year-old **Cnoc Freiceadain Chambered Cairns**, two vast overgrown long-cairns (slender stone burial chambers) with great views of the coast.

***Forss Country House Hotel** (☎ 01847-861201, fax 861301, Forss)* Singles/doubles from £57.50/90. This attractive country house is set in an area of woodland about 5 miles east of Reay and offers very good rooms and meals.

THURSO & SCRABSTER
☎ 01847 ● pop 7880

The most northerly town on the mainland, Thurso may seem a little bleak at first, but it has a number of historic ruins, a small surf scene and some excellent places to eat and drink. Most people just come here to pick up the ferry to Orkney, but there's plenty to see in the surrounding area.

Medieval Thurso was Scotland's major port for trade with Scandinavia – the name Thurso comes from the Norse *Thorsa* meaning 'Thor's River' – and was ruled as an annexe of the earldom of Orkney. After earl John of Orkney was murdered here in 1231, the town became part of Scotland and was made a royal burgh in 1633. The modern town was laid out in 1798 by Sir John Sinclair, one of the earls of Sinclair, whose family lived in the castle on the shore in Castletown. Thurso saw a long period of decline after WWII, but its fortunes were revived by the construction of the nearby Dounreay nuclear power station in the 1950s.

Ferries to Orkney cross from Scrabster, 2½ miles west of Thurso, a fairly plain little port with a pub, restaurant and lighthouse. North of the harbour, there's a fine cliff walk along Holborn Head (take care in windy weather).

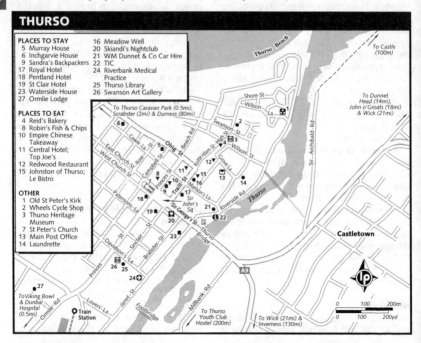

THURSO

PLACES TO STAY
5 Murray House
6 Inchgarvie House
9 Sandra's Backpackers
17 Royal Hotel
18 Pentland Hotel
19 St Clair Hotel
23 Waterside House
27 Ormlie Lodge

PLACES TO EAT
4 Reid's Bakery
8 Robin's Fish & Chips
10 Empire Chinese Takeaway
11 Central Hotel; Top Joe's
12 Redwood Restaurant
15 Johnston of Thurso; Le Bistro

OTHER
1 Old St Peter's Kirk
2 Wheels Cycle Shop
3 Thurso Heritage Museum
7 St Peter's Church
13 Main Post Office
14 Laundrette

16 Meadow Well
20 Skiandi's Nightclub
21 WM Dunnet & Co Car Hire
22 TIC
24 Riverbank Medical Practice
25 Thurso Library
26 Swanson Art Gallery

In September, Thurso co-hosts the North-lands Festival (☎ 603336) with Wick, staging loads of concerts, performances and exhibitions and a huge ceilidh.

Orientation & Information

Thurso is divided by the River Thurso but most places of interest are on the north-western bank. Traill St, which runs parallel to the river, is the main shopping street.

The TIC (☎ 892371), on Riverside Rd, opens from 10am to 5pm Monday to Saturday Easter to October (and on Sunday June to September). Thurso Library (☎ 893237), Davidson's Lane, offers free Internet access and opens 10am to 6pm Monday and Wednesday, 10am to 8pm Tuesday and Friday and 10am to 1pm Thursday and Saturday.

The Riverbank Medical Practice is in Janet St (☎ 892027), or there's the Dunbar Hospital (☎ 893263) on Ormlie Rd. There's a laundrette (☎ 893266) at Riverside Place, just beyond the TIC, open weekdays. The post office is on Grove Lane.

Things to See & Do

Thurso Heritage Museum (☎ 892459, *High St; adult/child £1/25p; open 10am-1pm & 2pm-5pm Mon-Sat June-Aug*), in Thurso Town Hall (☎ 892692), has Pictish carved stones and cross-slabs, fossils, the inevitable croft reconstruction and displays on Sir John Sinclair.

Beyond the ugly modern precinct at the western end of High St are the stately 17th-century ruins of **Old St Peter's Kirk**, originally founded around 1220 by Gilbert Murray, the bishop of Caithness. The small round building over the **Meadow Well** on Manson's Lane marks the site of the town's former water supply.

Near the end of Sinclair St, the **Swanson Art Gallery** (☎ 896357, *Thurso Library, Davidson's Lane; admission free; open 1pm-5pm Mon-Wed, 1pm-8pm Fri & 10am-1pm Sat*) features monthly exhibitions of crafts and fine art.

Thurso is an unlikely **surfing** centre, but the nearby coast has arguably the best and most regular surf on mainland Britain and there have been several big international tournaments here. There's an excellent right-hand reef break on the eastern side of town, directly in front of Lord Thurso's castle, and another shallow reef break 5 miles west at Brimms Ness. You'll need to bring all your own gear as Thurso has no surf shops.

Places to Stay

Thurso Caravan Park (☎ 805514, *fax 805508, Scrabster Rd*) Pitches from £7. The camp site is by the coast, at the western end of Thurso; the Stewart Pavilion cafe here serves good cheap meals.

Ormlie Lodge (☎/fax 896888, *Ormlie Rd*) Dorm beds without/with sheets £6.50/7.50. Singles/doubles £9/15, duvet hire £1. Open year-round. This hostel is also the halls of residence for the local community college and offers cheap but ageing rooms and dorms.

Thurso Youth Club Hostel (☎ 892964, e *t.y.c.hostel@btinternet.com, Millbank Rd*) Dorm beds £8, including breakfast. Open July & Aug. This basic hostel is housed in an old mill on the southern bank of the river.

Sandra's Backpackers (☎/fax 894575, *24-26 Princes St*) En-suite dorms from £8.50. This curious hostel is above a fish and chip shop and has clean rooms but no communal space. You can access the Internet in the chip shop downstairs.

Waterside House (☎ 894751, *3 Janet St*) B&B from £15 (from £17.50 en suite). Down by on the river, close to the TIC, this plush B&B has nice rooms and can arrange vegetarian breakfasts on request.

Murray House (☎ 895759, *1 Campbell St*) B&B from £20 per person (en suite £25). The rooms in this pretty town house are very comfortable.

Inchgarvie House (☎ 893837, *30 Olrig St*) Singles/doubles from £22/42 (doubles are en suite). This attractive stone house has well-cared-for rooms.

St Clair Hotel (☎ 896481, *fax 893730, 15 Sinclair St*) Singles/doubles from £32/60. This down-to-earth hotel has good rooms and is at the quiet end of Sinclair St.

Pentland Hotel (☎ 893202, *fax 892761, Princes St*) En-suite singles/doubles £35/60. The large, centrally located Pentland Hotel is housed in a partly modernised building and you can get adventurous food (mains £8 to £16, set dinner £17.50) at the attached restaurant.

Royal Hotel (☎ 893191, fax 895338, Traill St) En-suite singles £30-60, doubles £50-105 per person. This very dignified hotel is well run and has excellent rooms and a fine restaurant (dinner £12).

Places to Eat

Basic cafes in Thurso include *Reid's Bakery (☎ 891000, 3 High St)* and *Johnston of Thurso (893233, 10 Traill St)*.

For takeaways, try *Robin's Fish & Chips (☎ 895015, 15a Princes St)* or *Empire Chinese (☎ 896332, 20 Princes St)*.

Le Bistro (☎ 893737, 2 Traill St). Meals £6-15. Open lunch & dinner Tues-Sat. This intimate bistro serves excellent food, including the best steak we found in the Highlands. Desserts are also magnificent.

Central Hotel (☎ 983129, Traill St) Pub meals & grills £4-12. Open 7am-9pm. This friendly and popular pub serves good-value bar meals upstairs.

Redwood Restaurant (☎ 894588, Grove Lane) Bar meals £4-5.30. Open 9am-6.30pm. Opposite the Co-op supermarket, the Redwood Restaurant serves up a good selection of pub grub and there are live bands at weekends.

Royal Hotel (☎ 893191, Traill St) Meals £8-12. The attractive Royal Hotel's fine restaurant serves up salmon and various sea creatures, cooked in various styles. The set dinner costs £12.

The Upper Deck (☎ 892814, Scrabster) Mains £10-18. Open lunch & dinner daily. This upmarket seafood restaurant at the Ferry Hotel is a good posh choice while you're waiting for the ferry.

For cheaper food, try the *Fisherman's Mission (☎ 892402, Scrabster)* on the quay; most dishes are under £5.

Entertainment

Top Joe's (☎ 893129, Central Hotel, Traill St) Most of Thurso's young people crowd into this lively bar upstairs at the Central Hotel every weekend.

Viking Bowl (☎ 895050, Ormlie Rd; open daily) Bowling adult/child £1.70/1.40. Cinema £4-5. The Viking Bowl is a sign of the wealth brought to Thurso by the Dounreay reactor; it has a six-lane bowling alley, cinema, restaurant and bar.

Skinandi's (☎ 894526, Sir George's St) Admission £5. The town's nightclub is typically loud and boisterous and opens Thursday to Saturday.

Getting There & Away

Thurso is 290 miles from Edinburgh, 130 miles from Inverness and 21 miles from Wick. From Inverness, Citylink buses operate via Wick to Thurso (£10, 3½ hours); they stop in Sir George's St. Highland Country Buses/Rapsons (☎ 01847-893123) operates the daily Wick-Thurso route; buses also stop in Sir George's St. Harrold's Coaches (☎ 01955-631295) has four daily buses from Thurso railway station to John o'Groats.

There are two or three daily train services from Inverness in summer (£12.50, 3½ hours); space for bicycles is limited so cyclists should book ahead.

Getting Around

It's a 2-mile walk from Thurso train station to the ferry port at Scrabster, or there are buses from Olrig St (80p). In the grey mall at the end of the main street, Wheels Cycle Shop (☎ 896124), The Arcade, 35 High St, rents out mountain bikes from £10 per day.

Car hire is available from W M Dunnet & Co (☎ 893101) on Manson's Lane, near the TIC, from £22 per day plus 8p per mile.

DUNNET HEAD
☎ 01847

Forget John o'Groats – the beautiful heath-covered headland at Dunnet Head, a few miles west, is actually the most northerly point on the British mainland. The head is covered in peatland and finishes dramatically at a line of sheer cliffs. There are fine views across to Orkney over the Pentland Firth, one of the most dangerous stretches of water in Britain (tidal streams here can rip through at up to eight knots). Breeding birds such as puffins are seen in summer and there's a typical Stevenson lighthouse at the tip of the headland, built in 1831.

Just west of Dunnet Head is a magnificent stretch of sandy beach overlooking Dunnet Bay, which catches some good **surf** in the right winds. At the northern end of the beach is a **ranger station** with whalebones and displays on local natural history. Across the road, there are several walking trails in **Dunnet Forest**. At the other end of the beach lies the tiny harbour of **Castlehill**, where a heritage trail explains the evolution of the local flagstone industry.

Just north of the beach at Dunnet village is **Mary-Ann's Cottage** (☎ 603385; open 2pm-4.30pm Tues-Sun June-Sept), an old croft house that contains all the original fittings from its last owner Mary-Ann Calder, who lived here for 93 years! A few miles farther east at Mey is the 16th-century **Castle Mey**, the holiday home of the late Queen Mother (closed to the public at the time of writing).

Dunnet Bay Caravan Site (☎ 821319, Dunnet Bay) Pitches from £8.50. This pleasant camp site is right by the beach at Dunnet Bay.

Dunnet Head Tearoom (☎ 851774) Meals under £8. Open lunch & dinner daily. Situated on the road that leads to Dunnet Head, this place offers good, inexpensive food, including meals for vegetarians. B&B is available for £17 to £20 per person.

Castle Arms Hotel (☎/fax 851244, Mey) Singles £30-39, doubles £40-58. Close to the castle in Mey, this hotel has decent rooms and a gallery with photos of the Queen Mum.

JOHN O'GROATS
☎ 01955 ● pop 512

People making the epic 874-mile journey from Land's End to John o'Groats are likely to be a bit disappointed when they get here – it's quite a journey to make to have your photo taken in a car park surrounded by souvenir shops. Despite all suggestions to the contrary, John o'Groats isn't the most northerly point on the Scottish mainland (that honour goes to Dunnet Head) and the landscape slopes down to the sea in a fairly undramatic fashion. The original settlement here was at Huna, home to the Caithness lifeboat in the 19th and early 20th centuries, which set to sea on hundreds of occasions to rescue sailors from the Pentland Firth.

The name comes from Jan de Groot, one of three brothers commissioned by James IV to operate a ferry service to Orkney in 1496 – it's just coincidence that the fare for the crossing was originally one *groat* (a four-penny coin). About 3 miles west at Canisbay, **St Drostan's Church** was established in the 12th century on the mound of an ancient broch, and contains a tombstone of the de Groot family.

The TIC (☎ 611373), in the main car park in John o'Groats, opens 10am to 4pm daily Easter to October. Of interest is the **Last House & Museum** (☎ 611250; admission free; open 8am-8pm daily Mar-Sept, Tues-Fri 9.30am-4.30pm Oct-Feb) with lots of photos of local shipwrecks and the crofters of Stroma and the inevitable souvenir shop. Nearby, **Journey's End** (adult/child £2/1; open 10am-4pm daily April-Oct) is an audiovisual show on the history of Caithness. There's also a decaying hotel, post office and a chip shop, plus souvenir shops.

Organised Tours
For a short taste of what Orkney has to offer, **John o'Groats Ferries** (☎ 611353) offer full-day 'maxi' coach tours of Orkney mainland leaving John o'Groats at 9am daily May to September (adult/child £33/16.50, including ferry fare). A shorter 'highlights' tour leaves at 10.30am from June to August (£30/10). There are also 90-minute wildlife cruises to Stroma or Duncansby Head at 2.30pm (£12/6) daily June to August.

NorthCoast Marine Adventures (mobile ☎ 07867 666273) offers entertaining wildlife tours in a nippy inflatable boat, with trips to local skerries (semi-submerged rocks) and stacks.

Places to Stay & Eat
John o'Groats Caravan & Camping Site (☎ 611329) Tent & car £7.50. This site is right beside the car park and ferry pier.

John o'Groats Youth Hostel (☎ 611424) Beds £9/7.75. Open May-Sept. This SYHA hostel is 3 miles west of John o'Groats at Canisbay.

Caberfeidh Guest House (☎ 611219) B&B £15-20 per person. This is the better of the two guesthouses at John o'Groats.

Seaview Hotel (☎ 611220) B&B from £14.50. Across the road, the Seaview also does breakfast, lunch and dinner for non-residents.

The dilapidated *John o'Groats House Hotel* with its curious octagonal tower was closed for renovation when we visited.

Getting There & Away

Bus Highland Country/Rapsons runs up to seven buses daily between John o'Groats and Wick (£2.50, one hour) via the youth hostel at Canisbay, from Monday to Saturday. Harrold's Coaches (☎ 01955-631295) runs a bus from Thurso train station to John o'Groats several times daily, Monday to Saturday.

Boat From May to September the passenger ferry MV *Pentland Venture,* operated by John o'Groats Ferries (☎ 611353), shuttles across to Burwick in Orkney at 9am, 10.30am, 4pm and 6pm from June to August (in May there's just a 9am and 6pm service, while in September there are sailings at 9am and 4.30pm). The one-way fare to Burwick costs £16/8 and a return costs £26/13 (bicycles £3 extra each way).

See Organised Tours under Inverness in The Great Glen & the Western Highlands chapter for details of the John o'Groats Ferries bus-ferry-bus service, which takes you from Inverness to Kirkwall.

Pentland Ferries (☎ 01856-831226) operates a car ferry to St Margaret's Hope on Mainland Orkney from Gill's Bay, 2 miles west of John o'Groats. Ferries leave Gill's Bay at 9.45am, 1.45pm and 6.45pm for the 45-minute crossing (£10/5 one-way; car/motorcycle/bicycle £25/7/2.

John o'Groats to Wick

Two miles east of John o'Groats is **Duncansby Head**, a popular breeding ground

for seabirds at the start of summer. A clifftop path leads south to the **Duncansby Stacks** which soar over 60m above the sea. The grass-topped cliffs extend from Duncansby all the way to Wick.

Just south of Freswick bay are the overgrown ruins of the Norse stronghold of **Bucholly Castle**, while at Nybster, a narrow path leads along the cliffs to the **Three Follies**, a series of curious carved-stone monuments erected in the 1890s in honour of Sir Francis Tress Barry of Keiss, who excavated the nearby **Harbour Broch**, a ruinous tower.

Nearby in the old school at Auchengill is the **Northlands Viking Centre** (☎ 01955-607771; adult/child £1.70/1.30; open 10am-4pm daily June-Sept) with an audiovisual display and artefacts from local Viking sites. The ruins of the 16th-century **Keiss Castle**, a former Sinclair stronghold, cling precariously to the lip of a sheer cliff at Keiss, a few miles south. The path to the castle follows the cliffs from Keiss Harbour, which has several old stone buildings and a turf-covered ice-house once used to store fish. Keiss has a shop/post office and a hotel.

Sinclair Bay Hotel (☎ 01955-631233, fax 631492, Keiss) Singles from £16-25, doubles from 30-44. This tidy small hotel has good-value rooms.

WICK

☎ 01955 ● pop 7450

Wick, with its boarded-up buildings and general gloomy atmosphere, hasn't always been so dismal. The town was once the world's largest herring fishing port, with over 1100 fishing boats crammed into the harbour and dozens of tall ships standing by to carry the barrels of salted herring overseas. After WWI, the herring began to disappear, and trade ground to a halt when the market for herring in Eastern Europe collapsed in WWII.

Wick never really recovered, and today it's easily the most run-down place on the coast. Architecture buffs may be interested to know that Wick's massive harbour was the work of the engineer and canal pioneer Thomas Telford, who also designed Pulteneytown, the model town on the southern

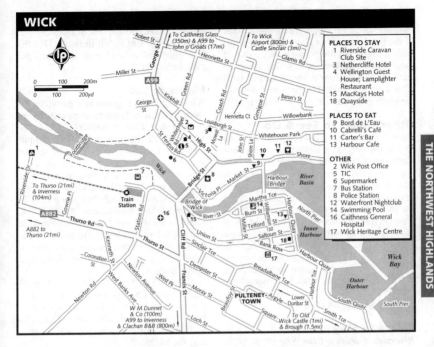

WICK

PLACES TO STAY
1 Riverside Caravan Club Site
3 Nethercliffe Hotel
4 Wellington Guest House; Lamplighter Restaurant
15 MacKays Hotel
18 Quayside

PLACES TO EAT
9 Bord de L'Eau
10 Cabrelli's Café
11 Carter's Bar
13 Harbour Cafe

OTHER
2 Wick Post Office
5 TIC
6 Supermarket
7 Bus Station
8 Police Station
12 Waterfront Nightclub
14 Swimming Pool
16 Caithness General Hospital
17 Wick Heritage Centre

bank of the river. A failed attempt to add a breakwater was the work of lighthouse-builder Thomas Stevenson.

The last clan battle fought on Scottish soil took place in 1680 at Altimarlach, 2 miles up the River Wick, between the Campbells of Glenorchy and the Sinclairs of Keiss (who were defeated). In September, Wick co-hosts the **Northlands Festival** (☎ 603336), with exhibitions, and lots of concerts and dancing.

Orientation & Information

Wick is split in two by the Wick River; the town centre is on the northern bank, but the more attractive harbour area is part of Pulteneytown to the south.

The rather inefficient TIC (☎ 602596, e wick@host.co.uk) is in Whitechapel Rd, which leads to the Safeway supermarket off High St, and opens 10am to 4.30pm Monday to Friday. The post office is on High St.

Wick Heritage Centre

The town's award-winning local museum (☎ 605393, Bank Row; adult/child £2/50p; open 10am-5pm Mon-Sat May-Sept) really deserves all the praise heaped upon it. It tracks the rise and fall of the herring industry, partly through the excellent Johnston photographic collection. From 1863 to 1977, three generations of Johnstons photographed everything that happened around Wick, and the 70,000 photographs are an amazing portrait of the town's life.

Castles

A path leads a mile south of town to the ruins of 12th-century **Old Wick Castle**, of which only a single tower survives, and the spectacular sea cliffs of the **Brough** and the **Brig**, or **Gote o'Trams** beyond. In good weather, it's a fine walk to the castle, but the final approach can be a bit of a scramble.

Three miles northeast of Wick are the magnificent cliff-top ruins of **Castle Sinclair** (also known as Castle Girnigoe). Dating from the late 15th century, this former seat of the Sinclair earls of Caithness was originally a single tall tower, but a succession of incumbents extended the structure along the clifftop. The castle was abandoned in 1690 after a family feud. The path here follows the cliffs from the car park at Noss Head.

Other Things to See & Do

On the northern side of town on the road to John o'Groats, it's worth popping into **Caithness Glass Visitor centre** *(☎ 602286; admission free; glass-making 9am-4.30pm Mon-Fri)*. While its main purpose is to sell glassware, there's a viewing gallery behind the shop where you can see dozens of glassblowers running around with hot gobbets of glass. The shop sells 'seconds' – glassware with small bubbles and other blemishes – at low prices and opens to 5pm (it also opens 11am to 5pm Sunday Easter to December).

The above-average **Wick Swimming Pool** *(☎ 603711, Burn St)* charges £2.20/1.10 per adult/child for a dip.

Places to Stay

Riverside Caravan Club Site *(☎ 605420, Riverside Drive)* Tents £5-12.50. This site is a half-mile west of the town centre, on the road to Thurso.

Wellington Guest House *(☎ 603287, fax 602237, 41 High St)* En-suite B&B £19-25 per person. This place is just around the corner from the TIC. There's a good restaurant upstairs and a cafe and takeaway downstairs (see Places to Eat below).

Quayside *(☎ 603229, 25 Harbour Quay)* En-suite singles/doubles from £22/32, with shared bathroom £15.50. This B&B is in the most attractive part of town by the harbour.

Clachan *(☎ 605384, South Rd)* Singles £25-30, doubles £40-44. This large cottage on the A9 at the southern edge of town is recommended.

MacKays Hotel *(☎ 602323, fax 605930, Union St)* Singles £58, doubles £80-90. The stylishly renovated MacKays is the best hotel in Wick, and sits at the end of 2.75m-long Ebenezer Place, the shortest street in Britain. Four-course dinners here cost £18.50.

Nethercliffe Hotel *(☎ 602044, fax 605691, Louisburght St)* Singles/doubles from £35/48. Just uphill from the TIC, this is a good-value hotel with the usual pub meals on offer.

Places to Eat

Wick is hardly a gourmet's paradise, but there are a few restaurants worth seeking out.

Bord de L'Eau *(☎ 604400, 2 Market St)* Mains £7-12. Open noon-2.30pm & 6pm-10.30pm Tues-Sun. Wick's finest restaurant, this upmarket French place serves up authentic continental dishes, such as maigret de canard (sautéed duck breast) and *escargots*, and is worth the splurge.

Lamplighter Restaurant *(☎ 603287, 41 High St)* Meals from £9-12. Open Fri & Sat evenings. Upstairs at the Wellington Guest House, this posh place serves great Scottish food. The cafe and tearoom downstairs opens daily.

Cabrelli's Café *(☎ 603155, 134 High St)* Mains under £5. Open 8.30am-11pm daily (until 10pm Sun). This place does good burgers and pasta dishes, and fish teas (fish and chips, bread and butter, and a cup of tea) for £4.99.

The simple **Harbour Cafe** *(☎ 602433, 21 Harbour Quay)* does fish suppers (£3).

Carters Bar *(☎ 603700, 2 Shore)* Meals under £4. This pub down on the riverfront serves very cheap pub meals daily, and is also a noisy nightspot.

Entertainment

Nightlife is fairly rough and ready in Wick, but there's a single nightclub.

Waterfront Nightclub *(☎ 602550, 4 Shore)* At weekends, party-goers head for this club by the river.

Getting There & Away

Wick Airport has daily flights to Edinburgh (Monday to Saturday) and flights to Kirkwall, Orkney every weekday. There's also a flight to Sumburgh, Shetland every Saturday. See the Getting There & Away chapter for further details.

There are regular train services from Inverness to Wick (£12.50, four hours) and from Wick on to Thurso (£3.90). Citylink buses from Inverness to Thurso also stop in Wick three to five times daily. Highland Country/Rapsons (☎ 01847-893123) runs the connecting service to John o'Groats for the passenger ferry to Burwick, Orkney.

Car hire is available from W M Dunnet & Co (☎ 602103) on Francis St, from £22 per day plus 8p per mile.

WICK TO LYBSTER
☎ 01593

There are several historic sites between Wick and Lybster.

About 2 miles south of Wick at Thrumster, a road leads inland to the **Yarrow Archaeological Trail**, a walking trail that runs around Loch Yarrow passing Neolithic roundhouses, several Bronze- and Iron-Age cairns and a partially submerged broch.

At Ulbster, 2 miles farther south, are the **Whaligoe Steps**, a spectacular staircase cut into the cliff face. At the bottom of the vertiginous descent is a tiny natural harbour ringed by vertical cliffs, echoing with the cackle of nesting fulmars. The path begins at the end of the minor road beside the telephone box, opposite the road signposted 'Cairn o'Get'. The **Cairn o'Get** itself is a partially reconstructed long-cairn, a quarter-mile off the A9, and then a 2-mile walk; you can continue from here to the Bronze-Age hill fort of Garrywhin over the Ulbster dam.

About a mile south, the **Hill o'Many Stanes** is a curious, fan-shaped arrangement of 22 rows of small stones probably dating from around 2000 BC. Its purpose is unknown, but similar monuments have been found in France, indicating a cultural link across northern Europe.

The quaint stone village of Lybster (pronounced **libe**-ster) was built as a planned fishing community in 1810 and there is still plenty of evidence of the wealth that the herring boom brought to the settlement. Overlooking the harbour is the **Waterlines Visitor Centre** (☎ 721520; admission free; open 11am-5pm daily May-Sept), with a heritage exhibition, a boatbuilder's workshop, and CCTV beaming live pictures of nesting seabirds from nearby cliffs.

Portland Arms Hotel (☎ 721721, fax 721722, ☑ info@portlandarms.com, Lybster) Singles/doubles £45/68, family rooms (up to four people) £80. The warm and welcoming Portland Arms, on the A9 main road in Lybster, has stylish and snug rooms and an excellent restaurant.

Bolton House (☎ 721228, Quatre Bras) B&B from £16. This simple B&B is in a stone house near the crossroads.

A mile east of Lybster, a turn-off leads to the **Grey Cairns of Camster**, 5 miles north of the A9. Dating from between 4000 and 2500 BC, these fine burial chambers are hidden in long, low mounds rising from an evocatively desolate stretch of moorland; a raised boardwalk links the tombs. The Long Cairn measures 60m by 21m and you can crawl into the central chamber where there's a skylight. The smaller Round Cairn has a corbelled ceiling and is also lit by a skylight (a torch is still useful).

Five miles to the northwest, on the minor road from Lybster to Achavanich and just south of Loch Stemster, are the 40 or so **Achavanich Standing Stones**.

LATHERON TO HELMSDALE
About 2 miles south of Lybster at Latheron, the **Clan Gunn Heritage Centre & Museum** (☎ 01593-731370; adult/child £1.50/75p; open 11am-1pm and 2pm-4pm Mon-Sat June-Sept, 2pm-4pm Sun July & Aug) is focused on the achievements of this famous clan; some claims, such as the assertion that it was really a Scot, not Christopher Columbus, who discovered America, need to be taken with a pinch of salt.

A little farther on is the **Laidhay Croft Museum** (☎ 01593-731244; adult/child £1/50p; open 10am-5pm daily Apr-Oct) which recreates crofting life from the mid-1800s to WWII. Its tearoom serves good soup and home baking.

In a deep glen about 1 mile farther south, **Dunbeath** was once a pretty little place, but the huge concrete road bridge has eroded the charm. There are good views of privately owned **Dunbeath Castle** from the harbour, and a hotel and shops inland from the A9.

THE NORTHWEST HIGHLANDS

On the hill south of the village is **Dunbeath Heritage Centre** (☎ 01593-731233, The Old School; adult/child £2/free; open 10am-5pm Easter-Oct), with displays about the history of Caithness, including crofting and fisheries.

At Berriedale, the A9 descends into a steep valley known as the **Berriedale Braes**, with steep gradients and hairpin bends. On the southern edge of the valley is a small crenulated folly tower with grand views; there are also nice walks along the valley, passing **Langwell House**, a private mansion with attractive gardens. The road south from here is sometimes closed by snow.

Kingspark Llama Farm (☎ 751202, Berriedale) B&B £16-18 per person. This friendly B&B is housed in a modern cottage on a working llama farm.

About 7 miles north of Helmsdale a 15-minute walk east from the A9 (signposted) takes you to **Badbea**, a clearance village with the remains of several crofts perched on the cliff top. Immediately before Helmsdale, the road climbs to a fine viewpoint at the **Ord of Caithness**, where there's also a ruined broch.

HELMSDALE
☎ 01431 ● pop 650

The delightful village of Helmsdale is a popular destination for anglers – the River Helmsdale is one of the premier salmon-rivers in the Highlands – and there's an excellent heritage centre. The village was established in the 19th century to house crofters who were evicted from Strath Kildonan by the duke of Sutherland. The appealing stone bridge (Old Bridge) was constructed by Thomas Telford and there's a 19th-century ice-house for storing salmon on the southern bank.

Helmsdale was also the centre of a minor gold rush in the 19th century, when small nuggets of gold were discovered in the Kildonan Burn at Baile an Or (Town of Gold), about 4 miles northeast on the Melvich road. Around 12,000lbs of gold was extracted in the first year of mining, but the source of the gold was never discovered and the duke of Sutherland closed the workings

down when local landowners objected to the shantytown that housed the workers.

Helmsdale has several supermarkets, an ATM and a number of bizarre chintzy restaurants, inspired by the larger-than-life romantic novelist Barbara Cartland, who used to holiday here annually. Helmsdale has Highland Games every August.

Things to See & Do
The excellent **Timespan Heritage Centre** (☎ 821327, Dunrobin St; adult/child £3.50/ 1.75; open 9.30am-5pm Mon-Sat & 2pm-5pm Sun Easter–mid-Oct, 9.30am-6pm daily July & Aug) has details of the 1869 Strath Kildonan gold rush and displays on Viking raids and Patrick Sellar, the duke of Sutherland's notorious henchman. There's a pleasant riverside cafe.

The salmon fishing at Helmsdale is legendary, but there's heavy competition for permits. Anglers should head for the **Bridge Hotel Tackle Shop** (☎ 821102, 1 Dunrobin St), which issues 24-hour permits for salmon and trout (£17.60 to £21.50); the season runs from 1 January to 30 September.

Small quantities of gold are still found in Kildonan Burn at Baile an Or, about a mile from Kildonan train station – if you fancy having a go, you'll need to obtain a licence (free) and rent a gold-panning kit (trowel, riddle and pan) for £2.50 from the **Strath Ullie souvenir shop** (☎ 821402, Shore St) in Helmsdale, open daily April to October.

Places to Stay & Eat
There are several B&Bs and hotels in town, plus a popular hostel.

Helmsdale Youth Hostel (☎ 821577, Stafford St) Beds £8.75/7.50. Open mid-May–Sept. This busy hostel is on the main road at the north end of town; book well ahead for July or August.

Belgrave Arms Hotel (☎ 821242, cnr Stafford & Dunrobin Sts) B&B from £18 per person (£21 en suite). This welcoming hotel on the A9 at Dunrobin St is friendly and great value.

Bridge Hotel (☎ 821100, fax 821101, 1 Dunrobin St) Singles/doubles £50/90. This regal hotel has been entirely redeveloped

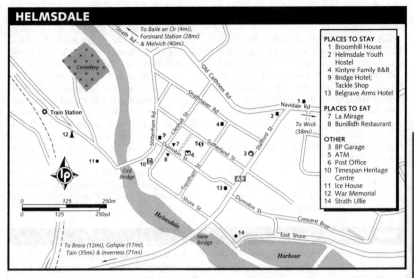

HELMSDALE

To Baile an Or (4mi),
Forsinard Station (28mi)
& Melvich (40mi)

Strath Rd

Cemetery

O Train Station

12

Old Caithness Rd

Strathnaver Rd

Navidale Rd

To Wick
(38mi)

Stittenham Rd

Lilleshall St

Strath Rd

9

11

10

8

Old
Bridge

Dunrobin St

5

6

7

4

Sutherland St

3

Stafford St

A9

13

Trentham St

Shore St

Dunrobin St

Crescent Brae

Helmsdale

New
Bridge

14

East Shore

Harbour

To Brora (12mi), Golspie (17mi),
Tain (35mi) & Inverness (71mi)

0   125   250m
0   125   250yd

PLACES TO STAY
1 Broomhill House
2 Helmsdale Youth
   Hostel
4 Kintyre Family B&B
9 Bridge Hotel;
   Tackle Shop
13 Belgrave Arms Hotel

PLACES TO EAT
7 La Mirage
8 Bunillidh Restaurant

OTHER
3 BP Garage
5 ATM
6 Post Office
10 Timespan Heritage
   Centre
11 Ice House
12 War Memorial
14 Strath Ullie

THE NORTHWEST HIGHLANDS

and the end result is spectacular – the collection of deer and elk heads in the wood-panelled dining room has to be seen to be believed. The Bridge Hotel also has its own angling shop that sells permits (see Things to See & Do earlier in this section).

There are a few B&Bs worth checking out.

Kintyre Family B&B (☎ 821590, Trentham St) B&B from £15, en-suite B&B £18 per person. There are pleasant and spacious rooms at this relaxed B&B.

Broomhill House (☎ 821259, fax 821259, Navidale Rd) En-suite B&B £17-19. This turreted house on the outskirts of Helmsdale has good rooms.

Both the *Belgrave Arms Hotel* and the pricier *Bridge Hotel* serve good food, plus there are a few eateries along Dunrobin St.

La Mirage (☎ 82165, 7-9 Dunrobin St) Mains £6-13. This incredible monument to chintz is run by Nancy Sinclair, a committed Barbara Cartland fan and lookalike, and is full of Cartland memorabilia and innumerable pink and fluffy ornaments. It's worth visiting just for the decor. The food – including fish and chips, posher seafood and Scottish meat dishes – is tasty and good value.

Bunillidh Restaurant (☎ 821457, 2 Dunrobin St) Meals from £5-12. Across the street, this place is full of fairy ornaments, in an attempt to out-chintz La Mirage, and serves inexpensive fish and chips, plus other dishes.

Getting There & Away

There are regular trains between Inverness and Helmsdale (£11.40, one hour) continuing on to Thurso (£10.40), and Citylink buses between Inverness and Thurso also stop here.

BRORA
☎ 01408 ● pop 1480

Located at the mouth of a river famed for its salmon, Brora has a fine beach, but the village itself is rather rundown. There are no particular sights here, but the village has two small supermarkets, a bank and a post office.

On the northern edge of town is **Clynelish Distillery** (☎ 623000; tours £3; open 9.30am-4.30pm Mon-Fri Apr-Oct, by arrangement Nov-Feb), the most northerly distillery in mainland Scotland.

The **Brora Golf Club** (☎ 621417) is well regarded and charges £25 to £30 per day.

There are camp sites nearby and plenty of B&Bs in town.

Glenaveron *(☎/fax 621601, Golf Rd)* B&B from £26 per person. Set in a nice garden near the gold course, this is a good B&B.

Rockpool Guest House *(☎ 621505, Rosslyn St)* B&B from £20. This is a friendly B&B down near the harbour.

Royal Marine Hotel *(☎ 621252, fax 621181, Golf Rd)* Singles/doubles from £68/110. The plush Royal Marine is popular with golfers and has an excellent restaurant (meals from £7 to £15).

Cheaper snacks and meals can be found at the ***Fountain Café*** *(☎ 621467, Rosslyn St)* and the ***Golden Fry*** *(☎ 62127, Memorial Square)* in the village centre.

Dunrobin Castle & Around

Dunrobin Castle *(☎ 01408-633177; adult/child £6/4.50; open 10.30am-4.30pm Mon-Sat, noon-4.30pm Sun Apr-Oct, 10.30am-5.30pm daily June-Sept)* is the largest house in the Highlands, with 187 rooms. This classic fairytale castle is adorned with towers and turrets and has beautiful formal gardens stretching down to the sea. In spite of its beauty, Dunrobin inspires mixed feelings amongst local people; the castle was once the seat of the cruel duke of Sutherland, who cleared a staggering 15,000 people from the far north of Scotland. The duke's estate was once the largest privately owned area of land in Europe, covering 1.5 million acres!

The Highland Clearances

Prior to the Jacobite Rebellion, Highland farmers had relied predominantly on cattle, but in 1762, Sir John Lockhart-Ross of Balnagown, Ross-shire, began to experiment with sheep farming, removing tenant farmers from parts of his estate and leasing the land to farmers from the lowlands. In terms of profitability, the project was a resounding success and the MacDonells of Glengarry followed suit, beginning large-scale evictions on their land in 1785.

Thus began the shameful Highland Clearances, which increased dramatically in 1792, when resilient Cheviot sheep were introduced into the Highlands. This hardy breed were able to tolerate Highland conditions and still produce large amounts of meat and wool, increasing the profits of sheep-farming exponentially. Henceforth 1792 became known as *Bliadhna nan Caorach* or 'Year of the Sheep', marking the beginning of the end for tens of thousands of tenant-farmers in the Highlands and islands.

Over the next century, village after village fell silent as clan leaders, landlords and their factors shifted the tenants to dismal crofts by the coast or onto emigrant ships bound for the New World. The brutality of some landlords, most famously the duke of Sutherland and his factors, James Loch and Patrick Sellar, became notorious; tenants were routinely beaten or threatened with illegal punishments to persuade them to leave their homes; some were even loaded onto ships at gunpoint.

There were frequent uprisings by tenants, but while judges condemned the cruelty of the landlords, there was nothing in Scottish law to prevent landlords from clearing their land. The forced emigrations carried out during the Potato Famine of the 1840s were even seen by many as a humanitarian action. Behind the scenes though, the idea of land reform was gaining more and more converts. With support from Edinburgh, the Highland Land Reform Association, an organisation of aggrieved crofters from across the region, eventually persuaded the government in Westminster to pass the Crofters' Holding Act in 1886, guaranteeing security of tenure, fair rents and crofters' rights to pass on their holdings by inheritance.

On 3 May 2000, the recently formed Scottish parliament voted unanimously to abolish feudal tenure, ending 900 years of feudalism. However, the legacy of the clearances can still be felt throughout the Highlands and islands. Two-thirds of Scottish land is still owned by just 1000 of its inhabitants, and many rural communities still suffer from the so-called 'Highland Problem' – low incomes, high unemployment and massive outward migration.

There has been a castle on this site since around 1275, but most of the present structure – including the ornate clocktower – was built in French style between 1845 and 1850, over the framework of a 17th-century castle. The interior is richly furnished and offers an intriguing insight into the opulent lifestyle of the Highlands' most notorious family. The house also displays innumerable gifts from farm tenants (probably grateful that they hadn't been asked to give up their homes for the duke of Sutherland's sheep welfare programme). The castle is reputedly haunted by the ghost of a green lady known as the *Ell-maid of Dunstuffnage*.

Tucked away in the magnificent formal gardens is an eclectic museum of archaeological finds, natural-history exhibits and more big-game trophies. The museum contains almost all the Pictish stones found in Sutherland, including the fine pre-Christian Dunrobin stone.

Nearby is **Carn Liath Broch**, a low ruined broch-tower overlooking the sea (there's a car park on the far side of the A9, or you can walk here along a coastal path from Golspie).

GOLSPIE
☎ 01408 ● pop 1460

Golspie is a pretty little village that has benefited over the centuries from the proximity of Dunrobin Castle. There are good facilities, including a couple of supermarkets, banks and a post office, and a pleasant beach just back from the main street. There are several nice walks around **Loch Fleet**, near the turn-off to Lairg, which has large populations of waterfowl.

Another interesting walk begins at the end of Fountain Rd, from where a path climbs steeply to the summit of Ben Bhraggie (394m), which is crowned by a massive monument to the duke of Sutherland. The statue was erected in 1834, supposedly by grateful tenants from the Sutherland estate. A more convincing statement of local feeling is the long-running campaign to have this memorial to the chief villain of the Highland Clearances torn down.

Sutherland Arms Hotel (☎/fax 633234, Old Bank Rd) B&B £28-35 per person. Golspie's best hotel at the northern end of town.

Granite Villa (☎ 633146, Fountain Rd) B&B from £16 per person. This attractive stone house contains a friendly little B&B.

Glenshee House (☎ 633254, Station Rd) Singles/doubles £24/40. South of the centre on the main road, this is another good B&B.

Buses and trains are the same as for Helmsdale (see Getting There & Away under Helmsdale earlier). The train station is just south of the centre.

LAIRG & AROUND
☎ 01549 ● pop 904

Lairg, at the southern end of Loch Shin, is a junction for roads across the interior to Tongue, Laxford Bridge (between Durness and Kylesku) and Ledmore (between Kylesku and Ullapool). There's no real reason to stop here, but you may pass through on your way across the central Highlands.

West of Lairg are the **Ord Hut Circles & Chambered Cairns**, a collection of prehistoric cairns and roundhouses, a short walk west of the Ferrycroft Countryside Centre (☎ 402160) on the far side of the river from the village, which also doubles as a TIC (open 10am to 5pm daily April to October, 9am to 6pm Monday to Saturday July to August). About 3 miles from Lairg on the back road to Invershin, you can watch salmon leaping the **Falls of Shin** on their way upstream to spawn from June to September.

Lairg has several shops, a bank (with ATM), post office and camp site. Every August, Lairg is home to the largest one-day lamb sale in Europe.

Dunroamin Caravan & Camping Park (☎/fax 402447, Main St) Pitches from £7. This camp site, east of the centre, also hires out bikes for £7/12 per half-/full day.

Lochview (☎ 402578, Lochside) B&B £18-20. Just west of the main junction, this is a decent B&B.

Nip Inn (☎ 402243, fax 402593, Main St) B&B £22-27 per person. On the main street, this modernised hotel is quite inviting and does bar meals from £5.50.

Shin Fry, also on Main St, is a fish and chip shop open Monday to Saturday.

Crask Inn (☎ 411241, Crask) B&B £20 per person. Dinner £8.50. The tiny and remote Crask Inn, 13 miles north of Lairg on the A836, is notorious for being the coldest place in Scotland. In December 1995 a record low of -30°C was recorded here, but peat-burning stoves and central heating keeps it cosy.

Sleeperzzz (☎ 01408-641343, [W] www .sleeperzzz.com, Rogart Station) Beds £9, 10% discount for cyclists and train travellers. Open Mar-Nov. Nine miles east of Lairg at Rogart train station is this charming and unique hostel. Ten compartments in two first-class railway carriages have been fitted with two comfy bunks in each; there's also an old two-bed gypsy caravan to let. Bike hire is available and costs £8 to £10.

Getting There & Around

Trains between Inverness and Thurso stop at Lairg (1½ hours) and Rogart (two hours) two or three times daily in each direction.

Coming from Inverness, there are hourly Stagecoach Inverness (☎ 01463-239292) buses to Tain (Monday to Saturday), from where you can pick up a MacLeod's Coaches (☎ 01408 641354) bus to Lairg (£2.50, 45 minutes, four daily Monday to Saturday). Postbus services (☎ 0845 774 0740) run from Lairg post office to Rogart, Lochinver (via Ledmore and Inchnadamph) and Tongue (via Altnaharra).

BONAR BRIDGE & AROUND

Heading southwards, the A9 crosses the Dornoch Firth to Tain, while the A836 cuts inland to **Ardgay**, where you'll find a train station, shop and a hotel. From here a single-track road leads 10 miles up Strath Carron to **Croick**, the scene of terrible evictions during the 1845 clearances. You can still see the tragic messages scratched by refugee crofters from the nearby crofting community of Glencalvie on the eastern windows of Croick Church.

North of Ardgay, the railway line passes **Carbisdale Castle**, a sumptuous youth hostel, built in 1914 for the dowager duchess of Sutherland, and gifted to the SYHA in 1943. Trains between Inverness and Thurso stop at Invershin, where a footbridge leads across the Kyle of Sutherland to Carbisdale. Close to the castle is the site of the Battle of Carbisdale, where the marquis of Montrose made his last stand in 1650.

Carbisdale Castle Youth Hostel (☎ 015 49-421232, Culrain) Beds £13.75/11.50, add 50p/£1.25 July & Aug. Open Mar-Oct. Carbisdale Castle is Scotland's biggest and most opulent youth hostel, with splendid decor throughout and all sorts of statuary along the halls. There are pleasant walks in the surrounding forest and a good cafe for a warming hot meal when you get back. Bookings are firmly recommended.

DORNOCH
☎ 01862 ● pop 1330

On the northern shore of the Dornoch Firth, about 2 miles from the A9, this attractive old market town is one of the most pleasant settlements on the east coast. Dornoch is best known for its championship golf course, but there are some fine old buildings, including **Dornoch Cathedral**, which was built from red sandstone in 1223, but extensively rebuilt over the years. Among other historical oddities, the last witch to be executed in Scotland was boiled alive in hot tar in Dornoch in 1722.

Down by the beach, the **Royal Dornoch Golf Club** *(☎ 01862 810219)* is the 9th-rated UK course and the 15th-rated course in the world. It's spectacularly located on the shore and charges green fees of £45 to £60 per round (£50 to £70 on Sunday) on the Championship course, and £9 to £18 per round on the less-impressive Struie Course. Green time should be booked well in advance.

There are some fine buildings on the main street, including 16th-century **Dornoch Castle**, the former home of the bishops of Caithness, and **Dornoch Jail**, built in 1840. Behind the castle is **Historylinks** *(☎ 811275; adult/child £2/free; open 10am-4pm Mon-Sat May-Sept)* with displays on local history from the Viking era to the present day.

The TIC (☎ 810400, 🅔 dornoch@host .co.uk), in the main square, opens 9am to 5pm Monday to Saturday.

Places to Stay & Eat

Camping is available for around £8 at *Pitgrudy Caravan Park (☎ 810001, fax 821382, Poles Rd)* and *Dornoch Caravan Park (☎/fax 810423, The Links)*.

Fearn House (☎ 810249, High St) B&B from £23 per person. This nice stone B&B is close to the cathedral.

Rosslyn House (☎ 810237, Castle St) B&B £15-18. On the main road through Dornoch, this is another good B&B.

Eagle Hotel (☎ 81008, fax 811355, Castle St) Rooms £24-35 per person. This very friendly and cosy hotel has good rooms and is a very popular place for lunch or dinner (meals cost £7 to £12).

Dornoch Castle Hotel (☎ 810216, fax 810981, Castle St) B&B £25-50 per person. Dinner £22. This comfortable hotel is housed in the castle and has a very nice restaurant (mains cost £7 to £15).

Royal Golf Hotel (☎ 810283, fax 810923, Royal Dornoch Golf Course) Singles/doubles from £86/108. If you want to tee off with the high flyers, this hotel is situated right there on the championship golf course.

Apart from the pubs, there are several cafes and restaurants.

Cathedral Café (☎ 810119, 2 High St) Light meals £3-6. Opposite the cathedral, this extremely pleasant cafe is popular and serves good snacks and coffee.

2 Quail (☎ 811811, Castle St) Open 7.30pm-9.30pm Thurs-Sat. 3-course dinners £30. This highly regarded restaurant serves particularly good Scottish food – bookings are advised.

Getting There & Away

Citylink buses between Inverness and Thurso stop in Dornoch three to five times daily. Alternatively there are numerous daily Stagecoach Inverness buses from Inverness, via Invergordon and Tain (less frequent on Sunday); buses continue on to Golspie and Helmsdale.

The Firthlands

The coastline between Dornoch and Inverness is split by three mighty inlets – the Dornoch, Moray and Cromarty Firths – creating a series of irregular peninsulas known as the Firthlands. Most visitors just whistle through as they head south along the A9 to Inverness, but there's plenty to see here if you leave the highway.

EASTER ROSS

Heading southwards from Dornoch, the A9 crosses the Dornoch Firth at Tain, entering the anvil-shaped peninsula of Easter Ross, an ancient tribal district known for its Pictish relics. The country here is mostly low-lying grassland, but it rises to red-sandstone cliffs (such as those near Cromarty on the Black Isle) around the coast that provide the stone for many of the area's buildings.

TAIN

☎ 01862 ● pop 3460

Tain is Scotland's oldest royal burgh and was once an important pilgrimage centre; James IV used to come here to clear his conscience after visiting his mistress in Moray. Today, it's best known for its excellent heritage centre and the Glenmorangie Distillery on the northern edge of town.

Amongst other unusual buildings, Tain has a curious 17th-century **tolbooth**, originally court offices and a jail, on the High St. The building was restored extensively by Oliver Cromwell during his siege of Scotland. Nearby, the 12th-century **St Duthac's Chapel** and 14th-century **St Duthac's Church** were built in honour of St Duthus, who was born in Tain and died in Armagh (Ireland) in 1065.

The church is now part of the **Tain Through Time (☎ 894089; adult/child £3.50/2.50; open 10am-6pm daily Apr-Oct, shorter winter hours)** heritage centre, which describes the history of Tain as a place of pilgrimage.

On the northern edge of town is the **Glenmorangie Distillery & Visitor Centre (☎ 892477; distillery tour £2; open 9am-5pm Mon-Fri year-round, plus 10am-4pm**

Sat & noon-4pm Sun June-Aug), which produces one of the Highlands' most distinctive single malts. There are regular guided tours of the distillery from 10.30am to 3.30pm, including a complimentary nip.

The attractive High St has a good range of shops plus a post office and several banks. The train station is down Castle Brae; turn-off the High St near the Sheriffs court.

Places to Stay & Eat

Royal Hotel (☎ 892013, fax 893450, High St) Singles/doubles from £45/70. This splendid Victorian hotel is opposite the tollbooth and has good rooms and tasty Scottish meals.

Mansfield House Hotel (☎ 892281, fax 892872, Morangie Rd) Singles £65-85, doubles £100-150. This fine old building is Tain's most regal country-house hotel.

Castlehill (☎ 894030, Castle St) B&B from £16. One street downhill from the High St, this is a good B&B.

Brambles Tearoom (☎ 892929, 5 High St) This pleasant tearoom serves teas, coffees and light meals.

Taste of India (☎ 894158, Queen St) Mains £5-9. This Indian restaurant, uphill from the High St, is in an old pub.

Getting There & Away

Citylink buses from Inverness to Thurso pass through Tain, or there are numerous daily Stagecoach Inverness buses (£5.50, one hour, hourly). There are three trains Monday to Saturday and one on Sunday to Inverness and Thurso.

PORTMAHOMACK

☎ 01862 ● pop 608

Portmahomack was once a busy fishing village but it's a quiet and relaxing place these days, with a strip of white-washed houses along the shore, plus a shop and post office.

The **Tarbat Discovery Centre** *(☎ 871351, Tarbatness Rd; adult/child £3.50/1; open 10am-5.30pm May-Sept, 2pm-5pm Mar, Apr & Oct-Dec)*, in the Tarbat Church, is home to some fine carved Pictish stones recovered from the Firthlands and there some interesting medieval grave-slabs in the kirkyard.

There are good coastal walks around the lighthouse at **Tarbat Ness**, 3 miles northeast of the village. On the far side of the headland at Rockfield, a path leads north along the shore to the ruins of the 16th-century **Ballone Castle**, formerly owned by the Dunbars of Tarbat.

Caledonian Hotel (☎ 872345, fax 871 757, Main St) Singles £29-35, doubles £45-59. The friendly and comfortable Caledonian overlooks the village's sandy beach and has a good restaurant.

The bright and cheerful *Oyster Catcher Restaurant (☎ 871560)* does inexpensive snacks during the day, and bistro meals in the evening; seafood pancakes and other snacks start at £5. It opens for lunch and dinner daily except Monday (closed February).

Every two hours from Monday to Saturday, Stagecoach Inverness has buses from Inverness to Portmahomack (£5.50, 1½ hours) via Fearn Hill, Hilton of Cadboll, Shandwick and Nigg, continuing on to Tain.

THE SEABOARD VILLAGES

Collectively known as the Seaboard Villages, the tiny settlements of Balintore, Shandwick and Hilton of Cadboll have a rich Pictish heritage, including a fine standing **Pictish stone** at Shandwick. The stone is covered by a glass conservatory to protect the carvings, which include some fearsome depictions of mythical beasts. Inland from Shandwick on the Hill of Fearn is **Fearn Abbey**, a 14th-century monastery; it looks great when floodlit at night.

A few miles farther south is the tiny village of **Nigg**, overlooking sandy Nigg Bay. The old parish church here contains another intricately carved Pictish cross-slab, featuring carvings of St Anthony and St Paul in the desert.

See under Portmahomack for bus details.

INVERGORDON

Invergordon is a fairly plain industrial centre, but it's worth driving though town to see the vast oil rigs being repaired in the firth. You may even get lucky and see one of the patched rigs being towed back out to sea.

Pictish Symbol Stones

Little is known about the ancient culture that occupied the Highlands during the Iron Age. During the Roman invasion of Britain, the Roman legions met fierce resistance in the area they called Caledonia at the hands of Picts – semi-naked warriors inked with elaborate tattoos who lived in communal dwellings and fought from chariots. These 'savages' would melt away into the swamps and mountains when attacked, surviving off roots and wild animals and sweeping down into the glens to stage guerrilla raids on Roman forts.

Although huge numbers of Picts died at the battle of Mons Graupius (near Inverness) in AD 84, it was the Irish who erased the Picts from the history books. After the annihilation of the northern tribes by the Vikings in the 9th century, the Picts were absorbed into the Irish Kingdom of Dàl Riata, losing their identity, language and their religion.

However, the Picts left behind an enigmatic record of their strange and ancient culture in the form of carved symbol stones, thought to record the lineages and alliances between the different Pictish tribes. The Pictish stones dramatically show the demise of pagan worship in Scotland. The first stones, known as Class I, are rough-hewn blocks carved with pagan symbols of snakes, fish, boar and mythical beasts, and strange abstract symbols known as V-rods, Z-rods and crescents.

During the 8th century, coinciding with the cultural dominance of the Dàl Riata kings, Class II stones began to appear, featuring both pagan symbols and Celtic crosses. Some later had their pagan symbols savagely defaced. By AD 790, the pagan symbols had vanished, and the neat stone slabs featured just carved Celtic crosses and human figures, backed by distinctive Celtic knotwork.

There are Pictish stones across the Highlands and islands, but you can see many in their original locations in Caithness, Sutherland and on Black Isle.

THE NORTHWEST HIGHLANDS

Just south of Invergordon on the edge of the A9 is the **Storehouse of Foulis** (☎ *01349 830000; adult/child £3.50/2; open 10am-4pm Mon-Fri, 11am-4pm Sat & Sun)* a converted grainhouse on the shore, which has displays on seals and other wildlife and the history of the Munro Clan.

ALNESS

Alness is a typical small town, with shops, banks, a supermarket and the friendly **Dalmore Distillery** (☎ *882362)*, across the A9; book ahead to arrange free tours.

On a hilltop just west of Alness, the Scottish military hero Sir Hector Munro commemorated his most notable victory, the capture of the Indian town of Negapatam from the Dutch in 1781, by erecting the **Fyrish Monument**. The curious group of arches, thought to be a representation of the gateway to Negapatam, is reached by a steep footpath through the woods. If you're coming by car, turn towards Boath off the B9176 just west of Alness.

EVANTON

Surrounded by towering hills, the village of Evanton is the base for walks to the **Black Rock of Novar**, an almost unfeasibly narrow gorge leading to Loch Glass. The chasm is rarely more than 3.5m wide, but in places is more than 30m deep; a local man is said to have once leapt it in a single bound, which would make for one of the longest-standing jumps in history! To get here, take the footpath west from the bunkhouse, from where it's 2½ miles to the gorge.

Black Rock Bunkhouse (☎ *830917)* Bunks £8-9. This good hostel is handy for the trail to the gorge.

Stagecoach Inverness buses run from Inverness to Tain (£2.90, 25 minutes, hourly) via Evanton from Monday to Saturday.

BLACK ISLE
☎ 01381

A peninsula rather than an island, the Black Isle is linked to Inverness by the modern **Kessock Bridge**, which carries the A9 across the Moray Firth. There's a TIC (☎ 01463 731920) at North Kessock, which opens 10am to 5pm Monday to Saturday and 10am to 4pm on Sunday, where there's a hide for spotting red kites (a breed of hawk) on the firth.

Getting There & Around

Highland Country/Rapsons (☎ 01463-222 244) runs regular buses (Monday to Saturday) from Inverness to Cromarty (55 minutes), via Munlochy, Avoch, Fortrose and Rosemarkie.

Cromarty

At the northern tip of the Black Isle, the delightful village of Cromarty guards the entrance to the Cromarty Firth and was the former site of the King's Ferry (named after James IV), part of the ancient coastal road to the northern Highlands. At one time the estate belonged to Macbeth, but it passed to several different clans before becoming a royal burgh in 1685. The Scottish crown established a colony of southern nobles here to subdue the Highland clans, and the village later became an important port for grain, herring, sandstone and later, for crofters fleeing the clearances for the New World. Most of the town's red sandstone houses were built by wealthy merchants.

The 18th-century **Cromarty Courthouse** (☎ 01381-600418, Church St; adult/child £3/2; open 10am-5pm daily Apr-Oct, shorter hrs Nov-Mar) is a fascinating old building which houses a thoroughly interesting local-history museum. The admission fee includes an audio tour of Cromarty's other historic buildings (available in French).

Next to the Courthouse is **Hugh Miller's Cottage** (NTS; ☎ 01381-600245; adult/child £2.50/1; open noon-5pm daily May-Sept). Miller (1802–56) was a local stonemason and amateur geologist who later moved to Edinburgh and became a famous journalist and newspaper editor. There's a statue of Miller on a tall plinth in the cemetery above town.

At the end of Church St is the wonderful 17th-century Presbyterian **East Church**, with an impressive 'poor loft', a wooden balcony

that the rich paid a contribution to sit in, providing money for local charity projects. In the western porch is a fine Pictish stone, with crosses, swords and a sun symbol.

From Cromarty Harbour, **Dolphin Ecosse** (☎ 01381-600323) runs boat trips to see bottlenose dolphins and other wildlife. The 2½- hour trips cost £20 per person (minimum four people). There are interesting displays and dolphin information at the Dolphin Ecosse office on Victoria Place.

Several places offer B&B from £16 per head including **Mrs Robertson** (☎ 01381-600488, 7 Church St).

For something to eat, try the pleasant **Country Kitchen** (Cnr Church St & Forsyth Place), open Tuesday to Sunday, or the **Cromarty Arms** (☎ 01381-600230, Church St), opposite the court house, which is a good pub with bar meals and live music.

Fortrose & Rosemarkie

Fortrose is known for the ruined **Fortrose Cathedral**, built for the bishops of Ross between the 13th and 15th centuries. Oliver Cromwell removed many of the stones to build his fortress in Inverness, but the southern aisle is still recognisable and dates from the 14th century. In the grounds is the vaulted crypt of a 13th-century chapter house and sacristy.

Chanonry Point, a mile and a half to the east, is a favourite dolphin-spotting vantage point. There's also a plaque here to the Brahan Seer (see the boxed text 'The Man Who Saw Too Much' opposite).

In Rosemarkie, the **Groam House Museum** (☎ 01381-620961; adult/child £1.50/ 50p; open 10am-5pm Mon-Sat & 2pm-4.30pm Sun Easter & May-Sept, 2pm-4pm Sat & Sun Oct-Apr) has a superb collection of Pictish stones incised with pagan and early-Christian designs. The pleasant **Fairy Glen walk** starts at the northern end of the main street (Bridge St), in Rosemarkie. The signposted trail leads you through gorges with waterfalls.

Places to Stay & Eat

Fortrose Caravan & Camp Site (☎ 620326, Fortrose) Pitches/caravans £6/8. At the end of Academy St in Fortrose, this pleasant camp site is right on the waterfront.

Royal Hotel *(☎/fax 01381-620236, Union St, Fortrose)* Singles/doubles from £30/44. This nice black and white hotel has comfortable rooms and serves good bar meals (£6 to £11).

Chanonry Restaurant *(☎ 620690, Fortrose)* Meals £4-8. Open 5.30pm-9pm Tues-Sun. This friendly little BYO restaurant serves a range of Scottish seafood and has a tearoom that's open all day.

Plough Inn *(☎ 620164, Rosemarkie)* Lunches & dinners from £5-9. This ancient leaning pub dates from 1691 and serves unusually adventurous food as well as locally produced organic beer.

Crofters *(☎ 01381-620844)*, on the waterfront in Rosemarkie, has bar meals from around £4.50.

Avoch & Around

The village of Avoch (pronounced och) is the last coastal settlement before the A9 and is a good spot for dolphin spotting. From Easter to September, ***Avoch Dolphin Trips*** *(☎ 620958)* runs daily dolphin-spotting boat trips on the Moray Firth for £9/6 adult/child.

Just before the A9 at Munlochy is the **Clootie Well**, an ancient shrine to St Boniface. Local people still come here to tie a cloot (piece of cloth) to the nearby tree and make a wish.

South of Munlochy, you can visit **Black Isle Wildlife & Country Park** *(☎ 731656; adult/child £4/2.75; open 10am-6pm daily Mar-Nov)*, with deer, snakes, raccoons, rabbits and other animals you can pet. Nearby is the **Black Isle Brewery** *(☎ 811871; free tours 10am-6pm Mon-Sat)*, which produces some fine organic beers and offers tours of the brewery.

The ***Station Hotel*** *(☎ 620246, Avoch)* offers pub meals for under £5.

MID ROSS

Inland from Easter Ross and the Black Isle, Mid Ross marks the start of Scotland's wild and desolate interior. Aside from a cluster of small towns around the Beauly Firth, the region is almost uninhabited. In the more

---

The Man Who Saw Too Much

The Brahan Seer, Còinneach Odhar, was Scotland's answer to Nostradamus, making a string of highly accurate predictions about the Highlands during the 17th century. Amongst other things, the seer predicted the arrival of rich landowners from the south, the Highland Clearances, steam railways and the construction of the Caledonian Canal. Like Nostradamus, his predictions were often mapped to later events, most notably his claim that a terrible disaster would befall the world when the River Ness could be crossed dryshod in five places, which became true just days before the outbreak of WWII.

Legend has it that Còinneach Odhar gained his powers after falling asleep in an enchanted glade, and was able to see the future and the truth by gazing through the hole in a magical stone. In 1660, the countess of Seaforth summoned the Seer to Brahan in order to find out what her husband, the earl, was up to while 'on business' in France, but flew into a rage upon hearing that the earl had another woman on his lap. She accused the seer of slander and ordered him burned alive in hot tar at Fortrose.

The seer left a parting prophesy of doom upon the Seaforth clan, predicting that the reign of the Seaforths at Brahan would end with a deaf-mute chief who would follow his four heirs to the grave. The prophesy came true in 1793, when the Seaforth title passed to Francis Humberston MacKenzie, who was left deaf-mute after contracting scarlet fever. Fishermen may be interested to learn that Còinneach predicted that his mystical stone would return to the world of men in the belly of a pike from Loch Ussie.

---

mountainous western part of the district there are several wild and beautiful glens, with plenty of wildlife. An autumn visit reveals the forest colours at their very best.

DINGWALL
☎ 01349 ● pop 4750

Dingwall is a fairly typical small town, dominated by a hill-top monument to the impressively named Sir Hector Archibald MacDonald. The town has lots of shops, but it's not the most exciting place in the area. Macbeth is believed to have been born at Dingwall Castle, but little of the building remains today except a doocot (dove-cote) on Castle St, built from scavenged stones.

The **Dingwall Museum** (☎ 865366, Eagle Court; adult/child £1.50/50p; open 10am-5pm Mon-Sat May-Sept) is housed in a regal Victorian church and has exhibits on the history of the royal burgh of Dingwall.

There are several places to stay and eat. **Dingwall Camping & Caravan Club** (☎ 862236, Jubilee Park Rd) Pitches from £10. This pleasant camp site is just across the railway from the High St.

Strathyre (☎ 867514, 6 Station Rd) B&B from £17.50. You can't miss this tidy B&B, just across the road from the station.

Hedgefield Guest House (☎ 864168, fax 867347, Castle St) B&B from £17 per person. This old-style guest house has neat rooms and a good central location.

National Hotel (☎ 862166, fax 865178, High St) Singles/doubles from £35/60. This charismatic Victorian hotel is easy to find and has good rooms and food; lunch and dinner is available for £4 to £12.

STRATHPEFFER
☎ 01997 ● pop 830

This charming old spa town rose to prominence during Victorian times, when fashion-conscious Englishmen and women flocked here in huge numbers to swim in, wash with and – egad! – drink the sulphurous waters from Morrison Well. The influx of tourists led to the construction of some grand Victorian hotels and architectural follies.

The 'Harrogate of the North' slipped into genteel decay after WWII, and the old spa baths were demolished in 1950. Recently, there's been a revival of interest in the spa and the newly renovated **Pump Room** (☎ 420124; adult/child £2.50/1; open 10am-5pm Mon-Fri Apr-Oct, 10am-6pm Sat May-Sept & 7pm-9pm Mon-Sat July-Aug) has some wonderful displays showing the bizarre lengths that Victorians went to in pursuit of good health. If you dare, you can

sample the waters yourself; the chalybeate (iron-rich) spring water is delicious, but the sulphurous Morrison Well water is for strong stomachs only… The derelict Spa Pavilion is to be renovated as a tearoom.

Half a mile downhill from the TIC, at the old Victorian train station, is the **Highland Museum of Childhood** (☎ 421031; adult/child £1.50/free; open 10am-5pm Mon-Sat & 2pm-5pm Sun May-Oct, 5pm-7pm Mon-Fri July & Aug). The old railway lines have been replaced by flowerbeds and the museum has a wide range of social history displays about childhood in the Highlands, from birth to school, toys to child labour.

In summer, there's Highland dancing and bagpipe-playing in the square, culminating in the **Strathpeffer Highland Gathering** in August up at Castle Leod (call ☎ 421348 for more details), with the usual piping, tug of war and caber tossing.

Activities
There are many good **walking trails** around Strathpeffer, a legacy of the days when brisk exercise was prescribed as part of the treatment for spa patients. One of the best follows the old carriage drive up to the remains of an Iron-Age fort on Knock Farrel (4½ miles, two hours). On the way back you can detour to the **Touchstone Maze**, a modern construction of 81 stones representing the various types of rock found in Scotland. In a field off Nutwood Lane, near the Highland Museum of Childhood, is a Pictish slab carved with pagan symbols.

Golfers should head to the 18-hole **Strathpeffer Spa Golf Club** (☎ 421219) on the hill above town; green fees are £15 per round. There are good views from here to Ben Wyvis (1046m).

Places to Stay & Eat
Strathpeffer Youth Hostel (☎ 421532) Beds £9/7.50. Open May-Sept. The SYHA hostel is in Elsick House at the southern end of the village, a short uphill stroll from the TIC.

White Lodge (☎ 421730, The Square) B&B £22-25. Rooms are comfortable in this attractively proportioned house right by the main square.

Craigvar (☎ *421622, The Square*) B&B £25-30 per person. This deluxe B&B is housed in a delightful Georgian stone building near the pumphouse.

Scoraig (☎ *421847, 8 Kinnettas Square*) B&B £15-25 per person. Out of the centre near the SYHA, this is a good, cheap B&B.

Mackays Hotel (☎ *421542, The Square*) Rooms £17-25 per person. Across from the TIC, this hotel covers two buildings and offers welcoming rooms and tasty pub meals for around £8.

Many of the old spa hotels have fallen into neglect, but a few have been taken over and renovated.

Highland Hotel (☎ *421457, fax 421033, Square*) Rooms from £32.50 per person B&B. Two-night breaks for £50 per person. This is the magnificent, European chateau-style building overlooking the TIC, with wood-panelled lobby and lounge, and lovely wooded grounds.

There are several tearooms in town; probably the best are the *Spa Tearoom* at the Mace supermarket in the main square and the *Museum Tearoom* at the Highland Museum of Childhood, which has tables out on the old station platform.

Getting There & Away

Stagecoach Inverness (☎ 01463-239292) operates an hourly bus service Monday to Saturday from Inverness to Strathpeffer via Dingwall, continuing on to Contin.

The Inverness to Gairloch and Durness buses, and some Inverness to Ullapool buses, also run via Strathpeffer.

BEN WYVIS & AROUND

This easily accessible Munro looms to the northwest of Strathpeffer and offers great hiking opportunities to the 1046m summit. The peak is usually climbed from **Garbat** or **Garve**, both west of Strathpeffer on the A835 to Ullapool. Trains from Inverness to Kyle of Lochalsh stop at Garve, while buses between Inverness and Ullapool can drop you at Garbat or the Ben Wyvis trailhead.

The summit bid takes about five hours return from Garbat; use OS map No 20 and carry plenty of food and drinking water

(there's no ground-water on the hill). Stout footwear is essential as some of the tracks through the forestry can be extremely wet.

Places to Stay & Eat

Inchbae Lodge Hotel (☎ *01997-455269, fax 455207, Inchbae, nr Garve*) Singles/doubles from £43/66. The Inchbae Lodge Hotel is just a mile from the start of the Ben Wyvis trail and serves excellent bar meals (from £6), including vegetarian dishes.

Aultguish Inn Bunkhouse (☎/fax *01997-455254,* e *richard@aultguish.co .uk, by Garve*) Bunkhouse beds £6, no kitchen, en-suite B&B £9-12 per person. Farther west, on the road to Ullapool, this friendly inn is just below the Glascarnoch dam. Rooms are great value and the bar serves hearty Scottish bar meals (from £4.50).

Back towards Strathpeffer, **Contin** has a Spar shop, a camp site, B&Bs and a couple of hotels.

Achilty Hotel (☎ *01997-421355, fax 421923, Achilty, Contin*) En-suite B&B singles £32-54, doubles £49-74. You can get good bar meals and decent rooms at this 18th-century former coaching inn.

Coul House Hotel (☎ *01997-421487, fax 421945, Contin*) Bar meals £4-8, restaurant mains £15-17. This excellent country mansion dates from 1821 and lies up a half-mile private drive from Contin. The meals include treats such as salmon and venison. This place also offers singles for £54 to £70 and doubles from £78 to £110.

MUIR OF ORD

This unremarkable village is known for the **Glen Ord Distillery** (☎ *872004; adult/under-18s £3/free; open 9.30am-5pm Mon-Fri Mar-Oct, 9.30am-5pm Sat & 12.30pm-5pm Sun July-Sept;*), which produces one of the Highlands' famous single malts. The brewery is an atmospheric place and the tours feature the inevitable free sample. On the outskirts of Muir of Ord, the 18-hole **Muir of Ord Golf Club** (☎ *01463-870825*) is the oldest course in the north.

The **Black Isle Show** held in August is Scotland's largest one-day agricultural show.

THE NORTHWEST HIGHLANDS

Ord House Hotel (☎/fax 870492, Muir of Ord) Singles/doubles from £38/86. Behind the Muir of Ord distillery, this regal white country house hotel offers nice rooms in a secluded location at the end of a private drive. A set dinner is also available for £24.

Dower House (☎/fax 870090, Highfield) B&B from £50 per person. This upmarket B&B is about a mile north of Muir of Ord, surrounded by gardens and woodland.

Regular buses run here from Inverness and Dingwall.

About 3 miles northwest of Muir of Ord at Marybank, *Fairburn Activity Centre (☎ 01997-433397, fax 433328, Marybank)* offers a vast range of activities, including archery, mountain-biking, canoeing, rafting and abseiling. Prices for a half-/full day of activities are £14/24 per adult and £10/16 for children, and accommodation is available (singles/doubles from £31/44).

BEAULY
☎ 01463 • pop 1230

In 1584, Mary Queen of Scots is said to have given this village its name when she exclaimed, in French, '*quel beau lieu*' (what a beautiful place). That would be overstating it today, but Beauly has some pleasant places to stay and the interesting red-sandstone **Beauly Priory**, founded in 1230 by the French Valliscaullian order. The church fell into disuse after the Reformation, but the impressive ruin contains some fine old tombs, including that of Sir Kenneth MacKenzie of Kintail (1491), a member of the clan who took over Lewis and Harris from the MacLeods.

There are some interesting things to see around Beauly. Five miles west, at the Aigas Dam (River Beauly), there's a **fish lift** *(open 10am-3pm Mon-Fri mid-June–early Oct)* where you can see migrating salmon take advantage of a dam bypass. East of Beauly, off the Inverness road, is **Moniack Wineries** *(☎ 831283, Moniack Castle; tours £2; open 10am-5pm Mon-Sat)*, one of the last fruit wineries in the Highlands.

Beauly has supermarkets, banks with ATMs, and a couple of camp sites.

Lovat Bridge Caravan Park (☎ 782374, Lovat Bridge) Pitches £9. This camp site, near the bridge east of the town, is the best.

Heathmount (☎ 782411, Station Rd) B&B from £20 per person. This is a comfortable and friendly B&B.

Lovat Arms Hotel (☎ 782313, fax 782862, High St) Rooms from £35 per person. This imposing Victorian hotel on the main street has comfortable rooms, a cosy bar and good meals (mains £6 to £16, three-course set dinner £22.50).

Priory Hotel (☎ 782309, fax 782531, ⓔ reservations@priory-hotel.com, The Square) Singles £45-52.50, doubles £84-99. The attractive and centrally located Priory has good rooms and an excellent restaurant.

Beauly Tandoori (☎ 782221, High St) Curries £5-11. This curry-house does good Balti dishes.

Beauly Coffee (☎ 783709, 11 High St) is a friendly little tearoom with a gift shop.

Stagecoach Inverness (☎ 01463-239292) operates hourly services Monday to Saturday (four on Sunday) from Dingwall and Inverness.

Orkney & Shetland Islands

Lying off the north coast of Scotland and exposed to the full ferocity of the Atlantic Ocean, the Orkney and Shetland Islands are the most northerly part of the British Isles. The Vikings conquered this area at around the same time as the Gaels arrived on the Scottish mainland, leaving indelible marks on the islands' language and culture.

Both groups of islands have long been the preserve of bird-watchers, with numerous migratory species and colourful native birds such as puffins, but increasing numbers of visitors are coming here for the islands' spectacular and varied archaeological heritage and rugged coastal scenery. The shipwrecks around the coast also provide the opportunity for some impressive, if chilly, scuba diving.

Although there are good air and ferry links to the mainland, transport between the islands can be slow and infrequent and flights and ferries are often cancelled in bad weather. However, the remoteness and inaccessibility of the islands contributes to their rugged appeal, and most people who make the trip out here find that the unique island atmosphere more than makes up for the inconveniences.

Orkney Islands

Just 6 miles off the north coast of the Scottish mainland, this scenic group of islands remains attractively remote, with some dramatic coastal scenery ranging from 300m-high sandstone cliffs to white, sandy beaches. Of course, many people just come here for the friendly, unhurried environment.

There are some 70 islands in the Orkney group, but only about 16 are currently inhabited. Although the landscape is almost entirely treeless, Orkney is blessed with good soil and the islands are surprisingly lush and green – a real change from the mainland's bleak brown heath. There are still some rugged areas of high ground,

Highlights

- Walk the winding flagstone lanes of the historic fishing port of Stromness
- Make a house call to Britain's earliest inhabitants at the Neolithic village of Skara Brae
- Dive into the waters of Scapa Flow and explore the wrecks of the German naval fleet
- Soak up the wonderful peace and quiet on remote Papa Westray
- Get back to nature – to about half a million birds to be more precise – on the isolated isle of North Ronaldsay
- Share a view with Celts and Vikings from magnificent Mousa Broch's 13m-high walls
- Walk through 2800 years of history in the ruins of Jarlshof

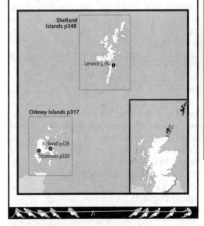

particularly on Hoy, the closest island to the Scottish mainland. Orkney is warmed by the Gulf Stream and the climate is often surprisingly mild, though fierce storms regularly lash the islands during winter. April and May are generally the driest months.

Prehistoric inhabitants here were forced to use stone rather than wood for their buildings, leaving behind a remarkable record of Neolithic, Bronze-Age and Iron-Age life. Over 1000 prehistoric sites have been identified, making this Europe's greatest concentration of ancient monuments. The most dramatic is Skara Brae on Mainland, a perfectly preserved Stone-Age village dating back 5000 years, which was exposed by a violent storm in 1850. Other impressive sites include the tomb of Maes Howe and the Ring of Brodgar (Mainland).

Orkney has always been the most fertile and hospitable of Scotland's islands, and migratory birds such as terns and puffins stop here in huge numbers from May to mid-July, attracting large numbers of migratory bird-watchers. The protected anchorage at Scapa Flow played a pivotal role in Britain's fortunes in WWI and WWII and there are numerous shipwrecks here.

HISTORY

Originally Celtic and Pictish, the islands were overrun by Viking marauders in the 8th century and absorbed into the Norwegian empire. For the next 300 years, the Norse colonies in Scotland were ruled from the earldom of Orkney in Kirkwall, and Norn (ancient Viking) became the main language of the Orcadians. The last Norse earl, Earl John, was murdered in Thurso in 1231, and the islands were governed by a string of 'caretaker' earls from the mainland, before passing to the Scottish crown in 1468 as part of a marriage agreement between James III of Scotland and Christian I of Norway and Denmark, the father of James' child-bride-to-be, Margaret. Even today, there are hints of those distant Scandinavian connections in the lilting accent with which Orcadians speak English.

Orkney was subsequently gifted to powerful lowland nobles, who imposed systems of land tenure and replaced the Norn language with Lallans (Lowland Scots). Perhaps the worst of these was Robert Stewart, the natural son of James V, who in 1564 was given the Royal Estates of Orkney and Shetland by his half-sister Mary Queen of Scots. Earl Robert embarked on a merciless campaign of oppression, continued by his son Earl Patrick, and the Stewarts became so hated that Patrick was forced to travel with a 50-man personal bodyguard. Bishop James Law eventually brought the Stewarts to justice, executing Earl Patrick and his son at Kirkwall in 1615. During the Reformation, the ruling nobles did their best to destroy the Episcopal church, replacing it with a Presbyterian kirk that was less threatening to their rule.

ORIENTATION & INFORMATION

The greatest concentration of people live on Mainland, the largest island in the group. Kirkwall is the capital and the seat of the Orkney Council, and is home to Orkney's main airport. Most visitors arrive by ferry at Stromness in the east of Mainland, or Burwick and St Margaret's Hope in the south.

The Orkney Tourist Board (☎ 01856-872856, W www.visitorkney.com), 6 Broad St, Kirkwall KW15 1NX, publishes a useful *Explore Orkney* brochure, detailing visitor attractions, services and accommodation options. It also has *The Islands of Orkney*, a very useful guide produced in conjunction with Orkney Ferries, which covers all the islands (except Mainland) in depth and contains ferry and flight schedules.

There are only two Tourist Information Centres (TICs), at Kirkwall and Stromness, but they're both open year-round.

The weekly *Orcadian* is the local newspaper and has entertainment listings. The paper also publishes a free paper, the *Visitor*, detailing lots of things to see and do.

Ordnance Survey (OS) Landranger maps covering Orkney include:

Landranger 5: Orkney – Northern Isles
Landranger 6: Orkney – Mainland
Landranger 7: Orkney – Southern Isles

ACTIVITIES

Orkney is delightful for **walking**, with fascinating historical ruins, fine beaches, gorgeous coastal scenery and plenty of wildlife. The walk on Hoy from Rackwick to the Old Man of Hoy sea stack must be one of the most scenic walks in Scotland. All the islands have something to offer and

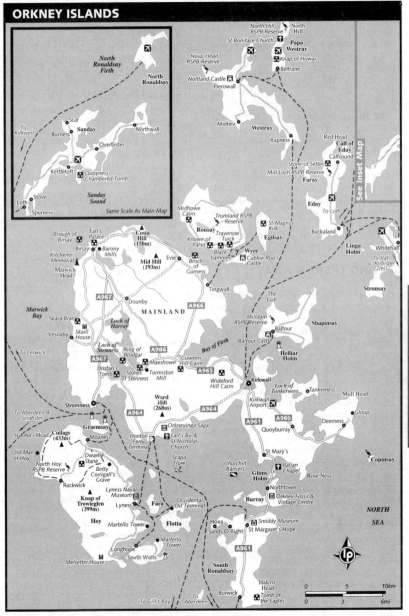

ORKNEY ISLANDS

many are so small that they can be walked around in a day; Papa Westray is particularly well set up for walkers.

Bird-watching is another major draw, and there are nature reserves at Mull Head (east Mainland), Copinsay, North Hoy, Milldam (Shapinsay), Mill Bay (Stronsay), Mill Loch and Ward Hill (Eday), Noup Head (Westray) and North Hill (Papa Westray).

The islands are perfect for **cycling**, and bikes can be carried inexpensively on all ferries. The wind can be a problem, but the islands are mostly low-lying and you'll stand a good chance of seeing wildlife from this quiet form of transport. You can rent bikes from various locations on Mainland, including Kirkwall and Stromness, and also on Hoy, Rousay, Sanday, Westray and Papa Westray.

For information on **scuba diving**, see Scapa Flow Wrecks in the Activities chapter.

GETTING THERE & AWAY
Air
Orkney is remarkably well connected to the rest of Scotland, and Kirkwall often seems less remote than many towns on the Scottish mainland. British Airways Express/ Loganair (☎ 0845 773 3377) fly to Kirkwall airport daily, except Sunday, from Aberdeen, Edinburgh, Glasgow, Inverness and Shetland's Sumburgh airport, with easy connections to London Heathrow, Birmingham, Manchester and Belfast. The cheapest return tickets (which must usually be bought 14 days in advance and require at least a Saturday night stay in Orkney) cost around £167 from Edinburgh or Glasgow, £124 from Aberdeen and £117 from Inverness. Kirkwall to Sumburgh costs around £90/73 one-way/return (the return price costs less).

Bus & Boat
Scottish Citylink (☎ 0870 550 5050) has daily coaches from Inverness to Scrabster (£10, three hours), connecting with the ferries to Stromness. Early morning departures from Glasgow or Edinburgh, and overnighters from London, connect with the Scrabster bus at Inverness.

John o'Groats Ferries (☎ 01955-611353) operates The Orkney Bus, a summer-only service between Inverness and Kirkwall. The ticket (single/return £28/40, five hours) includes bus travel from Inverness to John o'Groats, the passenger ferry to Burwick, and another bus from Burwick to Kirkwall. There's one bus daily in May and two daily from June to early September.

Boat
There are several car and passenger ferries from the Scottish mainland to Mainland Orkney, but services can be very busy and it's best to book ahead, particularly in July and August.

In October 2002, P&O ferry services to Orkney and Shetland will be taken over by NorthLink Ferries, a joint venture between Caledonian MacBrayne (CalMac) and the Royal Bank of Scotland. It will introduce three brand-new, purpose-built ferries, and plans to provide more frequent services with lower fares. Ferries from Aberdeen and Lerwick (Shetland) will dock at Kirkwall. For the latest details, visit the Web site at W www.northlinkferries.co.uk.

From Scrabster P&O Scottish Ferries (☎ 01224-572615, fax 574411, W www .posf.co.uk) operates a regular car ferry from Scrabster, near Thurso, to Stromness. (passenger/car £16.50/51, £15.50/45 September to May, two hours) one-way and £33/86 (£31/74 September to May) return. Motorcycles/bicycles cost £14/3 one-way and £28/6 return year-round.

Schedules vary slightly from month to month, but from April to October there are sailings from Scrabster at noon daily, plus at 6am weekdays and 5.45pm on Friday and Saturday. From Stromness there are sailings at 9am and 3pm daily, plus an extra 8pm sailing on Monday. The rest of the year there are sailings from Scrabster at noon daily plus at 6am weekdays, and from Stromness at 9am daily and at 3pm Monday to Thursday. You can book online at its Web site.

There are special vehicle rates for the Aberdeen-Stromness-Scrabster route: cars/ motorcycles/bicycles cost £118-132/34/7.

Foot passengers just pay the two single fares added together.

From Shetland P&O sails from Lerwick to Stromness (passenger/car/motorcycle/bicycle £40.50/95/21/4, eight to 10 hours) at noon on Friday year-round, and at noon on Wednesday and Friday from June to August.

Ferries from Stromness to Lerwick leave at noon on Sunday year-round and at 10pm on Tuesday and noon on Sunday June to August; return fares are £81/136/42/8.

From Aberdeen You can also get to Orkney on the P&O service from Aberdeen to Lerwick, which sails via Stromness (Aberdeen to Stromness takes eight to 14 hours). Ferries leave Aberdeen on Saturday, arriving at Stromness on Sunday and continuing to Lerwick on the same day. In the reverse direction, ferries leave Stromness on Friday continuing overnight to Aberdeen. From July to August there's an additional service from Aberdeen on Tuesday, returning from Stromness on Wednesday. Aberdeen to Stromness costs £43.50/87 one-way/return for passengers, £113/148 for cars, £21/42 for motorcycles and £4/8 for bikes. From September to May, it costs £40.50/81 for passengers and £95/136 for cars.

The minimum fare gets you a reclining seat; there's a supplement for a cabin-berth of £8.50 to £24 per person. You can use this service on the Aberdeen-Lerwick-Stromness-Scrabster route or vice versa.

From Gills Bay Pentland Ferries (☎ 01856-831226, Ⓦ www.pentlandferries.com) runs a shorter and less expensive car-ferry crossing from Gill's Bay, about 2 miles west of John o'Groats, to St Margaret's Hope on Mainland Orkney; see John o'Groats in The Northwest Highlands chapter for prices and times.

From John o'Groats During summer, John o'Groats Ferries (☎ 01955-611353, Ⓦ www.jogferry.co.uk) operates a passenger ferry from John o'Groats to Burwick, on the southern tip of South Ronaldsay – for details, see John o'Groats in The Northwest Highlands chapter.

GETTING AROUND

Highland Council (☎ 01463-702695) Glenurquhart Rd, Inverness IV3 5NS, publishes *The Highlands, Orkney, Shetland and Western Isles* (10p), a public transport map which lists air, bus and ferry services in Orkney. Also available is *North Highland and Orkney* (£1), an annual public transport guide which includes detailed timetables.

Air

British Airways/Loganair (☎ 0845 773 33 77 or ☎ 01856-872494) operates inter-island air services between Kirkwall airport and North Ronaldsay, Westray, Papa Westray, Stronsay, Sanday and Eday. For details, see the relevant island entries.

Bus

Orkney Coaches (☎ 01856-870555) runs a network of bus services on Mainland and South Ronaldsay. Few buses run on Sunday. A free timetable for all services is available from the TICs.

You can save money with Day Rover (£6) and 3-Day Rover (£15) tickets, which allow unlimited travel on bus routes operated by Orkney Coaches.

Postbuses are few and far between – the only regular postbus is the circular service around Rousay, which runs twice every morning Monday to Saturday.

Boat

The largest island, Mainland, is joined by causeways to Burray and South Ronaldsay. Orkney Ferries Ltd (☎ 01856-872044, Ⓦ www.orkneyferries.co.uk), Shore St, Kirkwall, operates car ferries from Mainland to the other islands: Houton (east of Stromness) is the port for ferries to Lyness (on Hoy) and Flotta; Stromness has ferries to Graemsay and North Hoy (for Rackwick and Old Man of Hoy); Kirkwall has ferries to Shapinsay, Westray, Papa Westray, North Ronaldsay, Eday, Sanday and Stronsay; and Tingwall has ferries to Rousay, Wyre and Egilsay. See the island entries for details.

Car

There are several car-hire companies on Mainland, which charge from £29 to £35 per day including VAT, insurance and unlimited mileage. See Getting Around under Kirkwall and Stromness for details.

Orkney Motorhome Hire (☎ 01856-874391, W www.orkney-motorhome-hire .co.uk) rents out camper vans – comfy for two adults, but will sleep two adults and three kids at a pinch – for £590 per week in July and August, £490 per week from April to June, September and October, and £390 per week in winter.

Organised Tours

Wildabout Orkney *(☎/fax 01856-851011, mobile ☎ 0777 637 8966, e wildabout@ orkney.com)* Tours £14-18.50 per person. Available Mar-Oct. This small tour company offers day trips covering archaeology, history, folklore and wildlife. The minibus tours pick up at Stromness ferry terminal, the TIC on Palace Rd in Kirkwall, and at Kirkwall Youth Hostel.

Discover Orkney *(☎/fax 01856-872865, 44 Clay Loan, Kirkwall)* Discover Orkney caters to individuals and small groups, and offers guided tours and walks throughout the islands in the company of a well-informed Orcadian guide.

Orcadian Reflections *(☎ 01856-781327, Midhouse, Holm)* Around £11.50 per hr. This operator offers custom-made tours of the islands with qualified guides.

Orkney Guides *(☎ 01856-811777, Asgard, Orphir)* From £65 for 5 hrs (£80 in a foreign language). Orkney Guides offers customised guided tours and the various guides can speak Spanish, French, German, Italian, Dutch, Norwegian, Swedish and Danish.

Also, ***Brass's Taxis*** *(☎ 01856-850750)* at the ferry terminal in Stromness and ***Peedie Cab*** *(☎ 01856-741398)* in Deerness offer taxi tours of Mainland from around £15 per hour for up to four people.

STROMNESS

☎ 01856 ● pop 1850

The appealing grey-stone port of Stromness is the very image of an island town, with a narrow, flagstone-paved main street and tiny alleys leading down to the waterfront between tall stone houses. The town has changed little since its heyday in the 18th century when it was a busy staging post for ships avoiding the troublesome English Channel during the European wars. In the 19th century, Stromness became an important herring and whaling port and was used as a depot by the Hudson Bay Company of Canada, which employed many local men.

Vikings had sheltered in the natural harbour at Hamnavoe since the 12th century, but Stromness wasn't formally founded

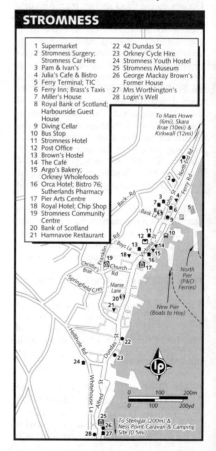

STROMNESS

1 Supermarket
2 Stromness Surgery; Stromness Health Centre
3 Pam & Ivan's
4 Julia's Cafe & Bistro
5 Ferry Terminal; TIC
6 Ferry Inn; Brass's Taxis
7 Miller's House
8 Royal Bank of Scotland; Harbourside Guest House
9 Diving Cellar
10 Bus Stop
11 Stromness Hotel
12 Post Office
13 Brown's Hostel
14 The Café
15 Argo's Bakery; Orkney Wholefoods
16 Orca Hotel; Bistro 76; Sutherlands Pharmacy
17 Pier Arts Centre
18 Royal Hotel; Chip Shop
19 Stromness Community Centre
20 Bank of Scotland
21 Hamnavoe Restaurant
22 42 Dundas St
23 Orkney Cycle Hire
24 Stromness Youth Hostel
25 Stromness Museum
26 George Mackay Brown's Former House
27 Mrs Worthington's
28 Login's Well

To Maes Howe (6mi), Skara Brae (10mi) & Kirkwall (12mi)

North End Rd

Ferry Rd

Back Rd

Bank La

Boys La

Franklin Rd

Christie's Brae

Church Rd

Springfield Cres

Manse Lane

North Pier

New Pier (Boats to Hoy)

North Pier (P&O Ferries)

Victoria St

Hellihole Rd

Dundas St

Whitehouse La

Alfred St

0   100   200m
0   100   200yd

To Stenigar (200m) & Ness Point Caravan & Camping Site (0.5mi)

The Shetlands boast a population of over 250,000 puffins.

Crab traps on Papa Stour

Ahoy there! The distant Isle of Hoy from the west coast of the Orkney Islands

Scalloway Castle, Shetland

Networking in Stromness: fishing trawlers prepare for sea.

Ancient Skara Brae is the best-preserved prehistoric village in northern Europe.

Orkney's enigmatic Ring of Brodgar, sited on a narrow isthmus, is over 4500 years old.

The chambered burial cairn at the summit of Ronas Hill (499m), the highest point in the Shetlands

until the 1620s when the bishop of Orkney established a series of fues (feudal plots) on the bay. When the *Discovery* and *Resolution* stopped here on their return from Captain Cook's fatal voyage to the South Seas, they found a busy village of at least 200 residents. Stromness became a Royal Burgh in its own right in 1817.

Stromness is the main arrival point for ferries from the Scottish mainland, but it still has the atmosphere of a working fishing village, with locals stopping to chat in the narrow streets and a handful of family-run general merchants, grocery and butchers shops. Stromness is also excellently located for trips to Skara Brae, Maes Howe, the Ring of Brodgar and the island of Hoy.

Orientation & Information

Almost everything can be found on the long, winding main road, which changes its name every few hundred yards. At the northern end of the village, near the TIC and ferry terminal, it's called Victoria St, changing to Graham Place, Dundas St, Alfred St and South End as it winds south towards Ness Point at the head of the bay.

The efficient TIC (☎ 872856, e info@ otb.ossian.net) is at the ferry terminal and its hours vary – you can rely on it being open 8.30am to 4pm weekdays and 10am to 4pm Saturday and Sunday, April to October (also 7.30pm to 8.30pm for late ferries). Winter hours are usually 8.30am to 10am weekdays and 1pm to 3pm Saturday. There's a bureau de change here and you can pick up the interesting *Stromness Heritage Guide* leaflet.

For Internet access, Stromness Community Centre (☎ 850712) at the top of Church Rd opens Monday to Saturday mornings and Monday and Tuesday evenings; it costs £2.50 per 30 minutes (£1.25 evenings and Saturday morning). Julia's Café & Bistro near the bus stop charges £1 per 10 minutes.

There's a Royal Bank of Scotland with an ATM on Victoria St, just behind the TIC, or a Bank of Scotland farther south on the same street.

Sutherland Pharmacy (☎ 873240), 30 Victoria St, is well stocked and also sells

camera film. Stromness Surgery (☎ 850205) is near the harbour on John St.

Things to See

The main occupation in Stromness is simply strolling along the narrow, atmospheric main street and watching island life unfold.

Pier Arts Centre (*☎ 850209, 30 Victoria St; admission free; open 10.30am-12.30pm*

The Amazing Dr Rae

One of Orkney's most famous sons was the inimitable Dr John Rae, a surgeon and explorer for the Hudson Bay Company who discovered the Northwest Passage between the Atlantic and the Pacific. Over the years, Dr Rae mapped hundreds of miles of the Canadian coast, travelling alone through the ice floes in a tiny inflatable dinghy and hunting or trading with Inuit Indians for food, before joining the search for the missing Franklin Expedition in 1848.

Led by Sir John Franklin, the lavishly funded expedition had set off from London to chart the Northwest Passage in 1845 and vanished without a trace near Baffin Island. In 1854 Dr Rae returned to England with 'melancholy tidings'; with the help of Inuit guides, he had discovered the bodies of nearly 40 sailors from the doomed expedition, frozen solid and bearing the obvious signs of human cannibalism.

This was too much for the 'civilised' English to contemplate. Dr Rae's reputation was shot down by Lady Franklin and other important establishment figures – including Charles Dickens – who refused to believe that such high-ranking socialites as Sir John could have fallen so low as to eat the bodies of their fallen comrades. Franklin was credited with the discovery of the Northwest Passage, and Dr Rae was marginalised, working as a physician in London until his death in 1893. Only posthumously were his incredible achievements given the recognition they deserved.

There's a fine memorial cenotaph to Dr John Rae in St Magnus Cathedral in Kirkwall.

& *1.30pm-5pm Tues-Sat)* is a progressive gallery exhibiting 20th-century British and international art, including works by Barbara Hepworth and Ben Nicholson. Farther south, the house at **42 Dundas St** was once the home of Eliza Frazer, who was shipwrecked in Queensland, Australia, giving her name to Fraser Island.

The wonderful **Stromness Museum** *(☎ 850925, 52 Alfred St; adult/student/child £2.50/2/50p; open 10am-5pm daily May-Sept, 10.30am-12.30pm & 1.30pm-5pm Mon-Sat Oct-Apr)* has an extraordinary collection of bits and pieces from the town's rich maritime heritage. Among the more unusual exhibits are South Sea Islander artefacts brought here by the survivors of Captain Cook's expedition and the tiny infboat used by Dr John Rae of the Hudson Bay Company in his Arctic explorations (see the earlier boxed text 'The Amazing Dr Rae'). Other displays cover whaling, natural history and the Scapa Flow wrecks.

Across the street from the museum is the house where local poet and novelist **George Mackay Brown** lived from 1968 until his death in 1996. Farther south on the main street is **Login's Well**, where famous ships such as the *Discovery* and *Resolution* stopped to take on water.

Special Events
The annual **Orkney Folk Festival** *(☎ 851331, **W** www.orkneyfolkfestival.com)* is a four-day event based in Stromness during the last weekend in May, with a programme of folk concerts and *ceilidhs* and informal pub sessions. Part of the **St Magnus Festival** is also held here every June, and the **Orkney Blues Festival** *(☎ 850325, **W** www.orkneyblues.com)* takes place in September. The **Tall Tales for Short Days** storytelling festival, held in October, is also interesting. For festival details contact the Kirkwall TIC.

Places to Stay
Ness Point Caravan & Camping Site *(☎ 873535 Alfred St, Ness Point)* Pitches £4. Stromness' breezy camp site overlooks the bay at the southern end of town, about 15 minutes' walk from the ferry.

Brown's Hostel *(☎ 850661, 45 Victoria St)* Beds £8. Open year-round. Brown's is a very popular 14-bed independent hostel, just five minutes' walk from the ferry. There's no curfew – knock at the house upstairs to check in.

Stromness Youth Hostel *(☎ 850589, Hellihole Rd)* Beds £9/7.75. Open May-Sept. This large and well-equipped Scottish Youth Hostels Association (SYHA) hostel is a 10-minute walk south of the ferry terminal.

Pam & Ivan's *(☎ 850642, 15 John St)* B&B £16-18 per person. This comfy B&B is directly opposite the ferry terminal. The basic rate includes a continental breakfast – a cooked breakfast costs an extra £2.

Miller's House *(☎ 851969, fax 851967, 13 John St)* Singles/doubles from £25/40. There are very comfortable rooms available here in the town's oldest house. The same owners also run the well-located ***Harbourside Guest House*** *(☎ 851969, 7 Victoria St).*

Mrs Worthington's *(☎ 850215, 2 South End)* B&B doubles from £36. This gorgeous, tall 19th-century house sits on its own pier not far from the museum and has a lovely waterside lounge. Great breakfasts are served in the charming old kitchen.

Stenigar *(☎ 850438, Ness Rd)* B&B £25-30. This fine former boatyard is at the end of the main street towards Ness Point, near the small park known as the Cannon.

Orca Hotel *(☎ 850447, **e** info@orcahotel.com, 76 Victoria St)* B&B from £22 per person. Formerly known as the Oakleigh, this central and friendly hotel has a great restaurant.

Ferry Inn *(☎ 850280, fax 851332 **e** lyall@ferryinn.com, John St)* Singles £18-30, doubles £42-50. The small Ferry Inn, opposite the ferry terminal, has a popular bar and good-value rooms.

Stromness Hotel *(☎ 850298, fax 850610, Pier Head)* B&B £30-39 per person (£19.50 Nov-Feb). The recently refurbished Stromness Hotel is a regal Victorian stone building that dominates the main street in front of the harbour. It has well-appointed rooms with harbour views and offers excellent meals at its *restaurant* (see Places to Eat) plus cheaper bar meals.

Places to Eat

Hamnavoe Restaurant (☎ 850606, 35 Graham Place) Mains £9-16. Open 7pm-late Mon-Sat Apr-Sept. The Hamnavoe is Stromness' gourmet choice, with a menu of steak and seafood dishes. Despite being fairly expensive, it doesn't accept credit cards.

Stromness Hotel (☎ 850298, Pier Head) Mains £10-20. The attractive restaurant at this fine old hotel serves up plenty of local produce – try the steak and smoked oyster pie.

Royal Hotel (☎ 850342, 55 Victoria St) Mains £6-17. This excellent and popular restaurant serves up treats such as steak stuffed with queenies (scallops) and flamed in whisky.

Bistro 76 (☎ 851803, 76 Victoria St) Mains £9-14. This reputable bistro in the basement of the Orca Hotel has great food including scallops and loch trout, and has occasional live bands.

Ferry Inn (☎ 850280, John St) Mains £5-14. This relaxed pub has good pub meals and more expensive steaks and seafood.

Julia's Café & Bistro (☎ 850904, Ferry Rd) Lunch mains £3-6, dinner mains £9-13. Bistro open evenings Wed-Sun; cafe open daily. This attractive eatery near the ferry terminal serves good cafe-style snacks and light meals during the day, and more formal dinners in the evening.

The Café (☎ 850368, 22 Victoria St) Snacks £1.50-5. Open daily. This friendly little place has a waterfront deck and does toasties, pizzas, burgers, lasagne and baked potatoes to eat in or take away.

The *Chip Shop (Victoria St)* sells deep-fried haggis and black pudding as well as fish suppers for £3.20.

Self-caterers should head to the large *Co-op supermarket (John St)* or *Argo's Bakery (Victoria St)*; there are also several traditional butchers and grocers for fresh meat and vegetables.

Entertainment

Although Orkney was 'dry' from 1920 to 1947, there are several nice drinking spots here now. The bar at the *Stromness Hotel* is recommended and often has live music.

Other pleasant drinking holes with live music include the *Ferry Inn* and *Bistro 76*. See Places to Eat earlier for further details of these venues.

Shopping

For local produce, *Orkney Wholefoods (☎ 850840, 36 Victoria St)* sells tasty fresh and smoked seafood, whisky-marinated herring, Orkney cheddar, Orkney ice cream and oatcakes.

Getting There & Away

For information on ferries to Scrabster, Lerwick and Aberdeen, see Getting There & Away under Orkney Islands near the start of the chapter. For boats to Hoy, see that section later.

For bus services, see Getting There & Away under Kirkwall later.

Getting Around

Orkney Cycle Hire (☎ 850255), 54 Dunas St, and Brass's Taxis (☎ 850750), North End Rd, both hire out bikes for £5 per day. Brass's Taxis also offers car hire (☎ 850850), or alternatively you can try Stromness Car Hire (☎ 850973), John St; rates vary from £25 to £31 per day.

NORTH FROM STROMNESS
☎ 01856

North of Stromness, the west coast rises into a truly dramatic series of cliffs and exposed sea stacks at **Yesnaby**, off the road to Skara Brae. It's a giddying feeling standing on the edge and looking down over the 150m drop to the boiling ocean below. You can walk south from here all the way to Stromness via the **Yesnaby Castle** sea stack. Take care on the cliffs in high winds, and in early summer watch out for nesting seabirds which may dive-bomb you to scare you away from their nests.

Skara Brae & Skaill House

Overlooking a beautiful sandy bay, 8 miles north of Stromness, is northern Europe's best preserved prehistoric village, Skara Brae *(owned by Historic Scotland, HS; ☎ 841815, Bay of Skaill; adult/child £3.50/1.20, joint* ticket with Skaill House £4.50/1.30; open 9.30am-6.30pm daily Apr-Sept, 9.30am-4.30pm Mon-Sat & 2pm-4.30pm Sun Oct-Mar). Built in around 3500 BC, this remarkable site was hidden under the sand dunes until 1850 when a severe storm blew away the sand and grass covering the stone huts. The local laird, William Watt, discovered the complex, which sits just half a mile from his mansion at Skaill, and made excavating the ruins his personal project for the next 18 years. Skara Brae was given World Heritage Listing in 1999.

The houses are in an incredible state of preservation. Even the stone furniture – beds, boxes and dressers – has survived the 5000 years since people last lived here. Among the buildings archaeologists discovered carved ceremonial stones, stone tools, bone pots and even tokens and primitive dice from ancient games. You can walk around on the banks between the huts and look down onto the village, but walking inside the huts is forbidden. The stylish visitors centre includes a museum, a good cafe, and a re-creation of House No 1 as it may have looked when it was inhabited. The official guidebook includes a good self-guided tour.

Skaill House (☎ 841501; adult/child £3/2.20, joint ticket with Skara Brae £4.50/1.30; open 9.30am-6.30pm daily Apr-Sept, 10am-4pm Thur & Sat Oct) is an early 17th-century mansion, the former home of the laird of Breckness, William Watt, who discovered Skara Brae. There are fine displays of period furniture and memorabilia, including Captain Cook's dinner service.

Places to Stay *Flotterston House* (☎ 841700, Sandwick) B&B from £18 per person. This neat square Victorian house is the closest B&B to Skara Brae – the ruins are a 1½-mile walk northwest.

Getting There & Away From May to September, bus No 8A runs twice daily to Skara Brae from Kirkwall and Stromness. Alternatively, it's possible to walk 9 miles along the coast from Stromness to Skara Brae via Yesnaby and the Broch of Borwick.

Historic Scotland Monuments

Orkney contains an amazing concentration of prehistoric monuments, many of them in the care of Historic Scotland (HS), which charges a small admission in exchange for their skilled conservation work. All the sites are well worth a visit and you can save money with a joint ticket that covers Maes Howe, Skara Brae, Skaill House, the Broch of Gurness, the Brough of Birsay, and the Bishop's Palace and Earl's Palace in Kirkwall; it costs £11/3.50 per adult/child April to September and £10/3 October to March.

Birsay
The small village of Birsay, with a shop and post office, is 6 miles north of Skara Brae. Birsay was a former stronghold of the despot Robert Stewart, who was appointed earl of Orkney by his half-sister Mary Queen of Scots. The ruins of the **Earl's Palace**, built using forced labour in 1574, dominate the village centre. Just beyond the palace is the *Heimdall Tearoom*, open 11am to 6pm daily, April to October.

About 1½ miles south along the cliffs is the dramatically located **Kitchener Memorial**, dedicated to Lord Kitchener of Khartoum who drowned when HMS *Hampshire* sank here in 1916.

Around 2½ hours either side of low tide (check times with a TIC) you can walk out across a causeway to the **Brough of Birsay** (☎ 841815; adult/child 1.50/50p; open 9.30am-6.30pm Apr-Sept), three-quarters of a mile northwest of the Earl's Palace. This windswept island is the site of extensive Norse ruins, including a number of longhouses and the 12th-century St Peter's Church. There's also a replica of a Pictish stone which was found here, carved with an eagle and human figures. St Magnus was buried here after his murder on Egilsay in 1117, and the island was a place of pilgrimage until a few centuries ago. You can continue across the headland to the attractive lighthouse, built in 1925, which has fantastic views along the coast.

Barony Mills (☎ 771276; adult/family £1.50/4; open 10am-1pm & 2pm-5pm daily Apr-Sept), 600m east of the Earl's Palace at the northeastern end of Loch of Boardhouse, is the last working, water-powered meal mill in Orkney, and you can see the miller at work.

Places to Stay Accommodation is scattered across the countryside around the village centre.

Birsay Hostel (☎ 873535 ext 2404, office hr only, fax 876327, Birsay) Beds £7.25/6.30. Open year-round. Formerly the village school, this 30-bed, council-run hostel now provides group accommodation for a minimum of 12 people, but you can camp and use the facilities for £2.75/2.

Primrose Cottage (☎/fax 721384, e iclouston@talk21.com, Birsay) Singles £14-19, doubles £34-38, dinner B&B £24-29 per person. Peaceful Primrose Cottage is a modern bungalow overlooking Marwick Bay, 2 miles south of the Earl's Palace.

Barony Hotel (☎ 721327, fax 721302, Birsay) B&B £25-30 per person. Open May-Sept. The Barony Hotel, overlooking Loch of Boardhouse about half a mile south of Birsay, is an angler's favourite, with a good restaurant serving steaks and seafood; it's also wheelchair friendly.

Evie

On an exposed headland at Aikerness, a 1½-mile walk northeast from the straggling village of Evie, you'll find the **Broch of Gurness** (☎ 751414; adult/child £2.80/1; open 9.30am-6.30pm daily Apr-Sept, 9.30am-4.30pm Mon-Sat & 2pm-4.30pm Sun Oct-Nov), an Iron-Age stone tower with walls still standing to 4m despite 2000 years of coastal erosion. Although not nearly as impressive as Mousa Broch in Shetland, this is certainly the best-preserved broch in Orkney and the main tower is surrounded by the remains of a number of well-preserved outhouses, including a curious shamrock-shaped building. The visitors centre has some interesting displays on the culture that built these remarkable fortifications.

Evie has a well-stocked shop and post office.

Eviedale Campsite & Bothy (☎/fax 751270, e colin.richardson@orkney.com, Dyke Farm, Evie) Pitches £3-4 plus £1/50p per adult/child, bothy beds £5. Open Apr-Sept. Clustered around the northern end of the village near the church, Eviedale comprises a small, basic bothy with four beds, a toilet and cooking equipment, plus a small camp site. Don't get this place confused with the run-down bothy hut farther south.

Woodwick House (☎ 751330, fax 751383, e woodwickhouse@appleonline.net, Evie) B&B £27-38 per person. This rather fine country house is set in beautiful wooded grounds overlooking a little sandy bay at the southern end of Evie. The food at the **restaurant**, where a three-course dinner costs £22, is superb.

STROMNESS TO KIRKWALL
☎ 01856

Heading east to Kirkwall, there are two roads from Stromness: the A964, which runs along the south coast via Houton; and the more direct A965 which passes several of Orkney's most famous archaeological sites, including the Standing Stones of Stenness, the Ring of Brodgar and Maes Howe. The A967, for Skara Brae, branches north off the A965 a mile north of Stromnessl; the A964 branches south at Loch of Stenness.

Stenness

The scattered village of Stenness sits at the end of a huge loch, about 4 miles east of Stromness. There's not much here, just a few houses, a petrol station and a hotel, but Stenness is surrounded by some of the most interesting prehistoric monuments on Orkney, easily accessible using the regular bus service between Stromness and Kirkwall (see Getting There & Away under Kirkwall later).

Closest to Stenness, on the B9055 about 500m north of the main crossroads, are the **Standing Stones of Stenness** (admission free; open year-round), a prehistoric stone circle dating from around 2500 BC. Only four of the original 12 mighty stones remain

ORKNEY & SHETLAND ISLANDS

erect, but one is over 5m high. Nearby, on a small promontory in the loch, is **Unstan's Tomb**, a chambered cairn from the 3rd millennium BC.

A short walk to the east are the excavated remains of **Barnhouse Neolithic Village**, thought to have been inhabited by the builders of Maes Howe, which includes the remains of six houses and a large ceremonial chamber.

Standing Stones Hotel (☎ 850449, fax 851262, Stenness) Singles/doubles from £40/76. This comfortable hotel sits right on the loch shore in the middle of Stenness and serves up good pub meals from around £5.

Mill of Eyreland (☎ 850136, fax 851633, Stenness) Singles £30-35, doubles £48-60. This wonderfully restored stone mill offers excellent rooms close to the archaeological action.

Ring of Brodgar

About a mile north of Stenness on the narrow isthmus of land between Loch Stenness and Loch Harray, the Ring of Brodgar *(admission free; open year-round)* is a wide circle of standing stones, some over 5m tall. Twenty-seven of the original 60 stones are still standing among the heather. These old stones, raised skyward 4500 years ago, still attract elemental forces – on 5 June 1980, one of the stones was split in two by a bolt of lightning. It's a powerful place, with the two lochs standing still and serene on either side. Legend has it that the stones are the petrified bodies of giants who danced here too long one night and were turned to stone by the rising sun.

Maes Howe

Constructed about 5000 years ago, Maes Howe *(☎ 761606; adult/child £2.80/1; open 9.30am-6.30pm daily Apr-Sept, 9.30am-4.30pm Mon-Sat & 2pm-4.30pm Sun Oct-Mar)* is the finest chambered tomb in Western Europe. From the outside, the grass-covered mound is nothing much to speak of, but once you enter the low stone passage leading into the central chamber, you step back several millennia to the dawn of man. The vast main chamber is over

6.7m high and 35m wide, and the entrance passage is aligned with the direction of sunset at the winter solstice.

No remains were found when the tomb was excavated in the 19th century, so it's not known how many people were originally buried here or whether they were buried with any of their worldly goods. What is known is that Vikings returning from the Crusades broke into the tomb in the 12th century, searching for treasure. They found none, but left a wonderfully earthy collection of graffiti, carved in runes on the walls of the tomb, including profundities such as 'Thorni bedded Helgi' and several 12th-century tags of the 'Ottarfila-was-here' variety – some things never change. There are some more artistic creations, including a crusader cross, a wonderful dragon-like lion, a walrus and a knotted serpent.

Maes Howe is about 10 minutes' walk east of the Stenness crossroads. Buy your ticket at **Tormiston Mill**, across the road from the tomb, where there's a cafe serving snacks and light meals, a gift shop, a small exhibition and a 15-minute video about Orkney's prehistoric sites. On site, a guide will take you through the history of Maes Howe and pinpoint the various bits of graffiti with a torch. The official guide is worth buying; it contains all the runes, mapped to the walls of the tomb.

Finstown

This scattered settlement on the Bay of Firth is the largest village between Stromness and Kirkwall, and marks the turn-off to the **Cuween Hill Chambered Tomb**, a Neolithic cairn in a splendid position overlooking the bay. The village has a shop and petrol station. About 4 miles east, overlooking Kirkwall, is **Wideford Hill Chambered Cairn**.

Sitting right on the lochside, *Atlantis Lodges (☎ 761581, fax 875361, Finstown)* is a complex of very comfortable modern chalets; the apartments all have sea views and kitchens and are available nightly (doubles cost £41 to £49) or weekly (rates for two/four/six people are £208/360/364).

THE SOUTH COAST

☎ 01856

There are a few things to see at Orphir, a scattered community with no shop, about 9 miles west of Kirkwall. From the main road, it's a 10-minute walk to the Orkneyinga centre.

The **Orkneyinga Saga Centre** *(admission free; open 9am-5pm daily)* has displays relating to the Orkneyinga Saga (a Norse historical text about Orkney dating from 1136 – see the Web site at Ⓦ www.orkney jar.com) and a widescreen video show. Translations of the saga are available from the Orcadian Bookshop in Kirkwall (see Information under Kirkwall later).

Just behind the centre is **The Earl's Bu**, the foundations of a 12th-century manor house belonging to the Norse earls of Orkney. There also are the remains of **St Nicholas' Church**, a unique circular medieval church built by Earl Haakon some time before 1136 and modelled on the rotunda of the Church of the Holy Sepulchre in Jerusalem. The church remained in use until 1705.

For accommodation, the attractive Scandinavian *Westrow Lodge (☎/fax 811360, Orphir)* offers cosy and comfy B&B for £22 per person, and overlooks Scapa Flow.

King Haakon of Norway beached his ship at **Houton** in 1263, after his defeat at the Battle of Largs, and he died in the Bishop's Palace in Kirkwall soon afterwards. There's not much at Houton apart from a ferry terminal.

Roving Eye Enterprises *(☎ 811360; adult/child £25/12.50; trips depart Houton pier at 1.20pm daily May-Aug)* offers boat trips on Scapa Flow, with the opportunity to view some of the wrecks of the German High Seas Fleet (see Scapa Flow Wrecks in the Activities chapter) using a video camera attached to a ROV (remotely operated vehicle) – a technology developed for use in the offshore oil industry. The trips, which must be booked in advance, last around three hours and include a visit to Lyness (see Hoy later in this chapter).

Bus No 2 runs from Kirkwall to Houton via Orphir (20 minutes, three or four daily except Sunday). For details of ferries from Houton to Hoy and Flotta, see Hoy later in this chapter.

KIRKWALL

☎ 01856 ● pop 6100

The capital of Orkney is a bustling market town, set back from a wide bay, but it's become a little frayed around the edges. Although Stromness is a prettier base from which to explore the island, Kirkwall's long, winding paved main street is still very atmospheric and the town is home to a handful of must-see attractions, including the Highland Park Distillery, the magnificent St Magnus Cathedral, and the ruins of the Bishop's Palace and the Earl's Palace, where so many of the power struggles between the church and the oppressive Stewart rulers of Orkney took place.

Kirkwall was established as a royal burgh in 1486 by James III, but its origins go back to the 11th century, when Earl Rognvald Brusson established his kingdom here. The name is derived from *kirkjuvagar* meaning 'church-bay'. The town has spread into the bay in the last few centuries, accounting for the plain modern buildings around the harbour; the shoreline used to run along Junction Rd.

Orientation

Kirkwall is fairly compact and it's easy enough to get around on foot. Ferries to the northern islands leave from Harbour St, while almost everything else is set back from the harbour on Albert St, which changes its name to Broad St and, later, Victoria St. The TIC, museum and cathedral are all along Broad St, while the Bishop's Palace and the Earl's Palace are up the hill on Palace Rd.

Information

Kirkwall's TIC (☎ 872856, info@otb.ossian .net), at 6 Broad St by the cathedral, opens 8.30am to 8pm daily June to September, and 9am to 5pm weekdays plus 10am to 4pm Saturday the rest of the year (from 8.30am weekdays in May). It's a helpful place with a good range of publications on Orkney for

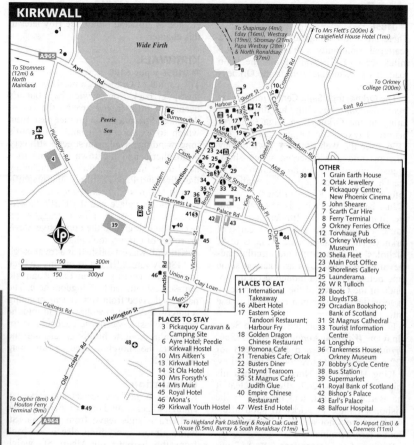

KIRKWALL

OTHER
1 Grain Earth House
2 Ortak Jewellery
4 Pickaquoy Centre;
 New Phoenix Cinema
5 John Shearer
7 Scarth Car Hire
8 Ferry Terminal
9 Orkney Ferries Office
12 Torvhaug Pub
15 Orkney Wireless
 Museum
20 Sheila Fleet
23 Main Post Office
24 Shorelines Gallery
25 Launderama
26 W R Tulloch
27 Boots
28 LloydsTSB
29 Orcadian Bookshop;
 Bank of Scotland
31 St Magnus Cathedral
33 Tourist Information
 Centre
34 Longship
36 Tankerness House;
 Orkney Museum
37 Bobby's Cycle Centre
38 Bus Station
39 Supermarket
41 Royal Bank of Scotland
42 Bishop's Palace
43 Earl's Palace
48 Balfour Hospital

PLACES TO EAT
11 International
 Takeaway
16 Albert Hotel
17 Eastern Spice
 Tandoori Restaurant;
 Harbour Fry
18 Golden Dragon
 Chinese Restaurant
19 Pomona Cafe
21 Trenabies Cafe; Ortak
22 Busters Diner
32 Strynd Tearoom
35 St Magnus Café;
 Judith Glue
40 Empire Chinese
 Restaurant
47 West End Hotel

PLACES TO STAY
3 Pickaquoy Caravan &
 Camping Site
6 Ayre Hotel; Peedie
 Kirkwall Hostel
10 Mrs Aitken's
13 Kirkwall Hotel
14 St Ola Hotel
30 Mrs Forsyth's
44 Mrs Muir
45 Royal Hotel
46 Mona's
49 Kirkwall Youth Hostel

---

sale. You can get free bus timetables here, as well as tide times for the Brough of Birsay crossing.

There are branches of Lloyds TSB, Bank of Scotland and Royal Bank of Scotland on Broad and Albert Sts. You can check email at Orkney College (☎ 569000) on East Rd, a 10-minute walk from the TIC, for £4 per hour (no minimum). The main post office, on Junction Rd, opens 9am to 5pm weekdays and 9.30am to 12.30pm Saturday, and has a bureau de change.

The Launderama (☎ 872982), 47 Albert St, does washing for £2.50 and drying for £1 per 20 minutes; it opens Monday to Saturday.

The Balfour Hospital (☎ 885400) is on New Scapa Rd.

The Orcadian Bookshop (☎ *879000, 50 Albert St*) has a wonderful collection of books about the islands, and for photographic supplies, your best bet is *Boots Pharmacy (Albert St)*.

St Magnus Cathedral

Founded in 1137 and constructed from local red sandstone and yellow Eday stone, St Magnus Cathedral (☎ *874894; admission free, but £1 donation requested; open 9am-6pm Mon-Sat & 2pm-6pm Sun Apr-Sept, 9am-1pm & 2pm-5pm Mon-Sat Oct-Mar, service at 11.15am Sun)* was built by masons who had previously worked on Durham Cathedral. As you might expect, the interior is magnificent and a powerful atmosphere of antiquity pervades the place, partly due to the appealingly uneven columns and medieval stonework.

Earl Rognvald Kolsson commissioned the cathedral in the name of his martyred uncle, Magnus Erlendsson, who was killed on the orders of Earl Haakon Paulsson on Egilsay in 1116. Work began in 1137, but the building is actually the result of 300 years of construction and alteration, and includes Romanesque, transitional and Gothic styles. The bones of St Magnus and St Rognvald are interred in the rectangular pillars in the middle of the cathedral.

Other memorials include the splendid cenotaph of John Rae, featuring a statue of the Arctic explorer sleeping on a bed of furs with his gun and bible, and the bell from HMS *Royal Oak*, torpedoed and sunk in Scapa Flow during WWII with the loss of 833 crew. There is also a memorial to William Balfour Baikie, a missionary who explored much of the Congo River.

Between the knave and apse, the walls are lined with medieval gravestones carved with hourglasses, coffins, skulls and crossbones, and other poignant symbols of mortality (the stones have never been exposed to the elements and are probably the best-preserved medieval slabs in Scotland). Hanging in the northern aisle is a sinister 17th-century *Mort Brod*, a wooden grave marker bearing an image of the grim reaper.

Bishop's Palace & Earl's Palace
Near the cathedral on Palace St are these two historic ruins *(HS; ☎ 875461, Palace Rd; adult/child £2/75p; open 9.30am-6.30pm daily Apr-Oct, 9.30am-4.30pm Mon-Sat & 2pm-4.30pm Sun Oct & Nov, closed Dec-March)* on either side of Watergate. The palaces were originally one building, but a road was run through the main gate after the place fell into disrepair.

The older Bishop's Palace to the west was built in the mid-12th century in order to provide suitable lodgings for Bishop William the Old. The floors have collapsed but the outer walls are remarkably intact and you can climb Bishop Reid's Tower, added in the 16th century, for wonderful views of the cathedral. Plaques show the different phases of the construction of the cathedral. On the outside of the tower is a small statue of Earl Rognvald.

Across the road, in a grassed-over quadrangle, is the ruin of the Earl's Palace, built by the tyrant Earl Patrick Stewart in 1600 using forced labour. The edifice is said to be the finest example of French-Renaissance architecture in Scotland, but the earl ran out of money and the palace was never completed. The ruins include several turrets with oriel windows and shot-holes, and the grand hall with its monumental stone fireplace.

Both palaces were repossessed by Bishop James Law in 1615 and Earl Patrick and his son were publicly executed. Remarkably, the despotic Patrick was found to be so ignorant that he was unable to even recite the Lord's Prayer; his execution had to be delayed by a day while priests taught him the words!

The palaces are covered by the Historic Scotland (HS) joint ticket (see the boxed text 'Historic Scotland Monuments' earlier in the chapter).

Tankerness House & Orkney Museum
This excellent restored merchant's house *(☎ 873191, Broad St; admission free; open 10.30am-5pm Mon-Sat, closed 12.30pm-1.30pm Oct-Mar & 2pm-5pm Sun May-Sept)* contains an interesting museum of Orkney life over the last 5000 years. Guided tours are available.

Orkney Wireless Museum
This museum *(☎ 871400, Kiln Corner; adult/child £2/1; open 10am-4.30pm Mon-Sat & 2.30pm-4.30pm Sun Apr-Sept)*, at the eastern end of the harbour, is a fascinating jumble of communications equipment dating from around 1930 onwards, especially relating to the Scapa Flow naval base.

Highland Park Distillery

Not only is Highland Park a very fine single-malt, but the tour of the world's most northerly whisky distillery (☎ 874619, Holm Rd; guided tour £3; open 1pm-5pm Mon-Fri Nov-Mar, 10am-5pm Mon-Fri Apr-Oct, also noon-5pm Sat & Sun July & Aug) is also one of the best. You'll see the whole whisky-making process – this is one of the few distilleries that still does its own barley malting – and the building is one of the most attractive of any distillery in Scotland. There are tours every half-hour from April to October, but one tour only at 2pm in winter.

Grain Earth House

This souterrain (stone-lined storage tunnel) was built in the Iron Age beneath a vanished stone hut complex. Today it sits in the middle of the Hatston industrial estate at the western end of the bay; get the key and a torch from the nearby Ortak Jewellery centre (☎ 872224), 10 Albert St, between 9am and 5pm Monday to Saturday.

Special Events

The St Magnus Festival (☎ 871445, Ⓦ www.stmagnusfestival.com) takes place in June and is a huge celebration of music and the arts. An interesting event called The Ba' takes place around Broad St – see the boxed text for more information.

Places to Stay

Camping There's a convenient camp site on the edge of town.

Pickaquoy Caravan & Camping Site (☎ 879900, Pickaquoy Rd) Pitches £3.50-4.40, caravans £6.60. Open year-round. This tidy site is situated on the western outskirts of Kirkwall, next to the town's leisure centre (you will have to use the toilets and showers at the leisure centre from October to March).

Hostels *Kirkwall Youth Hostel* (☎ 872243, Old Scapa Rd) Dorm beds £9.50/8.25. Kirkwall's large and well-equipped SYHA hostel is a 10-minute walk south from the bus station. The hostel is often booked out by youth clubs so book ahead.

Peedie Hostel (☎ 875477, 1 Ayre Houses, Ayre Rd) Beds from £10 per person. This relaxed place is on the waterfront next to the Ayre Hotel, a short walk west from the ferry terminal.

The Ba'

The boisterous and chaotic ball game known as The Ba' takes place every Christmas Day and New Year's Day, when Kirkwall residents chase a handmade cork-filled leather ball along the streets, with the aim of getting the ba' into their opponent's goal. Although it may seem like a free-for-all, there are actually two distinct teams: the 'Uppies', families from Up-the-Gates (ie, north of the cathedral) and the 'Doonies', who live Doon-the-Gates (ie, south of St Magnus).

At the stroke of 1pm, the ba' is thrown into the crowd from the Mercat Cross in front of the cathedral and the mad melee begins. The Uppies goal is a wall at the southern end of town, while the Doonies aim to get the ba' into the harbour at the northern end of town. All the shops barricade their doors and windows and the streets become a single heaving mass of people, striking this way and that as the ba' moves through the throng. It's not unknown for teams to take short cuts through shops and houses, or even across the rooftops, in their determination to get the ba' to goal.

The origins of The Ba' lie in the age-old battle between Church and state. In the 14th century, Kirkwall was divided into two departments, the Burgh, controlled by Earl Henry St Clair, and the Laverock, controlled by the bishop of Orkney. The boundary between the two was the kirkyard around St Magnus, and the original game grew from the rivalry between the Church's men (Uppies) and the King's men (Doonies).

The Ba' is an incredible spectacle, but be prepared to be jostled by the crowd.

B&Bs & Guesthouses There's a good range of cheap B&Bs, though most are very small and few have rooms with en-suite facilities.

Mrs Aitken's (☎ 874193, Whiteclett, St Catherine's Place) B&B from £16 per person. There are three doubles available at the central Mrs Aitken's.

Mrs Forsyth's (☎ 874020, 21 Willowburn Rd) B&B £13-18 per person, dinner B&B £21-23 per person. This small, friendly place is a 10-minute walk from the town centre.

Mrs Flett's (☎ 873160, Cumliebank, Cromwell Rd) B&B £15-16 per person. You'll get a warm welcome at this small B&B overlooking Kirkwall Bay, 10 minutes' walk east of the centre.

Mona's (☎ 872440, 7 Matches Square) B&B from £15-17 per person. Just off Junction Rd, Mona's is a comfortable, good-value B&B.

Mrs Muir (☎ 874805, 2 Dundas Crescent) B&B from £18. This delightful B&B is housed in a lovely old manse above the town.

Royal Oak Guest House (☎/fax 877177, Holm Rd) Singles/doubles from £26/44. The Royal Oak is a large, modern guesthouse with eight en-suite rooms; it's near the Highland Park Distillery on the southern edge of town.

Hotels There are several hotels along the harbourfront, immediately across from the ferry terminal.

Kirkwall Hotel (☎ 872232, fax 872812, e enquiries@kirkwallhotel.com, Harbour St) Singles £35-62, doubles £50-80. The imposing Victorian-era Kirkwall was once the island's finest hotel, though it's a little starchy and old-fashioned these days. It's still the grandest building on the harbourfront and some rooms have good views of the fishing boats on the quay.

St Ola Hotel (☎/fax 875090, Harbour St) Singles/doubles from £35/50. A few doors down, the stone-fronted St Ola is another good harbourside hotel.

Ayre Hotel (☎ 873001, fax 876289, e ayre.hotel@orkney.com, Ayre Rd) Singles/doubles from £66/90. The 200-year-old Ayre

Hotel is the most upmarket choice here and caters mainly to business travellers, though it's still family-run and quite intimate. The hotel is at the western end of the harbour near the curious round lake known as the Peerie Sea.

Royal Hotel (☎ 873477, fax 872767, e royalhotel@supanet.com, 40 Victoria St) Singles £30-60, doubles £50-90. The recently refurbished Royal is a friendly and homely hotel, on a quiet residential lane at the end of Kirkwall's winding main street.

West End Hotel (☎ 872368, Main St) Singles £40-45, doubles £58-64. This very appealing and tranquil hotel is tucked away on Main St. The hotel also serves tremendous bar meals.

Craigiefield House Hotel (☎ 872029, fax 872767, Carness Rd) B&B from £30-50. This appealing old country house is set in a secluded location at the eastern end of the bay towards Carness.

Places to Eat

Empire Chinese Restaurant (☎ 872300, 51 Junction Rd) Mains £5-7. Open for lunch & dinner daily. The Empire serves the usual Chinese dishes such as chop suey and foo yung and does a good-value all-you-can-eat buffet on Sunday (noon to 2pm) for £5.90.

Golden Dragon (☎ 872933, 25a Bridge St) Mains £5-7. Kirkwall's other Chinese choice is behind the Eric Kemp Sports Shop near the corner with Albert St and serves decent food.

Eastern Spice Tandoori Restaurant (☎ 878007, 7 Bridge St) Curries £6-10. Open 4.30pm-11pm daily (till midnight Fri & Sat). This is the only curryhouse in Orkney, and serves up tasty North Indian food till late.

Kirkwall Hotel (☎ 872232, Harbour St) Main courses £6-14. The attractive dining area retains some of the hotel's former splendour and dishes up intriguing creations such as lamb 'Grimbister' (lamb fillet stuffed with cheese, wrapped in bacon and cooked in Drambuie).

Albert Hotel (☎ 876000, Mounthoolie Lane) Bar meals £5.50-13. The welcoming bar at this hotel whips up great steaks and seafood.

ORKNEY & SHETLAND ISLANDS

West End Hotel (☎ 872368, Main St) Bar meals £6-7, restaurant mains £9-14. Bar meals noon-2pm Mon-Sat & 6pm-9pm daily. The West End Hotel serves great bar meals of the steak and seafood variety.

Busters Diner (☎ 876717, 1 Mounthoolie Lane) Burgers, pasta and tacos £3-5, pizzas from £3. Open 4.30pm-10pm Mon-Fri, noon-2am Thur-Sat & 4pm-10pm Sun. This is an American-style burger, Italian and Tex-Mex place serving the likes of pizzas and burgers to eat in or take away.

For fish and chips, try *Harbour Fry (☎ 873170, 3 Bridge St)*, open evenings plus lunchtime Monday to Saturday, or *International Takeaway (☎ 874773, 12 Bridge St)*, open lunch and dinner Monday to Saturday. A portion of fish and chips costs £3.30.

There are several popular and welcoming cafes and tearooms on the main street.

Trenabies Cafe (☎ 874336, 16 Albert St) Light meals & snacks £2-6. Open 9am-6pm Mon-Sat. This cheerful and cosy tearoom and cafe serves up good soups, sandwiches and baked potatoes.

Pomona Cafe (☎ 872325, 11 Albert St) Snacks £1-4. This cheap and cheery cafe has teas, cakes, sandwiches and hot meals such as baked potatoes and chips.

St Magnus Cafe (☎ 873354, Broad St) Snacks & light meals £1-3. Open 9.30am-4pm Mon-Sat. This cafe in the Kirkwall and St Ola Community Centre, across the road from the cathedral, has very good cheap food such as quiches and bacon rolls.

Strynd Tearoom (☎ 871552, The Store) Snacks £1-4. Open 10am-6pm Mon-Sat. Up an alley beside the TIC, this elegant tearoom is another good place for a cup of tea and a scone.

Self caterers should head for the large *Safeway* supermarket near the Pickaquoy Centre; it opens 8am to 9pm weekdays, 8am to 8pm Saturday and 9am to 6pm Sunday.

Entertainment

The local weekly newspaper, the *Orcadian*, has useful listings of what's on.

Torvhaug Inn (☎ 872100, Bridge St) This popular bar is the life and soul of the party on Friday and Saturday nights.

Albert Hotel (☎ 876000, Mounthoolie Lane) The Bothy Bar here is a lively place for a drink, with occasional live music in the evenings. On Thursday, Friday and Saturday evenings the Albert holds the Matchmakers Disco (admission £5).

Other good drinking places include the pleasant *West End Hotel*, and the bar at the *Ayre Hotel*, which has live fiddle music on Wednesday night.

The *New Phoenix Cinema (☎ 879900, Pickaquoy Rd)* is in the Pickaquoy Centre, known locally as 'the Picky'; there's a single movie nightly and tickets cost £4/2.70 per adult/child. The *Pickaquoy Centre* also offers all sorts of leisure activities including a gym, sports pitches and badminton courts.

Shopping

Ortak Jewellery (☎ 873536, 10 Albert St) sells unusually stylish jewellery in silver and gold, inspired by Pictish and Viking treasure. Other local jewellers include *Longship (☎ 873251, 7–9 Broad St)* and *Sheila Fleet (☎ 861203, 30 Bridge St)*.

For handmade wooden boats, ceramics, prints and the like, try *Shorelines Gallery (☎ 873821, 39 Albert St)* or *Judith Glue (☎ 874225, 25 Broad St)*; Judith also stocks knitted gifts from Westray, and local delicacies.

Getting There & Away

Air The airport (☎ 872494 for flight reservations) is 2½ miles east of the town centre and handles all flights into Orkney and on to the outlying islands. A new terminal is being built to replace the old porta-cabin terminal, and should have slightly better facilities. Currently, there's a postbox, payphone, cafe and a branch of the car-hire firm, W R Tulloch (☎ 875500), but no bureau de change. For details of flights see Getting There & Away at the start of the chapter as well as relevant island sections.

Boat There are ferries from Kirkwall to Shapinsay, Stronsay, Sanday, Eday, North Ronaldsay, Westray and Papa Westray. See the relevant island sections for ferries and fares. The Orkney Ferries office (☎ 872044),

Shore St, is down on the harbourfront and opens from 7am until 5pm Monday to Friday and 7am to 3pm on Saturday.

Bus The bus station for Orkney Coaches (☎ 870555) is southwest of the town centre; except for bus No 10, there are no services on Sunday. Bus No 1 runs from Kirkwall to Stromness direct (£2.35, 30 minutes, six to eight daily Monday to Saturday); No 2 runs to and from Orphir and Houton, connecting with the Hoy/Flotta ferry (20 minutes, three or four daily Monday to Saturday); No 6 runs from Kirkwall to Tingwall (35 minutes, four daily on weekdays plus one on Saturday), connecting with the Rousay, Egilsay and Wyre ferry; No 8 runs from Kirkwall to Stromness via Birsay (one daily, one hour, weekdays) – if you don't plan to stay in the north of Mainland, you're better off using the bus to day-trip to Birsay from Stromness. From June to September a special tourist service (No 8A) runs from Kirkwall to Stromness via Stenness Standing Stones, the Ring of Brodgar and Skara Brae, leaving Kirkwall at 9.30am and 1.30pm weekdays.

From May to September, bus No 10 runs from Kirkwall to the John o'Groats ferry at Burwick (50 minutes, three or four daily), via St Margaret's Hope. Causeway Coaches (☎ 831444) runs buses year-round from Kirkwall to St Margaret's Hope (30 minutes, four daily Monday to Friday plus two Saturday).

Getting Around

Bobby's Cycle Centre (☎ 875777) on Tankerness Lane charges £8 per day for bike hire.

Car hire is available from W R Tulloch (☎ 876262) on Castle St, Scarth Car Hire (☎ 872125) on Great Western Rd, or John Shearer (☎ 872950) on Burnmouth Rd from £32 per day, all inclusive.

For taxis, try Bob's Taxis (☎ 876543).

SOUTHEAST MAINLAND
☎ 01856

The land southeast of Kirkwall is mainly agricultural. The A961 heads south to the Churchill Barriers, while the A960 cuts

across towards Deerness, passing Kirkwall airport and the mysterious Iron-Age site of **Mine Howe** (☎ 861234; adult/child £2.50/ 1.50; open daily June-Sept, Wed & Sun late Sept & May), a deep multi-passaged souterrain – the Channel 4 TV series Time Team carried out an archaeological dig here in 2000 and concluded that it may have had some ritual significance.

On the far eastern shore of Mainland, a mile north of Skaill (at the end of the Deerness road), is **The Gloup**, a spectacular natural arch and sea cave, and farther north, the **Brough of Deerness**, a Norse or Pictish monastic complex.

There are large colonies of nesting seabirds at the nature reserve at **Mull Head**. Offshore here is the remote island of **Copinsay**, which you may be able to visit with permission from the RSPB (☎ 850176).

The attractive old *Quoyburray Inn* (☎ 861255, Quoyburray) serves excellent meals (£6 to £20) in its Kiln Bar. It opens 6pm to 9pm daily, plus noon to 2pm Saturday and Sunday. Quoyburray is around 5 miles southeast of Kirkwall.

The Churchill Barriers

For a long time the tight passages between Mainland and the islands of Burray and South Ronaldsay were blocked by a series of deliberately scuppered shipwrecks that were known as the 'blockships', but a German U-boat was still able to sneak through Kirk Sound into Scapa Flow in 1939 and torpedoed the battleship HMS Royal Oak, killing 833 seamen.

After the disaster, Winston Churchill set Italian POWs to work erecting vast causeways of concrete blocks across the channels on the eastern side of Scapa Flow, linking Mainland to the islands of Lamb Holm, Glimps Holm, Burray and South Ronaldsay. The Churchill Barriers, flanked by the rusting wrecks of the blockships which once guarded the channels, now carry the main road from Kirkwall to Burwick. There are good sandy beaches by Barrier Nos 3 and 4. Several diving companies (see Scapa Flow Wrecks in the Activities chapter) offer training and beach dives on the blockships.

Lamb Holm

On the tiny island of Lamb Holm, the **Italian Chapel** (☎ *781268; admission free; open daylight hr*) is all that remains of POW Camp 60, which housed the Italian POWs who worked on the Churchill Barriers. The prisoners built the chapel in their spare time, using two Nissen huts, scrap metal and their considerable artistic and decorative skills. In 1960, one of the original artists responsible for the exquisite trompe l'oeil painting, Domenico Chiocchetti, returned to restore the chapel to its original glory. It's an extraordinary monument to human ingenuity and definitely worth seeing.

Burray

The small island of Burray is linked to Mainland and South Ronaldsay by the Churchill Barriers and has a fine beach at Northtown, where you may spot seals. On the A961 at Echnaloch Bay, **Orkney Fossil & Vintage Centre** (☎ *731255, Viewforth; adult/child £2/1; open 10am-6pm daily Apr-Oct*) is a quirky collection of household and farming relics and 300-million-year-old fish fossils found in the local cliffs. There's a great coffee shop here.

Burray village, on the southern side of the island, has a general store with petrol, a post office and a hotel.

The *Sands Hotel* (☎/*fax 731298, Burray*), housed in a newly refurbished 19th-century herring station on the quayside, has en-suite doubles and family rooms, and there's a good bar and restaurant. B&B costs £20 to £25 per person.

Vestlaybanks (☎ *731305, fax 731401, *e* vestlaybanks@btinternet.com, Burray*) is a modern bungalow overlooking Scapa Flow that has two en-suite rooms (B&B £22 to £25 per person) and can provide evening meals for both carnivores and vegetarians.

SOUTH RONALDSAY
☎ 01856

This large, flat island is covered with a patchwork of fields and feels surprisingly remote, even though it's only 6 miles from the Scottish mainland. Most people come here to see the remarkable and thoroughly entertaining Tomb of the Eagles at the southern tip of the island. It's also worth detouring across to the immaculate white Sands O'Right on the road to Hoxa Head.

St Margaret's Hope

This pristine village of stone houses is the largest settlement on South Ronaldsay. The village was named after Margaret, the maid of Norway, who died here in 1290 on the way from her homeland to marry Edward II of England (the marriage was strictly a political affair; Margaret was only seven years old when she died).

It's a quiet place with an unhurried atmosphere, and on Cromarty Square there's the small **Smiddy Museum** (☎ *831567, Cromarty Square; admission free; open daily June-Aug*) with various hands-on displays about blacksmiths on the isles.

On the third Saturday in August, St Margaret's Hope hosts the unusual **Horse and Boys' Ploughing Match**, in which teenage boys compete to see who can make the most perfect plough tracks on the Sands O'Right, using exquisite miniature ploughs. Young girls make, and dress up in, elaborate copies of plough-horse harnesses. The competition is a real window on island life in times past.

St Margaret's Hope has a post office, two grocery shops and several friendly pubs.

Places to Stay & Eat *Wheems Bothy* (☎ *831537, Eastside*) Beds £6.50, camping £3 per person. Open Apr-Oct. Wheems, a mile southeast of St Margaret's Hope, is a very pleasant hostel offering basic accommodation and organic breakfasts.

Backpacker's Hostel (☎ *831205, St Margaret's Hope*) Beds £10. Housed in a nice stone cottage, this place is run by the neighbouring Murray Arms Hotel, and has good kitchen facilities and hot showers. The owners run a seasonal coffee shop next door.

Murray Arms Hotel (☎ *831205, St Margaret's Hope*) B&B £25-30 per person. This attractive stone hotel is on the main street through St Margaret's Hope and has comfy rooms and good pub food (from £5 to £9).

Bellevue Guest House (☎ *831294, St Margaret's Hope*) B&B £20-25 per person.

The two-room Bellevue, uphill from the road to the pier, is a lovely old stone-built house with great views.

Galley Inn & Anchorage (☎ *831456, Back Rd*) B&B from £20. Self-catering houses £200-250 per week. This old pub has decent rooms and a lovely cosy dining room with bar meals from £5 to £6.

Creel Inn & Restaurant (☎ *831311, Front Rd, St Margaret's Hope*) 3-course dinner £28. B&B singles/doubles £40-45/60-70. Open Apr-Sept. Arguably the best restaurant in Orkney, the Creel serves fresh local produce – fish, shellfish, beef, lamb, vegetables – simply but deliciously prepared. There are also five en-suite rooms available.

Getting There & Away Pentland Ferries (☎831226) operates a car ferry to St Margaret's Hope from Gill's Bay, 2 miles west of John o'Groats – see that section in The Northwest Highlands chapter for details.

Tomb of the Eagles
A visit to this tomb (☎ *831339, Liddle Farm, Isbister; adult/child £3/1.50; open 10am-8pm daily Apr-Oct, 10am-noon or by arrangement Nov-Mar*) at the southern tip of South Ronaldsay is highly recommended. The 5000-year-old chambered tomb was discovered by local farmers, the Simisons, who now run it privately as a visitor attraction. It's as interesting for their entertaining and informative guided tour as for the tomb itself. After handling some human skulls and sea-eagle talons found in the tomb, you walk across the fields, put on knee pads and crawl down the cramped entrance passage. It's possible that sky burials occurred here with the dead being placed on top of wooden platforms, just outside the tomb entrance, for eagles and carrion birds to pick clean. You'll also see a **burnt mound**, an impressive Bronze-Age midden mound. The tomb is a 20-minute walk east from Burwick, and you can continue around the headland to a gloup (natural arch) at Halcro Head.

Getting There & Away May to September, bus No 10 runs from Kirkwall to Burwick (50 minutes, four daily), or there's the

year-round service between St Margaret's Hope and Kirkwall (30 minutes, three or four daily except Sunday) run by Causeway Coaches (☎ 831444).

HOY
☎ 01856
Hoy (meaning 'high island') is the second-largest island in the Orkney archipelago, and is a wild and hilly place, with towering cliffs and high windswept hills covered in peat moorland. The highest point in Orkney is Ward Hill (479m), in the north, which is surrounded by desolate heath in every direction.

Northern Hoy
The vertical cliffs at the northern tip of Hoy are some of the highest in Britain – St John's Head on the northwest coast rises sheer from the ocean to 346m. Hoy's best-known sight is the spectacular **Old Man of Hoy**, a 137m-high rock stack that juts improbably from the ocean off the tip of an eroded headland. It's a humbling spot and it's worth just spending a moment contemplating the awesome power of the ocean. The Old Man was first scaled in 1966 by the eminent mountaineer Chris Bonington in the first ever televised rock-climb; it still attracts plenty of climbers, but climbing parties should be aware that there are no local rescue services. Keep an eye out for the Old Man as you pass by Hoy on the Scrabster-Stromness ferry. The surrounding area is wonderfully wild and woolly and has been maintained as a nature reserve by the RSPB since 1983; call the ranger on ☎ 791288 for details of guided walks.

The easiest approach to the stack is from Rackwick Bay, a two-hour walk from Moaness Pier through the beautiful **Rackwick Glen**. You'll pass the 5000-year-old **Dwarfie Stane**, the only example of a rock-cut tomb in Scotland, and, according to Sir Walter Scott, the favourite residence of Trolld, a dwarf from Norse legend. The hollowed-out stone block was dropped here by a glacier in the last Ice Age and features some interesting Victorian graffiti, including the words of the eccentric British spy Major Mouncey – 'I have sat two nights and so learnt patience' – carved in Persian. On your return, you can take the path via the **Glens of Kinnaird** and **Berriedale Wood**, Scotland's most northerly patch of native forest.

The most popular walk begins at **Rackwick**, a wonderful semi-deserted village of stone houses overlooking a secluded pebble bay with menacing cliffs rising on either side. Rackwick has a hostel and camping, and there's a clearly marked path across to Moaness. The trail to the Old Man starts from the hostel on the northern side of the bay and cuts westwards along the cliffs, turning north across the table-like moorland atop Rora Head before descending gradually to the edge of the cliffs opposite the Old Man of Hoy. It's a fine exhilarating walk, but allow about seven hours for the return trip from Moaness, or three hours from Rackwick.

South of Moaness, the main road skirts the edge of the high ground, passing a small white gravestone tucked among the heather on the hillside, the final resting place of **Betty Corrigall**. Betty was a Lyness girl who became pregnant to a visiting sailor in the 19th century and took her own life. The devout islanders refused to bury a suicide on hallowed ground, so the poor girl was interred in this lonely spot on the parish boundary.

Lyness

Lyness, on the eastern side of Hoy, was an important naval base during both world wars, when the British Grand Fleet was based in Scapa Flow. With the dilapidated remains of buildings, this isn't a pretty place, but the **Scapa Flow Visitors Centre** (☎ 791300; adult/child £2/1; open 9am-4.30pm Mon-Fri, plus 10.30am-4pm Sat & Sun mid-May–Sept) is well worth a visit. This fascinating naval museum is housed in the old pumphouse which once fed fuel to the ships, and features a fine collection of armaments, including a torpedo, plus photographs and memorabilia from various historic vessels which sailed from or sank in Scapa Flow. Included in the admission price is an evocative audiovisual show in a vast oil tank behind the centre.

On the way south from Lyness, look out for the curious stripey Deco facade of the old **Garrison Theatre**, now a private house.

South Hoy

Across a narrow isthmus, about 2 miles south of Lyness, is **South Walls**, a small low region with interesting historic relics. On either side of Longhope Bay, you'll see defensive **Martello Towers**, built to protect convoys heading for the Baltic in the Napoleonic Wars. At the head of the bay is **Melsetter House**, a laird's property with fine gardens that open Thursday, Saturday and Sunday by appointment (☎ 791352).

There are pleasant walks along the low cliffs at Cantick Head, where there's a Stevenson lighthouse and a poignant memorial to the crew of a Longhope lifeboat which was lost with all hands in 1969.

Places to Stay & Eat

There are two SYHA hostels on Hoy; bed linen isn't provided, but you can camp at both and use the facilities for £2.75/2. A few B&Bs dot the southern end of the island, but there is only one in Rackwick.

Hoy Youth Hostel (☎ 873535 ext 2415 office hrs only, Moaness) Beds £7.20/6.30. Open May-Sept. This place is a 15-minute walk from Moaness Pier. Bring your own sleeping bag and supplies.

Rackwick Youth Hostel (☎ 873535 ext 2415 office hr only, Rackwick) Beds £7.20/6.30. Open Mar-Sept. The Rackwick hostel, 6 miles from the ferry at Moaness, has eight beds in two dorms; bring your own sleeping bag and food. The hostel is uphill from the village, by the start of the footpath to the Old Man of Hoy. The warden comes by to collect your money each evening.

Stoneyquoy Farm (☎ 791234, Lyness) B&B from £18. A mile south of Lyness, this delightful farmhouse B&B is run by a charming Dutch-Orcadian couple and has good rooms and award-winning breakfasts and meals. Island tours are also available.

Mrs Hill (☎ 791240, St John's Manse, Longhope) £18 per person. Near Melsetter House, this fine stone manse offers comfortable rooms and a friendly welcome.

Mrs Rendall (☎ 791262, The Glen, Rackwick) B&B from £18. This simple place is the closest B&B to the Old Man of Hoy.

The Hoy Inn (☎ 791271, Moaness) Open noon-2pm, 6pm-9pm. Located near the ferry pier, this is a bar serves good seafood.

There's a friendly *cafe* serving snacks at the Scapa Flow Visitors Centre (see under Lyness earlier), and groceries can be bought at the shops in Lyness and Longhope.

Getting There & Away

Orkney Ferries (☎ 850624) runs a passenger ferry between Stromness on Mainland and Moaness pier (passenger/bicycle £2.65/1.30, 30 minutes) at 7.45am, 10am and 4.30pm weekdays, and 9.30am and 6pm at weekends, with a reduced schedule from mid-September to mid-May. These ferries also stop in Graemsay (£2.65/1.30). There are also services at 7pm and 9.30pm on Friday evening. In the other direction, the service departs five minutes after its arrival on Hoy.

There's also a car ferry to Lyness from Houton on Mainland that sails up to six times daily Monday to Saturday (passenger/car/bicycle £2.65/7.90/1.30, 45 minutes). There's a limited Sunday service from May to September. Some sailings go via Flotta.

Getting Around

Transport on Hoy is very limited. North Hoy Transport (☎ 791315 or ☎ 791261) runs a minibus service between Rackwick and Moaness, meeting the 10am weekday ferry from Stromness. Otherwise, call the same number for a taxi.

Louise Budge (☎ 791234) at Stoneyquoy Farm offers guided tours (in a VW people carrier) for up to six people, picking up from the ferry at Lyness; the price (£44) includes a light lunch at her farm.

Bike hire is available at Moaness pier (☎ 791225) for £6 per day. Hitching is possible, but sheep outnumber cars on the roads.

GRAEMSAY

This tiny low-lying agricultural island between Hoy and Stromness once supported a healthy population of crofting families but it's almost deserted now. The island has two

lighthouses, **Hoy Low** at the southern tip of the island, and the rather fine **Hoy High** in the north, a brilliant white 33m-high tower with a balcony supported by Gothic arches.

You can stop here on the way to Hoy and walk around the island. See Getting There & Away under Hoy for ferry details.

FLOTTA

This small, flat island is best known for the 68m flare stack that rises from the Occidental Oil Terminal in the north of the island like a medieval beacon. As a result of the oil industry, Flotta is fairly industrialised, but there are a few wartime relics dotted around the island, including a fine ruined stone building that housed the old YMCA in WWI, and some unusual sea stacks at **Cletts** at the southeastern tip of Flotta.

Car ferries stop here en route to Lyness and Longhope.

NORTHERN ISLANDS

The group of windswept islands that lies north of Mainland takes a bit of effort to reach – ferries are slow and infrequent and there is no public transport – but visitors are rewarded with beautiful scenery, including wonderful white sand beaches. Most islands are home to traditional Orcadian communities which give a real sense of what Orkney was like before the Scottish mainland infringed upon island life. The TICs in Kirkwall and Stromness have a useful brochure, *The Islands of Orkney*, with maps and details of these islands. Note that the 'ay' at the end of each island name (from the Old Norse for 'island') is pronounced 'ee' (eg, Shapinsay is pronounced **shap**-in-see).

Orkney Ferries (☎ 01856-872044, [W] www .orkneyferries.co.uk) operates an efficient service and you can day-trip from Kirkwall to most of the islands (except North Ronaldsay) on most days of the week. That said, it's really best to stay a few days and soak up the slow, easy pace of life.

Shapinsay
☎ 01856

Just 20 minutes by ferry from Kirkwall, Shapinsay is a low-lying and intensively cultivated island with a fine castle and good beaches along its western edge. The ferry here passes tiny Thieves Holm, formerly a prison for thieves and witches, and the lighthouse on Helliar Holm. The main settlement is made up of the former workers' cottages for Balfour Castle, overlooking Elwick Bay, where King Haakon's fleet sheltered before setting off for Largs. There are two general stores and a post office, and the island is only 6 miles long, making it easy to explore on foot.

Things to See Completed in 1848 in the turreted Scottish Baronial style, **Balfour Castle** *(☎ 872856; adult/child £16/8; guided tours Wed May-Sept)* dominates the southern end of the island. It was built by the Balfours who made a fortune in the British Raj in India, but now belongs to the Polish Zawadski family. In the grounds is the interesting **Dishan Tower** containing a saltwater shower and a doocot (dove-cote). Examples of the Balfours' civic projects include the neat line of cottages in the main village, the ornate gatehouse, now the *Gatehouse Pub* (☎ 711216), a sea-flushed public toilet near the jetty and the **Gasometer**, a castle-like folly which once provided the island with electricity. Guided tours should be booked in advance; the price includes the ferry, admission to the castle and afternoon tea.

Shapinsay Heritage Centre *(☎ 711258, The Smithy, Balfour Village; admission free; open noon-4.30pm daily Apr-Sept)* has a wide range of displays about the island's history, plus a cafe and craft shop.

Immediately north of the village is the wetland RSPB reserve of **Milldam**, with pintails, waders and the rarely seen water rail; there's a hide by the water that's wheelchair accessible.

About 4 miles from the pier, at the far northeastern corner of the island, is the Iron-Age **Burroughston Broch**, with a well-preserved central well. Seals are often seen on the beach here. Farther south on the east coast is the 12th-century ruin of **Linton Chapel**, from where a supposedly haunted lintel was removed and used to build a barn,

but returned when the farmer found several of his cows hanged in the byre.

Places to Stay *Girnigoe* *(☎ 711256, ⓔ jean@girnigoe.f9.co.uk, Girnigoe)* B&B £20 per person. This friendly farmhouse B&B, by the shore at the northeastern end of the island, serves excellent home-made breakfasts, and dinner for £12.

Hilton Farm *(☎/fax 711239, Hilton)* B&B £15-20 per person. Close to the RSPB reserve, this farmhouse B&B is comfortable and easy to find and serves evening meals for around £10.

Balfour Castle *(☎ 711282, fax 711283, ⓔ balfourcastle@btinternet.com, Balfour Village)* £70/100 per person without/with dinner. Comfortable old-fashioned rooms are available at Balfour Castle and the small private chapel is becoming popular for weddings. A boat is available for residents for island trips, bird-watching and sea fishing.

Getting There & Away There are about six ferries daily (plus three on Sunday May to September) between Kirkwall and Shapinsay (passenger/car £2.65/7.90, 20 minutes). The *Charles Ann* (☎ 711254) can be hired for trips to Helliar Holm or for emergency crossings to Kirkwall for around £35.

Rousay
☎ 01856 ● pop 200

This hilly island is famous for its numerous archaeological sites, earning it the nickname 'Egypt of the North'. Most of the island is classed as a Site of Special Scientific Interest (SSSI), but it also has the important RSPB **Trumland Reserve**, covering much of the heath-filled interior. The lochs of Peerie Water and Muckle Loch are good for trout fishing and attract plentiful birdlife. You can walk through the reserve to Blotchnie Fiold (250m), the highest point on the island.

Marion's shop, and a post office that looks like a hen coop, are at Sourin, 2½ miles north of the pier.

Things to See West of the pier are a number of prehistoric burial cairns and the ruins of at least four brochs. Close to the road and near the hostel, the two-storey **Taversoe Tuick** contained the remains of at least five people and a large amount of pottery; it's an interesting structure, but marred slightly by the concrete roof and skylight. Similarly, **Blackhammer**, a stalled Neolithic chambered cairn a mile west of Taversoe Tuick, was more atmospheric before the concrete cover was added. The **Knowe of Yarso** stalled cairn is a wet half-mile walk from the road; it contained the remains of 29 adults, and was used from 2900–1900 BC.

Dating from the 3rd millennium BC, **Midhowe Cairn**, the 30m-long 'Great Ship of Death' as it's called, is the longest chambered cairn in Orkney. The vast stone tomb is covered by a modern stone shelter, less intrusive than the glass and concrete skylights built into so many Scottish cairns, and has a suspended walkway allowing you to walk above the main passage and see the 12 stone 'stalls' where the bones of 25 people were discovered. As well as human remains, many bird and animal bones were found in the cave too, perhaps meant as food for the deceased. The cairn is 5½ miles west of the pier, and a steep 550m walk down from the road.

A short walk farther north is the atmospheric shoreside **Midhowe Broch**, with well-preserved outbuildings and numerous intact walls and partitions in the central well. The broch is one of three built here in the first century AD; **Northhowe Broch** is in the next field north, while **Southhowe Broch** is farther south along the shorefront **Westness Walk**, which runs to Westness Farm. Along the way you can see the ruins of the **Wirk**, a 13th-century palace, the chambered tomb of **Rowiegar** and a large Viking and Pictish cemetery, where the beautiful silver Gorie Rousay brooch was discovered. At the end of the walk, **Westness House** was the home of the Traill lairds of Rousay.

Along the northwest coast are dramatic cliffs and bleak moorland, where you may see short-eared owls and merlins. Tucked into Saviskaill Bay on the east coast of the headland is **Loch Wasbister**, with plenty of birdlife and ruined duns on two islands.

Organised Tours Operating from June to August, *Rousay Traveller History Tours (☎/fax 821234)* meets the 10.40am ferry from Tingwall and in six hours you'll be driven around the island in a minibus and given time to explore the main sites. Tours run Tuesday to Thursday and cost £15/6 per adult/child (not including the ferry). Shorter taxi tours to Midhowe are also available (£8 per person). Picnic meals can be provided for £2 to £5.

Places to Stay & Eat There are a couple of places to stay and you can get bar meals, including vegetarian choices, near the ferry jetty.

Rousay Farm Hostel (☎ 821252, Trumland Farm) Dorm beds £6-8, pitches £3. This hostel is half a mile from the ferry. There's excellent dormitory accommodation (bring a sleeping bag) and a small camp site.

Blackhamar (☎ 821333, fax 821421, e *jscott9616@aol.com, Rousay)* B&B £25 per person, dinner B&B £45 per person. Blackhamar is a delightfully remote 19th-century crofting cottage, near Wasbister in the north of the island. It's a 10-minute up-hill walk from the road (your bags are carried up by 4WD vehicle).

Pier Restaurant (☎ 821359) Meals under £5.50. Open 11.30am-9pm (to 6.30pm Wed & Sun). This cosy little cafe is good for a meal or a beer while you're waiting for the ferry.

Getting There & Around A small car ferry (☎ 751360) connects Tingwall on Mainland with Rousay (passenger/car/bicycle £2.65/7.90/1.30, 30 minutes) about six times daily, with most services stopping at the nearby islands of Egilsay and Wyre (trips between Rousay, Egilsay and Wyre cost £1.30 for passengers). Booking is recommended if you want to take a car.

Bikes can be rented for £6 per day from Arts, Bikes, Crafts (☎ 821398) near the pier; the island's single road makes a pleasant circuit of about 13 miles. Rousay also has Orkney's only postbus (☎ 01463-256228), which runs around the island twice daily Monday to Saturday.

ORKNEY & SHETLAND ISLANDS

Egilsay & Wyre

Egilsay is the larger of the two islands to the east of Rousay. Much of it is an RSPB reserve; listen for the corncrakes at the southern end of the island. A cenotaph erected in 1938 marks the spot where Earl Magnus was murdered in 1116 on the orders of Earl Haakon Paulsson. A few years later, Magnus' nephew Rognvald Kali seized the earldom and made his uncle into a saint, building the dramatic St Magnus Cathedral in his honour. Pilgrims were soon flocking to Egilsay seeking miracle cures and **St Magnus Kirk** was built, one of only two surviving Viking round-towered churches in Britain. There's a small shop and post office near the jetty.

Wyre was the domain of the Viking Baron Kolbein Hruga ('Cubbie Roo'); the substantial ruins of his castle (known as Cubbie Roo's Castle), built around 1145, stand dramatically above the northern shore. Either Cubbie Roo or his son Bjarni, bishop of Orkney, built **St Mary's Chapel**, which is still remarkably intact. From the jetty, you can walk west to a small **heritage centre** displaying photos of life in Wyre, passing the **Bu**, the former home of Scottish poet Edwin Muir. On the far western tip of the island, there's a small beach where you're almost guaranteed to see seals.

Getting There & Away Egilsay and Wyre are reached by the Rousay-Tingwall ferry (see Rousay earlier for details).

Stronsay & Papa Stronsay
☎ 01857

In the 18th century, the major industry on this island was the collection and burning of seaweed to make 'kelp', which was exported for use in the production of glass, iodine and soap. In the 19th century, herring whipped Stronsay into a frenzy; it was said that you could walk from Whitehall to the island of Papa Stronsay on the decks of the herring boats. However, the industry faded away after the collapse of the fisheries and these days Stronsay is a friendly, relaxed little island, with a patchwork of pastures and some good beaches.

Whitehall, in the north of the island, is the main settlement. The **Stronsay Fish Mart** by the jetty contains a hostel, a good cafe and a herring industry interpretation centre. The centre is currently closed due to the removal of most of the exhibits by a local contributor – call ☎ 616360 for an update.

There's a fine beach at St Catherine's Bay on the west coast, where you may see locals collecting 'spoots' (razor shells), an island delicacy. There's another fine beach at Rothiesholm Sand on the foot of land to the southwest. The heath-covered headland here was the source of the island's peat and is home to numerous seabirds.

Over on the east coast is a small bird reserve at **Mill Bay** run by the bird artist John Holloway, while the rugged southwest coast has some unusual rock formations, including the **Vat o'Kirbuster**, the best example of a gloup in Orkney. It's a dramatic spot, with a deep cauldron eroded by the ocean on the landward-side of the arch. A new nature trail leads from the road to the Vat or you can make the 10-mile round trip from Whitehall along the coast. There are pleasant beaches with plentiful seals around Holland Farm, which has a seal hide down on the shore, and you may see otters around nearby **Loch Lea-shun**.

Just across the harbour from Whitehall is the small island of **Papa Stronsay**, where Earl Rognvald Brusason was murdered in 1046. There's lots of wildlife and seals can be seen on the shore. In 1999 the island was purchased by the Transalpine Redemptorists, a breakaway sect from the Catholic Church, who built a new monastery here, continuing a tradition going back all the way to the 5th century. The monks are regularly seen on the main island and you can take boat trips to the monastery by prior arrangement (☎ 616389).

Places to Stay & Eat There are few good places to stay on the island.

Torness Camping Barn (☎ 616314, Holland Farm) £4 per person. At the southern end of the island, the environmentally friendly Holland Farm is run by a delightful couple and offers a simple camping barn only a few metres from the beach. It's a pleasant place, sleeping about eight, with kitchen and toilet, but you'll need a sleeping bag. Phone from the pier for a lift.

Stronsay Fish Mart Hostel (☎ *616360, Whitehall*) Beds £8. Part of the island's former herring station has been converted into a 10-bed hostel with shower and kitchen; bring your own sleeping bag or hire bedding for £2. The neighbouring cafe opens all day for takeaways, snacks and meals.

Stronsay Hotel (☎ *616473, fax 616465,* **e** *info@stronsayhotel.com, Whitehall*) B&B £25-35 per person. The island's hotel has been extensively refurbished and is bright and spotlessly clean. The bar serves recommended pub meals for £5 to £6.

Stronsay Bird Reserve (☎ *616363, Castle, Mill Bay*) B&B £16, pitches £5. John and Sue Holloway offer B&B and camping at this reserve, a 40-minute walk south from the ferry.

Getting There & Away British Airways/Loganair (☎ 01856-872494) has two flights a day on Monday, Wednesday, Friday and Saturday, from Kirkwall to Stronsay (single/return £31/64, 10 minutes).

A car-ferry service links Kirkwall with Stronsay (passenger/car/bicycle £5.25/11.75/2.10, 1½ hours, two daily) and Eday (1½ hours, two daily). There's a reduced service on Sunday (one daily; no run to Eday).

Eday
☎ 01857

This slender island was extensively cut for peat to supply the surrounding islands, and many of the farms here still use peat fires. The interior is hilly and covered in peat bog, while the coast and the north of the island are mostly low-lying and green. At the northern tip of Eday are the sandstone cliffs of **Red Head**, where much of the stone for St Magnus Cathedral in Kirkwall was mined. Eday has been occupied for at least 5000 years, with numerous chambered cairns, many of which can be reached by the well-signposted **Eday Heritage Walk**, starting from the Community Centre Shop in the middle of the island.

JANE SMITH

Getting to the otter side: watch out for local traffic signs.

The walk skirts the edge of brilliant blue **Mill Loch**, an RSPB reserve with a bird hide and a large population of red-throated divers, before cutting across Vinquoy Hill at the distinctive Stone of Setter, Orkney's largest standing stone. The path is marked by stakes and crosses the fields to **Braeside Chambered Cairn**, which is open to the sky, and **Huntersquoy Chambered Cairn**, which has two chambers reached by separate passages (you can wriggle into one of the chambers along a damp passage if you have a torch). More impressive is **Vinsquoy Chambered Cairn** on the hill top, with a beehive-shaped corbelled roof, reached through a narrow but dry tunnel. The path continues to the end of the headland, passing several ruined farm buildings and a small offshore lighthouse.

You can also start the walk near the early 17th-century **Carrick House** (☎ *622260; small admission charge; tours Sun afternoons June-Sept by appointment*) on the shore in the northeast of the island. The pirate John Gow, inspiration for Sir Walter Scott's *The Pirate*, was captured here in 1725 during a failed raid on the house (there's still a stain on the drawing room floor, said to be blood spilled during the raid). The arrest put an end to years of attacks on ships that sailed this way trying to avoid the dangerous English Channel. The pirates were later executed in London.

Bird-watchers may be interested in the **Warness Walk** at the southwestern tip of

ORKNEY & SHETLAND ISLANDS

the island (one hour), which has the scattered remains of **Stackel Brae**, an ancient Norse castle, several burned mounds and seabirds, including puffins at the Ward Hill RSPB reserve. There's a lovely beach walk along the Bay of Doomy, near London airport, the island's grass landing strip.

Across the fast-flowing waters of Carrick Bay is the little island of Calf of Eday, with a 17th-century saltworks, two chambered cairns and one stalled cairn and numerous seabirds and seals, particularly around Grey Head in the north. Boat trips can be arranged to the Calf through local B&Bs for around £12 return.

Organised Tours The *Eday Heritage Tour* (☎ 622248 or ☎ 622260) is a guided tour, using your own vehicle (Sunday only, July to mid-September). The guide meets you at Eday pier at 10.35am, and gives you a tour of the main sights until 5pm. Tours must be booked in advance; the price (£12 per person) includes refreshments and admission to Carrick House.

The *Eday Minibus Tour* (☎ 622206) runs on Monday, Wednesday and Friday from May to August (adult/child £17.50/11.75), beginning and ending at the ferry pier. The guided tour lasts two hours so you have the afternoon to yourself; the price doesn't include lunch and the tour doesn't include Carrick House, except by previous arrangement.

Places to Stay & Eat You can camp on the island provided you first ask permission from the local farmer.

Eday Hostel (☎ 622206 or ☎ 622311, Bay of London) Dorm beds £6.75/6. This recently renovated 24-bed hostel, run by the Eday Community Association, is 4 miles north of the ferry pier. You'll need your own sleeping bag.

Mrs Popplewell's (☎ 622248, Blett, Carrick Bay) Dinner B&B £26 per person. Mrs Popplewell's is a charming old-fashioned cottage overlooking Carrick Bay, opposite the Calf of Eday (take the road to the shore beside the coastguard station). She has one single and one double and a fully equipped self-catering crofthouse nearby, for up to

three people. Mrs Popplewell bakes fresh bread daily, and she serves snacks and meals at her craft shop.

Mrs Cockram's (☎ 622271, Skaill) Dinner B&B around £29 per person. This place is in a comfortable farmhouse at Skaill, near the church.

Getting There & Away There are two flights from Kirkwall (one-way/return £31/64, 30 minutes) to London airport – that's London, Eday – on Wednesday only. The ferry service from Kirkwall usually sails via Stronsay (passenger/car/bicycle £5.25/11.75/2.10, 1¼ to two hours), but occasionally it's direct. There's a link between Sanday and Eday (20 minutes) on Monday, Tuesday and Sunday.

Getting Around Alan Stewart (☎ 622206) runs a minibus and taxi service, charging about £3 for a trip along the length of Eday. Call Mr Burkett (☎ 622331) for bike hire.

Sanday
☎ 01857

This substantial island is aptly named, for Sanday consists of little more than a single giant sand dune, ringed by dazzling white sand beaches of the sort you'd expect in the Caribbean. The 12-mile-long island is almost entirely flat, apart from the cliffs at Spurness and is growing every year due to sand build-up. Although the beaches are good, and blissfully quiet, the island has suffered more from Highland syndrome than its neighbours, with a shrinking population and numerous old landowner's houses and crofts in various states of disrepair, creating a slight sense of decline.

Ferries now arrive at Loth at the very southern tip of Sanday, far from the main settlement at Kettletoft and the beaches. Almost everything of interest is in the north of the island, though you'll pass the ruins of a 19th-century **model farm** at Stove as you head north from the terminal. There's a fine sand beach at Backcaskaill, across a small headland from the pretty village of **Kettletoft**, home to the island's two hotels and the old ferry terminal. At the ruined church of **Lady Kirk**, north around the bay from Kettletoft, are a series of deep gouges in a stone set high in the wall; legend has it that the marks were made by the devil after the resident minister had his wicked way with a parishioner in the vestry of the kirk.

At the tip of the next headland is the **Quoyness chambered tomb**, similar to Maes Howe and dating from the 3rd millennium BC. It has triple walls, a main chamber and six smaller cells. Continuing northeast, there is a vast dramatic beach walk along the eastern shore from the Bay of Newark to the Bay of Lopness and around to the tip of the island, where a low-tide causeway leads over to the islet of Stuart Point, with its distinctive black-and-white lighthouse, built by the Stevenson brothers in 1802. Call the lighthouse keeper (☎ 600385) for permission to look inside. Beyond the loch, at the northeastern tip of Sanday, there's **Tofts Ness**, a largely unexcavated funerary complex with some 500 prehistoric burial mounds – when the area is finally excavated, it may radically alter the island's tourism potential!

There are shops and post offices at Kettletoft, Lady and Cross. A bank service is available at Kettletoft on Tuesday only. The island is known for its knitwear, which is sold in Lady village, at the Wool Hall. Also worth a visit is **Orkney Angora** (☎ 600421) at Upper Breckan, near Burness, which sells crafts made from Angora wool and has lots of long-coated Angora rabbits. Nearby is the ruined estate of **Scar**, formerly the main estate on Sanday. A fantastic Norse whalebone plaque was found in a Viking boat burial here in 1991.

Organised Tours *Bernie Flett (☎ 600418, Quivals Garage)* Adult/child £30/22. Tours 10.10am & 7.40pm Wed & Fri May-Sept. This operator runs minibus tours of the island for a minimum of four people. Tours leave from Kirkwall pier and the price includes the ferry fare.

Places to Stay & Eat With permission, you can camp anywhere on the island, but there's no hostel. There are several B&Bs charging around £15 per person, including *Margaret Groat (☎ 600396, North Myre)* and *Tina Flett (☎ 600467, Quivals)*, who also runs the island bus service.

Kettletoft Hotel (☎/fax 600217, Kettletoft) B&B £18-23 per person. The welcoming four-room Kettletoft is an old-style hotel and just along from the pier. Meals are available from £5 to £8.

Belsair Orkney Healing Retreat (☎ 600206, @ joy@sanday.quista.net, Kettletoft) B&B £17.50-23.50 per person. The Belsair, also at Kettletoft, offers comfortable accommodation combined with courses in 'spiritual healing, emotional clearance and personal insight through meditation'; a 1½-hour healing session costs £35.

The Kettletoft and Belsair are the only main places to eat out on the island; the *Kettletoft Hotel* also does takeaway fish and chips on Wednesday and Saturday evenings.

Getting There & Around

There are flights from Kirkwall on Mainland (single/return £31/64, 20 minutes) twice daily on Monday, Tuesday, Thursday and Saturday, plus one on Wednesday, landing on the grass strip near the school, north of Kettletoft.

There are at least two ferries daily from Kirkwall to Sanday (passenger/car/bicycle £5.25/11.75/2.10, 1½ hours), most of which permit a day trip allowing about eight hours on the island.

Quivals Garage (☎ 600418) operates a bus service to meet the ferries, running to Kettletoft, Lady village, the airport and Burness (£2.50/2 per adult/child; seats to Loth must be booked in advance).

Cars and taxis can be hired from Kettletoft Garage (☎ 600321) or Quivals, which also hires bikes.

Westray

☎ 01857 ● pop 700

This is the largest of the northern islands, with some fine places to stay, and the tangible high spirits of the locals make this one of the nicest islands to visit in Scotland. Most of the island is agricultural, but there's also a busy fishing industry for monkfish, haddock, crab and lobster, all of which fish are locally processed. The islanders have also been proactive in promoting tourism.

The ferry docks at Rapness in the south of the island but **Pierowall**, 7 miles to the north, is the main village and has one of the best natural harbours in Orkney. **Westray Heritage Centre** *(☎ 677414, Pierowall; adult/child £2/50p; open 10am-noon & 2pm-5pm Tues-Sat, 11.30am-5pm Sun -Mon May-Sept)* has displays on local history and interesting nature dioramas. Pierowall has two well-stocked general merchants, a post office and most of the island's places to stay. Call Westray & Papa Westray Tourist Association (☎ 677404) for local information.

Just west of Pierowall lie the impressive ruins of **Noltland Castle** *(adult/child £1.50/ 50p; open 9.30am-6.30pm daily June-Sept)*, a 16th-century fortified castle built by Gilbert Balfour, an aide of Mary Queen of Scots. Balfour was implicated in the murder of Mary's husband, Lord Darnley, and fled to Sweden where he was executed for plotting to kill the Swedish king! The castle is pockmarked with shot-holes but surprisingly intact. Upstairs, look for the great bread oven in the kitchen and the secret compartments in the windowsills. The spooky ruin is also said to be haunted; the ghostly baying of the Bocky Hound predicts a death in the Balfour family, and you might see the castle's resident brownie – see the boxed text below. Out of season you can visit free; get the key from the farm across the road.

In the northwest is the RSPB reserve at **Noup Head**, a dramatic area of sea cliffs which attracts vast numbers of breeding seabirds from April to July. There are big puffin colonies, plus fulmars, skuas and other familiar faces, and you can usually see dozens of seals hauled out on the sloping skerries to the north of the headland. You can walk from here to Netherhouse in the south of the island, passing the Bis Geo hostel. At the island's southeastern tip, there are more cliffs near Rapness, including the free-standing stack of **Castle o'Burrian**, site of an ancient hermitage.

Places to Stay & Eat With permission, you can camp almost anywhere. There are a couple of backpacker hostels, and several places offering B&B around Pierowall.

The Barn *(☎ 677214, e thebarn@ork ney.com, Chalmersquoy, Pierowall)* Beds £11.75/8.80. Pitches from £2 (2 campers in 1 tent). Open year-round. This wonderful 13-bed hostel is housed in a skilfully converted stone barn at the southern end of Pierowall village. There's an immaculate kitchen and a splendid wood-lined lounge with a stereo system and TV. The price includes bed linen and all the hot water you need, and there is one room with wheelchair access.

Bis Geos Hostel *(☎ 677420, w www.bis-geos.co.uk, Bis Geos)* Beds £9 per person. Open May-Sept. About 2 miles west of Pierowall, Bis Geos is a 16-bed bothy, with comfy bunks, Internet access, a kitchen and

Brownies, Gruagachs & Glaistaigs

As well as the ghosts of murdered chieftains and strangled maids, many ancient castles and noble houses in the Highlands and islands are said to be haunted by benevolent spirits or fairies, who tied their fate to the fate of a particular family. Traditionally, these useful characters performed beneficial acts around the clan estates, rescuing cattle or freeing beached boats, but would vanish forever if offered anything but food and drink for their labour.

The most common entities were brownies, short hairy male spirits who repaired fences and protected farms, but many castles were also blessed with gruagachs and glaistaigs, long-haired green women who specialised in caring for cattle. Glaistaigs had a dark side, however; these mischievous spirits would habitually misdirect travellers and often became harbingers of doom for the clans they were tied to, appearing in dreadful form to warn of impending death.

an attractive conservatory overlooking the sea. There are also self-catering cottages available year-round for £100 to £300.

Sand o'Gill *(☎ 677374, Pierowall)* B&B from £16. At the northern end of Pierowall, across from the road to Gill Harbour, this is a friendly and comfortable B&B and it also offers car and bike hire.

Mrs Groat *(☎ 677283, Arcadia, Pierowall)* B&B from £16. This modern B&B is set back from the shore on the way to the castle.

Kilnman's Cottage *(☎ 677447, fax 677780, Trenabie Mill)* Self-catering cottage £180 per week. At the southern end of the village is this fine stone cottage with a heated flagstone floor and traditional peat fire. There's a kitchen and bathroom and the cottage can sleep up to four, making it ideal for families. The owners are in the process of converting the lovely Trenabie Mill behind the cottage.

Pierowall Hotel *(☎ 677208, fax 677707, e pierowall.hotel@norsecom.co.uk, Pierowall)* B&B from £23 per person, en suites £28. The comfortable eight-room Pierowall Hotel is famous throughout Orkney for its fish and chips, which is produced from fish caught fresh by the hotel's own fishing boats and is available to eat in or take away.

Cleaton House Hotel *(☎ 677508, fax 677442, e cleaton@orkney.com, Cleaton)* Singles £50, doubles £64-80. The most comfortable place to stay on Westray is the Cleaton House Hotel, a refurbished Victorian manse about 2 miles southeast of Pierowall. There are also bar meals and a three-course set menu available for £5 to £8 and £22.50 respectively.

The only restaurants are at the ***Pierowall Hotel*** and ***Cleaton House Hotel***, but self-caterers can buy fresh crabs from Westray Processors at the northern end of the harbour, and fresh fish from the Pierowall Hotel in the afternoon.

Shopping Westray produces some very fine and original crafts.

Hume Sweet Hume *(☎ 677259, Pierowall)* This friendly souvenir shop produces sophisticated knitwear and cushions using local wool and collected beach pebbles; you can really see the inspiration of the islands in the work.

Getting There & Around There are Kirkwall to Westray flights twice daily on weekdays, and once on Saturday (£31/64 one-way/return), landing on the grass strip at Aikerness in the north of the island.

A ferry service links Kirkwall with Rapness (passenger/car/bicycle £5.25/11.75/2.10, 1½ hours) at least twice a day in each direction in summer, and once or twice a day from mid-September to mid-May. On Tuesday and Friday the boat also stops at Papa Westray.

There's also a passenger-only ferry from Pierowall to Papa Westray (passenger/bicycle £5.25/2.10, 25 minutes, two to six daily); the crossing is free if you've come direct from the Rapness ferry. From late October to May, the boat sails a limited schedule for schoolchildren and doctors – call ☎ 677216 for details.

The Barn hostel hires out bikes for £5 per day, and the Sand o'Gill B&B has bikes/cars to rent for £8/30 per day. Mrs Harcus (☎ 677450) runs a bus service to Rapness, but you'll need to book 24 hours in advance (£2/1 per adult/child).

Papa Westray

Known locally as Papay (pronounced **pa-pee**), this delightful island (4 miles long and a mile wide) is home to Europe's oldest domestic building, the **Knap of Howar** (built about 5500 years ago), and to Europe's largest colony of arctic terns (about 6000 birds) at North Hill. Even the two-minute hop from Westray airfield is featured in *The Guinness Book of Records* as the world's shortest scheduled air service.

The island is delightfully peaceful and unhurried and excellently set up for walking, with sturdy styles over all the fences. Starting from the ferry jetty at the south of the island (which has a nice Bothican beach where you can wait for the boat), you can walk around the east coast to the ruins of **St Tredwell's Chapel**, a medieval monastic complex on the site of an Iron-Age dun, on a wave-lapped island in Loch of St Tredwell. Farther north is the ruin of an ancient mill and a series of boat 'nousts' (stone landing bays) by the old pier.

About half a mile offshore is the **Holm of Papay**, a tiny islet with a series of fine stone cairns, including a vast **chambered cairn**, 21m long with 16 separate beehive-cells – entry is via a ladder and there's a torch so you can find your way around the gloomy interior. From May to September, *Jim Davidson (☎ 644259)* runs boat trips to the Holm for around £5 per person.

If you cross the island you'll pass the island community co-op shop, hostel and guesthouse at Beltane. At the main junction you can cross to the west coast, where you'll find the **Knap of Howar**, a pair of linked buildings built in around 3500 BC. The site has been sensitively restored and is very atmospheric. North on the junction is Holland Farm, which belonged to the Traill lairds for three centuries and is still a working farm. It's a real picture-postcard place, with a mill, doocot and corn kiln, and there's the informal **John Holland Museum** *(admission free; open year-round)* with old photos, farm machinery, and personal memorabilia, including a flea trap and a box from the first shipment of petrol to Orkney in 1919.

About half a mile north, a lane leads westwards to **St Boniface Kirk**, a low stone building with stepped gables, sitting on the site of an 8th-century monastery. Beyond the kirk, the entire northern end of Papa Westray, centred on North Hill, is a nature reserve with a huge Arctic tern breeding colony from May to August, as well as plentiful guillemots, kittiwakes, razorbills and puffins. The reserve was established too late to save one species – the very last great auk was killed here in 1813. **Katy Robinson** *(☎ 644240)* offers guided walks of the reserve at 1.30pm on Tuesday, Thursday and Saturday.

Owned by the local community co-op, *Beltane House Hotel (☎ 644267)* comprises a 16-bed SYHA-approved hostel and a guesthouse with four comfortable en-suite rooms; dorm beds cost £7/6.25 and B&B is

from £23 per person. There is also a small *shop* and *restaurant* here; evening meals are available for £16.50 (book in advance). It's about a mile north of the ferry.

On Tuesday, Thursday and Saturday, you can take a *Peedie Package Tour (☎ 644267)* of the island for £28/13 per adult/child, including tea at the Beltane's restaurant.

Getting There & Away Flying to Papa Westray from Kirkwall is good value compared with other flights in Orkney – about twice the distance for half the price. There are flights twice daily Monday to Saturday (£15/30 single/return).

The flight from Westray to Papa Westray is the world's shortest scheduled flight, lasting just two minutes, and as little as 45 seconds with a tailwind – the fare for this bit of fun is £19/38.

For ferry details, see Westray earlier. Call ☎ 644245 for bike hire.

North Ronaldsay
☎ 01857 ● pop 50

Pity the poor sheep on this remote, windswept island – they're kept off the rich farmland by a 13-mile-long wall all round the island, and forced to feed only on seaweed, which is said to give their meat a unique flavour. During the shearing and dipping seasons, the sheep are herded into communal 'punds' (stone enclosures), one of the last examples of communal farming in Britain.

North Ronaldsay sits right at the top of Orkney, north of Sanday, and has a real outpost atmosphere, surrounded by rolling seas and endless sky. Known locally as 'North Ron', the island measures just 3 miles long by a mile wide and is almost completely flat, reaching just 20m at its highest point. It attracts large numbers of bird-watchers who come to see rare migratory species from March to June and from August to November. Regular visitors include Arctic and sandwich terns, fulmars, guillemots, curlew, snipe and kittiwakes. At other times the island is blissfully quiet, and although there's not much to see or do, that may be just the reason to come here.

The island has Scotland's tallest land-built lighthouse (33m) at the Point of Sinsoss, and seal and cormorant colonies nearby. The beautiful **old lighthouse**, built in the 1780s, stands like a giant chess pawn at the headland south of Point of Sinsoss (the bauble on top replaced the lantern in 1809). The island also has some ancient relics, including a series of Neolithic villages at Bride's Ness and the extensive ruins of the **Broch of Burrian** at the island's southern tip.

There's a shop and a pub, which serves meals, a half-mile north of the ferry pier.

Powered by wind and solar energy, the **Bird Observatory** (☎ 633200, **e** warden@ nrbo.prestel.co.uk), next to the ferry pier, offers hostel (£18 per person) and B&B (£27.50 per person) accommodation and ornithological activities. All prices include breakfast, dinner and bed linen; under-15s are charged half-price, under-4s are free. There's also a shop, cafe and licensed lounge bar.

Mrs Muir's B&B, **Garso Guest House** (☎/fax 633244), is at the northern end of the island, about 3 miles from the pier. Dinner B&B costs £25 per head and she also has a self-catering cottage available, sleeping up to five, for £25 per night. Mr Muir offers a taxi and minibus service.

Getting There & Away Flights to North Ronaldsay cost £15/30 one-way/return, and leave twice daily Monday to Saturday. There's a weekly ferry (☎ 872044) from Kirkwall on Friday (passenger/car/bicycle £5.25/11.75/2.10, 1½ hours) – there's not really much point bringing a car.

Shetland Islands

These rugged and remote northern isles are only tenuously part of Britain; the islands were conquered by Viking marauders in the 8th century and remained under Norse rule until 1469, when they were mortgaged to Scotland as part of a Danish princess' dowry. Culturally, Shetland has always looked as much towards Scandinavia – the nearest mainland town is Bergen, on the Norwegian coast – as to the Scottish mainland. There were still over 10,000 Norse words in common usage here at the start of the 20th century and most place names have Viking rather than Celtic origins. Like Orkney, 60 miles to the south, Shetland was taken over by lowland Scottish nobles, so Lowland Scots rather than Gaelic became the main language of the islands.

Savage winds have battered the islands since around 3000 BC and there is almost no tree cover, except for a few tiny copses of stunted trees planted as windbreaks by the lairds of Shetland. The landscape in Shetland is far bleaker than in Orkney, but also grander, with sweeping glens, desolate peat bogs and fjord-like voes (sea inlets). You can see peat cuttings and drying stacks of peat blocks throughout the islands.

The rise of the oil and natural gas industries in the 1970s contributed a great deal of wealth to the Shetland economy; the general atmosphere of prosperity is quite tangible, particularly when compared to the other Scottish islands. Today, Shetland is the base for the North Sea oilfields, and pipelines feed Europe's largest oil refinery at Sullom Voe, in north Mainland. Shetland could have ended up considerably more wealthy, but much of the big money was filtered off back to England.

If you walk anywhere on the islands, chances are you will stumble across suspiciously regular piles of stones marking the site of some ancient building or burial cairn. Many have been excavated through the commendable work of Historic Scotland (HS), including Shetland's two most famous historic sites, the remarkable settlement of Jarlshof in the south – which features buildings dating from the Bronze Age right through to the 17th century – and Mousa Broch, near Sandwick, the most complete Iron-Age tower in Scotland.

Shetland's 552-sq-mile area consists of over 100 islands, of which 15 are inhabited. Mainland is by far the largest with its attractive stone capital at Lerwick; most other settlements are scattered villages. Budget accommodation includes six camping böds

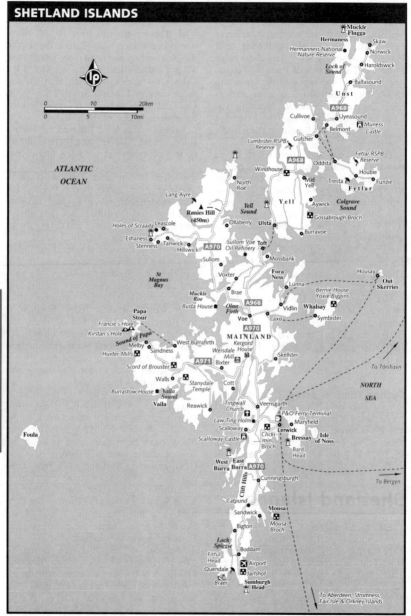

SHETLAND ISLANDS

ATLANTIC
OCEAN

Muckle
Flugga
Hermaness
Skaw
Hermanness National
Nature Reserve
Norwick
Haroldswick
Loch of
Sound
Baltasound
U n s t
A968
Cullivoe
Uyeasound
Muness
Belmont
Castle
Lumbister RSPB
Gutcher
Reserve
A968
Fetlar RSPB
Windhouse
Oddsta
Reserve
North Roe
Mid
Houbie
Yell
Tresta
Funzie
Yell Sound
Y e l l
F e t l a r
Lang Ayre
Aywick
Colgrave
Rønies Hill
Sound
(450m)
Ollaberry
Ulsta
Gossabrough Broch
Holes of Scraada
Leascole
Burravoe
Eshaness
Tanwick
A970
Sullom Voe
Toft
Housay
Stenness
Hillswick
Oil Refinery
Out
Sullom
Mossbank
Skerries
St
Voxter
Fora
Magnus
Ness
Lunna
Bay
Brae
Bernie Hoose
Muckle
Yoxie Biggins
Roe
A968
Vidlin
Busta House
Olna
Whalsay
Firth
To Tórshavn
Papa
Voe
Laxo
Stour
Symbister
Francie's Hole
MAINLAND
NORTH
Kirstan's Hole
Kergord
SEA
Sound of Papa
House
Melby
West Burrafirth
Sandness
Weisdale
Huxter Mills
Mill
Scord of Brouster
A971
Bixter
Skellster
Walls
Stanydale
Cott
Temple
Burrastow House
To Bergen
Vaila
Sound
Reawick
Vaila
Tingwall
Veensgarth
Church
P&O Ferry Terminal
Foula
Law Ting Holm
Maryfield
Scalloway
Clicki-
Lerwick
min
Bressay
Scalloway Castle
Broch
Isle
of Noss
Bard
West
East
Head
Burra
Burra
A970
Cunningsburgh
To Bergen
Cliff Hills
Catpund
Mousa
Sandwick
Mousa
Bigton
Broch
Loch
Spiggie
Boddam
Fitful
Head
Airport
Quendale
Jarlshof
Braer
Sumburgh
Head
To Aberdeen, Stromness,
Fair Isle & Orkney Islands

0   10   20km
0   5   10mi

(barns). The islands are far enough north to experience Scandinavian phenomena such as the Aurora Borealis and perpetual daylight – the 'simmer dim' – at the height of summer. Shetland has a vibrant tradition of folk music and storytelling, celebrated by annual festivals which bring hundreds of visitors to the islands.

ORIENTATION & INFORMATION

The islands have a single TIC (in Sumburgh – see that section later), but it compensates by selling an excellent selection of books on the islands. Well worth investing in is *Shetland* by Anna Ritchie, with detailed descriptions of almost all the islands' ancient monuments. The official Shetland Tourism Web site is at **W** www.visitshetland.com. BBC Shetland Radio (96.7MHz FM) broadcasts at 5.30pm weekdays.

The following Ordnance Survey (OS) Landranger maps cover Shetland:

Landranger 1: Shetland – Yell, Unst & Fetlar
Landranger 2: Shetland – Sullom Vow &
   Whalsay
Landranger 3: Shetland – North Mainland
Landranger 4: Shetland – South Mainland

ACTIVITIES

The main attraction in Shetland is the unparalleled **bird-watching** – see the boxed text 'Twitching in the Shetlands' later for information. Also, the lochs are great for **trout-fishing** and the TIC can help arrange permits for the various estates – daily permits cost £5.

The islands are beautifully undeveloped and excellent for **wild walking**. Shetland holds the annual Walk Shetland festival in August/September with a series of guided walks around little-seen parts of the islands (contact the TIC for details).

GETTING THERE & AWAY

Unlike Orkney, Shetland is relatively expensive to get to from mainland Scotland, although the transport links are excellent. Most visitors are involved in the oil industry and are travelling on expense accounts, so there's no pressure to bring down fares.

Air

Shetland's 'long haul' airport is at Sumburgh, 25 miles south of Lerwick. From Monday to Saturday, British Airways (BA; ☎ 0845 773 3377, **W** www.britishairways .com) has a morning flight from Inverness to Sumburgh, returning in the afternoon (£141 one-way, 1¼ hours) and flights from Sumburgh to Kirkwall (£80, 35 minutes). There's a single flight between Wick and Sumburgh on Saturday (£91, 45 minutes).

Travelling further afield, BA has several daily direct flights to Aberdeen (£155, one hour), with connections to London, Manchester, Birmingham and Bristol. There are two daily (one on Saturday and Sunday) flights to Glasgow (£221, one hour) and a single daily flight to Edinburgh (£198, 1½ hours). Note that returns are often cheaper than one-way fares.

Car hire, taxis and tourist information are available at Sumburgh, but there are no foreign exchange facilities. If you're killing time waiting for a flight, Sumburgh airport is just a short walk from the historic site at Jarlshof. From the airport, a taxi costs £27 to Lerwick, or there are regular Leask & Son buses (£2, less frequent on Sunday).

Boat

P&O Scottish Ferries (☎ 01224-572615, **W** www.posf.co.uk) operates over-night car ferries from Aberdeen to Lerwick (£60/120 one-way/return, 14 hours) on weekdays, departing at 6pm. Return trips operate from Monday to Saturday and leave Lerwick at 6pm (noon on Friday). From September to May the fare drops to £54/108. The surcharge for a cabin starts at £28 (£22.50 off-season) and there's a reasonably priced restaurant on board.

P&O also runs car ferries between Lerwick and Aberdeen via Stromness in Orkney (see Getting There & Away under Orkney for details), enabling you to travel Aberdeen-Lerwick-Stromness-Scrabster or vice versa. A high-season ticket on this routing costs £117/227 per passenger/car. Motorbikes/ bikes are £56/12.

For details of the ferry link between Lerwick, Tórshavn (Faroe Islands) and Bergen

ORKNEY & SHETLAND ISLANDS

Twitching in the Shetlands

Lying on the north–south and east–west migration routes, Shetland is one of Britain's top bird-watching locations, attracting huge numbers of dedicated twitchers – you can spot this rare breed by the binoculars and note books they habitually carry. As well as being a stopover for migrating Arctic species, there are large seabird breeding colonies, where you can see the elaborate mating rituals of creatures such as fulmars, skuas and puffins.

Out of the 24 seabird species that nest in the British Isles, 21 are found here; June is the height of the breeding season when all hell breaks loose around the isles. The bird population vastly outnumbers the human population of 24,000 – there are said to be around 30,000 gannets, 140,000 guillemots, 250,000 puffins and 300,000 fulmars.

The Royal Society for the Protection of Birds (RSPB; W www.rspb.org.uk) maintains reserves on south Mainland at **Sumburgh Head** and on the island of **Fetlar**, which supports the richest heathland bird community. There are also cliffs all around the islands with puffins, auks, gulls and shags.

There are national nature reserves (NNR) at **Hermaness**, where you can't fail to be entertained by the clownish antics of the almost tame puffins – known here as the tammy norrie – and on the **Isle of Noss**, which can be reached from Lerwick. **Fair Isle**, owned by the National Trust for Scotland (NTS), supports large seabird populations and offers accommodation at the bird observatory.

A useful Web site for bird-watchers is W www.wildlife.shetland.co.uk/birds/where.html. Birdwatchers are advised to take a few precautions. Many cliff-side nesting sites are dangerous in high winds and birds such as skuas (bonxies) will dive-bomb you if you go near their nests (they aim for the highest part of your body so a stick held above your head will get the brunt of their rage). Nesting fulmars have the gruesome habit of spitting caustic oily spittle over anyone who gets too close so give them plenty of space.

(Norway), see the Getting There & Away chapter for more information.

GETTING AROUND

The *Shetland Transport Timetable*, an invaluable publication listing all local air, sea and bus services, costs £1 at the TIC.

Air

Flights within the islands leave from Tingwall airport on Mainland. BA-affiliate Loganair (☎ 01595-840246) runs flights between Tingwall and Fair Isle, Foula, Papa Stour and Out Skerries – see the relevant island sections for further details. Flight timetables and special offer are available online at W www.loganair.co.uk.

Boat

Surprisingly inexpensive car and passenger ferries connect Mainland with the other Shetland Islands – see the individual island sections for details.

Bus

Several bus services operate from Lerwick's Viking bus station to all parts of Mainland, with connections meeting the ferries at Unst and Yell; for details call ☎ 01595-694100. Postbuses run on Fetlar (Monday, Wednesday and Friday) and Bressay (weekdays).

Car

The wide roads seem more like motorways after Orkney's tiny, winding lanes, though it's back to single lanes away from the main transisland highways. Beware of sheep on the roads at night.

Car hire is widely available. The main agent at Sumburgh airport is Bolts Car Hire (☎ 01950-693636), but it's cheaper to take the bus to Lerwick and hire a car there – see Getting Around under Lerwick.

Bicycle

If it's fine, cycling on the islands' roads can be an exhilarating way to experience the stark beauty of Shetland. It can, however, be very windy (wind speeds of up to 194mph have been recorded!) and there are few places to shelter. Bikes can be hired in Lerwick (see Getting Around in that section) and are carried free on Shetland ferries.

Shetland is part of the North Sea cycle route (W www.northsea-cycle.com), with connections by ferry in summer to Norway, providing access to the mainland European parts of the route.

Organised Tours
Several companies offer island tours. *Shetland Tours Charters* (☎ 692080) charges £22 per hour for customised car tours for up to four people.

On Tuesday from May to September, the TIC offers guided walking tours (£5.50/ 3.50 adult/child) of Lerwick led by guides in period costume. There are lunch tours (£35/20) to Busta House Hotel on Thursday and storytelling trips (£5/3.50) to the Crofthouse Museum at Boddam on Monday.

LERWICK
☎ 01595 ● pop 7280
This busy but surprisingly attractive town is almost entirely built of grey-stone and straddles a thin isthmus of land overlooking a natural harbour. Although it's full of atmosphere, Lerwick wasn't founded until the 17th century, making it almost a new town by Shetland standards. The original capital was on the west coast at Scalloway, which was better located for the narrow agricultural belt, but the arrival of Dutch herring fleets in the 17th century prompted a shift to the protected harbour at *leir vik* (from the Viking for 'mud bay'). Lerwick's position was guaranteed when Fort Charlotte was built in 1665 to keep a safe eye on British ships during the Anglo-Dutch wars.

At the height of the herring industry, in the late 19th century, Lerwick was the largest herring port in northern Europe, but the collapse of the Eastern European herring market during WWI led to a sharp decline in Lerwick's fortunes. The islands became something of a backwater until the discovery of oil in the 1970s.

Lerwick is the only settlement of any size in Shetland, and as such has a few 'big city' problems, mainly vandalism by bored youths (park your car in a well-lit street). The problems are all pretty low key, though you'll find a list of broken wing-mirrors in the weekly *Shetland Times*.

Orientation & Information
The old harbour, 20 minutes' walk south of the main ferry terminal, forms the focus of the town. Flagstone-paved Commercial St, one block back from the waterfront, is the main shopping street, dominated by the Victorian bulk of the Grand Hotel. The post office is on Commercial St and three or four banks with ATMs are along the same road.

You can use the Internet for free (30 minutes maximum) at the Shetland Library & Museum (☎ 693868), Lower Hillhead, or there's the Scottish Youth Information Centre (☎ 692002) at Da Cross (£1 per hour).

The TIC (☎ 693434, W www.visit shetland.com), Market Cross, opens 8am to 6pm weekdays, 8am to 4pm Saturday and 10am to 1pm Sunday, April to September (otherwise 9am to 5pm weekdays only). There's a bureau de change here and a very good range of books and maps, as well as brochures on everything from Shetland-pony stud farms to lists of safe anchorages for yachts. *Walks on Shetland* by Mary Welsh and *Walking the Coastline of Shetland* by Peter Guy are useful walking guides.

Diagonally opposite the post office, Shetland Times Bookshop (☎ 695531, 71–79 Commercial St) is commendably well stocked with books about the isles. For camera film try the Camera Centre (☎ 694345, Commercial St).

Several countries have consulates in Shetland. The consulates for Denmark, Iceland and Sweden can be contacted at Hay & Co (☎ 692533), 66 Commercial Rd; those for Finland, France, Germany and Norway at Shearer Shipping Services (☎ 692556) off Commercial Rd.

Lerwick Health Centre (☎ 693201) is on South Rd, opposite the Gilbert Bain Hospital (☎ 743000).

LERWICK

PLACES TO STAY
2 Shetland Hotel
11 Kumalang Guest House
13 Roseville B&B
15 Clickimin Caravan
   & Camp Site
16 Mrs Gifford's
17 Lerwick Youth Hostel;
   Isleburgh House Café
23 Fort Charlotte Guesthouse
27 Grand Hotel; Posers
41 Queen's Hotel
42 Kveldsro House Hotel
43 Bonavista Guest House
45 Solhelm Guest House;
   Carradale Guest House

PLACES TO EAT
8 Raba Indian Restaurant
12 Happy Haddock

24 Fort Café; The Street
   Sandwich Bar
25 Peerie Shop & Cafe
26 Osla's Café
37 Monty's Bistro
44 New Golden Coach

OTHER
1 Holmsgarth Ferry Terminal
3 Co-op Supermarket
4 Grantfield Garage
5 Bolts Car Hire
6 Shearer Shipping Services
7 Hay & Co
9 Viking Bus Station; Great
   Wall Chinese Restaurant
10 Lerwick Laundry
14 Up Helly Aa Exhibition
18 Shetland Library & Museum
19 Town Hall

20 Police Station
21 Garrison Theatre
22 Fort Charlotte
28 Bank of Scotland
29 Da Noost
30 Leasks Self Drive
31 Lloyds TSB
32 Camera Centre
33 Scottish Youth Information
   Centre
34 Captain Flint's
35 Tourist Information Centre
36 The Lounge
38 Post Office
39 Royal Bank of Scotland;
   Jamieson's Knitwear
40 Shetland Times Bookshop
46 Gilbert Bain Hospital
47 Lerwick Health Centre
48 Clickimin Broch

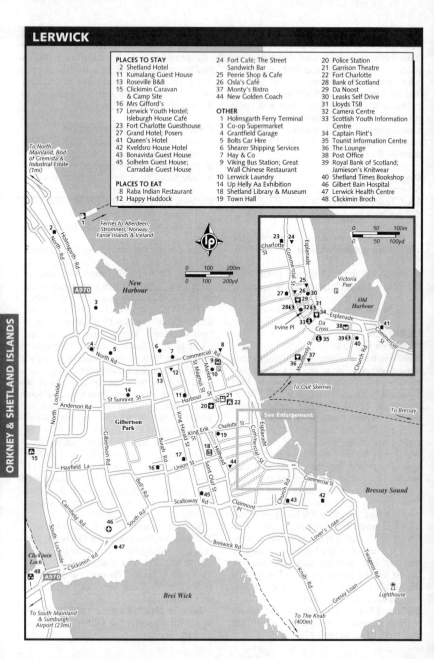

ORKNEY & SHETLAND ISLANDS

Lerwick Laundry (☎ 898043, Market St) charges £6.40 per load for washing and drying.

Things to See & Do

There are good views from the battlements of **Fort Charlotte**, built in 1665 to protect the harbour from the Dutch navy. There's not much to see in the fort itself, which housed the town prison (1837–75) and now provides the headquarters for the Territorial Army; it opens 9am to 10pm daily (until 4pm October to May).

The **Town Hall** (☎ 693535, Hillhead; admission free; open 9am-5pm Mon-Thur, 9am-4pm Fri) has stained-glass windows depicting local historical scenes, and a great view from the clock tower.

It's worth visiting the **Shetland Library & Museum** (☎ 695057, Lower Hillhead; admission free; open 10am-7pm Mon, Wed & Fri & 10am-5pm Tues, Thur & Sat) for an introduction to the islands' history and geology. There are replicas of the St Ninian's Isle treasure, carved Pictish stones and displays detailing the fishing, whaling and knitting industries, plus a curious 'chintz' room, with tacky memorabilia from the 1960s and '70s. Also here is a display by the Embroiderers Guild and a collection of 19th-century porcelain toilets (seriously!).

The **Up Helly Aa Exhibition** (St Sunniva St; adult/child £2.50/free; open 2pm-4pm Tues & Sat & 7pm-9pm Tues & Fri May-Sept), in the Galley Shed off St Sunniva St, explains the curious Viking fire festival (see Special Events). From June to August, you can take tours of the bay in a Viking longship every Monday evening (£5/2 – book with the TIC).

The fortified site of **Clickimin Broch**, about a mile west of the town centre, was occupied from the 7th century BC to the 6th century AD. The ruins are low and a little over-restored, but the walls give you a sense of how huge the broch was. It's always open; just follow the path opposite the BP service station.

The **Böd of Gremista** (☎ 695057, Gremista; adult/child £2/1.50; open 10am-1pm & 2pm-5pm Wed-Sun June–mid-Sept),

about a mile north of the ferry terminal, was the birthplace of Arthur Anderson, co-founder of P&O. It has been restored as an 18th-century fishing booth; there's also a small exhibition about Anderson.

There's a cliff-side **walk** south of Lerwick to the headland known as **The Knab**, where you can watch the ferries coming in.

Special Events

It's well worth being here for the **Folk Festival** (☎ 695381, W www.sffs.shetland.co.uk) in April/May, or for the wonderful **Fiddle and Accordion Festival** in October, when every pub on the island comes alive with duelling fiddles. The biggest spectacle of the year is the **Up Helly Aa** festival on the last Tuesday in January (see the boxed text below). A new addition to the calendar is the **Shetland Storytelling Festival** in September, honouring the islands' rich oral tradition. Contact the TIC for more information on all these festivals.

Note that beds can be hard to find during any of these festivals.

Places to Stay

Camping *Clickimin Caravan & Camp Site* (☎ 741000, fax 741001, Lochside) Pitches £4.40/6.20 for 1/2 people. Open

Up Helly Aa

Every January, islanders honour their Norse roots with a vast pageant and the ceremonial burning of a replica Viking longship. This festival for pyros dates back to Norse times, when Vikings celebrated the rebirth of the sun at yule by torching a longship in the bay. Over the centuries, Up Helly Aa has gone through several incarnations – during the 19th century barrels of burning tar were towed through the streets – but one feature that has been preserved across the years is *guizing* or fancy-dress. The tradition runs all the way back to pagan times and every year the head team at the longboat procession is a group of Vikings led by 'Guizer Jarl', elected annually by the celebrants.

ORKNEY & SHETLAND ISLANDS

May-Sept. This orderly site is on the western edge of town; it has its own shower and laundry block, but you may be able to stay and use the facilities at the attached leisure centre in winter.

Hostels *Lerwick Youth Hostel (☎ 692114, fax 696470, King Harald St)* Beds from £9.25/8. Open Apr-Sept. Housed in a fine old government building, Lerwick's only hostel is a mile from the ferry terminal, and reception stays open for late ferry arrivals. It's clean and well looked after and there's a cafe, which is just as well as the guests' kitchen is rather small.

B&Bs & Hotels Most of Lerwick's B&Bs and guesthouses are cosy affairs with just a few rooms.

Solheim Guest House (☎/fax 695275, 34 King Harald St) Singles £21-30, doubles £19-26 per person. This excellent place offers a good breakfast, colour TVs in every room, and is run by a welcoming family.

Carradale Guest House (☎ 692251, 36 King Harald St) B&B £20-25 per person. Next door to Solheim Guest House is Carradale, which is a similar place that also serves evening meals.

Roseville B&B (☎ 697128, 95 King Harald St) B&B from £22. Towards the waterfront, this is a cosy and well-located B&B.

Kumalang Guest House (☎ 695731, 89 St Olaf St) B&B £20-25 per person. This is another friendly place with dinner available on request.

Fort Charlotte Guesthouse (☎ 695956, 1 Charlotte St) Singles/doubles £25-35 per person. Squeezed between Commercial St and the fort, this narrow stone house is comfortable and excellently located.

Bonavista Guest House (☎ 692269, 26 Church Rd) Singles/doubles from £18/20. This relaxed option is uphill from the centre, and offers decent rooms and friendly service.

Queen's Hotel (☎ 692826, fax 694048, Commercial St) En-suite singles/doubles £65/90. This old stone hotel sits right on the water and some rooms have magnificent ocean views.

Grand Hotel (☎ 692826, fax 694048, 24 Commercial St) En-suite singles/doubles £65/90. This grand old Victorian hotel was once Lerwick's pride and glory, but the glory is a little faded these days. Rooms are still very comfortable though.

Kveldsro House Hotel (☎ 692195, fax 696595, Greenfield Place) Singles/doubles £70/94. This top-notch hotel is housed in an old building overlooking the harbour, but the small, narrow streets can make it difficult to find – the name is pronounced 'kelro' if you need to ask for directions.

Shetland Hotel (☎ 695515, fax 695828, Holmsgarth Rd) Singles/doubles from £69/90. This big modern hotel by the P&O ferry terminal is a good upmarket choice.

Places to Eat

Although there's good fresh fish, Shetland is no place for gastronomes. *Restit* is the best known local dish – lumps of mutton cured with salt and made into a soupy, salty stew traditionally eaten in the long winter months. It tastes quite as awful as it sounds and, consequently, rarely appears on menus.

New Golden Coach (☎ 692452, 17 Hillhead) Mains from £5. This decent Chinese restaurant offers a good range of Cantonese favourites to eat in or take away.

Great Wall Chinese Restaurant (☎ 693988, Commercial Rd) Mains £4-9. Perched above the bus station, this stylish restaurant serves very good Chinese food and less convincing Thai fare.

Raba Indian Restaurant (☎ 695585, 26 Commercial Rd) Mains £5-8. Just uphill from the bus station, this is a particularly fine Indian restaurant, with good vegetarian choices.

Monty's Bistro (☎ 696555, 5 Mounthooly St) Evening mains £8-12. Open Tues-Sat. This upmarket but informal bistro is highly recommended and serves lots of fine local produce such as lamb and monkfish. The bistro lunches (£2.50 to £6) are good value.

Queen's Hotel (☎ 692826, Commercial St) Bar meals £4-8, 3-course dinners £15.25. This place serves posh salmon and Angus beef creations and cheaper wholesome fare at the bar.

Kveldsro House Hotel (☎ 692195, *Greenfield Place*) 3-course dinner £17.50. The posh restaurant at the Kveldsro is a fine place to go for a really special occasion. The price includes tea or coffee.

Peerie Shop Cafe (☎ 692817, *Esplanade*) Sandwiches from £3. This very funky and upbeat coffee shop serves fine espresso and gourmet sandwiches.

Osla's Café (☎ 696005, *Commercial St*) Soup and snacks from £2. For snacks such as savoury pancakes and sandwiches, plus excellent coffees and teas, try this relaxed cafe on the main street.

The Street Sandwich Bar (☎ 694665, *124 Commercial St*) Sandwiches & tatties from £2. Closed Sun. This popular lunch stop serves good sandwiches and other snacks to eat in or take away.

Islesburgh House Café (☎ 692114, *King Harald St*) Mains around £4. Open 11am-9pm Mon-Thurs & 11am-5pm Fri & Sat. This place is in the same building as the youth hostel and serves good-value, wholesome food.

There are several takeaways in central Lerwick offering tasty portions of fish and chips made with freshly caught fish. *Fort Café* (☎ 693125, *2 Commercial Rd*) and *Happy Haddock* (☎ 692414, *59 Commercial Rd*) offer battered fish and chips for under £3.

Self-caterers can head for the large *Safeway* supermarket just south of the Clickimin Broch, near the Clickimin Rd roundabout, or the large *Co-op supermarket* on Holmsgarth Rd.

Entertainment

The Shetland Fiddlers play at a number of locations, and it's worth attending their sessions – enquire at the TIC.

The Lounge (☎ 692231, *4 Mounthooly St*) This wonderfully friendly bar is the best place to drink; there's live music several nights a week, from jazz and traditional fiddle nights to informal folk-music jams featuring dozens of local musicians.

Captain Flint's (☎ 692249, *Market Cross*) This lively pub has live music at weekends and serves bar lunches and dinners.

Da Noost (☎ 693446, *86 Commercial St*) This popular venue has live bands on Friday night and Saturday afternoon.

Posers (☎ 692826, *24 Commercial St*) Cover charge £5. Lerwick's only nightclub is at the Grand Hotel, which plays loud, but slightly dated, dance music.

There's a touring *cinema* (☎ 692114) several times a month at the Garrison Theatre in Fort Charlotte (adult/child £3.50/2.50).

Shopping

Best buys are the woollen jerseys, cardigans and sweaters for which Shetland is world-famous. There are numerous shops selling woollens, but for bargains you're best off going to the source – ask at the TIC for factories with outlet stores.

In the centre there is more expensive (from £40) but high-quality knitwear at the *Peerie Shop* (☎ 692816, *Esplanade*), with modern creations, and *Jamieson's Knitwear* (☎ 693114, *93 Commercial St*) has traditional Fair Isle sweaters with the distinctive OXOXO pattern.

Getting There & Away

See the introductory Getting There & Away section under Shetland Islands and the Getting There & Away chapter. Ferries dock at Holmsgarth terminal, 20 minutes' walk from the town centre (the terminal has been reconstructed to allow larger ships to dock). From Sumburgh airport, Leasks (☎ 693162) runs regular buses to meet flights (£2 one-way) and also handles bookings for flights within the islands and further afield.

Getting Around

Eric Brown (☎ 692709) at Grantfield Garage, North Rd, hires out bikes for £7.50/45 per day/week. Car hire is also available from £24 per day. Other car-hire options include Bolt's Car Hire (☎ 693636), 26 North Rd, and Leasks Self Drive (☎ 693162), Esplanade. Note that parking inspectors are ruthless here; there's a public car park on Victoria Pier.

If you need a taxi call Sinclair's Taxis (☎ 694617).

ORKNEY & SHETLAND ISLANDS

AROUND LERWICK
Bressay & Isle of Noss
☎ 01595 ● pop 353

Immediately across the Bressay Sound, the 21-sq-mile island of Bressay (pronounced bressah) shelters Lerwick from the North Sea, making the town's harbour one of the finest in Britain. Bressay was once an important port for Dutch herring boats, but just has a small local fleet these days. There are some interesting walks, especially along the cliffs at **Bard Head**, which has large seabird colonies, and up to Ward Hill (226m), which offers good views of the island. Ferries dock at Maryfield, which has a small **heritage centre** *(☎ 820638, Maryfield; admission free; open 10am-4pm Tues, Wed, Fri & Sat, 11am-5.30pm Sun)*, with exhibits on the herring industry.

For serious bird-watching, it's worth visiting the **Isle of Noss**, a national nature reserve (NNR), which has huge nesting colonies on its 183m cliffs. Noss can be visited 10am to 5pm mid-May to August (not Tuesday or Friday) when Scottish Natural Heritage (SNH) operates a visitors centre at Gungstie; boats run from the east coast of Bressay (£3/1.50 adult/child). Call the SNH (☎ 693345) before leaving Lerwick as the boat doesn't run in bad weather.

From Lerwick, *Bressaboats* runs two-hour cruises around Bressay and Noss daily except Wednesday, April to September (£25/15 adult/child); book with the TIC on ☎ 693434. The company also has a Bressay Sound cruise with an underwater camera (£25/15). The MV *Alluvion* charges £20 for Noss cruises (book with the TIC).

If you fancy staying over, *Maryfield House (☎ 820207, fax 820745)*, the grey farmhouse by the jetty, offers B&B (from £27.50) and good bar meals (£5 to £7).

A new böd is set to open in the *Bressay Lighthouse* – call ☎ 694688 to check if it's open.

Getting There & Away From the dock at the Albert Building, below Fort Charlotte on the Esplanade in Lerwick, there are hourly ferries (☎ 01426-980317) to Bressay (£1.30, £3.10 car and driver, five minutes, daily).

It's then 2½ miles across the island (some people bring rented bikes from Lerwick) to take the inflatable dinghy to Noss. There's a Monday to Saturday postbus service (☎ 820200) from the ferry terminal to Noss Sound and the lighthouse.

Scalloway
☎ 01595 ● pop 1053

The former capital of Shetland, Scalloway (pronounced scallowah), on the west coast 6 miles from Lerwick, has seen better days, but it's dominated by an imposing castle and has a small fishing industry. During WWII, the Norwegian resistance movement operated the 'Shetland Bus' from here, carrying arms and transporting refugees in fishing boats.

Things to See & Do The ruins of **Scalloway Castle** *(HS; Castle St)* rise above the port's warehouses. It was built in 1600 by the cruel Patrick Stewart, earl of Orkney and lord of Shetland, and consists of a four-storey rectangular main block, with a wing of the same height at one corner. The walls are full of shot-holes, manned at one time by the tyrant's 50-man bodyguard. If the gate is closed, you can get the key from the Shetland Woollen Company shop just up the hill.

The small, volunteer-run **Scalloway Museum** *(☎ 880675, Main St; donation requested; open roughly 10am-4.30pm Mon-Sat)* has interesting displays on the 'Shetland Bus', a bastion of anti-Nazi resistance during WWII, when Norwegian fishing boats were used to ferry weapons and fighters from Scalloway across the North Sea to the coast of Norway.

There are some pretty beaches and **walks** on the linked islands of Tronda and East and West Burra, south of Scalloway, with fine views of the Clift Hills.

Places to Eat The Scalloway Hotel is now leased to an oil company, but there are a few places to eat.

Kiln Bar (☎ 880444, Main St) Bar meals £4-10. This basic pub is near the Quay and has cheap food, but little atmosphere.

Da Haaf Restaurant (☎ 880747, Port Arthur) Fish dishes £5.50-9.50. Open 9am-8pm Mon-Fri. Located in the North Atlantic Fisheries College, this restaurant specialises in excellent local seafood, but also serves duck, beef and pasta dishes.

Getting There & Away Buses run every hour between Scalloway and Lerwick (20 minutes, daily except Sunday).

Tingwall Valley
☎ 01595

North of Scalloway, the B9074 follows the western shore of Loch of Tingwall through the fertile Tingwall Valley, where you'll find Tingwall airport (for flights within Shetland), The two lochs are good for trout fishing – call the Shetland Anglers Association (☎ 695903) for permits. Just south of **Veensgarth** village, at the northern end of Loch of Tingwall, is the site of **Law Ting Holm**, where Shetland's annual Norse parliament or *althing* was held in the 13th century. Criminals being tried here could gain amnesty if they managed to run through the crowd of spectators and touch nearby **St Magnus Kirk** without being caught. On the same site, **Tingwall Church** is more recent, but there's a burial vault from the original medieval kirk in the kirkyard, full of carved medieval graveslabs.

Herrislea House Hotel (☎ 840208, fax 840630, Veensgarth) Singles/doubles from £50/80. This fine hotel offers very comfortable rooms in an old mansion decked out with hunting souvenirs. Excellent bar meals (£5 to £7) are also available and there's a set menu for £10.75.

South Haven (☎/fax 830350, Nesbister) B&B £25-30. Over on the west coast near Whiteness, this lovely Scandinavian cottage has nice views over Whiteness Voe.

Weisdale
☎ 01595

Northwest of Tingwall, on the A971, there are great views of Shetland from **Wormadale Hill**, while below (past the Loch of Strom), the head of **Weisdale Voe** is a good spot for viewing wading birds. From here a road cuts inland up a broad glen to **Kergord**, with Shetland's only large significant area of woodland. In the middle of the tree plantations is **Flemington House**, the former *haa* (noble house) for the estate of Kergord. This attractive house was built from stones taken from crofthouses whose occupants were cleared out in the 1850s by the villainous David Dakers Black. During WWII, the house was the secret headquarters of the Shetland Bus operation. Today the tree plantations attract woodland birds such as the rook and chaffinch.

Nearby, the attractively restored **Weisdale Mill & Bonhoga Gallery** *(☎ 830400, Weisdale; admission free; 10.30am-4.30pm Tues-Sat, noon-4.30pm Sun)* is now a gallery with regular exhibitions by local artists, with a textile museum (£2/1 adult/child, closed Sun) in the basement. The bright and upbeat cafe here serves gourmet food from £1.50 to £5.

On the western shore of Weisdale Voe, in the copse of trees below Cott village, are the interesting ruins of the house where John Clunies Ross (1786–1853) was born. In 1827 Clunies Ross settled in the Cocos Islands in the Indian Ocean and proclaimed himself 'king' of the Cocos.

Inn on the Hill at The Westings (☎ 840242, fax 840500, Wormadale) Singles/doubles from £37.50/65. Camping £3 per person. This large comfortable hotel sits on the edge of the glen overlooking Whiteness Voe.

THE WEST SIDE
☎ 01595

The area west of Weisdale has some of the most dramatic scenery in the Shetlands. The moors are punctuated by blunt crags and dramatic coastal cliffs, and hundreds of cobalt-blue lochs and inlets. Few people make it out this way and it's a perfect area for walking, cycling and fishing.

Walls & Sandness

West of Weisdale, the A971 snakes through a remote moonscape of rocky bluffs and lochans to the village of Walls (pronounced Waas) overlooking Vaila Sound. The road forks right here, striking across the peninsula to Sandness which faces the rocky island of Papa Stour. The vast **Stanydale Temple**, a mighty Neolithic roundhouse thought to have been used for ceremonial purposes, is a steep 1½-mile walk above West Houlland – turn off the A971 just before Walls. The **Scord of Brewster**, a prehistoric farm, is on the hillside above Brig of Waas, near the turn-off to Walls. The countryside here is dotted with tiny abandoned crofts – it's hard to believe whole families lived in these miniature dwellings.

Burrastow House (☎ *809307, fax 809213, Walls)* Singles/doubles £60/120. This fine white haa sits on the western shore of Vaila Sound, about 2 miles around the bay from Walls. Burrastow has its own harbour with views across to Vaila Island, and also serves top-notch food.

Northwest from Walls, the road crosses desolate moorland, emerging at the crofting community of **Sandness**. The woollen spinning mill, **Jamieson's Spinning** (☎ *870285, Sandness)*, opens 8am to 5pm weekdays and sells knitted garments at factory prices (from £20). A short walk through the fields east of the village are the **Huxter Mills**, a series of traditional Norse watermills. There's a fine beach in front of the old laird's haa at **Melby**, just beyond Sandness.

There's good accommodation at the comfortable *Snarraness House* (☎ *809375, fax 809211, West Burrafirth)*, a working croft and fish-farm with its own private cove in West Burrafirth, where the ferry departs for Papa Stour. B&B costs between £18 and £20.

Papa Stour

Visible about a mile offshore from Sandness is the volcanic island of **Papa Stour**, home to huge colonies of auks, terns and skuas. The buckled volcanic strata has been wonderfully eroded by the sea to produce dramatic caves, arches, stacks and underground passages. Probably the most impressive is **Kirstan's Hole**, a partially collapsed gloup on the southwest coast. There are fine views from **Virda Field** in the northwest and several wrecks offshore which attract divers.

The island was once a leper colony, though the people sent here were actually suffering from a hereditary skin disease, caused by malnutrition. There's no shop, but the island has a B&B.

Mrs Holt-brook (☎ *873238, North House)* B&B from £16-19, dinner B&B £23-25. Boat trips around the caves can be arranged from this BB&B.

Access to the island is by ferry from West Burrafirth (east of Sandness), which runs four to seven times weekly (£4.40, £21.50 for a car and driver, one hour); book with W Clark (☎ 810460). Considering the fare, it's probably better to leave your car at West Burrafirth. Flights are also available from Tingwall on Tuesday (£32 return).

Foula

Out in the Atlantic Ocean, about 15 miles southwest of Walls, is the remote, windswept, 5-sq-mile island of Foula (Bird Island). It competes with Fair Isle for the title of Scotland's most isolated inhabited island, with just 42 human inhabitants and 1500 sheep, plus innumerable seabirds, including the rare Leach's petrel and Scotland's largest colony of great skuas. All this is amid dramatic cliff scenery, particularly the awesome, sheer Kame (372m). There's no shop on the island, but accommodation is available.

Mrs Taylor's (☎/fax *753226, Leraback)* Dinner B&B £28 per person. The island's B&B is just north of the airstrip near the post office; it's a comfortable place and serves home-cooked meals.

Foula is reached by twice-weekly ferries (£4.30 return, £21 for a car and driver, four hours) from Walls (☎ 753226) and flights (£42 return) from Tingwall airport.

SOUTH MAINLAND

From Lerwick, the main road south winds 25 miles down the eastern side of this long, narrow, hilly tail of land that ends at Sumburgh Head, with minor roads looping east to Sandwick, Levenwick and Boddam. Just south of Sandwick, a small road branches off to the west to Bigton before returning to the main road at Boddam.

Catpund

About 10 miles south of Lerwick, Catpund is an interesting archaeological site. From Norse to medieval times, this former large quarry was mined for soapstone, which was used to make various utensils and implements; evidence of the workings can be seen along the stream.

Sandwick & Around

☎ 01950 ● pop 1352

Opposite the small scattered village of Sandwick is the island of **Mousa**, a newly created RSPB reserve, on which stands the remarkable **Mousa Broch** (13m; see the boxed text 'Brochs & Wheelhouses'). This fantastically well-preserved broch was built in the Iron Age from local sandstone and features in two Viking sagas as a hideout for eloping couples! For fine views, climb the internal stairwells right to the top of the walls. Around 6000 storm petrels nest on Mousa, but they're only on the island at night. Common and grey seals can be seen on the beach and among the rocks at West Voe.

From mid-April to mid-September there are regular **boat trips** *(adult/child £7.50/3.50 return, 15 minutes)* from Leebitton harbour in Sandwick, allowing two hours on the island. Also available are ***porpoise-spotting trips*** *(from £20/10 per adult/child)*; contact Tom Jamieson (☎ 431367) in advance for reservations.

Solbrekke (☎ 431410, Park Rd, Sandwick) B&B £15-17 per person. Solbrekke only has one room for guests but it's comfortable and the owners are welcoming.

On the promontory on the west coast, **Hoswick** has the **Warp & Weft Heritage Centre** *(☎ 432215; admission free; open 10am-5pm Mon-Sat & 2-5pm Sun May-Sept)* with exhibits on the woollen industry.

Barclay Arms Hotel (☎ 431226, fax 431262, Hoswick) B&B £25-25 per person. This village inn has full en-suite facilities and also offers evening meals.

Farther south at Southpunds, there's a boggy but interesting walk to the ruined **Levenwick Broch**, a truly vast broch that has been scavenged to build the surrounding sheep punds (enclosures).

Brochs & Wheelhouses

The tiny isle of Mousa is home to the best-preserved broch in Scotland, which still towers to 13m after two millennia in Shetland's harsh environment. These remarkable defensive towers were built between 100 BC and AD 100 using rough hewn stones and were built up layer by layer, with a spiral stairwell made of stone slabs laid between the inner and outer walls. The brochs were used later by the Picts and Vikings; some, incredibly, were occupied right up to the 19th century!

Commonly associated with brochs are Iron-Age wheelhouses, communal dwellings with a central fire well and a series of chambers divided by vaulted partitions. The structures resemble a cartwheel from above, hence the name. These sophisticated dwellings were probably home to extended families with a high social status, perhaps the same people who later gave rise to the Highland clans. Tragically, many of Scotland's wheelhouses were destroyed by farmers, who saw the well-preserved chambers as a hazard to sheep; the best surviving examples can be seen at Jarlshof in southern Shetland.

Levenwick Campsite (☎ 422207, Levenwick) Camping from £5. Open May-Sept. This community camp site is off the A970.

There are two to nine buses daily from Lerwick to Sandwick (25 minutes).

Bigton & Around

☎ 01950

Buses from Lerwick stop twice daily (except Sunday) in Bigton on the west coast, but it's another couple of miles to the gorgeous sand **tombolo** (a narrow isthmus) that connects Mainland with St Ninian's Isle. It's the largest shell-and-sand tombolo in Britain – most other similar tombolos are made of gravel or shingle – and it's a breathtaking spot, rightly preserved as an SSSI. You'll often see land-yachts racing along the beach towed by kites.

Across the tombolo is **St Ninian's Isle** with the ruins of a 12th-century church, beneath which are traces of an earlier Pictish church. In 1958, during excavations, an incredible horde of 27 Pictish silver brooches, bowls, spoons and dishes, was found beneath a broken sandstone slab. They're now kept in the Museum of Scotland in Edinburgh, but you can see replicas in the Shetland Museum, Lerwick.

Farther south, an even smaller road branches off to the RSPB reserve of **Loch of Spiggie**, itself created by a sand tombolo. The loch is winter refuge for wildfowl, especially whooper swans, and kittiwakes, arctic terns, greylag geese and curlews are regularly seen. There's a wardens' hut for information at the southern end of the loch. There are two buses daily from Lerwick to Spiggie Monday to Saturday.

Spiggie Hotel (☎/fax 460409, Scousburgh) B&B from £35 per person. At the northern end of the loch, this friendly old-style hotel serves great meals for about £10.

Spiggie Lodge (☎ 460563, Scousburgh) B&B from £18. Nearby, this old farmhouse offers good-value B&B on the hillside overlooking the loch.

Boddam
☎ 01595

Over on the eastern shore, this small village is home to the **Shetland Crofthouse Museum** *(☎ 695057, South Voe; £1 donation requested; open 10am-1pm & 2pm-5pm daily May-Sept)*. Built in 1870, it has been restored, thatched and furnished with 19th-century furniture and utensils. The Lerwick–Sumburgh bus stops right outside.

Quendale
☎ 01950

At the far end of the headland is pretty **Quendale Beach**, a popular seal haul-out, where you'll find **Quendale Water Mill** *(☎ 460969; adult/child £1/50p; open 10am-5pm daily May-Sept)*, a nicely restored 19th-century mill with an interesting video display on the Shetland watermills.

There are fine cliffs and stacks at the southwestern tip of the island around **Fitful Head** and **Garth's Ness**, where you can see the infamous *Braer* shipwreck, which leaked 25 million gallons of oil into the Atlantic in the winter of 1993. Mercifully, hurricane-force winds and high seas churned most of the oil into a less harmful residue, but it still stands as Britain's worst ever oil spill.

Sumburgh
☎ 01950

At the southern tip of Mainland, the airport sits on a sandy isthmus separating the rocky mass of Sumburgh Head from the rest of Mainland. South of the airport is the incomparable **Jarlshof** *(HS; ☎ 460112; adult/child £2.80/1; open 9.30am-6.30pm daily Apr-Sept)*, Shetland's most impressive archaeological attraction. This site was continuously inhabited from the Bronze Age to the 17th century, and was revealed, like Skara Brae in Orkney, when a savage storm stripped back the turf in the 19th century. Among the ruins are Bronze-Age round-houses, Iron-Age wheelhouses, a large broch, a village of Viking longhouses and finally, atop it all, the laird of Sumburgh's 16th-century *haa* (noble house), with a corn-drying kiln and grand hall. You can climb the stairs at the haa for a fantastic overview of Jarlshof. Many of the structures are preserved almost up to their original height, giving a real sense of what life must have been like in these ancient houses. The name Jarlshof comes from Sir Walter Scott's novel *The Pirate*, which was set at Sumburgh. The 26-page guidebook (£2.50) available from the visitors centre interprets the ruins from a number of vantage points.

Near Jarlshof you can visit **Sumburgh Head**, an RSPB reserve. There's a fine old Stevenson lighthouse and cliff-top walks to view the many birds that nest here, including puffins (over 2000 pairs), from April to July, kittiwakes (1000 pairs), fulmars, guillemots (over 13,000 pairs), razorbills and cormorants (the best time to view most birds is April to September). It's a wonderful blustery spot and worth a visit just to watch the mighty waves crashing against the cliffs.

The other important bird-watching area is the **Pool of Virkie**, the bay just east of the airport. Nearby at Old Scatness, **Betty**

Mouat's Cottage is now a camping böd. Betty became famous in 1886 when, on a routine sailing trip to Lerwick on board the fishing smack *Columbine*, the captain was swept overboard and Betty was left alone when his two crewmen went to rescue him; the smack quickly drifted out of their reach and Betty survived nine days at sea before washing up on the coast of Norway.

Close by, a large archaeological dig is exposing the remains of several wheelhouses and a broch; there are regular historical re-enactments based on the artefacts found here.

East of the airport, **Grutness** is the port for the ferry to Fair Isle.

Places to Stay *Betty Mouat's Cottage (Old Scatness, Dunrossness)* Beds £5. Open Apr-Oct. This camping böd by the airport sleeps up to eight people. Book in advance at Lerwick TIC (see that section earlier).

Sumburgh Hotel (☎ 460201, fax 460394, Sumburgh) En-suite singles/doubles from £45/60. Next to Jarlshof and the airport, this former laird's house serves good meals for £6 to £11. Rooms are comfortable but cop a little noise from the airport.

Getting There & Away To get to Sumburgh from Lerwick take the airport bus (£2, 50 minutes) and get off at the stop before the airport (you'll see the Sumburgh Hotel from the road). You can easily walk from Sumburgh itself to the airport, which is across the isthmus.

FAIR ISLE
☎ 01595 ● pop 68

This lonely island, 24 miles southwest of Sumburgh and only 3 miles by 1½ miles in size, is still one of Scotland's most remote inhabited islands. It's suitably dramatic, with numerous caves, geos (fjord-like glacial inlets), rock arches and stacks around the coast and the imposing **Sheep Rock**, a wedge-shaped promontory rising to 135m cliffs, on the east coast.

The island was almost abandoned in the 1950s, but its owner George Waterson gave it to the National Trust for Scotland (NTS) in 1954. Today, bird-watchers come here in large numbers to spy on the island's huge population of migrating and breeding birds, which are monitored year-round by the **Bird Observatory**; visitors are welcome to participate. The island also has over 250 species of flowering plants, and grey and golden seals can be seen around the shores, especially in late summer.

The other big industry here is the production of the famous Fair Isle sweaters, using local wool and patterns dating back to Norse times. The sweaters are still produced in the island's co-operative, Fair Isle Crafts, and money from knitwear and tourism has paid for wind and diesel generators, providing the island with full-time electricity.

The small **George Waterson Memorial Centre** (*☎ 760244, Taft; donations welcome; open 2pm-4pm Mon, 10.30am-noon Wed, 2pm-3.30pm Fri)* has photos and exhibits on the island's natural history, crofting, fishing, archaeology and knitwear.

Places to Stay
Accommodation must be booked in advance and rates include meals.

Fair Isle Lodge & Bird Observatory (☎/fax 760258) Full-board dorms/singles/doubles £30/42/74. The bird observatory offers home cooking and free guided walks; it's located 400m from the ferry terminal.

Mrs Coull (☎ 760248, e kathleen .coull@lineone.net, Upper Leogh) Dinner B&B £30-34 per person. This peaceful B&B is located near the south harbour.

Getting There & Away
Air From Tingwall airport there are two return flights (£74 return, 25 minutes) on Monday, Wednesday and Friday year-round, plus one on Saturday from May to October. A day return allows about six hours on the island (eight on Monday, or 2½ hours on Saturday). There's also a return flight from Sumburgh on Saturday.

Boat From May to September, JW Stout (☎ 760222) runs a ferry service from Grutness (near Sumburgh) to Fair Isle (passenger/car £2.20/10.75, 2½ hours) on Tuesday,

ORKNEY & SHETLAND ISLANDS

For Peat's Sake

Until about 1000 BC, there was little or no peat in Shetland, but a dramatic change in the climate caused the soil to slowly become waterlogged, increasing its acidity and creating a sterile environment where bacterial activity was too slow to rot down the accumulating dead grass, sedge, heather and moss. Over the centuries, this undecayed plant matter built up in deep layers across the islands, trapping large amounts of energy-rich carbon in the soil. Given enough time, the peat would eventually break down to give crude oil.

The early inhabitants of the islands soon discovered that when dried, this brown bog soil could be burned, producing plenty of heat for cooking and warming their draughty dry-stone huts. Thus began a tradition which continues to this day on many islands.

Peat is cut year-round from sphagnum moss bogs in slowly advancing cuttings, which are then left fallow for many years, allowing more peat to accumulate. The peat is removed in rectangular blocks using a long-handled tool called a peat-iron – brutal back-breaking work that causes terrible blisters – but is initially extremely damp and takes months to dry out. To speed things up, the blocks are piled in orderly stacks on a grid pattern to allow the wind to pass through and dry the waterlogged soil.

Saturday and alternate Thursdays, and from Lerwick (£2.20/10.75, 4½ hours) on the remaining Thursdays. All sailings are return trips from Fair Isle, so day trips from Mainland Shetland aren't possible by boat.

NORTH MAINLAND

Mainland's rugged north has some of the most dramatic scenery on the island, with huge areas of wide-open moorland and fjord-like voes.

Voe
☎ 01806

The village of Voe (or more accurately Lower Voe) sits at the head of pretty Olna Firth and has a pleasant Scandinavian atmosphere. It's sheltered from the wind by the surrounding hills and has a bakery, a small salmon farm and a fishing jetty.

Selkie Charters (☎ 588297, e *selkie .charters@zetnet.co.uk*) offers diving trips, training courses and equipment hire.

Places to Stay & Eat *Sail Loft (Old Voe)* Beds £5 per person. Open Apr-Oct. In previous incarnations, this red-painted camping böd by the pier was a fishing shed and a knitwear factory.

Mrs Williamson (☎ 588206, Skol) B&B from £19. This comfortable modern house is located on the road down to the jetty.

Pierhead Restaurant & Bar (☎ 588332, Old Voe) Meals £5-9. Excellent fish dishes are available opposite the Sail Loft in this appealing wood-panelled pub.

Getting There & Away From Lerwick to Voe, there are six buses daily on weekdays and three on Saturday (also two on Sunday during school term).

Whalsay
☎ 01806 ● pop 1043

South of Voe, the B9071 branches east to Laxo, the ferry terminal for the island of Whalsay. This is one of the most prosperous of the Shetland Islands owing to its successful supertrawler fishing fleet, based at the modern harbour of **Symbister**. The imposing **Symbister House** above town was built by Robert Bruce, the tyrant landlord of Whalsay, reputedly to deprive his heirs of an inheritance; it now houses the Whalsay school.

The countryside is extensively cut for peat and there are scenic walks in the south and east where you can see the Iron-Age ruins of **Benie Hoose** and **Yoxie Biggins** and breeding colonies of seabirds. Whalsay is also popular for **sea angling** and **trout fishing**.

The Hanseatic League, a commercial association of German towns that existed between the 14th and early 18th centuries, set up trading booths at the harbour. One of these, **Pier House** (☎ *566362, Symbister; adult/child £1/free; open 9am-1pm & 2pm-5pm Mon-Sat Apr-Sept)*, has been restored and has an exhibition on the Hanseatic League and local history.

At **Sodom**, not far from Symbister, *Grieve House*, former home of famous poet Hugh MacDiarmid, is now a camping böd. Beds cost £5; book through Lerwick TIC.

Getting There & Away There are regular ferries (☎ 566259) daily between Laxo and Symbister on Whalsay (passenger/car £1.30/3.10, 30 minutes). Ferries sometimes leave from nearby Vidlin – call ahead to check.

Out Skerries
☎ 01806

As their name suggests, these rugged rocky isles lie far out to sea, northeast of Whalsay. The Out Skerries occupy just 2 sq miles and include the large islands of Housay and Bruray, connected by a road bridge, and Grunay, plus a number of islets. The cliffs here teem with birdlife.

Mrs Johnson (☎ *515228, Rocklea)* is a comfortable modern house on Bruray that offers good B&B from £18 (dinner and B&B £27).

There are ferries (☎ 515226) from Out Skerries to Lerwick on Tuesday and Thursday (2½ hours), and the rest of the week (except Wednesday) to Vidlin (1½ hours), 3 miles northeast of Laxo. The one-way fare costs £2.20 (£3.10 for a car and driver). You can fly from Tingwall on Monday, Wednesday, Thursday and Friday (£36 return).

Brae & Around
☎ 01806

The ugly modern settlement of Brae is a dormitory town for the Sullom Voe oil terminal and has little to recommend it. There's fine **walking** on the peninsula west of Brae, and to the south on the red-granite island of **Muckle Roe**, which is connected to the peninsula by a bridge. Muckle Roe also offers good **diving** off its west and north coasts.

Northeast of Brae, you can walk up the bleak Hill of Crooksetter for views over the surreal **Sullom Voe Oil Terminal**, Europe's largest, which looks like a set from Star Wars, with its own port and airport and three flaming flare stacks.

Brae has a petrol station, supermarket and post office, but most accommodation options in Brae itself cater to oil workers and are not very appealing.

Drumquin House (☎ *522621, Brae)* B&B £25-32. Friendly Drumquin House offers B&B in an unexpected older house in the middle of Brae.

Valleyfield Guest House (☎ *522563, fax 890257, Brae)* En-suite rooms £35 per person, pitches £4 per person. Overlooking a bleak moor, Valleyfield Guest House is useful for campers.

Busta House Hotel (☎ *522506, fax 522588, Busta)* En-suite singles/doubles from £70/91. The magnificent white haa of Busta House is reputedly haunted by a ghostly maid. It's a wonderful place to stay and has an extremely good restaurant, with set dinners for £28.50.

Mrs Wood (☎ *522368, Westayre, Muckle Roe)* B&B £20-22 per person. At the end of the road across Muckle Roe, this working croft offers home cooking and evening meals are available for £12.

Getting There & Away There are around five buses daily except Sunday between Lerwick and Brae (£2, 35 minutes).

NORTHMAVEN

From Brae, the A970 cuts north and west, across the tiny isthmus of **Mavis Grind**, where it's said you can throw a stone from the North Sea to the Atlantic, to the remote and beautiful Northmaven peninsula.

Eshaness & Hillswick
☎ 01806

About 11 miles northwest of Brae, the road ends at the red, basalt lava cliffs of Eshaness. There are fantastic views from the **lighthouse**, which is surrounded by vast boulders, ripped from the cliffs and thrown far inland by the Atlantic winds. Beside the

ORKNEY & SHETLAND ISLANDS

lighthouse, **Calders Geo** provides a cross section through an ancient volcano.

The most spectacular feature here is the **Holes of Scraada**, a tortured fissure far inland, lined by a black sand beach and linked to the sea by a long tunnel. The chasm was originally a cave, but the roof collapsed in 1873, when a local man rode across on his horse! If you follow the burn inland, you'll pass three ancient watermills and the ruins of a broch in Loch Houlland. The easiest route here is from the Leascole road – head across the fields in the direction of the lighthouse from the turn-off to Shetland Intense Smolts.

Just south of Eshaness is the ruined settlement of **Stenness**, a former herring fishing station that once catered to a fleet of 72 fishing boats. There are just a few ruined stone buildings now, but it's worth walking to the end of the headland for views of **Dore Holm**, a perilously thin arch out to sea.

A mile east, a side road leads south to **Tangwick Haa Museum** (*☎ 503389, Tangwick Haa; admission free; open 1pm-5pm Mon-Fri & 11am-7pm Sat & Sun May-Sept*) in a restored 17th-century house. The difficulties and dangers of fishing and whaling, and the hardships of island life, are shown through photographs and displays.

At **Hamnavoe**, reached by a small road branching north just east of Eshaness, is **Johnny Notions Camping Böd** (£5; book through Lerwick TIC). This was the birthplace of Johnny 'Notions' Williamson, an 18th-century blacksmith who inoculated several thousand people against smallpox using a serum and method he devised himself.

Offshore from **Hillswick**, 7 miles east of Eshaness, there's excellent **diving** around The Drongs, a series of finger-like sea stacks. This pretty village has some nice old houses and a hotel.

St Magnus Hotel (*☎ 503372, fax 503373, Hillswick*) Meals from £5. Built from timber brought from Norway in 1900, this charismatic hotel is usually rented to oil contractors, but the restaurant serves good bar food.

Booth Restaurant & Café (*☎ 503348, Hillswick*) Open daily May-Aug, plus Sat & Sun Sept. Down on the quay, this restaurant is in a 300-year-old Hanseatic trading post and serves vegetarian food. Proceeds go to the local wildlife sanctuary.

Beyond the turn off to Eshaness, the A970 continues north to the village of North Roe passing **Ronas Hill** (499m), the highest point in Shetland. The haunting cloud-shrouded peak can be climbed from the end of the dirt road to Collafirth Hill (near the turn off to Ollaberry). Allow about two hours for the 4-mile walk. Committed walkers can continue over the hill to the attractive beach at **Lang Ayre**.

Buses run Monday to Saturday evenings from Lerwick to Hillswick (£2, 1¼ hours), Eshaness (£2, 1 hour) and North Roe, returning in the morning; contact Rapsons (*☎ 01595 880217*).

THE NORTH ISLES

The North Isles are made up of the three islands of Yell, Unst and Fetlar, all connected to each other by ferry. These peat-covered isles have several wild nature reserves, the most important being Hermanness at the northern tip of Unst.

You can reach any of the islands within a few hours from Lerwick via the 8am bus to Toft on Mainland (£2, Monday to Saturday), which connects with the ferry to Ulsta on Yell; buses also pick up at the P&O terminal. Connecting buses run from Ulsta to Gutcher for the ferries to Unst and Fetlar.

Yell
☎ 01957 ● pop 1083

Yell is a desolate island covered mostly by heather moors atop a deep layer of peat. There are good coastal and hill walks, especially in the uninhabited northwest of the island. The island is also known for its large otter population.

Ferries from Toft arrive at **Ulsta**, which has a shop and not much else. From here the A968 leads north to Gutcher, where the ferry departs for Belmont on Unst. A more scenic route north from Ulsta leads 5 miles east to the village of Burravoe, which has the **Old Haa Visitor Centre** (*☎ 722339; admission free; open 10am-4pm Tues-Thur &*

Sat & 2pm-5pm Sun late Apr-Sept). This museum is housed in Yell's oldest building, built in 1672, and covers local flora, fauna and history; there's also a *tearoom*.

The road continues north, rejoining the main road just north of Mid Yell, the other large village on the island. On the way you can detour to a dramatically located broch at **Gossabrough**, and the **White Wife** at Queyon, the wooden figurehead of the German barque *Bohus*, wrecked here in 1924.

Just west of the junction, on the hillside above the main road, stands the menacing ruins of **Windhouse**, former home of the Swanieson family. Dating from 1707, this spooky house is said to be haunted by the ghost of a peddlar murdered by the Swaniesons and hidden in the walls of the house; a skeleton was found when the house was redecorated in the 19th century.

Immediately north of Windhouse is the RSPB reserve of **Lumbister**, where red-throated divers (called 'rain geese' in Shetland), merlins, bonxies, arctic skuas and other birds breed. Otters can sometimes be seen on the circular walking trail from Windhouse along the west coast. In the Daal of Lumbister, a narrow rocky gorge between the Loch of Lumbister and the west coast, there are bright displays of juniper, honeysuckle and thyme. The isolated area in the northwest of the island offers some exposed coastal walking.

The road north to Gutcher passes **Basta Voe**, where you may catch a glimpse of an otter, and continues beyond Gutcher to **Cullovoe**, the start of an attractive coastal walk to a fine **gloup**, passing the pretty **Sands of Brekken**.

Places to Stay & Eat *Windhouse Lodge (by the A968 in Mid Yell)* Beds £5. Below the haunted ruins of Windhouse you'll find this camping böd, popular with cyclists; book at Lerwick TIC.

Gutcher Post Office (☎ 744201, fax 744366, Gutcher) B&B £17 per person. This friendly pad is near the ferry terminal for Unst. Evening meals cost £8.

Mrs Leask's (☎ 722274, Hillhead, Burravoe) B&B £19 per person. This little white house, with well-maintained rooms, is on the hill top behind the church. It also offers good meals.

Hilltop Restaurant & Bar (☎ 702333, Mid Yell) Mains £2.50-5. This kit-house pub is the island's only restaurant and serves OK haddock and other Shetland standards till around 10pm.

While you're waiting for the ferry in Gutcher, you can snack at the *Seaview Café* where burgers start at just £1.20. There are general merchants in both Mid Yell and Ulsta.

Getting There & Away Yell is connected with Mainland by the car ferry (☎ 722259) that runs between Toft and Ulsta (passenger/car £1.30/3.10, 20 minutes). Although you don't need to book in advance, from May to September traffic is constant so it's wise to do so.

About six daily buses leave Lerwick every weekday for Toft ferry pier (£2, one hour). There are connecting buses at Ulsta for Burravoe, Mid Yell and Gutcher. There are fewer buses on Saturday, and Sunday buses only run during school terms.

Fetlar
☎ 01957 • pop 87

Fetlar is the smallest (5 miles by 2 miles) but most fertile of the North Isles – the name is derived from the Viking term for 'fat land'. Much of the island is given over to pasture, but on the higher ground you'll see numerous *planticrues*, walled enclosures covered by fishing nets and used for growing cabbages. There's great bird-watching, particularly on the 705-hectare **North Fetlar RSPB Reserve**, a region of grassy moorland around Vord Hill (159m). Large numbers of auks, gulls and shags breed in the cliffs, and common and grey seals can also be seen on the shores. The reserve is closed during the breeding season, which runs from May to August; contact the warden (☎ 733246) at Baelans.

Fetlar is home to three-quarters of Britain's red-necked phalaropes, which breed in the loch near **Funzie** (pronounced finnie), in the east. From April to November, you can view them from an RSPB hide in the nearby marshes. The whimbrel, a cousin of the curlew, also breeds here, and in summer, the ranger can arrange trips to view snowy owls.

There are several scenic walks around the island, including the hike around the Lamb Hoga headland, beginning at **Tresta Beach**, about a mile west of Houbie. You may see Shetland ponies, a diminutive breed used for carrying seaweed, roaming on the hills here. On the coast about a mile from the ferry port at Oddsta is **Brough Lodge**, a bizarre assembly of arches, buttresses and towers, built for the Nicolson family in the 1820s; there's an interesting **folly** on the hillock behind the lodge.

There's no petrol on Fetlar, but the main village of **Houbie** has a post office and shop. The excellent **Fetlar Interpretive Centre** (*☎ 733206, Houbie; admission free; open noon-5pm Tues-Sun May-Sept)*, near the post office, has photos, audio recordings and videos on the island and its history, including exhibits on Sir William Cheyne, a Fetlar resident who pioneered the use of antiseptics in medicine.

Places to Stay & Eat *Garth's Campsite* (*☎ 733227, Gord, Houbie)* Pitches £4-7.40. Garth's Campsite, with toilets and showers, overlooks the beach and lochan at Tresta.

Gord (*☎ 733227, Gord, Houbie)* B&B £23 per person. This is a comfortable B&B that can rustle up meals for £7.

The Glebe (*☎/fax 733242)* B&B £17-18 per person. This is a listed building in a small copse of trees overlooking Papil Water and Tresta Beach.

The *shop/cafe* in Houbie serves homemade food, including lemon chicken pie and pasta dishes.

Getting There & Away Regular ferries (passenger/car £1.30/3.10, 25 minutes) from Oddsta in the island's northwest connect with Gutcher on Yell and Belmont on Unst – call *☎ 722259*.

On Monday, Wednesday and Friday, there's a postbus (*☎ 733227)* from Oddsta to the post office at Houbie.

Unst
☎ 01957 • pop 1067

This appealing island rises from rolling grass-covered hills to desolate moorland at its northern tip and is Britain's northernmost inhabited island – Britain's most northerly *uninhabited* island, **Out Stack**, lies just off the coast. Nearby is the picturesque skerry of **Muckle Flugga**, crowned by a lighthouse built by Thomas Stevenson. His nephew Robert Louis Stevenson wrote *Treasure Island* while living on Unst; contrary to many later interpretations, the book was set here on Unst, rather than in some tropical island paradise! The island's unusual geology – serpentine and gabbro to the east and gneiss and schist to the west – contributes to the island's diverse vegetation, comprising over 400 different plant species. A few rare species such as Edmonston's Chickweed are only found in the 74-acre **Keen of Hamar** NNR northeast of Baltasound.

In the far northwest is the wonderfully wild and windy reserve of **Hermaness**, also an NNR. From the visitors centre, a bracing hour-long walk leads across the moors to the very edge of the British Isles. It's a peaceful, uplifting place and the land at the tip of Hermaness falls suddenly away, revealing an empty seascape stretching all the way to the Arctic Circle. During the birdwatching season (May to August), twitchers descend on the reserve to spy on the 56,000 puffins, 32,000 gannets, 28,000 fulmars and 26,000 guillemots which come here annually to breed. The impressive natural arch of **Humla Stack** lies just off the coast, home to a handful of gravity-defying sheep. For a scenic round trip, you can return to the visitor centre via the west coast.

Hermaness Visitor Centre (*☎ 711278, Shore Station, Burrafirth; admission free; open 8.30am-7pm daily late Apr–mid-Sept)*, near the reserve's entrance, has an entertaining seabird exhibit with lots of seabird noises, and provides information on the island's wildlife. There are guided walks in season – call for details.

On the way to Hermaness, you might want to pause to mail a card at Scotland's northernmost post box in **Haroldswick**, the main settlement. Most people here work at the nearby RAF radar complex at Saxavord. Haroldswick has a shop and leisure centre and the interesting **Unst Boat Haven** (☎ *711528, Haroldswick; admission free; open 2pm-5pm daily May-Sept)*, housing an interesting collection of restored wooden boats, including a traditional *sixareen* of the type used by whalers in the 19th century. Next door, the **Unst Heritage Centre** (☎ *711528, Haroldswick; admission free; open 2pm-5pm daily May-Sept)* houses a museum on geology and local history.

North of Haroldswick there's a wonderful sandy beach at **Norwick**, and another farther north at **Skaw** (accessible only on foot). Heading south, you'll pass Scotland's oddest **bus shelter** at Baltasound, maintained by local eccentric Bobby Macaulay. The shelter is fully furnished, with a sofa and net curtains, and must be the only bus shelter with it's own Web site (W www.unstbusshelter.shetland.co.uk).

In the south, about 3 miles east of Uyeasound, are the remains of **Muness Castle** (HS), a defensive towerhouse built for the vicious Laurence Bruce, brother of Earl Stewart of Orkney, in 1598.

Organised Tours *Shetland Wildlife* (☎ *01950-422483,* W *www.shetlandwildlife .co.uk)* runs popular 7½-hour tours from Mainland to Yell and onto Muckle Flugga and Out Stack on Wednesday in June and July for £65, including ferries from Toft.

Places to Stay & Eat Baltasound has the greatest range of accommodation on Unst.

Gardiesfauld Hostel (☎ *755259, fax 711211, Uyeasound)* Dorms £9.25/8. Pitch & 2 persons £6. Open Apr-Sept. This hostel has modern facilities and arranges bike hire.

Mrs Ritch (☎ *711323, Gerratoun, Haroldswick)* B&B £16-17 per person. Mrs Ritch offers B&B in a converted crofthouse. Dinner is available for an extra £7.

Mrs Firmin (☎ *755234, Prestegaard, Uyeasound)* Rooms £18 per person. This lovely white cottage has good rooms and sea views. Evening meals cost £8.

Clingera Guest House (☎*/fax 711579, Baltasound)* En-suite B&B £18-20 per person. This modern house has decent rooms and a quiet location overlooking the bay.

Buness Country House (☎ *711315, fax 711815, Baltasound)* Singles/doubles £36.50/63. The notorious Burke and Hare stayed at Buness House, but it's a fine old building and otters are often seen down on the shore. Dinner is an extra £20.

Baltasound Hotel (☎ *711334, fax 711358, Baltasound)* En-suite singles/doubles £39.50/59. This old square haa has extensions in nearby chalets and serves good meals from £5. Try the local real ale White Wife, produced by the Valhalla Brewery in Baltasound.

Getting There & Away Unst is connected with Yell by a small car ferry (☎ 722259) that runs between Gutcher and Belmont (passenger/car £1.30/3.10, 10 minutes).

Language

SCOTTISH GAELIC

Scottish Gaelic (*Gàidhlig* – pronounced *gallic* in Scotland) is spoken by about 80,000 people in Scotland, mainly in the Highlands and Islands, and by many native speakers and learners overseas. It is a member of the Celtic branch of the Indo-European family of languages which has given us Gaelic, Irish, Manx, Welsh, Cornish and Breton.

Although Scottish Gaelic is the Celtic language most closely associated with Scotland it was quite a latecomer to those shores. Other Celtic languages in the form of Pictish and Brittonic had existed prior to the arrival and settlement by Gaelic speaking Celts (Gaels) from Ireland from the 4th to the 6th centuries AD. These Irish settlers, known to the Romans as *Scotti*, were eventually to give their name to the entire country. Initially they settled in the area on the west coast of Scotland in which their name is perpetuated, Earra Ghaidheal (Argyll). As their territorial influence extended so did their language and from the 9th to the 11th centuries Gaelic was spoken throughout the country. For many centuries the language was the same as the language of Ireland; there is little evidence of much divergence before the 13th century. Even up to the 18th century the bards adhered to the strict literary standards of Old Irish.

The Viking invasions from AD 800 brought linguistic influences that are evident in many of the coastal place names of the Highlands.

Gaelic culture flourished in the Highlands until the 18th century and the Jacobite rebellions. After the Battle of Culloden in 1746 many Gaelic speakers were forced from their ancestral lands; this 'ethnic cleansing' by landlords and governments culminated in the Highland Clearances of the 19th century. Although still studied at academic level, the spoken language declined, being regarded as a mere 'peasant' language of no modern significance.

It was only in the 1970s that Gaelic began to make a comeback with a new generation of young enthusiasts who were determined that it should not be allowed to die. People from all over Scotland, and indeed worldwide, are beginning to appreciate their Gaelic heritage.

After two centuries of decline, the language is now being encouraged through financial help from government agencies and the EU. Gaelic education is flourishing from playgroups to tertiary levels. This renaissance flows out into the field of music, literature, cultural events and broadcasting.

The Gaelic language has a vital role to play in the life of modern Scotland.

Grammar

The usual word order in Gaelic is verb-subject-object; English, by comparison, has a subject-verb-object word order, eg, The girl (subject) reads (verb) the book (object). There are two forms of the pronoun 'you' in Gaelic: the singular *thu* and the plural form *sibh* which is also used as a formal (ie, polite) singular. The informal *thu* is used in the following phraselist.

English Borrowings from Gaelic

bard	*bard* (poet)
ben	*beinn* (hill)
bog	*bog* (soft, wet)
brogue	*bròg* (shoe)
claymore	*claidheamh mòr* (big sword)
dune	*dùn* (a heap)
galore	*gu leòr* (plenty)
loch	*loch* (loch)
Sassenach	*Sasannach* (Englishman)
strath	*strath* (mountain valley)

Pronunciation

Stress usually falls on the first syllable of a word. The Gaelic alphabet has only 18 letters:

Vowels There are five vowels: **a**, **e**, **i**, **o** and **u** – **a**, **o**, **u** are known as broad vowels, e, i are known as slender vowels. A grave accent indicates that a vowel sound is lengthened, eg, *bata* (a stick), *bàta* (a boat).

Consonants There are 12 consonants: **b, c, d, f, g, l, m, n, p, r, s, t**, and the letter **h** (only used to change other sounds).

Consonants may be pronounced in different ways depending on the vowel beside them. The spelling rule in Gaelic is 'broad to broad and slender to slender'. This means that if a consonant is preceded by a broad vowel it must be followed by a broad vowel, and if it's preceded by a slender vowel it must be followed by a slender vowel. Consequently, we speak about broad consonants and slender consonants, eg, *balach* (a boy), *caileag* (a girl).

Broad consonants sound approximately as their English equivalents. Slender consonants are often followed by a 'y' sound.

c	always a hard 'k' sound; never an 's' sound
d	when broad, thicker than English 'd'; when slender, as the 'j' in 'jet'
l, ll	when slender, as in 'value'
n, nn	when slender, as in 'new'
s	when slender, as 'sh'
t	when broad, thicker than English 't'; when slender, as the 'ch' in 'chin'

When consonants are followed by 'h', a change of sound occurs:

bh, mh	as 'v'
ch	when broad, as in *loch*; when slender, as the German *ich*; never as 'k'
dh, gh	when broad, voiced at the back of the throat; when slender, as 'y' – there's no English equivalent
fh	silent
ph	as 'f'
sh	as 'h' if before a broad vowel
th	as 'h'

There are a number of Gaelic sounds, especially vowel combinations and consonantal changes brought about by the addition of

the letter **h**, which cannot be reproduced satisfactorily in English. The help of a native speaker is invaluable in learning these. The italicised words and phrases in the following list are included as a pronunciation guide.

Greetings & Civilities

Good morning.
madding va
Madainn mhath.
Good afternoon/Good evening.
fesskurr ma
Feasgar math.
Good night.
uh eech uh va
Oidhche mhath.
How are you?
kimmer uh ha oo?
Ciamar a tha thu?
Very well, thank you.
gley va, tappuh let
Glè mhath, tapadh leat.
Please.
mahs eh doh hawl eh
Mas e do thoil e.
Thank you.
tappuh let
Tapadh leat.
Many thanks.
moe ran ta eeng
Mòran taing.
You're welcome.
sheh doh veh huh
'Se do bheatha.
I beg your pardon.
baaluv
B'àill leibh.
Excuse me.
gav mo lishk yal
Gabh mo leisgeul.
I'm sorry.
ha mee dooleech
Tha mi duilich.

Small Talk

Do you speak (have) Gaelic?
uh vil ga lick ackut?
A bheil Gàidhlig agad?
Yes, a little.
ha, beg an
Tha, beagan.

Not much.
chan yil moe ran
Chan eil mòran.
What's your name?
jae an tannam uh ha orsht?
De an t ainm a tha ort?
I'm ...
is meeshuh ...
Is mise ...
Good health! (Cheers!)
slahntchuh va!
Slàinte mhath!
Goodbye. (lit: Blessings go with you)
b yan achd let
Beannachd leat.
Goodbye. (The same with you)
mar shin let
Mar sin leat.

Travel & Accommodation

Can you tell me ...?
un yee ish oo ghoe ...?
An innis thu dhomh ...?
How do I get to ...?
kimmer uh yaev mee goo ...?
Ciamar a gheibh mi gu ...?

by bus
  ir uh vuss   air a' bhus
by train
  ir un tren   air an trean
by car
  a woon un car   ann an car

a hotel
  tuh ee awstu   taigh òsda
a bedroom
  roowm caddil   rùm cadail
a toilet
  tuh ee beck   taigh beag

Food

I'd like ...
boo tawl lehum
Bu toigh leam ...

That was good.
va shood ma
Bha siud math.
Very good.
gley va
Glè mhath.

bread
  aran   aran
broth, soup
  broht   brot
butter
  eem   ìm
cheese
  kashuh   càise
cream
  baahrr   bàrr
fish
  eeusk   iasg
meat
  fehyawl   feòil
oatcakes
  aran korkuh   aran coirce
porridge
  lee chuh   lite
potatoes
  boontahtuh   buntàta
salmon
  brahdan   bradan

Drinks

a cup of coffee
  coopa cawfee   cupa cofaidh
a cup of tea
  coopa tee   cupa tì
a drink of milk
  joch vahnyuh   deoch bhainne
a glass of water
  glahnyuh ooshkuy   glainne uisge
a glass of wine
  glahnyuh feeuhn   glainne fìon
beer
  lyawn   leann
whisky (lit: water of life)
  ooshkuy beh huh   uisge beatha

Glossary

bag – reach the top of (as in to 'bag a couple of peaks' or 'Munro bagging')
ben – mountain
böd – originally a simple trading booth used by fishing communities, today it refers to basic accommodation for walkers and so on
bothy – hut or mountain shelter
brae – hill
broch – defensive tower
burgh – town
burn – stream
cairn – pile of stones to mark path or junction; also peak
ceilidh – (pronounced **kay**-lee) informal entertainment and dance
clootie dumpling – steamed fruit pudding
craig – exposed rock
dirk – dagger
doocot – dove-cote
dram – whisky measure
dun – fort
firth – estuary
geo – gulley
glen – valley
gloup – natural arch
haa – noble house
hoagies – filled rolls
Hogmanay – New Year's Eve
HS – Historic Scotland
kirk – church
kyle – narrow strait of water
laird – estate owner
law – round hill
linn – waterfall
lochan – small inland loch
machair – grass and wildflower-covered dunes
manse – minister's house

muckle – big
Munro – mountain of 914m or higher
Munro bagger – a hillwalker who tries to climb all the Munros in Scotland
neeps – turnips
ness – headland
NNR – National Nature Reserve, managed by the SNH
NTS – National Trust for Scotland
Picts – early inhabitants of northern and eastern Scotland (from the Latin *pictus*, meaning painted, after their body paint decorations)
pund – enclsoure
queenies – scallops
rhinn or **rhin** – headland
RSPB – Royal Society for the Protection of Birds
sett – tartan pattern; also cobblestone
skerries – semi-submerged rocks
SMC – Scottish Mountaineering Club
SNH – Scottish Natural Heritage, a government organisation responsible for safeguarding and improving Scotland's natural heritage
souterrain – stone-lined storage tunnel
spoots – razor shells
sporran – purse worn around waist with the kilt
SRWS – Scottish Rights of Way and Access Society
SSSI – Sight of Special Scientific Interest
STB – Scottish Tourist Board
strath – valley
SYHA – Scottish Youth Hostel Association
tatties – potatoes
TIC – Tourist Information Centre
tolbooth – town hall; town jail
tombolo – narrow isthmus
voe – inlet (Shetland)

LONELY PLANET

You already know that Lonely Planet produces more than this one guidebook, but you might not be aware of the other products we have on this region. Here is a selection of titles that you may want to check out as well:

Scotland
ISBN 1 86450 157 X
US$16.99 • UK£10.99

Edinburgh
ISBN 1 86450 378 5
US$12.99 • UK£8.99

Walking in Scotland
ISBN 1 86450 350 5
US$17.99 • UK£11.99

Britain
ISBN 1 86450 147 2
US$27.99 • UK£15.99

Cycing in Britain
ISBN 1 86450 037 9
US$19.99 • UK£12.99

Walking in Britain
ISBN 1 86450 280 0
US$21.99 • UK£13.99

Western Europe
ISBN 1 86450 163 4
US$27.99 • UK£15.99

Read This First Europe
ISBN 1 86450 136 7
US$14.99 • UK£8.99

Europe on a shoestring
ISBN 1 86450 150 2
US$24.99 • UK£14.99

Edinburgh City Map
ISBN 1 74059 015 5
US$5.99 • UK£3.99

British Phrasebook
ISBN 0 86442 484 1
US$5.95 • UK£3.99

European Phrasebook
ISBN 1 86450 224 X
US$8.99 • UK£4.99

Available wherever books are sold

Lonely Planet Guides by Region

Lonely Planet is known worldwide for publishing practical, reliable and no-nonsense travel information in our guides and on our Web site. The Lonely Planet list covers just about every accessible part of the world. Currently there are 16 series: Travel guides, Shoestring guides, Condensed guides, Phrasebooks, Read This First, Healthy Travel, Walking guides, Cycling guides, Watching Wildlife guides, Pisces Diving & Snorkeling guides, City Maps, Road Atlases, Out to Eat, World Food, Journeys travel literature and Pictorials.

AFRICA Africa on a shoestring • Botswana • Cairo • Cairo City Map • Cape Town • Cape Town City Map • East Africa • Egypt • Egyptian Arabic phrasebook • Ethiopia, Eritrea & Djibouti • Ethiopian Amharic phrasebook • The Gambia & Senegal • Healthy Travel Africa • Kenya • Malawi • Morocco • Moroccan Arabic phrasebook • Mozambique • Namibia • Read This First: Africa • South Africa, Lesotho & Swaziland • Southern Africa • Southern Africa Road Atlas • Swahili phrasebook • Tanzania, Zanzibar & Pemba • Trekking in East Africa • Tunisia • Watching Wildlife East Africa • Watching Wildlife Southern Africa • West Africa • World Food Morocco • Zambia • Zimbabwe, Botswana & Namibia
Travel Literature: Mali Blues: Traveling to an African Beat • The Rainbird: A Central African Journey • Songs to an African Sunset: A Zimbabwean Story

AUSTRALIA & THE PACIFIC Aboriginal Australia & the Torres Strait Islands •Auckland • Australia • Australian phrasebook • Australia Road Atlas • Cycling Australia • Cycling New Zealand • Fiji • Fijian phrasebook • Healthy Travel Australia, NZ & the Pacific • Islands of Australia's Great Barrier Reef • Melbourne • Melbourne City Map • Micronesia • New Caledonia • New South Wales • New Zealand • Northern Territory • Outback Australia • Out to Eat – Melbourne • Out to Eat – Sydney • Papua New Guinea • Pidgin phrasebook • Queensland • Rarotonga & the Cook Islands • Samoa • Solomon Islands • South Australia • South Pacific • South Pacific phrasebook • Sydney • Sydney City Map • Sydney Condensed • Tahiti & French Polynesia • Tasmania • Tonga • Tramping in New Zealand • Vanuatu • Victoria • Walking in Australia • Watching Wildlife Australia • Western Australia
Travel Literature: Islands in the Clouds: Travels in the Highlands of New Guinea • Kiwi Tracks: A New Zealand Journey • Sean & David's Long Drive

CENTRAL AMERICA & THE CARIBBEAN Bahamas, Turks & Caicos • Baja California • Belize, Guatemala & Yucatán • Bermuda • Central America on a shoestring • Costa Rica • Costa Rica Spanish phrasebook • Cuba • Cycling Cuba • Dominican Republic & Haiti • Eastern Caribbean • Guatemala • Havana • Healthy Travel Central & South America • Jamaica • Mexico • Mexico City • Panama • Puerto Rico • Read This First: Central & South America • Virgin Islands • World Food Caribbean • World Food Mexico • Yucatán
Travel Literature: Green Dreams: Travels in Central America

EUROPE Amsterdam • Amsterdam City Map • Amsterdam Condensed • Andalucía • Athens • Austria • Baltic States phrasebook • Barcelona • Barcelona City Map • Belgium & Luxembourg • Berlin • Berlin City Map • Britain • British phrasebook • Brussels, Bruges & Antwerp • Brussels City Map • Budapest • Budapest City Map • Canary Islands • Catalunya & the Costa Brava • Central Europe • Central Europe phrasebook • Copenhagen • Corfu & the Ionians • Corsica • Crete • Crete Condensed • Croatia • Cycling Britain • Cycling France • Cyprus • Czech & Slovak Republics • Czech phrasebook • Denmark • Dublin • Dublin City Map • Dublin Condensed • Eastern Europe • Eastern Europe phrasebook • Edinburgh • Edinburgh City Map • England • Estonia, Latvia & Lithuania • Europe on a shoestring • Europe phrasebook • Finland • Florence • Florence City Map • France • Frankfurt City Map • Frankfurt Condensed • French phrasebook • Georgia, Armenia & Azerbaijan • Germany • German phrasebook • Greece • Greek Islands • Greek phrasebook • Hungary • Iceland, Greenland & the Faroe Islands • Ireland • Italian phrasebook • Italy • Kraków • Lisbon • The Loire • London • London City Map • London Condensed • Madrid • Madrid City Map • Malta • Mediterranean Europe • Milan, Turin & Genoa • Moscow • Munich • Netherlands • Normandy • Norway • Out to Eat – London • Out to Eat – Paris • Paris • Paris City Map • Paris Condensed • Poland • Polish phrasebook • Portugal • Portuguese phrasebook • Prague • Prague City Map • Provence & the Côte d'Azur • Read This First: Europe • Rhodes & the Dodecanese • Romania & Moldova • Rome • Rome City Map • Rome Condensed • Russia, Ukraine & Belarus • Russian phrasebook • Scandinavian & Baltic Europe • Scandinavian phrasebook • Scotland • Sicily • Slovenia • South-West France • Spain • Spanish phrasebook • Stockholm • St Petersburg • St Petersburg City Map • Sweden • Switzerland • Tuscany • Ukrainian phrasebook • Venice • Vienna • Wales • Walking in Britain • Walking in France • Walking in Ireland • Walking in Italy • Walking in Scotland • Walking in Spain • Walking in Switzerland • Western Europe • World Food France • World Food Greece • World Food Ireland • World Food Italy • World Food Spain **Travel Literature:** After Yugoslavia • Love and War in the Apennines • The Olive Grove: Travels in Greece • On the Shores of the Mediterranean • Round Ireland in Low Gear • A Small Place in Italy

Lonely Planet Mail Order

Lonely Planet products are distributed worldwide. They are also available by mail order from Lonely Planet, so if you have difficulty finding a title please write to us. North and South American residents should write to 150 Linden St, Oakland, CA 94607, USA; European and African residents should write to 10a Spring Place, London NW5 3BH, UK; and residents of other countries to Locked Bag 1, Footscray, Victoria 3011, Australia.

INDIAN SUBCONTINENT & THE INDIAN OCEAN Bangladesh • Bengali phrasebook • Bhutan • Delhi • Goa • Healthy Travel Asia & India • Hindi & Urdu phrasebook • India • India & Bangladesh City Map • Indian Himalaya • Karakoram Highway • Kathmandu City Map • Kerala • Madagascar • Maldives • Mauritius, Réunion & Seychelles • Mumbai (Bombay) • Nepal • Nepali phrasebook • North India • Pakistan • Rajasthan • Read This First: Asia & India • South India • Sri Lanka • Sri Lanka phrasebook • Tibet • Tibetan phrasebook • Trekking in the Indian Himalaya • Trekking in the Karakoram & Hindukush • Trekking in the Nepal Himalaya • World Food India **Travel Literature:** The Age of Kali: Indian Travels and Encounters • Hello Goodnight: A Life of Goa • In Rajasthan • Maverick in Madagascar • A Season in Heaven: True Tales from the Road to Kathmandu • Shopping for Buddhas • A Short Walk in the Hindu Kush • Slowly Down the Ganges

MIDDLE EAST & CENTRAL ASIA Bahrain, Kuwait & Qatar • Central Asia • Central Asia phrasebook • Dubai • Farsi (Persian) phrasebook • Hebrew phrasebook • Iran • Israel & the Palestinian Territories • Istanbul • Istanbul City Map • Istanbul to Cairo • Istanbul to Kathmandu • Jerusalem • Jerusalem City Map • Jordan • Lebanon • Middle East • Oman & the United Arab Emirates • Syria • Turkey • Turkish phrasebook • World Food Turkey • Yemen **Travel Literature:** Black on Black: Iran Revisited • Breaking Ranks: Turbulent Travels in the Promised Land • The Gates of Damascus • Kingdom of the Film Stars: Journey into Jordan

NORTH AMERICA Alaska • Boston • Boston City Map • Boston Condensed • British Columbia • California & Nevada • California Condensed • Canada • Chicago • Chicago City Map • Chicago Condensed • Florida • Georgia & the Carolinas • Great Lakes • Hawaii • Hiking in Alaska • Hiking in the USA • Honolulu & Oahu City Map • Las Vegas • Los Angeles • Los Angeles City Map • Louisiana & the Deep South • Miami • Miami City Map • Montreal • New England • New Orleans • New Orleans City Map • New York City • New York City City Map • New York City Condensed • New York, New Jersey & Pennsylvania • Oahu • Out to Eat – San Francisco • Pacific Northwest • Rocky Mountains • San Diego & Tijuana • San Francisco • San Francisco City Map • Seattle • Seattle City Map • Southwest • Texas • Toronto • USA • USA phrasebook • Vancouver • Vancouver City Map • Virginia & the Capital Region • Washington, DC • Washington, DC City Map • World Food New Orleans **Travel Literature:** Caught Inside: A Surfer's Year on the California Coast • Drive Thru America

NORTH-EAST ASIA Beijing • Beijing City Map • Cantonese phrasebook • China • Hiking in Japan • Hong Kong & Macau • Hong Kong City Map • Hong Kong Condensed • Japan • Japanese phrasebook • Korea • Korean phrasebook • Kyoto • Mandarin phrasebook • Mongolia • Mongolian phrasebook • Seoul • Shanghai • South-West China • Taiwan • Tokyo • Tokyo Condensed • World Food Hong Kong • World Food Japan **Travel Literature:** In Xanadu: A Quest • Lost Japan

SOUTH AMERICA Argentina, Uruguay & Paraguay • Bolivia • Brazil • Brazilian phrasebook • Buenos Aires • Buenos Aires City Map • Chile & Easter Island • Colombia • Ecuador & the Galapagos Islands • Healthy Travel Central & South America • Latin American Spanish phrasebook • Peru • Quechua phrasebook • Read This First: Central & South America • Rio de Janeiro • Rio de Janeiro City Map • Santiago de Chile • South America on a shoestring • Trekking in the Patagonian Andes • Venezuela **Travel Literature:** Full Circle: A South American Journey

SOUTH-EAST ASIA Bali & Lombok • Bangkok • Bangkok City Map • Burmese phrasebook • Cambodia • Cycling Vietnam, Laos & Cambodia • East Timor phrasebook • Hanoi • Healthy Travel Asia & India • Hill Tribes phrasebook • Ho Chi Minh City (Saigon) • Indonesia • Indonesian phrasebook • Indonesia's Eastern Islands • Java • Lao phrasebook • Laos • Malay phrasebook • Malaysia, Singapore & Brunei • Myanmar (Burma) • Philippines • Pilipino (Tagalog) phrasebook • Read This First: Asia & India • Singapore • Singapore City Map • South-East Asia on a shoestring • South-East Asia phrasebook • Thailand • Thailand's Islands & Beaches • Thailand, Vietnam, Laos & Cambodia Road Atlas • Thai phrasebook • Vietnam • Vietnamese phrasebook • World Food Indonesia • World Food Thailand • World Food Vietnam

ALSO AVAILABLE: Antarctica • The Arctic • The Blue Man: Tales of Travel, Love and Coffee • Brief Encounters: Stories of Love, Sex & Travel • Buddhist Stupas in Asia: The Shape of Perfection • Chasing Rickshaws • The Last Grain Race • Lonely Planet ... On the Edge: Adventurous Escapades from Around the World • Lonely Planet Unpacked • Lonely Planet Unpacked Again • Not the Only Planet: Science Fiction Travel Stories • Ports of Call: A Journey by Sea • Sacred India • Travel Photography: A Guide to Taking Better Pictures • Travel with Children • Tuvalu: Portrait of an Island Nation

Index

Text

Boxed Text

MAP LEGEND

BOUNDARIES

............International
............Provincial, State
............Regional, Suburb

HYDROGRAPHY

............Coastline
............River, Creek
............Lake
............Canal

ROUTES & TRANSPORT

............Freeway
............Highway
............Major Road
............Minor Road
............Unsealed Road
............City Freeway
............City Highway
............City Road
............City Street, Lane

............Pedestrian Mall
............Tunnel
............Train Route & Station
............Metro & Station
............Tramway & Tram Stop
............Cable Car or Chairlift
............Walking Track
............Walking Tour
............Ferry Route & Terminal

AREA FEATURES

............Building
............Urban Area

............Park, Gardens
............Cemetery

............Market
............Mountain Range

MAP SYMBOLS

🏛 Edinburgh ....Large City
◉ Glasgow ....City
◉ Inverness ....Large Town
◉ Wick ....Town or Village

● ....Point of Interest
■ ....Place to Stay
⛺ ....Camp Site
🚐 ....Caravan Park
⌂ ....Hut or Chalet
▼ ....Place to Eat
🍺 ....Pub or Bar
✈ ....Airport
............Ancient or City Wall

............Archaeological Site
............Bank
............Battle Site
............Beach
............Bird Sanctuary
............Bus Stop, Station
............Castle or Fort
............Cave
............Church or Cathedral
............Dive Site
............Cinema
............Embassy
............Golf Course
............Hospital

............Internet Cafe
▲ ....Mountain or Hill
............Museum
............Statly Home
............Parking
............Police Station
............Post Office
............Ship Wreck
............Ski Field
............Swimming Pool
............Telephone
............Theatre
............Tourist Information
🚶 ....Trail Head

Note: not all symbols displayed above appear in this book

LONELY PLANET OFFICES

Australia
Locked Bag 1, Footscray, Victoria 3011
☎ 03 8379 8000 fax 03 8379 8111
email: talk2us@lonelyplanet.com.au

UK
10a Spring Place, London NW5 3BH
☎ 020 7428 4800 fax 020 7428 4828
email: go@lonelyplanet.co.uk

USA
150 Linden St, Oakland, CA 94607
☎ 510 893 8555 TOLL FREE: 800 275 8555
fax 510 893 8572
email: info@lonelyplanet.com

France
1 rue du Dahomey, 75011 Paris
☎ 01 55 25 33 00 fax 01 55 25 33 01
email: bip@lonelyplanet.fr
www.lonelyplanet.fr

**World Wide Web: www.lonelyplanet.com *or* AOL keyword: lp
Lonely Planet Images: lpi@lonelyplanet.com.au**